BERKSHIRE
ENCYCLOPEDIA of SUSTAINABILITY
VOLUME 9

AFRO-EURASIA: ASSESSING SUSTAINABILITY

Editors Louis Kotzé, *North-West University;* Stephen Morse, *University of Surrey*

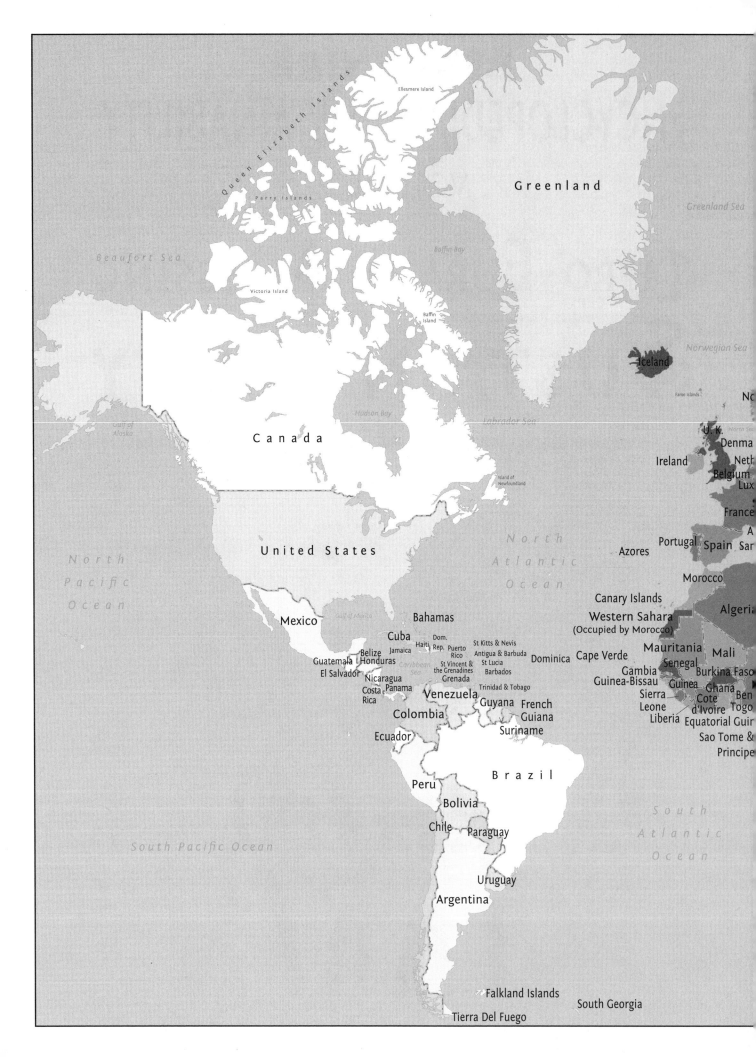

The darkened areas on this map indicate regions covered in this volume.

Digital editions

The *Berkshire Encyclopedia of Sustainability* is available through most major e-book and database services (please check with them for pricing). Special print/digital bundle pricing is also available in cooperation with Credo Reference; contact Berkshire Publishing (info@berkshirepublishing.com) for details.

For information, contact:
Berkshire Publishing Group LLC
122 Castle Street
Great Barrington, Massachusetts 01230-1506 USA
info@berkshirepublishing.com
Tel + 1 413 528 0206
Fax + 1 413 541 0076

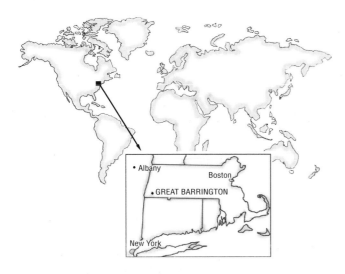

Library of Congress Cataloging-in-Publication Data

Berkshire encyclopedia of sustainability: / Afro-Eurasia: Assessing sustainability, edited by Louis Kotzé and Stephen Morse.
   v. cm.
   Includes bibliographical references and index.
   Contents: vol. 9. Afro-Eurasia: Assessing sustainability —
   ISBN 978-1-933782-19-5 (vol. 9 print : alk. paper)
   1. Environmental quality—Encyclopedias.   2. Environmental protection—Encyclopedias   3. Sustainable development—Encyclopedias.   I. Kotzé, Louis.   II. Morse, Stephen.

Berkshire encyclopedia of sustainability (10 volumes) / edited by Ray Anderson et al.
   10 v. cm.
   Includes bibliographical references and index.
   ISBN 978-1-933782-01-0 (10 volumes : alk. paper) — 978-1-933782-00-3 (10 volumes e-book) — ISBN 978-1-933782-15-7 (vol. 1 print : alk. paper) — ISBN 978-1-933782-57-7 (vol. 1 e-book) — ISBN 978-1-933782-13-3 (vol. 2 print : alk. paper) — ISBN 978-1-933782-55-3 (vol. 2 e-book) — ISBN 978-1-933782-14-0 (vol. 3 print : alk. paper) — ISBN 978-1-933782-56-0 (vol. 3 e-book) — ISBN 978-1-933782-12-6 (vol. 4 print : alk. paper) — ISBN 978-1-933782-54-6 (vol. 4 e-book) — ISBN 978-1-933782-16-4 (vol. 5 print : alk. paper) — ISBN 978-1-933782-09-6 (vol. 5 e-book) — ISBN 978-1-933782-40-9 (vol. 6 print : alk. paper) — ISBN 978-0-9770159-0-0 (vol. 6 e-book) — ISBN 978-1-933782-69-0 (vol. 7 print : alk. paper) — ISBN 978-1-933782-72-0 (vol. 7 e-book) — ISBN 978-1-933782-18-8 (vol. 8 print : alk. paper) — ISBN 978-1-933782-73-7 (vol. 8 e-book) — ISBN 978-1-933782-19-5 (vol. 9 print : alk. paper) — ISBN 978-1-933782-74-4 (vol. 9 e-book) — ISBN 978-1-933782-63-8 (vol. 10 print : alk. paper) — ISBN 978-1-933782-75-1 (vol. 10 e-book).
   1. Environmental quality—Encyclopedias.   2. Environmental protection—Encyclopedias.   3. Sustainable development—Encyclopedias. I. Anderson, Ray, et al.
   HC79.E5B4576   2010
   338.9'2703—dc22   2009035114

Editors

Editors
Louis Kotzé
North-West University

Stephen Morse
University of Surrey

Associate Editors
Irina Krasnova
Moscow State Academy of Law

Muhammad Aurang Zeb Mughal
Durham University

Anthony O'Connor
University College London

Fabienne Quilleré-Majzoub
University of Rennes 1

Mark Wilson
Northumbria University

Advisory Board
Ray C. Anderson, *Interface, Inc.;* Lester R. Brown, *Earth Policy Institute;* Eric Freyfogle, *University of Illinois, Urbana-Champaign;* Luis Gomez-Echeverri, *United Nations Development Programme;* Daniel M. Kammen, *University of California, Berkeley;* Ashok Khosla, *International Union for Conservation of Nature;* Christine Loh, *Civic Exchange, Hong Kong; Under Secretary for the Environment, Hong Kong;* Cheryl Oakes, *Duke University*

Production Staff

Publisher
Karen Christensen

Project Coordinator
Bill Siever

Copyeditors
Mary Bagg
Kathy Brock
Elaine Coveney
Cindy Crumrine
Kristen Greenberg
Carolyn Haley
Elizabeth Laederich
Kristen Osborne
Elma Sanders
Stephanie Schwartz Driver
Heidi Sias
Catherine Skeen
Susan Walker

Editorial Assistants
Ellie Johnston
Ginger Nielsen-Reed
Amanda Prigge

Design
Anna Myers

Information Management
Trevor Young

Composition and Indexing
Aptara, Inc.

Printer
Thomson-Shore, Inc.

Image Credits

continued on next page

S. *Angelica, southern Iceland*. Photo by Amy Siever.

T. *Lake Garda, Italy*. Photo copyright Eva-Maria Zetsche, project MAYA.

U. *Beach on the Isle of Harris, Outer Hebrides, Scotland*. Photo by Amy Siever.

V. *Volga River*. Photo by Sergei Mikhailovich Prokudin-Gorskii (1863–1944), taken 1910. World Digital Library.

W. *Water in motion, Red Sea*. Photo copyright Eva-Maria Zetsche, project MAYA.

Contents

List of Entries

Reader's Guide: Articles by Category

Note: most articles appear in more than one category

BUSINESS, ECONOMICS, AND INDUSTRY

Conflict Minerals

Corporate Accountability (Africa)

E-Waste

Ecotourism

Energy Security (Europe)

Fisheries

Microfinance

Mining (Africa)

Public-Private Partnerships (Africa)

Shipping and Freight

Travel and Tourism Industry

World Bank

ENVIRONMENTAL HISTORY

Afghanistan

Africa, Central

Africa, East

Africa, Southern

Africa, Western

The Balkans

Central Asia

Congo (Zaire) River

Danube River

France

Germany

Indus River

Lake Baikal

Lake Chad

Lake Victoria

Mediterranean Sea

Middle East

Nile River

Pakistan

Rhine River

Russia and the Soviet Union

Sahara

Sahel

List of Contributors

Abadie, Luis María
Basque Centre for Climate Change (BC3),
Spain
*European Union Greenhouse Gas Emission
Trading Scheme (EU ETS)* (co-author:
Ibon Galarraga)

Albright, Scott M.
University of Hawaii at Hilo
Warsaw, Poland

Anwana, EnoAbasi D.
University of Ghana
Migration (Africa) (co-authors: Samuel
N. A. Codjoe and Delali B. K. Dovie)

Awiti, Alex O.
Aga Khan University, Nairobi, Kenya
Education, Higher (Africa)

Bagaeen, Samer G.
University of Brighton,
United Kingdom
Dubai, United Arab Emirates

Barkemeyer, Ralf
University of Leeds, United Kingdom
Corporate Accountability (Africa) (co-author:
Jo-Anna Russon)

Barthel, Pierre-Arnaud
University of Paris-East—Marne-la-Vallée,
CNRS-Latts
Cairo, Egypt

Beinart, William
University of Oxford, United Kingdom
Africa, Southern

Birch, Eugenie L.
University of Pennsylvania
Urbanization (Europe) (co-authors:
Alexander M. Keating and Susan M.
Wachter)

Bleischwitz, Raimund
Wuppertal Institute for Climate,
Environment and Energy
Conflict Minerals (co-author: Lena Guesnet)

Bocchino, Clara
North-West University, Potchefstroom,
South Africa
Rural Development

Boone, Randall B.
Colorado State University, Fort Collins
Biological Corridors

Brade, Isolde
Leibniz Institute for Regional Geography,
Leipzig, Germany
Moscow, Russia (co-author: Tatyana G.
Nefedova)

Bromberg, Gidon
EcoPeace / Friends of the Earth Middle East
Transboundary Water Issues (co-author:
Jessica C. Marx)

Buckley, Ralf
Griffith University, Australia
Ecotourism

Castley, J. Guy
Griffith University, Australia
Parks and Preserves

Cater, Carl Iain
Aberystwyth University, United Kingdom
Travel and Tourism Industry (co-author:
   Tiffany Low)

Chiabai, Aline
Basque Center for Climate Change (BC3),
   Spain
Biodiversity Conservation

Cioc, Mark
University of California, Santa Cruz
Germany
Rhine River

Codjoe, Samuel N. A.
University of Ghana
Migration (Africa) (co-authors: Delali B. K.
   Dovie and EnoAbasi D. Anwana)

Conte, Christopher A.
Utah State University
Africa, East

Cumo, Christopher
Independent scholar, Canton, Ohio
Agriculture, Small-Scale
Diet and Nutrition

Davis, Diana K.
University of California at Davis
Middle East

Doevenspeck, Martin
University of Bayreuth, Germany
Goma, Democratic Republic of the Congo

Dovie, Delali B. K.
University of Ghana
Migration (Africa) (co-authors: Samuel N.
   A. Codjoe and EnoAbasi D. Anwana)

Eardley-Pryor, Roger
University of California, Santa Barbara
Lake Victoria

Eiselen, Sieg
University of South Africa
E-Waste

Enstad, Craig
Boston University
Lake Chad

Evered, Kyle T.
Michigan State University
The Balkans
Volga River

Forbes, William
Stephen F. Austin State University
London, United Kingdom

Fremuth, Michael Lysander
University of Cologne, Germany
European Union (EU) (co-author: Erik
   Pellander)

Galarraga, Ibon
Basque Centre for Climate Change (BC3),
   Spain
*European Union Greenhouse Gas Emission
   Trading Scheme (EU ETS)* (co-author:
   Luis María Abadie)

Giles-Vernick, Tamara
Institut Pasteur, France
Africa, Central

Grainger, Alan
University of Leeds,
    United Kingdom
Desertification (Africa)

Griffiths, Jesse
European Network on Debt and
    Development (Eurodad)
World Bank

Grobecker, Anna
EBS Business School, Germany
Shipping and Freight (co-author:
    Julia Wolf)

Guesnet, Lena
Bonn International Center for Conversion,
    Germany
Conflict Minerals (co-author: Raimund
    Bleischwitz)

Harms, Robert
Yale University
Congo (Zaire) River

Harper, Krista M.
University of Massachusetts,
    Amherst
Danube River

Hermanus, Mavis
University of the Witwatersrand,
    South Africa
Mining (Africa) (co-authors:
    Ingrid Watson and Tracy-Lynn
    Humby)

Humby, Tracy-Lynn
University of the Witwatersrand,
    South Africa
Mining (Africa) (co-authors: Ingrid Watson
    and Mavis Hermanus)

Ilesanmi, Adetokunbo O.
Obafemi Awolowo University, Ile-Ife, Nigeria
Lagos, Nigeria

Keating, Alexander M.
University of Pennsylvania
Urbanization (Europe) (co-authors: Eugenie
    L. Birch and Susan M. Wachter)

Kolb, Charles C.
National Endowment for the Humanities
Afghanistan

Lemanski, Charlotte
University College London
Cape Town, South Africa

Lide, James H.
History Associates, Incorporated
Scandinavia

Low, Tiffany
University of Bedfordshire, United
    Kingdom
Travel and Tourism Industry (co-author:
    Carl Iain Cater)

Lu, Jiang
Shanxi University, China
Energy Security (Europe)

MacKenzie, Catherine P.
University of Cambridge, United Kingdom
Rule of Law (Africa)

Majzoub, Tarek
Beirut Arab University, Lebanon
Urbanization (Western Asia and Northern Africa) (co-author: Fabienne Quilleré-Majzoub)

Malcolm, Rosalind
University of Surrey, United Kingdom
Rule of Law (European Union)

Marx, Jessica C.
EcoPeace / Friends of the Earth Middle East
Transboundary Water Issues (co-author: Gidon Bromberg)

McNamara, Nora
Missionary Sisters of the Holy Rosary
Microfinance

McNeill, J. R.
Georgetown University
Mediterranean Sea

Mughal, Muhammad Aurang Zeb
Durham University,
    United Kingdom
Pakistan (co-author: Anita M. Weiss)

Mwaniki, Fiona
Farmer Voice Radio (FVR), Nairobi, Kenya
Education, Environmental (co-authors: Robert B. Stevenson and Aravella Zachariou)

Nefedova, Tatyana G.
Institute of Geography, Russian Academy of Sciences
Moscow, Russia (co-author: Isolde Brade)

Njuki, Caroline Muthoni
Intergovernmental Authority on Development (IGAD)
African Union (AU) (co-author: J. Manyitabot Takang)
Immigrants and Refugees

O'Connor, Anthony M.
University College London
Tunis, Tunisia
Urbanization (Africa)

Oestigaard, Terje
The Nordic Africa Institute, Uppsala, Sweden
Nile River

Otiso, Kefa M.
Bowling Green State University
Nairobi, Kenya

Pattberg, Philipp
VU University Amsterdam
Public-Private Partnerships (Africa)

Pellander, Erik
University of Cologne, Germany
European Union (EU) (co-author: Michael Lysander Fremuth)

Pichura, Alexander
Pichura Consult—Architects
Architecture

Possehl, Gregory L.
University of Pennsylvania
Indus River

Poulsen, Bo
Aalborg University, Denmark
Fisheries

Quilleré-Majzoub, Fabienne
IODE—University of Rennes 1, France
Urbanization (Western Asia and Northern Africa) (co-author: Tarek Majzoub)

Qvenild, Marte
Norwegian Institute for Nature Research (NINA)
Svalbard Global Seed Vault

Reardon, Mitchell
Nordregio (Nordic Centre for Spatial Development), Stockholm, Sweden
Stockholm, Sweden (co-author: Peter Schmitt)

Russon, Jo-Anna
Queen's University Belfast
Corporate Accountability (Africa) (co-author: Ralf Barkemeyer)

Schmitt, Peter
Nordregio (Nordic Centre for Spatial Development), Stockholm, Sweden
Stockholm, Sweden (co-author: Mitchell Reardon)

Scholtz, Werner
North-West University, South Africa
Climate Change Refugees (Africa)

Smyntyna, Olena V.
Odessa I. I. Mechnikov National University, Ukraine
Ukraine

Stevenson, Robert B.
James Cook University, Cairns, Australia
Education, Environmental (co-authors: Fiona Mwaniki and Aravella Zachariou)

Takang, J. Manyitabot
University of Cologne, Germany
African Union (AU) (co-author: Caroline Muthoni Njuki)
International Conflict Resolution
Water Use and Rights (Africa)

Teplyakov, Victor K.
Seoul National University
Novosibirsk, Russia

Trumbull, Nathaniel S.
University of Connecticut
St. Petersburg, Russia

van Niekerk, Dewald
North-West University, South Africa
Disaster Risk Management

Vogiatzakis, Ioannis N.
Open University of Cyprus
Genetic Resources

Wachter, Susan M.
University of Pennsylvania
Urbanization (Europe) (co-authors: Alexander M. Keating and Eugenie L. Birch)

Washington, Sylvia Hood
Northwestern University
Africa, Western

Watson, Fiona J.
University of Dundee, United Kingdom
United Kingdom and Ireland

Watson, Ingrid
University of the Witwatersrand, South Africa
Mining (Africa) (co-authors: Tracy-Lynn Humby and Mavis Hermanus)

Weiner, Douglas R.
University of Arizona
Central Asia
Lake Baikal
Russia and the Soviet Union

Weiss, Anita M.
University of Oregon
Pakistan (co-author: Muhammad Aurang
   Zeb Mughal)

Wessels, Joshka
Lund University, Sweden
*Water Use and Rights (Middle East and
   North Africa)*

Whited, Tamara L.
Indiana University of Pennsylvania
France

Wolf, Julia
EBS Business School, Germany
Shipping and Freight (co-author: Anna
   Grobecker)

Zachariou, Aravella
Cyprus Pedagogical Institute, Nicosia
Education, Environmental (co-authors:
   Robert B. Stevenson and Fiona
   Mwaniki)

Berkshire Encyclopedia of Sustainability

Introduction to Afro-Eurasia: Assessing Sustainability

This volume—*Afro-Eurasia: Assessing Sustainability*—is the third of three *Encyclopedia of Sustainability* volumes devoted to a particular region. As with the previous two regional volumes, this volume covers a huge region in terms of both population and geographical size—so huge, in fact, that a large part of the region (China, India, and East and Southeast Asia) had to be covered separately in Volume 7. There are any number of conceivable ways to divide the world into three parts; none of them is wholly ideal and all inevitably involve compromise. As such, any division will seem somewhat arbitrary, which, in fact, it is—the same way that it is arbitrary that Australia is considered a continent, not a large island, while Greenland is considered an island and not a small continent.

What on Earth is Afro-Eurasia?

The term *Afro-Eurasia* designates the landmasses of Africa and Eurasia, together with their adjacent islands, as a single unit. Thinking about Afro-Eurasia as a large "system" may have its limitations, but it is nonetheless useful in the study of anything (such as ecology or, indeed, sustainability) where the conventional way of defining and separating the continents of Africa, Asia, and Europe is not particularly helpful. Attempting to study the complex ecology of a long-settled place such as the Mediterranean basin, for example, is not easy without looking at the European, African, and Asian—the Afro-Eurasian—shores as a functional unit. Some geographers have even gone so far as to suggest that sub-Saharan Africa should be considered its own continent; northern Africa should be included as part of the rest of Eurasia, separated as it is, both physically and ideologically, from sub-Saharan Africa by the Sahara. Plants, animals, and people have all migrated relatively easily within this region since the origins of the human species, which has had huge repercussions on everything from evolutionary ecology to warfare to the spread of ideas and immunity to disease—the last of which was to have disastrous repercussions when people from Afro-Eurasia encountered people living in the Americas who lacked immunity from the diseases the newcomers brought with them.

The Earth's single largest landmass has a name problem, though; "Afro-Eurasia" has yet to catch on with the general public. This is unfortunate, because geologists have named several large landmasses, such as Pangaea, Gondwana, and Laurasia, that existed before the Earth's tectonic plates settled into the continents with which we are familiar. The name Pangaea, especially, is relatively well known. Why, then, should the Earth's greatest current landmass not have a proper name?

It is not easy to summarize this region beyond geographic terminology. It encompasses some of the Earth's greatest deserts (the Sahara, the Kalahari, the Namib, the Taklimakan, the Arab, and the Gobi), the greatest mountain ranges (the Alps, the Atlas, the Caucasus, the Himalaya), and the greatest lakes (Lake Baikal in Russia, the Earth's most voluminous; the string of Great Lakes in Africa's Rift Valley). It is where Nobel Peace Prizes are awarded, and it has seen some of the planet's most brutal and destructive warfare and pillaging, from Chinggis (Genghis) Khan's rampages across Eurasia to those of Nazi Germany's Wehrmacht in World War II to the Balkans conflicts in the 1990s to today's child armies in war-torn parts of Africa.

Cooperation

Out of this shared sense of the disasters of war comes (we hope) a belief that cooperation is necessary. The European Union (EU), one of the world's foremost leaders in environmental policy and a subject of an article in this volume, was forged, in part, from the European Coal and Steel Community, a consortium of European industries intent on avoiding the warmongering mistakes of its members' collective recent past. The African Union (AU; also the subject of an article in this volume), meanwhile, came about as a desire on the part of pan-Africanists such as W. E. B. Du Bois to unite not only the nations of Africa but to include members of the far-flung African diaspora—largely separated by war and slavery—into the fold.

Not all cooperative unions have been entirely benign, however, especially where sustainability is concerned. The World Bank, also formed (in 1944, near the war's end) as a bulwark against the ravages of World War II, has an unfortunate history of favoring the interests of wealthy nations over those, particularly in Africa, that are not wealthy, although it can also be argued that the Bank has done much good and has been the subject of many reforms in recent years. Still, as author Jesse Griffiths writes in his article on the subject,

> high-income countries hold a majority of seats on the Bank's executive board. African countries hold only three board seats, while European countries currently hold nine. Indeed, Luxembourg (population 509,074) has a greater voting share than Uganda (population 35.9 million). This imbalance is most striking at the International Development Association, which lends to only low-income countries. Those countries have only 11 percent of the vote, and eleven countries in sub-Saharan Africa actually suffered a reduction of their voting shares in the 2010 reforms.

Clearly, there is a need for improvement in large development agencies such as the World Bank, which is where individuals and small organizations often come into play. This is a vast and diverse region, after all, with many talented people working to improve the common lot of humanity and our shared environment.

Cities Old and New, Dangerous and Green

Afro-Eurasia is simultaneously the site of some of what several compilers of sustainability indexes consider to be the "greenest," most "livable," and "sustainable" cities on Earth, such as Copenhagen, London, and Stockholm; some of the Earth's oldest—and therefore most sustainable in the basic sense that they've lasted for ages—cities, such as Rome, Cairo, and Tunis, the site of ancient Carthage, nemesis of Rome; and a number of the world's most dangerous cities, such as Mogadishu, the lawless (in relative terms) capital of Somalia, and Kinshasa, capital

of the Democratic Republic of the Congo (DRC). Even in Kinshasa, however, there are rays of hope: for example, a program organized by the United Nations Food and Agriculture Organization (FAO) to establish urban garden programs in cities of the developing world has had great success there. The FAO estimated, in its 2010 report *Growing Greener Cities,* that the program has helped thousands of urban vegetable gardeners improve their operations, and that urban gardeners in Kinshasa were able to meet 65 percent of the city's produce needs as a result. This is a case where, at times, the intervention of a large international body such as the FAO can help individuals help themselves in a very real way. The AU and the UN also have been instrumental in stemming some of the worst of the violence in war-torn regions.

Another, much smaller, city in the DRC, Goma, is the subject of an article in this volume; Goma was selected out of the galaxy of larger cities in tropical Africa due to the fact that it is an example of one of the least "sustainable" cities in the world. The majority of cities in tropical Africa—truly a galaxy of cities—are totally overlooked by the modern, connected global academic and business network; please see the article "Urbanization—Africa" for more on this fascinating topic. Contrary to the situation in other famously unsustainable cities such as Las Vegas, Nevada, or Phoenix, Arizona, however, this unsustainability has little to do with resource overconsumption by its residents. Rather, Goma is unique in facing the very real possibility of a massive natural cataclysm in the not-too-distant future. The rapidly growing city, its ranks swollen by the refugees from violent conflict in the region, abuts two active volcanoes and is built on a lake filled with potentially lethal gases dissolved in its depths as a result of the region's volcanism. The only places that potentially face a comparable dire future are those places faced with the possibility of nuclear assault by belligerent neighbors. People flock to Goma, however, because of the lure of jobs, relative safety from conflicts in the surrounding regions, and extremely fertile volcanic soil. There is ironically a well-known saying in Swahili that means, essentially, "Let's go to Goma to have a peaceful and easy life." It is, therefore, a classic case study for a book on sustainability.

Migration, Conflict, and Consumption

Why people choose to live where they live is part of the theme of this book, because it has everything to do with the "sustainability" choices that people make (or are forced to make). It is becoming increasingly less common for people to settle down in the place where they were raised. The forces that are behind this are varied and often interrelated, spanning environmental change through to economics. Indeed, migration in the modern era is made increasingly possible—and desirable—thanks in part to improved telecommunications that allow people to stay in touch easily with loved ones from afar. Also, as knowledge of the world outside spreads, either through improved education or better access to the Internet, or both, so does impatience with the status quo. The uprisings across the Arab world that started in 2010 that have come to be known as the Arab Spring are a case in point. The future of the region remains uncertain at the time of this writing, especially in Syria, which has descended into a civil war in all but name. One thing that is for certain is that, with a few exceptions (notably the wall erected by Israel to keep Palestinians contained), migration is getting easier and people will continue to move to, from, and within the Middle East, Africa, Europe, and beyond.

Africa was the site of the world's first mass migration, as hunter-gatherers left present-day Ethiopia for distant lands. The author Jared Diamond has made the point that because of the relative sameness of daylight and climate along Eurasia's long east-west axis, agricultural technologies have been able to pass more easily across the vast region over the millennia; migrants didn't have to make the repeated adaptations to new climatic conditions as they moved laterally across the continent that they would have had to make while traveling up and down, for instance, the Americas.

Migration continues apace today. In Europe this is made possible by the existence of the EU and its porous national borders. People from eastern Europe, Turkey, the Middle East, and Russia and its former satellites routinely travel to the wealthier nations of western and northern Europe for permanent or part-time work. In Africa the situation is a bit more complicated. As the authors of "Migration (Africa)" in this volume point out,

> Labor and trade mobility have traditionally dictated migration as a global phenomenon, although war and conflict in Africa have resulted in refugees as unintended migrants. Although many of the efforts to minimize migration in Africa have been through social and economic instruments such as welfare support programs, emigration laws, and trade regulations, the sustainability of these efforts may be constrained by the physical environmental resource base due to extensive

occupation and changing land use (i.e., land available for farming or agriculture).

The causes of these conflicts (and the migrations that they spawn) are, in many ways, directly related to the distribution of natural resources. For instance, the Darfur conflict that erupted in 2003, claiming between 200,000 and 500,000 lives, stems from interwoven religious, social, and political factors. The United Nations Environment Programme (UNEP) argues that climate change is at the heart of the conflict: prolonged periods of drought and famine, the spreading desertification toward the south, and decreases in rainfall have all forced nomadic herders to encroach on sedentary farmers' land, with disastrous results. The splitting of South Sudan from the rest of Sudan in July of 2011 appeared to be amicable and was initially met with much celebration within the new country, but the situation has since degenerated because of access to resources such as oil along disputed border territories.

The killing of thirty-four striking miners in August of 2012 by police forces in South Africa (regarded by many as the most progressive and stable nation in sub-Saharan Africa) demonstrates graphically that natural resources—and what the world's markets are willing to pay for them—can be of the utmost importance to a place's stability, even in a nation like South Africa, where the rule of law is relatively strong. This is a global problem, tied in, as it is, with global trade. As the authors of "Conflict Minerals" write,

> [T]he combination of open access to many natural resources and weakness of governments or institutions allows conflicts to arise far beyond normal market competition. "Lootable" commodities, in particular, offer to unscrupulous parties the means to enrich themselves and finance their operations. Such commodities are often categorized as contraband and contribute to prolonging wars.

It bears mentioning that many of these African nations whose citizens suffer such deprivation, often because of what has been called the "resource curse," are also, from a "carbon footprint" standpoint, some of the world's smallest consumers of resources. Europe, by contrast, while almost universally looked upon with admiration for many of its various nations' generally good environmental records, has, along with the United States, Canada, and Australia, one of the world's biggest carbon footprints. According to a report called "The Carbon Footprint of Nations," the tiny European nation of Luxembourg had the world's highest per capita carbon footprint, while

Ethiopia had the lowest. Such comparisons do need to be handled with some care, because Luxembourg has a small population of just over half a million people while Ethiopia has nearly 85 million, but it does nonetheless say something about the relationship between carbon emissions and wealth; those half-million people living in Luxembourg have nearly double the gross domestic product (GDP) of Ethiopia (US$58 billion versus US$31 billion in 2011). We all must learn this lesson to avoid slipping into complacency. A high quality of life, even for people with an enviable public transportation system, access to unpolluted landscapes, and a generally safe and healthy existence, does not necessarily equate to a squeaky clean carbon footprint. This is simply and algebraically a matter of wealth, population, and access to technology, all of which Europe has. As Richard York discussed in his article "I = P × A × T Equation" in Volume 6 of this series (*Measurements, Indicators, and Research Methods for Sustainability*), the I = P × A × T equation (pronounced eye-pat) specifies that environmental **I**mpacts are the multiplicative product of **P**opulation, **A**ffluence (per capita consumption), and **T**echnology (impact per unit of consumption). Another more recent and less technical sounding word for this phenomenon is "affluenza."

Although numbers don't lie, it helps us to identify where we have room for improvement. (It should be mentioned, however, that numbers can be misinterpreted any number of ways.) The lesson is that our ability to live sustainably is often the result of where we live—or where we've migrated to—and more critically this is often related to how we live. Equally important is the fact that individuals are able to make individual choices, at least within certain limits. The rich environmental, social, and economic diversity inherent within Afro-Eurasia thus provides a rich set of examples and issues that highlight just about every aspect of sustainability. We hope that readers will be able to absorb some of the material in these pages (as well as others in this series) to find new ways to make daily living a more sustainable thing: no matter if you live in Copenhagen, Tunis, St. Petersburg, Goma, or Kinshasa, a suburb in France, South Africa, or Egypt, or any of the multitude of places in between.

The Editors

Portions of this introduction were drawn from the article "Afro-Eurasia" by Ross E. Dunn, from the *Berkshire Encyclopedia of World History* (second edition). Berkshire Publishing, 2010.

Acknowledgments

Berkshire Publishing would like to thank the following people for their help and advice in various matters. In a project of this scope there are many to acknowledge, of course, but these people deserve our special thanks:

Dinara Ziganshina, *UNESCO Centre for Water Law, Policy and Science, University of Dundee*

Ibon Galarraga, *Basque Centre for Climate Change (BC3)*

Ralf Buckley, *Griffith University*

Marco Amati, *Macquarie University*

Terje Oestigaard, *The Nordic Africa Institute*

Frederick R. Steiner, *The University of Texas*

Elizabeth Allison, *California Institute of Integral Studies*

Nazim Muradov, *Florida Solar Energy Center*

Frank Rosillo-Calle, *Imperial College London*

Molly Anderson, *College of the Atlantic*

John Manyitabot Takang, *University of Cologne*

Riki Therivel, *Levett-Therivel Sustainability Consultants*

Warren Neilson, *World Green Building Council*

Tamara Bekefi, *Daedalus Strategic Advising*

Roshan Man Bajracharya, *Kathmandu University*

Christopher Cumo, *independent scholar, Canton, Ohio*

Evandro C. Santos, *Jackson State University*

Tony J. Pitcher, *University of British Columbia*

Anthony O'Connor, *University College London*

Alan Clarke, *University of Pannonia*

Verena Winiwarter, *University of Vienna*

Bob Stevenson, *The Cairns Institute & School of Education, James Cook University*

J. Andrew Grant, *Queen's University (Canada)*

Christine Richmond, *Queen's University (Canada)*

Charles Willner, *independent researcher*

Peter Schmitt, *Nordregio—Nordic Centre for Spatial Development*

David A. Sonnenfeld, *Wageningen University, State University of New York, College of Environmental Science and Forestry (SUNY-ESF)*

Richard J. T. Klein, *Stockholm Environment Institute*

James L. A. Webb Jr., *Colby College*

Afghanistan

30.4 million est. pop. 2012

Environmental management and sustainable development have not been a primary focus for the Afghan government, which has been engaged in international and civil conflict for the past thirty years. Despite substantial mineral resources and a newly expanded highway network, Afghanistan continues to struggle with a lack of environmental management programs, an absence of sustainable energy resources, and widespread disparities in income and the well-being of its people, all resulting in a discouraging outlook for sustainability.

Afghanistan (Land of the Afghans), formerly the Republic of Afghanistan (called Jomhuri-ye Afghanistan in Dari Persian, Da Afghanistan Jamhawriyat in Pashto), is a landlocked southwest Asian nation whose current boundaries were established during the late nineteenth century in the context of the "Great Game," a rivalry between the British, then occupying India on the Asian subcontinent, and the Russians in Central Asia; the British called Afghanistan the Northwest Frontier. It is bounded on the northeast by the People's Republic of China, on the north by three former Soviet republics—now members of the Commonwealth of Independent States (Turkmenistan, Uzbekistan, and Tajikistan)—on the east and south by Pakistan, and on the west by Iran. The total length of Afghanistan's borders with its six neighbors is 5,529 kilometers. The country covers 652,230 square kilometers, an area approximately the size of the US state of Texas or the United Kingdom. It is shaped similarly to a clenched right fist with the thumb extended to the northeast, the narrow Wakhan Corridor leading to China. Major physical features include the Amu Darya (the ancient Oxus) River, forming much of the northern international

border; the steppes and the Turkistan Plains in the north; a mountainous center and northeast dominated by the Hindu Kush mountain range (the western extension of the Himalaya) and the Pamirs; the Sistan Basin in the southwest, through which the Helmand River flows; and deserts to the far west (Dasht-i Margo) and south (Registan). Much of the rain that falls in Afghanistan does not make it to the sea. Except for the Kabul River, which flows eastward to join the Indus and goes from there to the Arabian Sea, the other rivers (including the Amu Darya, most of which flows northwestward into the rapidly diminished Aral Sea, although much of the water evaporates before reaching that point) end in inland seas, swamps, or salt flats.

Administratively, the nation has thirty-two *velayat* (provinces). United Nations (UN) data list the major ethnic groups as Pashtuns (54 percent of the population), Tajiks (concentrated in the north, 27 percent), Uzbeks (8 percent), and Hazara (7 percent) (US CIA 2012). Others include Kyrgyz, Arabs, Baluchis, Turkmen, Nuristani, Aimak, Brahui, Sikhs, and Jews. The Pashtun tribes, both sedentary farmers and nomadic pastoralists, inhabit principally the southern and eastern parts of Afghanistan. Tajik farmers and village craftspeople live in Kabul and Badakhshan *velayat* to the northeast and in Herat to the far west.

Demography and Poverty

Data on Afghanistan are not readily available. The US Central Intelligence Agency (US CIA), however, has compiled and published the following data in their 2012 *World Factbook:* the official languages of Afghanistan are Southern Pashto, spoken by 35 percent of the population, and the Dari dialect of Persian (Eastern Farsi or Dari), spoken by 50 percent of the population. Turkic languages (primarily Turkmen and Uzbek) are also spoken by 11 percent of the population, as are thirty other minor languages (US CIA 2012). A considerable proportion of the population is bilingual. Approximately 85 percent of the population are Sunni Muslim (Hanafi school), and 14 percent are Shiite (primarily in the north), with the remainder being Ismaili Muslims, Hindus, Sikhs, or of other religions.

There has never been an official, comprehensive census, but the 2012 population estimate for Afghanistan is 30.4 million with an annual population growth of 2.22 percent and a birthrate of 39.3 births/1,000 people (US CIA 2012). About 42.1 percent of the population is under the age of 14, 52.3 percent is between the ages of 15 and 64, and only 2.4 percent is 65 or older; life expectancy at birth is below 50 years for both sexes. A predominantly rural agrarian country, the urban population is 23 percent of the total. Kabul, the capital, had an estimated 3.573 million inhabitants in 2009, a 150 percent increase in ten years. A significant migration from rural to urban areas, primarily for economic reasons (environmental degradation and unemployment), has increased the numbers of inhabitants in Kabul, Kandahar, Herat, Mazar-i-Sharif, and smaller cities. At least 85 percent of Afghanistan's population was born since the Soviet invasion in 1969 (CSIS 2010). The percentage of the population that is classified as living in poverty has fluctuated but, in 2012, is at least 33 percent (World Bank 2012). In 2008, it was 36 percent; in 2007, it was 42 percent; and in 2005 it was 33 percent. Approximately 20 million people in Afghanistan are consistently impoverished.

Water and Irrigation

There are four hydrographic zones in Afghanistan: (1) the northern basin, which covers roughly a quarter of the territory, encompasses the Amu Darya River, its tributaries, and rivers north of the Hindu Kush that drain toward the Aral Sea; (2) the eastern basin, which covers around 12 percent of the territory, encompasses the Kabul River and its tributaries, which connect to the Indus River; (3) the southeastern basin, which covers roughly half of the territory, encompasses the Helmand River and tributaries draining into swamps in Sistan; and (4) the western basin, which covers around 12 percent of the territory, encompasses the Hari Rud and Murgab rivers, which drain into adjacent Turkmenistan. The region around Kabul faces a serious depletion of surface water and groundwater due to increasing exploitation by an expanding population, construction demands, and recent severe droughts (most recently in the summer of 2011). Only about 12 percent of Afghanistan's land surface is arable; agriculture, which is heavily dependent on irrigation, is

responsible for up to 99 percent of water consumption, mostly by floodwater irrigation. Rivers provide an estimated 85 percent of the irrigation water. There are four types of irrigation systems: (1) *kareze* or *qanat* (hand-dug unlined tunnels that tap underground aquifers for surface irrigation); (2) informal traditional communal systems (village-level, small-scale surface water systems); (3) informal highly structured communal systems (large-scale, multicommunal, valleywide surface water systems); and (4) formal highly structured systems (large-scale, "state oriented," surface water systems associated with major rivers, such as the Helmand River and the Hari Rud River) (Rout 2008). Violent flooding wreaks havoc on these types of irrigation; hence traditional stone and masonry walls are in constant need of maintenance, and there are only a few small modern concrete structures for flood control. Recent quantitative and qualitative data on water supplies and irrigation are nonexistent, and older information is unreliable at best. A national study and inventory of irrigation systems, management, flow rates, distribution, and sustainability must be undertaken as water is a critical, irreplaceable natural resource. Flood control and hydroelectric power capabilities must be assessed in order to determine the sustainability of water as a resource.

Ecology and Subsistence

The northern plains are a major agricultural region, accounting for 80 percent of the grain crops; the southwestern plateau is a desert and semidesert except for the irrigation agriculture associated with the Helmand River; the central highlands are dominated by the Hindu Kush and traversed by a few high mountain passes. Nearly half of the total land area lies above 2,000 meters and has a subarctic mountain climate with dry, cold winters and short, cool summers. The semiarid steppe lowlands, on the other hand, have cold winters and hot summers, and the southwest has a hot, arid, desert climate. Annual precipitation varies from 75 millimeters in the desert to 1,280 millimeters in the Hindu Kush. The elevation extremes are along the Amu Darya River (258 meters) and at Noeshak, the highest Hindu Kush peak in Afghanistan (7,485 meters). Climate, flora, and fauna vary with elevation, and temperatures range greatly. Agricultural products include wheat, rice, fruits, nuts, and vegetables; 14 percent of the land is arable, 46 percent consists of permanent pastures, 37 percent are deserts, and approximately 3 percent are heavily exploited forests. Even with the relatively small amount of arable land, agriculture remains the main occupation of most Afghans, despite the damage to cultivated land during nearly thirty years of warfare.

Grazing is also significant in the rural economy, with fat-tailed sheep, a staple of Afghan life, providing meat and fat for food and skins and wool for clothing. Soil degradation, deforestation, erosion, and overgrazing often result in severe flooding during seasonal rains and winter snowmelts. In northern Afghanistan, the World Food Programme distributed food to people who lost their harvest in 2011 due to a lack of rainfall. About 2.8 million people were affected by the drought in fourteen provinces of the country, and a harsh 2011–2012 winter made the situation even more difficult (WFP 2012).

Economy and Drugs

As of 2012, Afghanistan's economy is still recovering from decades of conflict but has improved significantly since 2001 largely because of the infusion of international assistance, the recovery of the agricultural sector, and growth in the service sector (US CIA 2012). Despite this progress, Afghanistan is extremely poor and, being landlocked, is highly dependent on foreign aid. Much of the population continues to suffer from shortages of housing, clean water, electricity, medical care, and employment opportunities above menial labor and agriculture.

Opium and hashish, fruits and nuts, handwoven carpets, Karakul lambskins, textiles, and gemstones are the main exports; machinery, foodstuffs, manufactured goods, and petroleum products are the main imports. Some small-scale manufacturers produce cotton and other fabrics, soap, furniture, shoes, fertilizer, cement, and processed agricultural goods. The opium poppy, grown mainly for the international illegal drug trade, is the most important cash crop, and the country is the world's largest producer of opium. Although poppy cultivation was relatively stable in 2010 (119,000 hectares were cultivated), a poppy blight affecting the major cultivation areas in that year reduced opium production to 3,200 tonnes, down more than 40 percent from 2009. An estimated 1.2 million Afghans—including 110,000 women—are addicted to heroin (UNODC 2011 and 2012; US CIA 2012). The Taliban, other antigovernment groups, warlords, and some corrupt sectors of Afghan society participate in and profit from this illicit trade.

Transportation

Much of the nation's road and highway network was built during the 1960s but was not maintained or was destroyed during ongoing wars starting in 1979. A new expanded highway network was built in the first decade of the millennium to accommodate the increase in domestic and international commerce and the exploitation of Afghanistan's mineral wealth. A road and tunnel under the Salang Pass, built by the Russians in 1964, still provides a short, all-weather route between northern and southern Afghanistan. By 2006, the road system covered nearly 42,000 kilometers (12,350 kilometers of paved and 29,500 kilometers of unpaved roads); this system must be sustained and expanded (US CIA 2012). Pack animals remain an important means of transport in the interior. Railroad construction in Afghanistan has consistently been hampered by the different gauges of track used in each of the surrounding countries (several Central Asian republics, India, Pakistan, Iran, and China). Currently the only completed line, begun in January 2010, is between Termez, Uzbekistan, and the northern Afghan city of Mazar-i-Sharif and is operated temporarily by Uzbekistan's national railway, Uzbekistan Temir Yulla. There are plans to extend the line to Kabul and then to Torkhan, on the eastern border, to connect with Pakistan Railways. China Metallurgical Group Corporation is financing the work, which is expected to be completed by 2014. The 1,200-kilometer-long Amu Darya River can accommodate riverine vessels up to 500 tonnes. Air transport in Afghanistan is provided by the national carrier, Ariana Afghan Airlines, and small private companies (Kam Air, Pamir, and Safi) as well as several international carriers. There are fifty-three major airports but fewer than twenty are paved and capable of handling modern commercial aircraft. By 2009, there were only 466 kilometers of gas pipelines in the country.

Mineral Wealth

Afghanistan's unexploited petroleum and ferrous and nonferrous mineral wealth is worth between $900 billion and $3 trillion (Ali and Shroder 2011; Brookings

Institution 2010). The US Geological Survey estimated in 2006 that northern Afghanistan has approximately 1.6 billion barrels of crude oil, 445 billion cubic meters of natural gas, and 562 million barrels of natural gas liquids. Afghanistan signed an oil exploration contract with China National Petroleum Corporation for the development of three oil fields along the Amu Darya. Substantial amounts of copper, gold, coal, iron ore, lithium, rare earth minerals, and gemstones (lapis lazuli, emeralds, amethyst, serpentine, and garnet) are also available for potential exploitation.

In 2007, a controversial thirty-year lease on the Aynak copper mine was granted to the China Metallurgical Group for $3 billion, making it the largest foreign investment and private business venture in Afghanistan's history (AGS and BGS 2005; Vogt 2010). This subterranean resource is also the locus of a major Hellenistic archaeological site and a Buddhist city currently undergoing archaeological excavation.

The Environmental Consequences of War

Decades of warfare have scarred Afghanistan's people and the environment in which they live. Some multilateral environmental agreements (MEAs)—international legal agreements regarding environmental conservation and management—are suspended, terminated, or are inapplicable in times of armed conflict. One such MEA, the Convention on Civil Liability for Damage Resulting from Activities Dangerous to the Environment (1993), explicitly states in article 8 that "[t]he operator shall not be liable under this Convention for damage which he proves . . . was caused by an act of war, hostilities, civil war, insurrection or a natural phenomenon of an exceptional, inevitable and irresistible character" (Council of Europe 1993). Gaps like this in international environmental laws make processing war crimes difficult.

Since the (re-)commencement of war in October 2001, over ten thousand villages in Afghanistan and their surrounding environments have been devastated by armed conflict. Destruction of water infrastructure has led to leaks, bacterial contamination, and water theft. Afghanistan was once one of the world's most important migratory thoroughfares for birds, but the frequent discharge of explosives has disrupted migratory patterns. Refugees taking shelter in the mountains use large, endangered, and potentially valuable animals such as leopards as bartering tools. Pollution from explosives has entered the air, soil, and water. People and livestock are vulnerable to substances such as cyclonite and rocket fuel, which have drastically increased cancer rates and thyroid damage, respectively. Land mines left behind in

Afghanistan continue to kill civilian men, women, and children (Enzler 2006). There is little substantive and reliable data, however, on the full extent of damage to Afghanistan's environment as a result of armed conflict. Some major research is still needed.

Sustainability and Outlook

The three pillars of sustainable development are environment, economy, and society. Afghanistan has significant problems in each. Environmental management is negatively impacted by the absence of national or regional management plans, by natural resource depletion, diminishing freshwater resources, and a lack of biodiversity due to the overexploitation of arable land and dependence on a few soil-depleting crops. Economically, there is an absence of sustainable energy resources, particularly electricity. Other problems threatening the country's economic sustainability are greenhouse emissions, toxic substance wastes, the absence of sustainable agricultural resources (causing food shortages), a need for food security (the nation struggles to produce sufficient crops to feed its growing population, and terrorist activities diminish supplies even further), and a shortage of educational and economic opportunities for Afghanistan's citizens. The social dimension is characterized by widespread disparities in the well-being of people (especially in terms of economy, ethnic background, and gender); substantial rural and urban poverty; increasing urban migration; a dearth of security and social justice; forced labor and sex trafficking; and increasing drug production and domestic consumption. Afghanistan's living standards are among the lowest in the world, and it is second only to Somalia on the Transparency International's Corruption Index (CSIS 2010).

Afghanistan's sovereignty is in peril due to a weak central government and an inability to extend the rule of law to all parts of the country, posing challenges to future economic growth. Criminality, economic corruption, the near collapse of Kabul Bank due to unsecured "loans," struggles over the control of opium production and distribution, feudal warlordism, and "on and off" expulsion of foreign aid and humanitarian nongovernmental organizations (NGOs) are paralleled by persistent incursions into Afghanistan by Taliban and Haqqani from Pakistan, resulting in the prolonged presence of US and North American Treaty Organization (NATO) troops in the country for security and the training of Afghan police and military. The outlook for sustainability in Afghanistan remains clouded.

Charles C. KOLB
National Endowment for the Humanities

See also Central Asia; Conflict Minerals; Immigrants and Refugees; International Conflict Resolution; Middle East; Pakistan; Rural Development; Russia and the Soviet Union; Water Use and Rights (Middle East)

FURTHER READING

Afghanistan Geological Survey (AGS), & British Geological Survey (BGS). (2005). Documents associated with Aynak Tender: Anyak information package. Kabul, Afghanistan: Afghanistan Geological Survey.

Ali, Saleem H., & Shroder, John F. (2011). *Afghanistan's mineral fortune: Multinational influence and development in a post-war economy*. (Research paper series C). Burlington, VT: Institute for Environmental Diplomacy and Security, University of Vermont. Retrieved April 15, 2012, from http://www.uvm.edu/ieds/sites/default/files/IEDSAfghanistan2011.pdf

Barfield, Thomas J. (2010). *Afghanistan: A cultural and political history*. (Princeton studies in Muslim politics). Princeton, NJ: Princeton University Press.

Brookings Institution. (2010, June 16). Deposits could aid ailing Afghanistan. Retrieved April 15, 2012, from http://www.brookings.edu/opinions/2010/0616_afghanistan_minerals_ohanlon

Center for Strategic and International Studies (CSIS). (2010, April 26). Agriculture, food, and poverty in Afghanistan. Retrieved April 15, 2012, from http://csis.org/publication/agriculture-food-and-poverty-afghanistan

Council of Europe. (1993). Convention on Civil Liability for Damage Resulting from Activities Dangerous to the Environment. Retrieved May 17, 2012, from http://www.ecolex.org/server2.php/libcat/docs/TRE/Multilateral/En/TRE001166.txt

Dupree, Louis. (1980). *Afghanistan*. (Rev. ed.). Princeton, NJ: Princeton University Press.

Enzler, S. M. (2006). Environmental effects of warfare. Retrieved May 10, 2012, from http://www.lenntech.com/environmental-effects-war.htm#ixzz1uU8gBzEd

Nytrop, Richard F., & Seekins, Donald M. (Eds.). (1986). *Afghanistan: A country study* (5th ed.). Washington, DC: United States Government Printing Office.

Rashid, Ahmed. (2010). *Taliban: Militant Islam, oil and fundamentalism in central Asia* (2nd ed.). New Haven, CT: Yale University Press.

Rout, Bob. (2008). *Water management, livestock and the opium economy: How the water flows: A typology of irrigation systems in Afghanistan*. Kabul, Afghanistan: Afghanistan Research and Evaluation Unit. Retrieved April 15, 2012, from http://www.areu.org.af/Uploads/EditionPdfs/811E-Typology%20of%20Irrigation%20Systems.pdf

United Nations Office on Drugs and Crime (UNODC). (2011). Afghanistan opium survey 2011. Retrieved April 15, 2012, from http://www.unodc.org/documents/crop-monitoring/Afghanistan/ORAS_report_2011.pdf

United Nations Office on Drugs and Crime (UNODC). (2012). Afghanistan. Retrieved April 15, 2012, from http://www.unodc.org/afghanistan/index.html

United States Central Intelligence Agency (US CIA). (2012). World factbook: Afghanistan. Retrieved April 15, 2012, from https://www.cia.gov/library/publications/the-world-factbook/geos/af.html

Vogt, Heidi. (2010, November 14). Chinese mine in Afghanistan threatens ancient find. Retrieved April 15, 2012, from http://www.msnbc.msn.com/id/40181935/ns/technology_and_science-science/t/chinese-mine-afghanistan-threatens-ancient-find/

World Bank. (2012). Afghanistan. Retrieved April 15, 2012, from http://data.worldbank.org/country/afghanistan

World Food Programme (WFP). (2012). Afghanistan: Food for drought-affected Afghans. Retrieved April 15, 2012, from http://www.wfp.org/countries/afghanistan

Africa, Central

Central Africa encompasses a huge expanse of territory of more than 7.7 million square kilometers stretching from the Sahara in the north to the Kalahari Desert in the south. This geopolitical region includes Burundi, the Central African Republic, the Republic of the Congo, the Democratic Republic of the Congo, Equatorial Guinea, Gabon, Rwanda, Angola, São Tomé and Príncipe, Zambia, and Zimbabwe. The region faces several environmental threats, including the unmanaged exploitation of the region's rain forest.

Central Africa's environment is marked by several defining geographic features: two major river basins, the Congo and the Zambezi; a vast equatorial rain forest; and two savannas bordering that forest, one in the north and one in the south. The rain forest is one of the world's largest, extending over 2 million square kilometers from southern Cameroon and the Central African Republic throughout the Congo River basin to the mouth of the Congo River. The northern savanna stretches from the edge of the Sahara through much of Cameroon, the Central African Republic, and Sudan and South Sudan (an independent nation as of July of 2011); the southern savanna extends from the mouth of the Congo to the Kalahari Desert.

Biological Diversity and History to 1400

Central Africa boasts great diversity in its plant and animal life and also has abundant mineral resources. The rain forests are of several types: monodominant (single-species) forest with very tall trees and scant understory; montane forest (moist, cool zones dominated by coniferous trees); semideciduous mixed forest of prized

mahoganies, ebony, and the edible bush mango; dense forest with tangled understories on marshy soil; and raffia palm forest in flooded areas (Richards 1996). The central African forest contains more than seven thousand species of flowering plants. Rainfall is generally very high, topping 1,800 millimeters annually in some locations. Animal populations include such charismatic species as elephants, bongo antelope, sitatunga (an aquatic antelope), forest buffalo, gorillas, and leopards. Gold and diamond deposits are found in some parts of the forest as well. The southern savanna is also varied; there are well-watered woodlands with highly fertile soils, semiarid zones prone to drought and food shortages, and highlands in Zimbabwe veined with rich gold reserves. The northern savanna ranges from open grasslands and dry forests, interspersed with lush gallery forests (forests that grow along waterways in areas otherwise devoid of forests), to more arid, scrubby zones closer to the Sahara. Elephants, lions, now-dwindling populations of rhinos, and baboons are among the savanna mammalian populations.

Biological diversity in central Africa is the result of long-term natural and human processes, and ecologists are only beginning to understand the complex interrelations between the forest, climatic and seasonal changes, wildlife, and people. Storms, landslides, flooding, and the migration and feeding of such mammals as elephants significantly affect the ecology of central Africa. Although most of central Africa has never been densely populated, its people have long interacted with and fundamentally shaped its diverse ecological features by hunting, trapping, gathering, farming, fishing, mining, and logging. Human beings have lived in and exploited central African environments since very early times. About eight thousand years ago, Sudanic peoples living in the northern savannas began to cultivate the first domesticated cereals in Africa (sorghum and millet), and they number among the first farmers in the tropics. Some scholars have hypothesized that while it took more than four thousand years for these farmers to begin intensive cultivation, they effectively transformed the region's dry woodlands into open grasslands. During this same period, some of these people acquired domesticated animals, including cattle, sheep, and dogs (Eggert 1993).

Human habitation in the rain forest has not been dated, but by the end of the last millennium BCE, forest inhabitants had developed a variety of ways of exploiting their diverse environment: They farmed bananas, yams, and other crops, hunted elephants and other game, raised animals, and gathered fruits, leaves, honey, medicinal plants, and building materials. They thus helped to influence the forest's composition by clearing lands, dispersing seeds, and encouraging particular plants to flourish. This history of cultivation is closely tied to the expansion of the Bantu-speaking peoples, a two-thousand-year process in which people, the Bantu language family, agriculture, and iron-making techniques expanded from western Africa through the equatorial rain forest and into the southern savannas, eastern Africa, and southern Africa (Bailey et al. 1989, 62–63). This process most likely ended sometime between 500 and 1000 CE. The introduction of iron tools throughout central Africa in farming regions caused populations to grow rapidly and to alter the social relationships that supported their environmental practices. By 1000 CE, forest specialists developed associations with Bantu-speaking agriculturalists, supplying forest products such as meat, honey, and fruits in exchange for iron implements and cultivated foods such as bananas, introduced from Southeast Asia or India (Klieman 2003).

The original hunter-gatherers of the southern savanna initially acquired Bantu speakers' techniques of farming and animal husbandry very gradually. The process of technological and linguistic change accelerated dramatically between 400 and 1400 CE, when people began to farm and herd more intensively, forge iron, and adopt the languages of Bantu speakers.

Global Connections and Environmental Change, 1400–1900

After 1400, some parts of central Africa encountered outside traders and experienced significant environmental, economic, political, and social change. The southwestern savanna was profoundly affected by the Portuguese, and later other Europeans, who arrived on the west coast of central Africa to acquire gold and silver but subsequently shifted to a trade in slaves for plantations and mines in the Americas (Birmingham and Martin 1983). Importantly, the Portuguese introduced

cassava (*Manihot esculenta*) from the Americas to Africa (Nweke 2005), and cultivation of the tuber spread throughout central Africa over the next six centuries. The historian Joseph Miller (1982) has argued that southwest central Africa's vulnerability to intermittent drought and food shortages fundamentally shaped its engagement with the Atlantic slave trade. Drought and famine drove people to concentrate in fertile, well-watered areas, which eventually produced considerable shortages in arable land. At the same time, some political leaders in these areas were able to centralize power in their own hands. Over the next four centuries, these rulers, their kin, and their successors, seeking to increase their power and to profit from a trade in weapons and luxury goods with European slave traders, expanded their slave raiding into the southern savanna's interior. Periodic drought and lack of food could also aggravate slave raiding, Miller has argued, because people enslaved during times of ecological crisis suffered more ill health and higher death rates than those captured in better times, and their increased death rates intensified demand for more captives.

The nineteenth century brought considerable upheaval to central Africa. During this century, equatorial Africa was increasingly incorporated into the global economy, a process fueled partly by an industrializing Europe, which needed African raw materials to produce its textiles, steel, and other products (Vansina 1990, 207–218). Africans in the Congo River basin forest took advantage of these opportunities, forming their own trading networks to exchange manioc, palm oil and wine, slaves, and ivory for such imports as firearms, beads, and cloth. Not all parts of the Congo basin were evenly affected by this international trade, and some forest peoples, although they engaged in small-scale, lively local trading, did not participate in long-distance trading caravans through the forest. Elsewhere, in the southern savanna, Africans shifted from sending slaves overseas in the Atlantic trade to keeping them to produce wax, ivory, rubber, and other valued resources to trade with European merchants. The northern savanna saw the development of slave and ivory raiding empires linked to the Nile River basin.

Generally, this burgeoning central African trade was based upon intensive environmental exploitation, and in many regions competition for valued resources sparked warfare, slave raiding, and mass migrations among central Africans. Elephant populations dwindled, overhunted to meet the Europeans' insatiable demands for ivory. Forests were cleared for agriculture to meet the needs of the increasing population. In the northern savanna, contact with a trans-Saharan slave and ivory trade precipitated the creation of large, concentrated trading posts and introduced new diseases—smallpox, syphilis, and measles—that became endemic among central Africans (Cordell 1985).

The Twentieth Century and Colonial Rule

European colonial rule introduced new ways of exploiting the forest, but also continued older ones. In the late-nineteenth century, central Africa became the focus of Belgian, French, British, and German dreams of commercial exploitation and immense wealth. Several European powers coped with limited finances, relatively sparse and intractable central African populations, and the enormous difficulties of communication and transportation in central Africa by delegating the responsibility for "developing" this wealth to private concessionary companies. Paying a fixed yearly rent and additional fees, these commercial enterprises held monopolies on valuable resources. They were supposed to build roads, customs posts, and telegraph lines in their concessions, but most did nothing. Instead, they sent armed guards into villages to conscript Africans to harvest rubber from trees and vines for months at a time, hunt for ivory and animal skins, and gather copal (a tree resin), tropical oils, and other products. Many companies, although they kidnapped, beat, cheated, and stole from workers, did not prosper, but others, such as that of the Belgian king Leopold II (1835–1909), known as the Congo Independent State (1885–1908), reaped enormous wealth (Hoschschild 1998). The changes these companies brought to central African environments were nevertheless significant: they depleted the savannas and the forest of its rubber-producing trees and vines, and they exhausted the once-plentiful elephant and game populations (Giles-Vernick 2002, 150–202). Widespread recruitment of laborers also helped to spread infectious diseases throughout central Africa. Epidemics of trypanosomiasis, or sleeping sickness, swept through much of central Africa in the early twentieth century, prompting a French medical service campaign to control them (Headrick 1994).

Even after European states put an end to the concessionary system, colonizers still welcomed the activities of companies that would "develop" central Africa's riches. Companies (and, at times, colonial administrators) avidly pushed cash cropping, diamond and gold mining, and logging, and the environmental consequences of these activities were considerable: farmers cleared more forest to expand cultivation, and hunters and trappers stepped up their activities to feed workers in the diamond camps and logging centers. Mining laid waste to forests and highlands and caused rivers to dry up during the dry season and to flood during the rainy season, and water pumps polluted these waters with oil and other chemicals. Elsewhere, large-scale colonial development projects transformed landscapes irrevocably. One of the most dramatic development interventions was the 1955–1959 construction of the Kariba hydroelectric dam—one of the world's largest—on what is now the Zambia-Zimbabwe border (formerly Northern Rhodesia and Southern Rhodesia). Supplying electricity to the Copperbelt in present-day Zambia as well as to parts of present-day Zimbabwe, the dam created a huge reservoir, Kariba Lake, and displaced fifty thousand people and significant numbers of wildlife from the area.

Postcolonial Dilemmas

Following independence from colonial powers in the early 1960s, central African states have maintained an uneasy relationship with the environment. On the one hand, environmental exploitation has continued to be at the foundation of their economies, a crucial source of export earnings. Hence, cash cropping, mining, oil exploitation, logging, and other activities of the colonial era continued (Butler 2006). Some states initiated large-scale development projects with finances from multi- and bilateral aid organizations that cleared wider expanses of forest and woodland and encouraged mechanized commercial agriculture. While much of central Africa is not highly urbanized, cities such as Brazzaville, Kinshasa, and Douala experienced rapid growth and have helped to redirect rural resources toward feeding, housing, and supplying the needs of growing urban populations. Road construction has facilitated both human mobility and extractive economic activities (logging, hunting, mining) within rain forests, even into relatively remote regions (Minnemeyer

2002). By their very nature, then, they promote activities that remain difficult to reconcile with forest protection.

On the other hand, there have been considerable efforts to protect central Africa's environment and resources. Colonial powers once took some measures to protect game and forests, creating hunting reserves and parks and implementing hunting permits for different classes of hunters. In the 1980s and 1990s, many African states revived, built upon, or expanded on such colonial measures, partly because conservation could earn much-needed tourism revenues, but also because states were under pressure from the World Bank to implement conservation programs as one condition for receiving loans. Many of the former colonial powers continue to play important roles in both regulating and exploiting forest resources (Forest Monitor 2001, 8–12). Conservation, however, has not been universally popular among ordinary Africans, who resent limits placed on where, what species, and how they can hunt, trap, fish, and gather. Others dislike the fact that conservation interventions limit mining, logging, and other activities within protected areas, thus reducing access to jobs, salaries, and consumer goods. Some central Africans, however, have found the small-scale development activities and provision of some services and jobs that go along with conservation projects a real boon.

Outlook

The twin demands of development and conservation pose a serious dilemma for central African states and their citizens. For many impoverished central African states and people, cash comes most readily through forms of environmental exploitation that are not always sustainable. Yet depleting central Africa of its valued resources and lands would also cause real losses. Balancing those twin demands will remain a critical problem for central Africa in the coming decades.

Tamara GILES-VERNICK
Institut Pasteur

See also Africa (*several articles*); African Union (AU); Agriculture, Small-Scale; Conflict Minerals; Congo (Zaire) River; Goma, Democratic Republic of the Congo; Lake Chad; Migration (Africa); Mining (Africa); Nile River; Parks and Preserves; Rural Development; Sahara; Sahel; Urbanization (Africa); World Bank

This article was adapted by the editors from Tamara Giles-Vernick's article "Africa, Central," in Shepard Krech III,

J. R. McNeill, and Carolyn Merchant (Eds.), the *Encyclopedia of World Environmental History*, pp. 11–14. Great Barrington, MA: Berkshire Publishing (2003).

FURTHER READING

Bailey, Robert C., et al. (1989). Hunting and gathering in tropical rain forests: Is it possible? *American Anthropologist, 91*(1), 59–82.

Birmingham, David, & Martin, Phyllis M. (Eds.). (1983). *History of central Africa: Vols. 1 & 2.* New York and London: Longman.

Birmingham, David, & Martin, Phyllis M. (Eds.). (1997). *History of central Africa: Contemporary years since 1960: Vol. 3.* New York & London: Longman.

Burnham, Phillip. (1980). *Opportunity and constraint in a savanna society: The Gbaya of Meiganga.* London: Academic Press.

Burnham, Phillip. (1996). *The politics of cultural difference in northern Cameroon.* Edinburgh, Scotland: Edinburgh University Press for the International African Institute.

Butler, Rhett Ayers. (2006). Congo rainforest. *Mongabay.com.* Retrieved January 5, 2012, from http://rainforests.mongabay.com/congo/

Coquery-Vidrovitch, Catherine. (1972). *Le Congo au temps des grands compagnies concessionnaires* [The Congo at the time of the great concessionary companies]. Paris: Mouton.

Cordell, Dennis D. (1985). *Dar al-Kuti and the last years of the trans-Saharan slave trade.* Madison: University of Wisconsin Press.

Eggert, Manfred K. H. (1993). Central Africa and the archaeology of the equatorial rainforest: Reflections of some major topics. In Thurstan Shaw, Paul Sinclair, Bassey Andah & Alex Okpoko (Eds.), *The archaeology of Africa: Food, metals and towns* (pp. 289–329). London: Routledge.

Forest Monitor. (2001). *Sold down the river: The need to control transnational forestry corporations: A European case study.* Cambridge, UK: Forest Monitor.

Giles-Vernick, Tamara. (2002). *Cutting the vines of the past: Environmental histories of the equatorial rain forest.* Charlottesville: University Press of Virginia.

Harms, Robert. (1987). *Games against nature: An eco-cultural history of the Nunu of Equatorial Africa.* Cambridge, UK: Cambridge University Press.

Headrick, Rita. (1994). *Colonialism, health and illness in French Equatorial Africa, 1885–1935.* Daniel Headrick (Ed.). Atlanta, GA: African Studies Association.

Hoschschild, Adam. (1998). *King Leopold's ghost.* New York: Houghton Mifflin.

Klieman, Kairn. (2003). *"The pygmies were our compass": Bantu and Batwa in the history of West Central Africa, early times to c. 1900 CE. The Social History of Africa* series. Portsmouth, UK: Heinemann.

Miller, Joseph C. (1982). The significance of drought, disease and famine in the agriculturally marginal zones of western central Africa. *Journal of African History, 23,* 17–61.

Minnemeyer, Susan. (2002). *An analysis of access to central Africa's rainforests.* Washington, DC: World Resources Institute.

Nweke, Felix I. (2005). The cassava transformation in Africa. FAO Corporate Document Repository. Retrieved January 5, 2012, from http://www.fao.org/docrep/009/a0154e/A0154E02.HTM

Richards, Primack W. (1996). *The tropical rain forest: An ecological study* (2nd ed.). New York: Cambridge University Press.

Vansina, Jan. (1990). *Paths in the rainforests: Toward a history of political tradition in equatorial Africa.* Madison: University of Wisconsin Press.

Africa, East

With a total area of 1.7 million square kilometers, East Africa is the geopolitical region consisting of Uganda, Kenya, Tanzania, Rwanda, and Burundi. It faces numerous threats to its extraordinary range of environments, including domestic sewage, solid domestic waste, habitat degradation, agrochemical pollution, and industrial waste pollution. Its biodiversity is also threatened by factors like illegal wildlife trade and overfishing.

East Africa contains a broad environmental diversity attributable to a range of historical idiosyncrasies and the interactions between humankind and nature. Given the evidence for the evolution of *Homo sapiens* in eastern Africa, the interactive processes involving culture and nature have likely been occurring for over 300,000 years. Until recently, however, historical analyses of ancient East Africa have portrayed a populace either struggling with nature for their very survival, or living with it in harmony. Neither characterization is correct.

Geography and Climate

Countries included in East Africa vary in size. Tanzania, with an area of 886,050 square kilometers (km²) is the largest; Kenya, covering an area of 567,000 km² is the second largest, and Uganda, with an area of almost 200,000 km² is the third. The two smaller countries, Rwanda and Burundi each cover about 25,000 km². The environment of East Africa is shaped, to some extent, by land-use patterns that incorporate combinations of hunting, agriculture, and pastoralism. Geologically, most of East Africa's landmass, aside from its coastal plain, consists of a raised plateau intersected by rift valleys—long narrow zones, such as the Great Rift Valley, that formed as the result of tensional stress in the Earth's crust. These

rifts formed during the Miocene Epoch (between about 24 million and 5 million years ago) and today are characterized by basins and lakes. At some points during the rifting, lava flowed from the fissures, forming basalt as it cooled. Highlands consisting of this basalt, of uplifted granitic massifs, of escarpments (long cliffs of weathering-resistant rock separating two areas that have been leveled by erosion), and volcanoes surround the rift valleys in dramatic contrast. The many volcanoes include Mt. Kilimanjaro, Mt. Kenya, Mt. Elgon, and Mt. Meru, among others.

East Africa's rainfall patterns are highly variable. The region's equatorial location and proximity to the Indian Ocean expose it twice annually to the abundant moisture that accompanies the passage of a tropical low-pressure zone, the Intertropical Convergence Zone (ITCZ). Not all the moisture reaches the mainland, however. Coastal winds, the speed of the passage of weather associated with the ITCZ, geographical features on the mainland, and the rain shadow effect of Madagascar, all limit rainfall distribution, creating a generally more arid climate than is found at comparable latitudes in West Africa. In East Africa, weather for the most part comes onshore in the form of a seasonal monsoon pattern. When it encounters the cooler highlands, rainfall covers the southern and southeastern slopes and diminishes as it moves west northwest. Thus, one finds mountains where annual rainfall varies from 2,000 millimeters on southern and eastern slopes, to 1,000 millimeters on northern and western slopes. One also finds very localized rain shadow effects—dry areas on the leeward side of elevated areas along the course of rain-bearing winds. Further variability results from sea surface temperature oscillations that precipitate El Niño and La Niña climatological events (WWF 2006). As a result, climate has been broadly stable over the long term, but annual weather patterns can diverge widely.

Making a Living

Given its capricious weather, East Africa's premodern environmental history was characterized by the development of complex production and exchange systems to facilitate survival under almost any environmental circumstances. The gradual transformation in foodways—food production and consumption patterns—constituted the most significant development in the area's environmental history before the first millennium CE. During the past two to three millennia, farming and herding have supplanted foraging as the dominant ways of making a living, with two separate husbandry traditions dominating the process. The most recent, some two thousand years ago, involved the introduction of a root-crop complex (agricultural production system based on taro and yams) that had evolved in central Africa and spread to the fertile and well-watered lakes region of Uganda and western Tanzania. A more ancient tradition extends back some three thousand years and concerns the spread southward—from Sudan and Ethiopia—of livestock herding and grain cultivation into the Central Rift Valley highlands. Both traditions involved complex transformations of aboriginal ideologies, languages, social organization, and technologies, whose nature and initial environmental effects remain only partially understood. Fortunately, archeologists and historical linguists have shed some light on the subsequent dynamics of technological and environmental change (Ehret and Posnansky 1982).

Pastoralists

In highland Kenya and Tanzania, where most elevations range between 1,500 and 3,000 meters above sea level, variations in rainfall and elevation created an ecological mosaic in which montane forests (those in cool, upland slopes, below the timberline dominated by large coniferous trees), rich savanna pasture, and fertile volcanic hills intersected. The environmental variety led to opportunities for numerous husbandry innovations. In drier reaches, pastoralism became the preferred means of subsistence. One of the most distinctive pastoral groups was the Sirikwa (twelfth to eighteenth century), the ancestors of today's Nilotic-speaking peoples who occupy western Kenya's Rift Valley highlands. The archeological remnants of these ancient herding communities lay scattered across the landscape in the form of thousands of saucer-like depressions, each about 10 meters wide. The depressions housed Sirikwa cattle, whose owners lived in attached structures facing outward from the cattle enclosure. The Sirikwa were neither the first nor the last pastoral society to occupy these grazing lands, but their adaptations represent part of a long East African pastoralist tradition that combined the milk production of their humped zebu cattle with the meat provided from sheep and goats. Furthermore, the demonstrated mobility (moving several times in a generation) of the Sirikwa and the defensive posture of their dwellings suggest they had learned that productivity of pastures fluctuates in response to climate and to human and animal population levels.

Under conditions of extreme drought, famine, disease, and marauding neighbors threatened herding communities. Therefore, East African pastoralists rarely relied on their herds alone. Nineteenth-century European observers reported extensive grain farming by pastoralists along the margins of the Rift Valley highlands where mountain streams discharged into the arid plains. Archeological remains suggest that this pattern is centuries old. One striking example is evident at Engaruka, an isolated village at the base of the Rift Valley's western escarpment in northern Tanzania. Researchers have uncovered a complex of irrigation furrows and terraces there dating to the twelfth and thirteenth centuries. Whereas some East African pastoralists clearly learned to farm on their own, others forged social relations with neighbors who occupied wetter montane environments with rain-fed agriculture.

Farmers

As pastoralists adapted their economy to the highland savannas, around two thousand years ago a horticultural tradition took hold on the forested hills of the Lake Victoria basin. This early agricultural transformation coincided with the incorporation of a new cultural complex into indigenous societies that included root crops, a new language (the ancestor of the Bantu languages now spoken across much of the region), new pottery styles, sedentary communities, and, eventually, ironworking. As the cultural and agricultural complex moved eastward, it brought from its origins in the Great Lakes of the Rift Valley a tendency to seek out places with abundant moisture and forest resources. When migrating peoples encountered new environments, such as lake shores, ocean coasts, and volcanic mountains, they fine-tuned their farming systems accordingly. Successful farming ultimately led to population growth, along with the often extensive environmental transformation that accompanied the process. Accumulations of evidence from linguistics, archeology, and paleoecology have revealed a pattern of large-scale deforestation and subsequent ecological change in the interlacustrine highlands beginning about two thousand years ago, a process tied closely to the industrial demands of ironworking. Similar circumstances, although perhaps smaller in scale, undoubtedly accompanied agriculture's intensification in other locales.

As demographic change brought herders and farmers into closer contact during the second millennium CE, the lines between pastoralism and agriculture sometimes became blurred. In some places pastoralists shifted completely into farming, whereas others with a herding tradition switched expertly back and forth between horticulture and herding as the climate allowed. In the Interlacustrine Zone (i.e., the region bounded by Lakes Victoria, Kyoga, Albert, Edward, and Tanganyika), where farmers had introduced and refined what became a highly successful farming system, immigrant herders introduced new notions of political power and prestige associated with cattle ownership. The result was the polarization of the two production complexes, where those with cattle garnered the social prestige necessary to form a ruling class and, in some cases, politicalized territories.

Globalization and the Coast, 1000–1800 CE

After the East African agricultural revolution reached the Indian Ocean coastal region at the end of the first millennium CE, its practitioners adapted to the coastal environment. In the early stages of their transformation, coastal villagers remained in many ways tied to their history of agricultural innovation, turning to the ocean simply to gather their subsistence during the dry seasons. By the middle of the second millennium CE, however, coastal settlements stretching from the Lamu archipelago in northern Kenya to Kilwa in southern Tanzania, shared a

language, Kiswahili, and a maritime economy that sharply differentiated them from other East Africans. The Swahili people had become expert boat builders and fishers whose skills enabled them to efficiently harvest the biologically rich offshore reefs. Coastal peoples also became international traders, welcoming and servicing ships and cargoes the seasonal northeast monsoon winds brought from the Red Sea, the Persian Gulf, and India. Some of the foreigners settled permanently in the growing coastal port towns to enhance their businesses, intermarried with the Swahili families (Nurse and Spear 1985), and introduced Islam (Pouwels 1987). As trade expanded, foreign demand grew for eastern and southern Africa's resources such as gold, slaves, ivory, and timber. With these commodities, Swahili merchants purchased luxury items and manufactured goods, increasing the wealth, architectural splendor, and prestige of the coastal towns. By the beginning of the nineteenth century the Swahili coast was dotted with urban landscapes.

As the commodity trade shows, the relationship between East Africa and Asia had ramifications far beyond the coastal region. The pattern was not exclusively extractive, however. For example, the introduction of bananas from the East Indies revolutionized agriculture across Africa's equatorial regions, helping to precipitate unprecedented population increases. In the seventeenth century, the scope of East Africa's ties to far-flung environments had grown when East Africans gained access to American crops such as maize, manioc, and potatoes, crops that in many places have come to dominate farming regimes in modern times.

The internationalization of East Africa's coastal region therefore touched both the coastal and the interior environments in profound ways. As trade flourished through the eighteenth and nineteenth centuries, a burgeoning slave trade began to decimate the productive capacity of communities in the interior. As it had in western and central Africa in previous centuries, the negative ramifications of East Africa's incorporation into the world economy became all too apparent.

The Colonial Era and Beyond

In the decades of the nineteenth century before European colonization, East Africa experienced a series of ecological disasters that decimated human and animal populations. The violence and dislocation of the slave trade had reduced the resiliency of farming and herding systems and created whole populations of refugees seeking protection. When drought and disease combined with regional violence, the agricultural environment fell apart. Terraces and irrigation systems collapsed in the highlands while tsetse fly–infested bush vegetation encroached on abandoned lowland gardens and pastures. In the 1880s and 1890s, colonial armies from Germany, Britain, and Belgium entered the devastated countryside and installed new authoritarian state systems and a complete reorientation of production systems along European lines. In places like Kenya's "white highlands," the new-comers claimed the finest highland pastures for them-selves for livestock and commodities like coffee and tea. Kenya's government forced the aggrieved pastoralists onto crowded reserves. On other huge swaths of seized land, European plantation companies produced cotton, sisal, and tobacco. Where African farmers remained on their land, tax burdens introduced by colonizers forced them to procure cash either by producing exportable commodities or providing labor on the settler's farms.

In the 1930s, colonial governments drew upon very preliminary scientific research to conclude that African farmers and herders had precipitated an ecological cri-sis manifest in deforestation and soil erosion. As an antidote, conservation programs in forestry and agri-cultural services were introduced (McClanahan and Young 1996). Sustained yield forestry systems, devel-oped in Europe, failed miserably in this tropical set-ting, however. Not only did the delineation of forest reserves displace many Africans, the system of forest exploitation devastated irreplaceable forest ecosystems (Lovett and Wasser 1993). After World War II, colo-nial governments across East Africa forced highland farmers to build terraces, plant hedge lines, and take other onerous soil erosion control measures. The pro-gram encountered stiff resistance, which helped to fos-ter a vocal anti-colonial sentiment.

Present Situation and Future Projections

The legacy of colonial environmental policy remains rooted in conservation and development programs now operating in eastern Africa. Administration and plan-ning remain top-down processes, although government and nongovernment development agencies now tend to recognize community participation as a worthwhile con-tribution. In the zones of biodiversity preservation, such as East Africa's highland forests and the famous savanna game parks of Kenya and Tanzania, the conservation community tends to view local use as anathema.

Over the past generation, episodic violence in Uganda, Rwanda, Burundi, Kenya, Somalia, and the eastern Democratic Republic of the Congo has increased pov-erty, vulnerability to famine, and daily threats to human safety (Oniang'o 2009). The periodic insecurity has fur-ther exacerbated the problems of dealing with the envi-ronmental issues at national and regional levels. Moreover, East Africa's farmers and herders continue to struggle with the climatic uncertainty that can bring flooding and drought to the same region in succeeding years.

The area is also vulnerable to global warming effects. In Kenya, for example, a small rise in temperature would drastically affect the country's lucrative tea industry, which depends on the prevailing cool and wet highland climate (Hussein 2011, 512). Long-term warming trends will likewise affect East Africa's food production across the entire region if temperatures rise 3 to 4°C by the year 2080, as one report predicts (The Select Committee on Energy Independence and Global Warming 2012).

Christopher A. CONTE
Utah State University

See also Africa (*several articles*); African Union (AU); Agriculture, Small-Scale; Conflict Minerals; Desertification; Goma, Democratic Republic of the Congo; Immigrants and Refugees; Lake Victoria; Mining (Africa); Nairobi, Kenya; Urbanization (Africa)

FURTHER READING

Anderson, David M. (1988). Cultivating pastoralists: Ecology and economy among the Il Chamus of Baringo, 1840–1980. In Douglas H. Johnson & David M. Anderson (Eds.), *The ecology of survival: Case studies from northeast African history* (pp. 241–260). Boulder, CO: Westview Press.

Anderson, David M., & Grove, Richard H. (1987). *Conservation in Africa: People, policies and practice.* Cambridge, UK: Cambridge University Press.

Ehret, Christopher. (2000). *An African classical age: Eastern and south-ern Africa in world history, 1000 BC to AD 400.* Charlottesville: University of Virginia Press.

Ehret, Christopher, & Posnansky, Merrick. (Eds.). (1982). *The archae-ological and linguistic reconstruction of African history.* Berkeley & Los Angeles: University of California Press.

Hussein, Muawya Ahmed. (2011). Climate change impacts on East Africa. In Walter Leal Filho (Ed.), *The economic, social and political elements of climate change.* Hamburg, Germany: Springer.

Johnson, Douglas H., & Anderson, David M. (Eds.). (1989). *The ecol-ogy of survival: Case studies from northeast African history.* Boulder, CO: Westview Press.

Kelly, Annie. (2009, March 12). Uganda's response to climate change "inadequate." Retrieved April 18, 2012, from http://www.guardian.co.uk/society/katineblog/2009/mar/12/uganda-climate-change

Kimbugwe, Kato; Perdikis, Nicholas; Yeung, May; & Kerr, William. (2012). *Economic development through regional trade: A role for the new East African community?* London: Palgrave MacMillan.

Lovett, Jon C., & Wasser, Samuel K. (Eds.). (1993). *Biogeography and ecology of the rain forests of eastern Africa.* Cambridge, UK: Cambridge University Press.

McClanahan, Tim R., & Young, Truman P. (Eds.). (1996). *East African ecosystems and their conservation.* Oxford, UK: Oxford University Press.

Nicholson, Sharon E. (1996). Environmental change within the his-torical period. In William M. Adams, Andrew S. Goudie & Antony R. Orme (Eds.), *The physical geography of Africa* (pp. 60–87). Oxford, UK: Oxford University Press.

Nurse, Derek, & Spear, Thomas. (1985). *The Swahili: Reconstructing the history and language of an African society, 800–1500.* Philadelphia: University of Pennsylvania Press.

Oniang'o, Ruth. (2009, October). *Food and nutrition emergencies in East Africa: Political, economic and environmental associations* (discussion paper 00909). Washington, DC: International Food Policy Research Institute.

Orindi, Victor A., & Murray, Laurel A. (2005). *Adapting to climate change in East Africa: A strategic approach* (Gatekeeper series 117). London: International Institute for Environment and Development.

Plisnier, Pierre-Dennis; Serneels, S.; & Lambin, E. F. (2000). Impact of ENSO on East African ecosystems: A multivariate analysis based on climate and remote sensing data. *Global Ecology and Biogeography, 9*(6), 481–497.

Pouwels, Randall L. (1987). *Horn and crescent: Cultural change and traditional Islam on the East African coast, 800–1900.* Cambridge, UK: Cambridge University Press.

Robertshaw, Peter. (1990). *Early pastoralists of south-western Kenya.* Nairobi, Kenya: British Institute of Eastern Africa.

Schmidt, Peter R. (1994). Historical ecology and landscape transformation in eastern equatorial Africa. In Carole L. Crumley (Ed.), *Historical ecology: Cultural knowledge and changing landscapes* (pp. 99–126). Santa Fe, NM: School of American Research Press.

Schmidt, Peter R. (1997). *Iron technology in east Africa: Symbolism, science, and archaeology.* Bloomington: Indiana University Press.

Schoenbrun, David Lee. (1998). *A green place, a good place: Agrarian change, gender, and social identity in the Great Lakes region to the 15th century.* Portsmouth, NH: Heinemann.

The Select Committee on Energy Independence and Global Warming. (2012). Impact zone: East Africa. Retrieved April 18, 2012, from http://globalwarming.house.gov/impactzones/eastafrica

Sutton, John E. G. (1990). *A thousand years of East Africa.* Nairobi, Kenya: British Institute in Eastern Africa.

Sutton, John E. G. (1994–1995). The growth of farming communities in Africa from the equator southwards (Special issue). *Azania, 29–30.*

Sutton, John E. G. (Ed.). (1989). The history of African agricultural technology and field systems (Special issue). *Azania, 24.*

Vansina, Jan. (1990). *Paths in the rainforest.* Madison: University of Wisconsin Press.

Vansina, Jan. (1994–1995). A slow revolution: Farming in subequatorial Africa. *Azania, 29–30,* 15–26.

World Wide Fund for Nature (WWF). (2006). Climate change impacts on East Africa: A review of the scientific literature. Gland, Switzerland: WWF. Retrieved April 18, 2012, from http://www.wwf.dk/dk/Service/Bibliotek/Klima/Rapporter+mv./Climate+change+impacts+on+east+africa.pdf

Xinhua News. (2012, February 21). Environmental destruction top threat to food security in E. Africa: UN. Retrieved April 18, 2012, from http://news.xinhuanet.com/english/world/2012-02/21/c_131423316.htm.

Zhou, Guofa; Minakawa, Noboru; Githeko, Andrew; & Yan Guiyun. (2004). Association between climate variability and malaria epidemics in the East African highlands. *Proceedings of the National Academy of Sciences of the United States of America, 101*(8), 2375–2380.

Africa, Southern

Southern Africa was settled by hunter-gatherers about 50,000 years ago. Settlement brought changes to the landscape, such as woodland cleared for habitation and agriculture. European colonization further changed southern Africa's environments; monocrop plantations (where one crop is grown on the same land every year) replaced native plants. Although rapid population growth and economic development stressed natural resources, southern Africa led conservation initiatives in the twentieth century.

Southern Africa, comprising the present states of South Africa, Namibia, Botswana, Lesotho, Swaziland, Zimbabwe, Zambia, Malawi, and Mozambique, is about half the size of the United States, including Alaska. Climatic and ecological conditions vary greatly. On the east coast, facing the Indian Ocean, and in the central highlands, which stand above 1,000 meters, rainfall exceeds 500 millimeters a year. In much of the western half of the subcontinent, however, precipitation is far less. Some of the world's great arid lands, such as the Namib (Namibia), the Kalahari (Botswana), and the Karoo (South Africa) are situated here. Most of the region experiences summer storm rainfall. In the north, around the Zambezi Valley, the climate is tropical; in the far south, a more temperate, Mediterranean climate prevails.

Precolonial Settlement

Environment played a key role in the peopling of southern Africa. Settlement by hunter-gatherers, using stone tools, dates back perhaps 50,000 years (Klein 2001). Its varied ecology is one reason the region was home to particularly diverse wildlife; antelopes especially were plentiful. About 2,500 years ago, Bantu-speaking Africans dispersed through the region: they worked iron, made pottery, kept cattle, and grew sorghum and millet grasses (Iliffe 1995, 100–130). This process of settlement was no sudden invasion, and earlier settlements sometimes were absorbed. Because they relied on rainfall for crops, these Africans did not move into the more arid western parts of the subcontinent. Hunter-gatherers, thus protected, survived as distinct communities until the colonial era. The Khoikhoi adopted cattle, herding them to scarce water sources and seasonal pastures.

Relatively open frontiers and small populations shaped African social and economic systems. Settlement was dispersed, and wealth and power lay in controlling people and livestock. A major African achievement, the US historian John Iliffe (1995) maintains, was to gain control of one of the most difficult environments on behalf of humankind. Several centralized political units developed, however, such as Great Zimbabwe (c. 1200 to 1500 CE) (Connah 1987, 224–254). It amassed large cattle herds, conquered its neighbors, conducted trade as far away as the coast, and was the first to exploit the area's rich gold deposits. Such systems were hard to sustain, and by the early nineteenth century, on the eve of colonization, few large kingdoms remained. The recently formed Zulu state, with perhaps 250,000 people, was the most powerful kingdom.

Africans changed the landscape of southern Africa. They burned pastures to renew them, exposing new growth to spring rains; cleared woodland for settlement and agriculture; and exploited timber for fuel. They hunted to find food and skins and to protect their livestock. Southern Africa shared in the Columbian Exchange (an exchange of animals, plants, culture, human populations, and ideas) with the Americas and introduced crops such as corn (maize), a staple by the early twentieth century. This exchange greatly enhanced agricultural productivity. African economies, however, had limited environmental impact; they depended largely on local produce, renewable natural products, long agricultural fallow periods (idle time), and a limited range of crafts. Tsetse flies, which carry trypanosomiasis, a disease fatal to cattle, restricted the buildup of livestock numbers in many tropical and lowland zones to the north of the Limpopo River.

Colonialism and Environmental Transformations

Colonial intrusions began when the Portuguese arrived on the Mozambican coast in the sixteenth century and the Dutch arrived at Cape Town in the seventeenth. By chance, the Dutch found themselves in some of the best terrain for European settlement, and they faced only the Khoisan people (McKenna 2011, 24), who failed to resist the intruders' firearms and diseases. Settlers followed game, water sources, and grazing routes into the semi-arid interior; in the nineteenth century, they went beyond it, to the high veldt (wide-open, rural spaces). They mastered this hostile environment and introduced new breeds, such as merino sheep, that vastly increased their wealth and capacity to invest. Unlike the settlers of North America and Australia, the Dutch were constrained more by indigenous Africans as they moved eastward and northward; the tsetse and malaria belts also hampered their progress.

Colonization transformed southern Africa's environments, as was widely recognized in the twentieth century: commercial grazing exhausted pastures; the limited native timber, as in western Zimbabwe, was felled for railway sleepers, mine props (lengths of lumber used to prop up the roofs of tunnels in coal mines), and flooring; some of the world's largest forest plantations, planted with exotic pine and eucalypts, spread along the northern Natal coast and through the Drakensberg watershed (Beinart and Coates 1995). Monocultural cash crops, such as sugar along the subtropical east coast, corn on the high veldt, and citrus in irrigated valleys, displaced significant numbers of native plants. Earth dams, boreholes (narrow shafts bored into the ground), and irrigation projects burgeoned in an attempt to tap southern Africa's water resources: the Zambezi projects of Kariba (Zimbabwe and Zambia in the 1950s) and Cahora Bassa (Mozambique in the 1970s), as well as South Africa's Orange (now Gariep) River Scheme, were major undertakings (Turton et al. 2004, 183–187). Much of the region's reticulated (recycled) water was funneled toward irrigation and industrial use, producing stark inequality in who could access tapped water. Yet control over this

most fundamental natural resource also has made it possible to provide for the region's rapidly growing cities.

Mining accelerated southern African economic growth starting in the late nineteenth century. Exploitation of diamonds in Kimberley and later Botswana, gold on the Witwatersrand and in Zimbabwe, and copper in Zambia all created urban enclaves and transport routes that demanded raw materials (McKenna 2011, 186–203). Coal—the second most important mining sector after gold—met energy needs and generated electricity for industries and cities. Lacking oil, and threatened by apartheid-era embargoes, South Africa built the world's largest oil-from-coal plant. Cheap coal does pollute, but it has brought a degree of energy self-sufficiency in key economic sectors.

African populations grew dramatically throughout the region in the twentieth century (McCann 1999), and by the 1960s, annual population growth of more than 3 percent was the norm. Growth in southern Africa, with perhaps 100 million people at the end of the century, may have been even faster. Old systems of peasant and smallholder production, dependent on sparse settlement and long fallow periods, put acute pressure on natural resources in rural areas, especially because the amount of land in black African hands had diminished in some countries. Although acute famine largely was conquered, except where violent conflict erupted, malnutrition and diseases of poverty became widespread. The percentage of people living off the land diminished sharply, and in some countries, more than half the population became urban. This urbanization increasingly was visible in the growth of large, unserviced, informal, and dense settlements that placed new environmental strains on urban hinterlands (the landscape between towns and rural areas).

Rapid economic development and population growth stressed natural resources, but still, southern Africa led conservation initiatives in the twentieth century. British colonial governments and the settler states of South Africa and Zimbabwe carved out wildlife reserves, where hunting and settlement were prohibited. These reserves are now key sites for preservation and tourism. The same authorities also tried to reshape African settlements and peasant economies to develop sustainable agricultural practices. Rural people often reacted with hostility to such interventions, which were seen to undermine local control over natural resources. In several countries, these conflicts fed into anticolonial struggles and remain an important feature of rural politics in the region.

Contemporary Environmental Issues

Southern Africa's population is growing with increasing speed, and international environmental agencies consider it an additional pressure on the natural resources. This growth is causing water and food insecurities, along with health issues (Swatuk 1996). The region risks a shortfall in freshwater due to the increasing demands of the growing population and other issues related to global climatic change. The water scarcity is due to many factors, including rainfall fluctuations, mismanagement, and other geological factors. The region has lost about 30 percent of its wetlands due to these adverse circumstances (Tarr 2003). The Zambezi River, one of the largest rivers in Africa, does not supply water to most of the water-scarce areas of Zimbabwe (FAO 2001). Its basin is under threat of floods and at a higher risk for droughts (Semu-Banda 2008). Similar conditions exist in Namibia, Botswana, and South Africa. In addition to limited and poor quality groundwater resources, South Africa has one of the world's lowest conversion ratios, with less than 10 percent rainfall available as surface water. Similarly, the country must clear the land for agriculture to meet the needs of the growing population, but many of the country's 8,500 species of vascular plants, 70 percent of which are endemic (found nowhere else in the world), are decreasing (WWF 2007).

Oil spills in the coastal areas of South Africa and Zimbabwe due to crude oil import for vehicles and industry are a serious threat to the region, as are overfishing and deforestation (Lange, Hassan, and Hamilton 2003). The region needs various regional and international measures to address these environmental issues and save the environment. Governments of southern African countries, working as the Southern African Development Community (SADC), are now realizing the need for such cross-border cooperation. In 2011, Angola, Botswana, Namibia, Zambia, and Zimbabwe created a transfrontier conservation area to allow humans and animals to cross over borders freely to protect the water resources; these countries now are planning to establish a regional climate-change research center to fill the gap in local expertise on environmental issues (Smith 2012).

William **BEINART**
University of Oxford

See also Africa (*several articles*); African Union (AU); Biological Corridors; Cape Town, South Africa; Climate Change Refugees (Africa); Conflict Minerals; Desertification (Africa); Fisheries; Migration (Africa); Mining (Africa); Public-Private Partnerships (Africa); Rule of Law (Africa); Urbanization (Africa); Water Use and Rights (Africa)

This article was adapted by the editors from William Beinart's article "Africa, Southern," in Shepard Krech III, J. R. McNeill, and Carolyn Merchant (Eds.), the *Encyclopedia of World Environmental History*, pp. 18–20. Great Barrington, MA: Berkshire Publishing (2003).

FURTHER READING

Beall, Jo; Beinart, William; McGregor, Joanne; Potts, Deborah; & Simon, David. (Eds.). (2000). African environments: Past and present. *Journal of Southern African Studies, 26*(4), 595–855.

Beinart, William, & Coates, Peter. (1995). *Environment and history: The taming of nature in the USA and South Africa*. London: Routledge.

Connah, Graham. (1987). *African civilizations: Precolonial cities and states in tropical Africa, an archaeological perspective*. Cambridge, UK: Cambridge University Press.

Food and Agriculture Organization of the United Nations (FAO). (2001). Global terrestrial observing system: Regional implementation plan for Southern Africa. Retrieved May 16, 2012, from http://www.fao.org/docrep/005/X9751E/x9751e00.htm

Iliffe, John. (1995). *Africans: The history of a continent*. Cambridge, UK: Cambridge University Press.

Klein, Richard G. (2001). Southern Africa and modern human origins. *Journal of Anthropological Research, 57*(1), 1–16.

Lange, Glenn-Marie; Hassan, Rashid M.; & Hamilton, Kirk. (2003). *Environmental accounting in action: Case studies from southern Africa*. Northampton, MA: Edward Elgar Publishing, Inc.

McCann, James C. (1999). *Green land, brown land, black land: An environmental history of Africa, 1800–1990*. Portsmouth, NH: Butterworth–Heinemann Ltd.

McKenna, Amy. (2011). *The history of Southern Africa*. New York: Britannica Educational Publishing.

Moyo, Sam; O'Keefe, Phil; & Sill, Michael. (1993). *The southern African environment: Profiles of the SADC countries*. London: Earthscan.

Murphy, Alan; Armstrong, Kate; & Bainbridge, James. (2010). *Southern Africa*. London: Lonely Planet.

Ramphele, Mamphela; McDowell, Chris; & Cock, Jacklyn. (Eds.). (1991). *Restoring the land: Environment and change in post-apartheid South Africa*. London: Panos.

Semu-Banda, Pilirani. (2008). Climate change threatens livelihoods. Retrieved May 16, 2012, from http://ipsnews.net/news.asp?idnews=45224

Smith, David. (2012, April 23). Southern African countries collaborate on plans for climate research centre. *The Guardian*. Retrieved May 16, 2012, from http://www.guardian.co.uk/global-development/2012/apr/23/southern-africa-climate-research-centre

Swatuk, Larry A. (1996). Environmental issues and prospects for southern African regional co-operation. In Hussein Solomon & Jakkie Cilliers (Eds.), *People, poverty and peace: Human security in southern Africa*. Retrieved May 16, 2012, from http://www.iss.co.za/pubs/monographs/No4/Swatuk.html

Tarr, Peter. (2003). *Environmental impact assessment in southern Africa*. Windhoek, Namibia: Southern African Institute for Environmental Assessment. Retrieved May 16, 2012, from http://www.saiea.com/saiea-book/

Turton, Anthony R.; Meissner, R.; Mampane, Patrick M.; & Seremo, O. (2004). A hydropolitical history of South Africa's international river basins (Report to the Water Research Commission, WRC Report No. 1220/1/04). Gezina, South Africa: African Water Issues Research Unit (AWIRU), University of Pretoria.

World Wide Fund for Nature (WWF). (2007). Environmental problems in South Africa: Water on the run. Retrieved May 16, 2012, from http://wwf.panda.org/who_we_are/wwf_offices/south_africa/environmental_problems__in_south_africa/

Africa, Western

West Africa, the westernmost region of the African continent, occupies an area of approximately 5 million square kilometers. This geopolitical region includes Benin, Burkina Faso, Chad, Cameroon, Cape Verde, Cote d'Ivoire, The Gambia, Ghana, Guinea, Guinea-Bissau, Liberia, Mali, Mauritania, Niger, Nigeria, Senegal, Sierra Leone, Togo, and sometimes includes the British overseas territory of the island of Saint Helena. The region, rich in minerals including gold, suffers from intensive logging and mining.

Most of western Africa is made up of plains lying less than 300 meters above sea level. Along the southern coast of the region, there are higher elevations in some countries, including Mt. Cameroon, a 4,095 meter active volcano whose lofty (and treeless) peak is a mere fifteen kilometers from the Atlantic Ocean. The region is diversified and includes arid deserts, mainly in the northern part, and tropical rain forest. The climate depends upon the interaction of two air masses; the maritime air mass originating over the Atlantic Ocean is associated with southwestern winds, and the continental air mass originating over the African continent is associated with the dry and dusty Harmattan winds (Windmeijer and Andriesse 1993, 15).

Geological History

Africa was originally part of the ancient supercontinent Gondwanaland, which also included contemporary Antarctica, South America, and Australia, as well as the Indian subcontinent. Gondwanaland underwent geological transformations that produced massive mountain ranges running southwest to northeast (Wright et al. 1985, 1–12). These ranges were eventually eroded to produce the peneplains (nearly flat surfaces that represent an advanced stage of erosion) of western Africa.

Geological transformations more than 5 billion years ago produced the mineral resources of ancient western Africa—iron, copper, and gold. Gold was deposited in part by Precambrian volcanism that produced granitic intrusions, and it was largely gold that motivated the trans-Saharan trade between western and northern Africans.

Humid and semiarid climates alternated. Abundant rain increased the percentage of land suitable for human habitation in some places, while arid periods made the Sahara desert into a climatic barrier that limited the penetration of Mediterranean influences in architecture, craft, and especially agriculture into the tropical regions of ancient western Africa.

Life Zones of Ancient Western Africa

Ancient western Africa, also referred to as the Sudan region, was situated to the south of the Sahara and extended west to the Atlantic Ocean, comprising the Chad and Niger basins, the Niger River, the present-day White Volta and Black Volta rivers, and the Fouta Djallon highland (Alagoa 1988). Ancient western Africa can be characterized by three major life zones (geographical regions characterized by distinctive terrain, climate, and natural vegetation): coastal, forest, and the Sudan savanna. Each of these zones yielded natural resources that were important in the emergence of the three famous ancient western African empires of Ghana, Mali, and Songhai (3000 BCE–700 CE).

The coastal zone extends from the Atlantic Ocean 30 to 130 kilometers inland, and the ancient peoples inhabiting it included the Jola, Pepel, and Serer of Senegambia and the Sherboro and Bulom of Sierra Leone.

These people produced salt for trade or consumption, and salt, along with gold, was an important trading commodity in Africa. The coastal inhabitants were initially nomadic, surviving by fishing, hunting, and gathering. They began radically transforming their environment when they learned the art of cultivation and entered the Early Iron Age (400 BCE–700 CE).

The forest zone is an area of tall trees and dense undergrowth stretching approximately 4,500 kilometers from Sierra Leone to Cameroon. Its ancient inhabitants included the Mende, Kru, Asante, Fon Yoruba, Edo, and Ibo peoples, who fall into two groups: the Gulf forest people near the gulf coast of Guinea and the western forest people near the Atlantic. This region was settled prior to 1000 CE, and the original inhabitants had a subsistence economy until the Stone Age. After learning how to make polished stone tools, they began to clear land, cultivate the soil, and domesticate animals. The Guinea forest people cultivated white and yellow yams, while the western forest people grew rice. Eventually plantain, bananas, and larger varieties of yam spread to this region from Asia.

Forest zone people were among the first in ancient western Africa to produce food surpluses for trade once they entered the Iron Age and began clearing forest for agriculture. Iron was used extensively in this zone, and archaeologists have found Iron Age settlements here as far apart as Senegambia and modern-day southern Ghana (Oliver and Fagan 1975) and ancient bronze works at Igbo-Ukwu in eastern Nigeria. Most of the iron ore in this region lay at the surface and was first mined using open-pit methods.

The Sudan savanna zone, characterized by tall savanna grasses and open woodland, covers vast fertile plains between the Sahara and Africa's tropical deserts. This was the most hospitable part of ancient western Africa for agriculture and the domestication of animals such as cattle, sheep, goats, and fowl. It also contains considerable gold resources, particularly in the Wangara mines of upper Senegal, the upper Niger River, Bonduku, and the area known as Elmina (Mabogunje 1981). Most of the gold in this region was alluvial and mined by panning. The Sudan also had abundant iron ore, but it lacked salt reserves. Early inhabitants of this area included the Wolof, Tukulor, Fulani, Soninke, Malinke, Songhai, and Hausa peoples. Early inhabitants of this area cultivated Guinea corn, millet, and rice. In the upper Niger basin, the Mandingo and Hausa peoples cultivated rice easily because they had developed heavy hoes for cultivating and ridging their crops. Their knowledge and expertise with iron protected their early empires and trade interests with North Africa (Diarra 1981).

Ancient Empires

Abundant natural resources—especially gold and iron ores—in the Sudan region led to the rise of the ancient empires of Ghana, Mali, and Songhai and to the emergence of trans-Saharan trade (Okyere 2000). All three empires used one or more of four primary trans-Saharan trade routes. The items transported along the first two routes were gold, salt, and horses, while the third carried a mixture of items including gold, salt, shells, skins, ivory, cloth, and kola nuts. The fourth route was primarily a slave-trading route supplying the Arabs through Tripoli and Benghazi. The most important exports to North Africa were gold, slaves (especially eunuchs), hides, ivory, ostrich feathers, kola nuts, gum, and manufactured goods (Stride and Ifeka 1971).

Environmental Problems

The abundance of natural resources in western Africa is reflected in its geographical names: the Gold Coast, Ivory Coast, and Slave Coast. The Gold Coast refers to a region rich in gold ore that encompasses both current and ancient Ghana. The Slave Coast was the center of slave traffic between the sixteenth and nineteenth centuries and was located between the Benin (now in Nigeria) and Volta rivers. The Slave Coast region—Nigeria in particular—is now exploited for petroleum, causing devastating environmental degradation. According to the Department of Petroleum Resources of Nigeria, 5,724 oil spills took place between 1976 and 1998, discharging more than 2.5 million barrels of crude oil into the environment (Aroh et al. 2010, 72–73).

Commercial logging has been part of the Ghanaian economy since the colonial era, and the country now faces the consequences of rapid deforestation. Pressures on the forests mounted with the initiation of the Economic Recovery Program in 1981 and with increased

European demand. Since 1981, deforestation in Ghana has proceeded at 2 percent per year, and only 25 percent of the original forests remain. Timber is Ghana's third most important export commodity after cocoa and minerals. Ghana's National Coalition of Civil Society Groups against Mining in Forest Reserves reported that Ghana's forest land amounted to about 8.2 million hectares in the early 1900s, but was less than 1.6 million hectares in 1995 (Forest Inventory and Management Project 1995).

Ghana has rich mineral resources, including gold, bauxite, manganese, limestone, diamonds, and salt. Gold now accounts for 80 to 90 percent of the country's total mineral exports, and Ghana is second only to South Africa in gold production in Africa. There are more than three hundred legal small-scale mines in Ghana. The gold mining operations are haphazard, leading to preventable environmental problems such as ground- and surface-water contamination (Sakyi-Addo 2003).

West Africa continues to attract international trade, including illegal trade in waste products. Many western African countries became favorite targets of international waste traders in the 1980s because they had weak environmental laws and limited state control over the customs officers who approved import shipments. These countries, like many others on the continent, accepted toxic and hazardous wastes because they had few economic options after the devastation wrought by war, poverty, and famine. By 1990, more than half of the countries on the continent had been approached to accept hazardous waste imports. Deforestation, soil erosion, and global climate change that put the region at the risk of severe droughts (Black 2009) contribute to the challenges facing the region.

Sylvia Hood WASHINGTON
Northwestern University

See also Africa (*several articles*); African Union (AU); Climate Change Refugees (Africa); Conflict Minerals; Lagos, Nigeria; Migration (Africa); Mining (Africa); Niger Delta; Rule of Law (Africa); Sahara; Sahel; Urbanization (Africa)

This article was adapted by the editors from Sylvia Hood Washington's article "Africa, Western" in Shepard Krech III, J. R. McNeill, and Carolyn Merchant (Eds.), the *Encyclopedia of World Environmental History*, pp. 20–22. Great Barrington, MA: Berkshire Publishing (2003).

FURTHER READING

Alagoa, Ebiegberi Joe. (1988). Introduction. In Ebiegberi Joe Alagoa & N. Newnan (Eds.), *The early history of the Niger Delta*. Hamburg, Germany: Helmut Buske Verlag.

Aroh, K. N., et al. (2010). Oil spill incidents and pipeline vandalization in Nigeria: Impact on public health and negation to attainment of Millennium development goal: The Ishiagu example. *Disaster Prevention and Management, 19*(1), 70–87.

Black, Richard. (2009, April 16). West Africa faces "megadroughts." BBC News. Retrieved January 5, 2012, from http://news.bbc.co.uk/1/hi/sci/tech/8003060.stm

Diarra, S. (1981). Historical geography: Physical aspects. In Joseph Ki-Zerbo (Ed.), *General History of Africa: Vol. 1* (pp. 316–332). Berkeley: University of California Press.

Forest Inventory and Management Project (FIMP). (1995). Timber yields from the forest reserves of Ghana: An analysis of the implications of sustainable forest management. Kumasi, Ghana: Forest Inventory and Management Project, Planning Branch, Forestry Commission. (Unpublished).

Harris, Joseph E. (1998). *Africans and their history* (2nd ed.). New York: Penguin Books.

July, Robert William. (1970). *A history of the African people*. New York: Charles Scribner's Sons.

Mabogunje, Akin L. (1981). Historical geography: Economic aspects. In Joseph Ki-Zerbo (Ed.), *General history of Africa: Vol. 1* (pp. 333–347). Berkeley: University of California Press.

McIntosh, Roderick James. (1998). *Peoples of the middle Niger: The island of gold*. Oxford, UK: Blackwell Publishers.

Okyere, Vincent. (2000). *Ghana: A historical survey*. Accra, Ghana: Vinojab Publications.

Oliver, Roland Anthony, & Fagan, Brian M. (1975). *Africa in the Iron Age, c. 500 B.C. to A.D. 1400*. Cambridge, UK: Cambridge University Press.

Sakyi-Addo, Kwaku. (2003, February 4). Ghana's gold dilemma. BBC News. Retrieved January 5, 2012, from http://news.bbc.co.uk/1/hi/world/africa/2724339.stm

Stride, George T., & Ifeka, Caroline. (1971). *Peoples and empires of West Africa. West Africa in history 1000–1800*. Nairobi, Kenya: Thomas Nelson and Sons.

Windmeijer, P. N., & Andriesse, W. (Eds.). (1993). *Inland valleys in West Africa: An agro-ecological characterization of rice-growing environments*. Wageningen, The Netherlands: International Institute for Land Reclamation and Improvement (ILRI).

Wright, J. B.; Hastings, D. A.; Jones, W. B.; & Williams, H. R. (1985). *Geology and mineral resources of West Africa*. London: George Allen & Unwin.

African Union (AU)

The African Union, originally known as the Organization of African Unity, is the continental organization of fifty-four nations that includes all African states except Morocco; it has been in existence since 2002. Pan-Africanism, or the union of all African nations, is a concept that dates to the nineteenth century. By working for peace, security, and respect for human rights, the AU is taking decisive steps toward the social, economic, and ecological sustainability of the African continent.

The African Union—the organization of fifty-four nations that includes all African states with the exception of Morocco—did not emerge out of a vacuum. The African Union must be understood as another phase in the quest for African unity as underscored by Pan-Africanism, which, according to the scholar W. B. Ofuatey-Kodjoe, is "the acceptance of a oneness of all people of African descent and the commitment to the betterment of all people of African descent" (1986, 388).

Geography, history, and politics have influenced the idea of Pan-Africanism. In their institutionalization attempts, protagonists have accentuated cultural, poetic, philosophical, or politico-economic aspects of Pan-Africanism. The African diaspora—the dispersal of Africans throughout the world, particularly by slavery—laid the groundwork for transforming the idea into an institutional form. In 1897 H. Sylvester William, a lawyer from Trinidad, founded the African Association in London and organized the Pan-African Conference of 1900 (Geiss 1974). The eminent African American scholar W. E. B. Du Bois promoted the idea through a series of Pan-African congresses in the early 1900s, while the Jamaican journalist and orator Marcus Garvey established the Universal Negro Improvement Association and African Communities League in the 1920s. Kwame Nkrumah and Jomo Kenyatta, both participants in the fifth Pan-African Congress in Manchester, England, in 1945, later became presidents of the independent Gold Coast (Ghana) and Kenya, respectively. Pan-Africanism thus reached continental Africa, where its leaders understood it as the unification of all African peoples, especially in their resistance against colonialism.

Then, like now, Pan-Africanism constitutes the framework within which African leaders envision Africa. Two dominant schools of thought soon emerged. Led by Kwame Nkrumah and the first president of Tanzania, Julius Nyerere, the progressives favored political integration based on a federation as the means to economic growth in Africa. The conservatives, led by Nigeria, argued that newly acquired sovereignty was still fragile, and they hence favored incremental economic, educational, scientific, and cultural cooperation as the proper approach to African unity (Adogamhe 2008).

In spite of these differences, thirty-two governments signed the agreement in 1963 in Addis Ababa, Ethiopia, to form the Organization of African Unity (OAU), the predecessor of the African Union (AU). Equity and social inclusion have always been at the heart of Pan-Africanism in all its resulting institutional forms. Social and economic sustainability therefore underlies the formation of the OAU and the AU.

Environmental sustainability followed soon afterward. In September 1968, some five years after the establishment of the OAU, African states adopted the African Convention on the Conservation of Nature and Natural Resources, which came into force in June 1969. Also known as the Algiers Convention, this comprehensive instrument addresses Africa's environmental issues, ranging from soil and water to the establishment and maintenance of protected areas.

Milestones

The OAU was a product of its time. Struggles for the self-determination of Africans marked its beginnings. The organization primarily focused on safeguarding the sovereignty of the newly independent African states and eradicating colonialism on the continent. With most states achieving political independence by the 1970s and South Africans dismantling the apartheid regime in 1990, the OAU was becoming redundant. In addition, the continent faced social, economic, environmental, and political challenges to which the OAU was ill equipped to respond.

African leaders adopted the Lagos Plan of Action and the Final Act of Lagos in 1980 on the premise that through industrialization and regional and continental integration, Africa would reduce its reliance on foreign aid and establish a common bargaining position on a global scale. In response to environmental degradation, African governments established the African Ministerial Conference on the Environment (AMCEN) in 1985 to provide guidance and enhance cooperation in tackling the environmental problems of the continent. AMCEN continues to play a crucial role within the AU structure today. The African Charter on Human and Peoples' Rights (ACHP), in force since 1986, was an important milestone. Article 24 of this charter grants the right to a "general satisfactory environment favorable to their development" to all Africans, thereby consolidating environmental sustainability as the basis of social and economic sustainability on the continent.

The Abuja Treaty of 1991, establishing the African Economic Community, is a fundamental step in the history of African regional integration. It came into force in 1994 and aims at establishing an African common market with the free movement of people and goods by building on Regional Economic Communities (RECs). Today, these include the Arab Maghreb Union, the Economic Community of Central African States, the Common Market for Eastern and Southern Africa, the Southern African Development Community, the Community of Sahel-Saharan States, the Economic Community of West African States, the East African Community, and the Intergovernmental Authority for Development (IGAD). The Abuja Treaty, moreover, highlights the importance of environment within the context of the sustainable development of Africa. African governments thus adopted the Bamako Convention on the Ban of the Import into Africa and the Control of Transboundary Movement and Management of Hazardous Waste within Africa in 1991 as part of the efforts to safeguard environmental sustainability. African governments, under the aegis of AMCEN, outlined an African Common Position on Environment and Development and presented it at the 1992 Earth Summit in Rio de Janeiro. This concerted African effort produced the 1994 United Nations Convention to Combat Desertification.

The thirty-sixth Summit of Heads of States and Governments of the OAU in Lomé, Togo, adopted the Constitutive Act of the African Union in 2000. The African Union began in Durban, South Africa, on 9 July 2002, the same year as the World Summit on Sustainable Development. A key development in this time line is the adoption of the New Partnership for Africa's Development (NEPAD) as a program of the AU to promote socioeconomic growth and sustainable development in Africa.

The African Union

Fifty-four member-states belong to the African Union. Article 3 of the Constitutive Act of the AU gives the objectives as regional integration, peace and security, and the protection of human rights. In contrast to the OAU's focus on sovereignty and nonintervention, the AU reserves the right to intervene in a member-state's internal affairs in instances such as war crimes, genocide, and crimes against humanity and to restore peace and stability. This focus clearly recognizes the interlinkages between peace and security, political stability, respect for human rights, and cooperation as the preconditions for the sustainable development of the continent.

The AU's headquarters are in Addis Ababa. The AU has created a myriad of institutions to meet the challenges of social, economic, and environmental sustainability in Africa.

The AU Assembly comprises the heads of state and government of all member states. It is the highest decision-making organ of the union. It elects a chairperson every year to head the assembly. Directly below the assembly is the Executive Council. Specialized Technical Committees (STCs) in Industry, Science and Technology, Energy, Natural Resources, and Environment prepare, coordinate, and follow up the union's programs. The Peace and Security Council is a decision-making organ of the AU on matters of prevention, management, and conflict resolution.

The African Court of Justice is the main judicial organ of the AU. In 2008 it merged with the African Court of Human and Peoples' Rights to form a single court, the African Court of Justice and Human Rights. Two nongovernmental organizations lodged a complaint (Communication 155/96) on behalf of the Ogoni People of Nigeria. The African Commission on Human and Peoples' Rights in 2001 found the government of Nigeria guilty of, among other things, violating Article 24 of the ACHP. The commission ruled that Nigeria's government had failed to uphold the peoples' right to a clean and healthy environment by virtue of its dealings with oil-exploiting companies and the resulting environmental pollution in Nigeria's Niger Delta.

The AU Commission is the main administrative organ of the AU. Other organs of the AU include the Pan-African Parliament, the Permanent Representatives Committee, the Economic, Social and Cultural Council (ECOSOCC), and the financial institutions.

Within the AU institutional arrangement, NEPAD is a comprehensive, holistic, and integrated framework for sustainable development that has three main components: peace, conflicts, political and economic governance; key sectors for economic growth; and mobilizing resources for growth. NEPAD thus stimulates sustainable development in Africa through investment in key sectors such as infrastructure, agriculture, human development, the environment, export diversification, and intra-African trade. NEPAD works in the area of social sustainability to develop human resource capacity in science and technology, health care, and education, to increase access to basic medicines and vaccines, and to combat HIV/AIDS and malaria.

NEPAD's environmental sustainability focus is significant, first through the Specialized Technical Committee on the Environment. In collaboration with AMCEN, the AU, the United Nations Environment Programme (UNEP), and the Global Environment Facility, NEPAD has produced an Action Plan for the Environment Initiative. This comprises six programs: combating land degradation, drought, and desertification; conserving Africa's wetlands; preventing, controlling, and managing invasive and alien species;

transboundary conservation or managing natural resources; conserving and sustainably using marine, coastal, and freshwater resources; and combating climate change on the continent.

Regional environmental agreements aside, several international environmental agreements to which AU members are party emerged from the 1992 Earth Summit in Rio de Janeiro, Brazil, and in the post-Rio era. Of particular relevance to Africa are the United Nations Framework Convention on Climate Change, the Convention on Biological Diversity, Agenda 21, and the Johannesburg Plan of Implementation. NEPAD's role in meeting the Millennium Development Goals in Africa thus cannot be overemphasized.

Today, the AU, especially in collaboration with AMCEN, NEPAD, and other partners, plays an important role in streamlining and implementing these agreements and in enhancing cooperation between African states. At the subregional level, most of the RECs have full-fledged environmental divisions, for instance, the IGAD Climate Prediction and Application Centre.

Widespread corruption and noncompliance with obligations under regional and international law, especially with regard to good governance, constitute serious obstacles to sustainable economic growth. It is in this regard that the African Peer Review Mechanism of the NEPAD serves as a system for monitoring corporate and governance practices.

Outlook

The AU interventions in recent conflicts such as in Darfur, Sudan, attest to the organization's commitment to regional peace and security. Critics contest the multistakeholder structure of NEPAD and its reliance on official development assistance and private investment, however. Some say that NEPAD seeks to integrate

Africa into a neoliberal global economy (an economy without any barriers such as tariffs, regulations, or restrictions on the flow of capital) and that its efforts will not result in the sustainable development of Africa (Murithi 2005). Other critics contend that the Regional Economic Communities that should be the building blocks of the AU are far from engaging in inter-regional trade. Whereas trade within individual regions is substantial, inter-regional trade is remarkably low (Bourenane 2002), largely due to the lack of infrastructure. Recent economic partnership agreements between African states or regions with the European Union might not favor inter-regional trade (Stevens and Kennan 2005). The British historian Basil Davidson (1992) might be right in his assertion that the "black man's burden" lies in maintaining colonial boundaries and using these as the basis for continental integration.

The political and intellectual elite are the primary drivers of Pan-Africanism and its current organizational outcome, the AU, as well as of regional integration in Africa. Although these elites diverge on the form such integration should take, plans for the next manifestation of Pan-Africanism, the United States of Africa, are indeed well under way. Political unity that bypasses real integration of the African people will run short of meeting the sustainable development goals of the AU. Although the AU structure provides for public participation through the engagement of civil society organizations in the ECOSOCC, grassroots Pan-Africanism, the indigenization of this idea, seems to present a viable option toward achieving social, economic, and environmental sustainability in Africa.

Synergizing the activities of AMCEN with those of NEPAD, the AU, its organs, and other institutions working on matters of sustainable development thus will be the key to attaining sustainability in Africa.

J. Manyitabot TAKANG
University of Cologne

Caroline Muthoni NJUKI
Intergovernmental Authority for Development (IGAD)

See also Africa (*several articles*); Climate Change Refugees (Africa); Conflict Minerals; E-Waste; Education, Higher (Africa); International Conflict Resolution; Migration (Africa); Mining (Africa); Rule of Law (Africa); World Bank

FURTHER READING

Adogamhe, Paul G. (2008, July). Pan-Africanism revisited: Vision and reality of African unity and development. *African Review of Integration, 2*(2), 1–34.

African Commission on Human and Peoples' Rights. (2001). Decision on Communication 155-96. Retrieved March 20, 2012, from http://www.achpr.org/english/Decison_Communication/Nigeria/Comm.155-96.pdf

Agyeman, Opoku. (2003). *The failure of grassroots Pan-Africanism: The case of the All-African Trade Union Federation.* Lanham, MD: Lexington Books.

Akokpari, John; Ndinga-Muvumba, Angela; & Murithi, Tim. (Eds.). (2008). *The African Union and its institutions.* Cape Town, South Africa: Center for Conflict Resolutions.

Berthélemy, Jean-Claude; Söderling, Ludvig; Salmon, Jean-Michel; & Lecomte, Henri-Bernard Solignac. (2001). *Emerging Africa: International development series, Development Centre seminars of the Organization for Economic Cooperation and Development (OECD).* Paris: OECD Publications.

Bourenane, Naceur. (2002). Regional integration in Africa: Situation and perspectives. In *Regional integration in Africa. International development series, Development Centre seminars of the Organization for Economic Cooperation and Development (OECD) AfDB* (pp. 17–46). Paris: OECD Publications.

Davidson, Basil. (1992). *The black man's burden: Africa and the curse of nation-state.* New York: Three Rivers Press.

Dosenrode, Søren. (2009). Obstacles to African unity: A Deutschian perspective. In Wolfgang Zank (Ed.), *Clash or cooperation of civilizations? Overlapping integration and identities.* (The International Political Economy of New Regionalism series; pp. 83–107). Surrey, UK: Ashgate Publishing.

Geiss, Imanuel. (1974). *The Pan-African movement: A history of Pan-Africanism in America, Europe and Africa.* (Ann Keep, Trans.). New York: Africana Publishing.

Heyns, Christopher. (Ed.). (2001). *Human rights law in Africa 1998* (Human Rights Law in Africa Series). The Hague, The Netherlands: Kluwer International.

Makinda, Samuel M., & Okumu, F. Wafula. (2008). *The African Union: Challenges of globalization, security and governance* (Global Institutions Series). London: Routledge.

Mazrui, Ali. (1977). *Africa's international relations: The diplomacy of dependency and change.* Boulder, CO: Westview Press.

Mkandawire, Thandika. (2005). African intellectuals and nationalism. In Thandika Mkandawire (Ed.), *African intellectuals: Rethinking politics, language, gender and development* (pp. 10–55). London: Zed Books.

Murithi, Timothy. (2005). *The African Union: Pan-Africanism, peace building and development.* Burlington, VT: Ashgate Publishing.

Musonda, Flora Mndeme. (2004). *Regional integration in Africa: A closer look at the east African community.* Munich, Germany: Helbing & Lichtenhahn.

New Partnership for Africa's Development (NEPAD) (2003). *Action Plan for the Environment Initiative.* Retrieved March 20, 2012, from http://www.nepad.org/system/files/Environment%20Action%20Plan.pdf

Ofuatey-Kodjoe, W. B. (1986). *Pan-Africanism: New direction in strategy.* Lanham, MD: University Press of America.

Organisation of African Unity (OAU). (1968). The African Convention on the Conservation of Nature and Natural Resources. Retrieved March 21, 2012, from http://au.int/en/sites/default/files/AFRICAN_CONVENTION_CONSERVATION_NATURE_AND_NATURAL_RESOURCES.pdf

Organisation of African Unity (OAU). (1980). Lagos Plan of Action for the economic development of Africa, 1980–2000. Addis Ababa, Ethiopia: OAU. Retrieved January 25, 2012, from http://www.uneca.org/itca/ariportal/docs/lagos_plan.PDF

Organisation of African Unity (OAU). (1981). The African (Banjul) Charter on Human and People's Rights. Retrieved on March 20, 2012, from http://www.africa-union.org/official_documents/treaties_%20conventions_%20protocols/banjul%20charter.pdf

Schmeisser, Iris. (2006). *Transatlantic crossings between Paris and New York: Pan-Africanism, cultural difference and the arts in the interwar years.* Heidelberg, Germany: Universitätsverlag Winter GmbH.

Schraeder, Peter J. (2004). *African politics and society: A mosaic in transformation* (2nd ed.). Belmont, CA: Wadsworth/Thomson Learning Press.

Stevens, Christopher, & Kennan, Jane. (2005). *EU-ACP economic partnership agreements: The effect of reciprocity* (Briefing paper). Brighton, UK: Institute of Development Studies. Retrieved January 7, 2012, from http://www.sarpn.org/documents/d0001254/EPA_reciprocity_BP2.pdf

Taylor, Ian. (2005). *NEPAD: Toward Africa's development or another false start?* Boulder, CO: Lynne Rienner Publishers.

Toure, Sekou, & Acquah, Peter. (Eds.). (2006). *History of the African Ministerial Council on the Environment: 1985–2005.* African Ministerial Council on the Environment (AMCEN) and the United Nations Environment Programme (UNEP). Retrieved March 20, 2012, from: http://www.unep.org/roa/Amcen/docs/publications/AMCENHistory.pdf

United Nations (UN). (2011). *United Nations Conference on Trade and Development (UNCTAD) handbook of statistics 2011.* Retrieved March 21, 2012, from http://www.onuitalia.it/images/file_articoli/2012/Jan2012/unctad_handbook_stats_2012.pdf

United Nations Economic Commission for Africa (UNECA). (1991, June 3). Treaty establishing the African Economic Community (AEC). Retrieved February 6, 2012, from http://www.uneca.org/itca/ariportal/abuja.htm

United Nations Economic Commission for Africa (UNECA). (2000, July 11). Constitutive Act of the African Union. Retrieved January 31, 2012, from http://www.uneca.org/daweca/conventions_and_resolutions/constitution.pdf

United Nations Economic Commission for Africa (UNECA). (2002). Charter of the Organisation of African Unity (OAU). Retrieved February 6, 2012, at http://www.uneca.org/itca/ariportal/oaucharter.htm

Agriculture, Small-Scale

Small-scale farmers are at the heart of the effort to feed more of the world's growing population. At the same time, they aim to conserve the environment and practice sustainable agriculture. In Africa and Eurasia, conservation agriculture, a diminution in the use of fossil fuels, the preservation of the soil, and the effort to minimize the use of chemicals and to protect biodiversity are all strategies for sustaining agriculture.

Concern about the sustainability of small-scale agriculture comes at a turbulent moment. The Green Revolution petered out in the 1980s, as grain yields began to fall worldwide. In the 1980s, the world lost 60,000 square kilometers of arable land per year to erosion. By 2050, the global temperature may increase 2°C to 6°C above 2010 levels. Rain may deluge areas where it is already abundant, and arid regions may lose what little they receive. Fossil fuels will likely be in short supply and consequently expensive. Yet in this time of crisis, a growing world population will demand 50 percent more food by 2025. Some experts believe that this 50 percent increase in food production will further degrade the environment. If farmers, small- and large-scale, denude the planet of forests to maximize arable land, they might squeeze 80 percent more food from the land, but the environment would suffer irreparable loss. To meet the demand by increasing yields, more fertilizer, pesticides, herbicides, and irrigation seem necessary; but all these inputs threaten the environment and will stretch the resources of small-scale farmers.

History

Agriculture arose independently in Eurasia and North America. Archaeologists have found very early agrarian settlements, surely of small-scale farmers, in the Middle East. In Mesopotamia, small-scale farmers were numerous in the north, although large estates arose near the Persian Gulf in the south. In Central Asia, farmers grew wheat and barley as early as 6000 BCE. In northern Africa, the rise of agriculture under the guidance of the pharaohs in Egypt established a pattern of landholding that continued into Roman antiquity. The pharaoh claimed ownership of all land, although in practice farmers worked small tracts along the Nile River. Egyptian agriculture was thus atomized into small units. The Romans, conquering Egypt in the first century BCE, preserved the practice of regal ownership of all land. The Roman emperors declared Egypt to be their personal property, although small-scale farmers continued to work the land.

The Romans may have been antiquity's boosters of small-scale agriculture. Roman agricultural writers believed that farmers were the backbone of civilization, and wherever they went, the Romans encouraged small-scale agriculture. In Roman North Africa, small farms coexisted with rangeland. In Roman Spain, small-scale farmers grew olives, although they also competed with large-scale farmers. In Turkey and Palestine, small-scale farmers grew grain and fruit. Small-scale farmers in Gaul grew the grapes that they fermented into wine, although here again, they competed with large estates.

On the one hand, small-scale farmers threatened the environment in antiquity. Their quest to bring land under the plow led to deforestation, especially in marginal environments. On the other hand, the Romans urged these farmers to conserve the environment, particularly the soil. Aware of the ruinous effects of soil exhaustion, the Romans counseled farmers to rotate grain with legumes and to use dung from livestock, birds, and even humans to enrich the soil. The fact that Rome had about one million inhabitants in the first century CE suggests that small-scale agriculture was productive enough to support a large urban population. These farmers must have been good stewards of the soil for agriculture to be so productive.

The decline of imperial Rome in the fourth and fifth centuries CE coincided with the rise of large estates in Europe. These estates, known as manors, used serfs to farm the land. The serfs were akin to small-scale farmers because each serf tended a long, narrow strip of land. The manor was thus atomized as Egypt had been. This kind of small-scale agriculture persisted into the Middle Ages, although careful Roman stewardship of the environment may have ebbed during this period. The diminution in the size of cities at this time suggests that agricultural productivity declined so that less food was reaching the urban centers. It seems possible that the small-scale farmers of the Middle Ages did not conserve the fertility of the soil as well as the Romans had. By the eighteenth century, though, Europeans were again mindful of the value of the soil. Small-scale farmers applied as much manure to the soil as their livestock could produce. Agricultural authorities touted the value of manure and crop rotation in increasing soil fertility. In conserving the soil, small-scale farmers conserved an important part of the environment.

One component of the environment is the biodiversity that it sustains. When humans migrated into central Europe, they brought both grasses for pasture and attractive, ornamental flowering plants. Thanks in part to the efforts of these migrants, the flora and fauna of central Europe were diverse into the nineteenth century. Thereafter, modern agriculture, with its emphasis on monoculture and the use of chemical herbicides and pesticides, has diminished this diversity. Farmers have been taking advantage of the bioengineering of herbicide-resistant soybeans, for example, to apply herbicide liberally to their fields without fear of injuring their soybean crop. The result is tracts of land clean of any vegetation except soybeans, leaving little forage for wildlife. This system of agriculture, a triumph of biotechnology and chemistry, has diminished wildlife populations and imperiled biodiversity. Although small-scale farming persists in some areas of the world, this large-scale monoculture is endangering the interconnected fabric of plants and animals in many places.

Toward Sustainability

As early as 1972, the United Nations warned that modern agriculture, reliant on fossil fuels and harmful chemicals, was not environmentally sustainable. The Food and Agriculture Organization of the United Nations (FAO) has championed the sustainability of small-scale agriculture. The FAO promotes conservation agriculture—farming that relies on minimum or no tillage (the practice of planting seeds without plowing fields beforehand) and aims to reduce farmers' reliance on fossil fuels and chemicals—in Africa, Europe, and West and Central Asia. To this end, the FAO established the Conservation Agriculture Working Group and convened international meetings to exchange research on conservation agriculture. In Africa, the FAO has recruited small-scale farmers in Malawi, Kenya, Eritrea, Ethiopia, Uganda, Tanzania, Guinea, Ghana, Burkina Faso, and Lesotho. Particularly attractive is the FAO's espousal of conservation agriculture as a way of saving labor in regions of Africa where deaths from AIDS have reduced the labor force. In addition to its work in Africa, the FAO sponsored conferences in 1999 in Kazakhstan and in 2000 in Altai to highlight the importance of conservation agriculture in that region.

In addition to pressing its own efforts, the FAO cooperates with other organizations globally. In 1998, the FAO and the Agricultural Research Council of South Africa organized an international conference in Harare, Zimbabwe. The venue was symbolic of the importance of small-scale agriculture in a nation of small farmers. In 1999, the FAO and its companion organizations formed the African Conservation Tillage Network (ACT) to promote minimum or no tillage as an environmentally sustainable practice. The ACT additionally recommends planting legumes for their ability to fix nitrogen in the soil, which lowers the need for chemical fertilizers. The legumes are used as green manure, and they are tilled into the soil rather than harvested. Some small-scale farmers have been reluctant, however, to spend time and energy tending a crop only to plow it under. The ACT aims to persuade African nations to create their own agencies to promote conservation. The organization compiles and disseminates information about best practices to sustain the environment and collects evidence that conservation tillage benefits small-scale farmers. It also publishes a monthly electronic newsletter, although it is unclear how many small-scale farmers, particularly poor ones, read it.

Another organization, the European Conservation Agricultural Federation (ECAF), counts among its members Belgium, Denmark, France, Germany, Greece, Italy, Portugal, Slovakia, Spain, Switzerland, and the United Kingdom. Chartered in 1999, the ECAF promotes the conservation of soil and biodiversity. It promotes environmentalism and increasing crop yields on the grounds that farmers will not pursue methods that do not sustain yields, no matter how environmentally sound.

Current Practices

As early as the 1970s, small-scale farmers in northern Kazakhstan practiced minimum or no tillage, protecting soil from wind erosion. By conserving the soil, these farmers maintained spring wheat yields at one tonne per hectare. Other areas of Central Asia, although slower to adopt conservation agriculture, have begun diversifying and rotating crops and practicing integrated pest management, a strategy that has reduced their reliance on pesticides. Because minimum- and no-tillage soil needs infusions of nitrogen, small-scale farmers in Central Asia have added legumes to their rotations. Rotation of chickpeas and small grains is a popular combination. In southern Kazakhstan, Kyrgyzstan, and Uzbekistan, small-scale farmers grow legumes and oilseed crops alternately with wheat. Small-scale farmers in Kyrgyzstan, Uzbekistan, Tajikistan, and Turkmenistan rotate cotton and wheat with forage crops. In other regions of Central Asia, small-scale farmers have diversified agriculture beyond the monoculture that robs soil of its fertility by growing sugar beets, corn, soybeans, peas, and safflower. Soybeans and peas are legumes that aid in fixing nitrogen in the soil. In northern Kazakhstan, small-scale farmers grow the legumes chickpeas, lentils, and peas. Where small-scale farmers had once fallowed land, tilling the fields without sowing a crop in them, they now rotate chickpeas with oats. This strategy reduces erosion because plant roots hold the soil in place whereas cultivated soil in fallow fields is liable to be washed away. In Kyrgyzstan, small farmers have also replaced fallow with forage, oilseed crops, and legumes.

In Africa, sustainable agriculture is particularly important. Soil in many parts of the continent is subject to erosion because the climate is extremely dry, and small-scale farmers are numerous and often poor and without access to current information and newer technologies. Since the 1980s, governments have aimed to strengthen small-scale farmers with the goal of making Africa self-sufficient in food production. Small-scale farmers are the majority of the population in most of Africa. In the eastern and southern part of the continent, for example, 80 percent of farmers have fewer than five hectares under cultivation. In Tunisia, 35 percent of date growers have farms of less than one hectare, and another 45 percent have just one to three hectares.

In Zimbabwe and Tanzania, large-scale farmers have been more eager to practice conservation tillage than have small-scale farmers. The dynamic is complicated in Zimbabwe, where the white minority monopolized the best land until the 1980s. White farmers held land in large estates, leaving blacks with small parcels of marginal land. Since the 1980s, however, the government has supported small-scale farmers by helping them market food, providing technicians and scientists to advise them, and extending credit. The reliance on corn, cotton, sunflower, and small grains has depleted the soil of nutrients, and the thin soils of Zimbabwe's marginal farms are vulnerable to overcropping, continuous cultivation until the soil's nutrients are completely depleted. Soil erosion, river siltation, and deforestation have also undermined the Zimbabwean environment. Many small-scale farmers lack money to buy fertilizer, and without fertilizer yields have declined on marginal land, especially in the southern and western parts of the country. Poor farmers, desperate for money, cut down trees to sell for fuel wood, exacerbating the problem of deforestation. In the twenty-first century, Zimbabwe's government, like many governments worldwide, has moved away from socialism and toward a free market economy. The World Bank and International Monetary Fund support these reforms, but little thought seems to go into what effect the reforms will have on the farmers or the environment. Without the support of a social safety net, the unemployed may turn to unsustainable practices, such as scavenging for wood and cutting trees on public lands or attempting to farm marginal land that is better left fallow. Increasing numbers of rural poor, barely able to eke out a living, may exploit the soil in ways that cannot be sustained.

In Ethiopia, traditional agricultural practices may not be sustainable. Teff, the most commonly grown grain, has such small seeds that farmers must pulverize the soil before planting to enable it to take root. It is customary to plow the soil five times before planting teff. Soil that has been cultivated to this degree is easily eroded; moreover, burning fossil fuels by plowing repeatedly with tractors exacerbates global warming. Conservation tillage may be a better practice in this environment. Moving to minimum or no tillage will reduce the amount of fossil fuel used, which will save money and the environment by putting less carbon dioxide in the atmosphere. (As a comparison, Greek small-scale farmers save sixty to eighty liters of fuel per hectare by practicing minimum or no tillage.)

As a ratio of yield to energy input from fossil fuels, yields have increased globally with the movement to conservation tillage. In many parts of Africa, yields have increased with the adoption of conservation tillage as they have in Kenya and Tanzania. In Tanzania, corn yields have risen as much as 50 percent. Yet some small-scale farmers who rely on cassava and sweet potatoes are reluctant to adopt minimum or no tillage because these crops do not direct-seed well. Another impediment for these farmers is that with no tillage techniques, it is difficult to manage the weeds that are numerous when farmers adopt the practice. Even farmers using conventional agriculture will not plant a crop until they have plowed under the invading weeds. To deal with the weed problem in the short term, farmers must use herbicides in large quantities on no-tillage land, a practice that harms the environment and is prohibitively expensive. As a result, one way small-scale farmers attempt to minimize weeds is to target fertilizer only to the crop rather than to broadcast it throughout a field, which enriches the soil for opportunistic weeds. The saving in fertilizer benefits the environment by leaving less of it to leech into groundwater or run off into streams and rivers. Small-scale date growers in Tunisia use no fertilizer, possibly because it is too expensive, but instead rely on manure, which enriches the soil and builds the quantity of organic matter. Soil rich in organic matter absorbs carbon dioxide from the atmosphere and so has the potential to slow global warming. Only 9.5 percent of Tunisia's small-scale date growers use pesticides. Ninety-five percent of these growers weed by hand rather than rely on herbicides. These traditional methods are sustainable practices. In Africa, there are nonetheless important impediments to the adoption of sustainable conservation practices. Because women do much of the labor on a small farm, their assent to conservation agriculture is essential for its success, but male dominated societies are reluctant to cede leadership to women. Many of the existing governmental agencies are reluctant, moreover, to embrace conservation agriculture.

In the 1990s, Europe began to focus attention on the relationship between agriculture and the environment. Conventional agriculture has not treated the continent kindly. In Europe, 16 percent of arable land has eroded. In southern Europe, as much as 75 percent of the land has eroded. In the worst instances, farmers are converting farmland to desert. By relying on inorganic fertilizers, farmers, small- and large-scale, have reduced the content of organic matter in the soil, making it less able to absorb carbon dioxide. As in other parts of the world, conservation agriculture has emerged as a way of protecting the environment and enhancing the sustainability of small-scale agriculture. Despite its potential, conservation agriculture has gained recruits very slowly. The United States, Canada, Brazil, Argentina, and Central Asia have all adopted conservation practices more quickly. The governments of Europe have been slow to offer small-scale farmers incentives to conserve fossil fuel, the land, and biodiversity. Spain, for example, did not begin to subsidize farmers who practiced conservation agriculture and planted cover crops to reduce erosion until 2001, while France now offers a disincentive to use irrigation water by charging farmers for it. Although small-scale farmers in Switzerland have only 3 percent of arable land in cultivation using no-tillage practices, even this small amount benefits the environment. This soil, for example, has more earthworms than conventionally tilled land. In an effort to increase conservation, Switzerland subsidizes farmers who adopt such practices.

As in Africa, European governments have expressed concern over the danger of fertilizer runoff. Some European farmers, usually small-scale, protect the environment by practicing organic farming, reducing the use of chemicals, converting cropland to pasture, rotating crops, and planting cover crops. Europeans seem committed to the idea that agriculture must be sustainable if it is to feed a growing population. Swedish small farmers speak not of conservation but of the care of nature. They wish to conserve the environment so that they can pass the family farm to their children. These farmers are knowledgeable enough to know that some farming practices harm the environment, although at times they put profit ahead of conservation. Some small-scale farmers, feeling constrained by regulations, resent the government for telling them how to manage their land. Climate change has produced different outcomes in different parts of Europe. Corn yields are high in much of Europe, but wheat yields are depressed in the Mediterranean basin. Small-scale farmers with limited resources are more vulnerable than large-scale farmers to climate change. Small-scale farmers in Europe feel caught between the public demand for environmental protection and the demands of the free market for the most economically efficient method of producing food regardless of environmental effects. German small farmers may be at the vanguard of the environmental movement. They conserve fossil fuels by using rapeseed oil as a substitute. Despite their good intentions, or perhaps because of them, however, small-scale farmers in Germany tend to be poorer than their counterparts in Denmark, the Netherlands, Belgium, northern France, and the United Kingdom.

The Future

In the future, globalization is likely to further impoverish small-scale farmers, many of whom do not have the financial or technological resources to adopt sustainable practices. These farmers are also faced with large multinational corporations that sell fertilizer, herbicides, and pesticides and continue to urge them to use their products. As the climate warms, pathogens and pests will migrate to higher latitudes, threatening the sustainability of small-scale agriculture. The oppressive heat of 2003, for example, caused crop failure even in temperate Europe and in parts of Africa and Asia. Small-scale farmers may be reluctant to plant corn in the future because it performed poorly in the hot, dry weather of 2003. In contrast, alfalfa yielded well in 2003, and it seems possible that farmers will plant it in the future as the legume of choice. Small-scale farmers are already making strides by confining intensive agriculture to the best lands with adequate rainfall and by planting legumes in rotation with other crops. For small-scale agriculture to thrive, scientists must develop drought-resistant crops and farmers must be encouraged to persist in minimum tillage and no-tillage methods.

Christopher CUMO
Independent scholar, Canton, Ohio

See also Africa (*several articles*); Central Asia; Desertification (Africa); Diet and Nutrition; Education, Environmental; Genetic Resources; Nile River; Transboundary Water Issues; Water Use and Rights (Africa); World Bank

FURTHER READING

African Conservation Tillage (ACT) Initiative. (2010, June 30). ACT e-newsletter, vol. 1. Retrieved September 15, 2011, from http://www.act-africa.org/publication/act_newsletter_vol1.pdf

Admassie, Yeraswarq; Mwarasombo, Lincoln I.; & Mbogo, P. (1998). *The sustainability of the catchment approach-induced measures and activities.* Nairobi, Kenya: National Soil and Water Conservation Program.

Alexandratos, Nikos. (1999). World food and agriculture: Outlook for the medium and longer term. *Proceedings of the national academy of sciences, 96,* 5908–5914.

Baland, Jean-Marie, & Platteau, Jean-Philippe. (1996). *Halting degradation of natural resources: Is there a role for rural communities?* London: Clarendon Press.

Bardham, Pranab K. (1984). *Land, labor and rural poverty.* New York: Columbia University Press.

Binns, Tony. (Ed.). (1995). *People and environment in Africa.* Chichester, UK: John Wiley & Sons.

Boyd, Charlotte, & Slaymaker, Tom. (2000). *Re-examining the "more people less erosion" hypothesis: Special case or wider trend? ODI Natural Resources Perspectives, Vol. 63.*

Burger, Kees. (Ed.). (2009). *Sustainable land management in the tropics: Explaining the miracle.* Surrey, UK: Ashgate.

Byiringiro, Fidele, & Reardon, Thomas. (1996). Farm productivity in Rwanda: Effects of farm size, erosion and soil conservation investments. *Agricultural Economics, 15,* 127–136.

Clay, Daniel C., et al. (1995). *Promoting food security in Rwanda through sustainable agricultural productivity: Meeting the challenges of population pressure, land degradation and poverty.* East Lansing: Michigan State University Press.

Clay, Daniel C., & Reardon, Thomas. (1994). *Determinants of farm-level conservation investments in Rwanda.* Milwaukee, WI: International Association of Agricultural Economists.

Clay, Daniel C.; Reardon, Thomas; & Kangasniemi, Jaakko. (1996). Sustainable intensification in the highland tropics: Rwandan farmers' investments in land conservation and soil fertility. *Economic Development and Cultural Change, 46,* 353–377.

Costin, Alec Baillie, & Coombs, Herbert Cole. (1982). Farm planning for resource conservation. *Search, 12*(12), 429–430.

Coxhead, Ian, & Jayasuriya, Sisira. (1995). Trade and tax policy reform and the environment: The economics of soil erosion in developing countries. *American Journal of Agricultural Economics, 77,* 631–644.

Deveze, Jean-Claude. (Ed.). (2001). *Challenges for African agriculture.* Washington, DC: The International Bank for Reconstruction and Development.

Dragon, Andrew K., & Tisdell, Clem. (Eds.). (1999). *Sustainable agriculture and environment: Globalization and the impact of trade liberalization.* Cheltenham, UK: Edward Elgar.

Earle, T. R.; Rose, C. W.; & Brownlea, A. A. (1979). Socio-economic predictors of intention towards soil conservation and their implication in environmental management. *Journal of Environmental Management, 9*(3), 225–236.

Ervin, Christine A., & Ervin, David E. (1982). Factors affecting the use of soil conservation practices: Hypothesis, evidence and policy implications. *Land Economics, 58*(3), 277–292.

Filho, Walter Leal. (2004). *Ecological agriculture and rural development in Central and Eastern European countries.* Amsterdam: IOS Press.

Garcia-Torres, Luis; Benites, Jose; Martinez-Vilela, Armondo; & Holgado-Cabrera, Antonio. (2003). *Conservation agriculture: Environment, farmers experiences, innovations, socio-economy, policy.* Boston: Kluwer Academic Publishers.

Gliessman, Stephen, & Rosemeyer, Martha. (Eds.). (2010). *The conversion to sustainable agriculture.* Boca Raton, FL: CRC Press.

Langeveld, Hans, & Roling, Neils. (Eds.). (2006). *Changing European farming systems for a better future: New visions for rural areas.* Wageningen, The Netherlands: Wageningen Academic Publishers.

Whiteside, Martin. (1998). *Living farms: Encouraging sustainable smallholder agriculture in southern Africa.* London: Earthscan Publications.

World Summit on Sustainable Development. (2002). Sustainable agriculture and rural development. Retrieved September 15, 2011, from http://www.fao.org/wssd/sard/index-en.htm

Architecture

Architecture is the interaction of humans with their built structures. Sustainable architecture accounts for the interrelations among humans, architecture, and the environment. Traditional architecture in such places as Africa is inherently sustainable, but mass production and industrial extraction of building materials and energy sources have led to high-tech, unsustainable architecture around the world. Many new technology-based approaches now promote sustainable architecture and urban planning.

Architecture and the built environment constitute the biggest noticeable interventions humans make on Earth. Buildings are immobile and fixed to their intended place and thus are exposed to the local natural environment. Because humans are sedentary, architecture and buildings are intended to have long life spans. Realizing and maintaining buildings requires a great expenditure of time and material.

Sustainability can be defined broadly as "methods, systems and materials that won't deplete resources or harm natural cycles" (Rosenbaum 1993). The characteristics of architecture greatly influence the environment and consequently affect sustainability, especially because a number of buildings are typically grouped together to form villages and towns. Architecture also inevitably shapes and influences social systems.

Although the terms *buildings* and *architecture* are often used as synonyms, they refer to different things. Whereas buildings include many types of physical structures humans create to serve a purpose, architecture is a planned structure aimed at fulfilling a balance of functionality, form, and usability (see the ancient Roman Vitruvius's architectural theories in Vitruvius Pollio 2001). Architecture includes the interaction of humans and the built structure.

Because architecture can extensively influence the natural environment, it can vary greatly in its degree of sustainability. Sustainable architecture ideally uses a low amount of energy to operate buildings; low embodied energy in building materials and the building process; and building materials that are healthy and nontoxic, recyclable, and durable enough to last the lifetime of the building. Sustainable buildings place low climatic demands on the surrounding environment (for example, by using natural ventilation) and do not take up excessive land. Their life cycle costs, including the costs of removing the buildings from service, are low. A process of civic participation is ideally part of the architectural process, which takes into account the mobility needs of its users. Sustainable architecture creates, identities, and reflects the human scale.

Sustainable architecture is not equivalent to energy efficient architecture nor does it mean reaching certain benchmarks. It also cannot be equated with carbon neutrality because scientists may detect future elements that have far greater influence on the atmosphere than carbon is suspected to have. Sustainability means not only being efficient but ethical. Sustainable architecture is a particular approach to solving architectural problems that takes into account the interrelations among humans, architecture, and the environment. It develops a balanced and lasting solution with minimal negative impacts on each system.

Sustainability responds to economic, ecological, and social preconditions and has to be understood as a relative performance dimension. The approaches to sustainable architecture in Africa, Asia, and Europe differ widely, as the aims and fundamental aspects of sustainability are subject to given local conditions and will vary according to culture and local resources.

Traditional architecture in Africa, originating mainly in traditional and vernacular (based on local needs and available materials) edifices, is largely sustainable. Extreme climates and the scarcity of certain natural resources like wood or stone led people in some areas to build mud and straw buildings. Such vernacular architecture is often completely recyclable and built with local material, often under minimum material application. The great strength of vernacular African sustainable architecture is the strict locality of solutions. Besides building technologies, the layout and spatial organization are important aspects of traditional African architecture; many African ethnic groups identify with their local building tradition as an expression of cultural identities.

Newly built sustainable architecture in Africa is comparatively scarce. There is a great technological gap between traditional, sustainable building methods and imported modern, less sustainable building technologies. Strong economic and population growth led to an abrupt implementation of modern building methods. The "sustainability gap" evolved from mass production and industrial extraction of building materials and energy sources. Cheap oil and gas made it easy to transport materials over long distances and to run heating and cooling systems. Cheap wood became an easily accessible building material. Pollution was not visible, and the pressure of rapid growth overshadowed the dimension of social responsibility. African countries and builders have not followed the imperative of sustainability for many decades. The central problem of today's approaches to sustainable architecture in Africa is that builders do not use traditional knowledge for present building assignments. On the contrary, Africa imports technology such as artificial building materials, high-performance glass, or advanced heating, ventilation, and air conditioning systems.

Once national states formed in Africa, often negating existing tribal areas, and border controls restricted migration to places with lower population density or better economic boundary conditions, the social dimension of architecture came back into focus. The Egyptian architect Hassan Fathy (1900–1989) transferred traditional African sustainable architectural approaches to twentieth-century buildings. His designs included considerations of energy efficiency in the form of natural cooling and ventilation. He used local materials like mud, embraced traditional craft skills, and focused on public health and poverty concerns. Fathy's buildings often achieved comfortable and healthy indoor climates without technical equipment. He received the first Right Livelihood Award (the "alternative Nobel Prize") in 1980, the Aga Khan Award for Architecture, and other honors. Fathy's social initiatives became an example for international development initiatives. His rediscovered building technologies are used in modern energy-efficient architecture. The perception that modern (less sustainable) architecture is more prestigious kept his approaches from gaining wider application, however.

The oil- and capital-rich Persian Gulf states were the first to carry unsustainable architecture to extremes in the late twentieth and early twenty-first centuries. Abundant and cheap oil and gas led to building types more suitable to areas with very different climates. These countries were also among the first to introduce sustainable high-tech architecture, however. Masdar City in Abu Dhabi typifies the latest sustainable approaches to architecture and urban planning in the Persian Gulf states. The initiating Abu Dhabi Future Energy Company and the general planners of Foster + Partners Architects aim to realize a city based entirely on solar energy and other renewable sources that achieves a zero-carbon and a zero-waste ecology. The social dimension of Masdar's architecture is oriented toward high-density structures including traditional building designs. A spatial mix of uses throughout the city and a non-carbon-dioxide-emitting public transportation system reduce land consumption and emissions.

Architectural and technological developments reached extremes in Europe and Asia, even more than in Africa, as industrialization in Europe, with its huge demands for energy and materials, influenced architecture and building for centuries. Europeans viewed unsustainable architecture as prestigious and a sign of power and wealth. Limited resources, however, especially land, in Europe have helped advance sustainable approaches. Germany's high population density and its traditional high esteem of forests and woods—frequently mentioned in literature, poetry, and chant—led the way to economical forest use that maintained the forests' structure and appearance. Strong legislation, which demands certain efficiency standards for architecture, has enhanced a technology-driven industry of sustainable building material producers and sustainability-oriented planners in most of Europe. Some of this knowledge of energy efficiency and sustainability in architecture and urban planning has been exported to Asia and Africa. Sustainable city projects have taken place in Dongtan and Anting near Shanghai, China.

Challenges and targets for sustainability approaches in Asia differ from in Europe. Population explosion and migration make the sustainability achievement in the middle term in Asia lower than that of more settled regions. Durability of architecture and urban structures is remarkably shorter due to persistent changes and fluctuation of users, functional requirements, and integrated building equipment and appliances. Sustainability targets of Asian architecture are reached by smaller, more frequent developmental steps.

Outlook

The future of sustainable building and architecture will vary from region to region. An effective reanimation of vernacular sustainability approaches to architecture is, unfortunately, unlikely to influence building on a greater scale. Most of traditional sustainability knowledge will not be continued as traditional building technologies and traditional building layouts are discontinued. New approaches are overwhelmingly technology based.

Many of these new technology-based approaches, however, are shedding light on the social dimension of sustainable architecture and urban planning. European harmonization will create comparable sustainability approaches in architecture all over Europe as many sustainability targets are set jointly, like the European Union Sustainable Development Strategy. Targets will likely be ambitious.

The outlook ahead includes expectations of great leaps of progress in the fast-developing countries of Asia, like South Korea, China, or Singapore, while other areas of Asia and Africa in general will see less uniform progress in sustainability developments. Highly developed and wealthy countries will establish—or already have done so—sustainability regulations and benchmarks. With international trade and worldwide competition of cities and regions, focal points that attract global business will establish comparable architectural sustainability standards.

Many countries have developed efficiency and sustainability labels. Leadership in Energy and Environmental Design (LEED) in the United States, the German Sustainable Building Council, Japan's Comprehensive Assessment System for Built Environment Efficiency (CASBEE), and the United Kingdom's Building Research Establishment Environmental Assessment Method (BREAAM) extend building and architecture from energy efficiency to sustainability. Standards such as these will likely be used for building certification worldwide.

These focal points with certified sustainable architectural projects hold promise of gradually spreading beyond the world's business hubs and bringing sustainable architecture to more of the world.

Alexander PICHURA
Pichura Consult—Architects

See also Dubai, United Arab Emirates; Energy Security (Europe); Germany; Rural Development; Urbanization (*several articles*)

FURTHER READING

BRE Environmental Assessment Method (BREEAM). (2011). BREEAM: The environmental assessment method for buildings around the world. Retrieved January 17, 2011, from http://www.breeam.org

Elleh, Nnamdi. (1996). *African architecture: Evolution and transformation.* New York: McGraw-Hill.

Fathy, Hassan. (2000). *Architecture for the poor: An experiment in rural Egypt.* Chicago, IL: University of Chicago Press.

German Sustainable Building Council. (2011). Homepage. Retrieved January 17, 2011, from http://www.dgnb.de/_en/index.php

Japan Sustainable Building Consortium (JSBC). (2011). An overview of CASBEE: Comprehensive Assessment System for Built Environment Efficiency. Retrieved January 17, 2011, from http://www.ibec.or.jp/CASBEE/english/overviewE.htm

Lauber, Wolfgang. (2005). *Tropical architecture: Sustainable and humane building in Africa, Latin America and South-East Asia.* Munich: Prestel.

Rosenbaum, M. (1993). Sustainable design strategies. *Solar Today,* March/April.

United States Green Building Council (USGBC). (2011). Homepage. Retrieved January 17, 2011, from http://www.usgbc.org

Vitruvius Pollio, Marcus. (2001). *Vitruvius: Ten books on architecture.* (Ingrid D. Rowland & Thomas Noble Howe, Eds.). Cambridge, UK: Cambridge University Press. (Original work 1st century BCE)

Williamson, Terry; Radford, Antony; & Bennetts, Helen. (2003). *Understanding sustainable architecture.* London: Routledge.

Yudelson, Jerry. (2007). *Green building A to Z: Understanding the language of green building.* Gabriola Island, Canada: New Society Publishers.

Yudelson, Jerry. (2009). *Green building trends: Europe.* Washington, DC: Island Press.

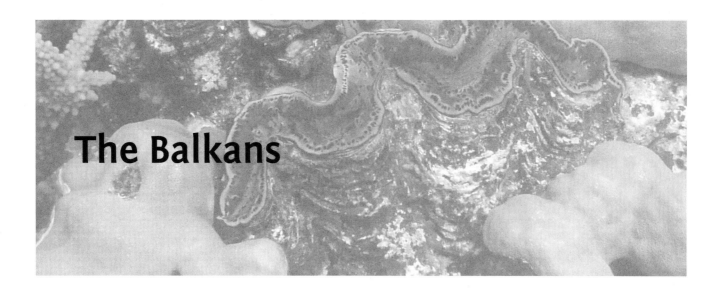

The Balkans

The Balkans is a region in the southeast of Europe. The term can refer either to the mountain range located inside Bulgaria or (more commonly) to the peninsula that shares its name, or to both. This region has a long history of agrarian traditions practiced by small landholders. The fall of communism in 1989 led to conflict and environmental problems, pertaining especially to pollution, deforestation, and water resources management, most of which remain unresolved.

The term *Balkans* generally refers to that region comprising either the mountain range found primarily in Bulgaria and on the Balkan Peninsula of southeastern Europe or the peninsula itself—or both. The mountains themselves often are considered to be part of a larger system that includes the Carpathian Mountains and the Transylvanian Alps to the north. In addition, other closer ranges often are included as subsystems or further extensions of the Balkan Mountains in this larger system; these ranges include the Dinaric Alps, the North Albanian Mountains, the Rhodope Mountains, and the Stara Planina. The range itself is almost 550 kilometers in length and runs approximately along the forty-third parallel north from the Belogradchik Pass in the west to the Black Sea in the east. Mount Botev is the highest peak in the Balkans at 2,376 meters above sea level, and the range's average height is just below 725 meters above sea level. From a geological perspective, the Balkans are mixed structurally, and this region has suffered significant earthquakes—sixty-two with catastrophic losses occurred between 1900 and 2010 (Abolmasov et al. 2011).

The Balkan Peninsula is one of three large peninsulas that define the geography of the southern European continent, and it is defined as the landed mass situated with the Mediterranean Sea to its south, the Aegean and Black seas to its east, the Adriatic and Ionian seas to its west, and the Danube River and its plains at its northern limit. Throughout the peninsula, rivers and associated valleys historically have constituted the main conduits for communications, trade, and transport.

The Balkans are home to a variety of peoples who are distinguished mostly by language and religious beliefs and who define their ethnicity and national aspirations in divergent ways. These peoples include Albanians, Bosnians, Bulgarians, Croats, Greeks, Jews (although their numbers are vastly reduced from their pre–World War II population), Macedonians, Muslims, Pomaks, Roma or Gypsies, Romanians, Serbs, Slovenes, and Turks.

The ecologies of the region reflect long-standing traditions of settled agriculture and various forms of animal husbandry (the care and breeding of domestic animals). Traditionally, peasant farmers have undertaken on small scales the vast majority of agricultural efforts throughout the region's history. The agrarian traditions of small landholders still prevail in the region into the twenty-first century, and most settlements throughout the Balkans are relatively small towns and villages.

Agriculture, Nature Resources, and Industry

Animal husbandry in the Balkans takes various forms and reflects variations both in herd/flock compositions and sizes, scales of production, and settlement preferences. Animals common in many parts of the region include sheep, goats, cattle, and pigs. Some regional traditions of livestock production historically have been depicted as causing both overgrazing and deforestation.

In addition to settled traditions of husbandry (in which herds remain in an established location), nomadic pastoralism (in which livestock are herded in irregular patterns to find fresh pastures) and transhumance (in which seasonal pastures are used) were also common in some periods.

Long-standing practices of extracting forest resources in the Balkans have caused deforestation, a common problem in some areas both historically and as of the early twenty-first century. Also, mining operations have focused on hard coal (anthracite) and other varieties of coal, as well as on copper and iron ores. Water resources are significant, both in their own right and as sources of power generation.

Although the Turkish Ottoman Empire controlled many parts of the region for almost five centuries (fifteenth to early twentieth century), the experiences of socialism and post-socialist conflicts in the latter half of the twentieth century made the greatest impact on the region's natural environments and cultural landscapes. Most processes of large-scale industrialization in the region took place during the socialist era. As in other parts of the Soviet and socialist realm, oversight was inadequate to regulate how the country developed and appropriated natural resources, as well as to consider how, and to what degree, these actions impacted the environment.

Environmental Issues in the Socialist and Post-Socialist Periods

Various environmental problems have their roots in the socialist period; these problems include situations related to urban and industrial contamination and overconsumption of water resources and its effects on associated environments (e.g., wetlands). Severe problems in the Danube River and its delta are among the most apparent to international observers, but many similar situations exist in the region's other rivers, lakes, and wetlands. Also harmful and widespread in the region are situations caused by numerous environmental problems, including contamination of land resources from improper disposal of solid wastes, unsafe air emissions, pollution of land and water resources associated with mining activities, deforestation, contamination of land and water resources by agricultural practices, erosion of soil resources, and associated losses in biodiversity (the existence of many different kinds of plants and animals in an environment). These problems have continued into the post-socialist era because resources are inadequate to devote to the needed reforms.

The conflict following the collapse of socialism in Eastern Europe and the former Soviet Union has exacerbated these environmentally and socioeconomically harmful situations. Significant difficulties emerging in the current Balkan environment have their roots in the violent conflicts that have raged in much of the former Federal Republic of Yugoslavia and at its peripheries. In addition to the loss of human life and the destruction of significant places in the region's built landscapes (features reflecting human occupation and use of natural resources), battles and violent episodes of ethnic cleansing have produced many problems arising from the large number of displaced persons throughout the region. Many refugees lack the bare necessities of life (e.g., fuel, food, homes), and their struggle to survive can create more environmental problems related to deforestation, erosion, and violation of land and water resources.

In 2010, national parks in the Balkans region protested against the illegal logging and lax enforcement that threatened the region's once-abundant forests. After years of neglect, authorities (including the governments of Romania and Croatia) and nongovernmental organizations (NGOs) in the region did begin to take action to reverse the decline in forest acreage (*The Independent* 2010). The environmental ramifications of civil war reveal themselves in other ways: areas littered with landmines, dangerous munitions (especially the depleted uranium munitions employed by NATO peacekeeping forces), and bombed facilities (e.g., factories, petrochemical plants) put people at risk and contaminate lands and water sources.

In 1988, the organization Green Balkans was created with a mandate for the conservation of rare species and habitats in Bulgaria (Green Balkans n.d.). It is a federation of nature conservation NGOs that is focused on the conservation of biodiversity and wildlife and has had success in raising public and government awareness of environmental issues.

Among other environmental problems, the Balkans region is susceptible to possible future droughts and heavy flooding. Albania is a particular flood risk from rising water levels because most of its surface and underground water is polluted. Bosnia's lack of infrastructure means that, increasingly, water there is undrinkable. Montenegro lost 48 million of the 54 million cubic meters of distributed water in 2005. Kosovo suffered a drought in 2007 that devastated whole communities, and more drought is expected in the future. Croatia has the best infrastructure, yet its many islands experience droughts most summers. Macedonia is thought to be the country that will be the worst affected by climate change in the region. Some 85 percent of Serbia's water originates outside of the country, the Danube being the core of the water system. Recent industrialization has led to increasing levels of contamination and less available drinking water (Delsere 2011).

The Future

In attempting to bring peace and long-term stability to the region, the United Nations is attempting to address fundamental questions of environmental security. The creation of the joint United Nations Environment Programme (UNEP) and United Nations Centre for Human Settlements (Habitat) Balkans Task Force (BTF) has been the first of such initiatives specifically concerned with natural and human environments in the area. While the Balkans region still faces many challenges emanating from its historic and contemporary contexts, this initiative seeks to resolve many of these problems and serve as a model for other regions of conflict (e.g., Afghanistan, Central Africa) in dealing with environmental challenges.

Kyle T. EVERED
Michigan State University

See also Agriculture, Small-Scale; Danube River; Mediterranean Sea; Russia and the Soviet Union; Ukraine

This article was adapted by the editors from Kyle T. Evered's article, "Balkans," in Shepard Krech III, J. R. McNeill, and Carolyn Merchant (Eds.), the *Encyclopedia of World Environmental History*, pp. 113–115. Great Barrington, MA: Berkshire Publishing (2003).

FURTHER READING

Abolmasov, Biljana; Jovanovski, Milorad; Ferić, Pavle; & Mihalić, Snježana. (2011). Losses due to historical earthquakes in the Balkan region: Overview of publicly available data. Retrieved June 5, 2012, from http://geofizika-journal.gfz.hr/vol_28/No1/28_1_abolmasov_et_al.pdf

Carter, Francis W. (Ed.). (1977). *An historical geography of the Balkans*. London: Academic Press.

Delsere, Lauren. (2011, June 2). Water in the Balkans: Too much, yet not enough. Retrieved April 16, 2012, from http://greengopost.com/water-balkans/

Green Balkans. (n.d.). Who we are? Retrieved April 11, 2012, from http://www.greenbalkans.org/category.php?language=en_EN&cat_id=57

The Independent. (2010, May 21). Balkans sound alarm over disappearing forests. Retrieved April 16, 2012, from http://www.independent.co.uk/environment/balkans-sound-alarm-over-disappearing-forests-1979367.html

Todorova, Maria N. (1997). *Imagining the Balkans*. New York: Oxford University Press.

United Nations Environment Programme (UNEP)/United Nations Centre for Human Settlements (Habitat) Balkans Task Force (BTF). (n.d.). Homepage. Retrieved April 16, 2012, from http://www.grid.unep.ch/btf/

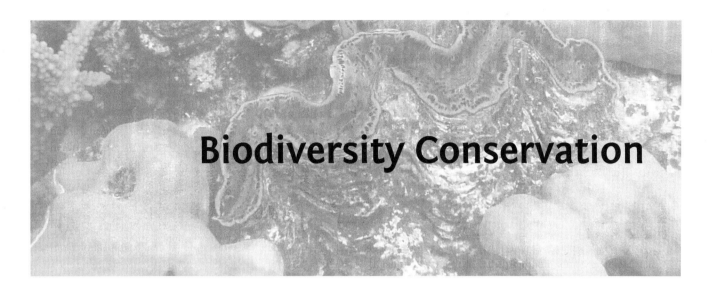

Biodiversity Conservation

Healthy ecosystems, characterized by a good biodiversity level, provide a multitude of services, some of them crucial for human life. Humans tend to overexploit natural resources because they often focus on short-term economic benefits rather than long-term environmental impacts. Conservation of biodiversity is the protection, preservation, management, and restoration of ecosystems, fauna, and flora in order to safeguard threatened species and habitats for current and future generations.

Conservation of biodiversity can be defined as *in situ* and *ex situ* conservation. In situ conservation is the preservation of ecosystems, habitats, plants, and animals in their natural environmental and biological location. Ex situ conservation takes place outside of the natural environment, in places such as zoos, botanical gardens, and seed banks. Conservation may involve the protection of threatened habitats or ecosystems, threatened animal or plant species, or biodiversity hotpots. Habitat degradation may cause species extinction.

The human influence on ecosystems is increasing the rate of species extinction. The International Union for Conservation of Nature (IUCN) assesses the global status of existing species. They publish the IUCN Red List of Threatened Species (IUCN n.d.), renowned as the most inclusive assessment of the conservation status of species, based on data that different conservation organizations provide. The IUCN bases its selection on biodiversity "hotspots," which helps it to define priorities. The term *hotspot* refers to a geographical area with high conservation value because of its high biodiversity richness and high risk of habitat and species extinction (Conservation International n.d.).

Linked with the concept of conservation is IUCN's (2011) definition of *protected area*: "A protected area is a clearly defined geographical space, recognised, dedicated and managed, through legal or other effective means, to achieve the long term conservation of nature with associated ecosystem services and cultural values." The IUCN defines a number of protected area categories: Strict Nature Reserves (for wilderness protection), National Parks (to protect natural ecosystems and recreation), Natural Monuments (for the conservation of specific features), Habitats (related to management interventions), Protected Landscapes (for conservation and recreation), and Managed Resources Protected Areas (for sustainable use). International protected areas include the following:

- Ramsar sites (international wetlands) under the Convention on Wetlands of International Relevance
- Biosphere reserves including terrestrial, coastal, and marine ecosystems internationally recognized under the United Nations Educational, Scientific and Cultural Organization (UNESCO) Man and the Biosphere Programme
- Biogenetic reserves under the Berne Convention
- World Heritage sites under the UNESCO Convention for Protection of World Cultural and Natural Heritage
- European sites and candidate European sites under the Habitats Directive (Special Areas of Conservation), and under the Wild Birds Directive (Special Protected Areas)
- European Diploma sites designated by the Council of Europe

Biodiversity Trends and Habitat Loss

The unsustainable use of the goods and services provided by an ecosystem depletes natural resources and related levels of biodiversity, with effects on the supply of ecosystem services that range from drinking water and food supplies to recreational uses. Sustainability can be assured only if natural resources are used in ways that do not exceed the threshold level of nature's recovery. Since the 1970s, human activities have exploited natural resources at unprecedented levels due to the rapid economic and population growth that has produced an increase in people's general welfare, at least in the richer countries. The costs of these changes are increased degradation of ecosystem services, substantial loss of biodiversity on Earth, and increased poverty of some groups. Scientists estimate that 60 percent of ecosystem services are degraded and exploited in an unsustainable way (MEA 2005). If this problem is not addressed, the global ecosystem's benefits to humans, including future generations, will be affected. Policies and institutions need to change significantly and set up conservation programs in order to reverse these negative impacts on the ecosystem while they take into account human necessities (MEA 2005).

Europe's demand for natural resources is higher than their provision (EEA 2010). There is no harmonized monitoring system of existing habitats and ecosystems. The limited data available do, however, show an alarming degradation of aquatic habitats and coastal zones and nutrient-poor terrestrial habitats (moorlands, marshes, wetlands) (EEA 2010). Ecologists consider forests, the major natural vegetation in Europe, to be critical ecosystems for the provision of ecosystem services and for the preservation of biodiversity levels. They are exploited mostly by human activities (e.g., logging); only about 5 percent remain untouched. Data from the Coordination of Information on the Environment (CORINE) Land Cover 2000 project show a dramatic decrease in the population of butterflies in wetlands (around 90 percent) and in grassland (around 50 percent) in the period 1970–2000. Forest birds have decreased by around 15 percent since 1990, although since 2000 the population has been stable. Unsustainable agricultural practices have led to a remarkable reduction in farmland birds in the 1980s (EEA 2010).

The Russian Federation insufficiently funds biodiversity inventories and assessment and lacks sufficient incentives and mechanisms to promote biodiversity conservation and sustainable land use. Protected areas represent around 2 percent of the territory of the Russian Federation, with 95 reserves, 33 national parks, 1,600 state game reserves, and 8,000 natural monuments (Caspian Environment Programme 2005). Most of the protected areas are situated in forest ecosystems. Unique marine ecosystems are insufficiently investigated and monitored and are at high risk because of oil pipelines constructed in southern and northern seas. Freshwater ecosystems are also under high threat as an increased number of species, mainly fish, become extinct (Caspian Environment Programme 2005). The Russian Federation Red Data Book, prepared by the Department of Biodiversity Conservation of the State Committee of Environmental Protection together with the Russian Academy of Sciences, lists rare and endangered species, both plants and animals, including 155 invertebrate, 39 fish, 8 amphibian, 221 reptile, 123 bird, and 65 mammal species (Marine Mammal Council 2000–2008).

In comparison with Europe and the Russian Federation and with other regions such as North America and Southeast Asia, Africa's biodiversity levels are in a relatively good state (UNEP 2006). Agriculture and urbanization nevertheless have contributed to losses of 50 percent of the African terrestrial eco-regions (Burgess et al. 2005; UNEP 2006) and more than 75 percent of the Mediterranean woodlands and forests, the rest of which are characterized by high fragmentation (Burgess et al. 2005). The main source of biodiversity loss is habitat loss (Sala et al. 2000). Savanna habitats are among the best protected areas, especially in eastern and southern Africa, while the areas with the lowest safeguards are located in northern Africa, in the drier areas of the Republic of South Africa, and in the deforested parts of western and eastern Africa. Some of the areas characterized by the highest biodiversity values are unfortunately also among the least protected, including, for example, Ethiopian montane (mountain or high elevation) forests, the lowland Fynbos (scrub) and Renosterveld (the Cape Floral region), the western Guinean lowland forests, and the east African montane forests (UNEP 2006).

Distribution of Biodiversity and Conservation

Biodiversity levels diverge widely across the world's main continents due to many aspects including latitude and altitude, temperature and precipitation patterns, and type of soil. Biodiversity tends to decrease with latitude, so that it is lower in the Polar Regions while it increases going toward tropical regions. This effect is known as the latitudinal diversity gradient.

A biodiversity hotspot is vulnerable to species extinctions and habitat loss. There are about twenty-five sites in the world particularly rich in biodiversity that have already lost 70 percent of their habitat. Conservationists estimate that the residual areas still support 60 percent of the total plant and animal species worldwide.

The Mediterranean Basin is an important hotspot in Europe. Its concentration of endemic vascular plant species (those having internal systems for flow of nutrients, as opposed to nonvascular plants such as mosses and algae) is four times higher than in the other regions of Europe. Its location at the intersection of Eurasia and Africa contributes to the existing high biodiversity levels. Many of the existing protected areas experience different forms of pollution as well as water scarcity. Conservation efforts include the European Union's Habitats Directive,

Natura 2000, requiring the design of conservation actions, the establishment of biosphere reserves, and the creation of the Mediterranean Action Plan based on a cooperative program to prevent pollution in the Mediterranean (Conservation International 2012c).

The Caucasus hotspot in the Russian Federation includes deserts, savannas, arid woodlands, and forests, and is home to a multitude of endemic plant species. The growing exploitation of forests for fuel wood, illegal hunting, and plant gathering threaten the region. Many conservation plans address this area. The federation has set up transboundary protected areas between Georgia, Azerbaijan, and Russia to alleviate the habitat fragmentation (discontinuities in a natural area, which can be produced by geological processes or human activity such as land use changes) that is altering ecosystems and threatening extinction of species. The Critical Ecosystem Partnership Fund invested in the region in 2003 to conserve threatened species, targeting five corridors: Greater Caucasus, Caspian, West Lesser Caucasus, East Lesser Caucasus, and Hyrcan (see Conservation International 2012b).

An important biodiversity hotspot in Africa is the Cape Floristic Region on the tip of South Africa, characterized by evergreen shrublands and registering the highest concentration of nontropical plants on Earth. About 14 percent of the area of the Cape Floristic Region is a protected area. Conservation efforts include the Working for Water Programme, which aims to preserve watersheds, the creation of new protected areas (e.g., the Cape Peninsula National Park), and the Cape Action Plan for the Environment for the sustainable conservation of plant and animal species (Conservation International 2012a).

Another hotspot is the Guinean forests of western Africa, which are populated by more than twenty species of primates and a quarter of the mammals in Africa. Only 9 percent of Africa's lowlands are protected areas, compared to 50 percent of the mountainous land, though lowlands are under greater threat and are among the most vulnerable regions.

Costs of Policy Inaction

The unsustainable use of ecosystem resources and related loss of biodiversity affects human well-being through the expected negative impacts on the provision of ecosystem services. Some studies affirm that by the year 2000 there was a total global terrestrial biodiversity loss of 27 percent from previous levels. The strongest declines occurred in temperate and tropical grasslands and forests. Researchers estimate that by 2050 another 11 percent will be lost (Braat and ten Brink 2008). Conservationists estimate biodiversity loss to cause annual losses in ecosystem services equaling about €14 trillion ($US18 trillion) by 2050.

If governments do not protect biodiversity in forest ecosystems, conservationists expect the impacts on

human welfare in the period 2000–2050 to be mixed depending on the geographical region affected and the ecosystem service affected. Developed countries such as in Europe might gain from the increased exploitation of forest plantations, while Russia and Africa might see a strong decline in carbon stocks (the amount of carbon stored in the forests) due to the increased loss of forest area (Chiabai et al. 2011). The conversion of natural forests to plantations, which are able to generate higher profits in the short run, is expected in the long run to harm the provision of important ecosystem services such as flood control, soil and water formation, and nutrient cycling provided by pristine areas.

Programs, Plans, and Legislation

Europe can currently count on a wide network of protected areas and plans to protect species under threat. Future action, however, should prioritize the conservation of biodiversity and ecosystem services in policy making, taking into account the needs in specific sectors that rely strongly on biological resources such as agriculture, fisheries, and forestry. This will be feasible with more involvement of local businesses and authorities and with consultations between European member states to identify major areas for action. The European Biodiversity Strategy for 2020 will have the objectives of reversing biodiversity loss and promoting the transition of Europe toward a green economy.

The Russian Federation's work program for the implementation of the Convention on Biological Diversity (CBD) affirms that by 2015 the existing protected areas should be integrated into broader landscape and seascape systems (WWF–Russia 2010). Both terrestrial and marine ecosystems should be included in the federal protected area network, as well as wetlands, important bird areas, forests, ecosystems with rare and endangered species, and key areas for plants having economic importance for the community. Other important goals include the establishment of regional networks and collaboration between protected areas and the preparation of management plans actively involving the different stakeholders implicated in the area (WWF–Russia 2010). The World Wide Fund for Nature (WWF n.d.) has analyzed the Russian Federation's vegetation types, biodiversity richness, and climatic conditions in protected areas, information that should help in formulating policies.

Compared to other parts of the world, Africa strongly depends on biological and natural resources such as agriculture, logging, fisheries, and livestock. The existing pressure on African ecosystems and their current degradation represents a serious threat to this region. There is nevertheless still a good store of biodiversity that would enable the recovery of losses to date. The conservation and preservation of the African ecosystems and biodiversity therefore represent a critical challenge for future decades. The strategies currently needed to preserve African biodiversity and ecosystems include, first, the involvement of local people of rural economies in the use and management of ecosystem services and biological resources. This strategy is in contrast to the past practice of creating national parks and reserves without the effort to integrate them with local societies. Second, the benefits arising from the ecosystems should be equitably shared among the population. Third, there is a need to integrate and combine biodiversity conservation with economic development in efforts to reduce poverty (UNEP 2006).

Outlook

Conservation entails the use of natural resources and ecosystems in ways that provide the highest benefit with sustainable consumption while preserving the capability of a healthy system to benefit future generations. Conservation must preserve biodiversity as well as ecosystem services and biological resources. Sustainable consumption requires policies and measures to preserve and maintain biodiversity and biological resources in the long run and to restore ecosystems when needed. Conservation programs set up in collaboration with local communities, taking into account local priorities for development and livelihood, are likely to be the most effective and sustainable.

Policies that will preserve biodiversity for the future involve the restoration of degraded ecosystems and maintenance of ecosystem services and biodiversity levels, a decrease in world population, decreases in the consumption of goods and services per person, and improved efficiency in goods and services production (WWF 2004).

Aline CHIABAI
Basque Center for Climate Change (BC3)

See also Biological Corridors; Climate Change Refugees (Africa); Corporate Accountability (Africa); Desertification (Africa); Ecotourism; Education, Environmental; Fisheries; Genetic Resources; Mediterranean Sea; Parks and Preserves; Russia and the Soviet Union; Svalbard Global Seed Vault

FURTHER READING

Amirkhanov, A. M. (Ed.). (1997). *Biodiversity conservation in Russia: The first national report of Russian Federation*. Moscow: Biodiversity Conservation Center of the Socio-Ecological Union (SEU).

Braat, Leon C., & ten Brink, Patrick. (Eds.). (2008). *The cost of policy inaction: The case of not meeting the 2010 biodiversity target* (Report of the COPI project). Wageningen, the Netherlands: Alterra, Wageningen University and Research Centre.

Burgess, Neil D., et al. (2005). Major gaps in the distribution of protected areas for threatened and narrow range Afrotropical plants. *Biodiversity and Conservation, 14*(18), 77–94.

Business & Biodiversity Resource Centre. (n.d.). Homepage. Retrieved May 6, 2012, from http://www.businessandbiodiversity.org

Caspian Environment Programme. (2005). National CBD reports: Russia. Retrieved March 9, 2012, from http://www.caspianenvironment.org/biodiversity/rus/preface.htm

Chiabai, Aline; Travisi, Chiara; Markandya, Anil; Ding, Helen; & Nunes, Paulo. (2011). Economic assessment of forest ecosystem services losses: Cost of policy inaction. *Environmental and Resource Economics, 50*(3), 405–445.

Conservation International. (n.d.). Biodiversity hotspots. Retrieved March 9, 2012, from www.biodiversityhotspots.org

Conservation International. (2012a). Cape Floristic Region. Retrieved May 6, 2012, from http://www.conservation.org/where/priority_areas/hotspots/africa/Cape-Floristic-Region

Conservation International. (2012b), Caucasus. Retrieved May 6, 2012, from http://www.conservation.org/where/priority_areas/hotspots/europe_central_asia/Caucasus

Conservation International. (2012c). Mediterranean Basin. Retrieved May 6, 2012, from http://www.conservation.org/where/priority_areas/hotspots/europe_central_asia/Mediterranean-Basin

European Environment Agency (EEA). (2010). *The European environment: State and outlook 2010: Synthesis*. Copenhagen, Denmark: EEA.

Gennad'evna, Khanina Larisa; Bobrosky, M. V.; Karjalainene, Timo; & Komarov, Alexander S. (2001). *A review of recent projects on forest biodiversity investigations in Europe including Russia* (Internal report no. 3). Joensuu, Finland: European Forest Institute.

Hillebrand, Helmut. (2004). On the generality of the latitudinal diversity gradient. *The American Naturalist, 163*(2), 192–211.

Hoekstra, Jonathan M.; Boucher, Timothy M.; Ricketts, Taylor H.; & Roberts, Carter. (2005). Confronting a biome crisis: Global disparities of habitat loss and protection. *Ecology Letters, 8*(1), 23–29.

International Union for Conservation of Nature (IUCN). (n.d.). Red List. Homepage. Retrieved November 10, 2011, from http://www.iucnredlist.org

International Union for Conservation of Nature (IUCN). (2011). About IUCN. Retrieved May 8, 2012, from http://iucn.org/about/work/programmes/pa/pa_what/

Marine Mammal Council. (2000–2008). Red data book of Russia. Homepage. Retrieved May 6, 2012, from http://2mn.org/engl/rdbrf_en.htm

Millennium Ecosystem Assessment (MEA). (2005). *Ecosystem and human well-being: Synthesis*. Washington, DC: Island Press.

Sala, Osvaldo E., et al. (2000). Global biodiversity scenarios for the year 2100. *Science, 287*(5459), 1770–1774.

United Nations Environment Programme (UNEP). (2006). Africa environment outlook 2: Our environment, our wealth. Nairobi, Kenya: UNEP.

Willig, Michael R.; Kaufman, Dawn M.; & Stevens, Richard D. (2003). Latitudinal gradients of biodiversity: Pattern, process, scales, and synthesis. *Annual Review of Ecology, Evolution, and Systematics, 34*, 273–309.

World Wide Fund for Nature (WWF). (n.d.). National protected areas of the Russian Federation: GAP analysis and perspective framework. Retrieved May 6, 2012, from http://www.wwf.ru/resources/publ/book/293

World Wide Fund for Nature (WWF). (2004). Living planet report 2004. Nairobi, Kenya: UNEP, WCMC.

World Wildlife Fund–Russia (WWF–Russia). (2010). Implementation of the Convention on Biological Diversity in the Russian Federation: Programme of work on protected areas. Retrieved March 9, 2012, from http://www.wwf.ru/resources/publ/book/448 (in Russian)

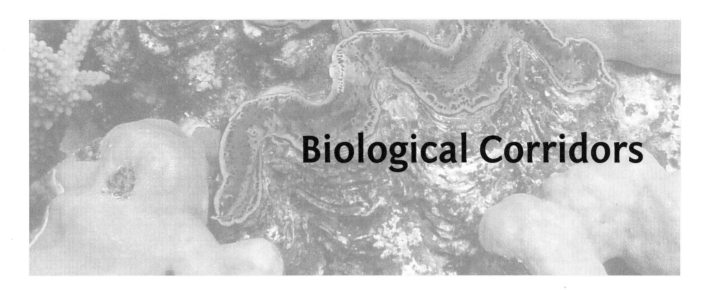

Biological Corridors

Pathways used by animals and landscapes that connect areas of natural vegetation are known as biological corridors. Corridors help conserve a mix of large mammals and allow movements in response to seasonal changes and long-term stresses. Modified landscapes and infrastructures limit movements of animals and shifts in ranges in response to climate change. International cooperation in Africa and Eurasia bodes well for biological corridors to contribute to sustainability.

Animals move between locations to access the diverse resources they need, such as food, water, or mates, to find suitable habitats, or to avoid predators or competition. Movements may include daily, seasonal, or annual round-trips, as well as permanent dispersals of animals to new locations. Plant populations also move across landscapes over generations, for example, by dispersal of seeds or by short-range sprouting of plant shoots. Whether the daily movement of individuals or a one-time dispersal of the young to distant locations, movements are most successful when made in an intact, suitable habitat.

Repeated use of these habitats by individuals or members of populations define biological corridors. The term *corridor* refers to a terrestrial pathway of a favored habitat within a matrix of lands that are less suitable (corridors used in bird migration are known as flyways and are not a focus here). The term serves a dual purpose in ecology— *biological corridor* is also used in conservation planning to refer to areas of intact vegetation connecting natural areas. These corridors are intended to provide habitats for movement of a variety of animal and plant species on a regional scale.

Populations of a given species can form groups termed metapopulations, with individuals that sometimes move between groups. Movements through corridors on regional scales allow areas where populations have gone locally extinct to be repopulated from more distant groups and allow metapopulation members to exchange genetic material. Corridors also allow organisms to make permanent shifts in ranges when areas become unsuitable over the long term.

As human land use intensifies, maintaining biological corridors is an increasingly difficult and pressing task. Fencing and habitat loss along corridors restrict seasonal movements of animals. As climates change due to increased greenhouse gases in the coming decades, shifts in the ranges of whole groups of species along biological corridors linking conservation areas will be important. Establishing broad-scale protections, however, is notoriously difficult.

A Diversity of Needs

The rationale for biological corridors may differ in some ways across regions. African landscapes are large, with high human population but little infrastructure and evolving land tenure approaches. High biodiversity includes large herbivores (plant-eating animals) that must access widely spaced resources. Some species are migratory, such as the white-eared kob (*Kobus kob leucotis*) of South Sudan and the great migration of the white-bearded wildebeest (*Connochaetes taurinus*), plains zebra (*Equus quagga*), and Thomson's gazelle (*Eudorcas thomsonii*) in the Serengeti Ecosystem of northern Tanzania and southwest Kenya. Migratory animals follow routes that are generally predictable from year to year. Drought increases the need for animals, whether migratory or not, to move to acquire sufficient food and water. To acquire sufficient resources to survive, animals must have the means to move transiently between areas that produce food and water. An inability to move the long distances required to access resources in drought is a frequent cause for the loss of African wildlife.

At the regional level, African countries have been forward thinking in their conservation planning. The reasons for planning are diverse, and corridors are typically secondary considerations, but the percentage of land in protected status in African countries is on par with that of wealthier nations (Chape, Spalding, and Jenkins 2008, 13). That said, many African protected areas were established in the colonial period, and planners identified and delineated areas that protected a limited resource, most often a permanent water source (e.g., Amboseli and Nairobi national parks in Kenya, Tarangire National Park in Tanzania). Political will to conserve large connected areas was lacking and would impact severely locals living in rural areas and others with a direct interest, so only the limited resource was conserved. Surrounding landscapes were open and presumably were viewed to be available for wildlife in perpetuity. But African rangelands are increasingly fragmented, and animals either must navigate divided and converted private lands or move through available biological corridors that remain or were created for the purpose.

In contrast to Africa, Eurasian landscapes have far fewer species, especially of large herbivores. Land ownership has a long history in Europe, and landscapes are finely divided into individual parcels. Human population density is high and infrastructure, such as fencing, roads, and railways, is common. For example, the Central Plateau of Switzerland, which includes Zurich and Geneva, has one of the highest densities of roads in Europe, at 3–4 kilometers of road per square kilometer of land (Trocmé 2005).

In Europe, arable land is mostly cultivated, and land is used intensively. Movement pathways are smaller in spatial scale and involve fewer individuals, such as European wildcats (*Felis silvestris silvestris*) moving between forest patches and reindeer (*Rangifer tarandus*) making short-range migrations. In Switzerland, dispersal patterns of red deer (*Cervus elaphus*), roe deer (*Capreolus capreolus*), Alpine ibex (*Capra ibex*), and other species were analyzed and simulated (Trocmé 2005), considering the spatial distribution of infrastructure, natural barriers, and agriculture. Marguerite Trocmé (2005), a senior scientist from the Swiss Department of the Environment, Transport, Energy and Communications, reported that 16 percent of 303 wildlife corridors were impassable, and more than half of the routes were moderately or severely impaired. That research identified 51 locations where connectedness may be restored, typically through incorporating overpasses with natural vegetation into ongoing highway widening projects.

In Europe, drought is not a major driver of movements or consideration for conservation planning. Instead, the shifts in species ranges to more northern latitudes and to higher elevations associated with the increased temperatures that climate change will bring are of concern. Considerations of the effects of future change on biodiversity in Europe are well developed, compared to Africa. For example, the Pan-European Ecological Network was established in 1995 (Bennett and Mulongoy 2006, 14), and some countries have their own plan for biological corridors linking their protected areas. The creation of the network spurred development of programs in many other countries. At the beginning of the twenty-first century, the Pan-European Ecological Network and the Pan-European Biological and Landscape Diversity Strategy are vital conservation programs.

Challenges

The maintenance of biological corridors is a challenge in Africa and Eurasia alike. In Africa, a quickly increasing human population and intensification of land use means that biological corridors are narrowed through land conversion to cultivation, home and business development, and fencing of private lands that were once communally held. For example, Nairobi National Park abuts the capital city of Nairobi, Kenya, and is separated by a fence. In past decades wildebeest would move to the south out of the park to the Kaputiei Plains for their wet season range. Development in and around a highway that bisects the area, plus construction of homes and fencing of pastures for agriculture or private grazing (Reid et al. 2008, 202), appears to have all but eliminated the migration. Another example on a far larger scale involves construction of veterinary fences in Botswana. In the 1950s, fence construction began with the purpose of isolating livestock from wildlife and allowing export of animals and meat to countries concerned about disease. During the droughts of the 1980s, many thousands of wildebeest died when they could not migrate to locate sufficient food and water, their paths cut off by the veterinary fences. Hartebeest (*Alcelaphus buselaphus*) and other animals have continued to die because their routes to locate resources in severe drought are truncated.

Elephants are a special case. Their range across Africa has declined dramatically in the last century, in part due to the hunting for ivory, but also due to land use intensification and the loss of biological corridors. Yet their size, appetite, and sometimes long-distance movements make maintaining corridors for their use difficult. Crops are destroyed by migrating elephants, and humans are at risk of injury and death from the animals. The long-distance movements some elephants make mean that the corridors pass through several governmental jurisdictions, which may have different, and sometimes contradictory, management goals. Transfrontier corridors do exist, however, where management objectives have been harmonized, such as the Selous-Niassa and Zambezi Valley corridors that link Tanzania, Mozambique, and Zimbabwe (Sebogo and Barnes 2003).

In addition to the advantages that biological corridors bring to conservation, there are costs and risks. In the same way that corridors promote movements of favorable species, corridors may also promote movements of invasive species. Predators or people may hunt animals in corridors, especially in areas known as "pinch points," where would-be prey must move through a confined area. Too much mixing of populations may dilute the influence of genetic selection for locally adapted traits. Finally, the spread of diseases may be promoted through corridors linking extensive habitats.

Outlook

One purpose behind establishing local and regional corridors is to allow humans to use landscapes in a sustainable way in order to benefit from the services ecosystems provide while conserving biological resources. The scientific and political will to create or maintain biological corridors is present in both Africa and Europe, at least at the national level. Wildlife tourism is a valued component of many African economies, and maintaining biological corridors will help maintain the resources on which this tourism is built while allowing other areas to be used to meet residents' needs. Transboundary initiatives in southern Africa restoring mobility to wildlife by removing fences that separate abutting protected areas provide further evidence of this political will.

In Europe, strong governments allow for the defense of biological corridors, and programs such as the Pan-European Ecological Network bode well for their maintenance. Landscapes heavily modified through history and high land prices make creating new corridors difficult. Creative solutions, however, are being devised. For example, naturalists on the ground and analysts using satellite images identified a swath of uninhabited land along what used to be the Iron Curtain, the defended border between Eastern European countries once affiliated with the Soviet Union and Western democratic countries. This was essentially no-man's-land, where natural processes were less altered than in other parts of Eurasia. Old-growth forests and continuous forest patches were relatively common in some areas of the border. In other areas, vegetation was kept short to spot people in the forbidden area, which favored species that use open spaces. Few roads or human settlements are present within the area. In 1989, German interests met to develop a greenbelt—a biological corridor—through Germany. In the first decade of the twenty-first century, that idea expanded as the International Union for Conservation of Nature (IUCN) European Green Belt Initiative, a plan to conserve lands in a strip from the Arctic to the Black Sea, 8,000 kilometers through twenty-two countries (Fraser 2009). The fact that the "Death Zone" created by fences, bunkers, and weapons now provides opportunities for conserving European wildlife is extraordinary.

Rapid human population growth in Africa is the main threat to the sustainable use of resources, and economic worries in Europe and elsewhere that started in 2008 point to less concern for conservation interests. In Africa erratic leadership, civil war, fledgling economics, and corruption have weakened governments' abilities to defend encroachment into biological corridors with conservation status, but a changing climate will make the need for both local and regional biological corridors more pressing. More frequent and severe weather events will make movements of animals to more favorable areas critical to their survival. Over the long term, regional movements of populations of plants and animals will be required for some species to persist. Networks of natural areas, surrounding mixed-use lands that buffer natural areas from intensive use, and corridors connecting natural areas are designed to help in long-term shifts in ranges.

There are still reasons to be optimistic about the contributions biological corridors make to sustainable use of landscapes. In Africa, expanding opportunities and family planning options are related to slower human population growth, and economic development promotes sustainable planning by societies. In Eurasia, strong governments and a concerned citizenship suggest that conservation of biological corridors will strengthen as economic conditions improve; in Europe an environmental ethic is mainstream. Throughout Afro-Eurasia, involvement of local and distant people with a direct interest through research, nongovernmental organizations, and local, regional, and national governments will strengthen biological conservation.

Finally, people in the scientific, management, and policy realms increasingly recognize the value of the landscape matrix, the lands containing the biological corridor passages. For example, David Western (1998), chairman of the African Conservation Centre in Nairobi, estimates that three-quarters of wildlife in Kenya are outside of protected areas. The more of the matrix that can be made suitable for animals and plants, the less reliant we must be on regional biological corridors for the conservation of biological diversity.

Randall B. BOONE

Colorado State University, Fort Collins

See also Biodiversity Conservation; Ecotourism; Education, Environmental; Genetic Resources; Migration (Africa); Nairobi, Kenya; Parks and Preserves; Public-Private Partnerships (Africa)

FURTHER READING

Bennett, Graham, & Mulongoy, Kalemani J. (2006). *Review of experience with ecological networks, corridors and buffer zones.* Montreal: Secretariat of the Convention on Biological Diversity, Technical Series No. 23.

Berger, Joel. (2004). The last mile: How to sustain long-distance migration in mammals. *Conservation Biology, 18*(2), 320–331.

Boone, Randall B., & Hobbs, N. Thompson. (2004). Lines around fragments: Effects of fencing on large herbivores. *African Journal of Range & Forage Science, 21*(3), 147–158.

Chape, Stuart; Spalding, Mark; & Jenkins, Martin D. (2008). *The world's protected areas.* UNEP World Conservation Monitoring Centre. Berkeley & Los Angeles: University of California Press.

Fraser, Caroline. (2009). *Rewilding the world: Dispatches from the conservation revolution.* New York: Metropolitan Books, Henry Holt and Company.

Galvin, Kathleen A.; Reid, Robin S.; Behnke, Roy H.; & Hobbs, N. Thompson. (Eds.). (2008). *Fragmentation of semi-arid and arid landscapes: Consequences for human and natural systems.* Dordrecht, The Netherlands: Springer Publishing.

Hannah, Lee. (2001). The role of a global protected areas system in conserving biodiversity in the face of climate change. In G. Visconti, et al. (Eds.), *Global change and protected areas.* Dordrecht, The Netherlands: Kluwer Academic Publishers.

Jones, Trevor; Caro, Tim; & Davenport, Tim R. B. (Eds.). (2009). *Wildlife corridors in Tanzania.* Arusha, Kenya: Tanzania Wildlife Research Institute. Retrieved November 5, 2011, from http://www.wildlife-baldus.com/download/TAWIRI%20WCS%20 WildlifeCorridors%20TZ.pdf

Reid, Robin S., et al. (2008). Fragmentation of a peri-urban savanna, Athi-Kaputiei Plains, Kenya. In Kathleen A. Galvin, Robin S. Reid, Roy H. Behnke & N. Thompson Hobbs (Eds.), *Fragmentation of semi-arid and arid landscapes: Consequences for human and natural systems.* Dordrecht, The Netherlands: Springer Publishing.

Root, Terry L., et al. (2003). Fingerprints of global warming on wild animals and plants. *Nature, 421*, 57–60.

Rouget, Mathieu; Cowling, Richard M.; Lombard, Amanda T.; Knight, Andrew T.; & Kerley, Graham I. H. (2006). Designing large-scale conservation corridors for pattern and process. *Conservation Biology, 20*(2), 549–561.

Sebogo, Lamine, & Barnes, Richard F. W. (Eds.). (2003). *Action plan for the management of transfrontier elephant conservation corridors in West Africa.* Quagadougou, Burkina Faso: IUCN/SSC African Elephant Specialist Group. Retrieved November 5, 2011, from www.african-elephant.org/tools/pdfs/apn_wcor0306_en.pdf

Toteu, Sadrack F.; Anderson, John M.; & de Wit, Maarten. (2010). "Africa Alive Corridors": Forging a new future for the people of Africa by the people of Africa. *Journal of African Earth Sciences, 58*, 692–715.

Trocmé, Marguerite. (2005). *The Swiss defragmentation program—reconnecting wildlife corridors between the Alps and Jura: An overview.* Davis: Road Ecology Center, John Muir Institute of the Environment, University of California, Davis.

Western, David. (1998). Letters to the editor. *Science, 280*, 1507.

World Bank. (2010). *Convenient solutions to an inconvenient truth.* Washington, DC: World Bank.

Cairo, Egypt

20 million est. pop. 2012

A metropolis of nearly 20 million people, Cairo is Africa's largest city. Based on current rates of urban growth (with approximately 500,000 new residents per year), the population will likely reach 25 million in 2020 and 35 million by 2050. Given the uncertain political climate following the end of the long rule of Hosni Mubarak in 2011, the future of the city and its people and environment is uncertain. Law enforcement, governance, participation, and decentralization remain huge challenges.

Despite being at a critical developmental stage, urban sustainability is not an unreachable strategy for the future of Cairo. The question is how to understand and implement sustainability in this booming world city of the global South, where challenges, culture, and governance are not the same as those of the global North. ("Global" North and South refers to the division of the world, contested by some geographers, into the more developed North and the less developed South; Australia and New Zealand are considered outliers of the developed North in this development model.) The contemporary development of Cairo cannot be solved with recipes and "best practices" from abroad; instead it must invent its own form of sustainability.

Developmental Failures and Pessimism

Tracing Cairo's history regarding sustainable development is quite challenging. As with Egypt in general, it is undergoing a multifaceted crisis, giving cause for concern.

Climate change projections indicate that a sea-level rise may pose a threat to the Nile Delta, a vital region for the country. In addition, there are political pressures on drinking-water sources. The 1959 Nile Waters Agreement (between Egypt and Sudan) giving Egypt privileged access to the Nile is contested by the states of Ethiopia, Uganda, Rwanda, and Tanzania. Also as a result of rapid urbanization, Egypt is subject to agricultural land decay, as well as a loss in biodiversity due to tourism development on its shorelines. Pressure on resources is increasing due to the continuous population growth, which is confined to the "usable" land of the valley and the Nile Delta (only 10 percent of the territory) that is bordered by the desert. Energy reserves are also dwindling. Egypt will likely have consumed all its oil by 2030, so there will not be a lot of gasoline available (JCEE 2009). Given the low per capita carbon footprint of the developing countries, Egypt remains one of the highest polluters in Africa, after Tunisia and South Africa, producing 2.3 gigatons of carbon dioxide per capita in 2010, while ten years earlier the value was only 1.3 gigatons (UN-Habitat 2012).

For Cairo, expert and academic literature is abundant on the risks associated with a continued strong population pressure and an excessive concentration of people in the central area of the city bordered by Ring Road (the major freeway circling Cairo) in the absence of an efficient national development strategy that aims to strengthen secondary regional urban centers.

In 2006, Cairo's population was about 17 million people, but it is estimated to be close to 20 million in 2012. There will likely be 25 million in 2020 and 35 million in 2050, based on current rates of urban growth (approximately 500,000 per year). In some areas, levels of residential densities are among the highest in the world and generate traffic congestion, structural air pollution, and conflicts of multiple uses. These negative externalities and the highly sustained population growth in the late 1970s prompted the Egyptian authorities to establish the first new towns in the desert surrounding the capital. This resulted in a misappropriation of public land, which was sold to the highest bidder, and the creation of unfinished areas, which were highly segregated between gated communities and social housing units built by the state until the 1980s. Cairo is now ringed by newly built, artificially green, low-density desert communities, which contrast with the hyper-compact, vertically oriented, traditional city center built along the Nile. Social and environmental inequalities have increased—while poor communities living in informal settlements or neighborhoods are increasingly exposed to multifaceted health risks, well-off households are sheltered in their gated communities (a hundred are under construction or have already been constructed in the Greater Cairo area), keep to themselves, and invent strategies to avoid the negative externalities.

Egypt is far from being destitute, which is reflected in the annual figures of economic growth. This growth, however, has done little to solve environmental problems head on. On the contrary, industrialization, mass consumption, and progressive motorization of households have increased the pressure on resources and increased health problems tenfold. These trends are noticed by investors (including foreigners) and represent obstacles to development for them.

The literature explaining Cairo's developmental failures is prolific. Issues about urban governance are not easy. State authoritarianism, an extreme centralization of technical and political power in the hands of successive governments and ministries, an absence of powerful elected local powers, and a lack of midlevel metropolitan authority between the local and national levels create difficulties in government–public relations. The corollary is twofold: an "urban silence" in which citizens keep to themselves instead of banding together to form civil society groups that fill the void of a governmental presence, and often a public denial of urban problems as well (Myllyla 2001). Some examples of the public's silence include ignoring the worsening urban air pollution, refuting of resource scarcity, and denying the increasing differentiation between social classes of urban residents regarding access to basic services (water, sanitation, electricity).

Property is the first engine of growth in the capital, and the annuity constitutes a collusion of interests between economic and political elites around the sale of the desert as well as some other well-located land reserves (Denis 2006). Bureaucracy and corruption accompany this urban production, which is the subject of an overly technical and financial investment from the Egyptian state. Conversely, under-investment by public authorities in the slums forces residents (assisted by some nongovernmental organizations [NGOs]) to self-sufficiency in an advanced decaying environment at the metropolitan level. Worse, the policy discourse consists of demolishing and relocating the slums, even if the task is so immense that it is unrealistic. Finally, the legislative context is itself conducive to waste and deterioration of urban fabric: energy sources (such as electricity and oil) are still heavily subsidized, suggesting to Egyptians that it will be endless; locked rents in central areas inhibit any rehabilitations; laws for construction are inadequate; and there is a culture of zone planning, which just started to evolve in 2007.

More Sustainable than One Thinks?

In his recent book, *Understanding Cairo: The Logic of a City out of Control*, the US economist and urban planner David Sims (an expert in housing and urban strategy, established in Cairo since 1974) goes against the current regarding the numerous issues and challenges facing the Egyptian capital. He revisits the history of Cairo and puts some qualities of its development into perspective. Sims readily acknowledges that the Egyptian capital is completely out of control with regard to Western modes of urban management. He counters the Western discourse on chaotic megacities of the third world with the example of Cairo, which has avoided the chaos. Here, the ironic combination of an authoritarian state, offering nothing to poor households, and the tenacity and the ingenuity of small family entrepreneurs has, despite contravening laws, fostered effective mechanisms for building neighborhoods qualified by decision makers as "informal." It is true that a good majority of these developed areas, accounting for more than 60 percent of the urban superficy (the built-up area), were achieved at the expense of agricultural land. Sims shows, however, that the urban sprawl generated by the planning of these spontaneous urban neighborhoods proved to be a consumer of little space, unlike the new towns of the desert. In essence, they are a continuation of the urban agglomeration, filling in the gaps between the village centers surrounding the central area of Cairo. The original compactness of the historic areas has been maintained in these neighborhoods built in the 1970s to 2000s. Rising residential density, mixed functions of structures, and pedestrian and motorized tricycle (called tuk-tuk and microbus) movement within the area are all examples of growth occurring in the same limited space. David Sims and a handful of other Egyptian experts consider the ability of Cairenes to live in densely built and vertical environments, to rely on highly developed local social networks, and to borrow skills from both tradition and modernity to be the building blocks of a resilient and sustainable urban matrix created by and for the families living there (Shehayeb 2009).

The context of Cairo offers a case study for stimulating research. How can sustainable development be approached in such a framework, culturally non-Western (its roots are found mainly in an Arab background) and marked by extremely serious failures of urban governance? How is sustainable development being implemented in a megapolis that is subject to the challenge of population size, inducing immediate complexity, but also having advantages and potential relations to its "DNA" (in the form of compactness and resilience)?

Sustainable Agenda under Construction

The urban agenda in Cairo in the 1990s and the 2000s reflects an undeniable spread of sustainable development adopted in a multiplicity of definitions and recipients (Barthel and Monqid 2011). The challenge, however, is how to measure the most profitable change from the neoliberal forces (since the former Egyptian president Anwar Sadat's structuring of the development of the Egyptian capital, and in particular the significance of a laissez-faire of the authorities) to the benefit of a private sector that supports the areas of urban action. Are urban actors all engaged deeply in the dynamics of sustainable development beyond the increasing of official speeches? Indeed sustainable development "may not be successful if genuine political commitment for change does not exist and if the activities are not based on strategies that strengthen the capacity of public administration, support cooperation between civil society and authorities as well as enhance more equal resource allocation amongst city residents" (Myllyla and Kuvaja 2005, 235–236).

There are at least two prominent urban agendas on strong issues of sustainable development: the green agenda and the brown agenda (Satterthwaite 2001). The green agenda focuses on reducing the societal impact on natural resources and ecosystems, in particular the impact of production, consumption, and waste generation. Meanwhile the brown agenda includes health issues related to the degradation of the living environment. The dichotomy is not relevant in the case of megacities of the South, where both agendas are extremely mixed on the issues of resource depletion, poverty, and pollution (Leitmann 1999). The sustainable agenda reflects coalitions between public actors (ministries and governorates in the lead), foreign donors, international agencies, the private sector, and civil society. The reduction of industrial pollution involves the Egyptian Ministry of Environment, the Federation of Egyptian Industries, the Egypt National Cleaner Production Center (ENCPC), and the United Nations Industrial Development Organizations (UNIDO). Several programs are focusing on the Helwan industrial zone and the newly built 6th of October City, site of several information technology and finance companies; its name refers to the date of commencement of the 1973 Arab–Israeli War. Other innovative action includes the development of renewable energy through the creation of a Joint Committee on Energy Efficiency (in 2007) involving the Egyptian Agency for Renewable Energy and the Deutsche Gesellschaft für Technische Zusammenarbeit (German Agency for Technical Cooperation; formerly GTZ, now GIZ). All the key sectors (consumption, clean production, energy, waste management, air pollution) are therefore taken into account through these actors and coalitions.

Multiple methods of sustainable urban action are identifiable through these coalitions of actors. It is also accompanied by the institutionalization of sustainable development at the national level, such as the 1994 law of environmental protection, updated in 2009 (for a more complete history of environmental laws relating to industry, energy, development, and irrigation, and the problems with their enforcement, see Wahaab 2003), the creation of the Ministry for Environmental Affairs in 1997 along with new public agencies responsible for waste and beautification, the protection of historic districts or clean production, the launching of a National Environmental Action Plan (2002–2017), and finally, the preparing of a National Sustainable Development Strategy Framework since 2008. Public actors are thus caught in a time of the preparation or revision of laws for heritage (valuable built environment), energy, and urban planning; codes for green building and energy efficiency in construction; guides for recommendations of open spaces, materials, and green space management; and standards such as the Green Pyramids Rating System created in 2010 to certify the performance of new buildings.

Sustainable development is spreading as much with this institutional policy making as with market forces. To give one example, Egyptian companies are forced by the European Union (EU) to comply with its regulations (including high standards of quality and industrial processes) if they want to export agricultural and industrial products on the EU market. This economical approach to sustainable development should not be underestimated in Egypt. The recycling economy is another example. Whereas recycling in Europe is a business as well as an "eco-gesture" revealing a voluntary practice by consumers to self-segregate their waste, the waste in Cairo is simply a source of income for garbage collectors (a social group highly stigmatized). So far there is no meaningful public awareness in Cairo regarding separation of garbage at home.

In this evolving context, without communication or knowledge sharing, NGOs and foreign and private actors also participate in the renewal of action and policies. For example, the Egyptian Six of October Development and Investment Company (SODIC), in partnership with the Lebanese Société Libanaise de Développement et de Reconstruction (Solidere)—a company in charge of the reconstruction of downtown Beirut—challenged the Egyptian New Urban Communities Authority (NUCA) to get more rights to build structures with a higher floor–area ratio (the total floor area of a building in relation to the parcel of land the building is on) to test ecofriendly neighborhood projects. The transnational Aga Khan Foundation came to Egypt to make a park instead of a historical dump, and furthermore exposed to the Egyptian authorities in the 2000s that a sustainable model of Islamic Cairo revitalization was possible. Also, the French/Belgian nun

Sister Emmanuelle (1908–2008) served Cairo's slums for over twenty years and gave rise to a powerful NGO called Association Soeur Emmanuelle (ASMAE); Sister Emmanuelle's work in Cairo's slums often has been compared to the work of Mother Theresa. Lastly, the Solar Cities NGO has set up solar water heaters and biogas units in poor neighborhoods and demonstrated the viability of the economic model to the Egyptian authorities.

Once sustainable urban programs and policies are outlined and described, through both the procedures and the results, it can still be difficult to assess the changes they make, especially given the prevalence of market-based regulations that govern urban development in Cairo, which can cause interference. Even before the resignation of former Egyptian politician and military commander Hosni Mubarak in February 2011, the status of sustainable development was already uncertain and shifting, uncertain because the decision makers, primarily politicians, did not firmly grasp the information, and because sustainability is still not in line with the interests, values, and lifestyles of both economic and political elites. It is also uncertain due to the fact that the regression of sustainable development can be observed in light of other narratives, mobilizing the concepts of progress and modernization that are measured in car ownership and household air-conditioning equipment. And the legacy is there with its inertia. The exploitation of land assets will still justify an advance in job creation linked to the real estate industry and infrastructure works, even if the vacancies or unfinished housing continues.

The challenges to sustainability must be met to change the current course taken, in order to truly enter into a new developmental cycle. In this case, sustainable development is challenged by Cairo, and not vice versa.

Sustainable Development Paradigm Challenged

Regarding the issue of urban governance, it is clear that the prerequisites for sustainable development are far from being established in Cairo, as mentioned earlier. From this point of view, the effectiveness of sustainable development should begin firstly with improvements of political issues, thus addressing the issue of corruption, the excessive centralization of political and technical power, and routines of government. It's a prerequisite for making sustainable policies that aim for a better distribution of resources and minimize the vulnerabilities of the poorest households. The challenge is that of the decentralization of government and the greater interaction between urban actors (from public authorities to civil society) in order to work on shared values. In a "revolution" context, it is difficult to say whether Cairo will empower a real break with authoritarian political legacy. A Franco-Egyptian joint seminar relaunched the project of decentralization in May 2011, and the election of representatives of local councils could become a reality in the near future (Arab Republic of Egypt 2011). And some Egyptian environmentalists call for a green constitution in the near future:

> The greater challenge, I believe, is to lobby for a constitution that is environmentally conscious. This requires focusing on writing a constitution that is intended to serve the people through sustainable development and environmental perspectives, not just to safeguard the interests of a specific party that dominates Parliament. (Mansour 2012)

Improving dialogue with civil society is another challenge. Just on environmental issues alone, on one hand an entrenched network of NGOs with a proven track record of training local entrepreneurship to solve local problems and classical issues of daily environment has been identified. On the other hand, since 2008 a new generation of activists has been marshalling new and fashionable themes such as climate change, solar energy, and carpooling or city biking (Barthel and Monqid 2011). In braving the oil and electricity subsidies by the authorities and valuing local knowledge, these minority groups believe that policies must change now. For the moment, this "street environmentalism" (Myllyla 2001) faces the problem of visibility across a city as big as Cairo, and the low culture of collaborative work with decision makers who relay very little of their actions.

Lastly, changing urban cultures by the elites is also a critical challenge. It seems closely related to the challenge of sharing power, and shifting from a market-driven and top-down vision for the city currently prevailing in Cairo to a more sustainable model based on the potentials and strengths of the capital (Sims 2010). The vision about informal settlements on the part of the technical staff appears to be changing in recent years, however, and the redesign of the development of "new towns" is another encouraging sign. Also what about, for example, the speeches that appear in the construction of the development strategy known as "Greater Cairo 2050" on the priority to be given to nature, on the intensification of collective transportation projects, and on the need for a unified regulatory "Greater Cairo" authority? Are they indicating, at most, a willingness from the Egyptian policy makers to resume the international agencies' expectations? A proclamation of sustainable development will not be enough, especially if the metropolitan governance does not change in depth.

Change, however, is not simple. As stated above, there are isolated calls for a green constitution and ongoing work for a more decentralized governance with the technical support of UN-Habitat. Khaled Ali, an Egyptian activist and lawyer who ran for president in 2012, is fighting for environment and social justice. Manifestos for a change in planning and policies have been released in 2012. Transition is slow, though, many projects are on hold, and certain issues such as traffic congestion (especially when areas like Tahrir Square or Abbassiya are closed down due to riots and demonstrations) and informal constructions are increasing rapidly.

Pierre-Arnaud BARTHEL
University of Paris-East—Marne-la-Vallée,
CNRS–Latts

See also Desertification (Africa); Dubai, United Arab Emirates; Lagos, Nigeria; Mediterranean Sea; Nile River; Sahara; Transboundary Water Issues; Tunis, Tunisia; Urbanization (Africa); Urbanization (Western Asia and Northern Africa); Water Use and Rights (Middle East and North Africa)

FURTHER READING

Arab Republic of Egypt. (2011, May 24). Prime minister's speech in a seminar titled "Towards new local system in Egypt: Lessons learned from the French experience." Retrieved March 21, 2012, from http://www.egyptiancabinet.gov.eg/Media/NewsDetails.aspx?id=2397

Barthel, Pierre-Arnaud. (2010a). Arab mega-projects: Between the Dubai effect, global crisis, social mobilization and a sustainable shift. *Built Environment* (special issue), *36*(2), 133–145.

Barthel, Pierre-Arnaud. (2010b). First experiences of sustainable neighborhoods in Arab Mediterranean countries: Reproducing the European model? In Steffen Lehmann, Husam Al Waer & Jamal Al-Qawasmi (Eds.), *Sustainable architecture and urban development: Vol. 3* (pp. 121–136). Amman, Jordan: The Center for the Study of Architecture in the Arab Region (CSAAR).

Barthel, Pierre-Arnaud. (2011). The new metropolitan strategy "Cairo 2050": Whose vision? In Christopher Horwood (Ed.), *Cairo: A city in transition* (pp. 152–155). Nairobi, Kenya: UN-Habitat.

Barthel, Pierre-Arnaud, & Monqid, Safaa. (2011). *Le Caire, réinventer la ville* [Cairo, reinventing the city]. Paris: Autrement.

Barthel, Pierre-Arnaud, & Zaki, Lamia. (Eds.). (2011). *Expérimenter la "ville durable" au sud de la Méditerranée* [Experiencing "urban sustainability" in the south Mediterranean countries]. La Tour d'Aigues: France: Editions de L'Aube.

Denis, Eric. (2006). Cairo as neo-liberal capital? From walled city to gated communities. In Diane Singerman & Paul Amar (Eds.), *Cairo cosmopolitan: Politics, culture, and urban space in the new Middle East* (pp. 47–71). Cairo: The American University in Cairo Press.

Egyptian-German Joint Committee on Renewable Energy, Energy Efficiency and Environmental Protection (JCEE). (2009). *Impact of energy demand on Egypt's oil and natural gas reserves: Current situation and perspectives to 2030*. Cairo: Deutsche Gesellschaft für Technische Zusammenarbeit.

Hopkins, Nicholas S.; Mehanna, Sohair; & el-Haggar, Salah. (2001). *People and pollution: Cultural constructions and social action in Egypt*. Cairo: American University in Cairo Press.

Leitmann, Joseph. (1999). *Sustaining cities: Environmental planning and management in urban design.* New York: McGraw-Hill.

Lorrain, Dominique. (Ed.). (2011). *Métropoles XXL en pays émergents.* Paris: Sciences Po Press.

Mansour, Waleed. (2012, February 12). A call for a green constitution. Retrieved March 29, 2012, from http://www.almasryalyoum.com/node/652361

Myllyla, Susanna. (2001). *Street environmentalism: Civic associations and environmental practices in the urban governance of third world megacities.* Tampere, Finland: Tampere University Press.

Myllyla, Susanna, & Kuvaja, Kristiina. (2005). Societal premises for sustainable development in large southern cities. *Global Environmental Change, 15,* 224–237.

Nour, Ayman M. (2011). Challenges and advantages of community participation as an approach for sustainable urban development in Egypt. *Journal of Sustainable Development, 4*(1), 13.

Satterthwaite, David. (2001). Environmental governance: A comparative analysis of nine city case studies. *Journal of International Development, 13*(7), 1009–1014.

Shehayeb, Dina K. (2009). Advantages of living in informal areas. In Regina Kipper & Marion Fischer (Eds.), *Cairo's informal areas: Between urban challenges and hidden potentials. Facts. Voices. Visions.* Cairo: Deutsche Gesellschaft für Technische Zusammenarbeit (GIZ).

Sims, David. (2010). *Understanding Cairo: The logic of a city out of control.* Cairo: The American University in Cairo Press.

Singerman, Diane. (Ed.). (2009). *Cairo contested: Governance, urban space and global modernity.* Cairo: The American University in Cairo Press.

United Nations Human Settlements Programme (UN-Habitat). (2012). *The state of Arab cities 2012: Challenges of urban transition.* Nairobi, Kenya: UN-Habitat.

Wahaab, R. Abdel. (2003). Sustainable development and environmental impact assessment in Egypt: Historical assessment. *The Environmentalist, 23*(1), 49–70.

Zetter, Roger, & Al-Moataz, Hassan. (2002). Urban economy or environmental policy? The case of Egypt. *Journal of Environmental Policy and Planning, 4*(2), 169–184.

Cape Town, South Africa

3.4 million est. pop. 2010

Cape Town is a city of extremes: unparalleled natural beauty, stunning tourist attractions, and incredible wealth alongside environmental degradation and desperate poverty. Like the rest of South Africa, Cape Town is faced with the difficulties of overcoming the spatial and socioeconomic legacies of segregation and inequality. To create a sustainable community, the city will have to improve the quality of life for its poorest citizens.

Located on Africa's south-western tip, Cape Town is South Africa's oldest city, established in 1652 as a trading post for the Dutch East India Company. In recent decades, the city has become a popular international tourist destination, with the majestic Table Mountain towering over its beautiful beaches, celebrated vineyards, and diverse fauna and flora. In Cape Town, natural beauty, unique biodiversity, and cultural history are juxtaposed with sprawling informal settlements and desperate poverty. The city is facing problems of waste production, water pollution, biodiversity destruction, and resource exploitation.

Cape Town is often colloquially called Africa's European city due to its diverse ethnic composition and cosmopolitan buzz. The city's population of 3 million is ethnically divided: one-third Black African, one-fifth White, and nearly half Coloured. (*Coloured* is the official South African term that refers to the offspring and descendants of mixed unions among Europeans settlers, slaves brought south from other parts of Africa and the world, and indigenous peoples such as the Khoisan. During the apartheid era the descriptors *White*, *Black*, *Coloured*, and *Indian* were designated by law, and

capitalized, as the country's four official racial groups, and are spelled as such in this article. Because Cape Town is recognized as the birthplace of the Coloured population, it is also called the Mother City.)

Cape Town's composition differs radically from South Africa as a whole, where Black Africans are by far the most numerous group (approximately 80 percent), and where Coloureds and Whites are a tiny minority (approximately 9 percent each). Cape Town's demographic is gradually changing, however, as the absolute number of Black Africans in the city has grown significantly since the end of apartheid, leading social geographer John Western (2001) to comment that "Africa is coming to the Cape."

The (Post) Apartheid City

South Africa's contemporary cities cannot be understood without reference to their apartheid history. The National Party came to power in 1948 and introduced a barrage of legislation to preserve White supremacy. The Group Areas Act (Act No. 41 of 1950) established race-based residential segregation, which radically restructured Cape Town both spatially and socially. Cape Coloureds were forcibly removed to the unconsolidated Cape Flat scrublands, with virtually nonexistent public services, inadequate housing, and long commutes to employment. Cape Town's Black Africans remained where they were, in already segregated, underserviced and overcrowded peripheral townships. The Coloured Labour Preference Area Act of 1955 (repealed in 1985) subsequently restricted Black Africans from entering Cape Town, as it gave preference to Coloured labor. In contrast, Cape Town's White population enjoyed secluded prosperity throughout the apartheid period, being spatially and socially distanced from other races and the socioeconomic problems associated with their marginalization.

Following the demise of apartheid in the late 1980s, repeal of the Group Areas Act in 1991, and the country's first democratic elections in 1994, Cape Town's previously stringent segregation policy and practice were open to change. Nonetheless, apartheid's spatial and socioeconomic segregation and inequality remain a powerful legacy that is difficult to overcome. Ivan Turok, a professor of urban economic development, describes post-apartheid Cape Town as a "starkly polarized city" (2001) exemplified by the juxtaposition of centrally located affluent suburbs and economic centers with poverty-stricken and overcrowded settlements located on the city's edges. Since 2000, however, significant resources have been invested in tackling social and spatial inequality, particularly through housing and service delivery programs. For example, in 2007 only 15 percent of Cape Town's households still resided in informal dwellings such as shanties (down from 19 percent in 1996) and more than 93 percent of all households had access to electricity, piped water, adequate toilet facilities, and weekly garbage pickup, compared to 88 percent in 1996 (City of Cape Town 2008). Nevertheless, Cape Town remains a city of extreme socioeconomic and spatial inequality.

Economic Development

South Africa's post-apartheid re-entry into international markets affected the country's economy in various ways. For example, the city's already struggling manufacturing industries, such as textiles, clothing, and food production, were negatively impacted by international competition and the removal of tariff barriers. More than 50,000 jobs were lost in the clothing and textile industries in the mid-1990s. At the same time, contemporary Cape Town has experienced an expansion in service-provider and finance-based firms, the film industry, and investment corporations.

While Cape Town's transition from a manufacturing-based to a service-based economy has spurred the city's economic growth, it has polarized the workforce between highly paid skilled professionals and un(der)employed unskilled and semiskilled workers (Lemanski 2007). Although it has been argued that Cape Town is experiencing a growing professionalism rather than polarization of the workforce as a new middle-income occupational class has emerged (Borel-Saladin and Crankshaw 2009), this assessment arguably sidesteps the extent of unemployment in the city. Approximately a quarter of Cape Town's economically active population is unemployed. Furthermore, economic polarization is race-based and spatially determined. Predominantly White areas of affluence are centrally located in Cape Town's leafy suburbs with large homes, schools, and shopping centers; in contrast, Black African townships located on the urban periphery host mass unemployment and poverty. Thus, despite economic growth and development, like the rest of South Africa, Cape Town remains a highly divided city.

Environmental Challenges

Cape Town's outstanding environmental beauty has economic implications, attracting tourists and businesses to invest in its magnificent natural setting. At the same time urban sprawl, accompanied by inadequate services and infrastructure to meet the needs of Cape Town's rapidly growing population, has consequences for the city's environment; Cape Town thus faces a situation that potentially threatens the very basis of its economic success. One of the city's major environmental concerns, the pollution of freshwater and coastal ecosystems from poorly treated wastewater and polluted stormwater runoff, highlights the interconnectedness of the city's problems. For example, limited access to sanitation for the urban poor causes pollution of the natural environment, with potentially negative consequences for tourism, a major element of the city's economic base. This deterioration of water quality is a serious environmental problem that requires urgent attention, but for which resources are limited. Environmental success stories, however, may be evident on the horizon: the city has reduced water use and improved its solid waste management (City of Cape Town 2010).

A further environmental concern is the destruction of biodiversity. Nearly two-thirds of the city's original vegetation has been destroyed by human action, and the remaining vegetation is considered highly vulnerable. Given that Cape Town is home to globally unique biodiversity, it is critical that action be taken to protect the city from further environmental destruction. For example, the city is currently undertaking a major culling of alien vegetation, which has for a long time threatened the city's biodiversity and water resources. Cape Town authorities are strongly promoting the development of a more environmentally sustainable city, balancing this goal with the challenge of providing an infrastructure that meets the needs of the poor, the building of which has been a major cause of the city's biodiversity destruction (City of Cape Town 2010).

Future

Cape Town is a city full of contradictions and incongruities: a city with unparalleled natural beauty alongside environmental destruction; a city that attracts foreign tourists and international investment, yet is home to desperate poverty and mass unemployment; a city of social, economic, spatial, and environmental extremes. Moving into the future, the city will be faced with the challenges of reducing inequality and unequal access to public services and resources. If these are successfully overcome, Cape Town may become a model for development throughout the country.

Charlotte LEMANSKI
University College London

See also Africa, Southern; Biodiversity Conservation; Lagos, Nigeria; Nairobi, Kenya; Urbanization (Africa)

FURTHER READING

Besterman, Catherine L. (2008). *Transforming Cape Town*. Berkeley: University of California Press.

Borel-Saladin, Jacqueline, & Crankshaw, Owen. (2009). Social polarisation or professionalisation? Another look at theory and evidence on deindustrialisation and the rise of the service sector. *Urban Studies, 46*(3), 645–664.

City of Cape Town. (2008). Demographic and socio-economic trends for Cape Town: 1996 to 2007. Retrieved November 28, 2011, from http://www.capetown.gov.za/en/stats/CityReports/Documents/2007%20Community%20Survey%20Summary.pdf

City of Cape Town. (2010). City of Cape Town state of the environment report 2009. City of Cape Town Environmental Resource Management Department.

Cook, Gillian P. (1991). Cape Town. In Anthony Lemon (Ed.), *Homes apart: South Africa's segregated cities* (pp. 26–42). Cape Town, South Africa: David Philip.

Haferburg, Christoph, & Oßenbrügge, Jurgen. (Eds.). (2003). *Ambiguous restructurings of post-apartheid Cape Town*. Hamburg, Germany: Lit Verlag Münster.

Lemanski, Charlotte. (2007). Global cities in the south: Deepening social and spatial polarisation in Cape Town. *Cities, 24*(6), 448–461.

Robins, Steven. (2002). At the limits of spatial governmentality: A message from the tip of Africa. *Third World Quarterly, 23*(4), 665–689.

Turok, Ivan. (2001). Persistent polarisation post-apartheid? Progress towards urban integration in Cape Town. *Urban Studies, 38*(13), 2349–2377.

Western, John. (1981). *Outcast Cape Town*. London: George Allen and Unwin.

Western, John. (2001). Africa is coming to the Cape. *Geographical Review, 91*(4), 617–640.

Central Asia

The former Soviet republics in Central Asia are suffering the consequences of decades of poor water management, uncontrolled pollutants from industrial centers, and radiation from nuclear testing. Efforts to grow grain and cotton in the arid steppes and the destruction of traditional irrigation systems and farming practices have led to desiccation of many of the area's lakes, most notably the Aral Sea.

Central Asia consists of the republics of Turkmenistan, Kazakhstan, Uzbekistan, Kyrgyzstan, and Tajikistan, all formerly part of the Soviet Union (USSR) and, before that, of the Russian empire. The total area of the five republics is over 2.48 million square kilometers, about half that of the continental United States. Some experts also include Afghanistan, Mongolia, Tibet, and Sinkiang (Chinese Turkestan) as part of Central Asia.

Since the Neolithic period, Central Asia has been home to concentrated areas of urbanites and agriculturalists in a land of pastoralists. Cities and agriculture clustered around oases and the floodplains of rivers (the Amu Dar'ya, Syr Dar'ya, Murghab, Tejen, and Zaravshan). Irrigated orchards formed the basis for wealthy sedentary empires such as that of Khorezm (Khwarizm), centered in the cities of Urgench, Bukhara, and Samarqand during the ninth to thirteenth centuries. Despite the destruction of the urban, agricultural, and political infrastructure by the Mongols in the thirteenth century, the local economy slowly recovered, and by the fifteenth century the Turkic conqueror Timur (Tamerlane), who claimed descent from the Mongol conqueror Chinggis (Genghis) Khan, made Samarqand the capital of his empire. With the breakup of Timur's empire, the region fragmented into smaller khanates and emirates.

Russian military conquest of the region began in the 1860s, spurred by the notion of converting Central Asia into a center for cotton growing. Supplies of cotton from the southern states of the United States were not reaching Europe because of the Civil War, and the czarist regime saw an opportunity not only to meet its own needs for cotton but also to become a competitive exporter.

By 1889 the conquest was complete. The extensive network of canals and small-scale agriculture was not affected. Farmers practiced water-conserving practices, including crop rotation, and were attentive to proper drainage of their irrigated fields. Village leaders oversaw the decisions of the *mirab*, or water master, who held responsibility for maintenance of the canal and for the equitable distribution of water.

Beginning in the 1930s, however, the collectivization and industrialization campaigns of Joseph Stalin (1878–1953) transformed the face of the region. Small-scale traditional systems of irrigation were completely destroyed as independent farms were dissolved and merged into gigantic collective and state farms (*kolkhozy* and *sovkhozy*). With construction of the Great Fergana Canal in 1939 and the irrigation of the Hungry Steppe of Uzbekistan (between Tashkent and Samarqand), Chechens, Crimean Tatars, and ethnic Korean rice and orchard farmers, deported from the Caucasus and the Soviet Far East, were resettled in those areas.

On the steppes and semidesert pasturages that had dominated northern and central Kazakhstan, herders were ordered to pool their flocks into new livestock collective farms. Brutal implementation and resistance led to the deaths of about 1.5 million Kazakhs, 25 percent of the population (Sindelar 2008). Nomadic herding as a cultural and economic form of livelihood was brought to an end.

Migration to the Steppe

On the newly emptied portions of the northern Kazakh steppe, ethnic Germans deported during World War II to create an agricultural base joined an appreciable number of Great Russians (members of the dominant Slavic-speaking ethnic group of Russia) and Ukrainians who had migrated to the region since its conquest. In 1954 Nikita Khrushchev (1894–1971), Soviet Communist Party First Secretary, announced a Virgin Lands Campaign to turn the steppe into a grain factory. Despite initial successes, however, inappropriate tilling practices and the absence of crop rotation led to enormous soil erosion and serious dust storms (in 1963, 1965, 1968, and 1974).

In the hillier eastern region of Kazakhstan, Stalin's revolution was industrial, with the creation of gigantic mining, refining, and manufacturing centers at Ust-Kamenogorsk, Ekibastuz, and Semipalatinsk (Semei). Although air pollution has decreased since 1991 because of the general economic decline in the area, it is still a serious issue, as is water pollution. In 2010, over 2 million tonnes of air-polluting emissions were discharged, accounting for a large majority of all pollutants in Kazakhstan that year. In the years immediately previous to this, the air pollution levels had decreased (Kazakhstan Agency of Statistics 2010, 40–41). The Irtysh River, which flows north from eastern Kazakhstan, is heavily polluted by industrial effluents.

One of the grimmest environmental legacies of the Soviet regime is that of the extensive nuclear testing that was conducted in Kazakhstan from 1949 to 1989. Testing was ended partly in response to the emergence of a powerful grassroots antinuclear movement in Kazakhstan led by author Olzhas Suleimenov. An alliance, Nevada-Semipalatinsk, was formed with those exposed to nuclear tests in the western United States during the 1940s and 1950s. Because most of the victims in Kazakhstan were rural ethnic Kazakhs and the tests were ordered from Moscow, the movement acquired an anticolonial tenor. Over 450 explosions, including 119 above ground, left expanses in western Kazakhstan (Kapustin Yar) and eastern Kazakhstan (near Semipalatinsk) as disaster areas. Hundreds of thousands of people were exposed to dangerous levels of radiation in those areas, and the incidence of birth defects and cancers is many times higher than the averages for the rest of the country and for the former Soviet Union. Because of the tests, 190,000 square kilometers of land—about the size of the US state of South Dakota—have become unusable as well. Extensive areas in southern and central Kyrgyzstan, where uranium was mined, are also heavily polluted by mining residue.

By 1900 the oil fields in the southern Caspian Sea near Baku, Azerbaijan, made the Russian empire among the world's leaders in oil production. In recent decades, the discovery of oil and natural gas in the shallow, northern, Kazakh portion of the Caspian Sea and its coastal region (especially the Tengiz fields) has led to intensive exploitation by multinational corporations (such as Chevron). The water level in the Caspian Sea has risen notably since 1970, and protective dikes have failed to prevent breaching of well caps and other facilities. As a consequence, petroleum products in the waters of the northeastern Caspian Sea are thirty times permissible levels, and the soil cover of the coastal region has been polluted. The sturgeon catch, which amounted to 27,000 metric tons in 1985, was a mere 1,890 metric tons in 1994, although part of this decline is also a consequence of the hydropower dams on the Volga River and its tributaries and the resultant inability of sturgeon to reach their spawning streams.

Caspian Sea Mining

Another attempt to mine the Caspian Sea also led to environmental problems. In 1980 the Kara-Bogaz Gol, a shallow gulf of the Caspian, was dammed off to permit its water to evaporate. This was to allow the mining of mineral salts on the floor of the gulf. Windstorms deposited great quantities of the salts on irrigated fields in Turkmenistan, however, and in 1984 authorities ordered that the dam be blown up and the gulf reflooded.

Arguably the most important environmental issue in Central Asia is the availability of water. On the eve of World War II, in 1939, plans for a vast expansion of cotton growing were accelerated. Russian czarist authorities had eyed the region for this purpose in the 1860s, and the goal of cotton self-sufficiency for the USSR was posed early on by Russian Communist leader Vladimir Lenin (1870–1924) in 1918. It was under Stalin that the regime undertook to harness the Amu Dar'ya and Syr Dar'ya Rivers to irrigate the cotton fields. In 1950 planning commenced for the Karakum Canal in Turkmenistan. By the 1970s Central Asia could no longer feed itself because cotton replaced food crops against the backdrop of rapid population increase (the population of the Central Asian republics more than doubled between 1959 and 1987). Moreover, the combination of decades of huge withdrawals of water from the river systems of the region for cotton irrigation, overwatering, indiscriminate application of fertilizers and pesticides, and poor drainage management has resulted in one of the most ruinous regional environmental catastrophes of modern history.

Desiccation of the Aral Sea

East of the Caspian Sea lies the Aral Sea, which in the 1960s was the fourth-largest lake in the world, with an area of 66,000 square kilometers (an area roughly the size of Latvia or Lithuania), a volume of 1,061 cubic kilometers, and a salinity level of 10 parts per 1,000 (Weiner 2009, 295). The Aral Sea is rapidly drying up, like Lobnor in China and Lake Chad in Africa. By 1994 the area of the lake—segmented into "large" and "small" seas at this point—was under 32,000 square kilometers (less than half its former size) and in 1998 it was only 29,000 square kilometers with a volume of 181 cubic kilometers, less than one-fifth of its former size (Kubo et al. 2009; Weiner 2009, 295). By 2008 the Aral Sea as a whole amounted to a mere 10,400 square kilometers (Lauener 2010). During that period salinity in the lake increased dramatically, and the fish catch, which once amounted to over 40,000 metric tons annually, diminished to zero (The Aral Sea Crisis 2008). A public health emergency followed, caused by receding water causing salt- and pesticide-covered lands to emerge. Because the Central Asian republics have been unable to shift their agricultural economies away from cotton and rice to more traditional orchard crops, the Aral Sea is in serious danger of disappearing within a few decades.

By 1980, after years of water being diverted to grow cotton, inflow of the Amu and Syr Dar'ya rivers into the Aral Sea had effectively dwindled to nothing, while the evaporation rate continued apace. The Karakum Canal in Turkmenistan proved particularly wasteful.

Other geographical changes included the vast expansion of the human-made Lake Sarykamysh, which is a basin for the discharge of drainage water from the cotton fields, and the disappearance of the *tugai* (dense floodplain) habitat along the rivers and in their deltas. The *tugai*, with its reedy tall grasses, tamarisks, poplars, willows, and oleasters, once formed a rich habitat for a large variety of fishes, birds, and mammals. Like the Amu Dar'ya tiger, they, too, face extinction as halophytic (growing in salty soil) vegetation takes over and then itself disappears, yielding to the cracked, crusty *takyr* desert (desert areas of low relief, often composed of thick

clay deposits that serve as catchment areas for precipitation).

The most serious consequences of the desiccation of the Aral Sea have been those connected with human health. Because much of the seabed is now exposed, large quantities of sand laden with salts, pesticides, fertilizers, and other chemicals are blown across fields and human settlements each year. This has been exacerbated by an increasing frequency of days with dust storms, thought to be related to a regional climate change caused by the shrinking of the lake. The surrounding Karakalpak Autonomous Republic (in Uzbekistan), whose livelihood was once dependent on Aral Sea fishing, has been most severely affected. According to the Asian Development Bank, deficient water quality is responsible for the widespread poor health in the region. Large numbers of women and children suffer from anemia, and the incidence of viral hepatitis, tuberculosis, cancer, and typhoid fever is increasing.

Cotton Hopes and Water Crisis

Although self-sufficiency in cotton supply was a goal of Soviet leaders, they also believed that cotton would be an enduring source of export income, but cotton prices on the world market fell steeply from the 1960s to the 1980s. Ironically, despite the expansion in irrigation, cotton production, although doubling in Central Asia from 1960 to 1980, began to decrease thereafter as more and more irrigated land was damaged by salinization.

During the 1970s increasing recognition of the water crisis led Central Asian Communist Party leaders to call for a transfer of water from northward-flowing Siberian rivers such as the Irtysh and Ob' to their region. The Sibaral canal, dubbed "the project of the century," was first discussed by the Aral-Caspian Expedition of the USSR Academy of Sciences in 1950. It would have stretched 2,200 kilometers across the Turgai uplands, terminating north of the Aral Sea. This project had entered the planning stage along with a parallel project to divert northward-flowing European rivers and waters southward to irrigate Ukraine, Kalmykia, and the northern Caucasus and to halt a feared further drop in the level of the Caspian Sea. These projects elicited a crescendo of opposition from scientists, writers, nature protection advocates, and Russian nationalists who objected to exporting "Russian" water to Central Asia. In 1986 all work on the diversion projects was cancelled—providing Russian leader Mikhail Gorbachev's first major signal to the educated public that he sought to be viewed as a reformer.

Protected Land

While Central Asia was a part of the Soviet Union, environmental protection chiefly took the form of *zapovedniki*, nature reserves set aside for the protection of unique, significant, or endangered ecological communities. Chief among the people who conducted important ecological field investigations and promoted nature protection were Abram L'vovich Brodskii, Daniil Nikolaevich Kashkarov, and Nina Trofimovna Nechaeva.

Enforcement of protection in the reserves in all of the republics is not effective, however, because of inadequate funding. Additionally, Turkmenistan has a government policy of selling licenses to hunt rare animals in reserves, and in Tajikistan an ongoing civil war has taken a heavy toll on wildlife. Over the past century, despite the establishment of *zapovedniki* and *zakazniki* (other protected areas), species loss in Central Asia has been significant, including the Amur tiger and the leopard. Currently, of large mammals, the cheetah and the urial, mouflon, Marco Polo, and other mountain sheep and goats are endangered. Finally, reacclimatization of native animals into the wild from zoos, breeding farms, and *zapovedniki*, as well as acclimatization of exotic species, were pursued during the Stalin and subsequent regimes. Reacclimatized fauna include the *saiga* (large Eurasian steppe antelope) released near Almaty, *dzheiran* (Central Asian desert gazelle) released on Barsa Kelmes Island *zapovednik* in the Aral Sea, *arkhar* sheep released in northern Kazakhstan, and the *kulan*, or Asiatic wild ass (onager), removed from the Barsa Kelmes *zapovednik* beginning in 1981 to other parts of Central Asia because of the increased salinity of the Aral Sea and the degradation of the habitat on the island.

Outlook for the Aral Sea

After the Central Asian states gained their independence in 1991, it was hoped that they would deal with the serious ecological situation of the Aral Sea, but in 2010 the United Nations Secretary General was still calling the leaders to come together and discuss the problem. While other nations seem uninterested, Kazakhstan's portion of the sea has been increased thanks to its efforts. At The Hague, Netherlands, in 2000, the United Nations Educational, Scientific and Cultural Organization (UNESCO) water management plan, Vision 2025, was developed to prevent the Aral Sea's continued desiccation (Wegerich 2001). The Kokaral dam project has made an ironic contribution to the health of the Small Aral Sea: where most dams cause environmental upheaval, the Kokaral has aided in steadily refilling the Small Aral and bringing indigenous fish species back to the once-dead sea. Fish populations have increased so rapidly that, as of 2010, the Small Aral Sea was divided into ten licensed fishing districts. This rebound, however, comes at the cost of the Large Aral Sea (Lauener 2010). An organization called the International Fund for Saving the Aral Sea was created to rescue the dying sea and has to balance the rival water demands of Kazakhstan, Uzbekistan, Kyrgyzstan, Tajikistan, and Turkmenistan (Lauener 2010). What is left of the Aral Sea, however, is still very much at risk, with much international concern about whether it will survive into the future (Inter Press Service 2012). With populations expected to rise, the demand for water in the central Asia region will require innovative programs and plans to avoid catastrophic outcomes.

Douglas R. WEINER
University of Arizona

See also Afghanistan; Biological Conservation; Indus River; Lake Chad; Moscow, Russia; Novosibirsk, Russia; Pakistan; Russia and the Soviet Union; Transboundary Water Issues; Ukraine; Volga River

This article was adapted by the editors from Douglas R. Weiner's article "Asia, Central" in Shepard Krech III, J. R. McNeill, and Carolyn Merchant (Eds.), the *Encyclopedia of World Environmental History*, pp. 69–73. Great Barrington, MA: Berkshire Publishing (2003).

FURTHER READING

The Aral Sea Crisis. (2008). Environmental impacts. Retrieved May 9, 2012, from http://www.columbia.edu/~tmt2120/environmental%20impacts.htm

Bissell, Tom. (2002, April). Eternal winter: Lessons of the Aral Sea disaster. *Harper's Magazine*, 41–56.

Chesnokov, Nikolai Ivanovich. (1989). *Dikie zhivotnye meniaiut adresa* [Wild Animals Change Their Addresses]. Moscow: Mysl.

Daly, John C. K. (2000, November 8). Global implications of Aral Sea desiccation. *Central Asia—Caucasus Analyst*.

Feshbach, Murray, & Friendly, Alfred, Jr. (1992). *Ecocide in the USSR: Health and nature under siege.* New York: Basic Books.

Fipps, Guy. (2003). The Aral Sea disaster. Retrieved May 9, 2012, from http://gfipps.tamu.edu/Publications&Papers/Professional%20Papers/Aral%20Sea.pdf

Glantz, Michael H. (Ed.). (1999). *Creeping environmental problems and sustainable development in the Aral Sea basin.* Cambridge, UK: Cambridge University Press.

Grote, Ulrike. (Ed.). (1997). *Central Asian environments in transition.* Manila, Philippines: Asian Development Bank.

Inter Press Service. (2012, March 22). Kazakhstan, Uzbekistan take differing approaches on Aral Sea. Global Issues. Retrieved March 26, 2012, from http://www.globalissues.org/news/2012/03/22/13092

Kazakhstan Agency of Statistics. (2010). Kazakhstan in 2010. Retrieved March 27, 2012, from http://www.eng.stat.kz/publishing/DocLib/2011/Statyear2010.pdf

Kubo, Hirokazu; Tateno, Kodai; Watanabe, Akira; & Kato, Yuri. (2009). Human and environmental symbiosis in Central Asia: Through the water management of the Aral Sea Basin crisis. *Transition Studies Review, 16*(2), 467–478.

Lauener, Paul. (2010). A sea returns to life, a sea slowly dies. Retrieved May 7, 2012, from http://www.newint.org/features/2010/11/01/aral-sea/

Micklin, Philip P. (Ed.). (1992). The Aral crisis. *Post-Soviet Geography, 5.*

Pryde, Philip Rush. (1991). *Environmental management in the Soviet Union.* Cambridge, UK: Cambridge University Press.

Sindelar, Daisy. (2008, December 8). Keeping count when the numbers are staggering. Radio Free Europe/Radio Liberty. Retrieved March 26, 2012, from http://www.topix.com/forum/world/russia/T4SI5PNE5QVONE375

Wegerich, Kai. (2001). Not a simple path: A sustainable future for central Asia. Retrieved May 7, 2012, from http://www.soas.ac.uk/water/publications/papers/file38371.pdf

Weiner, Douglas R. (2009). The predatory tribute-taking state: A framework for understanding Russian environmental history. In Edmund Burke & Kenneth Pomeranz (Eds.), *The environment and world history* (pp. 276–315). Berkeley: University of California Press.

Weinthal, Erika (2002). *State making and environmental cooperation: Linking domestic and international politics in central Asia.* Cambridge, MA: MIT Press.

Climate Change Refugees (Africa)

Climate change has already caused the forced displacement of people on the African continent; these people are known as climate change refugees. The African Union has taken steps to confront this challenge through the Kampala Convention of 2009. The convention contains several provisions that protect displaced people and serves as a good example of a regional effort to address the plight of vulnerable displaced populations.

In 1990 the Intergovernmental Panel on Climate Change projected that climate change is likely to result in forced migration of vulnerable people throughout Africa. The relationship between climate change and forced migration is not a direct one, because environmental factors are only part of a multifaceted configuration of the economic, social, and political factors that cause migration. Most experts, however, recognize that climate change contributes to the displacement of people. British environmentalist Norman Myers, for instance, has predicted that the dire impacts of climate change may result in the future displacement of 200 million people by 2050 (Myers and Kent 1995). As a result of the recognition of this link between climate change and forced migration, scholars in a variety of disciplines have begun to investigate the various aspects of the plight of so-called climate change refugees.

The African continent is particularly vulnerable to the consequences of climate change because the continent lacks the capacity to pursue adaptation measures. It is ironic that Africa, a relatively undeveloped continent, is the victim of the unsustainable lifestyles of the developed world that have contributed so much to global climate change. In fact, the consequences of climate change have already resulted in the emergence of so-called climate refugees on the African continent. Nomadic societies of the Sahel, Kalahari, and Karoo are examples of the way that climate change affects migration. These people have traditionally migrated because of changes in annual and seasonal rainfall patterns. They have been able to adapt to fluctuating and extreme climates as long as they have sufficient scope for movement and other necessary supports remain intact. Their vulnerability has been exposed, however, by the prolonged drying trend in the Sahel since the 1970s. The wetter end of their traditional migration route is already densely occupied, and when the permanent water points at the drier end fail, these societies have no place to go. The ongoing drought has resulted in a widespread loss of human life and livestock, as well as a change in the social system of these nomadic groups. Ultimately, the displacement of people on the African continent puts extreme pressure on governments that have few resources and may result in conflicts over scarce water and food resources. This potential instability has made the issue of climate change refugees a great concern for the African Union (AU).

The Role of International Law

The term *climate change refugees* has become a frequently used label. It is important to bear in mind, however, that legally speaking this term is incorrect, because climate change refugees do not fit with the definition of refugees in terms of Article 1 of the United Nations Refugee Convention of 1951.

Nonetheless, this group of refugees does fall under the generic classification of environmental refugees, which the United Nations Environment Programme (UNEP) researcher Essam El-Hinnawi defined as "those people who have been forced to leave their traditional habitat, temporarily or permanently, because of a marked environmental disruption (natural and/or triggered by people) that jeopardised their existence and/or seriously affected the quality of their life" (El-Hinnawi 1985, 4).

Forced migration is a very important characteristic of climate change refugees. One difficulty with the designation, though, is the determination of a threshold for forced migration. The South African legal scholar Werner Scholtz proposed the more specific definition that "people who are forced to migrate permanently or temporarily because of the consequences of climate change (e.g., floods or drought) in order to survive or to meet their basic needs will be thought of as climate change refugees" (Scholtz 2010, 40).

Several proposals have been made for the protection of climate change refugees through international law. Some scholars have advocated broadening the definition in the UN refugee convention in order to accommodate climate change refugees. Most, however, concur that this is not a viable option because the refugees defined in the convention need a completely different kind of protection from very different threats. It is important to note, for example, that these refugees often cross national borders, while climate change refugees often migrate within countries. Other scholars have advocated the establishment of treaties and protocols to protect climate change refugees. These proposals often address preventive as well as reactive measures. Various proposals deal with the relocation and resettlement of refugees and related funding by the international community.

The Guiding Principles on Internal Displacement developed for the United Nations Commission on Human Rights may apply to climate change refugees, because this document does refer to displacement that occurs mostly within national borders. The identification of displaced persons in paragraph 2 of the text of the guiding principles is broad enough to accommodate climate change refugees, because it describes internally displaced persons as "persons or groups of persons, who have been forced or obliged to flee or to leave their homes or places of habitual residence, in particular as a result of or in order to avoid the effects of armed conflict, situations of generalized violence, violations of human rights or natural or human-made disasters, and who have not crossed an internationally recognized State border" (UNHCR 2011b).

The guiding principles are a synthesis of human rights and humanitarian and refugee law, and they provide protection against displacement as well as during and after it. Although the guiding principles are not binding law, the principles may be used to develop legislation for the protection of displaced people. (The following states have adopted national policies that reflect the internally displaced persons [IDPs] guidelines: Burundi, Colombia, the Philippines, Sri Lanka, and Uganda. Peru and Angola have legislation based on the IDP guidelines.) Because of

their widespread adoption, the guiding principles may become customary international law in the future.

The African Union and Climate Change Refugees

The Guiding Principles on Internal Displacement may play an important role in addressing the plight of climate change refugees on the African continent. Africa has the largest number of internally displaced persons in the world, and the enormity of the problem led to the adoption of the Convention for the Protection and Assistance of Internally Displaced Persons in Africa (also known as the Kampala Convention) by the African Union 2009 (African Union 2009a). Article 2(b) of the convention states that its goal is to "establish a legal framework for preventing internal displacement, and protecting and assisting internally displaced persons in Africa" and to "promote and strengthen regional and national measures to prevent or mitigate, prohibit and eliminate root causes of internal displacement" (article 2[a]). Under article 3(2)(a), the parties have an obligation to incorporate the convention into domestic law. Under article 4, the parties have obligations to prevent and avoid arbitrary displacement. Furthermore, article 4 lists nonexclusive prohibited categories of arbitrary displacement. Subarticle (f) is relevant for the discussion of climate change refugees because it refers to "forced evacuations in cases of natural or human made disasters." Article 5 includes the primary obligations of countries toward the assistance and protection of IDPs, and article 9 stipulates the obligations of parties during displacement. Subarticle (4) obliges parties to the convention to assist and protect IDPs who have been displaced due to natural or human made disasters, "including climate change." The Kampala Declaration on Refugees, Returnees and Internally Displaced Persons in Africa (African Union 2009b), adopted by the African Union, urges member states to adopt the Kampala Convention and further affirms that climate change may cause forced displacement. The preamble deplores the fact "that large numbers . . . are displaced . . . as a result of natural disasters, and increasingly climate change," and further, it calls "upon the international community to continue to support the African Union as it addresses . . . the increasing incidence of displacement caused by environmental factors, including climate change."

The convention provides that when a party is unable to fulfill its primary obligations toward IDPs because of inadequate resources, the party is compelled to "cooperate in seeking the assistance of international organizations, and humanitarian agencies, civil society organizations and other relevant actors" (article 5[6]). Article 11 lays out obligations concerning the return, integration, and relocation of IDPs. Article 12 provides for compensation in the event of damages incurred because of the displacement. Article 14 provides for monitoring of compliance through the Conference of the Parties established by the convention, the submission of reports to the African Commission on Human and People's Rights under article 62 of the African Convention on Human and People's Rights, and the African Peer Review Mechanism.

For the Kampala Convention to enter into force, it has to be ratified by fifteen parties. As of 2011, this requirement had not been met, which means that the convention is not legally binding. Several countries are already pursuing the implementation of the IDP guidelines through national legislation and programs, but it is important that all fifteen parties follow through.

Outlook

The fact that the Kampala Convention has not been ratified does not mean that it is of no value. The convention affirms the importance of the IDP guidelines and serves as a catalyst for regional efforts to protect climate change refugees. Because regional organizations, such as the African Union and the European Union, are closer to the problem, they may be able to facilitate the cooperation of member states. In this regard, the Kampala Convention may be viewed as a progressive milestone. It may ensure that climate change refugees on the African continent receive adequate help in establishing sustainable lives. The Kampala Convention may also serve as an important example for other regional organizations, which will have to protect persons displaced by climate change in other parts of the world. Regional organizations may also play an important role in the dissemination, recognition, and enforcement of the guidelines.

One shortcoming of the Kampala Convention is that it applies only to internally displaced people, while many climate change refugees will cross national boundaries. A holistic solution to the displacement of climate change refugees, irrespective of national borders, is needed. The African Union is the most suitable organization to facilitate a viable solution.

Werner SCHOLTZ
North-West University, South Africa

See also African Union (AU); Agriculture, Small-Scale; Desertification (Africa); European Union (EU); Immigrants and Refugees; International Conflict Resolution; Migration (Africa); Rule of Law (Africa); Sahel

FURTHER READING

African Union. (2009a). African Union convention for the protection and assistance of internally displaced persons in Africa (Kampala Convention). Adopted by the special summit of the Union held in Kampala, Uganda, 22nd October 2009. Retrieved February 6, 2012, from http://www.unhcr.org/refworld/docid/4ae572d82.html

African Union. (2009b). Kampala declaration on refugees, returnees and internally displaced persons in Africa of 2009 (Ext/Assembly/AU/PA/Decl. (I)). Retrieved February 6, 2012, from http://www.unhcr.org/refworld/publisher,AU,,,4af0623d2,0.html

Biermann, Frank, & Boas, Ingrid. (2007). Preparing for a warmer world: Towards a global governance system to protect climate refugees (Working paper No. 33). *The Global Governance Project.* Retrieved November 1, 2011, from http://www.glogov.org/

El-Hinnawi, Essam. (1985). *Environmental refugees.* Nairobi, Kenya: United Nations Environmental Programme (UNEP).

Global Database: Guiding principles on internal displacement. (2007). Homepage. Retrieved November 1, 2011, from http://www.idpguidingprinciples.org/

Intergovernmental Panel on Climate Change (IPCC). (1990). IPCC first assessment report 1990 (FAR): Working group II report: Impacts assessment of climate change. Retrieved November 1, 2011, from http://www.ipcc-wg2.gov/publications/Reports/index.html#AR

Intergovernmental Panel on Climate Change (IPCC). (2007). IPCC fourth assessment report (AR4): Climate Change 2007: Working group II report: Impacts, adaption and vulnerability. Retrieved November 1, 2011, from http://www.ipcc-wg2.gov/publications/Reports/index.html#AR

McAdam, Jane. (Ed.). (2010). *Climate change and displacement: Multidisciplinary perspectives.* Oxford, UK: Hart Publishing.

Myers, Norman, & Kent, Jennifer. (1995). *Environmental exodus: An emergent crisis in the global arena.* Washington, DC: The Climate Institute.

Piguet, Paul; Pecoud, Antoine; & de Guchteneire, Paul. (2011). *Migration and climate change.* Cambridge, UK: Cambridge University Press.

Scholtz, Werner. (2010). The day after no tomorrow? Persons displaced environmentally through climate change: AU law to the rescue? *South African Yearbook of International Law, 35,* 36–55.

United Nations High Commissioner for Refugees (UNHCR). (2011a). The 1951 Refugee Convention. Retrieved November 15, 2011, from http://www.unhcr.org/pages/49da0e466.html

United Nations High Commissioner for Refugees (UNHCR). (2011b). Guiding Principles on Internal Displacement. Retrieved February 6, 2011, from http://www.unhcr.org/43ce1cff2.html

Conflict Minerals

Conflict minerals are those that are exploited, controlled, or used to finance the purchase of supplies by armed actors in a conflict. Commonly involved minerals include cassiterite and coltan, used in electronics, as well as diamonds and gold. These minerals are rarely the cause of the conflict they "support" but do affect its duration and intensity. Because conflict minerals are bought worldwide, there are international repercussions for economies, natural resources and security, and sustainable resource management on a global scale.

Conflict minerals have become a prominent subject through protest or awareness campaigns such as "blood diamonds" and "blood on your mobile." Questions thus arise about how to define conflict minerals, and what national and international dynamics trigger what kinds of conflict, and how they can be minimized or avoided. According to the political economist and geographer Philippe Le Billon (2003, 216), conflict minerals are those minerals "whose control, exploitation, trade, taxation, or protection contribute to, or benefit from the context of, armed conflict."

The actors directly involved in these activities can be warlords, rebel groups, a country's regular national army, or renegade members of the army. The armed actors use the profits derived from conflict minerals to finance their purposes (e.g., purchasing weapons, ammunition, and supplies) and in some instances to enrich them. In such cases, conflict minerals are a main driver for perpetuating armed conflicts. Conflict minerals may thus not cause a conflict, but they are a factor in how a conflict evolves and how long it lasts.

As the minerals are usually sold to international customers, a number of external actors become indirectly involved in the conflicts by way of using the associated minerals.

Conflict Minerals and Security

Many of today's conflicts are nontraditional, in the sense that they are typically not a military conflict between nations. Instead, most of them are internal violent conflicts involving secessionist groups or rebels opposing a government. Since the end of the Cold War, and with the onset of globalization, the characteristics of conflict have changed substantially. In 1994 the United Nations Development Programme (UNDP) introduced the notion of "human security" to address the dimension of people and development rather than just territories and arms, leading some people to call these conflicts "new wars" (Kaldor 1999; Duffield 2001; Münkler 2002). Regardless of what these wars are called, socioeconomic factors play an increasingly important role in them; and mining activities producing so-called conflict minerals often form part of a region's socioeconomic factors.

A scholarly debate on the link between natural resources and conflict emerged in the 1990s (Gleditsch 1997; Homer-Dixon 1995 and 1999; Levy 1995; see also Myers 1989 and Pirages 1978). The debate first focused on the likelihood of an outbreak of violent conflict over a country's richness in natural resources (Collier and Hoeffler 1998; Collier 2000). The term "resource curse" was coined to address poor economic performance of resource-rich countries (Auty 1993). Research by the economists Paul Collier and Anke Hoeffler (2004) analyzed the incentives of those who aim to profit by starting a violent conflict that stems from characteristics of natural resources. Subsequent research broadened the focus of the debate to include state and military, as well as outside economic actors (Snyder and Bhavnani 2005; Humphreys 2005), and the environmental dimension (Dinar 2011).

It can be concluded that the combination of open access to many natural resources and weakness of governments or institutions allows conflicts to arise far beyond normal market competition. "Lootable" commodities, in particular, offer to unscrupulous parties the means to enrich themselves and finance their operations. Such commodities are often categorized as contraband and contribute to prolonging wars (Ross 2004; Samset 2009; WTO 2010, 95).

The links between natural resources and violent conflicts can be seen as a dual relationship: "armed conflicts motivated by the control of resources, and resources integrated into the financing of armed conflicts" (Le Billon 2001, 580). Alternatively, the relationship can be considered two sides of the same coin: resource conflicts and conflict resources. While resource conflicts are caused at least partly by opposing interests fighting over a scarce resource, such as a particular mineral, conflict resources are mainly a means of carrying out a conflict which has other root causes (Le Billon 2001, 561; Mildner 2011, 13).

The Case of the Democratic Republic of the Congo

Mining in the eastern Kivu regions (North and South) of the Democratic Republic of the Congo (DRC) has often been viewed as a case of conflict over minerals. Owing to specific geological conditions—deposits are too small to be suitable for large-scale industrial mining—mining in eastern DRC is mainly artisanal and small scale. In this region, there is robust evidence showing how rebel groups are profiting from the minerals extraction and trade. For instance, a recent United Nations report (UNSC 2010) establishes evidence showing that Congolese national army units have gained control over mineral-rich areas in North and South Kivu provinces and are competing among themselves for control over such areas; moreover, they collude with armed groups in order to attack rival commanders. Table 1 (below) shows large sums earned by the military from a North Kivu mine.

In the Kivu provinces, fighting over the control of mining sites is not the dominant feature in which minerals are linked to conflict. Added to this are numerous opportunities for these actors to accrue resource rents—profits derived from a resource—throughout a number of subsequent transportation stages and intermediaries at local markets within the region. The International Peace Information Service (IPIS) offers reports and maps, showing how armed actors make use of conflict minerals.

The number of actors involved in the commodity chain, and the fact that official representatives and armed groups often cooperate with each other, create a nontransparent situation. As well, market prices of those commodities are much lower than those of reliable competitors (e.g., one of the DRC's mineral products, coltan, has been offered at one-third the price of comparable Australian tantalum products).

Therefore, many players in the originating country and downstream benefit from the current situation, and there is little incentive to change it. Thus failing states get locked into a self-perpetuating situation that extends through a mineral's value chain across countries.

Conflict Minerals as Part of a Broader Natural Resources Picture

Minerals are but one type of natural resource that can be linked to conflict. According to the UN Expert Panel, the armed groups in eastern DRC finance themselves through the illegal exploitation of other natural resources, such as timber, meat, and fish (UN IFTPA 2010). In Côte d'Ivoire (Ivory Coast), rebels and the government both acquired funding for their fight from the cocoa business (Global Witness 2007; Guesnet, Müller, and Schure 2009; Klare 2001). Some analysts underline the likelihood of war in countries that possess oil (Soysa 2002; Fearon and Laitin 2003). Others point to agricultural

TABLE 1. Military Earning from Bisie (a Tin Mine in North Kivu)

Source	Earnings per Month ($US)
Mineral production of nearly 250 tonnes per month going through the military	$1.14 million to $2.25 million
Taxes on diggers outside mines	$45,600 to $90,000
Taxes on porters going to Bisie	$3,300 to $16,800
Total from all known sources	**$1.2 million to $2.4 million**

Source: Global Witness (2010, 8).

The military in North Kivu province in the Democratic Republic of Congo levy taxes not only on the production of tin in the Bisie mine but on outside laborers and porters as well.

commodities in general, and coffee in particular, as sources of conflict (Humphreys 2005; Dube and Vargas 2006).

According to the Heidelberg Institute for International Conflict Research's 2010 conflict barometer, natural resources rank second as a source of conflicts worldwide. In this ranking, natural resources comprise extractive resources and agricultural products as well as land, habitats, and water (HIIK 2010). Research thus should increasingly look at the nexus between different natural resources and conflicts rather than spot single minerals.

The Social and Political Dimension

From the viewpoint of nongovernmental organizations (NGOs) that work with local communities, human rights are a major concern amid these natural resource–related conflicts. The NGO Global Witness defines conflict resources as a broad category embracing conflict minerals: "natural resources whose systematic exploitation and trade in a context of conflict contribute to, benefit from or result in the commission of serious violations of human rights, violations of international humanitarian law or violations amounting to crimes under international law" (Global Witness 2011).

This definition takes into account the different forms of violence surrounding minerals extraction and trade. It refers to situations of abuse, such as people being forced to work under slave-like conditions, threatened by armed overseers. Even if an armed conflict is not involved, minerals are often mined under violent conditions.

Furthermore, the extraction of natural resources can trigger new conflicts. At the local level of extraction sites, the livelihood of the residents of the area can be badly affected (e.g., by pollution of land, water, and air). If their grievances are ignored, this can spark violent protests and acts of sabotage and can lead into violent confrontations with security forces. At the national level, conflict over the use of revenues from natural resources can occur. This is particularly likely where nondemocratic governance is combined with corruption (Paes 2009, 5). Such conflicts have materialized, for instance, in the oil-abundant Niger Delta region in Nigeria.

The Environmental Dimension

Environmental consequences of mining can spark conflicts at the local level, mostly between residents and those exploiting the mineral (artisanal miners or a mining company). For instance, pollution may result from unsafe mine tailings and waste dumps, acid mine drainage, improper closure of pits and mines, dumping of toxic effluent into the water, mining waste, and the like.

Landscape alterations are often irreversible, with secondary effects on local agriculture that will become both economically and environmentally devastating if peasants hire themselves out as diggers.

Sound planning through a strategic environmental assessment (SEA) depends by and large on voluntary efforts, especially in countries with weak governments, legislation, and enforcement. International standards on such SEAs have been formulated (SEA-info.net 2011). Attempts to measure such environmental pressures along the life cycle of materials are called "ecological rucksacks" (Bringezu and Bleischwitz 2009).

In many cases, environmental pressures result from mining outside the requirements of law, failing to perform proper assessments, not having to comply with environmental laws and standards, and making no plans for their rehabilitation. As an example of such negative environmental impact, in the Kahuzi Biéga National Park, one of the last resorts of mountain gorillas worldwide, mining activity itself destroys natural habitat and is exacerbated by the presence of armed groups controlling several areas. At the same time, local agriculture and subsistence farming suffer from lack of continuous activities and inappropriate interventions into local ecosystems.

Which Minerals Are Conflict Minerals?

The minerals most commonly involved in resource conflicts are cassiterite (tin), coltan (tantalum and columbite-tantalite), diamonds, gold, and wolframite (tungsten).

Cassiterite is needed to produce tin. It is also used in the manufacture of electronic goods, such as MP3 players. The world's largest cassiterite producers are China and Indonesia, followed by Peru, Bolivia, and Brazil. For eastern DRC, however, cassiterite is the most important mineral in terms of quantity and price.

Coltan, the nickname of a mineral extracted in Central Africa, belongs to a group internationally known as tantalum. It is mainly used for capacitors in electronic devices, such as mobile phones, pagers, and personal computers. Future demand is expected to grow. For a long time Australia dominated the world market, but the production situation has changed significantly. Since late 2008, Africa (i.e., the lakes region including Mozambique) has become a major, if not the largest, supplier of tantalum on the world market, followed by Brazil and a few other suppliers.

Diamonds are used in jewelry and for some industrial applications. They were the first officially recognized conflict commodity, following observations of brutal civil wars in Sierra Leone, Liberia, and Angola. In response, the Kimberley Process on certification emerged (see the section on Response Options, below).

Gold is used in jewelry, electronics, and dental products. It is also present in some chemical compounds used in semiconductor manufacturing. Major gold suppliers are South Africa, the United States, Australia, Russia, and Peru; and gold is an important export good in countries such as Uzbekistan, Ghana, and Papua New Guinea. For eastern DRC, almost all gold exports are illicit and undeclared; no reliable statistics are available.

Wolframite, an important source of tungsten, has a wide range of uses. It is also used in the metals industry, wherein composites are used as a substitute for lead (e.g., in some gasoline refineries). Almost 78 percent of the world's production of tungsten occurs in China, but Europe imports large shares from Kenya and Tanzania. Tungsten's economic importance is very high, since substitutes are rarely available and impose much higher costs.

This list of conflict minerals is incomplete, but it forms part of a wider context of natural resources that drive economic and political conflicts. Typically, conflict minerals (except diamonds and gold for jewelry) pass through a variety of intermediaries internationally before being purchased by multinational companies (e.g., electronic manufacturers) and consumers. Not all mineral suppliers, however, are involved in conflicts. In most cases, conflict regions act as buffer suppliers during peak times but not as main suppliers over a longer period. But rubies from Myanmar (Burma), which are being mined under inhuman conditions and profit the Burmese dictatorial regime, can be seen as a case where 90 percent of the world market originates from one conflict region.

Whether a given mineral and region are involved in conflict depends partly on prices, since price peaks attract revenue-seeking actors. Some conflicts—especially nonviolent ones—are a typical side effect of most extractive industries and their commodities; hence, good governance, including sound environmental management practices and control as well as the respect of social standards, can influence the scale of conflict or whether it even arises. Good governance at the national level and within extractive industries and sustainable resource management is needed to prevent negative consequences of minerals extraction and related conflicts (Feil et al. 2010; Bringezu and Bleischwitz 2010).

International Interaction

Since most conflict minerals are indispensable for a number of high-tech applications including green technologies and sustainable energy (Graedel 2011), the dimension of international trade is of vital strategic importance (WTO 2010).

The recent discovery of minerals in Afghanistan (worth approximately US$1 trillion) suggests the possibility of extended conflicts in the future, potentially with severe international consequences. The US National Intelligence Council (NIC 2008) develops some gloomy scenarios about how international repercussions of such conflicts could jeopardize international security.

The mineral production facilities in Asia are probably the main routes for illicit mineral chains. Involvement of the Asian processing industry has been subject to investigations by UN Expert Panels and surveys (e.g., RESOLVE 2010). Accordingly, the consumer electronics assembly industry in China and other Asian countries can be seen as a main source of demand for conflict minerals, though many companies of Europe and the United States have also been named in reports as being involved—at least on a temporary basis. The end consumers of those products, however, are located worldwide.

Response Options

Countries' current main options in responding to the conflicts related to minerals are to establish regulations aimed at enhancing transparency and due diligence, both in the extractive industries themselves and along international mineral chains (Bannon and Collier 2003). A Model Mining Development Agreement (MMDA) is available. Initiatives have been undertaken by:

- international organizations (OECD 2010; UN Interagency Framework Team for Preventive Action 2010)
- international and regional policy-makers (Analytical Fingerprint, Certified Trading Chains, the International

Conference of the Great Lakes Region certification program in the Great Lakes Region of Africa, the STAREC plan to establish local marketplaces in the DRC)
- NGOs such as the Extractive Industries Transparency Initiative and Publish What You Pay
- particular industries (e.g., iTSCi—an initiative driven by the smelting industry, and GeSI/EICC—an initiative driven by electronics industry); the International Council on Mining and Metals (ICMM) supports related activities
- advanced institutional hybrids such as the Kimberley Process for diamond certification with all major industries, governmental administrations, and NGOs involved.

In July 2010, the US government introduced legislation (the Dodd-Frank Act) requiring oil, gas, and mining companies registered with the US Securities and Exchange Commission to disclose tax and revenue payments made to host governments in the countries of operation. This law is still under discussion (as of September 2011) and would affect eight of the world's ten largest mining companies. In June 2010, the Hong Kong stock exchange introduced a similar regulation for listed mining companies, which affects major players in the Asian market. The US law also requires companies that manufacture products containing cassiterite, coltan, wolframite, or gold to disclose whether these are sourced from the DRC or surrounding countries, and to demonstrate what steps are being taken to avoid sourcing from armed groups.

On 16 June 2011, the UN Human Rights Council endorsed the "Guiding Principles on Business and Human Rights: Implementing the United Nations 'Protect, Respect and Remedy' Framework" proposed by UN special representative John Ruggie, which provides guidance for businesses to act in accordance with human rights.

Taken together, these initiatives and forthcoming legal requirements lay the groundwork for establishing a minimum global standard of transparency for extractive companies and manufacturers of critical minerals. If well coordinated, properly enforced, and complemented by expanding civil society initiatives, these initiatives could set a precedent for greater transparency and accountability toward the goal of sustainable resource management (Bringezu and Bleischwitz 2009). Improved supply chain management and materials stewardship across industries will further strengthen these efforts. In a broader sense, all efforts to increase resource efficiency along the life cycle of products and minerals, as well as for economies, promote a business interest to lower demand for minerals (Bleischwitz, Welfens, and Zhang 2010) and decrease the ensuing conflict risks.

Tracing value chains in a comprehensive manner and according to standards of accountability will be challenging, given that many actors are involved. Besides profit-seeking behavior and vested interests entrenched in the conflict regions, many knowledge gaps downstream still prevail that also hinder effective regulation. It remains to be seen to what extent consumers will become engaged, as long as uncertainties and the tiny percentage of conflict minerals in any product make a consumer's responsibility difficult to understand and accept.

For that reason, global governance with new and legally binding mechanisms seems necessary to promote accountability against corruption and in favor of sustainability. Proposals for an international metals covenant and an agreement for sustainable resource management have been made (Bleischwitz 2009; Wilts, Bleischwitz, and Sanden 2010). Following a suggestion made by Paul Collier and a fellow economist Anthony Venables (2010, 15), the anti-bribery legislation that the Organisation for Economic Co-operation and Development now requires of its membership could also be a requirement of World Trade Organization membership—a compliance issue for China and elsewhere.

National governance of conflict minerals in the respective regions—such as an effective mining law, general macroeconomic and political stability, and social sector reforms; a fair share of revenues between the local and national governments; and integrated land-use planning towards sustainable development—needs to be instituted as well.

Outlook for the Future

Conflict minerals continue to support financing of armed conflicts around the world, and especially in parts of Africa. While attention was initially focused on rebel groups financing their fights through extraction and trade in these minerals, it became clear over time that state armies sometimes use/abuse minerals in the same way. Since conflict minerals appear on the world market and in consumer goods, the private, public, and civil actors doing business in or purchasing their minerals from conflict regions carry a responsibility in how those minerals are handled. The economic dimension of the problem originates from low-cost supply-driven competition not covering the enormous social costs, and international trade hiding its responsibility through the World Trade Organization principle of neutrality toward process and production methods. High volatility (e.g., measured on an annual basis compared to other goods) aggravates the risks for producers and users.

The challenge for international business and policy makers to cope with these issues hence is enormous. In order to eliminate the conflicts surrounding the minerals discussed here (as well as other minerals), governments and corporations must act on principles of social responsibility, good citizenship, and material stewardship—and they must initiate and adhere to certification and legal mechanisms—along every link in the material value chains (Bringezu and Bleischwitz 2009; Feil et al. 2010). The high probability of rising raw material prices, and greater efforts toward building a green economy, should promote international efforts toward sustainable resource management at a global scale.

Raimund BLEISCHWITZ
Wuppertal Institute for Climate, Environment and Energy

Lena GUESNET
Bonn International Center for Conversion

See also Afghanistan; African Union (AU); Corporate Accountability (Africa); E-Waste; Goma, Democratic Republic of the Congo; International Conflict Resolution; Mining (Africa); Rule of Law (Africa)

Note: The authors used the following sources for their data, in addition to those found in the Further Reading section:

- Armed Conflict Dataset, provided by Uppsala Conflict Data Program (UCDP) and the Centre for the Study of Civil Wars, International Peace Research Institute, Oslo (PRIO);
- Conflict Information System (CONIS, formerly KOSIMO) provided by the Heidelberg Institute for International Conflict Research, University of Heidelberg;
- Correlates of War (COW) established by Melvin Small and J. David Singer at the University of Michigan.

This article originally appeared in Volume 4 of the *Encyclopedia of Sustainability*: *Natural Resources and Sustainability*.

FURTHER READING

Auty, Richard M. (1993). *Sustaining development in mineral economies: The resource curse thesis*. London: Routledge.

Bannon, Ian, & Collier, Paul. (Eds.). (2003). *Natural resources and violent conflict: Options and actions*. Washington, DC: World Bank.

Bleischwitz, Raimund. (2009). Ein internationales Abkommen als Kernelement eines globalen Ressourcenmanagements: Ein Vorschlag an die Politik [An international agreement as pillar for sustainable resource management: A proposal]. In Raimund Bleischwitz & Florian Pfeil (Eds.), *Reihe EINE WELT: Bd. 21. Globale Rohstoffpolitik: Herausforderungen für Sicherheit, Entwicklung und Umwelt* [A World Series: Vol. 21. Global resource politics: Challenges for security, development and environment] (pp. 147–161). Baden-Baden, Germany: Nomos Verlag.

Bleischwitz, Raimund; Welfens, Paul J. J; & Zhang, Zhong Xiang. (Eds.). (2010). *International economics of resource efficiency: Eco-innovation policies for a green economy*. Heidelberg, Germany: Physica-Verlag.

Bringezu, Stefan, & Bleischwitz, Raimund. (Eds.). (2009). *Sustainable resource management: Trends, visions and policies for Europe and the world*. Sheffield, UK: Greenleaf.

Collier, Paul. (2000). Economic causes of civil conflict and their implications for policy. Washington, DC: World Bank.

Collier, Paul, & Goderis, Benedikt. (2007). Commodity prices, growth, and the natural resource curse: Reconciling a conundrum. The Centre for the Study of African Economies (CSAE) Working Paper Series 2007-15. Oxford, UK: University of Oxford.

Collier, Paul, & Hoeffler, Anke. (1998). On economic causes of civil war. *Oxford Economic Papers, 50*(4), 563–573.

Collier, Paul, & Hoeffler, Anke. (2004). Greed and grievance in civil war. *Oxford Economic Papers, 56*(4), 563–595.

Collier, Paul, & Venables, Anthony J. (2010). International rules for trade in natural resources. World Trade Organization (WTO) Staff Working Paper (Economic Research and Statistics Division) ERSD-2010-06. Geneva: WTO.

De Soysa, Indra. (2002). Paradise is a bazaar? Greed, creed, and governance in civil war, 1989–99. *Journal of Peace Research, 39*(4), 395–416.

Dinar, Shlomi. (Ed.). (2011). *Beyond resource wars: Scarcity, environmental degradation and international cooperation*. Cambridge, MA: MIT Press.

Dube, Oeindrila, & Vargas, Juan F. (2006). Resource curse in reverse: The coffee crisis and armed conflict in Colombia. Royal Holloway, University of London: Discussion Papers in Economics 06/05, Department of Economics, Royal Holloway University of London. Retrieved September 23, 2011, from http://economia.uniandes.edu.co/publicaciones/d2006-46.pdf

Duffield, Mark. (2001). *Global governance and the new wars: The merging of development and security*. London: Zed Books.

Fearon, James D., & Laintin, David D. (2003). Ethnicity, insurgency, and civil war. *American Political Science Review, 97*(01), 75–90.

Feil, Moira; Tänzler, Dennis; Supersberger, Nikolaus; Bleischwitz, Raimund; & Rüttinger, Lukas. (2010). Rohstoffkonflikte nachhaltig vermeiden: Forschungs- und Handlungsempfehlungen [Avoiding resource conflicts in a sustainable way: Recommended procedure and research]. Berlin: Adelphi. Retrieved August 2, 2011, from http://www.adelphi.de/files/uploads/andere/pdf/application/pdf/rohkon_bericht_5_empfehlungen.pdf

Gleditsch, Nils Petter. (Ed.). (1997). *Conflict and the environment*. Dordrecht, The Netherlands: Kluwer Academic Publishers.

Global Witness. (2007, June 8). Hot chocolate: How cocoa fuelled the conflict in Côte d'Ivoire. Retrieved August 1, 2011, from http://www.globalwitness.org/library/hot-chocolate-how-cocoa-fuelled-conflict-c%C3%B4te-d%E2%80%99ivoire

Global Witness. (2010, December 14). The hill belongs to them: The need for international action on Congo's conflict minerals trade. Retrieved August 1, 2011, from http://www.globalwitness.org/library/hill-belongs-them-need-international-action-congos-conflict-minerals-trade

Global Witness. (2011). Conflict. Retrieved September 15, 2011, from http://www.globalwitness.org/campaigns/conflict

Graedel, Thomas. (2011). On the future availability of the energy metals. *Annual Review of Materials Research, 41*, 323–335.

Guesnet, Lena; Müller, Marie; & Schure, Jolien. (2009). Natural resources in Côte d'Ivoire: Fostering crisis or peace? The cocoa, diamond, gold and oil sectors. BICC Brief 40. Bonn, Germany: Bonn International Centre for Conversion.

Heidelberg Institut für Internationale Konfliktforschung e.V. [Heidelberg Institute for International Conflict Research e.V.] (HIIK). (2010). *Conflict barometer 2010*. Heidelberg, Germany: HIIK.

Homer-Dixon, Thomas F. (1995). The ingenuity gap: Can poor countries adapt to resource scarcity? *Population and Development Review, 21*(3), 1–26.

Homer-Dixon, Thomas F. (1999). *Environment, scarcity, and violence.* Princeton, NJ: Princeton University Press.

Humphreys, Macartan. (2005). Natural resources, conflict, and conflict resolution: Uncovering the mechanism. *Journal of Conflict Resolution, 49*(4), 508–537.

International Peace Information Service (IPIS). (n.d.). Mapping conflict motives in war areas. Retrieved September 23, 2011, from http://www.ipisresearch.be/mapping.php

Kaldor, Mary. (1999). *New and old wars: Organized violence in a global era.* Stanford, CA: Stanford University Press.

Klare, Michael T. (2001). *Resource wars: The new landscape of global conflict.* New York: Metropolitan Books.

Le Billon, Philippe. (2001). The political ecology of war: Natural resources and armed conflict. *Political Geography, 20*(5), 561–584.

Le Billon, Philippe. (2003). Getting it done: Instruments of enforcement. In Ian Bannon & Paul Collier (Eds.), *Natural resources and violent conflict: Options and actions* (pp. 215–286). Washington, DC: World Bank.

Le Billon, Philippe. (2005). Fuelling war: Natural resources and armed conflicts. Adelphi Paper 373. London: IISS & Routledge.

Levy, Marc A. (1995). Time for a third wave of environment and security scholarship? In *The Environmental Change and Security Project Report, No. 1* (pp. 44–46). Washington, DC: Woodrow Wilson Center.

Mildner, Stormy-Annika. (2011). Konfliktrisiko rohstoffe? Herausforderungen und chancen im umgang mit knappen ressourcen [Potential conflicts from resources? Challenges and chances out of scarce resources], SWP-Studie S 05. Berlin: Stiftung Wissenschaft und Politik (SWP), Deutsches Institut für Internationale Politik und Sicherheit.

Münkler, Herfried. (2002). *Die neuen kriege* [The new wars]. Reinbek, Germany: Rowohlt.

Myers, Norman. (1989). Environment and security. *Foreign Policy, 74*, 23–41.

National Intelligence Council. (2008). Global trends 2025: A transformed world. Washington, DC: National Intelligence Council. Retrieved September 23, 2011, from http://www.dni.gov/nic/PDF_2025/2025_Global_Trends_Final_Report.pdf

Organisation for Economic Co-operation and Development (OECD). (2010). OECD Due diligence guidance for responsible supply chains of minerals from conflict-affected and high-risk areas. Retrieved August 1, 2011, from http://www.oecd.org/document/36/0,3746,en_2649_34889_44307940_1_1_1_1,00.html

Paes, Wolf-Christian. (2009). *Preface.* In Lena Guesnet, Jolien Schure & Wolf-Christian Paes (Eds.), *Digging for peace: Private companies and emerging economies in zones of conflict* (pp. 4–6). Bonn, Germany: Bonn International Center for Conversion. BICC Brief 38.

Pirages, Dennis Clark. (1978). *The new context for international relations: Global ecopolitics.* North Scituate, MA: Duxbury Press.

RESOLVE. (2010). Tracing a path forward: A study of the challenges of the supply chain for target metals used in electronics. Washington, DC: RESOLVE.

Ross, Michael L. (2004). How does natural resource wealth influence civil war? Evidence from thirteen cases. *International Organization, 58*(1), 35–67.

Samset, Ingrid. (2009). Natural resource wealth, conflict, and peacebuilding. New York: Ralph Bunche Institute for International Studies, City University of New York.

SEA-info.net. (2011). Minerals and waste. Retrieved September 26, 2011, from http://www.sea-info.net/content/sectors.asp?pid=68

Snyder, Richard, & Bhavnani, Ravi. (2005). Blood, diamonds, and taxes: Lootable wealth and political order in sub-Saharan Africa. *Journal of Conflict Resolution, 49*(4), 563–597.

United Nations Interagency Framework Team for Preventive Action (UN IFTPA). (2010). Extractive industries and conflict: Guidance note for practitioners, Draft 2010. New York: UN IFTPA.

United Nations Security Council (UNSC). (2010). Final report of the Group of Experts on the Democratic Republic of the Congo, DRC Report S/2010/596.

Wilts, Claas Henning; Bleischwitz, Raimund; & Sanden, Joachim. (2010). Ein Covenant zur Schließung internationaler Stoffkreisläufe im Bereich Altautorecycling [A covenant for closing material cycles in the recycling of end-of-life vehicles]. Ressourceneffizienz Paper 3.5. Wuppertal, Germany: Wuppertal Institute. Retrieved August 2, 2011, from http://ressourcen.wupperinst.org/downloads/MaRess_AP3_5.pdf

World Trade Organization (WTO). (2010). *World trade report 2010: Trade in natural resources.* Geneva: WTO.

Congo (Zaire) River

The Congo River is named after the Kingdom of Kongo (1390–1914), which was located in the area at the mouth of the river, and it presently gives its name to both the Democratic Republic of the Congo and the Republic of Congo. The river and its basin play a vital role in the ecological balance of the continent of Africa. The Congo rain forest is reported to be one of the most threatened ecosystems in the world.

With a length of more than 4,377 kilometers, the Congo River is the fifth longest river in the world and the second longest in Africa, after the Nile (Heale 1999, 12–13). It is also the second most powerful river in the world, discharging nearly 34,000 cubic meters of water per second. So powerful is the Congo River that its brown waters surge nearly 144 kilometers out into the Atlantic Ocean. The city nearest its mouth is Banana, in the Democratic Republic of the Congo. The river's width ranges from 0.8 kilometers to 16 kilometers, and it contains more than four thousand islands.

The Congo River crosses the equator twice while cutting an arc through the basinlike depression in the equatorial African rain forest known as the *cuvette* (basin). The river's drainage basin covers almost all of the Democratic Republic of the Congo (formerly Zaire), the Republic of the Congo, the Central African Republic, and parts of Zambia, Angola, Cameroon, and Tanzania (Campbell 2005). Because it receives water from tributaries both north and south of the equator, the river maintains a strong flow all year.

The river can be divided into three sections. From its source in the savannas of Shaba Province in the Democratic Republic of the Congo (DRC), it is called the Lualaba, and it flows northward for more than 1,600 kilometers to Wagenia Falls, in the heart of the equatorial

rain forest near Kisangani. There it takes the name Congo and flows in a lazy arc through the rain forest. The banks are not always clearly delineated, and during periods of high water the river spills over into floodplains that stretch as far as 19 kilometers from the river's usual course. The third section begins at Malebo Pool, where the two national capitals of Kinshasa (DRC) and Brazzaville (Republic of the Congo) face each other across the river. Between the pool and the Atlantic Ocean, the river plunges nearly 304 meters, creating the largest reserve of waterpower in the world.

Economic Significance and Hydroelectric Power

The river has about thirty-two cataracts (i.e., areas of rapids). Along the lower Congo, these provided a barrier to European penetration during the era of the slave trade, although there was a lively river trade along the upper Congo that was dominated by networks of indigenous traders such as the Bobangi, the Boloki, and the Ngombe. Control of the Congo River was seen as crucial by the French and the Belgians, who were trying to establish colonies in equatorial Africa beginning in the late nineteenth century (Forbath 1977). They transported steamboats piece by piece from the Congo estuary to Malebo Pool for use on the upper Congo, and they used conscripted African labor to build railroads that bypassed the cataracts. With riverboat transportation in place, the Congo River became the major transportation artery in equatorial Africa. The railway now bypasses the three major falls at Matadi-Kinshasa, Kisangani-Ubundu, and Kindu-Kongolo. River steamers operate throughout the year between the chief ocean port, Kinshasa, and the chief river port, Kisangani. The Congo River and its tributaries form a system of navigable waterways approximately 14,480 kilometers long, which allow the trade of goods such as copper, palm oil, sugar, coffee, cotton, and others for central Africa.

The Congo River is the richest source of hydroelectric power in Africa. Since independence from Belgium in 1960, the government of the Democratic Republic of the Congo has attempted to harness some of the water power of the lower Congo's rapids by building dams. As of 2011, there were forty hydropower plants on the Congo River, with the largest at Inga Falls, about 200 kilometers southwest of Kinshasa. There two dams, Inga I and Inga II, provide more electricity than the country is able to consume. The entire Congo basin accounts for 13 percent of global hydropower potential, which can provide power for all of the electricity needs of sub-Saharan Africa (Nubourgh 2010).

Environmental Issues

The Congo River and its basin play a vital role in the ecological balance of the entire continent of Africa. Due to difference in the level of rainfall in different regions, the water flow in the Congo's tributaries fluctuates. Because the Congo has a large basin area, the change in rainfall level in one region does not affect too much the overall flow of the river, and the river usually has a regular flow except for a few years in the second half of the twentieth century (Nkounkou and Probst 1987). The DRC and the Republic of the Congo have not developed industrial centers along the banks of the Congo, and therefore it remains one of the world's least polluted rivers (according to a survey conducted in 1999 by the World Commission on Water for the 21st Century, a Paris-based group supported by the World Bank and the United Nations).

Unrestricted and careless extraction of oil and minerals has created some of the recent environmental threats to the river and its vast watershed. The river's basin holds the world's second largest contiguous rain forest and is biologically so diverse that it anchors more than 200 species of fish. The entire Congo basin area is estimated to contain 700 fish species, 500 of them endemic, 227 amphibian species, four sites recognized by the Ramsar Convention on Wetlands of International Importance, twenty-one areas identified by BirdLife International as wetland-dependent important bird areas (IBAs), and six endemic bird areas (Watersheds of Africa 2003). The Congo basin is home to the endangered Mountain Gorilla (one of the two subspecies of Eastern Gorillas). Although it also contains a protected area that comprises 4.7 percent of the total 3,730,881-square-kilometer basin

area, some illegal fishing, hunting, and poaching of large mammals continue with the demands of increasing population.

The Congo rain forest is reported to be one of the most threatened ecosystems in the world (Butler 2006). Deforestation due to hasty urban expansion, as well as to logging by poor farmers who rely on forest land for agriculture and fuel wood, threatens the river basin's ecosystem. The ecological health of the Congo and its basin are of central concern if the environmental stability of the African continent is to be maintained.

Robert HARMS
Yale University

See also Africa, Central; Agriculture, Small-Scale; Mining (Africa); Nile River; Parks and Preserves; Transboundary Water Issues; Water Use and Rights (Africa)

This article was adapted by the editors from Robert Harms' article "Congo (Zaire) River" in Shepard Krech III, J. R. McNeill, and Carolyn Merchant (Eds.), the Encyclopedia of World Environmental History, pp. 261–262. Great Barrington, MA: Berkshire Publishing (2003).

FURTHER READING

Butler, Rhett Ayers. (2006). Congo rainforest. Retrieved January 5, 2012, from http://rainforests.mongabay.com/congo/

Caputo, Robert. (1991). Lifeline for a nation: Zaire River. *National Geographic, 180*(5), 35.

Campbell, D. (2005). The Congo River Basin. In Lauchlan H. Fraser & Paul A. Keddy (Eds.), *The world's largest wetlands: Ecology and conservation* (pp. 149–165). Cambridge, UK; Cambridge University Press.

Devroey, Egide. (1941). *Le bassin hydrographique congolais* [The hydrographic basin of Congo]. Brussels, Belgium: G. Van Campenhout.

Forbath, Peter. (1977). *The River Congo: The discovery, exploration and exploitation of the world's most dramatic river.* New York: Harper & Row.

Harms, Robert. (1981). *River of wealth, river of sorrow: The central Zaire Basin in the era of the slave and ivory trade.* New Haven, CT: Yale University Press.

Heale, Jay. (1999). *Cultures of the world: Democratic Republic of the Congo.* New York: Marshal Cavendish Corporation.

Miracle, Marvin P. (1967). *Agriculture in the Congo Basin: Tradition and change in African rural economies.* Madison: University of Wisconsin Press.

Nkounkou, Renard-Roger, & Probst, Jean-Luc. (1987). Hydrology and geochemistry of the Congo River system. *SCOPE/UNEP Sonderband, 64*, 483–508.

Nubourgh, Alain. (2010). Belgian Technical Cooperation (BTC). Retrieved January 5, 2012, from http://weetlogs.scilogs.be/index.php?op=ViewArticle&articleId=331&blogId=27&utm_source=twitterfeed&utm_medium=twitter

Veatch, Arthur Clifford. (1935). *Evolution of the Congo Basin.* New York: The Society.

Watersheds of Africa: A02 Congo. (2003). Water Resources eAtlas. Retrieved January 6, 2012, from http://pdf.wri.org/watersheds_2003/af3.pdf

Corporate Accountability (Africa)

The corporate accountability of multinational corporations (MNCs), particularly those from the developed nations of the world, has become a prominent area of concern in sub-Saharan Africa. MNCs are increasingly held accountable for aspects that go beyond their immediate economic performance and conduct, and toward their wider societal impacts. Views differ on which issues are central to corporate accountability in 2012, however promise remains for the ongoing development of African corporate accountability in the future.

Corporate accountability refers to a system of checks and balances designed to hold companies accountable for their economic, social, and environmental impacts. In recent years, the term has gained prominence in particular as a counterweight to the unprecedented rise of large multinational corporations (MNCs). The idea of corporate accountability is firmly rooted in any theorizing about the role of business in society, including corporate governance (how society governs its corporations), corporate social responsibility (CSR) (the social responsibilities of business), corporate citizenship, stakeholder theory, integrated social contract theory, and organizational legitimacy theory. These theories examine issues related to the role of business in society, such as how they are governed, what society regards as legitimate business behavior, and what corporations are responsible for and to whom they are responsible. These theories build on the underlying assumption that a company needs to take its stakeholders' interests and concerns (i.e., the interests and concerns of everyone who has a stake in the outcome of or is affected by an enterprise) into account in order to maintain its "social license to operate." This includes the provision of information that enables society and relevant institutions to hold these companies accountable and to evaluate their performance.

One Term, Different Meanings

Very different opinions exist about how accountability should be implemented. At one end of the spectrum, theory and practice linked to CSR have promoted the voluntary, beyond-compliance (e.g., a company doing more than what is strictly required by law) provision of (sustainability) performance information as a core element. The dissemination of corporate sustainability reporting, which has become mainstream practice in particular among large MNCs, is positioned at the forefront of this view. Beyond sustainability reporting, other potentially important channels that serve to promote and enhance accountability include (a) investor-side instruments such as shareholder (as opposed to stakeholder) activism or socially responsible investment (SRI); (b) consumer-side instruments through eco-labels and fair trade labels; (c) demand-side measures such as the external verification of management systems such as ISO 14001 and SA 8000 (systems developed by the International Organization for Standardization and Social Accountability International, respectively); and (d) internal measures such as corporate codes of conduct or whistle-blowing mechanisms to combat corruption.

At the other end of the spectrum, a range of actors and initiatives reject this current wave of mainstream CSR instruments for their voluntary, beyond-compliance, corporate-led character, in essence arguing that it largely leads to various forms of "greenwashing" (Greer and Bruno 1996) or "hijacking corporate environmentalism" (Welford 1997). This so-called corporate accountability movement (Bendell 2004) calls for binding regulation to fill governance gaps, and therefore favors a "post voluntarist" (Utting 2005) regime, thereby dismissing corporate lead voluntary practices under the concepts of CSR or corporate citizenship. In this post-voluntarist regime, existing pieces of (home country) legislation such as the US Foreign Corrupt Practices Act and Alien Tort Claims Act, which are aimed at preventing misconduct of US companies operating abroad, as well as existing international mechanisms such as the complaint procedures of the Organisation for Economic Co-operation and Development (OECD) Guidelines for Multinational Enterprises are seen as starting points on which to build a functioning system of binding regulation.

Northern MNCs and Sub-Saharan Africa

For a number of decades, large MNCs in the developed countries of the global North (i.e., generally the Northern Hemisphere, where most of the world's more developed countries are located) have been the focal point of attempts to further corporate accountability, in particular with regard to their conduct in developing countries. In recent years, however, the widely perceived role of these companies has changed substantially; rather than seeing business as a source of environmental and socioeconomic problems in the developing world, it is increasingly seen as part of the solution to these problems. Given their resource base and technological capabilities, MNCs are expected to make a positive contribution toward sustainable development throughout their operations as well as their supply chains. In zones of comparatively weak governance, this may apply to an even greater extent. For example, the Nigerian industrial economist Foluso Phillips concludes that "in Africa, the motivations for CSR come from the failures of government to do right for its people" (2006, 24). Large MNCs have held dominant positions in sub-Saharan African economies for nearly a hundred years, and are now generally regarded as one of the main actors involved in solving global development issues.

Given the fact that sub-Saharan Africa has received more than its fair share of high-profile environmental and socioeconomic disasters involving large MNCs from the developed world, doubts exist whether these companies are able or willing to fulfill this new role in global governance. At the same time, however, calls are made by various actors—including international organizations such as the World Bank, the International Labor Organization, or the United Nations Development Programme—for greater MNC involvement in sub-Saharan Africa (Kolk and van Tulder 2006). Markets largely respond to profit potential and economic demand rather than need, thus areas of greatest absolute poverty such as sub-Saharan Africa tend to hold the least interest for the international market economy (Collier 2008; Steidlmeier 1993). Furthermore, investment in Africa

remains at levels that are inadequate for the attainment of the international Millennium Development Goals (MDGs), which set certain goals such as eliminating poverty and limiting the spread of HIV/AIDS (Anyanwu 2006).

Accountable for What?

The scope of MNC responsibility and accountability has broadened considerably in recent years. While corporate accountability has traditionally focused on its direct *sphere of responsibility*, such as misconduct inside the company gates, recent years have seen a trend toward holding large MNCs accountable for misconduct within their *sphere of influence*, as shown by, for example, large-scale consumer boycotts directed at Nike, H&M, or Mattel based on problems within their supply chains. In the 1990s and 2000s, all three companies were criticized for issues such as child labor, working conditions, and paying below a living wage—situations existing within their supply chains. It should be noted that there does not necessarily have to be a causal relationship between a company's impacts and societal problems. One such example is a campaign targeted at Coca-Cola by HIV/AIDS activists in 2002—not for misconduct, but rather because its highly visible brand name positioned it to potentially play an important role in combating HIV/AIDS: Coca-Cola's highly sophisticated and efficient distribution network in sub-Saharan Africa made the company ideally suited to provide the rural population with medication (Kytle and Ruggie 2005).

In very general terms, companies tend to be held accountable for a number of issues, including transparency and disclosure, poverty, health, environmental impacts, labor standards, and human rights.

Transparency and Disclosure

Many countries in sub-Saharan Africa have been dominated by socio-political contexts of weak governance, poor regulatory frameworks, limited trade union power, and ineffective or nonexistent modes of corporate accountability. Corporate governance and accountability in sub-Saharan Africa are relatively new. This is partly due to the fact that the separation of the management and ownership of modern corporations is a fairly recent development in many African countries, which until recent years were dominated by state-owned enterprises that are both owned and managed by governments (UNECA 2007). While state-owned enterprises (SOEs) are decreasing in number, they still comprise approximately one-quarter of southern African economies. SOEs often lack accountability for their performance, particularly where there are political involvement and weak board and management structures (UNECA 2007). Such governance gaps have been partly filled by nongovernmental organizations (NGOs). There is, however, increasing attention on the extent to which private corporations are responsible for engaging in transparent dealings with the host country governments where they operate.

The Norwegian economists Arne Wiig and Ivar Kolstad point out that in resource-rich countries, such as Angola or Nigeria where MNCs are dominant players within the economy, acting in ways that address institutional or governance problems may not necessarily be in a company's best interest. This is because institutional reform has distributive consequences that can shift access to resource rents from oil companies to host country populations (Wiig and Kolstad 2010). This illustrates the conflicting issues companies may face when the voluntary adoption of transparency mechanisms in their dealings with host country governments may reduce a company's ability to gain contracts or operating licenses, through patronage for example.

Nevertheless, the increasing demands and expectations of local populations have been integral in driving corporations like Shell in Nigeria to actively address governance problems, and to provide resources and knowledge transfer in a wide range of areas, including transport infrastructure, healthcare, and education. Multistakeholder initiatives such as the Publish What You Pay (PWYP) initiative and the Extractive Industries Transparency Initiative (EITI) are two well-known initiatives that aim to improve financial transparency and accountability mechanisms in the extractive industries.

Some still challenge, however, the extent to which these changes benefit more marginalized groups within society. For example, while transparency in oil contracts and oil revenues increases revenues for host country governments, the private sector does not typically have a mandate to address how host country governments use these revenues (Frynas 2005). For example, at the beginning of the twenty-first century, the Nigerian government on average received 70–80 percent of total oil revenues generated in the country (Frynas 2005). It could therefore be argued that it should be the responsibility of the state—rather than the private sector—to address governance gaps and to better address the demands and expectations of local populations.

Poverty

The problem of poverty illustrates some of the critical issues in accountability mechanisms that are based on voluntary compliance with principles and codes. It has been argued that business-based notions of corporate social responsibility and accountability are inadequate for addressing poverty alleviation because they fail to address some of the root causes of poverty where business has an impact, such as tax avoidance, the abuse of market power, or the destruction of community livelihoods and resources (Blowfield and Frynas 2005; Newell and Frynas 2007).

The traditional view of the role of business in poverty alleviation is that business contributes through job creation and taxation, and governments are responsible for the redistribution of wealth. This approach, however, is often inadequate where host country governance structures are weak, nonexistent, or corrupt, enabling corporations to "race to the bottom" by driving down the terms and conditions that govern their business activity such as negotiating favorable labor conditions or reduced taxation schedules. For example, in Cameroon it was found that investors were given exemptions from price control mechanisms, tax holidays for up to ten years, and favorable terms related to labor and finance (Orock 2006). Furthermore research has shown that African governments keen to compete in attracting foreign direct investment (FDI) are more likely to accept terms and conditions that are exploitative. In contrast, others argue that MNCs actually create a "race to the top" by raising operational efficiency, driving up standards, and improving local skills (Bhagwati 2004).

One of the most comprehensive studies of the linkages between a corporation and poverty alleviation was conducted jointly by the international aid and human rights organization Oxfam and the Unilever corporation in Indonesia (Clay 2005). This research found that the greatest potential for impact on poverty lay within mainstream operations and supply chains through the generation of employment and income, and opportunities to develop basic skills. Participation in these linkages, however, did not guarantee improvements in the living conditions of poor people, who remained vulnerable to poor and unfair working conditions (Clay 2005). While not based in Africa (and therefore somewhat outside the scope of this volume), this research highlighted the difficulties in agreeing on areas of accountability in relation to host country poverty alleviation.

Corporate accountability in relation to poverty is hampered by difficulties in identifying causality and attributing responsibility to individual businesses, hence reporting guidelines such as the Global Reporting Initiative (a nonprofit organization that promotes economic sustainability throughout the world) and company codes of conduct tend to ignore poverty as a specific issue (van Tulder 2008). There are calls for research and business practice to be improved by developing established methodologies for social accounting in the area of poverty alleviation (Kolk and van Tulder 2010).

Health

The failure to solve the issues of health care access and disease control and prevention continue to take a toll on Africa's growth and development. The pharmaceutical industry faces criticism for failing to address these needs. One study found that seven out of eleven companies reported spending less than 1 percent of their research and development budget on either sleeping sickness, leishmaniasis, Chagas' disease, malaria, or tuberculosis, all diseases that disproportionately affect developing nations (Eaton 2001). Furthermore, solutions to some basic healthcare issues can sometimes be antithetical to corporate interests. Voluntarily agreeing to increase access to medicines for the poor can mean giving up intellectual property rights and reducing prices relative to the purchasing power of those in poverty in favor of serving the poor. While some would argue that it is primarily the obligation of governments and donor agencies (not pharmaceutical companies) to fairly distribute aid and welfare services to the poor (Leisinger 2005), large pharmaceutical companies have been criticized by Oxfam for denying poor people access to affordable drugs (O'Dowd 2007).

The AIDS pandemic is a good example of the complex interplay between corporations, the public sector, and the nonprofit sector. Many governments and pharmaceutical companies were slow to respond to the AIDS pandemic, although this has changed drastically. In countries where HIV prevalence was greater than 20 percent, the majority of businesses surveyed by the World Economic Forum in 2005 had dedicated HIV prevention policies (WEF 2005). Companies such as Bristol-Myers Squibb, Merck, Pfizer, and Abbott have all launched significant corporate foundations and initiatives aimed at tackling HIV and AIDS since the turn of the new millennium.

Once again, however, the notion of voluntary corporate accountability as an overall agent of social development is challenged on the basis that a company's actions are driven by corporate objectives rather than social development. A pharmaceutical company can be engaged in philanthropic activities that contribute to health issues such as HIV, while simultaneously challenging host country government patent rights, taxation, or trade policies—actions that reduce costs for the corporation but raise costs or reduce income for host country governments (Hartwig, Rosenberg, and Merson 2006).

Environmental Impacts

Given the persistently high levels of poverty and underdevelopment in Africa, social issues tend to dominate the responsibility agenda there. Negative impacts on the environment, however, are of grave concern in Africa, particularly as many economies are dependent on the extractives sector (industries that extract resources, such as the oil and mining industries) notorious for its damage to the environment. In addition, environmental degradation often goes hand-in-hand with poor sanitation, negative impacts on public health, and poor working conditions (cf. Hayes 2006).

Accountability for environmental impacts has largely been driven by external pressure on the extractive industries. It is often based on self-regulation through voluntary measures that involve environmental management systems, impact assessments, environmental reporting, and efforts to improve long-term environmental performance (UNECA 2007).

Another driving force for environmental accountability is the emergence of litigation as a tool of persuasion. Victims of oil pollution from Shell's installations in Nigeria have in 2011 filed a number of class action suits against Royal Dutch Shell in the United Kingdom, the United States, and the Netherlands (Vidal 2011; Muchlinski 2011). In the UK case, Shell eventually accepted liability for two large-scale oil spills that occurred in 2008 and 2009 in the Ogoniland region of the Niger Delta, and they face a potential payout of hundreds of millions of dollars for the damage caused to river ecosystems and mangrove forests in the area (Vidal 2011).

Labor Standards

Real wages have lagged behind productivity growth in many African countries, and jobs created by multinationals are often low skilled, low paid, temporary, and have historically been associated with exploitative and risky working conditions (Orock 2006). The increased use of labor standards on issues related to worker rights and the use of sweatshop, forced, and child labor often involve the monitoring of MNCs through labor codes, although labor standards can also be imposed through trade agreements.

Companies are expected to disclose information on employee rights to be represented by and engage in negotiations with trade unions, contributions to the effective abolition of child labor and all forms of forced or compulsory labor, health and safety, and the employment and training of local personnel (UNECA 2007).

Labor standards are criticized, however, for failing to address issues such as the right to a living wage, wider economic issues relating to investment and disinvestment, or price fluctuations. Typically, smallholders in developing countries are most vulnerable to these types of uncertainties within the market economy (Jenkins and Sen 2006). Research on the supply chain of Kenyan cut flowers to UK markets concluded that while there are signs of improvements in labor conditions on some farms, downward pressures in buyer-controlled supply chains fail to address problems of sexual harassment of female workers, workplace insecurity and vulnerability due to the use of temporary contracts, compulsory unpaid overtime, and chemical exposure. This research also highlighted difficulties in monitoring such issues without the use of intensive social auditing processes (Hale and Opondo 2005).

Human Rights

Companies are expected to exercise their responsibility to respect human rights through the adoption of a human rights policy, periodic assessment of human rights impacts, and proper reporting and grievance procedures that address the interests of those affected by a company's actions. According to Peter Muchlinski, professor of international commercial law and globalization at the University of London, international law is increasingly seen as an avenue for the extension of human rights responsibilities to corporate actors (2011). Innovative public interest lawyers are going beyond traditional national and corporate laws, challenging corporate wrongs and human rights abuses through tort law or criminal law. In 2006, it was reported that there were growing possibilities that the US Alien Tort Statute could be used to litigate against US companies who violate human and environmental rights in Equatorial Guinea and Angola (Puppim de Oliveira and Ali 2006). The 2011 case of Shell in Nigeria (as reported in relation to environmental accountability) also demonstrates developments within the corporate accountability movement.

Finally, while global norms and standards, such as the United Nations Global Compact (an initiative that encourages companies to adopt sustainability into their daily operations), represent a worldwide consensus on human rights standards, the US business ethics professor Patricia Werhane (2010) outlined some of the difficulties companies may face operationalizing them in everyday practice, such as decisions that involve a trade-off between the right to work and the right to a decent environment. Companies also face moral and ethical challenges when human rights–based codes and principles do not translate where deeply ingrained cultural traditions separate people on the basis of gender, race, or ethnic divisions. Additionally, these standards do not protect the human rights of African farmers to free trade, where farmers are prevented from exporting crops to Western nations by tariff restrictions. Hence, progress is needed on how human rights–based standards can be operationalized in diverse settings (Werhane 2010).

Future Prospects

There are critical issues pertinent to MNC activity in Africa that fail to receive sufficient attention in current corporate accountability practices. Some observers suggest that the CSR agenda is largely shaped by Northern MNCs, with a clear lack of participation or integration of actors from developing countries (Barkemeyer 2009; Fox 2004; Schepers 2006; Utting 2001). Currently, normative corporate guidelines as well as CSR practice tend to reflect Northern interests and priorities (Barkemeyer et al. 2011). Consequently, corporate accountability largely fails to address important aspects such as tax avoidance and transfer pricing (Jenkins 2005). Among the wider issues that need to be addressed are corporate power and policy influence, the negative effects of economic liberalization (Prieto-Carron et al. 2006; UNRISD 2003), or the risk of deindustrialization as a result of these revenues derived from natural resources: it has been argued that an over-reliance on extractive industries typically has a negative impact on other sectors within an economy, in particular manufacturing and agriculture (Corden and Neary 1982). The concept of corporate accountability to stakeholders is also dependent on which people are considered to be the stakeholders, as certain groups such as home workers, those engaged in labor in the informal economy, or the poor may not be regarded as corporate stakeholders.

Development and economic theorists have shifted toward the view that market-based solutions to development do not work without supporting policies and institutions (Besley and Burgess 2003), which further supports the view that the incorporation of both market and nonmarket business channels in accountability mechanisms is essential.

Notwithstanding these critical issues related to voluntary compliance and regulated corporate accountability, current developments aimed at building up internal accountability mechanisms both within and between African countries may pave the way for future progress. Some scholars believe that corporate governance developments in South Africa may act as a catalyst for the development of country-specific governance across the rest of Africa (Lund-Thomsen 2005; Vaughn and Ryan 2006). There is a particular promise for progress through the South African King Reports, the most recent of which (2009) promotes integrating corporate accountability with the Global Reporting Initiative.

The African Peer Review Mechanism (APRM) established by the New Partnership for Africa's Development (NEPAD) also represents a significant change in the thinking of African leaders as they seek to reverse the trends of lack of accountability, political authoritarianism, state failure, and corruption by promoting and consolidating democracy and transparent economic management (Hope 2005). Many nations across sub-Saharan Africa have set up stock exchanges, which may play a role in making standards, codes, and principles easier to enforce among listed companies, and in increasing shareholder empowerment, which in Nigeria is seen as a potential avenue for influencing corporate attitudes to CSR (Amao and Amaeshi 2008).

The activities of multinational corporations in sub-Saharan Africa remain a double-edged sword. Nevertheless, hopes prevail that good governance in sub-Saharan African nations, combined with recently established accountability mechanisms such as the aforementioned EITI or PWYP, will help to steer multinationals toward enhanced accountability and transparency.

Ralf BARKEMEYER
University of Leeds

Jo-Anna RUSSON
Queen's University Belfast

See also African Union (AU); Conflict Minerals; E-Waste; International Conflict Resolution; Microfinance; Mining (Africa); Rule of Law (Africa); World Bank

FURTHER READING

Amao, Olufemi, & Amaeshi, Kenneth. (2008). Galvanising shareholder activism: A prerequisite for effective corporate governance and accountability in Nigeria. *Journal of Business Ethics, 82*(1), 119–130. doi:10.1007/s10551-007-9566-2

Anyanwu, John C. (2006). Promoting of investment in Africa. *African Development Review, 18*(1), 42–71.

Barkemeyer, Ralf. (2009). Beyond compliance—below expectations? CSR in the context of international development. *Business Ethics: A European Review, 18*(3), 273–289.

Barkemeyer, Ralf; Holt, Diane; Preuss, Lutz; & Tsang, Stephen. (2011). What happened to the "development" in sustainable development? Business guidelines two decades after Brundtland. *Sustainable development, early view* (available online). doi:10.1002/sd.1521

Bendell, Jem. (2004). Barricades and boardrooms: A contemporary history of the corporate accountability movement. *Programme on Technology, Business and Society, Paper No. 13.* Geneva: United Nations Research Institute for Sustainable Development (UNRISD).

Besley, Timothy, & Burgess, Robin. (2003). Halving global poverty. *The Journal of Economic Perspectives, 17*(3), 3–22. doi:10.1257/089533003769204335

Bhagwati, Jagdish. (2004). *In Defense of Globalization.* Oxford, UK: Oxford University Press.

Blowfield, Michael, & Frynas, Jedrzej George. (2005). Setting new agendas: Critical perspectives on corporate social responsibility in the developing world. *International Affairs, 81*(3), 499–513.

Clay, Jason. (2005). Exploring the links between international business and poverty reduction: A case study of Unilever in Indonesia. An Oxfam GB, Novib, Unilever, and Unilever-Indonesia joint research project. Oxford, UK: Oxfam GB, Novib Oxfam Netherlands, and Unilever.

Collier, Paul. (2008). *The bottom billion: Why the poorest countries are failing and what can be done about it.* Oxford, UK: Oxford University Press.

Corden, W. Max, & Neary, J. Peter. (1982). Booming sector and deindustrialization in a small open economy. *Economic Journal, 92,* 825–848.

Eaton, Lynn. (2001). Drug companies neglect research into diseases affecting the poor. *British Medical Journal, 323*(7317), 827.

Fox, Tom. (2004). Corporate social responsibility and development: In quest of an agenda. *Development, 47*(3), 29–36.

Frynas, Jedrzej George. (2005). The false developmental promise of corporate social responsibility: Evidence from multinational oil companies. *International Affairs, 81*(3), 581–598.

Greer, Jed, & Bruno, Kenny. (1996). *Greenwash: The reality behind corporate environmentalism.* New York: Apex Press.

Hale, Angela, & Opondo, Maggie. (2005). Humanising the cut flower chain: Confronting the realities of flower production for workers in Kenya. *Antipode, 37*(2), 301–323. doi:10.1111/j.0066-4812.2005.00494.x

Hartwig, Kari; Rosenberg, Alana; & Merson, Michael. (2006). Corporate citizenship, AIDS and Africa: Lessons from Bristol-Myers Squibb Company's Secure the Future. In Wayne Visser, Malcolm McIntosh & Charlotte Middleton (Eds.), *Corporate citizenship in Africa: Lessons from the past; paths to the future* (pp. 127–138). Sheffield, UK: Greenleaf.

Hayes, Karen T. A. (2006). Grounding African corporate responsibility: Moving the environment up the agenda. In Wayne Visser, Malcolm McIntosh & Charlotte Middleton (Eds.), *Corporate citizenship in Africa: Lessons from the past; paths to the future* (pp. 93–105). Sheffield, UK: Greenleaf.

Hope, Kempe Ronald, Sr. (2005). Toward good governance and sustainable development: The African Peer Review Mechanism. *Governance, 18*(2), 283–311. doi:10.1111/j.1468-0491.2005.00276.x

Jenkins, Rhys. (2005). Globalization, corporate social responsibility and poverty. *International Affairs, 81*(3), 525–540.

Jenkins, Rhys, & Sen, Kunal. (2006). International trade and manufacturing employment in the South: Four country case studies. *Oxford Development Studies, 34*(3), 299–322.

Kolk, Ans, & van Tulder, Rob. (2006). Poverty alleviation as business strategy? Evaluating commitments of frontrunner multinational corporations. *World Development, 34*(5), 789–801.

Kolk, Ans, & van Tulder, Rob. (2010). International business, corporate social responsibility and sustainable development. *International Business Review, 19*(2), 119–125.

Kytle, Beth, & Ruggie, John Gerard. (2005). Corporate social responsibility as risk management: A model for multinationals. *Corporate Social Responsibility Initiative Working, Paper No. 10.* Cambridge, MA: John F. Kennedy School of Government, Harvard University.

Leisinger, Klaus M. (2005). The corporate social responsibility of the pharmaceutical industry: Idealism without illusion and realism without resignation. *Business Ethics Quarterly, 15*(4), 577–594.

Lund-Thomsen, Peter. (2005). Corporate accountability in South Africa: The role of community mobilizing in environmental governance. *International Affairs, 81*(3), 619–633.

Muchlinski, Peter. (2011). The changing face of transnational business governance: Private corporate law liability and accountability of transnational groups in a post-financial crisis world. *Indiana Journal of Global Legal Studies, 18*(2), 665–705.

Newell, Peter, & Frynas, Jedrzej George. (2007). Beyond CSR? Business, poverty and social justice: An introduction. *Third World Quarterly, 28*(4), 669–681.

O'Dowd, Adrian. (2007). Drug companies are ignoring health crisis in poor countries. *British Medical Journal, 335*(7630), 1111.

Orock, Rogers Tabe Egbe. (2006). An overview of corporate globalisation and the non-globalisation of corporate citizenship in Africa. In Wayne Visser, Malcolm McIntosh & Charlotte Middleton (Eds.), *Corporate citizenship in Africa: Lessons from the past; paths to the future* (pp. 250–260). Sheffield, UK: Greenleaf.

Phillips, Foluso. (2006). Corporate social responsibility in an African context. *Journal of Corporate Citizenship, 24,* 23–27.

Prieto-Carron, Marina; Lund-Thomsen, Peter; Chan, Anita; Muro, Ana; & Bhushan, Chandra. (2006). Critical perspectives on CSR and development: What we know, what we don't know, and what we need to know. *International Affairs, 82*(5), 977–987. doi:10.1111/j.1468-2346.2006.00581.x

Puppim de Oliveira, Jose A., & Ali, Saleem H. (2006). Can corporate power positively transform Angola and Equatorial Guinea? In Wayne Visser (Ed.), *Corporate citizenship in Africa* (pp. 158–170). Sheffield, UK: Greenleaf.

Rossouw, G. J. (2005). Business ethics and corporate governance in Africa. *Business & Society, 44*(1), 94–106.

Schepers, Donald H. (2006). The impact of NGO network conflict on the corporate social responsibility strategies of multinational corporations. *Business and Society, 45*(3), 282.

Steidlmeier, Paul. (1993). The business community and the poor: Rethinking business strategies and social policy. *The American Journal of Economics and Sociology, 52*(2), 209–221.

United Nations Economic Commision for Africa (UNECA). (2007). *An overview of corporate governance and accountability in Southern Africa.* Addis Ababa, Ethiopia: UNECA.

United Nations Research Institute for Social Development (UNRISD). (2003). Corporate social responsibility and development: Towards a new agenda? *UNRISD Conference News.* Geneva: UNRISD.

Utting, Peter. (2001). Promoting socially responsible business in developing countries. The potential and limits of voluntary initiatives. *Report of the UNRISD Workshop 23–24 October 2000.* Geneva: UNRISD.

Utting, Peter. (2005). Corporate responsibility and the movement of business. *Development in Practice, 15*(3–4), 375.

van Tulder, Rob. (2008). *The role of business in poverty reduction: Towards a sustainable corporate story?* Geneva: UNRISD.

Vaughn, Melinda, & Ryan, Lori Verstegen. (2006). Corporate governance in South Africa: A bellwether for the continent? *Corporate governance: An international review, 14*(5), 504–512. doi:10.1111/j.1467-8683.2006.00533.x

Vidal, John. (2011, August 3) Shell accepts liability for two oil spills in Nigeria. *The Guardian.* Retrieved May 23, 2012, from http://www.guardian.co.uk/environment/2011/aug/03/shell-liability-oil-spills-nigeria

Welford, Richard. (1997). *Hijacking environmentalism: Corporate responses to sustainable development.* London: Earthscan.

Werhane, Patricia H. (2010). Principles and practices for corporate responsibility. *Business Ethics Quarterly, 20*(4), 695–701.

Wiig, Arne, & Kolstad, Ivar. (2010). Multinational corporations and host country institutions: A case study of CSR activities in Angola. *International Business Review, 19*(2), 178–190.

World Economic Forum (WEF). (2005). *Business and HIV/AIDS: Commitment and action?* Geneva: WEF, Global Health Initiative in co-operation with UNAIDS.

Danube River

The Danube is Europe's second-longest river, passing through eight countries with a catchment area inhabited by millions of people. Its floodplains and wetlands are important in supporting European biodiversity. The Danube is used for many purposes, including generating electricity, irrigating land, and disposing of industrial waste. These activities have harmed the environment and caused diplomatic conflict between states jockeying for control of the river.

The Danube River originates with the meeting of the Brig and Brigach streams at Donauschingen in Germany's Black Forest, and flows southeast through central and southeastern Europe into the Black Sea. At 2,850 kilometers, it is the second-longest river in Europe after the Volga; its major tributaries include the Inn, Morava, Tisza, Drava, Sava, and Prut rivers. The Danube is the world's most international river, passing through eight countries—Germany, Austria, Slovakia, Hungary, Yugoslavia, Bulgaria, Romania, and Ukraine. These countries, along with parts of Switzerland, Slovenia, Croatia, Bosnia and Herzegovina, and Moldova form the Danube basin's catchment area (the area drained by a river). This area consists of 816,000 square kilometers and is inhabited by 83 million people, a figure that is not expected to increase significantly by 2020 (UNDP n.d.).

The Danube basin has three subregions: the Upper Danube (from Germany to the Devin Gate in Slovakia), the Middle Danube (from the Devin Gate to the Iron Gates on the Serbian-Romanian border), and the Lower Danube (from the Iron Gates to the Romanian-Bulgarian border). The 6,000-square-kilometer Danube Delta spans the Black Sea coast of Romania and Ukraine. Approximately two-thirds of the delta is submerged seasonally, and the alluvial floodplains and wetlands of the Danube are important areas for European biodiversity. Important wildlife include the pygmy cormorant (*Phalacrocorax pygmeus*), red-breasted goose (*Branta ruficollis*), and the European otter (*Lutra lutra*). Several rare karst (an area of limestone formations) hydrogeological ecosystems exist along the Danube, and these areas are especially vulnerable to ecological degradation.

Social History of the River

Humans have inhabited the Danube basin for at least seven thousand years. Neolithic Danubian society lived along the river between 5000 and 4000 BCE. The Danube was an important trade artery in the Middle Ages and Renaissance, carrying grain, people, and goods between central and southeastern Europe.

Floods occur regularly on the Danube in the early spring and early summer of each year. The 1501 flood remains one of the worst ever recorded. Composer Franz Liszt gave a concert to benefit the Hungarian victims of the catastrophic flood of 1838. Serious floods occurred again in 1876, 1884, 1954, 1965, 1999, and 2000.

Human regulation of the river began as early as 1426, when Hungarian villages on the riverbanks instituted a small-scale irrigation system. Prior to large-scale regulation of the Danube, the river shifted its course often and split into a number of smaller channels in many stretches. The 1856 Danube Convention, signed after the Crimean War (1853–1856), guaranteed free international navigation and laid the groundwork for twentieth-century international collaborations such as the Danube Commission and the International Commission for the Protection of the Danube River (ICPDR). Armed conflicts and embargoes disrupted river transit during the First and Second World Wars, and again during the Yugoslavian civil war of the 1990s.

River Protection Issues

The countries through which the Danube flows before entering the Black Sea have harnessed the river for generating hydroelectricity, cooling nuclear power plants, irrigating agricultural land, and providing a sink for waste material from chemical plants, paper mills, and oil refineries. Nitrogen and phosphorus pollution from agriculture and industries along the Danube has caused eutrophication (lack of oxygen due to an overabundance of plant life, which feeds on the nitrogen and phosphorus) and other environmental problems in the Black Sea.

Rising environmental awareness has set in motion waves of citizens' actions in population centers along the Danube. In 1984, thousands of activists lodged a successful protest against a proposal by the Austrian government to site a hydroelectric dam at Hainburg, a large wetland east of Vienna. In Ruse, an industrial city on the Danube, Bulgarian citizens rallied against chemical plant emissions in 1987.

In the 1980s, plans for a dam on the border of Hungary and Czechoslovakia provoked a mass movement in Hungary. At the peak of the movement in 1988, forty thousand protesters demonstrated in Budapest against the dam. The Hungarian government abandoned construction after the collapse of state socialism in 1989, but the newly formed Slovak government diverted 80 percent of the river's flow to make its part of the dam system operable. For Hungary, the protest movement became a symbol of its emergence from state socialism, while Slovakia considered the dam a symbol of national development.

Communities along the river have had to contend with contamination from industrial accidents as well. In 2000, the Danube was affected by a major cyanide spill on the Tisza, its largest tributary. The spill originated at a gold-mining operation in Romania but also affected Hungary, Yugoslavia, and Bulgaria. Cyanide from the accident eventually reached as far as the Danube Delta. In 2010, a company called MAL Hungarian Aluminium discharged toxic red sludge into the river when one of its reservoirs burst. Although Hungarian politicians played down the effects of the spill, several people died (BBC 2010a and 2010b), mainly by drowning, and several dozen people were treated for chemical burns. Hungary's state secretary for the environment, Zoltan Illes, described the flood as the worst chemical accident in Hungary's history (BBC 2010c).

Environmental Protection Initiatives

Policy makers in the Danube region have responded to these environmental problems by establishing several international nature preserves along the river, including the Danube-Ipel between Slovakia and Hungary, and the Danube-Drava between Hungary and Croatia. The 1971 Ramsar Convention on Wetlands helps to protect the Danube Delta, and UNESCO created the Danube Delta Biosphere Reserve in Romania in 1979. Meanwhile, ongoing citizens' actions, state-level environmental protection, and international environmental coordination ventures all bolster efforts to protect the Danube's ecosystems for future generations.

Krista M. HARPER
University of Massachusetts, Amherst

See also Disaster Risk Management; Germany; International Conflict Resolution; Mediterranean Sea; Parks and Preserves; Rhine River; Rule of Law (European Union); Transboundary Water Issues; Ukraine; Volga River

This article was adapted by the editors from Krista M. Harper's article "Danube River" in Shepard Krech III, J. R. McNeill, and Carolyn Merchant (Eds.), the *Encyclopedia of World Environmental History*, pp. 284–286. Great Barrington, MA: Berkshire Publishing (2003).

FURTHER READING

British Broadcasting Company (BBC). (2010a, October 8). The company behind Hungary's toxic spill. Retrieved November 30, 2011, from http://www.bbc.co.uk/news/business-11501441
British Broadcasting Company (BBC). (2010b, October 8). Hungary calms Danube sludge fears as death toll rises. Retrieved November 30, 2011, from http://www.bbc.co.uk/news/world-europe-11498884
British Broadcasting Company (BBC). (2010c, October 5). Hungary battles to stem torrent of toxic sludge. Retrieved April 16, 2012, from http://www.bbc.co.uk/news/world-europe-11475361
Carter, F. W., & Turnock, David. (1993). *Environmental problems in Eastern Europe.* New York: Routledge.
Commission of the European Communities. (2001). *Environmental cooperation in the Danube-Black Sea region.* Brussels, Belgium: Commission of the European Communities.
Cousteau Society. (1993). *The Danube: For whom and for what?* Paris: Cousteau Foundation.
Fitzmaurice, John. (1996). *Damming the Danube.* Boulder, CO: Westview.
Held, Joseph. (Ed.). (1994). *Dictionary of East European history since 1945.* Westport, CT: Greenwood.
United Nations Development Project (UNDP). (n.d.). Danube regional project: Population. Retrieved December 31, 2011, from http://www.undp-drp.org/drp/danube_population.html

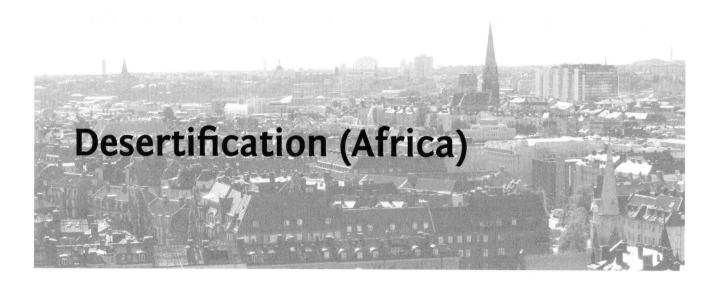

Desertification (Africa)

Desertification is the degradation of drylands and is symptomatic of unsustainable development. Estimates of its extent are still uncertain, but Africa is thought to contain a third of all desertified land. Proper global monitoring is essential for learning more about this complex phenomenon, and for controlling it through the UN Convention to Combat Desertification and national integrated environmental management.

The term *desertification* is used to describe the degradation of land in dry areas, not the expansion of natural desert as is commonly thought. Land degradation is a long-term process resulting from human overuse, and it can occur anywhere in the world as one of the most visible terrestrial symptoms of unsustainable development. Desertification is treated as a distinct phenomenon because dry areas are highly susceptible to degradation, which can be accelerated by extended droughts. Africa, with the Sahara desert at its core, contains about one-third of all desertified land in the world and a slightly higher proportion of the global arid zone.

History

The concept of desertification originated in the mid-1970s when the United Nations Environment Programme (UNEP) coordinated a response to a drought that had afflicted the Sahel region of western Africa since 1968. For various reasons, UNEP transformed a problem resulting from the natural hazard of drought into one having a human cause as well. It convened the UN Conference on Desertification (UNCOD) in Nairobi, Kenya, in 1977, at which delegates negotiated the UN Plan of Action to Combat Desertification,

building on the results of two years of scientific research (UN 1977).

UNEP chose the term *desertification* from a range of alternatives. It was originally devised by the French botanist André Aubréville (1949) to refer to desert expansion. But UNCOD contradicted this, and referred instead to land degradation "pulling out" deserts, since desertification can occur far from natural deserts. Nevertheless, the term remains controversial owing to its earlier meaning. Many scientists working in this field often refer to "dryland degradation" instead.

Following a recommendation by the UN Conference on Environment and Development (UNCED), in Rio de Janeiro, Brazil, in 1992, negotiations began on the UN Convention to Combat Desertification (UNCCD). The negotiations concluded in 1994, and the UNCCD came into force in 1996 (UN 1994). The UNCCD is framed by the principle of sustainable development, like the UN conventions on climate change and biological diversity signed at UNCED.

Definitions

UNCOD had a clear understanding of desertification as a long-term process of land degradation catalyzed by relatively short-term droughts. Yet its definition was not concise: "the diminution or destruction of the biological potential of the land . . . [that] can lead ultimately to desert-like conditions—an aspect of the widespread deterioration of ecosystems under the combined pressure of adverse and fluctuating climate and excessive exploitation" (UN 1977).

Following UNCOD, various definitions were proposed, each with a different balance between the roles of human overuse and climatic variation. A consensus definition was finally achieved at UNCED in 1992 and adopted in the text of the UNCCD: "land degradation in arid, semi-arid and dry sub-humid areas resulting from various factors, including climatic variations and human activities" (UN 1994).

Forms and Direct Causes

Desertification involves the degradation of both soil and the vegetation that covers it. Soil degradation is evident in five main forms: water erosion, wind erosion, compaction, waterlogging, and salinization/alkalinization. A number of these may affect any dry area at the same time. Principal direct (or proximate) causes include deforestation, woodland degradation, overgrazing, overcropping, and poor irrigation management.

Reducing vegetation cover makes soil more vulnerable to degradation. Vegetation cover may be reduced by clearing woodland for agriculture or other purposes, as in deforestation elsewhere. Since tree cover in dry areas mainly comprises open (savanna) woodland, which has an open canopy in contrast to the closed canopy found in more humid areas, a reduction in tree canopy cover, density, height, and biomass rather than outright clearance is more common. This change in the quality of woodland cover is called *woodland degradation* and can occur for different reasons, including expansion of grazing land, browsing of trees by livestock, and fuelwood cutting.

Grassy vegetation is also degraded through overgrazing by livestock. Large areas of dryland comprise mixtures of pasture, trees, and shrubs in varying proportions. These multiple layers of vegetation are used for multiple purposes, often simultaneously, and overgrazing can affect all three layers.

Overcropping occurs when crops are grown too frequently and without adequate fallow periods or fertilizer applications. Overcropping and overgrazing make soil more prone to wind and water erosion by reducing its vegetation cover and organic matter content. Soil can also be compacted by trampling, either by livestock or agricultural machinery.

Irrigation has many benefits in terms of improved crop yields in drylands, but if too much water is applied, the soil can become waterlogged. Evaporation of water from waterlogged soil can leave upper soil layers abnormally rich in sodium chloride (salinization) or other chemical compounds (alkalinization). Use of saline or otherwise poor-quality irrigation water can also lead to these problems.

Underlying Causes

Desertification has several underlying causes, including population growth and economic growth, which drive agricultural expansion; poverty, which constrains sustainability; and irregular climatic variation, which affects the other causes and sustainability of land use itself.

In the early years of desertification research, links between socioeconomic and climatic driving forces and dryland degradation were portrayed as simple and deterministic. Drought was thought to reduce vegetation growth, which in turn encouraged people to overcrop or overgraze land, thereby degrading it, which fed back to raise the intensity of use, which increased the degree of degradation in a vicious circle (Grainger 1990).

A less deterministic view has been adopted. Research suggests that single-factor causation is rare, and that multiple-factor causation is common, with three to five underlying causes driving two to three direct causes (Geist and Lambin 2004). The drylands development paradigm characterizes desertification by a complex array of spatio-temporal processes comprising coupled, dynamic, and co-adapting human–environment systems; interactions between variables that change slowly (e.g., soil fertility), and those that change more quickly (e.g., crop yields linked to strongly fluctuating precipitation); the switching of some environmental features to a new state if they pass a critical threshold; and cross-scalar processes, so the ultimate cause of degradation in a very dry area may be agricultural expansion hundreds of miles away in a more humid area (Reynolds et al. 2007).

Distribution

Early assessments of desertification divided it into degrees of degradation: slight, moderate, severe, and very severe (Dregne 1977). Terms have changed with successive assessments, but the same general approach is still used.

TABLE 1. Varying Estimates of Continental Areas Suffering at Least Moderate Desertification (in millions of hectares)

	Dregne	Mabbutt	UNEP Atlas
Africa	490	741	201
Asia	769	748	214
Australia	403	112	4
North America	399	208	66
South America	174	162	37
Europe	20	30	86
Total	2,255	2,001	608

Source: Dregne (1983); Mabbutt (1984); UNEP, Middleton, and Thomas (1997).

Note: These figures relied on subjective estimates by UN experts, not actual measurements. A proper measurement of the global extent of desertification is still needed.

Two early estimates put the extent of at least moderately desertified dryland at 2,255 million hectares (Dregne 1983) and 2,001 million hectares (Mabbutt 1984). (See table 1 above.) This represented over 40 percent of the total area of dryland in the world and 17 percent of world land area.

The latest global estimate of at least moderately desertified dryland, published in UNEP's *World Atlas of Desertification* in 1997, was 608 million hectares, less than one-third of the 1980s estimates. Of these, 201 million hectares were in Africa (UNEP, Middleton, and Thomas 1997). The total was revised slightly from 607 million hectares in the first edition of the atlas (UNEP, Middleton, and Thomas 1992).

All these figures relied on subjective estimates by UN experts, not actual measurements. A proper measurement of the global extent of desertification is still awaited.

Key Debates

Desertification is one of the more contentious of all global environmental change phenomena.

Political Ambiguity

One reason for contention may be that the UNEP devised desertification as an ambiguous concept, acceptable to developing countries concerned about how drought constrains development, as well as to developed countries concerned with environmental degradation. Conflicting views about desertification continue to hinder the work of the UNCCD (Ortiz and Tang 2005).

Reality or Myth?

There is still much skepticism in the scientific community about the reality of desertification, fueled by widespread lack of global empirical data and the complexity of the phenomenon, which facilitates misinterpretation (Thomas and Middleton 1994). In spite of this, scientific investigation continues at the highest level (MEA 2005).

Global Environmental Monitoring

Lack of global empirical data is a consequence of lack of global monitoring. There are occasional remote-sensing studies of the extent of desertification, but often their results have limited applicability because they rely on satellite sensors whose resolution is too low to give reliable results (Turner 2003). Scientists convened by the UNCCD, however, have begun examining the requirements for continuous monitoring of desertification (Verstraete et al. 2011).

Contextuality

Another reason why large-scale empirical data about desertification is hard to obtain is that it varies so much from place to place. Desertification may be found in some parts of an area but not in others (Tiffen and Mortimore 2002). A new research growth area involves finding new ways to incorporate contextuality in assessing dryland livelihoods by combining scientific and lay contextual knowledges (Raymond et al. 2010).

Political Economy of Desertification

Simple apolitical generalizations about relationships between environmental deficiencies and threats to human livelihoods often prove to be misleading when inspected more closely. The economist Amartya Sen (1984) argued that a link between drought and famine is not inevitable. Some groups are affected more than others, since society allows them insufficient "entitlements" to cope with social, economic, or environmental hazards.

Vulnerability and Resilience

Research is shedding new light on how dryland populations respond to drought. Some communities are more "vulnerable" than others, as they differ in land rights and other entitlements, their ability to cope with stresses, and in their "resilience"—the ability to return to their former mode when stresses end (Turner et al. 2003). A study of Senegal's silvopastoral zone found that Peul (an ethnic group) pastoralists cope much better with drought, because their livelihoods have built-in adaptability resulting from long experience. They can switch seamlessly into a "survival mode" that ensures an easy return to their long-term livelihoods when conditions improve. Conversely, Wolof croppers are much less resilient, so when drought strikes they often leave the area (Bradley and Grainger 2004).

Climate Change and Desertification

In the 1990s there was growing appreciation that while global climate change may not cause the prolonged droughts that have affected Africa in recent decades, it does have generic similarities with desertification (Williams and Balling 1996). Global climate change is expected to raise mean temperature worldwide and, in some areas, reduce mean rainfall, thereby increasing aridity. It will also cause climatic variability to move toward that seen in drylands. So countries outside the arid zone can best prepare themselves to adapt to future global climate change by learning more about how people in dry areas respond to drought and desertification (Grainger et al. 2000).

Science and Policy

The involvement of science in preparing for UNCOD in 1977 was long regarded as a model for later international environmental agreements. Yet even in the 1970s, scientists had to work within closely defined political constraints in synthesizing and presenting scientific knowledge to policy makers (Dregne 1987). When the UNCCD was negotiated, the panel of scientific experts appointed by the UN General Assembly was sidelined by negotiators for fear that they would disrupt the negotiations (Corell 1999). Rules in the text of the UNCCD restrict the ability of its parties to access the state of the art of scientific knowledge on dryland degradation, so they are still incapable of monitoring the extent and rate of change of desertification and how the UNCCD is reducing both of these variables (Bauer and Stringer 2009; Grainger 2009).

Outlook

Desertification is a major feature of African environments. It threatens the livelihoods of its peoples and is symptomatic of the unsustainability of their development. Too often in the past, desertification has been compartmentalized, even within developing countries, instead of being treated as part of a larger environment and development picture. If developing countries and donor agencies could integrate their attempts to combat desertification, achieve sustainable development, and adapt to climate change, they could make better use of limited resources and be more effective in tackling these great challenges. Better monitoring is essential for this.

Alan GRAINGER
University of Leeds

See also Agriculture, Small-Scale; Climate Change Refugees (Africa); Disaster Risk Management; Immigrants and Refugees; Nairobi, Kenya; Sahara; Sahel; Water Use and Rights (Africa)

FURTHER READING

Aubreville, André. (1949). *Climats, forets et désertification de l'Afrique tropicale* [Climates, forests and desertification in tropical Africa]. Paris: Societe d'Edition Geographiques, Maritimes et Coloniales.

Bauer, Steffen, & Stringer, Lindsay. (2009). The role of science in the global governance of desertification. *Journal of Environment and Development, 18*(3), 248–267.

Bradley, Daniel, & Grainger, Alan. (2004). Social resilience as a controlling influence on desertification in Senegal. *Land Degradation and Development, 15*(5), 451–470.

Corell, Elisabeth. (1999). *The negotiable desert: Expert knowledge in the negotiations of the Convention to Combat Desertification* (Linköping Studies in Arts and Sciences, Vol. 19.). Linköping, Sweden: Linköping University.

Dregne, Harold. (1977). *Map of the status of desertification in the hot arid regions.* Nairobi, Kenya: United Nations Environment Programme.

Dregne, Harold. (1983). Evaluation of the implementation of the Plan of Action to Combat Desertification. Nairobi, Kenya: United Nations Environment Programme.

Dregne, Harold. (1987). Reflections on the PACD. *Desertification Control Bulletin, 15,* 8–11.

Geist, Helmut, & Lambin, Eric. (2004). Dynamic causal patterns of desertification. *Bioscience, 54*(9), 817–829.

Grainger, Alan. (1990). *The threatening desert: Controlling desertification.* London: Earthscan.

Grainger, Alan. (2009). The role of science in implementing international environmental agreements: The case of desertification. *Land Degradation and Development, 20*(4), 410–430.

Grainger, Alan; Stafford Smith, Mark; Glenn, Edward; & Squires, Victor. (2000). Desertification and climate change: The case for greater convergence. *Mitigation and Adaptation Strategies for Global Change, 5*(4), 361–377.

Mabbutt, Jack. (1984). A new global assessment of the status and trends of desertification. *Environmental Conservation, 11*(2), 100–113.

Millennium Ecosystem Assessment (MEA). (2005). *Ecosystems and human well-being: Desertification synthesis.* Washington, DC: Island Press.

Ortiz, Even, & Tang, Guangting. (2005). Review of the management, administration and activities of the UN Convention to Combat Desertification (UNCCD). Geneva: Joint Inspection Unit, United Nations.

Raymond, Christopher, et al. (2010). Integrating local and scientific knowledge for environmental management. *Journal of Environmental Management, 91*(8), 1766–1777.

Reynolds, James, et al. (2007). Building a science for dryland development. *Science, 316*(5826), 847–851.

Sen, Amartya. (1983). *Poverty and famine: An essay on entitlement and deprivation.* Oxford, UK: Clarendon Press.

Thomas, David, & Middleton, Nicholas. (1994). *Desertification: Exploding the myth.* Chichester, UK: John Wiley.

Tiffen, Mary, & Mortimore, Michael. (2002). Questioning desertification in dryland sub-Saharan Africa. *Natural Resources Forum, 26*(3), 218–233.

Turner, Billie Lee, II, et al. (2003). A framework for vulnerability analysis in sustainability science. *Proceedings of the National Academy of Sciences USA, 100*(14), 8074–8079.

Turner, Matthew. (2003). Methodological reflections on the use of remote sensing and geographic information science in human ecological research. *Human Ecology, 31*(2), 255–279.

United Nations (UN). (1977). Plan of Action to Combat Desertification (PACD). Nairobi, Kenya: United Nations Environment Programme.

United Nations (UN). (1994, September 12). Elaboration of an international convention to combat desertification in countries experiencing serious drought and desertification, particularly in Africa. Retrieved May 24, 2012, from http://www.preventionweb.net/files/5650_convunccdeng.pdf

United Nations Environment Program (UNEP); Middleton, Nicholas; & Thomas, David. (Eds.). (1992). *World atlas of desertification.* London: Arnold.

United Nations Environment Program (UNEP); Middleton, Nicholas; & Thomas, David. (Eds.). (1997). *World atlas of desertification* (2nd ed.). London: Arnold.

Verstraete, Michel, et al. (2011). Towards a global drylands observing system: Observational requirements and institutional solutions. *Land Degradation and Development, 22*(2), 198–213.

Williams, Martin, & Balling, Robert. (1996). *Interactions of desertification and climate.* London: Edward Arnold.

Diet and Nutrition

Diet and nutrition are cornerstones of good health and a sustainable environment. The earliest hunter-gatherer and the modern suburbanite depend on a nutritious diet to function in different worlds. An inadequate diet may shorten life, and a superabundant diet may be no less problematic. An optimal diet contains sufficient, but not excessive, calories, vitamins, and minerals.

In the modern world the word *diet* has an unappealing connotation. It is a regime of deprivation to be endured only long enough to shed unwanted weight. Its true meaning, however, is much broader and includes all the food that one consumes. Diet is culturally constructed. Whereas many Africans eat cassava and cocoyams, for example, these foods are virtually absent from the diet of Europeans. Diet and nutrition are also intertwined with the environment. In much of Central Asia the soil lacks iodine, for instance, so iodine was once deficient in the diet of many people there. Global warming may also make an adequate diet harder to obtain in affected parts of Africa and Asia.

History

Anatomically modern humans arose in Africa perhaps 200,000 years ago, although some paleoanthropologists posit an earlier date. No later than 40,000 years ago they migrated into Asia and Europe (O'Neil 2012). At their inception humans were hunter-gatherers. They depended on game and edible plants. Meat was a welcome addition to their diet, supplying protein, vitamins, and minerals. The saturated fat and cholesterol in meat, however, were not nourishing. The lifespan of early humans was brief, so they did not live long enough to develop the coronary

diseases that can accompany the consumption of meat. In the Mediterranean basin the people of North Africa and southern Europe supplemented their diet with fish, whose protein and omega-3 fatty acids were nourishing. The consumption of fish was part of the diet of the people on the coasts of Africa and Eurasia and of river dwellers. If meat was not an everyday item in the diet, plants were. Humans gathered roots, tubers, nuts, berries, and leaves. This varied diet must have been nutritious because the anatomically modern hunter-gatherers of Europe were larger and more robust than the agriculturalists who followed them (Norwood 2012). Although it is true that many factors, genetics among them, determine a person's size, diet also plays a role in determining the size and shape of a person's body. Hunting and gathering were an environmentally sound strategy for maximizing calories with minimal effort. Hunter-gatherers did not depopulate the fauna of Africa and Eurasia as they may have in North America (Cooper 2011). Hunter-gatherers in Africa, Asia, and Europe also did not wipe out the flora. Perhaps because the population of humans was small, their effect on the biota and the environment was benign, making their effect on the environment sustainable.

The Advent of Agriculture

As successful as hunting and gathering were, they gradually ceded ground to agriculture, beginning about 10,000 years ago. The transition from gathering wild barley and wheat in the Middle East to the domestication of these plants took centuries, and there is no doubt that hunting and gathering coexisted with farming for generations. The effect on diet and nutrition due to the transition to agriculture is not easy to gauge. Farmers were smaller than their hunter-gatherer forebears, suggesting an impoverished diet (Norwood 2012). The people of the Mediterranean basin, including the Egyptians, who subsisted on a diet of grains, were smaller and slighter than the hunter-gatherers who predated them (The Animal Attraction n.d.). Yet the fact that populations grew in North Africa, Asia, and Europe suggests that the diet of farmers was adequate to ensure procreation. The grains humans ate contained carbohydrates, vitamins, and minerals, but little protein. In the Middle East and Europe, farmers remedied this deficiency by planting peas. Peas are protein-rich legumes that complemented grains and boosted the nutrition of Eurasia's agriculturalists. A diet dependent on farming in antiquity did not imperil the environment. To be sure, farmers cleared forests to plant crops, and burned wood for warmth and to cook their food, a process that liberated some nutrients, making them easier to digest. The burning of wood put carbon dioxide into the atmosphere but in such small quantities as not to cause global warming. The lifeways of early farmers were environmentally sustainable.

The Columbian Exchange

The Columbian Exchange—the term used to describe the exchange of crops, livestock, and other plants and animals that occurred as a result of European colonization of the Americas—sent crops both ways across the Atlantic Ocean. Africa, Asia, and Europe received from the Americas the potato, corn, peanuts, tomatoes, peppers, and cacao, diversifying the diet of the inhabitants of these continents. The potato is a good example of the far-reaching effects of the Columbian Exchange on diet and nutrition. The potato is rich in vitamin C and potassium and has a better balance of amino acids, the building blocks of protein, than any food except egg whites. The people of Africa, Asia, and Europe, however, were not quick to adopt it. The potato did not thrive in tropical Africa because it was a crop that needed the cool climate it had known in the Andes Mountains. Europeans were suspicious of the potato, having little experience in growing tubers. The potato showed its value, however, in warfare. Armies that lived off the land took farmers' grain and fruit, but did not bother to dig for potatoes (Messer 2000). Northern Europe, especially Ireland, had a climate favorable to the potato, and its cultivation dramatically increased the country's population. In 1800 Ireland had 4.5 million people, and in 1845 it had more than 8 million people (Walsh 2009).

The Irish tenant, working arduously in the field, consumed as many as 6.3 kilograms of potatoes per day along with cabbage, milk, and occasionally pork. This diet, monotonous though it may seem, was nourishing. The Irish became so dependent on the potato that they suffered when the crop failed. In 1845 and 1846, a fungus swept though the fields, rotting potatoes in the ground. With little to eat, the Irish became malnourished. The starving ate tree bark in an attempt to satisfy their hunger. One million died during these years, and another 1.5 million fled their homeland (Barber 2006, 193). The nutritious potato, once the staple of the diet in northern Europe, gave way to malnutrition, sickness, and death. Because the potato, corn, and peanuts had caused an increase in the population, farmers cleared more land, worsening deforestation. Although it is true that the peanut enriched the soil with nitrogen, it was the only legume to come from the Columbian Exchange. The other crops depleted the soil to varying degrees. The potato monoculture had led to ecological ruin.

Africa in Modernity

In sub-Saharan Africa people eat a variety of foods, including cassava and sweet potato. Cassava, once detoxified, provides carbohydrates but little protein and beta-carotene, the precursor of vitamin A. The sweet potato also supplies carbohydrates, chiefly in the form of starch, and the orange-fleshed varieties contain beta-carotene.

According to the Food and Agriculture Organization (FAO) of the United Nations, sub-Saharan Africa was home to 236 million undernourished people in 2007 (FAO 2008). In 2008 the estimate rose to 263 million people. According to the World Bank, Africa must import 45 percent of its rice and 85 percent of its wheat to feed its population (World Bank 2011). To meet this crisis of undernourishment, the developed world sends food to Africa. Western governments, however, have not been alone in aiding Africa. The Bill and Melinda Gates Foundation has created the Alliance for a Green Revolution in Africa to increase food production so that Africans have access to food adequate in calories and nutrition (AGRA 2012). Also active in Africa, the World Bank is committed to the notion that better nutrition can decrease poverty; between 1982 and 2001 it gave African governments $2.8 billion to improve nutrition and health (World Bank 2005, 40). With this goal in mind, the governments of Mali, Madagascar, Malawi, Namibia, Niger, Chad, and Ethiopia invest a portion of their domestic budget on agricultural development.

As is the case elsewhere, the quality and quantity of the diet of Africans is inversely correlated with income. In 2000, 47 million African children were malnourished, which caused 56 percent of childhood deaths in Africa. Malnourished children are less likely to attend school, and those who do attend school tend to be poor students. Iron deficiency causes anemia in 50 percent of children ages one to fourteen years and pregnant women. Vitamin A deficiency is more acute in Africa than elsewhere, causing more than 20 percent of all childhood deaths (World Bank 2005, 10–11). Stagnant income and increases in population may mean less food for all but the most affluent Africans.

In Ghana one-third of children are malnourished, although the fraction may be as high as two-thirds, and between the ages of six months and twenty-four months, boys tend to be more malnourished than girls. The people of Ghana consumed 87 percent of the recommended daily allowance of calories in 1965, but the percentage fell to 76 in 1985 (Asenko-Okyere, Benneh, and Tims 1997, 187 and 208). Thereafter strides were rapid, with the people of Ghana averaging 93 percent of the recommended daily allowance of calories in 1990. In the early twenty-first century only 2 percent of adults are chronically malnourished.

The whole story of the African diet, however, is not merely a lack of calories. In South Africa and Egypt, 60 percent of urbanites consume so many calories that they have become obese (Lawrence, Lyons, and Wallington 2010, 115). Whereas South Africans consumed 2,800 calories daily in 1980, they ate 3,000 calories per day in 2000. During these same years the number of calories in the diet of Nigerians increased from 2,100 to 2,800 per day. The quantity of calories has increased as the affluent have adopted Western diets. The affluent in Africa eat processed food high in sugar and vegetable oil. Eager to order large portions, they eat fast food and dine at restaurants, consuming food high in saturated fat (Lawrence, Lyons, and Wallington 2010, 117). In many families the parents are obese and the children are malnourished (2010, 146).

Surprisingly, some rural economists perceive malnutrition as a desideratum (i.e., something needed or wanted). Deficiencies in vitamin E and iron appear to lessen the symptoms of malaria because the red blood cells collapse before the malaria parasite has had an opportunity to multiply. The nomads of Somalia live on camel's milk, which has little iron, and there is little incidence of malaria among these people. When aid workers gave them iron supplements, the nomads suffered from malaria and brucellosis. Here a diet deficient in vitamin E and iron may have given humans a selective advantage in an environment conducive to the Anopheles mosquito. In this way diet and the environment are intertwined. The Maasai of Kenya and Tanzania consume the milk and blood of animals. They seldom have hypertension, diabetes, or heart disease. Those who moved to the city and adopted a Western diet, however, fared poorly. Half developed diabetes and 30 percent hypertension (Ruttan 1994, 66–67).

Changes to the environment may worsen the diet of Africans. Climate change may exacerbate malnutrition in sub-Saharan Africa. Climate change will likely imperil the food supply, and thus diet and nutrition, by exacerbating drought in tropical Africa. Sub-Saharan Africa may lose arable land through drought, making food scarce and more costly and, in turn, impoverishing the diet and nutrition of the poor. A temperature increase of 1°–2°C may be enough to decrease the availability of food. Between 1970 and 2000, climate change caused malnutrition severe enough to kill some 160,000 people, many of them in Africa and Asia (Clapp and Cohen 2009, 131–132). In much of the developing world, including Africa and Asia, food production may decline 10 to 20 percent by 2080 because of climate change. A temperature increase of more than 3°C may cause food prices to rise 40 percent. By 2080, 100 to 380 million people, many in Africa and Asia, will likely have inadequate diets and nutrition (Cohen et al. 2008, 5 and 38). The degradation of the environment has led farmers to plant crops on what had been pastureland to secure an adequate diet, but this has led to conflict with pastoralists. Meat may become less prevalent in the diet as those who raise livestock switch to native breeds that are better adapted to high temperatures but yield less meat.

Eurasia in Modernity

Affluent Europeans eat too much fat and too few fruits and vegetables. The World Health Organization (WHO), working with European leaders, aims to convince Europeans to eat a variety of foods and to derive their calories and nutrients chiefly from plants rather than animals (WHO, Europe 2011). The derivation of nutrients and calories from organically grown food might be one way to bring the diets of Europeans, Africans, and Asians in harmony with the environment. In parts of Europe children under age five are already deficient in iron and therefore have anemia (World Bank 2006, 53). Others ages six to twelve years are deficient in iodine (Andersson et al. 2007, 9). Lack of iodine, vitamin A, and iron are the crucial deficiencies of European children and pregnant women, particularly the poor.

Central Asians eat wheat and oats, although the chickpeas, peas, lentils, and soybeans that are part of Central Asian cuisine are more nutritious because they contain more protein than wheat or oats, and therefore complement a diet rich in grains. In Central Asia, as elsewhere, legumes improve the soil by enriching it with nitrogen. Land that was once fallow is rotated with oats and chickpeas. Legumes make Central Asians, like Africans and Europeans, good stewards of the land, and their way of life appears to be environmentally sustainable.

In Central Asia, however, as many as 50 percent of women and 32 to 70 percent of children are anemic because of inadequate iron in their diet (IRIN 2008a). Children in Tajikistan are deficient in iron, iodine, and vitamin A. In the 1990s, the fragmentation of the Soviet Union left Central Asia no means of producing iodized salt. Without iodine, children were developmentally disabled and their growth was hindered. In Central Asia fewer than 25 percent of families used iodized salt, the world's lowest consumption rate (Gill 2003). The governments of Azerbaijan, Kazakhstan, the Kyrgyz Republic, Mongolia, Tajikistan, and Uzbekistan have articulated the goal of providing more iodine in the diet. The environment plays a role in this lack of iodine in the diet. The soil of Central Asia once contained iodine, but erosion and the leeching of iodine by rain has left the soil bereft of iodine. The crops that farmers grow cannot therefore contain iodine. The nutrient must be supplied by some other means, and the most common is the iodization of salt. The United States has given the republics of Central Asia $6.85 million to increase the supply of iodine in the diet (Gill 2003). Also participating in this effort is the United Nations International Children's Emergency Fund and the Kazakh Academy of Nutrition. Thanks to progress in this endeavor, the people of Turkmenistan and Kazakhstan are no longer deficient in iodine. In 2004 Turkmenistan was the first country in Central Asia and the fourth worldwide to iodize all of its salt. Ninety-two percent of the people of Kazakhstan consume iodized salt, yet nutritional problems remain. In the Kyrgyz Republic two-thirds of children take vitamin A tablets twice per year (IRIN 2008a). In Central Asia 50 to 60 percent of women and children are deficient in iron

and vitamin A (IRIN 2008b). Three million women in Tajikistan take vitamin A and iron pills. In Uzbekistan the National Flour Fortification Program has added vitamins and minerals to 1.9 million tons of flour per year, enough to feed 90 percent of the population (IRIN 2008a and 2008b).

The Future

Climate change, it seems, may worsen the diet and nutrition of Africans and Asians because it may cause food production to decrease. As population grows, the world will face the challenge of providing an adequate diet for all its inhabitants. Without increases in yields, the environment could suffer because farmers may plant crops on marginal land and increase the use of fertilizer, herbicides, and pesticides, chemicals that harm the environment. On the other hand, an increase in the demand for organic food in Europe may spare the continent these chemicals, although the use of fertilizers, herbicides, and pesticides remains high. The emphasis on eating fresh, locally grown food may benefit the environment because food that is grown and consumed locally is not trucked long distances with the attendant burning of fossil fuel and the warming of the planet. In rural districts in Africa and Asia food is grown and consumed locally, and this may be the trend in the future. Wholesome food may benefit not only the diet and nutrition of the people of Africa and Eurasia; it may also benefit the environment. Sound dietary and environmental policy is badly needed in today's world. It will be even more important in the future.

Christopher CUMO
Independent scholar, Canton, Ohio

See also Africa (*several articles*); Agriculture, Small-Scale; Central Asia; Climate Change Refugees (Africa); Desertification (Africa); Education, Environmental; Rural Development; Shipping and Freight; Svalbard Global Seed Vault; United Kingdom and Ireland; World Bank

FURTHER READING

Alliance for a Green Revolution in Africa (AGRA). (2012). About the Alliance for a Green Revolution in Africa. Retrieved May 16, 2012, from http://www.agra-alliance.org/section/about

Andersson, Maria; de Benoist, Bruno; Darnton-Hill, Ian; & Delange, François. (Eds.). (2007). Iodine deficiency in Europe: A continuing public health problem. Geneva, Switzerland: World Health Organization (WHO). Retrieved May 17, 2012, from http://www.who.int/nutrition/publications/VMNIS_Iodine_deficiency_in_Europe.pdf

The Animal Attraction. (n.d.). Program 2: The animals that conquered the world. Retrieved May 16, 2012, from http://www.abc.net.au/animals/program2/factsheet2.htm

Asenso-Okyere, W. Kwadwo; Benneh, George; & Tims, Wouter. (Eds.). (1997). *Sustainable food security in West Africa*. Boston: Kluwer Academic Publishers.

Barber, Shelley. (Ed.). (2006). *The Prendergast letters: Correspondence from famine-era Ireland, 1840–1850*. Amherst & Boston: University of Massachusetts Press.

Clapp, Jennifer, & Cohen, Marc J. (Eds.). (2009). *The global food crisis: Governance challenges and opportunities*. Waterloo, Canada: Wilfrid Laurier University Press.

Cohen, Marc J.; Tirado, Cristina; Aberman, Noora-Lisa; & Thompson, Brian. (2008). Impact of climate change and bioenergy on nutrition. Food and Agriculture Organization of the United Nations (FAO). Retrieved October 2, 2011, from http://www.fao.org/docrep/010/ai799e/ai799e00.htm

Cooper, Dani. (2011). Ice age animals not wiped out by humans. Retrieved April 3, 2012, from http://www.abc.net.au/science/articles/2011/11/03/3354353.htm

European Commission. (2003). Monitoring public health nutrition in Europe: Nutritional indicators and determinants of health status. Retrieved October 2, 2011, from http://ec.europa.eu/health/ph_projects/2000/monitoring/fp_monitoring_2000_frep_02_en.pdf

Food and Agriculture Organization of the United Nations (FAO). (2008, December 9). Media Centre: Number of hungry people rises to 963 million. Retrieved April 3, 2012, from http://www.fao.org/news/story/en/item/8836

Gill, Ian. (2003, June 9). Nutrition project in Central Asia: Making progress against micronutrient deficiency. Asian Development Bank (ADB). Retrieved October 2, 2011, from http://kan-kaz.org/newsite/adb.html

Integrated Regional Information Networks (IRIN). (2008a, April 9). Central Asia: Iodised salt, fortified flour: What are the next nutritional challenges? *ReliefWeb*. Retrieved October 2, 2011, from http://reliefweb.int/node/261986

Integrated Regional Information Networks (IRIN). (2008b, May 5). Central Asia: Nutritional problems remain despite improvements. Retrieved October 2, 2011, from http://www.irinnews.org/report.aspx?reportid=78040

Knudson, Jeannie. (2011). Do all excess vitamins get excreted from the body? Retrieved April 3, 2012, from http://www.livestrong.com/article/451616-do-all-excess-vitamins-get-excreted-from-the-body

Lawrence, Geoffrey; Lyons, Kristen; & Wallington, Tabatha. (2010). *Food security, nutrition and sustainability*. London: Earthscan.

McMichael, Anthony J., et al. (Eds.). (2003). *Climate change and human health: Risks and responses*. Geneva: World Health Organization (WHO).

Messer, Ellen. (2000). Potatoes (white). In Kenneth F. Kipel & Kriemhild Conee Ornelas (Eds.), *The Cambridge world history of food* (pp. 187–200). Cambridge, UK: Cambridge University Press. Retrieved April 3, 2012, from http://www.cambridge.org/us/books/kiple/potatoes.htm

Nomdo, Christina, & Coetzee, Erika. (Eds.). (2002). *Urban vulnerability: Perspectives from southern Africa*. Oxford, UK: Periperi Publications.

Norwood, F. Bailey. (2012). Cavemen in the Garden of Eden: A natural and human history of man and his farm animals. Retrieved April 3, 2012, from http://asp.okstate.edu/baileynorwood/Bailey/essays/livestock.htm

O'Neil, Dennis. (2012). Early modern *Homo sapiens*. Retrieved May 16, 2012, from http://anthro.palomar.edu/homo2/mod_homo_4.htm

Ruttan, Vernon W. (Ed.). (1994). *Health and sustainable agricultural development: Perspectives on growth and constraints*. Boulder, CO: Westview Press.

Vogtmann, Hartmut, & Dobretsov, Nikolai. (Eds.). (2004). *Environmental security and sustainable land use: With special reference to Central Asia*. Dordrecht, The Netherlands: Springer.

Walsh, Dennis. (2009). Ireland's history in maps. Retrieved May 16, 2012, from http://www.rootsweb.ancestry.com/~irlkik/ihm/ire1841.htm

World Bank. (2005). *Improving health, nutrition, and population outcomes in sub-Saharan Africa: The role of the World Bank*. Washington, DC: The World Bank.

World Bank. (2006). How serious is malnutrition? And why does it happen? In World Bank (Ed.), *Repositioning nutrition as central to development* (pp. 42–61). Retrieved May 17, 2012, from http://www.google.com/url?sa=t&rct=j&q=&esrc=s&source=web&cd=1&ved=0CGoQFjAA&url=http%3A%2F%2Fsiteresources.worldbank.org%2FNUTRITION%2FResources%2F281846-1131636806329%2FNutritionStrategyCh2.pdf&ei=KQGoT5z8M8SZiQKJ9OyqAg&usg=AFQjCNGpDofnGvOV7yVrxe5uHtgo1yXC_Q

World Bank. (2011). The effects of high food prices in Africa: Q&A. Retrieved May 16, 2012, from http://web.worldbank.org/WBSITE/EXTERNAL/COUNTRIES/AFRICAEXT/0,,contentMDK:21753440~menuPK:258657~pagePK:2865106~piPK:2865128~theSitePK:258644,00.html

World Health Organization (WHO), Europe. (2011). A healthy lifestyle. Retrieved October 2, 2011, from http://www.euro.who.int/en/what-we-do/health-topics/disease-prevention/nutrition/a-healthy-lifestyle

Yue, Chengyan, et al. (2011). Investigating consumer preference for organic, local, or sustainable plants. *HortScience*, *46*(4), 610–615.

Disaster Risk Management

Disasters in Africa and Eurasia result in significant loss of life and economic damage. Since the 1990s, a global shift in the understanding and actions linked to disasters has occurred. Disaster risk management has changed the traditional focus on disaster response to more proactive measures. The integration of disaster risk reduction into sustainable development planning is widely recognized as the way forward in reducing disasters globally.

Disaster! The word conjures up images of injury, death, and destruction. It instills feelings of helplessness, chaos, and dependence on external intervention. A disaster can undo years of hard-earned development. It can increase poverty; it can topple governments; it can change a familiar landscape; and it can destroy the systems on which humans depend to survive.

In times of disaster, low-income countries often sustain the most loss in human lives, while high-income countries often experience the highest economic losses. The International Disaster Database shows that for the period 1980–2008, Africa reported 3,656 disasters, Eurasia 3,210, and Europe 1,976. The total number of people killed in Africa was approximately 300,000, in Eurasia 87,476, and in Europe 55,736. The estimated damage in Africa was US$5.2 billion, in Eurasia, US$85 billion, and in Europe, US$20 billion (CRED 2010). Disasters are clearly a very costly affair. In Africa, disasters are primarily the result of hydrological hazards (such as droughts and floods), in Eurasia, of geophysical hazards (for example, earthquakes) and meteorological hazards (flash floods and storm surges), and in Europe, of climatological hazards (such as heat waves and severe weather events). Disasters result from natural hazards, but hazards do not create disasters; vulnerability does.

Well-planned, sustainable development initiatives can address vulnerability.

Disaster and Disaster Risk Defined

Contemporary thought in disaster risk reduction emerged from the realization that decades of emphasis on disaster preparedness, disaster management, and disaster response have not significantly curtailed either the number of disasters that occur or their social, physical, and economic impact. In the field of disaster and risk management, the basic definition of a disaster is highly debated. Scholars have expressed diverse views. The literature shows that the determination that an event is a disaster closely relates to the level of development in a specific country. Developing countries once linked the existence of a disaster to a specific number of losses sustained (for example, the number of people killed and injured); others held that an event was a disaster if a certain predefined threshold was reached (for example, once a trigger to a certain contingency measure, such as the maximum unacceptable level of water in a floodplain, was reached). Most developed countries assessed disasters relative to geographical extent and variation from "normal" conditions, and a few expressed a disaster in terms of both direct and indirect monetary losses.

Since the International Decade of Natural Disaster Reduction (1990–1999), however, the various scientific understandings for disaster have come together in a globally accepted definition. The United Nations International Strategy for Disaster Reduction (UNISDR) defines a disaster as "a serious disruption of the functioning of a community or a society involving widespread human, material, or environmental losses and impacts which exceeds the ability of the affected community to cope using only its own resources" (UNISDR 2009).

Whether an event is a disaster or not depends on people's ability to cope with the consequences of the event. One should therefore ask why it is that people cannot cope. The answer lies in the level of a community's vulnerability to natural phenomena such as flood, drought, or other severe weather conditions. It is the combination of vulnerability and hazardous conditions that determines the level of disaster risk. Vulnerability is defined by the UNISDR (2009) as the characteristics and circumstances of a community, system, or asset that make it susceptible to the possible damaging effects of a hazard. Vulnerability can be explained as a set of prevailing conditions arising from various physical, social, economical, political, and environmental factors that increase the susceptibility of a community to the impact of hazards. Human beings and their interaction with their environment create the conditions of vulnerability. Successful risk management needs to address vulnerability to prevent hazards from turning into disasters because people are unable to deal with their consequences. Vulnerability also explains why certain areas and countries are more prone to disasters than others. This is particularly true in a comparative analysis of regions such as Africa and Eurasia. The diverse effects and types of hazards in these regions also mean that the management of disaster risks varies greatly.

Disaster risk can be expressed as the likelihood that a hazard of a specific nature can exploit a certain level of vulnerability within a given time frame. Disaster risk reflects both vulnerability (prevailing and continuous unsafe conditions) in communities and the likelihood of hazardous threats. Disaster risks can be managed successfully.

Risk Management

Disaster risk management involves understanding how disaster can be avoided. It is the "systematic process of using administrative directives, organizations, and operational skills and capacities to implement strategies, policies and improved coping capacities in order to lessen the adverse impacts of hazards and the possibility of disaster" (UNISDR 2009). This generally accepted definition clearly indicates the strategic focus of disaster risk management. It signals that successful disaster risk management implementation can occur only through a multisector and multidisciplinary approach.

Internationally, the Hyogo Framework for Action 2005–2015 (a global agreement on disaster risk reduction under the auspices of the United Nations, signed by more than180 countries) guides countries in achieving disaster

risk management through sustainable development. Its goal is to ensure that disaster risk reduction is a national and local priority. The Hyogo Framework puts forward five guiding principles to provide direction for reducing disasters and risk:

- Ensure that disaster risk reduction is a national and a local priority with a strong institutional basis for implementation.
- Identify, assess, and monitor disaster risks and enhance early warning.
- Use knowledge, innovation, and education to build a culture of safety and resilience.
- Reduce underlying risk factors.
- Strengthen disaster preparedness for effective responses.

While the Hyogo Framework embodies a global understanding, disaster risk management remains a government and public sector function. Georgia, South Africa, Mongolia, and Germany are good examples of countries in the context of this volume that have implemented strong disaster risk management in the public sector. These countries have made a significant paradigm shift away from pure disaster preparedness and response to a decentralized implementation of disaster risk management measures linked to development objectives. Regional coordination for disaster risk management remains imperative, however, because disasters know no borders.

Regional Cooperation for Risk Reduction

Since 2005, a number of regional organizations in Africa, such as the Economic Community of West African States, the Intergovernmental Authority on Development in East Africa, the Southern African Development Community, the Economic Community of Central African States, and the Indian Ocean Community, have developed plans and policies aimed at disaster risk reduction related to climate change and adaptation. The Regional Disaster Risk Reduction Policy and Plan of Implementation of the African Union supports these plans. In Europe, the European Union, as the overarching regional economic community, as well as a number of other regional organizations, such as the Parliamentary Assembly of the Mediterranean and the South-East European Cooperation Process, support disaster risk reduction efforts on their continent. Similarly, in Eurasia the Economic Cooperation Organization and the League of Arab States have made significant progress in addressing the international disaster risk reduction agenda.

Issues of climate change are dominating the public policy debate in these regions. Disaster risk management of the possible impacts of climate change and variation is essential. Around the world, evidence shows that a changing climate is influencing the frequency and severity of natural hazards. The disaster risk related to these hazards is thus heightened. Faced with the global threats, countries are compelled to address disaster risks through a combined, cross-border approach. Addressing both disaster risk and climate change requires an emphasis on sustainable development. Using sustainable development as the foundation, it is possible to prevent natural hazards from becoming disasters through integrated planning for the future. By focusing on sustainable development, the root causes of disaster risks can be addressed. For example, well-planned settlements (sometimes in at-risk areas such as flood-prone regions), built according to a national building code and aligned with environmental concerns (such as protection of biodiversity through urban layout), make their inhabitants safer, protect the environment, and contribute to sustainable use of natural resources. Development, however, especially urban development, can in itself also become hazardous.

Risk and Development

Years of development and progress can be wiped away by a disaster. The seminal work of the US disaster relief specialist Frederick Cuny in the 1980s ushered in a new era and focus on disasters as the outcomes of failed development. Many scholars, especially in the United Kingdom and the United States, were very active in the 1980s and 1990s in developing the body of knowledge that links the sustainable development and disasters discourse.

The logic in this argument centers around the principle that well-planned development of all kinds will reduce the risks of disasters occurring. Elements such as land use planning, zoning, enforcing building codes, spatial planning, urban development, and integrated planning can all take into consideration limiting the population's vulnerability to hazards. Even the UN statements about disaster reduction emphasize the need for this reduction to be grounded in sustainable development and for risk reduction and sustainable development to be mutually reinforcing. Development by human beings can lead to disasters (poorly built, low-cost housing or settlement planning below flood levels, for example), but it can also reduce the possibility of disasters (such as ecofriendly housing, water catchment management, and conservation of natural barriers). The development of economic opportunities in cities, for example, leads to urbanization in many African countries. This in turn stresses the existing infrastructure, settlement patterns, and the ability of municipalities to protect their citizens against harm. The United Nations Development Assistance Framework 2010–2015 for Armenia (UNESCO 2010) is one example

of a plan that emphasizes the need for the integration of environmental management, poverty reduction, democratic governance, basic social services, and disaster risk reduction. The Ninth Development Plan 2007–2013 for Turkey (Turkey 2006) mentions disaster management as a thematic and cross-sector issue that is not adequately included in development planning. In southern African countries such as Zambia, Zimbabwe, and South Africa, the integration of disaster risk reduction measures has become a legislative requirement. No development may take place that does not contribute to reducing the disaster risk profile of the area in question. Each municipality is compelled by various laws to integrate disaster risk reduction and development into its planning, for example. This integration in turn is linked to the budget of the municipality. Such checks and balances now also form part of development planning in European countries such as Germany, Sweden, the Netherlands, Greece, and Switzerland.

Future Disaster Risks

Uncertainty linked to climate change, the greenhouse effect, the rate of urbanization and use of natural resources, changing ecosystems, and the loss of biodiversity raises the level of disaster risk humans face. It is now well known that all the listed factors heighten the probability of disasters occurring. This in turn makes implementing timely and effective disaster risk reduction measures urgent. Disaster risks that arise in the future will also have a profound impact across national borders. Closer cooperation and joint solutions between nations will become imperative. The mitigation and reduction of disaster risks will also become a central focus in planning for the future for governments, civil society, and the private sector.

Reducing future disasters will require that African, Eurasian, and European countries understand all of the dynamics and variables contributing to disaster risks. The solutions are possible only once all the systems in which disaster risks are created are understood.

Dewald VAN NIEKERK
North-West University, South Africa

See also Biodiversity Conservation; Climate Change Refugees (Africa); Desertification (Africa); Education, Environmental; Immigrants and Refugees

FURTHER READING

Anderson, Mary B. (1985). A reconceptualization of the linkages between disasters and development. *Disasters, 9*(S1), 46–51.
Anderson, Mary B., & Woodrow, Peter J. (1998). *Rising from the ashes: Development strategies in times of disaster.* London: Lynne Rienner Publishers.

Bates, Frederick L.; Dynes, Russell R.; & Quarantelli, Enrico L. (1991). The importance of the social sciences to the International Decade of Natural Disaster Reduction. *Disasters, 15*(3), 288–289.

Benson, Charlotte, & Clay, Edward J. (2004). *Understanding the economic and financial impact of natural disasters* (Disaster Risk Management Series No. 4). Washington, DC: The World Bank.

Carr, Lowell Juilliard. (1932). Disasters and the sequence-pattern concept of social change. *American Journal of Sociology, 38,* 207–218.

Centre for Research on the Epidemiology of Disasters (CRED). (2010). EM-DAT: *International Disaster Database.* Retrieved November 16, 2011, from http://www.cred.be/

Chen, Liang-Chun; Liu, Yi-Chung; & Chan, Kuei-Chi. (2006). Integrated community-based disaster management program in Taiwan: A case study of Shang-An Village. *Natural Hazards, 37*(1–2), 209–223.

Cuny, Frederick C. (1983). *Disasters and development.* Oxford, UK: Oxford University Press.

Cuny, Frederick C. (1999). *Famine, conflict and response: A basic guide.* Bloomfield, CT: Kumarian Press.

Cutter, Susan L. (Ed.). (1994). *Environmental risk and hazards.* Upper Saddle River, NJ: Prentice Hall.

Doughty, Paul L. (1971). From disaster to development. *Americas, 23,* 23–35.

Gilbert, Claude. (1995). Studying disasters: A review of the main conceptual tools. *International Journal of Mass Emergencies and Disasters, 13,* 231–240.

Glantz, Michael. (1976). *The politics of natural disaster: The case of the Sahel drought.* New York: Praeger.

Global Network of Civil Society Organisations for Disaster Reduction (GNDR). (2009). *Clouds but little rain . . . : Views from the frontline: A local perspective of progress towards implementation of the Hyogo Framework for Action.* Teddington, UK: Global Network of Civil Society Organisations for Disaster Reduction.

Hewitt, Kenneth. (1997). *Regions of risk: A geographical introduction to disasters.* London: Longman Publishing Group.

Lavell, Alan. (1999, July 5–9). *The impact of disasters on development gains: Clarity or controversy.* Geneva: IDNDR Programme Forum.

La Trobe, Susan, & Davis, Ian. (2005). *Mainstreaming disaster risk reduction: A tool for development organisations.* Teddington, UK: Tearfund.

Lewis, James. (1999). *Development in disaster-prone places: Studies of vulnerability.* Trowbridge, UK: Cromwell Press.

McClean, Denis. (Ed.). (2010). *World Disasters Report 2010: Focus on urban risk.* Geneva: International Federation of Red Cross and Red Crescent Societies.

O'Keefe, Phil; Westgate, Kenneth N.; & Wisner, Ben. (1976). Taking the naturalness out of disasters. *Nature, 260.*

Pelling, Mark, & Wisner, Ben. (2009). *Disaster risk reduction: Cases from urban Africa.* London: Earthscan.

Quarantelli, Enrico L. (Ed.). (1998). *What is a disaster? Perspectives on the question.* London: Routledge.

Quarantelli, Enrico L., & Perry, Ronald W. (2005). *What is a disaster? New answers to old questions.* Bloomington, IN: Xlibris.

Shaw, Rajib, & Krishnamurthy, R. R. (Eds.). (2009). *Disaster management: Global challenges and local solutions.* Himayatnagar, India: Universities Press.

South Africa (Republic). (2003). *Disaster Management Act No 57 of 2002.* Pretoria, South Africa: Government Printer.

South Africa (Republic). (2005). *National disaster management policy framework.* Pretoria, South Africa: Government Printer.

Thomalla, Frank; Downing, Tom; Spanger-Siegfried, Erika S.; Han, Guoyi; & Rockström, Johan. (2006). Reducing hazard vulnerability: Towards a common approach between disaster risk reduction and climate adaptation. *Disasters, 30*(1), 39–48.

Turkey (Grand National Assembly). (2006). *Ninth Development Plan 2007–2013.* Ankara, Turkey: Turkish Grand National Assembly.

Twigg, John. (2004). *Good practice review: Disaster risk reduction: Mitigation and preparedness in development and emergency programming.* London: Humanitarian Practice Network.

United Nations (UN). (1994, May 23–27). *Yokohama strategy and plan of action for a safer world: Guidelines for natural disaster prevention, preparedness and mitigation.* World Conference on Natural Disaster Reduction. Yokohama, Japan: United Nations.

United Nations Educational, Scientific and Cultural Organization (UNESCO). (2010.) United Nations Development Assistance Framework 2010–2015: Armenia. Retrieved February 9, 2012, from http://planipolis.iiep.unesco.org/upload/Armenia/Armenia_UNDAF_2010-2015.pdf

United Nations International Strategy for Disaster Reduction (UN/ISDR). (2005). *Hyogo Framework for Action: Building the resilience of nations and communities to disaster.* Geneva: UN.

United Nations International Strategy for Disaster Reduction (UN/ISDR Africa). (2005). *Guidelines for mainstreaming disaster risk assessment in development.* Nairobi, Kenya: UN.

United Nations International Strategy for Disaster Reduction (UNISDR). (2009). *Terminology on disaster risk reduction.* Geneva: UNISDR. Retrieved February 6, 2012, from http://www.unisdr.org/we/inform/terminology

Van Niekerk, Dewald. (2006). Disaster risk management in South Africa: The function and the activity: Towards an integrated approach. *Politeia, 25*(2), 95–115.

Wisner, Ben; Blaikie, Pearce; Cannon, Terry; & Davis, Ian. (2004). *At risk: Natural hazards, people's vulnerability and disasters* (2nd Ed.). London: Routledge.

Berkshire's authors and editors welcome questions, comments, and corrections. Send your emails about the *Berkshire Encyclopedia of Sustainability* in general or this volume in particular to: sustainability.updates@berkshirepublishing.com

Dubai, United Arab Emirates

2 million est. pop. 2012

In 1971, free from the sovereignty of Britain, seven emirates including Dubai and Abu Dhabi formed the United Arab Emirates. Dubai's capital, the city of Dubai, has ambitions to decrease its dependence on oil and become a hub of global commerce and a top tourist and a shopping mecca. To achieve these goals, Dubai has spent billions of dollars transforming its image and urban landscape by investing in ambitious infrastructure and logistics facilities, mixed-use urban developments, and entertainment complexes.

The economic and urban development of Dubai—the capital city located on the northern coast of the emirate of Dubai (a part of United Arab Emirates)—has evolved from its advantageous position midway between Europe and Asia. During the period from 2000 to 2008, Dubai and the United Arab Emirates (UAE) as a whole have experienced high growth rates thanks, in great part, to surging oil income and an active real estate market. All of the emirates, as well as the other Gulf States, are making significant strides in diversifying their economies so that before the oil supply is depleted, a larger portion of oil and gas surplus revenue will have been invested in the region. Although Dubai remains solidly in the hands of its founder's family, the al-Maktoum dynasty, it has shown that it has the ability to diversify and reinvent its role in response to external needs. It has, for example, already developed its economy to the point where oil accounts for only 7 percent of the gross domestic product (GDP).

Another emirate, Abu Dhabi, has followed in Dubai's footsteps. It is building a portfolio of projects in the arts (it is set to become the home of the world's largest Guggenheim Museum, designed by Frank Gehry) and has invested through the Masdar (a commercially driven enterprise established in 2006; in English it means "resource") in renewable energy and sustainable technologies. Masdar is a wholly owned subsidiary of the Abu Dhabi government-owned Mubadala Development Company, a catalyst for the economic diversification of the emirate. Masdar's flagship project is Masdar City, a high-density, pedestrian-friendly development where current and future renewable energy and clean technologies are showcased, marketed, researched, developed, tested, and implemented.

A Brief History

Dubai was a small trading port that had grown gradually from a fishing village inhabited in the eighteenth century by members of the Bani Yas tribe. By the turn of the twentieth century, Dubai had been for some eight years under the sovereignty of the United Kingdom and was a sufficiently prosperous port to attract settlers from Iran, India, and Baluchistan; by the 1930s, nearly a quarter of its population of 20,000 was foreign. Some years later the British also made it their center for administrative agency on the coast, establishing a political agency in 1954. In 1971, the British withdrew from the Persian Gulf and the emirate of Dubai joined with Abu Dhabi, Sharjah, Ajman, Fujairah, Umm al-Quwain, and later Ras al-Khaimah to create the Federation of the United Arab Emirates. Toward the end of the century, it was the third most important re-export center in the world. Only Hong Kong and Singapore surpass Dubai in the volume of their imported and then re-exported foreign goods.

Dubai Properties, a member of Dubai Holding, is the world's fastest growing global real estate development investment firm. Even so, the 2008 financial crisis and real estate crash, coupled with low oil prices, forced a reality check upon the ambitions of Dubai and made it imperative to reestablish cordial relations with its oil-rich neighbor, Abu Dhabi. This turn of events has relieved some of the pressure on the emirate associated with its oversaturated roads and with its housing affordability. The real estate boom in Dubai has had a significant impact on the cost of living in the city and in the adjacent emirates over the last couple of years. For example, residential rents rose between 20 and 40 percent in 2005, and again by up to 50 percent in some parts of the city during the following year (Westley 2006). During the boom years, properties were sold "off plan" (i.e., sold before being fully developed or built). Today, instead, vacation homes being bought in Dubai are occupant-ready. Throughout 2010 and 2011, the general surplus of new properties has translated into an increased availability of housing and a downward pressure on rents. The market is becoming realistic in terms of prices as tenants have an increasingly wide array of choices. Things remain uneasy, however, about off-plan offerings, given that many projects across the UAE are either on indefinite hold or have been canceled altogether.

A Logistics Hub

For Dubai, Singapore has been the model that has already proved that combining business with tourism can be a successful formula for a city-state. To follow this model, Dubai has marketed itself as a city-state and turned itself into a transport hub.

As a new city, Dubai has invested in state-of-the-art infrastructure, technology, airports, ports, and public utilities. It has also invested in "soft infrastructure"—the laws, regulations, and institutions that enable businesses to prosper. Modern Dubai can be described as an *aerotropolis*—a city whose focus and infrastructure highlight its airports as the main drivers for business creation, urban growth, and global economic integration. In Dubai, this urban form, which connects its workers, suppliers, executives, and goods to the global marketplace, contributes some $2.5 billion to the GDP (Saidi 2011). In addition to Dubai International Airport, Dubai has also built the al-Maktoum International Airport at Dubai World Central, the world's largest passenger and cargo hub.

Sustainable, Tempered Growth

The frenetic pace and character of Dubai's unprecedented growth, particularly between 2000 and 2008, had suggested a future likely marred by environmental and sustainability problems. Development projects during that period generally ignored such fundamental environmental factors as climate or geography. Viewed from the air, the Palm Islands project (initiated in 2001 and consisting of three palm-tree-shaped residential and commercial settlements built by dredging and redepositing sand off Dubai's coast), created a highly visible impression and generated a lively debate about its merits and about its impacts on marine life. At the heart of the matter were questions about potential damage to the marine habitat and about the burying of coral reefs, oyster beds, and subterranean fields of sea grass, with resulting threats to local marine species and to other species dependent on them for food.

In 2012, the "Dubai of tomorrow" is a much wiser city, one that allows for tempered growth and that is the product of a carefully devised and strategically planned economy in which tourism, construction, banking, commerce, logistics, and trading all act as levers for a type of progress that is no longer measured by the oil barrel. The signs are promising, with passenger numbers at Dubai International Airport in the first half of 2011 marking the busiest six months in the past fifty years. Dubai is at a critical junction in its history and development trajectory as it seeks to recover the dynamism that characterized the two decades up until the crash of 2008. One thing is for certain: the emirate remains externally oriented. This is crucial to its development given its size, and this is why Dubai's links with China feature heavily in its future plans. The ongoing financial crisis may not lead to the fall of Wall Street (New York) or The City (London), but the accelerating trend toward a shift in financial centers favors metropolises in the East such as Hong Kong, Shanghai and, of course, Dubai.

Samer G. BAGAEEN
University of Brighton

See also Cairo, Egypt; London, United Kingdom; Middle East; Shipping and Freight; Tunis, Tunisia; Urbanization (Western Asia and Northern Africa); Water Use and Rights (Middle East and North Africa)

FURTHER READING

Aalbers, Manuel. (2009). Geographies of the financial crisis. *Area*, *41*(1), 34–42.

Aerotropolis Business Concepts, LLC. (n.d.). Aerotropolis. Retrieved March 9, 2012, from http://www.aerotropolis.com

Ahmed, Ameen. (2006, July 8). Frank Gehry to design Guggenheim museum. *Gulf News*. Retrieved December 19, 2011, from http://gulfnews.com/news/gulf/uae/leisure/frank-gehry-to-design-guggenheim-museum-1.243948

'Ahmed, Ashfaq. (2005, August 9). Study on water taxi service between Dubai and Sharjah gets under way. Retrieved December 19, 2011, from http://gulfnews.com/news/gulf/uae/traffic-transport/study-on-water-taxi-service-between-dubai-and-sharjah-gets-under-way-1.296843'

Ahmed, Ashfaq. (2007, May 21). Authority dispels fears of clogged Dubai roads. *Gulf News.* Retrieved December 19, 2011, from http://gulfnews.com/news/gulf/uae/traffic-transport/authority-dispels-fears-of-clogged-dubai-roads-1.179295

Bagaeen, Samer. (2007). Brand Dubai: The instant city; or the instantly recognizable city. *International Planning Studies, 12*(2), 173–197.

Davis, Mike. (2007). Sand, fear and money in Dubai. In Mike Davis & Daniel Bertrand Monk (Eds.), *Evil paradises: Dreamworlds of neoliberalism* (pp. 48–68). New York: The New Press.

Dubai Government. (n.d.). *The official portal of the Dubai government.* Retrieved March 9, 2012, from http://www.dubai.ae/en/pages/default.aspx

Dubai Statistics Center. (2012). Population clock. Retrieved March 29, 2012, from http://www.dsc.gov.ae/en/pages/home.aspx

Krane, Jim. (2010). *Dubai: The story of the world's fastest city.* London: Atlantic Books.

Nicolson, Adam. (2006, February 12). Boom town. *The Guardian.* Retrieved December 19, 2011, from http://www.guardian.co.uk/business/2006/feb/13/unitedarabemirates.travel

Oxford Economics Report. (2011). *Explaining Dubai's aviation model.* A report for Emirates and Dubai Airports. Oxford, UK: Oxford Economics.

Saadiyat Island. (2010). Homepage. Retrieved March 29, 2012, from http://www.saadiyat.ae/en/masterplan/saadiyat-cultural-district.html

Saidi, Nasser. (2011). Joining the dots. Retrieved March 29, 2012, from http://vision.ae/special_report/articles/joining_the_dots

Westley, David. (2006, March 13). Is Dubai still good value? *Gulf News.* Retrieved December 19, 2011, from http://gulfnews.com/business/features/is-dubai-still-good-value-1.228554

E-Waste

Redundant electronic products, e-waste, have become an environmental problem of huge proportions, not only in developed countries, but also in developing countries such as Nigeria, Kenya, and other African countries where hazardous e-waste is being dumped or recycled in adverse conditions. E-waste contains highly toxic substances, which necessitate special care to prevent health hazards to humans and environmental damage. International conventions and national legislation are regulating the handling and recycling of e-waste as the focus shifts from dealing with toxic waste to the recycling of valuable resources.

E-waste refers to electronic products ranging from calculators, cell phones, and computers to television monitors, microwaves, and refrigerators that have become redundant. Most of these products have a relatively short life span of between three and five years because constant technological innovation renders older products obsolete very quickly. E-waste is the fastest growing stream of waste in developed countries, placing greater strain by sheer volume on already overburdened waste disposal systems and sites.

A Worldwide Problem

E-waste is a dual problem in Africa and Europe. Developed countries such as Germany, the United Kingdom, and France have limited space for waste disposal generally but especially for e-waste. A 2009 report indicated that the United Kingdom alone generated more than 4 million tonnes of e-waste annually.

E-waste contains a number of highly toxic substances such as lead, mercury, and cadmium, which all have the potential to seriously harm the environment and human health. This ideally requires these products to be dealt with separately from normal household waste in order to prevent the harmful chemicals and heavy metals from contaminating the environment, water sources, and the air. The cost of recycling e-waste has led developed countries to export their e-waste to developing countries that often do not have the capability to properly treat e-waste

Developed countries often export and dump e-waste in developing countries. Crime syndicates export a significant amount of e-waste illegally (INTERPOL 2009, 2–3). They dump e-waste in developing countries in Africa and Asia, often under the guise of exporting secondhand reusable goods. It is also a growing problem as high-tech goods such as televisions, computers, and cell phones become more commonplace in the consumer markets of Africa.

The facilities for the recycling of these goods are either nonexistent or primitive in most African countries or not yet well developed, as in South Africa. The e-waste either is dumped without treatment, damaging the environment, or recycled in conditions hazardous to humans and the environment because these facilities lack regulation and use cheap labor.

European countries have been dumping e-waste in African and Asian countries such as Nigeria, India, and China, but this is now more strictly regulated under the European Waste Electrical and Electronic Equipment (WEEE) Directive of 2002 (Directive 2002/96/EC). Despite the regulation, there is still a significant level of illegal export and dumping of this waste in developing countries.

The Nature of E-Waste

E-waste includes a wide range of domestic devices ranging from refrigerators, washing machines, and television sets to mobile phones, personal computers, fax machines, printers, and toys. Apart from their use in normal households, these products are also specifically featured in the health, education, communication, security, and entertainment industries and in businesses in general. The steady growth in e-waste is set to continue as emerging markets catch up to the markets in the developed world (UNEP 2009a, 1–2).

An estimated 20 to 50 million tonnes (depending on inclusions and exclusions of products) of electronic waste are generated each year (ETBC 2012b, 3). These huge volumes of waste, which decay much slower than household waste, take up space in waste dumps that are already stretched to their limit by other forms of household waste (Hull 2010, 5–6).

E-waste consists of a wide range of components. Some of these components are bulky such as the steel and aluminum in refrigerators and washing machines, the plastic compounds in televisions, computer and printer housings and keyboards, and the glass in television sets. Some components make up minor parts of e-waste bulk but contain significant amounts of valuable or toxic materials. Modern electronics can contain up to sixty different elements. Printed wiring boards and mobile phones contain the most complex mix of substances and are major consumers of base metals such as copper and tin, many precious metals such as gold, silver, and palladium, and special metals such as cobalt, indium, and antimony. A tonne of mobile phones without batteries contains 130 kilograms of copper, 3.5 kilograms of silver, 340 grams of gold, and 140 grams of palladium. The lithium-ion batteries add another 3.5 kilograms of cobalt (UNEP 2009b, 7–8).

Some e-waste is highly toxic because it contains significant amounts of metals such as lead, mercury, cadmium, hexavalent chromium, beryllium, barium, and nickel. Many of the plastic compounds as well as the brominated flame retardants used in computer and television housings, cables, and printed circuit boards cause toxic fumes upon incineration, creating health hazards for workers in informal recycling processes (Templeton 2009, 766–768).

E-waste also contains a number of valuable resources such as gold, silver, copper, and palladium. As of 2012, 90 percent of these valuable nonrenewable resources go to waste because e-waste is not being recycled. The focus of e-waste treatment has steadily shifted to the recycling of these resources. The United Nations Environment Programme (UNEP) has played an important part in this process.

Recycling Need and Potential

The UNEP states that "e-waste is usually regarded as a waste problem, which can cause environmental damage if not dealt with in an appropriate way. However, the enormous resource impact of electrical and electronic equipment (EEE) is widely overlooked" (UNEP 2009a, 6). The amount of e-waste must be reduced and the toxic elements kept from polluting the environment or creating health hazards. The valuable minerals, which are not a renewable resource, need to be recycled. Although it requires significantly lower amounts of energy to recycle these metals than to mine them, resulting in much less carbon emission, it is still much more expensive to recycle these materials than to mine them.

The electronics industry is a major consumer of base metals, precious metals, and special metals, which are mined at great environmental cost by primary producers in places such as Canada, China, Australia, Russia, and South Africa. The use of special minerals, called rare earth elements (REEs), in the production of electronic products has become contentious because China mines 95 percent of these minerals and exports them to the rest of the world (Hurst 2010). Although significant new deposits have been found in South Africa, Greenland, and in the seabed near Hawaii, and will be developed by countries including South Korea and Japan, the current shortage of REEs and the dependence on China will last for a number of years; REEs are likely to be in short supply until these sources are exploited (*Yahoo! Finance* 2011; Greenland Minerals and Energy Ltd. 2012a and 2012b; Arthur 2011; Humphries 2011, 3–4).

The electronics industry consumes the following estimated amounts of metals produced annually: gold, 3 percent; silver, 3 percent; palladium, 13 percent; cobalt, 15 percent; indium, 80 percent; ruthenium, 80 percent; and antimony, 50 percent (UNEP 2009a, 7–8). Potentially there are more than 40 million tonnes of base and precious metals that can be recycled annually based on 2009 volumes.

Recycling in Africa and Europe

The recycling of e-waste consists of collection, dismantling, processing, and end processing. To recycle e-waste consumers must be educated and aware and must cooperate in sorting their waste and disposing of e-waste separately. Consumers must use special containers and municipal authorities must collect e-waste, and sellers or producers must collect their e-waste. The WEEE Directive places the primary responsibility for the collection and treatment of e-waste on producers. (See the section "The European WEEE Directive" below for more on this subject.) Dismantling and preprocessing consists of sorting e-waste into different components, removing hazardous materials and valuable items such as chips and processors that can be reused, and shredding and crushing bulk materials. This can be a very labor-intensive process. End processing usually requires expensive high-tech equipment relying on big volumes to be economically viable. Regionalization of such facilities therefore makes economic sense. Low-tech informal end processing often leads to the kind of environmental damage and health risks illustrated by Guiyu, China, where a large-scale informal recycling industry has poisoned local water supplies and caused widespread air pollution (BAN 2004).

Although not strictly dealing with e-waste, the Probo Koala scandal in 2006 illustrates the dangers of dumping toxic waste in developing countries that have insufficient infrastructure to deal with such waste. A Swiss multinational company dumped more than 500 tonnes of a mixture of fuel, caustic soda, and hydrogen sulfide at twelve different sites around Abidjan in the Côte d'Ivoire (Ivory Coast). Several deaths and thousands of injuries resulted from this environmental disaster. There have been similar reports of wide-scale environmental damage and damage to human health due to inadequate recycling facilities in India and China.

Because responsible recycling is expensive, there is a lucrative illegal trade in e-waste; primary producers responsible for recycling simply export their e-waste to developing countries to be dumped or recycled. Recycling costs in these countries are much lower due to lower labor costs and far fewer, if any, regulations imposed on recycling operations (Templeton 2009, 763–764). The primary destinations for recycling are India and China, and significant amounts have been dumped in West African countries such as Nigeria as well. The restrictions of international and national regulations, aimed at preventing the cross-border export of hazardous waste, have led to a lucrative illegal trade in e-waste that is hard to contain.

The market for recycling e-waste is enormous. For example, it is estimated that the treatment of e-waste produced in the United States alone is worth in excess of $5 billion annually (Majmudar 2011). This estimate provides a strong indication of the size of the e-waste

recycling market as a whole and will increase as the price of REE rises. Stricter controls and decreasing costs of recycling may lead to the development of viable recycling industries in the developed nations, and a decrease in the illegal trade and dumping of e-waste.

International Agencies

A number of international agencies and organizations promote responsible recycling of e-waste. The United Nations established the United Nations Environment Programme (UNEP) in 1972 to advocate global environmental protection. The responsible recycling of e-waste has become an important part of UNEP's focus. As part of their Solving the E-Waste Problem (StEP) initiative, UNEP published a 2009 report, *Recycling: From E-waste to Resources*, a major contribution to the debate and knowledge about the responsible treatment of e-waste.

The Basel Action Network (BAN) is a nongovernmental environmental action group based in the United States but focused on confronting the global environmental injustice and economic inefficiency of toxic trade (toxic wastes, products, and technologies) and its devastating impacts. BAN first raised awareness about the plight of the Guiyu residents. It has reported on similar situations elsewhere (BAN 2004).

The e-Waste Association of South Africa (eWASA) is an example of a locally based voluntary organization established to promote environmentally sound e-waste management within a country where there are no specific e-waste regulations, but where e-waste is treated within the more general and less effective environmental legislation. The association has made an impact in South Africa as members establish e-waste collection and recycling programs and raise awareness about e-waste. It commissioned and published a 2007 in-depth review of the regulatory landscape in South Africa (Dittke 2009). The Electronics TakeBack Coalition (ETBC) is a similar US organization promoting green design and responsible recycling in the electronics industry. These and many other similar organizations play an important role in raising the awareness of the responsible treatment of e-waste and confronting the illegal dumping of e-waste in developing countries.

Regulatory Landscape

A number of international, regional, and national regulations are relevant for the management of e-waste.

The International Regulatory Landscape

There is no international convention specifically aimed at e-waste. Instead there are a number of conventions that deal generally with the cross-border transportation of toxic waste. E-waste is a fairly new phenomenon that can be dealt with within the scope of the broader definition of toxic waste contained in international conventions. The problem has not been a lack of regulation, but a lack of proper implementation.

Basel Convention 1989

The Basel Convention on the Transboundary Movement of Hazardous Waste is the most important multilateral convention for controlling the movement of hazardous waste across international boundaries. It entered into operation in 1992 (Pratt 2011, 156ff.). Its main objective is to ensure that the export of hazardous waste between countries is done in a way that is environmentally responsible. There are 179 parties to the convention, but three original signatories—Afghanistan, Haiti, and the United States—have not ratified it yet. A 1995 amendment to the convention, the Basel Ban Amendment, aims at a ban of all export of hazardous waste between developed and developing countries. Due to its controversial nature, which in part concerns the lack of regulations about what constitutes recycling, it had not yet been in force by the end of 2011.

The Basel Convention has not yet been successful in eliminating the large-scale exportation of e-waste, partly because the United States is not a party to the convention and partly due to strategies circumventing the convention, such as exporting e-waste under the guise of equipment destined for reuse in the importing country. The US legal associate Shaza Quadri (2010, 468–469) remarks that e-waste continues to be dumped in India despite India's ratification of the convention.

Bamako Convention 1991

African nations were not satisfied with the Basel Convention because it did not contain a total ban on the export of toxic waste. They believed that the recycling exception created a loophole that would be exploited by unscrupulous parties in developed countries (Tladi 2000, 213). The Bamako Convention of 1991, Convention on the Ban of Import into Africa and the Control of Transboundary Movement and Management of Hazardous Wastes within Africa, mirrors the Basel Convention in many respects, but contains an all-out ban on the importation of toxic waste into Africa. The convention entered into force in 1998 and has been ratified by twenty-four African nations. Due to poor implementation, the convention has also not yet achieved the desired objectives.

The European WEEE Directive 2002/96/EC

The European Union (EU) has a three-pronged approach to the management of e-waste:

- The WEEE Directive is aimed at transferring the responsibility for e-waste from the government to the private sector. Consumers are entitled to return redundant products to retailers who must accept them and become responsible for their recycling (Hagen 2006, 8–9). The directive has been made law in all member states of the EU. Although the directive has been less successful than hoped, efforts to amend the directive in 2008 have not yet been implemented (EU 2008).
- The Restriction on Certain Hazardous Substances Directive 2002/95/EC (RoHS Directive) is aimed at prohibiting makers of electronic goods from manufacturing goods containing certain substances such as lead, mercury, cadmium, and hexavalent chromium.
- The Energy Using Products Directive 2005/32/EC is aimed at the design stage of most energy using products in order to regulate the product from conception to grave.

The inter-relationship between the three directives is legally complex and sometimes confusing. They form a comprehensive body of legislation that regulates not only electronic waste but electronic products from the outset in order to minimize electronic waste and its negative by-products. The EU aims at recycling 85 percent of e-waste by 2016 instead of 33 percent in 2011. The directives not only have been implemented by all member states of the EU, but also have had an impact on regulations in China, Japan, and the United States (Kuschnik 2008, 1).

Africa

The importation of toxic waste from developed countries has been recognized as far back as 1988 with the Council of Ministers declaring that "the dumping of wastes in Africa is a crime against Africa and the African people" (Tladi 2000, 213). This concern was also the background to the adoption of the Bamako Convention. Very little has been done in African countries, however, to stem e-waste dumping.

South Africa has quite comprehensive environmental legislation supported by a constitutional provision guaranteeing a safe environment, but it has no regulations dealing specifically with e-waste. The treatment of e-waste has instead relied on the voluntary cooperation by manufacturers with initiatives like eWASA. Large-scale recycling is unlikely to take place in the absence of more specific regulations or programs.

Kenya is the first African country to have introduced specific measures to manage e-waste. The National Environment Management Authority published guidelines for the management of e-waste in December 2010. The guidelines stress the need for an appropriate regulatory framework for e-waste management to augment the voluntary aspects of the present guidelines. The guidelines aim at the provision of a framework for the development of regulations and policies with the participation of key participants in the sustainable management of e-waste in Kenya.

Outlook

There is a growing awareness of the problems that e-waste poses to waste management in general, the management of toxic waste, and the export to and dumping of e-waste in developing countries that do not have the capacity to properly deal with such waste. There is a need for better enforcement of the existing international and national regulations that restrict the dumping of e-waste. Consumer awareness will play a key role in the more effective collection and recycling of e-waste, as will organizations like UNEP. There are indications that the United States, one of the largest producers of e-waste, will exercise stricter control over the dumping of e-waste in developing nations. This will have a similar beneficial effect to the stricter measures that have been imposed by the members of the European Union.

Sieg EISELEN
University of South Africa

See also Africa (*several articles*); African Union (AU); Conflict Minerals; European Union (EU); Corporate Accountability (Africa); France; Germany; Mining (Africa); Rule of Law (Africa); Rule of Law (European Union); Shipping and Freight; United Kingdom and Ireland

FURTHER READING

Arthur, Charles. (2011, July 4). Japan discovers "rare earth" minerals used for iPads. *The Guardian*. Retrieved February 13, 2012, from http://www.guardian.co.uk/technology/2011/jul/04/japan-ipads-rare-earth

Basel Action Network (BAN). (2004). Dante's digital junkyard. Retrieved March 28, 2012, from http://www.ban.org/ban_news/dantes_digital_040406.html

Basel Action Network (BAN). (2011). Homepage. Retrieved February 13, 2012, from http://www.ban.org/

Boon, Joel. (2006, Spring). Stemming the tide of patchwork policies: The case of e-waste. *Transnational Law and Contemporary Problems*, *15*(2), 731–757.

Chung, Soo-Wu, & Murakami-Suzuki, Rie. (2008). A comparative study of e-waste recycling systems in Japan, South Korea and Taiwan from the EPR perspective implications for developing countries. In Michikazu Kojima (Ed.), *Promoting 3Rs in developing countries: Lessons from the Japanese experience* (pp. 125–145). Chiba, Japan: Institute of Developing Economies (IDE). Retrieved June 12, 2012, from http://www.ide.go.jp/English/Publish/Download/Spot/pdf/30/007.pdf

Courtney, Rob. (2006, July). Evolving hazardous waste policy for the digital era. *Stanford Environmental Law Journal*, *25*, 199–227.

Dittke, Mark. (2009, August). A review of South African environmental and general legislation governing e-waste. Retrieved December 14, 2011, from http://www.ewasa.org/downloads/files/ewasa%20legal%20review.pdf

Drayton, Heather L. (2007, Fall). Economics of electronic waste disposal regulations. *Hofstra Law Review*, *36*(1), 149–183.

E-waste hazardous to human life. (2010, February). *ReSource*, *12*(1), 37–39, 41.

Electronics TakeBack Coalition (ETBC). (2010). States Summary. Retrieved December 14, 2011, from http://www.electronicstakeback.com/wp-content/uploads/Compare_state_laws_chart.pdf

Electronics TakeBack Coalition (ETBC). (2012a). Brief comparison of state laws on electronic recycling. Retrieved March 28, 2012, from http://www.electronicstakeback.com/wp-content/uploads/Compare_state_laws_chart.pdf

Electronics TakeBack Coalition (ETBC). (2012b). E-waste facts and figures. Retrieved March 28, 2012, from http://www.electronicstakeback.com/wp-content/uploads/Facts_and_Figures_on_EWaste_and_Recycling.pdf

European Union (EU). (2008, March 11). Official journal of the European Union: Directive 2008/35/EC of the European Parliament and of the Council of 11 March 2008. Retrieved May 28, 2012, from http://eur-lex.europa.eu/LexUriServ/LexUriServ.do?uri=OJ:L:2008:081:0067:0068:EN:PDF

Ezroj, Aaron. (2010). How the European Union's WEEE & RoHS directives can help the United States develop a successful national e-waste strategy. *Virginia Environmental Law Journal*, *28*, 45–72.

Fehm, Sarah. (2011, Fall). From iPod to e-waste: Building a successful framework for extended producer responsibility in the United States. *Public Contract Law Journal*, *41*(1), 173–192.

Greenland Minerals and Energy Ltd. (2012a). Rare earth elements at Kvanefjeld. Retrieved February 13, 2012, from http://www.ggg.gl/rare-earth-elements/rare-earth-elements-at-kvanefjeld/

Greenland Minerals and Energy Ltd. (2012b). Kvanefjeld: REEs, uranium, zinc. Retrieved February 13, 2012, from http://www.ggg.gl/projects/kvanefjeld-rees-uranium-zinc/

Hagen, Paul E. (2006). Product-based environmental regulations: Europe sets the pace. *ABA Trends*, *37*(3), 8–10.

Hull, Eric V. (2010). Poisoning the poor for profit: The injustice of exporting electronic waste to developing countries. *Duke Environmental Law and Policy Forum*, *21*(1), 1–48.

Humphries, Marc. (2011, September 6). Rare earth elements: The global supply chain (Congressional Research Service Report). Retrieved February 13, 2012, from http://www.fas.org/sgp/crs/natsec/R41347.pdf

Hurst, Cindy. (2010, November 15). The rare earth dilemma: China's rare earth environmental and safety nightmare. *The Cutting Edge*. Retrieved February 13, 2012, from http://www.thecuttingedgenews.com/index.php?article=21777

International Business Times. (2010, November 3). China's dream for rare earths rests on grim costs. Retrieved February 13, 2011, from http://www.ibtimes.com/articles/78461/20101103/rare-earth-china.htm

International ICT Policies and Strategies. (2011, June 25). E-waste law and regulatory framework in India. Retrieved February 13, 2012, from http://ictps.blogspot.com/2011/06/e-waste-law-and-regulatory-framework-in.html

INTERPOL Pollution Crime Working Group. (2009, May). Electronic waste and organized crime: Assessing the links. Lyon, France: INTERPOL.

Kellner, Rod. (2009). Integrated approach to e-waste recycling. In Ronald E. Hester & Roy M. Harrison (Eds.), *Issues in environmental science and technology: Vol. 27. Electronic waste management.* London: Royal Society of Chemistry.

Knee, Jeremy. (2009, Fall). Guidance for the awkward: Outgrowing the adolescence of state electronic waste laws. *Environs: Environmental Law and Policy Journal, 33*(2), 157–187.

Kuschnik, Bernhard. (2008). The European Union's energy using products: EUP–Directive 2005/32 EC. *Temple Journal of Science, Technology & Environmental Law, 27*, 1–33.

Kutz, Jennifer. (2006). You've got waste: The exponentially escalating problem of hazardous e-waste. *Villanova Environmental Law Journal, 17*, 307–329.

Lee, Soo-cheol, & Na, Sung-in. (2010). E-waste recycling systems and sound circulative economies in East Asia: A comparative analysis of systems in Japan, South Korea, China and Taiwan. *Sustainability, 2*(6), 1632–1644.

Luther, Linda. (2007, September 10). Managing electronic waste: An analysis of state e-waste legislation (CRS Report for Congress). Washington, DC: Congressional Research Service.

Majmudar, Nishad. (2011, September 18). E-waste: Recyclers, scrap haulers vie to keep U.S. computer trash home. *Washington Post.* Retrieved May 29, 2012, from http://www.washingtonpost.com/business/economy/e-waste-recyclers-scrap-haulers-vie-to-keep-us-computer-trash-home/2011/09/15/gIQAJi7EdK_story.html

Manasvini, Krishna, & Kulshrestha, Pratiksha. (2008). The toxic belt: Perspectives on e-waste dumping in developing nations. *U.C. Davis Journal of International Law and Policy, 15*(1), 71–93.

McCrea, Hannah. (2011, Summer). Germany's take-back approach to waste management: Is there a legal basis for adoption in the United States? *Georgetown International Environmental Law Review, 23*(4), 513–529.

National Environmental Management Authority (NEMA). (2010). *Guidelines for management of e-waste in Kenya.* Nairobi, Kenya: NEMA. Retrieved February 13, 2012, from http://gesci.org/assets/files/Knowledge%20Centre/E-Waste%20Guidelines_Kenya2011.pdf

Pratt, Laura A. W. (2011, Winter). Decreasing dirty dumping? A re-evaluation of toxic waste colonialism and the global management of transboundary hazardous waste. *Texas Environmental Law Journal, 35*(2), 147–178.

Proactive Investors Australia. (2009, June 18). Greenland Minerals and Energy confirms huge rare earth resource in Greenland. Retrieved February 13, 2012, from http://www.proactiveinvestors.com.au/companies/news/1767/greenland-minerals-and-energy-confirms-huge-rare-earth-resource-in-greenland-1767.html

Quadri, Shaza. (2010). An analysis of the effects and reasons for hazardous waste importation in India and its implementation of the Basel Convention. *Florida Journal of International Law, 22*(3), 468–493.

Royal Society of Chemistry (RSC). (2011, July 13). Manufacturers targeted by India's e-waste laws. Retrieved December 14, 2011, from www.rsc.org/chemistryworld/News/2011/July/13071101.asp

Templeton, Nicola J. (2009 Spring/Summer). The dark side of recycling and reusing electronics: Is Washington's e-cycle program adequate? *Seattle Journal for Social Justice, 7*(2), 763–797.

Tladi, Dire. (2000). The quest to ban hazardous waste import into Africa: First Bamako and now Basel. *Comparative and International Law Journal of South Africa, 33*(2), 210–222.

Towle, Holly K.; Dyer, Andrew H.; & Evans, Michael W. (2005). The European Union directive on waste electrical and electronic equipment: A study in trans-Atlantic zealotry. *Rutgers Computer and Technology Law Journal, 31*(1), 49–156.

United Nations Environment Programme (UNEP). (2009a, January 28). Solving the e-waste problem (StEP) white paper: E-waste take-back system design and policy approaches. Retrieved December 14, 2011, from http://www.google.com/url?sa=t&rct=j&q=&esrc=s&source=web&cd=1&ved=0CE4QFjAA&url=http%3A%2F%2Fwww.step-initiative.org%2Ftl_files%2Fstep%2F_documents%2FStEP_TF1_WPTakeBackSystems.pdf&ei=dsK7T5idNrT8iQLhgaGGDg&usg=AFQjCNEnRzPZzWgUamR2z9AWnZigH2aRlw

United Nations Environment Programme (UNEP). (2009b, July). *Recycling: From e-waste to resources.* Retrieved December 14, 2011, from http://www.unep.org/PDF/PressReleases/E-Waste_publication_screen_FINALVERSION-sml.pdf

Widawsky, Lisa. (2008). In my backyard: How enabling hazardous waste trade to developing nations can improve the Basel Convention's ability to achieve environmental justice. *Environmental Law, 38*(2), 577–626.

Yahoo! Finance. (2011, December 5). Frontier Rare Earths and Korea Resources Corporation sign definitive strategic partnership agreement. Retrieved February 13, 2011, from http://finance.yahoo.com/news/Frontier-Rare-Earths-Korea-cnw-1531259259.html

Yoon, Hyunmyung, & Jang, Yong-Chul. (2006, May 8–11). The practice and challenges of electronic waste recycling in Korea with emphasis on extended producer responsibility (EPR) In *Proceedings of the 2006 IEEE International Symposium on Electronics and the Environment, 2006* (pp. 326–330). Scottsdale, AZ: IEEE.

Ecotourism

The conservation of biodiversity is severely threatened in many parts of the world, including Africa and Europe, with species extinctions continuing despite international efforts to prevent them. Ecotourism has the potential to make a positive contribution to conservation of the natural environment. Africa in particular has a number of commercial tourism operations that contribute to the conservation of the natural landscape.

The underlying concept of ecotourism is that commercial tourism can make a positive net contribution to conservation of the natural environment by creating financial and political capital and incentives that outweigh its own direct impacts; some would argue that this makes ecotourism unlike any other industry sectors. This is a concept with long historical antecedents in many cultures, including the Western model of national parks and wilderness areas not only as reservoirs of biodiversity, but as places that can provide opportunities for visitors to appreciate nature.

The term "ecotour" was first used in the 1960s, with the first formal definitions appearing in the 1980s. During the 1990s, government tourism planning documents began to mention ecotourism with increasing frequency, and many commercial tourism operations began to claim themselves as ecotourism (Buckley 2003). The United Nations International Year of Ecotourism in 2002 provided mainstream intergovernmental recognition. Plans produced by government and financial donor agencies now refer routinely to ecotourism, mainly as a mechanism to provide economic and political opportunities for impoverished peoples in developing nations. Both the practical examples and the political influence of ecotourism have continued to expand in recent years. In Africa in particular, there are now a number of commercial tourism operations that contribute to conservation (Buckley 2009, 2010a, and 2011) or community development (Spenceley 2008; Saarinen et al. 2009; Nelson 2010).

Significance for Sustainability

No matter how sustainability is defined, conservation of the natural environment is a key component. In its most fundamental and meaningful sense, namely the continuing ability of the planet to support populations and societies of humans as well as other species, there are two key components to sustainability. The first is to stabilize and reduce both the size of the global human population and per capita consumption and pollution of natural resources and environment. The second is to maintain biological diversity and ecosystem services and functions, including the fundamentals of edible food, drinkable water, breathable air, and stable climate.

Currently, conservation of biodiversity is under particularly severe threat in many parts of the world, with species extinctions continuing despite international efforts to prevent them. Many individual species are under threat from a wide range of human activities and related disturbances. Two types of threat are particularly severe. The first is large-scale logging and clearance of native vegetation for industrialized agriculture in developing nations with high biodiversity. The second is the targeted poaching of individual rare species for the illegal international trade in animal parts. Both of these activities are driven ultimately by networks of wealthy, powerful, and unscrupulous individuals, with local residents either coerced or co-opted.

Ecotourism can, in some instances at least, help to counteract these threats to sustainability by providing a local source of income that depends on intact natural ecosystems and biodiversity and provides means and incentives to protect them. These means may include financial capital, which can be used directly on the ground or used to gain political capital through lobbying or lawsuits. The means may also include political capital, generated both by regional economic activity and by international publicity from tour operators and their clients, which in turn can generate financial capital through government budget processes.

Worldwide, there are as yet relatively few private tourism companies that make a demonstrable net contribution to conservation of threatened species and ecosystems and hence to this key aspect of sustainability (Buckley 2010a). There are, however, a number of public national park systems that now rely heavily on revenue from individual visitors to the parks concerned. There are also many private companies that claim to use minimal-impact practices or contribute to human social welfare but whose net overall effect on sustainability is nonetheless negative.

Regional Patterns and Dynamics

The structure of the ecotourism sector differs considerably between Africa and Europe. The term ecotourism is not widely used within the African tourism industry itself. It is used largely by international nongovernmental organizations (NGOs) aiming to establish community tourism ventures. Mainstream tourism operations keen to demonstrate compliance with South Africa's laws for Black Economic Empowerment commonly use the term *responsible tourism*, which originated in South Africa. Most commercial operators use terms that reflect key features of their products, such as game, wildlife, birdwatching, or natural history. Many of these operators have also adopted measures to minimize impacts, but these measures are rarely promoted much in marketing.

In much of Africa, a longstanding history of international wildlife watching and hunting safaris in colonial times has evolved, in modern postcolonial times, into a large and complex industry of wildlife- and nature-based tourism on public, private, and communally owned lands. Much of this can qualify as ecotourism. Indeed, some of the world's best examples of conservation tourism—tourism that makes a net positive contribution to the conservation of biodiversity—are in sub-Saharan Africa (Buckley 2010a). Many of the models for modern ecotourism enterprises worldwide, both those that are entirely private sector and those that involve public, community, and nongovernment organizations, originated in sub-Saharan Africa.

It is in this region, perhaps more than anywhere else worldwide, that ecotourism has demonstrated its practical ability to contribute to conservation and rural communities on a relatively large scale. In this region, ecotourism has successfully demonstrated its political and practical feasibility and economic viability, and is now grappling with a new set of issues associated with expansion to mainstream industry. These issues include, for example, the complexities of commercial structures for large-scale ecotourism enterprises operating across numerous countries; the details of legal frameworks for land tenure and ownership of wildlife and their consequences for the design and outcomes of wildlife tourism products; and the ability and mechanisms for tourism to fund not only isolated private reserves but also entire nationwide protected area systems, including antipoaching measures; and difficulties associated with political patronage in countries where it is commonplace for senior government officials to have personal stakes in major commercial enterprises (Nelson 2010).

At present, ecotourism in Africa is strongly concentrated in the eastern and southern parts of the continent. In the east, it includes the long-standing safari industries of Kenya and Tanzania and to a lesser degree also Uganda and, most recently, Ethiopia. This region also provides the gateway to the gorilla-watching sites in the Virunga Mountains of Uganda and Rwanda. Gorilla watching, however, although very well known and in high demand, is economically far smaller than wildlife tourism in the savannah grassland regions.

Also in the east African region, but marketed somewhat separately, are the island nations of Madagascar and the Seychelles. Madagascar is an internationally known destination for birdwatching and wildlife tourism, with a focus on lemurs and chameleons (Buckley 2010b). The Seychelles are principally a beach, sun, and sea destination for Europeans, but there are also several island reserves, funded by ecotourism, that contribute significantly to the conservation of endangered endemic bird species. Some of these are privately owned and operated, whereas others are run by NGOs.

In southern Africa, the principal international gateway is Johannesburg in South Africa, and the wildlife safari industry is strongly focused in South Africa, Botswana, and Namibia. There are differences between and within these three nations in ecosystems, social structures, infrastructure and access, and laws relating to ownership of land and wildlife. All these differences influence the design of ecotourism products and enterprises. Similar models are also operational, although on a somewhat smaller scale, in neighboring Zambia, Mozambique, and Malawi, and historically also in Zimbabwe. These approaches could also be adopted in other countries such as Angola if political conditions become sufficiently stable and safe for international tourism.

In most of northern Africa, as indeed along the southern coast of South Africa, the emphasis is principally on large-scale coastal resort tourism. There are, however, some well-known enterprises that are marketed as ecotourism, typically including both adventure and Arabian cultural components. Best known of these is Al Maha near Dubai in the United Arab Emirates, but there are also lower-key examples in countries such as Oman. The scale of these enterprises, however, is very small in comparison to the megadevelopments along the coastlines. There is also an extensive dive tourism industry in the Red Sea, and a smaller and more diffuse industry along the coastlines of eastern and southern Africa.

In West Africa there is enormous potential for ecotourism, but to date most of this region is perceived as too risky either for commercial tourism entrepreneurs or for individual tourists. There are very large-scale international commercial operations in the mining, logging, and hydroelectric sectors, most of them involving powerful political patronage and some of dubious legality. There are a small number of long-standing ecotourism enterprises in this region, including a canopy walkway at Kakum in Ghana and birdwatching operations in the Gambia; and there are former village homestays, no longer operational, in Senegal (Buckley 2003 and 2010a). There is also at least one newly constructed upscale wildlife lodge in the Republic of the Congo, operated by the large southern African conservation tourism company Wilderness Safaris. Many species of wildlife in West Africa are endangered through logging and land clearance, and many international NGOs, African ecotourism enterprises, and conservation organizations such as African Parks are keen to develop ecotourism operations in this area. Until they have reasonable access, security of land tenure, protection of forests and wildlife in key areas, and safety for staff and clients, such developments are unlikely to go ahead.

Ecotourism in Europe differs considerably between countries, with a broad distinction between Scandinavia, the Alps, and the Mediterranean. There are some continent-wide initiatives, such as PAN Parks and the European Union's tourism ecolabel programs, but individual nations have very different legal and cultural contexts. Ecotourism in Scandinavia has been analyzed by researchers Stefan Gössling and Johan Hultman (2006) and seems to focus principally on the reindeer-herding cultures of the northern Sami peoples and on traditional small-scale farming practices. There are also ecotourism initiatives in the Karelia region in eastern Finland and adjacent areas of far western Russia (TACIS Project 2001). Initiatives in the alpine region include: a number of transboundary trekking trails; a high concentration of local-scale ecocertification programs; and so-called soft mobility programs such as the "Alpine Pearls" destinations, which aim to reduce dependence on fossil fuels. In France, Italy, and Greece there are extensive networks of small-scale farm tourism operations, some of which may qualify as ecotourism; and NGO-initiated conservation projects that include ecotourism components (Buckley 2003; Ollenburg 2008). In France, ecotourism has been used as a mechanism to overcome a degree of rural antipathy to national parks (Priskin and Sarrasin 2010).

Organizations and People

As on other continents, national government agencies are the most influential organizations for ecotourism policy and practice in both Africa and Europe. These include agencies relating to tourism, national parks, wildlife, land tenure, and rural and community development. In Namibia, for example, the legislative foundation for community-based natural resource management (CBNRM) has proved critical to the development of ecotourism, and the coordinating Namibian Association of CBNRM Support Organisations has gained prominence in consequence. In South Africa, legislation for Black Economic Empowerment has driven a range of organizational and social changes within many industry sectors, including tourism.

For ecotourism specifically, the South African National Parks agency SANParks has played a major role, particularly because the national government has continually reduced its central funding and forced it to rely increasingly on revenue from tourism. Other important organizations include Ezemvelo KZN in the South African province of KwaZulu-Natal, a leader in breeding and trading wildlife of high value in conservation and tourism. In the Madikwe region adjacent to Botswana, the North West Parks and Tourism Board plays a critical role in the Madikwe multiowner syndicated private reserve, which is funded by tourism and makes significant contributions to conservation in this part of the country (Castley 2010).

Throughout eastern and southern Africa, individual private tourism enterprises that fund conservation on private or community reserves have played a key role in ecotourism. Perhaps the largest and best known are the two companies & Beyond and Wilderness Safaris, each with several dozen operations spread throughout the region (Buckley 2010a). In addition, there are numerous single-site enterprises that follow similar approaches (Castley 2010). A number of international NGOs are involved in promoting and cofunding individual ecotourism enterprises, principally those with strong involvement from local communities. In addition, the private conservation organization African Parks is playing an increasingly important role in helping impoverished African nations to maintain their protected-area systems more effectively for conservation, by establishing revenue streams from tourism. These private organizations, which have successfully harnessed tourism in conservation, have been established and expanded by dedicated and visionary individuals with the persistence and charisma to enlist others successfully. Kenya has also established its own ecotourism association (Ecotourism Kenya 2010).

In Europe, different countries have rather different legal arrangements and social traditions relating to national parks, forestry and farming, and hunting and fishing, all of which influence the shape and structure of the modern ecotourism subsector. There are a number of national-scale ecotourism associations and several transnational NGOs and related programs such as PANParks. There have been several attempts at European Union–wide ecocertification programs, the most recent under the name Travelife. None seem to have been particularly successful to date. The United Nations World Tourism Organisation (UNWTO) is based in Madrid, and perhaps in consequence, UNWTO programs such as the Tour Operators Initiative for Sustainable Tourism are focused largely within Europe. This program, however, is aimed more at environmental management in mainstream tourism, than at ecotourism specifically. A number of university research groups, consultants, and government agencies throughout Europe also have interests in various aspects of ecotourism, and a considerable proportion of the academic literature in this field originates within Europe (Weaver and Lawton 2007).

Outlook

The outlook for ecotourism in both Europe and Africa depends strongly on the future financial and social costs of different forms of travel, as a result of increasing fuel prices and carbon taxes and public concerns over climate change. In Europe, most tourist destinations are served by road and rail links as well as airports, so substitution between travel modes is possible. It has been argued that European tourists will take more local and fewer international holidays and rely more on rail travel, but as of 2012 this trend has not appeared in practice.

The successful African ecotourism model relies heavily on international long-haul tourists from the northern hemisphere, plus the self-drive market from South Africa into neighboring countries. There are African safari and wildlife-watching opportunities available to suit all budgets, from backpacker to luxury. At the upper end of the market, the cost of international travel makes up only a small proportion of the total cost of a tour, because the top-tier lodges charge $1,000 per person per night or more. At the bottom end of the commercial market, so-called overlander tours travel in large converted trucks or buses, and per capita travel costs are low. For the large family-oriented sector in the middle of the market, however, air-travel costs are a major component, so this market may be hard hit by cost increases. Private conservation reserves rely principally on the upper end of the market, but national parks systems in a number of African countries receive over 50 percent of their total funding from visitor entry fees, and thus rely heavily on the large mid-market family package holiday sector. Climate change and fuel costs thus pose a significant risk to ecotourism and conservation in Africa.

The other major risk in the African region is political instability, corruption, or patronage. Safety and security are prerequisites for a successful tourism sector. There are many African nations with the natural resources to maintain a successful wildlife tourism industry that are too insecure for tourists to visit or for tourism entrepreneurs to invest. Even in those countries that are relatively stable, there is a growing problem of political patronage (Nelson 2010), under which powerful government officials routinely co-opt a major share in any large-scale and commercially successful enterprise. Early ecotourism initiatives were too small to attract attention, but now that the sector is larger, especially where it attracts international donor or investment funding, it can be difficult for companies to retain the commercial independence they need to reinvest profits into expansion.

While Europe has large-scale inbound, outbound, and domestic tourism sectors, African ecotourism caters principally to international inbound visitors, and, to a smaller degree, internal regional travelers from South

Africa. International visitors to Africa come principally from the richer European and North American nations. In particular, there are former colonial links that are now perpetuated through tourism, largely through linguistic mechanisms; thus although Europe and Africa are very different continents, in an ecotourism context there are still some powerful links. In terms of practical mechanisms, Europe and Africa exhibit differences: in Europe, cross-national government and NGO initiatives seem to be particularly significant, while ecotourism in Africa relies heavily on public national parks, community conservancies, and private conservation reserves.

Ralf BUCKLEY

Griffith University, Australia

See also Africa (*several articles*); African Union (AU); Agriculture, Small-Scale; Biodiversity Conservation; Biological Corridors; Dubai, United Arab Emirates; European Union (EU); France; Mediterranean Sea; Parks and Preserves; Public–Private Partnerships (Africa); Rural Development; Scandinavia; Travel and Tourism Industry

FURTHER READING

Buckley, Ralf C. (2003). *Case studies in ecotourism.* Wallingford, UK: CAB International.

Buckley, Ralf C. (2009). *Ecotourism: Principles and practices.* Wallingford, UK: CAB International.

Buckley, Ralf C. (2010a). *Conservation tourism.* Wallingford, UK: CAB International.

Buckley, Ralf C. (2010b). Ethical ecotourists: The narwhal dilemma revisited. *Journal of Ecotourism, 9*(2), 169–172. doi:10.1080/14724040903142190

Buckley, Ralf C. (2011). Tourism and environment. *Annual Review of Environment and Resources, 36,* 397–416. doi:10.1146/annurev-environ-041210-132637

Castley, J. Guy. (2010). Africa. In Ralf C. Buckley (Ed.), *Conservation tourism* (pp. 145–175). Wallingford, UK: CAB International.

Ecotourism Kenya. (2011). Homepage. Retrieved November 2, 2011, from http://www.ecotourismkenya.org/

Gössling, Stefan, & Hultman, Johan. (Eds.). (2006). *Ecotourism in Scandinavia: Lessons in theory and practice.* Wallingford, UK: CAB International.

Nelson, Fred. (Ed.). (2010). *Community rights, conservation and contested land: The politics of natural resource governance in Africa.* London: Earthscan.

Ollenburg, Claudia. (2008). Regional signatures and trends in the farm tourism sector. *Tourism Recreation Research, 33*(1), 13–24.

Priskin, Julianna, & Sarrasin, Bruno. (2010). France and Francophone nations. In Ralf C. Buckley (Ed.), *Conservation tourism* (pp. 110–124). Wallingford, UK: CAB International.

Saarinen, Jarkko; Becker, Fritz; Manwa, Haretsebe; & Wilson, Deon. (Eds.). (2009). *Sustainable tourism in southern Africa: Local communities and natural resources in transition.* Bristol, UK: Channel View Publications.

Spenceley, Anna. (2008). *Responsible tourism: Critical issues for conservation and development.* London: Earthscan.

TACIS Project. (2001). *Ecotourism on the way to Russia.* Karelia Parks Development, Project No. ENVRUS9704. Petrozavodsk, Russia: TACIS.

Weaver, David B., & Lawton, Laura J. (2007). Twenty years on: The state of contemporary ecotourism research. *Tourism Management, 28*(5), 1168–1179. doi:10.1016/j.tourman.2007.03.004

Education, Environmental

Since the 1960s and 1970s, a series of (mainly) UNESCO-sponsored international conferences produced reports and policy statements that have shaped the goals and principles of environmental and sustainability education and have been influential in shaping national policies. A historical analysis of these statements reveals evolving views of education's role in improving the environmental and the human condition. Several environmental and sustainability education issues confront Africa, Europe, and Central and Western Asia.

Environmental education (EE) evolved from the environmental movement in the late 1960s and early 1970s and focused attention on increasing concerns about environmental degradation, including the unsustainable exploitation of natural resources. These concerns led to a call for education that would inspire present and future generations to alter their habits of misusing the environment. Two significant developments in this area were the Belgrade Charter, adopted in 1975 in a working meeting of people actively involved in EE, and the Tbilisi Declaration (1978), a product of the first Intergovernmental Conference on Environmental Education, which was attended by high-level government representatives. The latter conference ratified (with some modifications) principles and objectives for EE that had been identified in the Belgrade Charter. These guiding principles espoused lifelong, interdisciplinary, and holistic learning aimed at increasing people's awareness, knowledge, attitudes, skills, and participation (with an emphasis on the development of problem solving, critical thinking, and decision making) in addressing environmental issues and at actively working toward their resolution (Tbilisi Declaration 1978). The term *environment* now came to include the built environment (such as buildings and roads), in addition to its natural, social, cultural, economic, political, and biophysical factors. Educational aspirations also expanded beyond merely developing students' and citizens' awareness and knowledge of environmental concerns to include their active involvement in investigating and working toward the resolution of environmental problems (Stevenson 1997).

The Brundtland Commission report (World Commission on Environment and Development 1987, also widely known as *Our Common Future*) introduced the concept of *sustainable development* to describe the link between the environment and development. The report argued the need for equity between and within generations, noting that development trends were leaving increasing numbers of people poor and vulnerable while degrading the natural environment. Agenda 21 (the United Nations Action Plan that was a product of the 1992 Earth Summit in Rio de Janeiro, Brazil) called for a reorientation of EE education toward education for sustainable development or a sustainable future. This resonated with some policy makers and scholars who were concerned that the policy objectives and principles for environmental education had come to be associated only with environmental problems and lacked an orientation that looked toward the future (Smyth 1995). Education for sustainable development (ESD) or education for sustainability (EfS) became the preferred terms in international and many national policy circles, particularly in Africa, Europe, and Asia.

Five years after Agenda 21 was adopted, Declaration 10 (which came out of the 1997 United Nations Educational, Social and Cultural Organization–United Nations Environment Programme [UNESCO-UNEP] conference in Thessaloniki, Greece) introduced an, again, expanded concept of sustainability to encompass "not only the environment but also poverty, population, health, food security, democracy, human rights, and peace" (UNESCO-EPD 1997, 6). Subsequently, the text of Declaration 11 stated that EE had evolved from its conceptualization, defined at the Tbilisi conference, to address all of the global issues included in Agenda 21, and now had also become recognized as education for sustainability (Sato 2006).

The concept of EE was broadened, therefore, in several dimensions, evolving from conservation education (with its focus on understanding the management of natural systems) to environmental education (which addresses understandings, values, and skills related to the biophysical, sociocultural, economic, and political factors that affect the use of the natural environment) to education for sustainability or sustainable living for everyone on the planet (with its explicit concern for socially just and peaceful approaches to development). One concern remained, however—that educational practices did not match the rhetoric of EE or ESD/EfS.

The Role of Education

Statements on EE objectives made in the Tbilisi Declaration (1978) and the Brundtland Report (1987) and on education in Agenda 21 tend to acknowledge EE's instrumental role in achieving the goals of sustainable development. Many policy makers and practitioners, and, indeed, researchers, have believed that EE's purpose is to recommend changes in individuals' behavior. They called for a raised awareness of environmental issues, assuming that greater awareness would change attitudes and behaviors—an assumption that many scholars have challenged because they believe it does not take into consideration the complex nature of behavioral change (e.g., Trainer 1994; Kollmuss and Agyeman 2002) and is premised on the questionable belief that only individual behavioral change is necessary to address sustainability issues. This instrumental approach to education also raises questions and concerns about whether people have the right to decide what counts legitimately as environmentally appropriate behavior and if education should focus on building people's capacity to think for themselves (Jickling 1992).

Instead of the view that education has such an instrumental function, the role of EE/EfS has been conceptualized to empower people by developing their individual and collective capacities to become informed and active participants who can contribute to the creation of ecologically, economically, and socially sustainable and just communities. EE and ESD can be treated as social processes of learning how to live within environmental limits in which all people have sustainable livelihoods (Stevenson 2007). This suggests the

necessity to build the learning capacities of individuals, organizations, and communities—a task that would greatly benefit from educators' contributions. Part of this complex undertaking requires that individuals and communities explore "the complexity and implications of sustainability as well as the economic, political, social, cultural, technological, and environmental forces that foster or impede sustainable development" (Fien and Tilbury 2002, 10).

Despite the differences in educational ideologies, national policies use similar language and (ambiguous) concepts of ESD/EfS. There is considerable convergence in these policies across a range of different historical, cultural, political, and economic contexts. The differences that do exist emphasize, however, the need to translate policies into practice in ways that are appropriate to specific issues and circumstances in local contexts. Those differences also suggest that educational approaches adopted should encourage the participation and help build the capacity of stakeholders (those people who have an interest in the outcome of an enterprise), local groups, organizations, and communities to respond to local and regional issues. The importance of such approaches is revealed when different regional influences and controversies, in addressing sustainability in the context of global concerns such as climate change, are examined.

Climate-Change Education Issues in Africa

Africa, and particularly sub-Saharan Africa—where in 2007 an estimated 30 percent of the population suffered from food insecurity and extreme poverty (Balasubramanian et al. 2007)—is likely to be severely affected by climate change. The very limited scientific expertise on climate change in Africa (with the exceptions of South Africa and parts of West Africa) and the newness of the concept of climate-change education have led to a general lack of awareness of climate change, especially in the farming community, which is the most vulnerable. A challenge for education on climate-change mitigation and adaptation stems from the fact that a majority of people believe it is not caused by human activities (that is, it is not anthropogenic), but results from natural processes. Fortunately, many organizations are working in Africa toward mitigating and building community resilience to climate change, such as the International Center for Research in Agroforestry, the Africa Technology Policy Studies Network, the Consultative Group on International Agriculture Research, World Vision, ActionAid International, the International Development Research Center, the

Global Climate Observing System, Farmer Voice Radio, the Nigeria Integrated Rural Accelerated Development Organisation, Environnement et Développement pour le Tiers Monde, the World Wide Fund for Nature (WWF), and the Food and Agriculture Organization of the United Nations, among others (UNEP 2009).

According to the Economic Commission for Africa (2002), Africa's rising population (growing by 2.5 percent annually and estimated to exceed 1.2 billion people by 2025) is putting pressure on the continent's natural resources, leading to competition for land and other resources. This pressure, together with the effects of climate change (such as prolonged droughts), has led to serious land degradation, where communities encroach on forests and engage in illegal logging and charcoal burning and use slash-and-burn methods to clear large tracts of bushland for agricultural activities. Conflicts over human-wildlife interactions and over water and pastoral-land rights are a common occurrence. Some cultural beliefs exacerbate the situation: for example, Kenya and Tanzania's Masai pastoral communities believe that keeping a huge herd of cattle is a sign of wealth—even under the prevailing drought conditions. Women in Africa are particularly affected by climate change because, in their role as primary caretakers of children and the home, they spend most of their time fetching firewood and water and less on education and other development work. Yet they are excluded from or underrepresented in climate-change policy-development processes and debates.

Climate change also threatens Africa's economy, which is highly dependent on agriculture (representing 30 percent of the continent's gross domestic product) (Nampinga 2008). Most rural farmers in Africa rely on rain-fed agriculture. The general lack of reliable meteorological data across the continent has caused uncertainty about changes in future rainfall and water availability (Williams and Kniveton 2011). This uncertainty means that most countries in Africa cannot make area-specific predictions on the future effects of climate change. Technologies that would mitigate the effects of climate change (such as preventing crop disease) and drought-tolerant crop varieties developed through conventional plant breeding are expensive for the farmers to adopt. Other ideas such as the use of *Jatropha* (a

genus of succulent plants, shrubs, and trees), and specifically *Jatropha curcas* for biodiesel and genetically modified foods, are highly controversial (Chakeredza et al. 2009, 14–15).

Addressing climate-change issues in Africa may be of interest, but is not a priority in countries such as Sierra Leone, Somalia, Egypt, Libya, Nigeria, and the Democratic Republic of the Congo, which are either suffering from or recovering from civil war, political instability, poverty, and diseases (among other issues). The involvement of the grassroots population, which is minimally represented in policy formulation meetings in countries developing climate-change education policies and strategies, should be encouraged so as to not exclude the most affected and vulnerable communities from participating.

Environmental and Sustainability Education Issues in Europe

Driven by the state of the its environment, Europe has been very active in addressing environmental and sustainability issues such as air pollution, biodiversity decline, unsustainable production and consumption patterns, energy demands, climate change, and the improper management of resources (EAA 2007). Several initiatives at the political and policy levels have given environmental and sustainable development issues a central place within the education process, while recognizing that environmental and sustainability education constitutes lifelong learning processes that extend beyond formal education (CEU 2006; UNECE 2005).

Each European country examines the key issues (such as consumption and production patterns and models, natural resource management, pollution, sustainable transportation, climate change, energy efficiency, biodiversity, and urban and rural development) according to its priorities and needs. They are examined as part of schools' curricula and in various formal, informal, and nonformal educational activities and programs at the national, regional, and European levels. Various parties and organizations, schools, and communities also participate and cooperate. Although these issues are examined interchangeably—as mentioned in the evaluation report from the United Nations Economic Commission for Europe, *Learning from Each Other: Achievements, Challenges, and Ways Forward* (UNECE 2012)—the dominant component of sustainability education issues is the environmental component. Given the three dimensions of sustainability (environmental, economic, and social/cultural), a more integrative conceptualization of sustainability education would give equal focus to socioeconomic and cultural aspects. In light of the global financial and economic crises (beginning in 2008), which have also affected Europe, greater emphasis has been made on the economic and social components of environmental sustainability education. These two components are being implemented, taking into consideration the green economy, citizenship, community cohesion, equal opportunities, and the development of human capital.

These issues are all being addressed through various national, bilateral, and European programs and networks in formal and informal education. In Romania, a national initiative, entitled the Second Chance Program, was established to address the social dimension of sustainable development by focusing on providing disadvantaged pupils (who dropped out of school) with an additional opportunity to gain formally recognized skills and competencies (Directorate-General [DG] Education and Culture 2008). In France, Germany, Greece, Italy, and the Netherlands, however, the environmental and sustainability education priorities are sustainable consumption and lifestyles along with sustainable transportation solutions (UNECE 2009). Students, teachers, the business sector, and local communities examine these topics through their participation in joint initiatives and activities. Overall, it can be argued that EE and ESD issues occupy a significant place at both the national and regional levels in Europe. Challenging questions remain, however: What are the appropriate learning contexts in which these issues can be examined effectively in a systematic and holistic manner? And how can these become mainstream rather than marginal issues?

EE and ESD Issues in West and Central Asia

The countries of West and Central Asia must be examined in light of their vast differences in needs, education systems, and environmental, cultural, and economic conditions and in the context of the political instability and conflicts that exist in the region. Within this framework, environmental and sustainability education is a mosaic of contrasts. For some countries, these issues are marginal or at an embryonic stage, while for others they constitute vital parts of the formal, nonformal, and informal educational curricula and are closely connected with a qualitative improvement in their educational systems.

Countries such as Syria, Jordan, Lebanon, Iraq, and the Palestinian territories face common problems related to peace and human security, conflict resolution, the role of women in the workplace and in the production sector, and biodiversity and climate change (UNESCO 2008), but, unfortunately, the slow reformation of these countries' educational systems and the absence of a clear policy on sustainability has not allowed them to introduce these matters as key educational issues (Hamad 2010). Israel, Armenia, and Cyprus, on the other hand, examine environmental and sustainability education issues in the context of holistic educational approaches. EE and ESD are incorporated in school curricula, mainly using an interdisciplinary method or integrating them within other subject matter (rather than by segregating EE as a separate subject) (UNECE 2012). They also attempt to connect schools with society by studying questions of global, regional, and national interest, such as waste management, water supplies, production processes dependent on nonrenewable resources, consumerism, biodiversity, climate change, and desertification.

By considering the specific regional context and the problems common to all who live there, the development of cooperation for the implementation of environmental and sustainability education provides a platform for building relations of mutual understanding and respect among peoples and nations and contributes to peace—a necessary foundation for moving toward a sustainable future.

Implications

Given the complexity of these educational issues, it is clear that the challenges that environmental and sustainability education face are numerous, especially in the Afro-Eurasia region, given the enormity of the poverty and cultural conflicts that are endemic there. This fact underscores the importance of examining the interrelationships among the environmental, social, and economic aspects of sustainability. It is also critical that educators be responsive to the diversity of stakeholders' perspectives and the sociocultural and political contexts in which education takes place. Any future orientation for EE/EfS should address the need to empower all citizens, young and old, by encouraging their engagement in investigating, debating, and taking action on sustainability issues. In addition, in the face of potentially overwhelming global threats (such as climate change), educators need to foster hope by accenting local stories that demonstrate creative approaches to building the adaptive capacities of individuals and communities.

Robert B. STEVENSON
James Cook University, Cairns, Australia

Fiona MWANIKI
Farmer Voice Radio, Nairobi, Kenya

Aravella ZACHARIOU
Cyprus Pedagogical Institute, Nicosia, Cyprus

See also Africa (*several articles*); Central Asia; Climate Change Refugees (Africa); Education, Higher (Africa); Immigrants and Refugees; Microfinance; Rural Development

FURTHER READING

Balasubramanian, Vethaiya; Sie, Moussa; Hijmans, Robert J.; & Otsuka, Keijiro. (2007). Increasing rice production in the sub-Saharan Africa: Challenges and opportunities. *Advances in Agronomy, 94*(6), 55–133.

Brundtland Commission. (1987). *Our common future: Report of the World Commission on Environment and Development.* Oxford, UK: Oxford University Press.

Chakeredza, Sebastian; Temu, August B.; Yaye, Aissetou; Mukangwa, Steven; & Saka, John D. K. (2009). Mainstreaming climate change into agricultural education: Challenges and perspectives (ICRAF working paper no. 82). Nairobi, Kenya: World Agroforestry Centre.

Council of European Union (CEU). (2006). Review of the EU Sustainable Development Strategy. Retrieved June 15, 2012, from http://register.consilium.europa.eu/pdf/en/06/st10/st10917.en06.pdf

Directorate-General (DG) Education and Culture. (2008). Inventory of innovative practices in education for sustainable development—final report. Brussels, Belgium: GHK.

Economic Commission for Africa. (2002). Harnessing technologies for sustainable development. In Bruce Ross-Larson et al. (Eds.), *Sustaining natural assets and reducing human vulnerability* (pp. 21–44). Washington, DC: Communications Development Incorporated.

European Environment Agency (EAA). (2007). *Europe's environment—the fourth assessment.* Copenhagen, Denmark: EEA.

Fensham, Peter. (1976). *A report on the Belgrade workshop on environmental education.* Canberra, Australia: Curriculum Development Centre.

Fien, John, & Tilbury, Daniella. (2002). The global challenge of sustainability. In Daniella Tilbury, Robert Stevenson, John Fien & Danie Schroeder (Eds.), *Education and sustainability: Responding to the global challenge* (pp. 1–12). Geneva: International Union for Conservation of Nature (IUCN).

Hamad, Shafik. (2010, January 28–30). *National seminar: Towards an educational strategy for sustainable development.* Damascus, Syria: Department of Ecumenical Relations and Development & Minster of State for Environmental Issues in Syria.

Jickling, Bob. (1992). Why I don't want my children to be educated for sustainable development. *Journal of Environmental Education, 23*(4), 5–8.

Kollmuss, Anja, & Agyeman, Julian. (2002). Mind the gap: Why do people act environmentally and what are the barriers to pro-environmental behavior? *Environmental Education Research, 8*(3), 239–260.

Nampinga, Rachael. (2008, February 25–March 7). Gender perspectives on climate change: Commission on the Status of Women fifty-second session (Emerging Issues panel). New York: Commission on the Status of Women.

Sato, Makiko. (2006, May 1–3). Evolving environmental education and its relation to EPD and ESD (Paper presented at the UNESCO Expert Meeting on Education for Sustainable Development [ESD]: Reorienting education to address sustainability). Kanchananaburi, Thailand: UNESCO.

Smyth, John. (1995). Environment and education: A view of a changing scene. *Environmental Education Research, 1*(1), 3–20.

Stevenson, Robert B. (1997). Schooling and environmental/sustainability education: From discourses of policy and practice to discourses of professional learning. *Environmental Education Research, 13*(2), 265–285.

Stevenson, Robert B. (2007). Schooling and environmental/sustainability education: From discourses of policy and practice to discourses of professional learning. *Environmental Education Research, 13*(2), 265–285.

Tbilisi Declaration. (1978). Toward an action plan: A report on the Intergovernmental Conference on Environmental Education. Washington, DC: US Government Printing Office.

Trainer, Stuart. (1994). If you really want to save the environment. *Australian Journal of Environmental Education, 10*(1), 59–70.

United Nations Economic Commission for Europe (UNECE). (2005). UNECE strategy for education for sustainable development. Retrieved March 12, 2012, from http://www.unece.org/fileadmin/DAM/env/documents/2005/cep/ac.13/cep.ac.13.2005.3.rev.1.e.pdf

United Nations Economic Commission for Europe (UNECE). (2009). Addressing sustainable consumption, production and transportation through education for sustainable development: Analysis of good practices. Retrieved March 12, 2012, from http://www.unece.org/fileadmin/DAM/env/documents/2009/ECE/AC.25/ece.ac.25.2009.4.e.pdf

United Nations Economic Commission for Europe (UNECE). (2012). *Learning from each other: Achievements, challenges and ways forward.* Retrieved March 12, 2012, from http://www.unece.org/fileadmin/DAM/env/esd/7thMeetSC/Official_Docs/SynthesisReport/ece.cep.ac.13.2012.3e.pdf

United Nations Educational, Scientific and Cultural Organization (UNESCO). (2008). *Regional guiding framework of education for sustainable development in the Arab Region.* Beirut, Lebanon: UNESCO Regional Bureau for Education in the Arab States.

United Nations Educational, Scientific and Cultural Organization's Educating for a Sustainable Future: Environment, Population and Sustainable Development Program (UNESCO-EPD). (1997, December 8–12). Thessaloniki Declaration (International conference). Environment and society: Education and public awareness for viability. Thessaloniki, Greece: UNESCO-EPD.

United Nations Environment Programme (UNEP). (2009). A preliminary stocktaking: Organisations and projects focused on climate change adaptation in Africa. In Musonda Mumba & Brian Harding (Eds.), *Stocktaking report contributing to the Africa Adaptation Network as an integral part of the Global Adaptation Network facilitated by UNEP* (pp. 16–22). Nairobi, Kenya: UNEP.

Williams, Charles, & Kniveton, Dominic. (Eds.). (2011). *African climate and climate change: Physical, social and political perspectives. (Advances in global research 43).* Dordrecht, the Netherlands: Springer Science+Business Media.

Education, Higher (Africa)

Africa's higher education is critical to promoting the sustainability of the continent's environment, although there are anxieties about its capacity to educate and equip citizens with the skills necessary for life and well-being on a continent beset by complex and interdependent socioeconomic and environmental challenges. These challenges can provide a framework for revitalizing higher education, though several paradigm shifts will also be critical to enhancing the contribution of higher education to sustainability.

Expansion in gross domestic product (GDP) in sub-Saharan Africa (SSA) has accelerated from a low annual average of 2 percent in the 1990s to more than 5 percent between 2002 and 2009. This remarkable economic turnaround is the result of economic reforms that have evened out market imperfections and reduced trade barriers, hence accelerating global demand for exports of Africa's natural resources. Consequently, increased earnings have stimulated investments in Africa's primary sector, fueling demand for skilled labor, energy, food, urban housing, and other services.

Despite these impressive gains, Africa's growth is fragile. Real and sustainable growth will be stymied by persistent difficulties that emerge from interactions and feedback among complex political, social, economic, institutional, and environmental factors. These factors include (1) poor governance, (2) low agricultural productivity, (3) unplanned urbanization, (4) natural resource scarcity (water, land, vegetation, and biodiversity), (5) poverty, (6) hunger and malnutrition, (7) climate change, and (8) high disease burden. A critical mass of an educated citizenry is urgently needed to deal with these problems. Higher education can be the engine that drives Africa's development in the twenty-first century and beyond.

Africa's socioeconomic and environmental challenges present unprecedented opportunities for integrated solutions that are sustainable and resilient over time. Incorporating advances in science, engineering, social sciences, humanities, and the arts is a crucial primary mechanism to catalyze the development of viable solution options for sustainable development in Africa's higher education.

Current State

Africa's higher education has suffered deep stagnation. For many decades, African governments and donor agencies have placed more emphasis on primary and adult literacy. For instance, the World Education Forum in Dakar, Senegal, in 2000 generated a movement called Education for All, which prioritized basic education and adult literacy as key drivers of social welfare. The reason for the historically low emphasis on higher education is partly because earlier studies by economists, including the US economist Milton Friedman, suggested there was no evidence that higher education yielded social benefits over and above those accrued by the individual students (Friedman and Friedman 1980).

In a review of twenty-two Poverty Reduction Strategy Papers (PRSPs) and nine interim PRSPs from African countries, the US public health economist David Bloom and colleagues (2005) observed that only two countries planned to increase tertiary education budgets, while six countries explicitly planned to cut funding. International donor agencies have abetted, inadvertently, African governments' neglect of higher education. Africa is starved of resources. For example, international aid in support of higher education is on average US$600 million annually, or one-quarter of all aid to the education sector in sub-Saharan Africa (World Bank 2010).

Persistent underinvestment in higher education in Africa is evidenced by low enrollment rates. Gross enrollment in Africa's higher education was just 5 percent in 2005, compared to 11 percent in India, 20 percent in China, and 70 percent in the Organisation for Economic Co-operation and Development (OECD) countries (UNESCO 2009). The 5 percent average belies large differences among countries. For instance, the gross enrollment rate in higher education was 1 percent in Tanzania, 4 percent in Kenya, 8 percent in Cote d'Ivoire, 10 percent in Nigeria, 15 percent in South Africa, and 31 percent in Tunisia (UNESCO-UIS 2009).

The issues of enrollment, retention, and completion of education must be understood in the wider socioeconomic context, however. For instance, the introduction of free primary education led to an upsurge in enrollment but that does not guarantee retention and completion, especially among children from marginalized communities, particularly girls. Moreover, the persistent low public investment in education is a contributing factor to poor educational infrastructure and poor quality of teaching.

Low public investment and spending in higher education has precipitated further declines in quality and relevance of curricula, the quality of the graduate, and the output of scientific as well as artistic products such as peer reviewed publications or products or design prototypes. Africa's published research papers only amount to 0.7 percent of the global total (TFHE 2000). This means Africa's scholars are not doing enough to generate local knowledge that could provide potential homegrown solutions to Africa's urgent social, institutional, technological, and environmental problems.

The economic growth benefit of higher education is only one dimension. An equally important but often ignored dimension is education's contribution to enhancing capability of the state through robust governance and effective service delivery. This can only be delivered through a cadre of well-educated and skilled civil service workers. But decades of underinvestment in higher education have caused what the US economist Lant Pritchett and colleagues (2010) have described as state capability traps because state bureaucracy is largely dominated by poorly educated personnel. A 2011 audit of higher education revealed that, nearly fifty years after independence, only 10 percent of Kenya's public servants had attained higher education. Similarly, in 1998, less than 3 percent of Mozambique's national public administration staff had higher education (Republic of Mozambique 2001).

In Zambia, a country with a population of about thirteen million, the current patient-doctor ratio is 1:15,000, which is far lower than the ratio of 1:5,000 recommended by the World Health Organization (Mukasa 2009). This is partly explained by the fact that Zambia has a single

medical school, at the University of Zambia, which graduates about fifty physicians each year. In Zambia, deaths from preventable diseases are rising and life expectancy is falling. Similarly in Ghana, one of Africa's more progressive countries, low quality and quantity of critical, high-level skills give cause for concern. Weak capacity is a major problem in most African countries, affecting all tiers of government, and is likely to get worse (Commission for Africa 2005, 137–138). Africa's capacity to deliver on its commitments to global development goals is therefore at risk.

Besides low investment and low enrollment and academic output, higher education in Africa suffers from programs in universities being out of touch with the needs of their countries. The report of the United Nations Economic Commission for Africa *Youth, Education, Skills and Employment* observed that Africa's youth face many challenges in gaining an education that equips them with the skills and knowledge needed by the labor market, which thus leads to high rates of unemployment among university graduates (UNECA 2005). The yawning supply-demand gap exacerbates the problem of graduate unemployment and further undermines the efficiency of public investment in tertiary education (Boateng and Ofori-Sarpong 2002).

The diminishing return on investment in basic education is now widely recognized. With this recognition comes the imperative to direct attention toward the hitherto neglected area of higher education. A critical motivation for the need to revitalize Africa's higher education is the growing dominance of the so-called knowledge economy. Based on research, intensive discussion, and hearings conducted over a two-year period, the Task Force on Higher Education and Society (TFHE), convened jointly by the World Bank and the United Nations Educational, Scientific and Cultural Organization (UNESCO), concluded that without more and better higher education, developing countries will find it increasingly difficult to benefit from the global knowledge-based economy (TFHE 2000). A key component of a knowledge-based economy is the premium value of high intellectual capability of citizens, as opposed to natural resources such as mineral ore or oil (Powell and Snellman 2004).

Rationale and Framework for Revitalization

A key issue that merits serious examination is the role Africa's higher education can play in developing and nurturing the knowledge, skills, and other attributes needed by professionals, teachers, and leaders to support equitable and sustainable development in the twenty-first century and beyond.

All regions of the world with the exception of Africa have recorded remarkable progress in key indicators of poverty reduction, food and nutrition, health (especially maternal and child health), and overall economic growth (Chen and Ravallion 2007). Moreover, Africa's raw material or commodity boom and the associated large resource receipts are unlikely to mitigate this exceptionalism due to low levels of governance capacity. Understanding the key factors or interventions that are necessary to reverse this exceptionalism is a top priority in the pursuit of sustainability for the African continent.

Africa is plagued by persistent conditions of extreme poverty, hunger, malnutrition, high disease burden, vulnerability to climate change, and weak governance. Higher education has a critical role to play by training professionals—including teachers, policy makers, and business leaders—to address these development obstacles. A study of four universities in four sub-regions revealed, however, that higher education in Africa currently contributes insufficiently to poverty reduction, and improvement of other levels of the education system (United Nations University 2009).

The broad consensus on the critical value of higher education in Africa's economic development has prompted action to revitalize and reform higher education, albeit to make it more responsive to contemporary societal needs. The Commission for Africa report recommended an investment of $500 million in institutions of higher education and $3 billion over ten years to develop centers of excellence in science and technology (Commission for Africa 2005). Revitalization of African universities was a major agenda item of the African Union's Plan of Action for 2004–2007. Moreover, a key objective of the African Union is to transform the African university into a "development university," responsive to local needs, while enhancing Africa's competitiveness in the global knowledge economy.

The difficulties that beset Africa require more than interventions that merely address the supply-demand gap in critical technical skill areas like engineering, medicine, information technology, and management. In addition to training in critical technical skill areas, professionals must possess sustainability literacy. Sustainability literacy is a paradigm shift from an emphasis on disciplinary expert knowledge to that of a systemic worldview, which encompasses a deep understanding of interdependence and interconnection between nature and socioeconomic development. Central to sustainability is the idea that decisions made today affect future socioeconomic and environmental outcomes, which in turn are critical determinants of human well-being.

The goal of educating a cadre of African professionals in skills related to a globalized and competitive workplace is noble, but it is inadequate to the broader aims of achieving equitable and sustainable development. Africa can progress rapidly on a sustainable development pathway if citizens, politicians, and professionals, including teachers, understand the principles of sustainability, and possess the skills necessary to critically evaluate information and propose options for action.

As they exist in 2012, however, Africa's higher education programs are ill equipped to cultivate the knowledge, skills, values, and life practices necessary to meet the challenges of sustainability. Any serious call for a truly transformative approach to higher education for sustainability will require change in the structural conventions of curricula, pedagogy, and assessments that underpin Africa's higher education systems. The World Summit on Sustainable Development (WSSD), held in Johannesburg, South Africa, in 2002 recognized the need to reorient national education systems to a vision of sustainability, linking economic growth with respect to social (human rights, identity, and security) and environmental (water, energy, land productivity) issues. According to the environmental scientists Gerd Michelsen of Germany and Peter Blaze Corcoran of the United States (2007, 296), recognition of the need to advance sustainability and include it in higher education curriculum promulgates two outcomes: the creation of dedicated courses that focus on sustainability, and the integration of sustainability into existing curricula.

The United Nations Decade of Education for Sustainable Development (DESD) and the Agenda 21 action plan—a product of the UN's Conference on Environment and Development (UNCED), held in Rio de Janeiro, Brazil, in 1992—both provide rich contexts for engaging the urgent need to advance sustainability education. At its fifty-seventh session in December 2002, the UN General Assembly declared 2005–2014 the DESD, emphasizing the critical role of education in achieving sustainable development (UNESCO 2003). Africa launched the DESD and its regional *Strategy of Education for Sustainable Development for Sub-Saharan Africa* in 2006 at the Association for the Development of Education in Africa's biennial meeting in Libreville, Gabon. Little has been done, however, to incorporate the concepts of sustainable development or education for sustainability into the higher education curricula.

Chapter 36 of Agenda 21, Education, Training, and Public Awareness, recognizes that education is critical for achieving environmental awareness, values, and attitudes consistent with sustainable development. The DESD draft proposal by UNESCO of August 2003 describes sustainable development as essentially an educational enterprise. Sustainability in the African context can be understood as harnessing social, economic, scientific, technological, and ecological resources to meet the needs of the present generation without compromising the capacity of future generations to meet their needs.

The major problems that beset Africa in 2012—poor governance, unplanned urbanization squalor, land degradation, high disease burden, poverty, vulnerability to climate change, hunger, and malnutrition—are not bound neatly within any single academic discipline. Current curriculum and degree requirements for a majority of African universities are determined by isolated departments or schools, and designed to satisfy national accreditation authorities. Moreover, conventional pedagogical methods give priority to didactic approaches centered on memorization and regurgitation and are built on the belief that knowledge is simply transferred from the professor to the student. This is inconsistent with contemporary views of epistemology and learning theory, which treat knowledge as constructed by the individual based on his or her prior knowledge and mental models. As such, pedagogies based solely on didactic approaches are thought to stifle processes like analytical reasoning, critical thinking, problem solving, and self-reflection (Dewey 1938).

Agenda 21 emphasizes the importance of new pedagogical approaches, including systems thinking, exposure to issues of equity and justice, and optimal strategies such as interdisciplinary learning and hands-on activities. Hence, higher education must not produce students of some subject matter, but students of problems (Popper 1963, 88). Curricular and pedagogical approaches, especially in higher education, must represent the complexity of the real world. Narrow disciplinary simplification would amount to abdication of intellectual duty.

To be relevant to its context and meet urgent societal needs, Africa's higher education must bring together, through interdisciplinary approaches, different epistemologies, including local knowledge, that mutually enrich each other. In particular, the variety of forms and systems of traditional knowledge across the African continent are vital assets in the pursuit of sustainability. For example, the Chagga home gardens are an indigenous multistrata agroforestry system practiced by smallholder farmers on the slopes of Mt. Kilimanjaro in Tanzania. These farming systems have remained sustainable because of the high degree of nutrient cycling and the continuous ground cover that they provide (Fernandes, Oktingati, and Maghembe 1983). Examples such as these provide relevant case study material for education for sustainability. Building coherence or consilience among different disciplines and epistemologies is critical in order to foster a systems-thinking framework for understanding the real world, which is increasingly governed by complex, interconnected systems that are dynamic and uncertain.

Systems thinking examines various complex systems and how they relate to one another. A systems-thinking approach to education imparts knowledge not as isolated facts on social, economic, technological, or environmental phenomena, but as an experience in holistic understanding of the complex and existential interdependence between humankind and the Earth's finite resources. Such an approach is central to education for sustainability because it enables the fusion of concepts and fact-based theory across disciplines to create a unifying framework for understanding the relationships between critical socioeconomic and environmental issues.

If Africa is to create conditions that will ensure a more sustainable future, higher education must enable the construction of knowledge, acquisition of skills, and cultivation of attitudes necessary to prepare college and university graduates to tackle the difficulties presented by population growth, poverty, climate change, resource scarcity (water, land, and vegetation), disease, and loss of biodiversity. As an essential part of sustainability literacy, Africa's higher education curricula must challenge old, inaccurate paradigms such as "maximum sustainable yield" and "man subduing nature" (Larkin 1977). Such paradigm shifts are singularly important for Africa at a time when sustainability is central to social, economic, political, and environmental progress.

The four pillars of education (Delors 1996)—learning to know, learning to do, learning to be, and learning to live—represent an intuitive framework for articulating the action competences, against which to evaluate learning outcomes in sustainability education. Action competence relates to a capacity for planning, participation, and emotional response as well as critical thinking and reflection. The growing relevance of competence-based outcomes in education, especially in education for sustainability, is based partly on the quest for an education model that is focused on producing graduates who have agency for and orientation to grappling with the problems that face society.

Way Forward

The Kenyan ecosystems ecologist Alex O. Awiti proposes five paradigm shifts, each considered critical to enhancing the contribution of Africa's higher education to socioeconomic and environmental sustainability.

The first paradigm shift involves ensuring that the fundamental goal of higher education is sustainability literacy through acquisition of knowledge, skills, and attitudes that enhance sustainable development. Graduates literate in sustainability are likely to be individuals with motivations and action competence, which enables them to make choices that do not deplete vital environmental resources.

The second paradigm shift places greater emphasis on problem-based approaches to teaching and learning, which encourage cooperative, inquiry-based, and experiential learning, along with reflective practice. These approaches support retention and application knowledge, leading to action competence needed for sustainability.

Placing greater emphasis on knowledge integration, rather than reductionist and disciplinary focus, in curriculum design is the basis for the third paradigm shift. For instance, curricula of such fields as engineering, religion, artistic design, biotechnology, and Earth sciences must require students to understand the complex dynamic interplay among real-world issues like ethics, politics, economics, governance, and environmental change.

Greater adoption of technology is the fourth paradigm shift, and it will expand access to higher education through distance learning, enhance the quality of teaching and learning, and increase collaboration among African universities and with the rest of the world. More importantly, technology supports active learning, allowing students to be much more engaged in constructing their own knowledge.

The fifth paradigm shift involves encouraging partnership in education for sustainability through effective community engagement, where the university works in collaboration with the community to define and solve problems at the local level. Professional and continuing education should focus on increasing the knowledge, skills, and understanding needed to develop attitudes and moral reasoning necessary to promote sustainability. Students and faculty must grapple with real-world problems, which are brought to them by societal stakeholders, while simultaneously learning about and contributing to sustainable changes in society.

Alex O. AWITI

Aga Khan University, Nairobi, Kenya

See also Africa (*several articles*); African Union (AU); Biodiversity Conservation; Education, Environmental; Genetic Resources; Microfinance; Migration (Africa); Public-Private Partnerships (Africa); Rule of Law (Africa); World Bank

FURTHER READING

Bloom, David; Canning, David; & Chan, Kevin. (2005). *Higher education and economic development in Africa.* Cambridge, MA: Harvard University Press.

Boateng, Kwabia, & Ofori-Sarpong, E. (2002). *An analytical study of the labor market for tertiary graduates in Ghana.* Washington, DC: World Bank/ National Council for Tertiary Education and the National Accreditation Board Project.

Chen, Shaohua, & Ravallion, Martin. (2007). Absolute poverty measures for the developing world, 1984–2004. *Proceedings of the National Academy of Sciences, 104*(43), 16757–16762.

Commission for Africa. (2005). *Our common interest: Report of the Commission for Africa.* London: Commission for Africa.

Delors, Jacques, et al. (1996). *Learning: The treasure within, report to UNESCO of the International Commission on Education for the Twenty-First Century.* Paris: UNESCO Publishing Press.

Dewey, John. (1938). *Experience and education.* New York: Macmillan.

Friedman, Milton, & Friedman, Rose. (1980). *Free to choose: A personal statement.* New York: Harcourt Brace Jovanovich.

Fernandes, E.C.M.; Oktingati, A.; & Maghembe, J. (1983). The Chagga home gardens: A multi-storeyed agro-forestry cropping system on Mt. Kilimanjaro, northern Tanzania. *Agroforestry Systems, 1*(3), 269–273.

Larkin, Peter A. (1977). An epitaph for the concept of maximum sustained yield. *Transactions of the American Fisheries Society, 106*(1), 1–11.

Michelsen, Gerd, & Corcoran, Peter Blaze. (2007). Epilogue. In Joop de Kraker, Angelique Lansu & Rietje van Dam-Mieras (Eds.), *Crossing boundaries: Innovative learning for sustainable development in higher education: Vol. 2* (pp. 295–299). Frankfurt, Germany: VAS.

Mukasa, Emmanuel. (2009). The human resource crisis in the Zambian Health Sector: A discussion paper. *Medical Journal of Zambia, 35*(3), 80–87.

Popper, Karl R. (1963). *Conjectures and refutations: The growth of scientific knowledge.* New York: Harper Torchbooks.

Powell, Walter W., & Snellman, Kaisa. (2004). The knowledge economy. *Annual Review of Sociology, 30*(1), 199–220.

Pritchett, Lant M.; Woolcock, Michael; & Andrews, Matthew. (2010). *Capability traps? The mechanisms of persistent implementation failure* (CGD Working Paper 234). Washington, DC: Center for Global Development.

Republic of Mozambique. (2001). *Action plan for the reduction of absolute poverty (PARPA) (2001–2005).* Maputo, Mozambique: Republic of Mozambique.

Task Force on Higher Education and Society (TFHE). (2000). *Higher education in developing countries: Peril and promise.* Washington, DC: World Bank.

United Nations Economic Commission for Africa (UNECA). (2005). *Youth, education, skills and employment.* Addis Ababa, Ethiopia: UNECA.

United Nations Educational, Scientific and Cultural Organization (UNESCO). (2003). *United Nations decade of education for sustainable development (2005–2014): The first two years.* Paris: UNESCO. Retrieved June 5, 2010, from http://tinyurl.com/6m88jg7

United Nations Educational, Scientific and Cultural Organization Institute for Statistics (UNESCO-UIS). (2009). *Global education digest 2009.* Montreal: UIS.

United Nations University. (2009). *Revitalizing higher education in sub-Saharan Africa: A United Nations university project.* Tokyo: United Nations University.

World Bank. (2010). *Financing higher education in Africa.* Washington, DC: World Bank.

Energy Security (Europe)

The European Union (EU) plays an important role in Europe's energy security. To ensure Europe's energy security, the EU has strengthened relations with Russia and other oil- and gas-supplying states and also has tried to build a sustainable and competitive internal energy system, but to increase its energy independence, the EU must pay more attention to sustainable development and the development of low-carbon energy and technology.

Europe plays a very important role in global energy security. Although European integration has made great progress, the energy security situation in Europe has not been changed fundamentally since 2000. Of course, the idea of sustainable development brings new understanding to Europe regarding energy security, especially for the European Union (EU). The EU has started to link energy security to sustainable development.

Energy Security since 2000

Generally speaking, energy supply, price, and energy structure are the primary factors impacting energy security. Of these three factors, the most severe threat to energy security would be an abrupt disruption in energy supply. As far as energy price is concerned, prices that are too high or too low would have similarly significant adverse effects, which can make energy production unstable. Energy structure also holds a key position in energy security. When energy production or consumption unduly relies on a certain kind of energy, such as coal or oil, it is more vulnerable to varying energy trends.

Since 2000, the energy security situation in Europe has not been changed fundamentally, especially in the external environment. The EU is a net import area in

energy, which puts it in a very unstable situation. (See figure 1 on page 124.)

Increasing Conflicts in Oil- and Gas-Supplying Areas

Energy supply for the EU comes mainly from five areas: Russia, Norway, the Middle East, Africa, and Latin America. Since 2000, conflicts in some of these areas have been increasing. Russia is the largest energy supplier for the EU, for example, providing 33 percent of oil imports and 40 percent of gas imports (Europe's Energy Portal 2009).Gas disputes between Russia and Ukraine thus directly impact EU energy security. Conflicts in the Middle East and Africa as well as energy nationalism in Latin America have also had some influence on European energy security.

International Crude Oil Prices

After the oil crisis in the 1970s, international crude oil prices hovered at a relatively low price, although during the Gulf War in 1991 and the Asian financial crisis in 1999, crude oil prices fluctuated wildly. Crude oil prices continued to rise from 1999 to 2001, which was the longest period of increasing oil prices since 1861. In July 2008, oil prices soared to a record US$145 per barrel. In December 2008, the price rapidly declined to US$32 per barrel. (See figure 2 on page 124.)

This rapid and sharp fluctuation of international oil prices resulted in the reduction of energy investment and new energy development slowdown. The EU was severely affected, which sparked extensive debate about whether to continue to research and develop renewable energy technology.

Figure 1. Import Dependency of the European Union (Percentages)

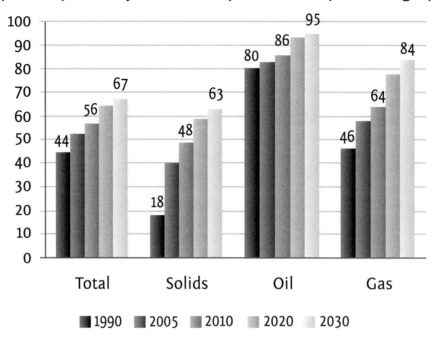

Source: European Commission (2008).

The percentages of energy resources the European Union imports, projecting to the year 2030. Reliance on external sources puts the EU's energy security at risk.

Figure 2. International Oil Prices in USD per Barrel/Year

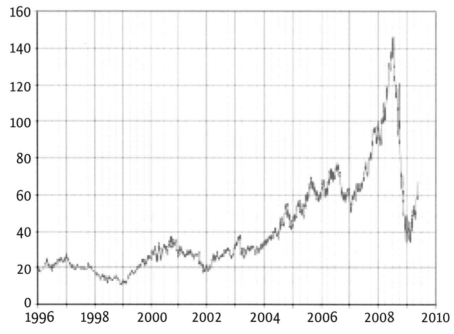

Source: OilPrices.org (2010).

Oil prices increased to the record US$145 per barrel in 2008 followed by a sharp decrease, mainly due to the worldwide economic downturn. Such sudden and extreme changes in price can make energy production unstable.

Laws and Policies

The earliest EU law concerning energy security dates back to the basic treaties of the European Community. Article 3 of the treaty establishing the European Coal and Steel Community states, "The institutions of the Community shall, within the limits of their respective powers, in the common interest: . . . (d) ensure the maintenance of conditions which will encourage undertakings to expand and improve their production potential and to promote a policy of using natural resources rationally and avoiding their unconsidered exhaustion" (ECSC 1951). The treaty did not, however, reflect the energy supply security in detail because at that time energy security was not a real problem for the European countries. In the 1970s, two oil crises struck Europe. The EU started to strengthen its laws and policies to ensure energy security. Efforts fell into two main categories: building up the EU internal energy market and strengthening external energy relations with oil- and gas-rich countries.

Internal Energy Market

The establishment of the EU internal energy market can be traced to the Single European Act of 1987. The EU member states agreed to adopt measures to progressively establish a common market over a period that would conclude on 31 December 1992.

In 1988, the idea of a well-functioning internal energy market was first spelled out by the European Commission. A commission working document regarding the internal energy market was put forward. The document envisioned a common carrier system for gas and electricity across the member states in which any consumer could purchase energy from any supplier across the Community, regardless of ownership of the intermediary grid structures. Member states, however, had different views as to how far the integration and liberalization of the energy sector should be pursued.

During the period of 1988–2006, the EU passed several laws based on two energy packages put forward regarding internal energy market regulation. The first energy package included the 1990 directive concerning a Community procedure to improve the transparency of gas and electricity prices charged to industrial end users, the 1991 directive on the transit of natural gas through grids, the 1996 electricity directive, and the 1998 gas directive. The second energy package included the 2003 electricity directive and the 2003 gas directive. These directives have helped to strengthen further the EU internal energy market, especially in electricity and gas market integration.

The two energy packages were a necessary but insufficient step toward achieving the end goal of a functional EU internal energy market. Many issues remained unresolved even after the directives were enacted. First, all EU gas markets, except in the Nordic countries, were still controlled at the national level in the economic field. Second, in the absence of well-developed cross-border competition, the structure of national markets has problems. Third, many member states were late in implementing the directives, and some of the member states still have not done so as of 2012 (European Commission 2011, 3). The EU needs a new energy package to tackle these problems.

External Energy Relations

To ensure energy security, in addition to building an internal energy market, the EU has worked to establish external relations with oil- and gas-rich countries. The EU entered into the Energy Charter Treaty (ECT), a multilateral treaty that went into effect in 1998. The ECT provides rules on energy trade, foreign investment protection, energy transport, energy efficiency, and energy dispute settlement. The purpose of the ECT is to reduce cross-border energy investment risk and to ensure that producers, consumers, and transit states apply common rules. In fact, the ECT is mainly for strengthening energy investment and transport with Russia and eastern European countries. The EU made ratification of the ECT a requirement for becoming an EU member state. As of 2012, the members of the ECT are negotiating about the charter protocol regarding energy transit.

The EU has made great efforts to strengthen energy cooperation and energy dialogue with oil- and gas-rich countries. Russia, as a large energy supplier, has always been of major importance to the EU in external energy relations, but since 2006, disputes between Russia and Ukraine have had indirect effects on EU energy security. Although Russia signed the ECT, its parliament did not ratify the ECT. Also, on 20 August 2009, Russia informed the depository of the ECT that it did not intend to become a contracting party of the treaty, thereby terminating Russia's provisional application of the ECT.

In 1994, the EU and Russia established the Partnership and Co-operation Agreement (PCA), which entered into force in 1997 and expired in 2007. Both parties seek to negotiate a new agreement to replace the PCA, but it is not easy for the EU and Russia to find common ground in political and economic negotiations. The EU chooses to engage Russia in a dialogue about energy, rather than other issues, to ensure energy supply security.

In addition to negotiations with Russia, the EU also strengthened energy cooperation with other oil- and gas-rich countries. In 2008, the EU and sixteen Mediterranean countries concluded the plan on the Barcelona Process: Union for the Mediterranean, which would further ensure EU energy supply security. Barcelona Process aims to inject a renewed political momentum into Euro-Mediterranean relations; the members decided to launch a number of initiatives, including Alternative Energies: Mediterranean Solar Plan (Council of the EU 2008).

Sustainable Development

With the widespread concern about environmental issues, the idea of sustainable development has become important in the field of energy security. Energy security includes not only energy supply and price safeguards but also needs to consider the environmental impact of energy use. In other words, although there may be sufficient fossil energy, such as oil, coal, or gas, to ensure energy security for the immediate future, it is not sustainable for long-term energy security. Sustainable development in the energy field not only can decrease air pollution but also may improve energy independence and sufficiency. Renewable energy may extend energy supply. Energy-saving technology may decrease energy consumption. Development of such resources therefore would help to ensure energy security. At present, sustainable energy is still only a small part of energy production and consumption. It cannot completely replace fossil energy yet because of outside and inside limitations for sustainable energy, such as incomplete marketization, disadvantageous energy technology, and some negative policies.

In 1997, sustainable development was included in the Treaty of Amsterdam as a fundamental objective of the EU. At the Gothenburg Summit in 2001, EU leaders launched the first EU sustainable development strategy. From 2006 to 2009, the EU revised and reviewed its sustainable development strategy. Based on this review, the idea of the sustainable development was included in the EU's climate change and energy policies.

In 2006, the European Commission published "A European Strategy for Sustainable, Competitive and Secure Energy," in which sustainable development was established as a pillar of the EU energy strategy (EU 2006). This paper proposed that balancing the goals of sustainable energy use, competitiveness, and security of supply would need to be done on the basis of a thorough impact assessment. The paper also suggested establishing a benchmark for assessing the EU's developing energy mix to help stem the increasing dependence on imports.

In 2007, the European Commission adopted a third package of legislative proposals to liberalize energy markets. Sustainable development is an important component of the third package, which specifically includes provisions for increasing sustainability and low-carbon energy by developing renewable energy resources,

biofuels, and sustainable fossil-fuel technologies. In addition, the third package promotes sustainability by stimulating energy efficiency and guaranteeing that small companies, particularly those investing in renewable energy, have access to the energy market.

In November 2008, the European Commission proposed a new strategic energy review, the EU's second, that primarily dealt with three challenges: the internal energy market, energy efficiency, and international energy policy. This strategic energy review required measures to make transport more efficient and improve the energy performance of buildings, to promote international agreement on energy efficiency, and to increase the use of renewable resources in the EU's overall energy mix. The European Commission also suggested increased research into sustainable fossil fuels.

In 2010, the European Commission put forth the Energy 2020 strategy, which focused on reducing energy consumption, implementing the internal market, developing infrastructure, improving technology, protecting consumers, and reinforcing the external dimensions of energy policy. These goals will be achieved by a series of legislative proposals. Energy 2020 also stresses the importance of renewable energy and development of better energy technology.

Climate Change

Since the 1990s, global climate change has become increasingly important in the international community. It is necessary to reduce greenhouse gas (GHG) emissions in the energy field because carbon emission from energy consumption is the main cause of global warming. In 1997, the Kyoto Protocol was passed, which obligated the EU to reduce GHG emissions by 8 percent. This binding environmental obligation has put more pressure on EU energy security.

In January 2008, the European Commission put forth an integrated proposal for climate action. This package of proposals emphasized the EU's climate change targets, which required promoting the development of renewable energy. In April 2009, a concomitant new directive entered into force regarding promotion of the use of energy from renewable sources. This directive provides stable and predictable support strategies to promote the needed investments in clean, renewable energy technologies. The approach of maintaining well-known and effective national support strategies and gradually implementing a voluntary trading mechanism secures important and needed investment stability for the coming years. Moreover, it increases transparency and provides investors and the industry with a clear indication of renewable development in all countries through the development of national action plans and ongoing reporting to the European Commission. It also helps overcome many of the barriers for the development of clean energy technology in Europe in connection with the development of grid connection and the improvement of the national planning processes.

According to the EU climate and energy package, many member states have drawn up their own national plans. For example, in 2009, the United Kingdom enacted its Climate Change Act. Germany also revised its Renewable Energy Act in 2008. These national legislations undoubtedly contribute to sustainable energy development in the EU.

Outlook

Both the EU's internal energy market and its external relations are being strengthened through its energy laws and policies, but if the EU wants to fundamentally change its energy security situation, it must pay more attention to sustainable development. Only through development of low-carbon energy and technology can the EU increase its energy independence. Fortunately, the EU is already working toward this goal. The proportion of renewable energy in the EU energy mix rose to 10 percent of the gross final energy consumption in 2008. In 2009, 62 percent of newly installed electricity generation capacity in the EU was from renewable sources, mainly wind and solar (EU 2010). In December 2011, to further reduce the EU's GHG emission, the European Council put forth Energy Roadmap 2050, providing the framework for long-term action in the energy sectors. The future of the EU's energy system development will be driven by the need for energy security, sustainability, and competitiveness in a changing global energy context.

Jiang LU
Shanxi University

See also European Union (EU); European Union Greenhouse Gas Emission Trading Scheme (EU ETS); France; Germany; Mediterranean Sea; Middle East; Rule of Law (European Union); Russia and the Soviet Union; Scandinavia; Shipping and Freight; Ukraine

FURTHER READING

Bamberger, Craig S.; Linehan, Jan; & Wälde, Thomas. (2000). Energy charter treaty in 2000: In a new phase. *Journal of Energy & Natural Resources Law, 18*(4), 331–352.

Cameron, Peter. (2005). *Legal aspects of EU energy regulation: Implementing the new directives on electricity and gas across Europe.* Oxford, UK: Oxford University Press.

Council of the European Union (EU). (2008, November 4). Barcelona Process: Union for the Mediterranean ministerial conference. Retrieved June 12, 2012, from http://www.consilium.europa.eu/ueDocs/cms_Data/docs/pressData/en/misc/103733.pdf

de Jong, Jacques, & Weeda, Ed. (2008). *Europe, the EU and its 2050 energy storylines.* The Hague, The Netherlands: 2007 Clingendael International Energy Programme.

Eikeland, Per Ove. (2008). *EU internal energy market policy: New dynamics in the Brussels policy game?* Lysaker, Norway: Fridtjof Nansen Institute.

Emerson, Michael; Tassinari, Fabrizio; & Vahl, Marius. (2006). A new agreement between the EU and Russia: Why, what and when? In Michael Emerson (Ed.), *The elephant and the bear try again: Options for a new agreement between the EU and Russia.* Brussels, Belgium: The Centre for European Policy Studies.

Europe's Energy Portal. (2009). Homepage. Retrieved May 18, 2012, from http://www.energy.eu

The European Coal and Steel Community (ECSC). (1951). Treaty. Retrieved June 12, 2012, from http://personal.ashland.edu/jmoser1/ecsc.htm

European Commission. (2008). European energy and transport, trends to 2030—Update 2007. Retrieved June 8, 2012, from http://www.e3mlab.ntua.gr/reports/energy_transport_trends_2030_update_2007_en.pdf

European Commission. (2011). *2009–2010 report on progress in creating the internal gas and electricity market.* Brussels, Belgium: European Commission.

European Union (EU). (2006). *Green paper: A European strategy for sustainable, competitive and secure energy.* Brussels, Belgium: The EU. Retrieved June 8, 2012, from http://europa.eu/documents/comm/green_papers/pdf/com2006_105_en.pdf

European Union (EU). (2008). *Second strategic energy review: An EU energy security and solidarity action plan.* Brussels, Belgium: The EU.

European Union (EU). (2010). *Energy 2020: A strategy for competitive, sustainable secure energy.* Brussels, Belgium: The EU.

European Union (EU). (2011a). *EU-Russia energy dialogue.* Brussels, Belgium: The EU.

European Union (EU). (2011b). *Energy roadmap 2050.* Brussels, Belgium: The EU.

Glachant, Jean-Michel. (2005). *Implementing the European internal energy market in 2005–2009: A proposal from academia.* Paris: ADIS Working Paper.

Klachenberg, Dag. (2004). *Rethinking the EU regulatory strategy for the internal energy market.* Brussels, Belgium: Centre for European Policy Studies.

OilPrices.org (2010). Oil price trends. Retrieved February 23, 2012, from http://www.oilprices.org/oil-price-trends.html

Rühl, Christof. (2008). *BP statistical review of world energy 2008.* London: BP Company. Retrieved May 18, 2012, from http://www.bp.com/liveassets/bp_internet/china/bpchina_english/STAGING/local_assets/downloads_pdfs/SR_SpeechAsia_ENG.pdf

Schmidt, John R. (2008). Why Europe leads on climate change. *Survival, 50*(4), 83–96.

Vasconcelos, Jorge. (2005). Towards the internal energy market: How to bridge a regulatory gap and build a regulatory framework. *European Review of Energy Markets, 1*(1), 1–17.

Wälde, Thomas W. (1996). *The energy chart treaty: An east-west gateway for investment and trade.* London: Kluwer Law International.

European Union (EU)

The European Union (EU) is a confederation of states that was formed in the mid-twentieth century. At its founding, the union's primary purpose was economic integration, but even then environmental protection was recognized as a limiting factor on market freedom. Since the 1990s the political mandate of the EU has expanded, with the expectation that its policies and activities will be guided by the ideal of sustainable development—both in Europe and throughout the world.

The European Union (EU) is a pioneer when it comes to sustainability, in that it is acting to meet the needs of the present without compromising the ability of following generations to meet the needs of the future. The EU traces its history to the beginning of European integration in the mid-twentieth century, when the European Communities (since absorbed into the EU by the Lisbon Treaty of 1 December 2009) created a Common Market for its participating states. Economic integration was the main intention then, but it was never the only intention: besides reconciliation among the former enemies of World War II, the founders of European integration also expected that economic integration would foster political integration. In a revolutionary act, they voted for a supranational model for the European Communities, and this model today governs most parts of the EU.

The EU is not just an international organization; it has independent organs and powers that go beyond what is customary for such a body under international law. Its laws and orders enjoy supremacy, and it can also intervene in the domestic sphere of its member states to address individuals and private legal entities directly. The nature of the EU's power is reflected in the various forms of action it can take, as specified in Article 288 of the Treaty on the Functioning of the European Union (TFEU). The most important legislative acts among these forms of action are regulations, directives, and decisions.

A regulation is comparable to an Act of Parliament: it is presented in general, abstract terms and immediately becomes law within all member states without requiring an implementing act on the part of the individual states. A regulation thus can be said to constitute a "European bill." In contrast, a directive is binding as to the results required, but member states are left with the choice of form and methods, and therefore an act of implementation is required. Finally, decisions are binding upon those states and individuals covered, but they may need both legislative and executive laws for enforcement. As a result of these supranational powers, EU policy has a tremendous impact on its member states, which has led to a high degree of coherence and consistency among their legal systems. Meanwhile, the political mandate of the EU has expanded since the 1990s, and within the scope of this statelike agenda the EU is charged with being guided by sustainability—in particular when it comes to environmental protection.

Sustainability Mandate

Sustainability is specifically included in the treaties as one of the EU's goals. Article 3(3) of the Treaty on European Union (TEU) requires the EU to work for the sustainable development in Europe and to balance economic and social aims with "a high level of protection and improvement of the quality of the environment." Paragraph 5 requires the EU even to contribute to "the sustainable development of the Earth." These mandates, although not granting powers in themselves, confer binding force in that they influence the interpretation of the entire treaty, including provisions that grant authority to the EU. This is especially true for the provisions concerning the environment, since Title XX of the TFEU, which addresses development cooperation, surprisingly does not refer to sustainability. It does, however, define the policy objectives of the EU on the environment—namely, the protection of the environment, the protection of human health, the rational utilization of natural resources, and international cooperation. Moreover, Article 191(2) introduces five principles to guide EU policy: (1) the *high level of protection principle*, according to which the EU must aim to ensure a high level of environmental protection; (2) the *precautionary principle*, which obliges member states to foresee and assess environmental threats, to warn potential victims, and to prevent and mitigate such threats; (3) the *preventive principle*, which mandates early intervention on behalf of the environment; (4) the *source principle*, which aims to rectify environmental damages at their source; and (5) the *polluter pays principle*, which stipulates that polluters should bear the cost of environmental damage. These objectives and principles do, in fact, serve the purpose of sustainability.

With regard to international relations, Article 21(2) of the TEU requires that the EU "shall define and pursue common policies and actions . . . in order to foster the sustainable economic, social and environmental development of developing countries." Furthermore, Article 37 of the EU Fundamental Rights Charter states that a "high level of environmental protection and the improvement of the quality of the environment must be integrated into the policies of the Union and ensured in accordance with the principle of sustainable development." Consequently, even though individual rights are not covered explicitly, addressing environmental concerns within a human-rights document underlines the close relationship between the environment, sustainable development, and human rights. Sustainability, therefore, is not only an objective aim in itself but is also supported from a natural-rights perspective.

Environmental Law and Sustainability

How do the general commitments presented above come into play in the law and policy of the EU? First, secondary legislation amplifies these commitments and provides additional specifics—like, for example, the regulations and directives on the protection of freshwater and marine living resources. Second, these commitments need to be taken into account not only with regard to the law and policy of the EU on environmental matters, but also in other areas, such as the free trade of goods. Finally, the EU seeks to promote the principle of sustainable development on the international level through its role as a party to multilateral environmental agreements (MEAs).

Secondary Legislation

Environmental damages do not respect national boundaries. For example, the pollution of freshwater is not a national but rather a European concern because nearly all EU member states share water resources. A decline in fish stocks—which often straddle thousands of kilometers—is another example of an environmental threat that affects all EU member states. Because common concerns require common policies, the EU has adopted a wide range of secondary legislation that covers transboundary environmental matters. Freshwater and fisheries are examples of the approaches taken by the EU on these matters, which include the prescription of general strategies, financial support to environmentally friendly initiatives, the active involvement of stakeholders and those affected by damage to the environment, and the establishment of firm standards and limits.

Freshwater

According to 2010 figures, 20 percent of Europe's land mass is seriously threatened by pollution, European groundwater resources are overexploited by up to 60 percent, and 50 percent of European wetlands are endangered (European Commission 2010b). In order to protect and preserve European freshwater, the EU adopted the far-reaching and innovative Water Framework Directive in 2000. According to this document, "[w]ater is not a commercial product like any other, but rather a heritage which must be protected, defended and treated as such." In contrast to previous legislative acts covering water, the Water Framework Directive does not establish emission limits or quality standards. Instead, it contains general strategies—such as creating basin-management plans or actively involving all parties affected by a particular issue—which member states must then implement to reach the stated goal of using inland surface water, groundwater, and coastal water (up to one nautical mile) sustainably. Through implementing the measures provided for in the Water Framework Directive, member states are expected to be able to achieve "good" ecological status (as defined by the Water Framework Proposal) of freshwater by 2015.

Fisheries

Because most European fish stocks are overexploited (European Commission 2010a), EU fisheries policy obviously has failed to ensure that marine living resources are used sustainably. The European Commission therefore has come up with a proposal that radically reforms fisheries policy and aims to bring all fish stocks to sustainable levels by 2015. This proposal introduces a decentralized ecosystem approach, with plans for long-term management that are based on scientific evidence. It includes clear targets and time frames, but allows member states to determine which conservation measures are the most appropriate to achieve these goals. According to the commission, these measures should aim to bring the size of fleets in line with fishing quotas, provide financial support to environmentally friendly initiatives, and provide information for consumers on the sustainability of the fish they buy. Finally, the proposal acknowledges the need to promote the sustainable use of marine living resources not only in the EU, but also in the rest of the world.

Sustainability and Free Trade

Article 11 of the TFEU stipulates that environmental protection requirements must be integrated "into the definition and implementation of the Union's policies and activities, in particular with a view to promoting sustainable development." That provision goes beyond an assurance of commitment; it establishes environmental protection and sustainability as general, cross-sectional responsibilities that govern the entire conduct of the EU and its member states within the scope of EU law. Under Article 11, environmental concerns have to be taken into consideration and balanced against conflicting interests before any measure is adopted, and these concerns must be integrated into the general agenda of the EU. Article 11 also includes a provision that allows for court review if necessary, meaning that within the purview of EU law, a country cannot escape environmental protection and sustainability.

Environmental protection had been recognized as a limiting factor on other principles of EU law, such as market freedom, even before the Treaties of the European Union had established clear mandates. In *Commission v. Denmark*, the European Court of Justice accepted environmental protection for the first time as a mandatory requirement that could restrict the free movement of goods. The court has emphasized that any measure, including those intended to protect the environment, must be proportional (*Radelberger v. Baden-Württemberg*)—although a total denial of market freedoms, like the absolute ban on the transboundary movement of hazardous waste, may be justified in situations that pose real danger to the environment (*Commission v. Belgium*). Often, though, market freedoms are concretized by EU secondary laws (regulations and directives), which exhaustively strike the balance between freedoms and environmental protection.

Multilateral Environmental Agreements

The EU, as a global player in the international environmental arena, is party to several MEAs. These include the Convention on Long-Range Transboundary Air Pollution, the Vienna Convention for the Protection of the Ozone Layer, the Basel Convention on the Control of Transboundary Movements of Hazardous Wastes and Their Disposal (known as the Basel Convention), and the United Nations Framework Convention on Climate Change (the UNFCCC). The EU is therefore bound to implement these commitments in its policies. The EU currently represents twenty-seven nations, among them economic giants like Germany as well as France and the United Kingdom, and consequently brings strength to the bargaining table in the negotiation of MEAs. It was successful in including an amendment to the Basel Convention that bans the transboundary movement of hazardous waste from developed to developing countries. Unfortunately, its voice was not heard at the conference of the parties to the UNFCCC in Copenhagen, Denmark. China and the United States in particular sidelined the EU and prevented the negotiation of a strong climate-change agreement. Ultimately, it is up to member states to grant the EU the ability to speak with one voice so that it may promote environmental protection in the international arena.

Model for Tomorrow

Sustainability is a principle that crosses all branches of government. It is a cause that governments must respect and serve, because not to address environmental problems may threaten the very existence of life on Earth—at least of the human race. Yet environmental challenges transcend national borders and the ability of the single state to find solutions, and so sustainability and environmental protection (as efforts to handle climate change exemplify) have become international concerns and crucial issues in world politics. Accordingly, a collective approach on the part of governments, in conjunction with international organizations, nongovernmental organizations (NGOs), and civil society, seems to be essential. The EU is a model of how to address sustainability on a supranational level and how to integrate it in policies that reconcile national political agendas. Time is against us, and other international actors should have a closer look at the EU's example—for a better tomorrow and for the sake of our children.

Michael Lysander FREMUTH and Erik PELLANDER
University of Cologne

See also African Union (AU); E-Waste; European Union Greenhouse Gas Emission Trading Scheme (EU ETS); Fisheries; France; Germany; International Conflict Resolution; Rule of Law (European Union); Transboundary Water Issues

FURTHER READING

Commission of the European Communities v. Kingdom of Belgium, Case C-2/90 (1992).

Commission of the European Communities v. Kingdom of Denmark, Case 302/86 (1988).

Dross, Miriam, & Bloch, Felix. (2004). The reform of the EU common fisheries policy: A step towards greater precaution in the conservation of fishery resources. *Environmental Law Network International Review, 1,* 17–25.

European Commission. (2009, April 22). Reform of the common fisheries policy (green paper). Brussels, Belgium: Commission of the European Communities. Retrieved August 29, 2011, from http://eur-lex.europa.eu/LexUriServ/LexUriServ.do?uri=COM:2009:0163:FIN:EN:PDF

European Commission. (2010a). *Facts and figures on the common fisheries policy.* Luxembourg: Publications Office of the European Union. Retrieved August 31, 2011, from http://ec.europa.eu/fisheries/documentation/publications/pcp_en.pdf

European Commission. (2010b). Water is for life: How the water framework directive helps safeguard Europe's resources. Luxembourg: Publications Office of the European Union. Retrieved August 31, 2011, from http://ec.europa.eu/environment/water/pdf/WFD_brochure_en.pdf

Fremuth, Michael Lysander. (2010). *Die Europäische Union auf dem weg in die supranationalität* [The European Union on its way to supranationality]. Berlin: LIT Verlag.

Jans, Jan H., & Vedder, Hans H. (2008). *European environmental law* (3rd ed.). Groningen, The Netherlands: Europa Law.

Kallis, Giorgos, & Butler, David. (2001). The EU water framework directive: Measures and implications. *Water Policy, 3*(2), 125–142.

Krämer, Ludwig. (2007). *EC environmental law* (6th ed.). London: Sweet & Maxwell.

Lee, Maria. (2007). Sustainable development in the EU: The renewed sustainable development strategy 2006. *Environmental Law Review, 9*(1), 41–45.

Marauhn, Thilo, & Boehringer, Ayse Martina. (2011). Environmental law: Europe. In Klaus Bosselmann, Daniel S. Fogel & J. B. Ruhl (Eds.), *Berkshire encyclopedia of sustainability: Vol. 3. The law and politics of sustainability.* Great Barrington, MA: Berkshire Publishing.

Radlberger Getränkegesellschaft mbH & Co. & S. Spitz KG v. Land Baden-Württemberg, Case C-309/02 (2004).

Vedder, Hans. (2010). The treaty of Lisbon and European law and policy. *Journal of Environmental Law, 22*(2), 285–299.

European Union Greenhouse Gas Emission Trading Scheme (EU ETS)

The European Union Emission Trading Scheme is the European Union's main climate policy instrument. It was designed and revised with a view to reducing greenhouse gas emissions in the least financially expensive way possible. Since it was first developed, policy makers have adjusted the plan to take into account the behavior of the industries covered under the regulations.

The European Union Emission Trading Scheme (EU ETS) was established by a directive of the European Union in 2003 (Directive 2003/87/EC) and was amended in 2004 (Directive 2004/101/EC). It regulates emissions by about eleven thousand facilities in thirty countries (the twenty-seven in the European Union plus Iceland, Liechtenstein, and Norway), making it the biggest emission trading program in the world. It includes all power stations and other combustion plants, oil refineries, coke ovens, and iron, steel, cement, glass, lime, brick, ceramics, pulp, paper, and board facilities more than a given minimum size.

How the System Works

The system sets a maximum amount of carbon dioxide these facilities are permitted to emit (a so-called cap). Each facility receives a certain number of allowances (EU Allowance, or EUA), and each allowance entitles the facility to emit one ton of carbon dioxide per year. Initially, these allowances were distributed free of charge (a system known as grandfathering), which in some cases resulted in windfall profits when costs were passed on (for example, through higher electricity prices), even though the allowances had been provided free of charge. Since this initial distribution, an ever-increasing proportion of allowances have been auctioned. Because pollution emitters are required to pay for the allowances, carbon costs are factored more into product costs in two ways: the quantity of pollutants emitted during the production process is lowered and the price of the electricity consumed in production is raised.

The auction system, however, sometimes leads to an effect known as *carbon leakage*, in which production is transferred to other countries or sectors with less stringent environmental regulations, so that worldwide emissions actually increase (Abadie and Galarraga 2011). To reduce this effect, emission allowances will continue to be provided free of charge to industries in the EU that are most likely to transfer production outside the regulated zone. An alternative policy would be to penalize imports of products from countries with weaker environmental regulations, but this is no easy matter, because such measures may be classed as protectionism and may therefore be challenged.

The allowance mechanism is effective because there are more industries that want to pollute than the total quantity of allowances will permit. The relative scarcity of allowances as compared with needs determines their market price. The players in the carbon market are mainly energy and industrial firms and financial intermediaries. Regulated facilities have three options. They can invest in abatement so that they do not need to purchase allowances (they may even sell allowances they possess but do not need), purchase allowances at market prices, or simply stop producing. The most efficient solution—which should also be the cheapest solution—may be different for each firm. Improving energy efficiency is one form of abatement available to these firms. The price of allowances has fluctuated a great deal, however, which leads to uncertainty in planning and has a negative impact on investment in abatement (Abadie and Chamorro 2008).

Futures contracts on EUAs are traded in several markets, among them the IntercontinentalExchange (ICE). The existence of these futures markets enables the costs of energy and the allowances needed to produce to be hedged. This significantly reduces the risk of prices changing in the future. Futures contracts that mature in 2020 are currently in place. Spot prices can be consulted on BlueNext.

The EU ETS is being carried out in three phases. During Phase I—the learning phase—(2005–2007), allowances were considerably overallocated. This was discovered in 2006, when real emissions were checked. At this point, the existing allowances lost all their value because there was no market for them. (They could not be used in the following phase because the system did not provide for banking between phases.)

Phase II (2008–2012) is known as the Kyoto phase. During both phases I and II, allowances were generated on the basis of the National Allocation Plan (NAP) for each country that was provided in the directive, but many difficulties arose: EUA price volatility was high (though less so in Phase II than in Phase I), and there was still considerable regulatory uncertainty. Phase II did provide for banking between phases (which helped bring down volatility), but borrowing was still not permitted.

Phase III features a number of improvements intended to achieve greater reductions in emissions in a more effective way and to minimize damage to vulnerable sectors. Specifically, the target set for this phase is a 21 percent reduction from 2005 emission levels for the sectors covered by the 2004 directive. (Phase III has become known as the European Union's 20/20/20 package: reduce greenhouse gas emissions by 20 percent from 1990 levels, with the possibility of an additional 10 percent reduction if other developed countries second the proposal; reduce energy consumption 20 percent through energy efficiency; and increase energy production from renewable resources 20 percent, including a strong boost for carbon capture and storage technologies.)

Directive 2004/101/EC

In the 2004 directive, several changes were made that would increase the effectiveness of the existing program. More sectors were brought into emission trading, including aeronautics, and aluminum and ammonia producers. Nitrous oxide and perfluorochemicals (PFCs) were added to the list of regulated gases. To reduce regulatory uncertainty, this phase, Phase III, was scheduled to last eight years (Phase II lasted five years).

A centralized distribution system for all of Europe replaced distribution by individual member states.

National Allocation Plans (NAPs) were eliminated. This new distribution structure eliminated distortions in competition between the same sectors in different countries (previously, the same sector had different allocations in France and Spain, for example).

The cap on allowances drops in linear fashion by 1.74 percent per year on the amounts available in Phase II. This year-on-year decrease is scheduled to continue beyond 2020. In addition, an auction system replaced the free distribution of allowances. In 2012, 20 percent of the allowances were auctioned, and the percentage of allowances to be auctioned increases in stages: 20 percent by 2013, 70 percent by 2020, and 100 percent by 2027 (CMS Cameron McKenna 2009). The goal was to stop providing free emission allowances to the most heavily polluting facilities; the free allowances that are given out in this phase are based on benchmarks involving emissions from the top 10 percent of most efficient facilities.

The energy industry was required to obtain all its allowances from auctions, and this eliminated windfall profits that had been captured in earlier phases. Certain exceptions were incorporated, however, for the energy generating industry in countries with poor connections to the European electricity grid. These industries were allowed reductions of up to 30 percent in the proportion of emission allowances that they must obtain by auction by 2013. The proportion of allowances they must obtain by auction grows gradually to 100 percent by 2020 (CMS Cameron McKenna 2009, 9).

Under this plan, it may be possible to protect sectors that are vulnerable to carbon leakage (defined as those sectors for which purchase by auction increases costs by more than 5 percent of gross added value and for which more than 10 percent of trade is with non–European Union countries). Such sectors could reduce their emissions if market prices are high enough to cover costs and uncertainty levels are low enough.

Outlook

In the future, the possibility of linking EU ETS with other compatible systems will be planned. Examples of similar initiatives are the California Emissions Trading Scheme and the Regional Greenhouse Gas Initiative, both in the United States, and the emission market in New Zealand (New Zealand Emissions Trading Scheme).

Luis María ABADIE and Ibon GALARRAGA
Basque Centre for Climate Change (BC3)

See also Climate Change Refugees (Africa); Energy Security (Europe); European Union (EU); Rule of Law (European Union); Shipping and Freight

FURTHER READING

Abadie, Luis María, & Chamorro, Jose M. (2008). European CO$_2$ prices and carbon capture investments. *Energy Economics, 30,* 2992–2015.

Abadie, Luis María, & Galarraga, Ibon. (2011). The European Emission Trading Scheme: Implication for long-term investment valuation. *Climate Change Economics, 2,* 129–148.

BlueNext. (2011). Homepage. Retrieved July 8, 2011, from http://www.bluenext.eu/

Chevallier, Julien. (2009). Carbon futures and macroeconomics risk factors. *Energy Economics, 31*(4), 614–625.

CMS Cameron McKenna. (2009). Phase III of the EU emissions trading scheme: Your Q&A guide. Part of the 2020 climate package series. Retrieved July 24, 2012, from http://www.law-now.com/cmck/pdfs/nonsecured/phase3.pdf

Ellerman, A. Denny, & Buchner, Barbara K. (2007). The European Union Emissions Trading Scheme: Origins, allocation and early results. *Review of Environmental Economics and Policy, 1*(1), 66–87.

Ellerman, A. Denny, & Joskow, Paul L. (2008). Carbon futures and macroeconomics risk factors. *Energy Economics, 31*(4), 614–625.

European Union Emissions Trading Scheme (EU ETS). (2011). Homepage. Retrieved July 6, 2011, from http://ec.europa.eu/clima/policies/ets/index_en.htm

González-Eguino, Mikel; Galarraga, Ibon; & Ansuategi, Alberto. (2011). The future of old industrial regions in a carbon constrained world. *Climate Policy, 12*(2), 164–186.

IntercontinentalExchange market data. (2011). Homepage. Retrieved July 8, 2011, from https://www.theice.com/homepage.jhtml

Kyoto Protocol to the United Nations Framework Convention on Climate Change. (2011). Retrieved July 8, 2011, from http://unfccc.int/resource/docs/convkp/kpeng.html

Mansanet-Bataller, María, & Pardo, Ángel. (2008). What you should know about carbon markets. *Energies, 1,* 120–153.

Official Journal of the European Union. (2004, November 13). Directive 2004/101/EC of the European Parliament and of the council of 27 October 2004. Retrieved July 8, 2011, from http://eur-lex.europa.eu/LexUriServ/LexUriServ.do?uri=OJ:L:2004:338:0018:0023:EN:PDF

Fisheries

Humans have been fishing for more than 100,000 years, and until about 1900 most fishing practices were sustainable. During the last 100 years, almost every corner of the oceans has been heavily impacted by modern industrial fishing. The amount of wild-caught fish peaked in 1980, but due to the rapidly emerging aquacultural sector, total production of fish had doubled as of 2011.

Wild-living fish stocks are a finite resource and renewable only through natural processes, whereas the success of those who make their living from fishing is dictated by their ability to locate, catch, preserve, and subsequently market the end product. This nature of fisheries has presently and historically caused a number of sustainability issues, foremost the concern that a growing number of fishermen are extracting more fish from the oceans than can be replaced through natural growth and dispersal of fishes.

During the nineteenth century, though, French scientists and fishermen greatly improved the ancient idea of artificially rearing fish—aquaculture, which since 2009 has replaced catching from the wild as the world's primary source of fish. While aquaculture may solve some of the immediate problems of overexploiting wild fish stocks, other issues of sustainability related to pollution, parasites and diseases, ecological footprints, mixing up of natural species characteristics, and invasive species, as well as socioeconomic and nutritional problems, have arisen from the growth of the aquacultural industry. These sustainability issues are global in scale and impact, but the problems first arose in Europe several centuries ago.

History

The earliest records of marine fishing anywhere, found in South Africa, date from 165,000 to 120,000 years ago, and fishing is now the last major human enterprise reminiscent of a hunter-gatherer society (Rick and Erlandson 2008). In Europe, the first documented fishery is that which resulted in Neanderthal kitchen middens (heaps of discarded waste) in caves on the Iberian Peninsula, while a bounty of fish species have been found in association with remains of *Homo sapiens* occupation from the last 20,000 years. More than forty species have been found, along with sharpened bones that suggest the use of hooks.

In the seventh century BCE, the Phoenicians, who dominated Mediterranean trade, also fished for tuna (*Thunnus thynnus*); archaeological findings from Roman times suggest that the pan-Mediterranean trade in fermented fish sauce, the so-called garum, was as prominent as the wine trade, and large-scale fermentation sites have been excavated along the Black Sea coast.

Northern Europe is probably the best-excavated area in terms of fish archaeology. While 7,000-year-old remains of Atlantic cod (*Gadus morhua*), haddock (*Melanogrammus aeglefinus*), and ling (*Molva molva*) have been extracted from sites in the Orkney Islands, a truly international trade in cod from Lofoten in northern Norway developed about 1000 CE. Around the same time, Northern Europeans started fishing at sea with open boats, using long-line hooks for the so-called benthic species (such as cod and ling), and gill nets for herring (*Clupea harengus*) and other pelagic species (those swimming in the upper layers of the water column). The sudden upsurge in fishing might be linked to an increase in demand for marine products from the growing urban population, as well as the increased practice of fasting (i.e., abstinence from eating meat), which accompanied the spread of Christianity. In addition, the technique of salting herring in barrels was invented in the Øresund strait, the narrow waters separating Denmark and Sweden. For inland fisheries, such as those for salmon (*Salmo salar*) and trout (*Salmo trutta*), research has shown that catches were gradually being hindered by the building of dams and dikes, while medieval legislation shows signs of a clear awareness of protecting fry and larvae from damaging gear practices. Knowledge is lacking, however, as to whether or not fisheries caused the abundance of inland species to decline, but their relative importance on the European dinner table was waning compared to rising interest in marine products. The per capita consumption of fish in Europe seems to have reached a high point in the fourteenth and fifteenth centuries, and the few surviving records of long-term fish prices suggest that, relative to other food items, herring and cod were much higher priced in this period compared to more recent centuries.

The limits to growth were also dictated by technology insofar as medieval fishing practices necessitated that the fish be landed within a matter of a few days in order to be processed, either through salting, drying, or smoking. Offshore fish stocks, therefore, were only targeted within a day's sailing distance from the shore. This technological barrier was broken in the early 1400s as Flemish and later Dutch fishermen started to catch herring all over the North Sea using decked vessels containing salt, barrels, large drift nets, and provisions, which enabled the fishermen to process the herring onboard and continue to search the fishing grounds for many weeks at a time. The same technique was introduced in cod fishing, which soon involved the entire North Atlantic.

In theory, all known waters of the world could now be fished, and they gradually would be. Around 1500, Basque, and later English and French, fishermen pioneered the Great Banks of Newfoundland, which soon became the world's largest cod fishery. Dried cod can last for years under the right conditions and became a flexible, easily transportable, and nutritious supplement to the diet of the Atlantic world. African fisheries are little known from the time before the European colonization of the continent. By the 1700s, cod exports from Newfoundland to the Caribbean slave plantations were an integral part of the triangular trade between Africa, Europe, and the Americas. Fish consumption was going global.

Another novelty of European fish consumption from around 1600 onwards was a growing interest in a greater variety of species and preservation techniques. Russian caviar from sturgeon (*Acipenser sturio*) was exported westward all over Europe, while oysters were shipped south and east from France and the Low Countries. In the 1700s, natural oyster beds became early telling signs that marine resources could be depleted.

Foremost though, the interest in fresh fish grew at the expense of salted and dried fish, although Eastern Europe and the Iberian Peninsula continued to consume large quantities of salted herring and bacalao (dried and salted cod), respectively. Fish ponds, especially for carp (*Cyprinus carpio carpio*), were set up all over Europe following inspiration from the Turkish court, which had learned of the technique from China. Flatfish were kept alive in dams aboard fishing vessels and sailed directly to the marketplace. In spite of local cases of depletion, European fisheries were by and large sustainable, and only from the latter half of the nineteenth century did total landings (quantities of fish brought in) start to increase with the rate of the general population.

The development of railroads opened new markets for the consumption of fresh fish, and incentives grew to invest in steam and motor propulsion of fishing vessels. British vessels first introduced steam, and soon France, Germany, and the Netherlands followed suit before 1900. Catches soared once people could fish more or less unhindered by the changing weather, aided by the engine power added to trawling. Motor propulsion was introduced in Japan just after 1900, and soon South Africa hosted the first modern industrialized fishery in sub-Saharan waters. This marks the beginning of large-scale industrial fishing in South African waters, in which the banks of the Benguela Current Upwelling System, flowing north from the Cape of Good Hope to present-day Namibia, provide the most prolific fishing grounds. These fisheries relied mainly on snoek (*Thyrsites atun*) caught with line until the mid-twentieth century.

By the outbreak of World War II, European fisheries had already had a serious impact on the abundance of many commercial species. This is evident from centennial scale records of catch per vessel, where after 1945 the so-called Mexican wave phenomenon was observed—that is, catch rates were much higher immediately after the war, following six years when the fish were left in peace a few meters below the turmoil of naval warfare.

Challenges of Modern Practices

In many ways the modern era of fishing began in the 1950s. Following the introduction of echo sounding and sonar, the fishes of the ocean became much more locatable from the deck of a vessel. The implementation of nylon was another leap in technology, as it enabled stronger, lighter, and consequently bigger nets to be used. The purse seine, by which a school of, for instance, sprat (*Sprattus sprattus*) can be circled and scooped in one haul, was a result of the combined sonar and nylon revolutions.

Another factor that has been enormously influential on the growth of the fishing industry has been the ability to freeze or refrigerate fish caught at sea. Although mechanical equipment to freeze goods was developed in the mid-eighteenth century, it was not until the mid-nineteenth century that commercial freezing equipment was produced. The US inventor Clarence Birdseye brought about the first breakthrough in frozen foods; Birdseye launched a series of frozen consumer products under the brand name Birds Eye Frosted Foods in 1930 (Sonesson 2011, 156).

During the 1950s and 1960s, following the introduction of the aforementioned technological innovations, large stocks of main commercial species became depleted, such as North Sea herring. Following the implementation of the European Common Fisheries Policy, a moratorium on herring was imposed in 1977. The ban was lifted only gradually during the 1980s, and today North Sea herring is considered a success in terms of marine restoration (Karlsdottir 2005). The Scando-Atlantic herring, North Sea cod, and Baltic cod, however, have not reached the peaks in catches that were seen in the 1960s and 1970s. With regard to Baltic cod, environmental factors such as inflow rates of salt water into the Baltic Sea play a major role; but in every case, fishing pressure has been intense.

European restrictions within the territorial waters of Europe led to a widening of the fishing area, with fleets from many European countries, not the least of which were Russian and Spanish trawlers, beginning to prowl the unregulated waters off the coast of West Africa. In addition to the environmental effect of this practice, social sustainability was also affected as a local and nutritious natural resource like fish by-passed the local economy. In a similar move toward more fish-rich, less restricted areas, much fishing has taken to the grounds of the Mid-Atlantic Ridge. Several times during the first decade of the twenty-first century, scientists discovered new species and fish stocks living in previously uncharted areas, only to find that their abundance had already been disturbed by fishing.

Off the South African and Namibian coast, purse-seine fishing for sardines (*Sardinops sagax*) became the main fishing practice after World War II until the stock collapsed in the 1960s. Thereafter, hake (*Merluccius paradoxus*), anchovy (*Engraulis encrasiolus*), and horse mackerel (*Trachurus* spp.) have made up the bulk of catches. Hake is an important export commodity to Europe and North America, and compared to many others their ecosystem is still very productive.

The Black Sea has suffered a great deal more. Following a combination of eutrophication from river runoff, jellyfish invasions, and inefficient management, life in the upper trophic levels (large and mid-size fish) has nearly disappeared. This had led to a complete shift in the controls of the local ecosystem, which is now dominated by low-order species such as jellyfish (scyphozoans). An ecosystem already impacted by conditions such as eutrophication is more prone to be affected by environmental changes, such as the arrival of the comb jelly (*Mnemiopsis leidyi*) in ballast tanks. The larger Mediterranean Sea is not as severely impacted, but recent studies of the Adriatic Sea reveal that the larger late-maturing species have declined in importance relative to smaller species over the twentieth century (Fortibuoni et al. 2010).

Another novelty, already invented before World War II, was fisheries for fodder instead of human consumption. Worldwide, Peru and Chile are leading nations in fishmeal production, and within Europe, Denmark and

Norway are dominant players in this industry, where the catches are processed and turned into a powder suitable for feeding pigs as well as farmed fish.

Almost all fish are carnivorous, so even though fish farming relieves the fishing pressure on the farmed species, such as cod or halibut (*Hippoglossus hippoglossus*), the rearing of fish depends on large catches of other fish, which in turn become in danger of overfishing. Such has been the case for fish like sand eel (*Ammodytes tobianus*) and sprat, which are now fished under quota regulations in the same way as fish for direct consumption. One of the present challenges of fish farming is to genetically engineer fish that will thrive on vegetable proteins.

The mixing of distinct stocks is another problem, when, for instance, salmon escape the farms and blend with the natural stocks differing from river to river. In Norway, it is estimated that hardly any "clean" stock is left. While many European fish farms work under fierce regulations in terms of what to feed the fish, and how much nutrient outflow is allowed, the rapidly growing African aquaculture sector is posing a serious problem. Since 2000, Nile perch (*Lates niloticus*) has become a major African export commodity, especially for the European market. While this undoubtedly benefits several African economies, in many lakes and rivers Nile perch has completely disrupted the original fauna. Positive introduction of new species occur as well, such as the introduction of freshwater sardines (*Limnothrissa miodon*) into the artificially constructed Lake Kariba, which consequently has come to support a large commercial fishery (Marshall 1991).

Another downside is that fish, a nutritious and healthy food item, is becoming less readily available to the local consumers around the shores and lakes of Africa, while European and North American consumers are not affected by the rapid changes in how and where fish are obtained for consumption. Relatively cheap shipping costs have facilitated a booming market for frozen fish in the developed countries. Sushi restaurants serving expensive raw fish, such as tuna, have become a global craze.

Invasive species create still other problems. Fish have been successfully transplanted from one area to another for more than a century, exemplified by Danish fisheries scientist C. G. J. Petersen's effort to relocate plaice (*Platessa platessa*) from the Danish Limfjord onto Dogger Bank in the North Sea, now an important fishing ground for plaice. A more recent invader is red king crab (*Paralithodes camtschaticus*), which Russian fishermen moved from the Pacific Ocean to the Barents Sea, from where it is now spreading into the North Atlantic. In other cases, the invasion is accidental, such as that of Pacific oysters (*Crassostrea gigas*), which probably entered European waters through ballast water. They are gradually replacing the resident European flat oysters (*Ostrea edulis*) along the shores of the European continent, which is seen as a mixed blessing.

In summary, most preindustrial fishing activities from the Paleolithic Era onward took place in a sustainable fashion, whereas increasingly since the latter half of the nineteenth century fisheries have had serious impact on the abundance and diversity of commercial fish species in Afro-Eurasia. With the rapid increase in world population during the twentieth century, as well as the development of preservation techniques such as freezing and the opening of new fish markets via railroads, trucks, and air transport, the demand for seafood has outstripped the natural supply of the Earth's oceans. An important response to this situation has been the increased development of aquaculture, which has risen to prominence in recent decades, now surpassing wild-caught fish as the main source of seafood.

Bo POULSEN
Aalborg University

See also Biodiversity Conservation; Diet and Nutrition; Education, Environmental; Mediterranean Sea; Nile River; Parks and Preserves; Shipping and Freight

FURTHER READING

Bekker-Nielsen, Tonnes. (2005). *Ancient fishing and fish processing in the Black Sea region* (Black Sea studies, 2). Langelandsgade, Denmark: Aarhus University Press.

Fortibuoni, Tomaso; Libralato, Simone; Raicevich, Saša; Giovanardi, Otello; & Solidoro, Cosimo. (2010). Coding early naturalists' accounts into long-term fish community changes in the Adriatic Sea (1800–2000). *PLoS ONE*, 5(11), e15502. Retrieved June 26, 2012, from http://www.plosone.org/article/info%3Adoi%2F10.1371%2Fjournal.pone.0015502

Gertwagen Ruthy, et al. (Eds.). (2009). *HMAP international summer school: When humanities meet ecology: Historic changes in Mediterranean and Black Sea marine biodiversity and ecosystems since the Roman period until nowadays. Languages, methodologies and perspectives*. Retrieved January 11, 2012, from http://hmapcoml.org/documents/When_Humanities_Meet_Ecology_english.pdf

Hoffman, Richard C. (1996, June). Economic development and aquatic ecosystems in medieval Europe, *American Historical Review*, 101(3), 631–669.

Holm, Poul; Marboe, Anne Husum; Poulsen, Bo; & MacKenzie, Brian R. (2010). Marine animal populations: A new look back in time. In Alasdair D. McIntyre (Ed.), *Life in the world's oceans*. Hoboken, NJ: Wiley-Blackwell.

Karlsdottir, Hrepna M. (2005). *Fishing on common grounds: The consequences of unregulated fisheries of North Sea herring in the postwar period*. Göteborg, Sweden: Ekonomisk-Historiska institutionen vid Göteborgs universitet.

Kideys, Ahmet E. (2002, August 30). Fall and rise of the Black Sea ecosystem *Science*, 297(5586), 1482–1484. doi:10.1126/science.1073002

Kinsey, Darin. (2006). Seeding the water as the earth: The epicentre and peripheries of a western aquacultural revolution. *Environmental History*, 11(3), 527–566.

Pauly, Daniel, et al. (2002). Towards sustainability in world fisheries. *Nature, 418*(6898), 689–695.

Pinnegar, John K., & Engelhard, Georg H. (2008). The "shifting baseline" phenomenon: A global perspective. *Reviews in Fish Biology and Fisheries, 18*(1), 1–16.

Rick, Torben C., & Erlandson, Jon M. (Eds.). (2008). *Human impacts on ancient marine ecosystems: A global perspective*. Berkeley: University of California Press.

Roberts, Callum. (2007). *The unnatural history of the sea. The past and future of humanity and fishing*. London: Gaia Books.

Rozwadowski, Helen M. (2002). *The sea knows no boundaries: A century of marine science under ICES*. Seattle & London: International Council for the Exploration of the Sea/University of Washington Press.

Sicking, Louis, & Abreu-Fereira, Darlene. (Eds.). (2008). *Beyond the catch: Fisheries of the North Atlantic, the North Sea and the Baltic, 900–1850*. London & Boston: Brill Academic Publishers.

Sonesson, Ulf. (2011). Food, frozen. In Sarah Fredericks, Lei Shen, Shirley Thompson & Daniel Vasey (Eds.), *The Encyclopedia of Sustainability: Vol. 4. Natural Resources and Sustainability*. Great Barrington, MA: Berkshire Publishing.

Watermeyer, K. E.; Shannon, L. J.; Roux, J-P.; & Griffiths, C. (2008). Changes in the trophic structure of the northern Benguela before and after the onset of industrial fishing. *African Journal of Marine Science, 30*(2), 383–403.

France

France's long history at the crossroads of European development has resulted in much change across the landscape as people have found ways to meet their resource demands. This story is told through the prism of four particular resources: agricultural land, water, forests, and energy, specifically coal. While many environmental challenges persist, the French have taken great strides toward sustainability.

Ecosystems and societies have interacted in France, a historic nation bridging the Mediterranean Sea and northern Europe in the western part of the continent, for at least fourteen millennia. Changing relationships between ecosystems and societies over time in France can best be examined through the lens of four crucial resources—agricultural land, water, forests, and energy.

Agricultural Land

People of the Mesolithic period (beginning 12,000 BCE) began to reshape the dense deciduous forests through burning and sheepherding. The Neolithic (beginning c. 7000 BCE) way of life combined grain cultivation with small livestock raising and hunting and gathering; large and continuously cultivated open fields became a feature of ancient Gaul long before Romans arrived. In the Bronze and Iron Ages (3500–500 BCE), migrations of Celts resulted in an extension of cultivated areas, and eventually iron plows were introduced to work the heavier soils of the north. By the time of the Roman conquest in 58–51 BCE, Gaul had a population of at least 10 million people, and estimates have ranged up to 30 million.

Romans inaugurated a slave-based agricultural system, organized around villas (estates). They maintained open fields and the "old" grains—soft wheat, barley, and millet—and introduced new crops; namely olives, vines, cherries, and peaches. Spreading gradually, vine cultivation led to the export of wines from present-day Bordeaux to Roman Britain by the first century CE. In subsequent centuries, the feudal system reshaped the agrarian landscape through strip farming in the north of France and, after 1250, widespread crop rotation systems that incorporated fallow (leaving unsown) periods and thus helped to regenerate soils. Long-term demographic pressure made land the most contested resource in France, yet "wastes" (uncultivated land), forests, fallow land, and harvested land could be as fiercely defended or coveted as cultivated land. Collective rights—to glean; to graze on unenclosed fields, stubble, or fallow land; to access meadows after haymaking; to cut wood—could assure survival for the rural poor and helped those better off to turn a profit. The French Revolution's Rural Code of 1791 maintained key collective rights, and although partition of the commons (common land for all villagers) was authorized in 1793, little partition actually occurred. On balance, however, revolutionary policies promoted agrarian individualism by vindicating private property but *not* by redistributing land, thus setting the legal and social basis for agrarian capitalism in France.

Both public and private efforts have promoted greater agricultural productivity and regional specialization in modern times. The massive planting of vineyards in the Midi region in the nineteenth century best exemplifies the trend toward monoculture (cultivation of only a single crop) spurred by the demands of national and international markets. The vast vineyards of the south became prey to a louse that attacks root stock called *phylloxera*, which was first detected in 1863. An environmental catastrophe for winegrowers, *phylloxera* spread from south to north, destroying 30 percent of the surface area of French vineyards. Ultimately, the crisis was resolved by grafting resistant US root stock to French plants. France did, however, remain a mosaic of small and large properties. The post–World War II era saw increasing mechanization, chemical applications, and plot consolidation. Beginning in the mid-1950s, the Common Market's Common Agricultural Policy guaranteed a market for surpluses at higher than world prices. The largest growers benefited most from these policies—and polluted water, soils laden with heavy metals, destroyed hedge rows, and erosion have been their ecological legacy. Meanwhile, smaller growers were abandoning approximately 72,000 hectares per year by the late 1990s. Roughly half of this land ultimately comes back into cultivation or pasturage, whereas the rest becomes either part of the built environment—buildings, streetscapes, and related structures—or a semi-wild ecosystem.

Agribusiness, subsidized by France and the European Union (EU), has been contested since 1987 by the Confédération Paysanne, a union supporting the interest of independent small farmers. The union fights for fair pricing for farmers, and against the use of genetically modified organisms (GMOs) in agriculture. As of 2009, France was receiving one-fifth of the Common Agricultural Policy (CAP) subsidies issued by the EU. Most CAP subsidies are awarded to large agribusiness firms, and many smaller farmers who have received fixed sums (a maximum of about 30,000 euros) have continued to go out of business. In addition, the EU has ordered French farmers to reimburse the French government for subsidies issued illicitly by the latter (i.e., on top of EU subsidies). In short, agribusiness continues to alter the landscape by eliminating traditional hedgerows in favor of massive fields given over to water- and chemical-intensive crops such as corn (Reuters 2012; Taylor 2009).

Water

Agriculture always has and always will depend on freshwater resources, but just as consequential has been France's exposure to two seas. No point in France is more than 400 kilometers from a sea, and extensive Atlantic and Mediterranean coastlines go far to explain the country's historic orientation to both northern and southern Europe. Efforts to connect the two coastal areas helped forge France's political identity, as did the presence of an impressive network of rivers. The Loire and Seine Rivers cut through the old provinces, whereas the Rhone and Saône functioned as barriers, and the Rhine often marked part of the northeastern border. Historian Fernand Braudel called the Rhone River corridor the "French isthmus," for it formed part of the great commercial artery that connected northern Italy to the Low Countries (now Belgium and the Netherlands), reaching

into the French interior by tributaries of the Loire and Seine (Braudel 1988, 265).

Water directly influenced urban development by allowing for both commerce and early manufacturing. In the well-watered north, canal building in the eleventh century followed by marsh draining in the twelfth reshaped Caen, Rouen, Amiens, Beauvais, Troyes, and Reims into "mini-Venices" (Guillerme 1988, 51). The constant flow of diverted water and a benign textile industry kept these northern cities relatively clean. For their part, waterwheels represented a stable energy potential until the early nineteenth century.

The association between urban waters and disease originated in the fourteenth century, when warfare prompted the building of large moats that filled with stagnant water. Moats and ramparts cut cities off from the countryside and its flowing waters. Incidences of fevers and pulmonary diseases were worsened by the greater humidity caused by a general lowering of temperature from the early fourteenth to the late nineteenth century. This Little Ice Age saw an annual dip of 1.5° C during its coldest periods, which also led to a number of grain-scarcity crises and a decline in freshwater fishing. Eighteenth-century concern over stagnant water and noxious vapors helped create the Pasteurian mentality (so-named after the founder of microbiology, Louis Pasteur, 1822–1895) of the nineteenth century, which sought to analyze the bacterial content of water in order to find a way to purify it. The goal of providing clean water to cities and eliminating foul water played a major role in nineteenth- and twentieth-century urban improvement efforts, starting with the renovation of Paris's infrastructure during the Second Empire (1851–1870). The Public Hygiene Act of 1902 promised significant state involvement in order to provide pure water throughout France. Ironically, the dismantling of walls, ramparts, and moats made French cities vulnerable to free-flowing water in the form of floods.

Free-flowing water has been subject to greater control during the past two centuries in the interests of irrigation and a well-maintained canal network. France has led in the commodification of water through the marketing of mineral water, and modern industry has depended on water as well, especially along the Rhone—the site of numerous hydroelectric and nuclear power plants. In nuclear power plants, water functions to cool spent fuel rods for two to three years in the initial stage of treating nuclear waste. Spent fuel is then shipped from French (and foreign) reactors to the controversial facility run by Cogema at Cap de la Hague in Normandy. There, untreated waste cools for another six to seven years before chemical treatment separates unburned uranium from plutonium and fission byproducts. These highly radioactive materials are then vitrified—turned into glass—prior to permanent storage in canisters underground. Bure, in France's northeast, has been explored as a potential site for a new, geological storage method of nuclear waste. A blueprint will be presented to the government, which, if approved, would be implemented in 2025 (Nature 2010).

Tourism, secondary residences, port development, and pleasure boats have compromised France's coastal ecology, yet the proportion of French beaches and lakeside swimming areas meeting the EU's water purity criteria had increased dramatically by the late 1990s. Through land purchases, the national Conservatoire du Littoral assured the conservation of 13 percent of France's coastline by the 1990s (Bess 2003, 167). France's freshwater ecosystems have perhaps fared worse, with eutrophication (the process by which water becomes enriched with nutrients) from agricultural runoff threatening lakes and rivers in the north and west (particularly in Brittany). The provision of pure water to many rural communes has remained an elusive goal. Measures have been taken under environmental laws (known as Grenelle 1, 2, and 3, adopted between 2008 and 2010) to dedicate 10 percent of state-owned marine areas as marine preservation zones. The amount of clean water at catchment sites (for the extraction of potable water) in France is slated to double by 2015. Other measures seek to limit access to water for gardening, car washing, and irrigation when the government deems the supply too low (Écologie, Énergie, Développement Durable & Mer 2009).

Forests

The deciduous forest is the fundamental biome of France—a forest typically harboring a multilayered understory (i.e., the vegetative layer and especially the trees and shrubs between the forest canopy and the ground cover) of shrubs, ferns, grasses, mosses, and mushrooms. Pine, spruce, and larch reign in the upper elevations of the Alps and the Pyrenees, and thinner oak forests dominate in the highly eroded soils of the Mediterranean region. The composition of France's deciduous forests has been very unstable over time because of changes in the soil, climate, and human activity. Since the Middle Ages, pressure to cultivate land has steadily relegated forests to marginal, often acidic, soils, with forest clearance reaching its peak during the twelfth century. Only in the mid-nineteenth century did forest begin to replace inland waters as state foresters carried out a massive reforestation of the extensive Sologne and Landes wetlands. Using trees to control water also justified the ambitious project, begun in 1860, to reforest the Alps, Pyrenees, and Massif Central. Blanketed with evergreens, the mountains would in theory retain their waters and soils and consequently not threaten lowlands with flooding and debris flows. These two modern examples illustrate a long historical association between forest management and state power.

There is an even longer history pointing to the fundamental role that forests have played in the peasant economies of France. Use rights to the forest included gathering firewood, construction wood, plants for barn litter, and human food such as berries, mushrooms, and honey. Rights to graze livestock in forests stemmed from the structural shortage of meadows and fallow land. The peasants' forest—marked by the presence of livestock and people—contrasted greatly with royal and aristocratic forests, kept off limits to all but elite hunters and their wild game. The common tendency to sacrifice forest for more arable land threatened the equilibrium of the forest-field-pasture ecosystem. From the passage of the landmark Forest Ordinance of 1669 until the tightening of official control over forests in the nineteenth century, the state limited, and even eradicated, use rights. France's first national forestry school (established in 1824) deepened the state's imprint on forests by teaching even-aged (i.e., having a difference in age among trees in a given stand of forest usually no greater than twenty years), single-species management. Rural communities vigorously contested both the state's jurisdiction and methods of management, especially during the revolutions of 1830 and 1848.

Many other factors tolled heavily on French forests. Cities required wood for building, heating, and cooking even after other European urban populations had turned to coal for domestic needs. Charcoal-powered iron forges consumed vast quantities of wood. The state demanded thousands of oaks to build naval ships until the later nineteenth century. During the Old Regime (France's period of absolute monarchy, roughly 1600–1789), the state routinely sold forests on the royal domains to shore up its finances. Approximately 200,000 hectares of forest in northern France suffered damage ranging from degradation to obliteration during World War I, and the military effort itself devoured wood.

In all, though, during the twentieth century there was a significant, spontaneous return of forest to previously cultivated land in areas of severe depopulation. Land abandonment alone presently increases forest cover by about 1 percent every two years. Forests and more lightly wooded land covered nearly 28 percent of the surface area of metropolitan France (i.e., the part of France located in Europe, not including its overseas territories) by 2010; France's 17 million hectares of forested land have increased by over 400,000 hectares since 2000 (European Commission, Eurostat 2011). Voluntary reforestation has also continued; since the 1950s, foresters have begun favoring mixed plantations over single-species coniferous forests because of alarming soil acidification and the lack of resistance of single-species forests to wind, fire, and pathogens. The capacity of a diverse forest to resist high winds was, in a negative sense, brought home in December 1999 when Hurricane Lothar swept across France, felling the equivalent of three years' wood production; it was cited by climate historians as France's most destructive storm since 1739. Recent concern has also focused on the pine forests of Provence—dense, low forests with a heavy understory, that are highly susceptible to fire. Finally, the popularity of forests for outdoor recreation has created new imperatives for management and has exposed more vulnerabilities.

Past and Future Energy

The amount of energy supplied by waterwheels and charcoal forges remained sufficient into the early nineteenth century. The chief disincentive to fully harness coal for industry was its poor distribution across a relatively large national territory. Eventually, heavily exploited forests drove up the price of charcoal, and the introduction of the steam engine resulted in a new use for coal: it was put to use in France's cotton industry, which was the nation's first industry to mechanize using coal-fired steam engines after 1811.

Traditionally, manufacturing had been highly dispersed throughout the French countryside. Industry based on coal led to the existence of distinct industrial regions because transportation cost more in France than in smaller England or Belgium. Coal deposits, concentrated in the north (Pas-de-Calais) and the center (Saint-Étienne/Le Creusot), existed far from iron deposits,

concentrated in Lorraine. Moreover, the high phosphorous content of Lorraine's iron limited its appeal to steel manufacturers. Two developments made French coal and iron compatible: railroads, which linked them profitably to each other, and the Thomas converter (1878), which purified iron sufficiently for steel production. The mass production of steel in Lorraine exemplifies the regionalization of industry based on coal, as does the cotton industry around Mulhouse, fed by coal brought from Le Creusot by canal. The largest industrial belts, however, ultimately depended more on the benefits offered by cities than on the location of natural resources: Paris, with its intellectual and material resources and huge market; Lyon, the hub along the French isthmus; and Marseille, with its port-based trade, all spawned industrial complexes.

Railroads spurred coal production and industrialization in general. France's first rail line (1827) extended from Saint-Étienne to Andrézieux, connecting the coal basin to the Loire River. Had mining engineers prevailed, France's rail system would have continued to link manufacturing and resource extraction, but such was not the case. Mimicking the royal highways of the mid-eighteenth century, the main lines of France's railway system radiated from the capital and famously defied natural landforms and property boundaries. The railroads helped create a national market in the years 1850–1900, furthering the specialization of agriculture.

Coal indisputably helped create a modernized, industrialized France. The amount of coal mined in France increased from 4.4 million tons to 13.3 million tons in the two decades between 1851 and 1871—production increases that mirrored those in neighboring western European countries during that period (Landes 1969, 203). But compared to England and Germany, France was notoriously deficient in this fossil fuel. Imported petroleum became cheaper than domestic coal for industrial use shortly after World War II, and France's turn to nuclear power in the postwar era represented a quest for renewed geopolitical power in light of pressing energy needs.

As of 2012, France is a leader in the nuclear power industry, with 80 percent of the nation's electricity coming from its fifty-eight nuclear power plants (Viscusi and Patel 2011). While the country's present dependence on nuclear power is not without challenges, it has led France to become one of the world's largest net exporters of electricity and has reduced the country's greenhouse gas emissions. The Fukushima nuclear disaster (caused by the March 2011 tsunami that devastated Japan's northeast coast) rattled French public support for nuclear power, and the 2012 presidential election of François Hollande may spell changes in France's focus on nuclear energy development over renewable energy.

Industry based on fossil fuels has brought environmental degradation but also popular consciousness of environmental risks. Early efforts at regulation—a Paris ordinance of 1898 prohibiting prolonged emissions of black smoke over the capital, a national law of 1917 instituting inspections of polluting businesses—are more noteworthy for their dates than their real effects. After the 1860s, French industrialists constructed tall brick smokestacks to disperse emissions and resisted regulation until recent decades. Even hydroelectricity, nicknamed "white coal" in the 1870s, compromised the aesthetic value of the mountains and reduced the alluvial deposits of alpine rivers. Daily emissions from aluminum and electrochemical plants in the Maurienne Valley in the northern Alps equaled those produced by a large city such as Lyon by the 1970s. Since the 1960s, though, overall emissions of the major polluting gases—hydrocarbons, sulfur dioxide, nitrous oxides—have declined as France has imposed tighter regulations and heeded those of the EU. France has ratified the Kyoto Protocol and contributed to the passing of the EU's greenhouse gas emissions legislation, both of which compel the country to reduce its greenhouse gases.

Outlook for the Future

The French have reacted to ongoing threats to flora, fauna, air, and water in ways that parallel developments in other Western countries. The Ministry of the Environment, created in 1971—which, after several name changes, as of 2012 is called the Ministry of Ecology, Sustainable Development, Transport, and Housing (Ministère de l'Ecologie, du Développement durable, des Transports et du Logement, or MEDDTL)—has spawned legislation on a wide range of issues including air pollution, species conservation, and water conservation. The French government responded with enthusiasm to the EU's Natura 2000 initiative of 1992, an ambitious project to create a network of parks and nature reserves across what were at the time the EU's fifteen member states. By 2008 a variety of natural areas—from pristine alpine habitats to natural regional parks embracing farms and villages—had acquired varying degrees of legal protection, and over 20 percent of French territory was shielded by protective statutes (Martinez 2008). France is active in the negotiation and support of international environmental treaties. At home, vibrant local and regional associations advocate for specific causes.

In 2007, President Nicholas Sarkozy instigated the roundtable Grenelle Environment Forum (*Grenelle de l'environnement*) discussions, the name deliberately echoing the multiparty Grenelle Accords negotiated during the crisis of May 1968. The government consulted with state and local officials, nongovernmental organizations (NGOs), and businesses (both employers and employees) on a proposed plan to address the environment and sustainable development in several areas: buildings and energy; transportation; biodiversity, agriculture, forests, and seas; health and the environment; waste management; and governance, information, and training. After additional consultations with the broader public, the plan was officially launched by Jean-Louis Borloo, France's then Minister of Ecology. Between 2008 and 2010, the French parliament adopted two laws titled Grenelle 1 and Grenelle 2. (The Grenelle 3 bill was abandoned prior to adoption and its measures incorporated into Grenelle 2.) These laws address numerous issues from a multitude of angles, for example embedding sustainability in urban planning and mandating the reporting of any nanomaterial in consumer products, among others (Grenelle Environnement 2012).

France is also renowned for its modern train system and its extensive, ever-expanding, and widely used public transit system. The French government continues to take great strides both domestically and on a European level to address its environmental challenges. How the country (as of 2012 with a new socialist president and still battling a lengthy global recession) addresses its environment in the future remains to be seen, although it is to be hoped that the French people and their leaders will continue finding ways to contribute to local, regional, and global endeavors toward sustainability.

Tamara L. WHITED
Indiana University of Pennsylvania

See also Agriculture, Small-Scale; European Union (EU); Germany; Mediterranean Sea; Parks and Preserves; Rhine River; Rule of Law (European Union); Urbanization (Europe)

This article was adapted by the editors from Tamara L. Whited's article "France" in Shepard Krech III, J. R. McNeill, and Carolyn Merchant (Eds.), the *Encyclopedia of World Environmental History*, pp. 557–561. Great Barrington, MA: Berkshire Publishing (2003).

FURTHER READING

Bess, Michael. (2003). *The light-green society: Ecology and technological modernity in France, 1960–2000*. Chicago: University of Chicago Press.
Braudel, Fernand. (1972). *The Mediterranean and the Mediterranean world in the age of Philip II* (Sian Reynolds, Trans.). New York: HarperCollins.
Braudel, Fernand. (1988). *The identity of France: Vol. 1* (Sian Reynolds, Trans.). New York: Harper & Row.
Clout, Hugh D. (1977). *Themes in the historical geography of France*. London: Academic Press.

Clout, Hugh D. (1996). *After the ruins: Restoring the countryside of northern France after the Great War.* Exeter, UK: University of Exeter Press.

Corvol, Andrée. (1987). *L'Homme aux bois: Histoire des relations de l'homme et de la forêt, XVIIIe–XXe siècles* [Man in the woods: A history of human-forest relations, eighteenth to the twentieth centuries]. Paris: Fayard.

Delort, Robert, & Walter, François. (2001). *Histoire de l'environnement européen* [History of the European environment]. Paris: Presses Universitaires de France.

Duby, Georges, & Wallon, Armand. (Eds.). (1976). *Histoire de la France rurale* [History of rural France]. Paris: Seuil.

Écologie, Énergie, Développement Durable & Mer [Ecology, Energy, Sustainable Development and the Sea]. (2009). Le Grenelle Environnement: La première loi du Grenelle [The Grenelle environment: The first law of the Grenelle]. Retrieved May 18, 2012, from http://www.developpement-durable.gouv.fr/IMG/pdf/La_premiere_loi_du_Grenelle.pdf

Ecology, Sustainable Development, Transport and Housing. (2010). Grenelle 2 law. Retrieved June 4, 2012, from http://www.developpement-durable.gouv.fr/IMG/pdf/Grenelle_Loi-2_GB_.pdf

European Commission, Eurostat. (2011). Forestry in the EU and the world: A statistical portrait. Retrieved June 4, 2012, from http://epp.eurostat.ec.europa.eu/cache/ITY_OFFPUB/KS-31-11-137/EN/KS-31-11-137-EN.PDF

Green, Nicholas. (1990). *The spectacle of nature: Landscape and bourgeois culture in nineteenth-century France.* New York: Manchester University Press.

Grenelle Environnement [Grenelle Environment]. (2012). Homepage. Retrieved May 15, 2012, from http://www.legrenelle-environnement.fr/spip.php (in French)

Goubert, Jean-Pierre. (1989). *The conquest of water: The advent of health in the industrial age* (Andrew Wilson, Trans.). Cambridge, UK: Polity Press.

Guillerme, André E. (1988). *The age of water: The urban environment in the north of France, A.D. 300–1800.* College Station: Texas A&M University Press.

Harrison, Robert Pogue. (1992). *Forests: The shadow of civilization.* Chicago: University of Chicago Press.

Hecht, Gabrielle. (1998). *The radiance of France: Nuclear power and national identity after World War II.* Cambridge, MA: MIT Press.

Landes, David S. (1969). *The unbound Prometheus: Technological change and industrial development in western Europe from 1750 to the present.* Cambridge, UK: Cambridge University Press.

Martinez, Carole. (2008). Les Espaces protégés français: Une diversité d'outils au service de la protection de la biodiversité [Protected places in France: A variety of tools for the protection of biodiversity]. Retrieved June 4, 2012, from http://www.uicn.fr/IMG/pdf/UICN_France_-_espaces_proteges.pdf

McPhee, Peter. (1999). *Revolution and environment in southern France: Peasants, lords, and murder in the Corbières, 1780–1830.* Oxford, UK: Oxford University Press.

Nature. (2010). France digs deep for nuclear waste. *Nature, 466,* 804–805. doi:10.1038/466804a (updated online August 13, 2012).

Neboit-Guilhot, René, & Davy, Lucette. (1996). *Les Français dans leur environnement* [The French and their environment]. Paris: Nathan.

Osborne, Michael A. (1994). *Nature, the exotic, and the science of French colonialism.* Bloomington: Indiana University Press.

Planhol, Xavier de (with Claval, Paul). (1994). *An historical geography of France* (Janet Lloyd, Trans.). Cambridge, UK: Cambridge University Press.

Pritchard, Sara B. (2011). *Confluence: The nature of technology and the remaking of the Rhone.* Cambridge, MA: Harvard University Press.

Reuters. (2012, May 9). States accused of hiding data on EU farm subsidies. Retrieved May 18, 2012, from http://uk.reuters.com/article/2012/05/09/eu-agriculture-data-idUKL5E8G98Q620120509

Taylor, Paul. (2009, August 10). Order to pay back farm subsidies comes at a bad time for France. Retrieved May 18, 2012, from http://www.nytimes.com/2009/08/11/business/global/11inside.html

United Nations Conference on Sustainable Development. (2012). Homepage. Retrieved May 1, 2012, from http://www.franceonu.org/spip.php?article5232

Viscusi, Gregory, & Patel, Tara. (2011, May 30). France criticizes German retreat from nuclear power in wake of Fukushima. Retrieved May 15, 2012, from http://www.bloomberg.com/news/2011-05-30/areva-s-lauvergeon-says-germany-will-import-nuclear-power.html

Whited, Tamara L. (2000). *Forests and peasant politics in modern France.* New Haven, CT: Yale University Press.

Genetic Resources

Genetic resources, worldwide, are sources of income, food security, health, and nutrition. Manipulation of genetic resources allows farmers and breeders to improve quality and productivity. Although genetic modification of organisms is a controversial issue and the regulation of access to and benefits from genetic resources is a complicated process, the use of these resources might play a key role in adaptation to global climate change.

The term *genetic resources* is a collective one that refers to the genetic material in plants and animals that determines useful traits people can use to meet their needs. These resources range from genes encoded in DNA to particular expressions of the genes that have undergone selection by farmers, scientists, and plant breeders. Europe, Africa, and Asia together have more than eighty centers of plant diversity, as identified by the World Wide Fund for Nature (WWF) and the International Union for Conservation of Nature (IUCN), and the highest numbers of local animal breeds (Davis, Heywood, and Hamilton 1995; FAO 2007b). Naturally, genetic resources are a source of income and food security, health, and nutrition and provide the means to combat environmental degradation. Particularly for developing countries in Asia and Africa, genetic resources are among their main assets and a foundation for growth and stability. Although worldwide food production depends on relatively few major crops at the local and regional level, many more crops are needed for a number of other services including food and forage provision, industrial applications, and cultural practices. The contribution of agriculture to the total gross domestic product is 18 percent in Africa and 13 percent in Asia, compared with less than 4 percent in Europe.

The importance of Africa, Asia, and Europe in the global mosaic of genetic resources was recognized as early as the 1920s by the Russian scientist Nikolai Vavilov. Vavilov (1994) identified the following four centers of plant origin in these continents: southwestern Asia, southeastern Asia, the Mediterranean, and Egypt and Abyssinia (the modern nations of Ethiopia and Eritrea). Following continental exploration and subsequent colonization, there has been a continuous gene flow between continents. In the mid-twentieth century, technological advances facilitated the process. In addition, other factors such as the demand for optimal performance and health and hygiene standards have caused changes in consumer preferences (mainly in Europe), which influences markets in Africa and Asia as well as government policies that support farmers through export of genetic resources. The use, conservation, and erosion of genetic resources are influenced by a number of factors including demographics, technological developments, national policies, and economic, social, and cultural factors. In Africa, for example, epidemics, civil conflict, and population migration have resulted even in recent times in genetic erosion.

Population growth that exerts pressure on resources is higher in Africa and Asia compared with Europe, pushing toward an increase of agricultural production in order to meet food demands. The so-called Green Revolution has had a significant impact on the growing populations of India and China, as the advances that came along (fertilizers, irrigation systems, and high-yield varieties) made crop growth possible in marginal environments (Everson and Gollin 2003). Africa, however, has failed to benefit much from the Green Revolution because of the lack of infrastructure, governmental transparency, and security across much of the continent. Genetic material transfer, with its link to economic development, has been a major driver of land-use change in these three continents, which in turn has affected biological diversity as a whole.

Africa and Asia, despite a low investment in infrastructure for genetic research, have a repository of indigenous genetic resources—potential reservoirs of adaptive and functional genes that may serve in the future in terms of adaptation to changing conditions or substances for medical purposes. Bioprospecting is "the search for new plant and microbial strains that may serve as sources for new natural products such as food or pharmaceuticals" (Mannion 2007). The fact that some of these genetic resources are currently localized and scarce means that, with development, they might have great economic potential. For example, research has estimated that the value of increases in crop yields derived from new genes and genetic modification since 1945 has translated into billions of US dollars per year.

Regulating the access to and benefits from the use of genetic resources is a complex process, especially in the case of developing countries where it is complicated by resource and capacity shortages. As a result, legitimate access is jeopardized, and the interests of developing nations in these continents are not served. Although the Convention on Biological Diversity in 1994 recognized the sovereign rights of countries over their biological resources, the fair and equitable sharing of the benefits arising from access to and use of genetic resources (access and benefit sharing) has proven difficult to achieve.

The genetic modification of organisms is a controversial issue that has attracted much interest by media, academia, and in the political arena since the 1980s (Mannion 2007). Among the three continents examined here, Europe has not adopted genetically modified (GM) crops, India and China are among the biggest players worldwide, and South Africa was the first country on the African continent to allow their commercial release. Changes in intellectual property rights systems have lead to the privatization of genetic resources and subsequently to the proliferation of new agricultural biotechnology products. On one hand, these innovations have the potential to increase agricultural production while limiting environmental degradation. There is a fear, however, that private sector domination of the development of new products may skew the distribution of benefits away from the origin of these resources in developing countries. Similarly to development of GM plants the current development of GM animals is related mainly to improved food security and medical purposes. Since there has been limited commercial release of GM animals, however, the examples which can be used as an aid to risk assessment are few (FERA and University of Leeds 2010).

The recent changes in plant and animal genetic diversity have been summarized in two reports by the United Nations Food and Agriculture Organization (FAO) (FAO 2007a and 2007b). The main issues emerging from these reviews include the need for collaboration between various sectors (government, research and development institutions, and indigenous and local communities) and the need to accept global responsibility for management of shared resources while at the same time safeguarding ownership. Moreover, it is becoming evident that shifts in climate worldwide will have dramatic implications for crop improvement and genetic resources conservation in developing countries, suggesting that international movement of germplasm (the collection of genetic resources for an organism) will be necessary for adaptation (Burke, Lobell, and Guarino 2009). In addition, the demand of the food industry for raw material consistency forces more genetic and ecological uniformity, exerting huge pressure on farmers and breeders worldwide, with those in developing countries being the most vulnerable.

Ioannis N. VOGIATZAKIS
Open University of Cyprus

See also Africa (*several articles*); African Union (AU); Agriculture, Small-Scale; Biodiversity Conservation; Biological Corridors; Central Asia; Diet and Nutrition; European Union (EU); Fisheries; Middle East; Migration (Africa); Parks and Preserves; Svalbard Global Seed Vault

FURTHER READING

Burke, Marshall B.; Lobell, David B.; & Guarino, Luigi. (2009). Shifts in African crop climates by 2050, and the implications for crop improvement and genetic resources conservation. *Global Environment Change, 19*(3), 317–325.

Davis, Stephen D.; Heywood, Vernon H.; & Hamilton, Alan Charles. (Eds.). (1994). *Centres of plant diversity: Vol. 1. Europe, Africa, South West Asia and the Middle East: A guide and strategy for their conservation.* Gland, Switzerland & Washington, DC: IUCN & WWF.

Davis, Stephen D.; Heywood, Vernon H.; & Hamilton, Alan Charles. (Eds.). (1995). *Centres of plant diversity: Vol. 2. A guide and strategy for their conservation. Asia, Australasia and the Pacific.* Gland, Switzerland & Washington, DC: IUCN & WWF.

Everson, Robert E., & Gollin, Douglas. (2003). Assessing the impact of the Green Revolution, 1960 to 2000. *Science, 300*(5620), 758–762.

The Food and Environment Research Agency (FERA), & University of Leeds. (2010). Defining environmental risk assessment criteria for genetically modified mammals and birds to be placed on the EU market (Scientific/Technical Report submitted to EFSA). London & West Yorkshire, UK: FERA & University of Leeds.

Mannion, Antoinette M. (2007). Biotechnology. In Ian Douglas, Richard John Huggett & Chris Perkins (Eds.), *Companion encyclopedia of geography: From the local to the global: Vol. 1* (2nd ed.) (pp. 263–277). London: Routledge.

United Nations Food and Agriculture Organization (FAO). (2007a). The second report on the state of the world's plant genetic resources for food and agriculture. Rome: FAO.

United Nations Food and Agriculture Organization (FAO). (2007b). The state of the world's animal genetic resources for food and agriculture. Rome: FAO.

Vavilov, Nickolai Ivanovich. (1994). *Origin and geography of cultivated plants* (Doris Love, Trans.). Cambridge, UK: Cambridge University Press.

Germany

81.3 million est. pop. 2012

Germany is Europe's second most populated country, with one of the world's strongest economies. Although Germany leads the world in many ways in the fields of environmental technology and sustainable development, with high levels of recycling and renewable energy use, there are also issues with pollution, particularly in the eastern part of the country (the former East Germany) and the coal-rich, densely populated Ruhr region in the west. The term Ökologie (ecology) was coined by a nineteenth-century German to highlight the relationship between an organism and its environment.

The Federal Republic of Germany occupies an area of 357,000 square kilometers (slightly smaller than the US state of Montana) in north-central Europe. It is bounded by nine countries and two bodies of water: by Poland and the Czech Republic in the east, by Austria and Switzerland in the south, by France, Luxembourg, Belgium, and the Netherlands in the west, and by Denmark, the North Sea, and the Baltic Sea in the north. The official language is High (or Standard) German, but regional variations and dialects are widespread.

As of 2012, Germany is Europe's second most populated country behind Russia, with an estimated population of 81.3 million (US CIA 2012). Its population density, almost 228 persons per square kilometer, is among the highest in Europe. Germany has only four cities with more than 1 million inhabitants: Berlin (3.4 million), the nation's capital and largest city; Hamburg (1.8 million), a major port city on the mouth of the Elbe River; Munich (1.3 million), the fast-growing capital of Bavaria, Germany's largest state; and the cultural center

of Cologne, with one of Europe's largest (and oldest) universities, with just more than 1 million people (US CIA 2012). Most Germans live in small (100,000 to 500,000) and medium-sized (500,000 to 1 million) cities situated close to each other. The Ruhr region, in the state of North Rhine-Westphalia, is a network of cities that includes Cologne, Düsseldorf, Duisburg, Essen, and Dortmund, where approximately 10 percent of the population of Germany lives. Other important networks include Frankfurt-Mainz-Wiesbaden and Mannheim-Ludwigshafen. Bremen, Hannover, Stuttgart, Leipzig, and Dresden are also important urban-industrial centers.

The birthplace of Martin Luther (1483–1546), Germany remains a religiously divided country, with around 40 percent professing Protestantism and 35 percent Catholicism. Most Protestants live north of the Main River, most Catholics south of it. Before Adolf Hitler (1889–1945) seized power in 1933, Germany had a vibrant Jewish community of around 600,000, about 1 percent of the country's population. The estimated 2005 population stood at around 115,000 (JPPPI 2005). Germany has a fast-growing Muslim population; many are of Turkish descent who came to the country as part of the guest worker (*Gastarbeiter*) program.

Geographical and Environmental Features

Geographically, Germany consists of three zones: the north lowland plain, the central uplands, and the southern alpine foreland. The north lowland plain, which covers about one-third of German territory, is part of the broad plain that stretches from the Netherlands to

Russia. The central uplands is a hilly and forested area that includes the Harz and Thüringer mountains in the north, the Erzgebirge Mountains and the Bohemian Forest in the east, the Swabian and Franconian Jura mountains in the south, and the Eifel Mountain and Hardt and Black forests in the west. The southern alpine foreland is situated in the southern tip of Germany just north of the Alps. It contains Germany's highest peak, the Zugspitze (2,962 meters), and largest lake, the Bodensee (Lake Constance).

Germany's principal rivers cut across these geographical zones. They include the Rhine in the west, the Danube in the South, the Weser in the center, and the Elbe and Oder in the east. All flow northwesterly from the Alps or central uplands to the North or Baltic seas except the Danube, which flows easterly from the Alps to the Black Sea. The German government reengineered most German rivers in the nineteenth and twentieth centuries to promote land reclamation, flood control, and navigation. Nearly all also became polluted with industrial effluents, urban sewage, and agrochemicals. Government-mandated cleanup efforts have greatly improved water quality since the 1980s.

Germany was blanketed in old-growth forest two millennia ago, but the spread of agriculture, towns, wood-based industries, and roads over the centuries has expunged all but around one-quarter of its forest cover. Since the eighteenth century Germans have been in the forefront of scientific forest management, establishing some of the world's first forestry schools and promoting the practice of sustainability (*Nachhaltigkeit*) long before it became a watchword of modern conservationism. Although oak, birch, beech, chestnut, and walnut trees are still found in Germany, the foresters' preference for fast-growing commercial timber has tipped the balance in favor of conifers (principally pine and fir), which now account for about two-thirds of remaining forest cover. In the 1980s there was widespread concern that acid rain was causing *Waldsterben* (forest death), especially in the fabled Black Forest. Closer inspection, however, revealed that monocultural practices, exotic species introductions, underbrush removal, and soil exhaustion also explain why so many of Germany's forests are disease ridden.

Before the Industrial Revolution, natural resource utilization—land reclamation, forest management, and similar activities—was known as *Naturpflege* (the cultivation of nature). In the late nineteenth century, as Germany began experiencing unprecedented air, water, and soil pollution from coal-fired industries, the botanist Hugo Conwentz (1855–1922) popularized an alternate term, *Naturschutz* (nature protection), and lobbied in favor of state-sponsored conservation of the country's resources. Derivative coinages include *Tierschutz* (animal protection), *Landschaftsschutz* (landscape protection),

Denkmalschutz (monument protection), and even *Naturdenkmalschutz* (natural monument protection). About the same time, the early Darwinist Ernst Haeckel (1834–1919) coined the term *Ökologie* (ecology) to highlight the relationship between an organism and its environment.

For the past two centuries most German conservationists have championed the establishment of nature reserves, monument landmarks, and national parks (an idea borrowed from the United States), with the goal of protecting certain important bioregions and historical sites from the impact of industrial and urban growth. It is largely through their efforts that Germany now has an extensive network of protected areas throughout the country. Some conservationists, however, took a more anti-technological and pro-nationalist stance, notably the musician Ernst Rudorff (1840–1916), founder of the *Heimatschutz* (homeland protection) movement; the ethnographer Wilhelm Heinrich Riehl (1823–1897), advocate of a folk-based (*völkisch*) nationalism that links nature with Germandom; and the geographer Friedrich Ratzel (1844–1904), popularizer of the term *Lebensraum* (living space). From there it was a short step to the race-based "blood and soil" (*Blut und Boden*) brand of conservationism that R. Walther Darré (1895–1953) and other prominent Nazi leaders used to justify the extermination of Jews and the appropriation of agricultural land in eastern Europe.

The Nazi government did pass one significant piece of nature-protection legislation—the Reich Conservation Law of 1935, which standardized conservation practices among the states and established bureaucratic oversight by a reich forest chief (one of the Nazi leader Hermann Göring's many positions). In reality, however, the Nazis were committed to breakneck economic recovery and military expansion, not nature protection, and their twelve-year reign of terror left a legacy of air and water pollution of breathtaking proportions in addition to their more well known atrocities against the human race.

History, Politics, and Economy

The terms *German* and *Germany* are of Latin derivation. Germans use the terms *Deutsch* and *Deutschland*. Historically, Germans lacked political unity and well-defined borders; language and ethnicity ("bloodlines") functioned as the main cultural unifiers. In modern times, the German empire (or "Second Reich" to distinguish it from the Holy Roman Empire that preceded it) was characterized by rapid industrial growth, socialist-led labor unrest, and rabid militarism, especially after William II (1859–1941) assumed the emperor's throne in 1888. Germany's defeat in World War I (1914–1918) was followed by a brief period of extreme political and economic instability under the Weimar Republic (1919–1933), then the establishment of Hitler's Third Reich (1933–1945). The Nazi goal of conquering Europe and exterminating its Jewish population came close to success during World War II (1939–1945) until thwarted by a combination of forces from the Soviet Union, the United States, and the United Kingdom.

The Cold War politics of the post-1945 period led to the division of Germany into two states: the Federal Republic of Germany (established in1949), also known as West Germany, and the German Democratic Republic (1949–1990), also known as East Germany. The latter's environmental record would prove to be dismal compared with that of its neighbor to the west. A satellite state of the Soviet Union, East Germany collapsed in the wake of Soviet Premier Mikhail Gorbachev's reforms and was absorbed by West Germany in 1990. Since 1990 the unified nation has continued to be known as the Federal Republic of Germany.

Today the reunified Germany is a federal republic consisting of sixteen *Länder* (thirteen states and three city-states) with a parliamentary form of government and a bicameral legislature. The powerful Bundestag (federal diet, or assembly) consists of delegates (the number varies) elected to four-year terms; as of 2012 the number of delegates stands at 620. The Bundestag selects the chancellor, the country's most powerful political figure, and passes all legislation. The less-powerful Bundesrat (federal council), composed of around sixty-eight delegates elected by the states, has veto power only over legislation that relates to education, culture, law enforcement, and other state prerogatives. Germany also has a largely ceremonial president, elected to a five-year term by the Bundestag and representatives of the state governments. The Federal Constitutional Court, composed of sixteen justices elected to twelve-year terms, has the power to declare legislation unconstitutional.

Germany's two largest political parties—the conservative Christian Democratic Union / Christian Social Union (CDU/CSU) and the left-leaning Sozialdemokratische Partei Deutschlands (Social Democratic Party or SPD)—have dominated national, state, and local politics since 1949. The current German chancellor (as of 2012) is Angela Merkel, who first took power in 2005, leading the CDU. In 2009, the CDU achieved another victory at the polls, giving the party another mandate for four years, this time with enough votes to drop the alliance they had held in the first term with the SPD, in favor of a pro-business party, the Free Democratic Party (FDP) (BBC 2012). The FDP frequently has been part of the governing coalition, more often with the CDU/CSU than with the SPD. Founded in 1979, the environmentalist Alliance 90/Greens (Green Party) has been represented in the Bundestag since 1983. The Party of Democratic Socialism, successor to the Socialist Unity Party (Communist Party) of the former East Germany, has also enjoyed a modicum of electoral success since 1990.

The ruling CDU's statement pertaining to the environment says that "environmental policy needs convincing strategies offering effective long-term incentives to develop and implement environmentally acceptable technologies and thus form the basis for a change of attitude in individuals and society" (CDU n.d.). The party believes in the "polluter pays" principle, placing all costs of pollution prevention and environmental damage on the originator. The party advocates using the economy to tackle environmental issues, such as introducing a vehicle tax relating to emission levels, tax allowances for environmentally friendly investment, and levies to encourage the reduction of emissions and pollutants. The party also aims to increase environmental awareness within society, protect and promote rural work such as farming and conservation, encourage an ecologically sound transport system, and increase international cooperation on environmental targets (CDU n.d.).

Germany has a strong economy compared to other European nations (such as Greece). In the wake of the financial crisis in 2008 the country's export-led economy was initially hit hard; by 2010, however, its exports had helped it to rebound from the lengthy recession that hit other countries (BBC 2012). The US Central Intelligence Agency's (CIA's) *World Factbook* lists Germany's economy as the strongest in Europe and the fifth strongest in the world (US CIA 2012). The country possesses extensive deposits of coal and lignite as well as modest deposits of iron ore, natural gas, timber, uranium, copper, potash, and nickel (US CIA 2012). Its export-driven economy depends on the production of high-quality manufactured goods, including motor vehicles (Daimler-Chrysler, BMW, Audi, Volkswagen, Opel), chemicals (Bayer, BASF, Aventis, Agfa), and machine tools and electronics (Bosch, Siemens). It also possesses an extensive transportation network that includes an efficient railway, high-speed autobahns (expressways), navigable rivers (Rhine, Elbe), and large seaports (Hamburg, Bremen, Bremerhaven). Germany has an abundance of arable land, but agriculture accounts for a very small percentage of its gross national product. Crops include barley, oats, wheat, sugar beets, vegetables, fruits, and wine grapes. Cattle, pigs, sheep, and poultry are the principal livestock.

Postwar Economic Policies

The economic policies of the immediate post–World War II era served only to exacerbate the problems inherited from the Nazi era. In West Germany the "economic miracle" of the 1950s resulted in the utter befoulment of the Ruhr region. When the Christian Democratic government under Chancellor Konrad Adenauer (in office 1949–1963) failed to address this issue, the Social Democrats launched their "Blue Skies over the Ruhr" campaign, which helped bring Chancellor Willy Brandt (in office 1969–1974) to power. Meanwhile, the Green Party emerged over issues such as nuclear-reactor safety, river pollution, urban congestion, airport runway expansion, and nuclear-weapons modernization by the North Atlantic Treaty Organization (NATO). In 1983 the Greens won 5.6 percent of the national vote and joined the Bundestag for the first time. Starting in 1998 the party was in coalition with the SPD-led government of Chancellor Gerhard Schröder (b. 1944, in office 1998–2005). Some ministers in Schröder's SPD-led government were (and still are, although they are no longer ministers) members of the Green Party, such as the foreign minister of that government, Joschka Fischer (b. 1948), and the environmental minister Jürgen Trittin (b. 1954). In Merkel's current government, the federal minister for Environment, Nature Conservation and Nuclear Safety, until recently was Norbert Röttgen, who is a member of Merkel's own party, the CDU. In mid-May 2012, Merkel fired Röttgen, due to a poor election result, and replaced him with Peter Altmaier (*Der Spiegel* 2012b).

In East Germany, Soviet-style economic practices entailed a concentration on heavy industry—coal, lignite, steel, chemicals—especially in the urban centers of East Berlin, Leipzig, Dresden, and Chemnitz (Karl-Marx-Stadt). The country's Communist system stifled any significant civic and political discourse, so government leaders were free to pollute with little fear of public backlash. As a consequence, East Germany's land, air, and water continued to deteriorate for the duration of the country's existence. The two most visible symbols of the country's environmental mismanagement were the once-ubiquitous Trabant, a small car made mostly of plastic and equipped with a two-stroke engine that spewed a trail of toxins from its tailpipe; and Bitterfeld, nicknamed "the filthiest city of Europe," which lies close to some of Europe's largest lignite strip mines. (Lignite, sometimes called "brown coal," is a low quality form of coal akin to peat.) Fortunately, air and water quality improved tremendously in the former East Germany after 1990 as the Trabants were gradually phased out and the worst-polluting mines, factories, and power plants shut down. Paradoxically, the buffer zone that once separated East and West Germany (and the wall that once divided Berlin) functioned as an unofficial nature refuge, in a similar manner as the demilitarized zone between the two Koreas; industrial and agricultural development now threatens this open space.

Nuclear Power and Renewable Energy

In general, Germans have been less enthusiastic about nuclear energy than have their neighbors to the west, the French. In June 2000 the Greens secured an agreement that foresees the total phasing out of Germany's nineteen nuclear power plants as early as 2021 (thirty-two years after the last plant became operational in 1989). Since the Fukushima nuclear disaster in March 2011, which occurred after an earthquake and its resulting tsunami devastated the northeastern coast of Japan, Germany has announced an acceleration of its efforts to wean itself from nuclear power. In 2011, Merkel announced that eight of the country's seventeen remaining reactors would close immediately, with the rest closing by 2022. According to the CIA Factbook, before this shutdown, the country relied on nuclear power for about 23 percent of its energy needs, and double that for its base-load electrical production (US CIA 2012). In a recent interview, the former environment minister, the aforementioned Norbert Röttgen, stated that renewable energies were growing and that there was no doubt solar energy would be competitive in Germany in the near future (*Der Spiegel* 2012a). By 2050 it has been legislated, through the Renewable Energy Act of 2012, that 80 percent of electricity will come from renewable sources (German Energy 2012). Merkel's energy plans have made little progress, however, since announcing the phase-out of nuclear power (Medick and Wittrock 2012).

Pollution and Other Environmental Issues

Within Europe, West Germany was in the forefront (and, following reunification, Germany as a whole is in the forefront) of antipollution legislation. Notable laws include the 1957 Federal Wastewater Act, the 1974 Federal Air Pollution (Emissions) Act, the 1976 Hazardous Waste Disposal Act, and the 1991 Packaging Disposal Act. Chancellor Helmut Kohl (in office 1982–1998) was also instrumental in forcing other European governments to ban the use of leaded gasoline in automobiles. Internationally, Germany has participated in forums such as the 1972 Stockholm Conference on the Human Environment and the 1992 Rio Conference on Environment and Development. Germany is party to most major international treaties, including the 1973 Convention on International Trade in Endangered Species, the 1979 convention on Long-Range Transboundary Air Pollution, and the 1992 Framework Convention on Climate Change (as well as the 1997 Kyoto protocols).

Severe environmental problems nonetheless continue to plague Germany. Its economy is highly dependent on oil (imported from Russia, Norway, the United Kingdom, and Libya), coal, and lignite, which generate large quantities of carbon dioxide, sulfur, and ozone. This dependency on fossil fuels will undoubtedly grow, at least in the short term, as the country's nuclear plants are shut down. Air pollution is especially problematic in the densely populated Ruhr region and in the vicinity of the German-Czech-Polish border (known as the Yellow Triangle). Water pollution remains a problem as well, especially along the heavily industrialized stretches of the Rhine, Main, Emscher, Erft, and Elbe rivers. It may take decades to develop more-benign energy sources, clean up the country's industrial regions, and mitigate the damage caused by East German authorities. Air pollution in 2011 was also at excessive levels of particulate matter and nitrogen dioxide pollution. The mean level of particles recorded was higher than levels of the previous four years, and nitrogen dioxide pollution remained high. Averages recorded daily for particulate matter were above allowable limits at 42 percent of stations near roads (UBA 2012a).

Outlook

Despite these environmental problems, Germany is one of the world's leading innovators for environmental technology, with Hamburg being nominated the European Green Capital in 2011. The country is number one in the field of renewable energies, and wind farms play an important part in energy production. It is also leading the way with solar technology, for which it has the largest European market by a wide margin (Travel Daily News 2011). A recent report declared Germany to be a leading recycler in Europe (German Missions in India 2012a). Renewable energy jobs are also being increased. A study published recently by the German Ministry of Environment states that renewable technologies development and production as well as the supply of renewably generated electricity, heat, and fuel in 2011 already have provided employment for approximately 380,000 people in Germany. This is an increase from 2004 of about 4 percent (German Missions in India 2012b).

The German Council for Sustainable Development, known as RNE, was established in 2001 to support Germany on its way toward sustainability and to promote sustainability in Germany. Preparing for the United Nations Conference on Sustainable Development in Rio de Janeiro, Brazil—known as Rio+20, which took place in June 2012—has been a large part of RNE's work. At the heart of the matter is the call for a green economy. The Vision 2050 program is another important aspect of RNE's work. Vision 2050 is a roadmap to sustainability by 2050. RNE aims to deal with the absence of an overarching vision of sustainability and the lack of a dialogue on sustainability being a guiding principle (RNE n.d.) Vision 2050 is being led by the International Network for Sustainable Europe, INFORSE-Europe. This model aims to have 100 percent of energy produced from renewable sources in twenty to forty years, beginning in 2010 (INFORSE-Europe n.d.).

Mark CIOC
University of California, Santa Cruz

See also Energy Security (Europe); European Union (EU); France; Parks and Preserves; Rhine River; Rule of Law (European Union); Urbanization (Europe)

FURTHER READING

Ardagh, John. (1988). *Germany and the Germans*. London: Penguin.

Berghahn, Volker R. (1982). *Modern Germany: Society, economy, and politics in the twentieth century*. Cambridge, UK: Cambridge University Press.

British Broadcasting Company (BBC). (2012, March 13). Country profile: Germany. Retrieved May 20, 2012, from http://www.bbc.co.uk/news/world-europe-17299607

Carr, William. (1969). *A history of Germany, 1815–1990*. London: Edward Arnold.

Christian Democratic Union (CDU). (n.d.). Continuing environmental policy in Germany. Retrieved May 20, 2012, from http://www.cdu.de/english/gru-prog/gp6c.htm

Craig, Gordon A. (1980). *Germany, 1866–1945*. New York: Oxford University Press.

Detwiler, Donald S. (1989). *Germany: A short history*. Carbondale: Southern Illinois University Press.

Der Spiegel. (2012a, March 6). SPIEGEL interview with German Environment Minister: "Germans are willing to pay" for renewable energies. Retrieved May 20, 2012, from http://www.spiegel.de/international/germany/spiegel-interview-with-german-environment-minister-germans-are-willing-to-pay-for-renewable-energies-a-819413.html

Der Spiegel. (2012b, May 16). Aftermath of election debacle: Merkel fires Environment Minister Röttgen. Retrieved May 20, 2012, from http://www.spiegel.de/international/germany/chancellor-angela-merkel-sacks-environment-minister-norbert-roettgen-a-833614.html

Dominick, Raymond H. (1992). *The environmental movement in Germany: Prophets and pioneers, 1871–1971*. Bloomington: Indiana University Press.

Fischer, Klaus P. (1996). *Nazi Germany: A new history*. New York: Continuum.

German Energy Blog. (2012). Overview Renewable Energy Sources Act. Retrieved May 20, 2012, from http://www.germanenergy-blog.de/?page_id=283

German Missions in India. (2012a, April 24). Germany among Europe's top waste recyclers. Retrieved April 24, 2012, from http://www.india.diplo.de/Vertretung/indien/en/__pr/Climate__Sustainability__News/Germany__recycle.html?archive=3255528

German Missions in India. (2012b, April 3). Renewable energy in Germany creates jobs. Retrieved April 24, 2012, from http://www.india.diplo.de/Vertretung/indien/en/__pr/Business__News/Germany-renewables-study.html?archive=3255528

INFORSE-Europe. (n.d.). Sustainable energy visions: Visions for a renewable energy world. Retrieved April 24, 2012, from http://www.inforse.org/europe/Vision2050.htm

Jewish People Policy Planning Institute (JPPPI). (2005). Annual assessment. Retrieved May 7, 2012, from http://www.policyarchive.org/handle/10207/bitstreams/16548.pdf

Lees, Charles. (2000). *The red-green coalition in Germany: Politics, personalities, and power*. Manchester, UK: Manchester University Press.

Mayer, Margit, & Ely, John. (Eds.). (1998). *The German greens: Paradox between movement and party*. Philadelphia: Temple University Press.

Medick, Veit, & Wittrock, Philipp. (2012, March 12). Energy revolution stalls: Berlin struggles to realize nuclear-free ambitions (Jan Liebelt, Trans.). *Der Spiegel*. Retrieved May 20, 2012, from http://www.spiegel.de/international/germany/energy-revolution-stalls-berlin-struggles-to-realize-nuclear-free-ambitions-a-820427.html

Papadakis, Elim. (1984). *The green movement in West Germany*. New York: St. Martin's Press.

Rat für Nachhaltige Entwicklung (RNE) [German Council for Sustainable Development]. (n.d.). Homepage. Retrieved April 24, 2012, from http://www.nachhaltigkeitsrat.de/en/home/?size=1%C3%83%E2%80%9A%C3%82%C2%A8blstr%3D0%2Ftrackback%2F

Rollins, William H. (1997). *A greener vision of home: Cultural politics and environmental reform in the German Heimatschutz movement, 1904–1918*. Ann Arbor: University of Michigan Press.

Travel Daily News. (2011, May 13). Germany leads the way in sustainability and green meetings. Retrieved April 17, 2012, from http://www.traveldailynews.com/pages/show_page/43246-Germany-leads-the-way-in-sustainability-and-green-meetings

Umwelt Bundes Amt (UBA). (2012a, March 28). Press release 006/2012: How good is air quality in Germany? Retrieved April 17, 2012, from http://www.umweltbundesamt.de/uba-info-presse-e/2012/pe12-006_how_good_is_air_quality_in_germany.htm

Umwelt Bundes Amt (UBA). (2012b, April 19). Air and air pollution: What's new? Retrieved April 17, 2012, from http://www.umweltbundesamt.de/luft-e/index.htm

United States Central Intelligence Agency (US CIA). (2012). The world factbook: Germany. Retrieved April 10, 2012, from https://www.cia.gov/library/publications/the-world-factbook/geos/gm.html

Goma, Democratic Republic of the Congo

1 million est. pop. 2012

Goma in many ways epitomizes the many issues of sustainability facing Africans. The population is simultaneously threatened by two active volcanoes (which lure people to their slopes with their highly fertile soils) and potentially lethal explosive gases dissolved in the water of Lake Kivu; one of the volcanoes is the most active in Africa. Persisting armed conflict in the Democratic Republic of the Congo (DRC), and state institutions incapable of providing basic infrastructure, have had a severe impact on the quality of life of the rapidly growing population. Despite the hazardous environment, however, Goma is a dynamic city of opportunities for migrants fleeing warfare and seeking economic opportunity.

The fast-growing city of Goma is the capital of the province of North Kivu, in the east of the Democratic Republic of the Congo (DRC). At an altitude of 1,500 meters above sea level, Goma is located on the north shore of Lake Kivu, at the border with Rwanda, and covers an area of about 75 square kilometers. The city receives 1,260 millimeters of rain annually and is close to Virunga National Park in the north, with the Masisi hills, also called "Africa's Switzerland," in the west.

Since the beginning of the still ongoing violent conflict in the area of North and South Kivu in the early 1990s that turned into an international war with the Rwandan occupation of eastern Congo from 1996 onward, Goma's population has shot up from 170,000 inhabitants to an estimated one million, making it in 2012 the tenth most populous city in the DRC (Büscher 2011, 87). The enormous influx comprised refugees from war-torn rural areas and migrants attracted by the new job market created by the concentration of international

humanitarian organizations (Büscher and Vlassenroot 2010), as well as a construction boom, in which much money from the mineral trade (especially coltan and cassiterite) was reinvested. Goma had always attracted immigrants from other provinces because its strategic location as a regional trade center offered income opportunities and because the fertile volcanic soils in the highly productive rural areas surrounding the town guaranteed low food prices. "Twanjingoma" is a well-known saying in Swahili and means essentially: "Let's go to Goma to have a peaceful and easy life."

Volcanic Threat

From Goma, there is nothing to obstruct the view of the volcano Nyiragongo, so people in the city have daily visual experiences of its activity. Together with Nyamulagira, Nyiragongo belongs to the Virunga volcano chain in the western branch of the East African rift system. Nyiragongo's summit caldera is 1.2 kilometers wide and contains the world's largest and most voluminous persistent lava lake. The summit looms 2,000 meters above Goma, which is only 18 kilometers away. With an average of one eruption every two years since 1980, Nyamulagira is the most active volcano in Africa and one of the most active worldwide. Because of its less-steep slopes, however, and also because Nyiragongo forms a natural barrier for lava streams, Nyamulagira is less dangerous for Goma. As a result of permanent volcanic activity on Lake Kivu's north shore, people are continually affected by creeping hazards such as acid rain, endemic fluorosis, diarrhea, and other diseases caused by polluted drinking water. Ash and gas emissions during the frequent eruptions of Nyamulagira and acid rain from the gas plume released by the lava lake of Nyiragongo pose severe risks for human health and for agriculture, especially given prevailing winds, and particularly in the area west of Goma (Smets et al. 2010).

The first known description of Nyiragongo reports permanent activity (von Goetzen 1895) that was only interrupted for a short period between 1924 and 1926. Since 1927, the lava lake has been continually active (Tazieff 1975), but during the eruption of January 1977 it drained through fissures in the flanks, and huge, very fast lava flows covered an area of about 20 square kilometers, killed about seventy people, and stopped just before the airport. In June 1994, Nyiragongo showed signs of activity at a time when more than a million Rwandan refugees were living in Goma and in nearby camps, causing fears of a disaster. No eruption occurred, however, and the lava lake remained active until in January 2002, in the middle of the so-called "Second Congo War," a renewed flank eruption started after a major series of earthquakes in the Kivu rift. An extensive network of fractures extended downward, and two major lava flows devastated the city center almost entirely, leaving tens of thousands of people homeless, killing about one hundred, and causing the flight of 400,000 inhabitants to higher ground in Rwanda. This eruption "constitutes the most outstanding case ever of lava flow in a big town." The eruptions in 1977 and 2002 are the only ones worldwide "in which people were directly killed by lava flows," and that in 2002 is the first that occurred in a civil war context (Favalli et al. 2009, 363).

Gas in Lake Kivu

As part of the western branch of the African rift valley, Lake Kivu was formed about 500,000 years ago in the course of the emergence of the Virunga volcano chain. The lake is unique in the world because its deeper waters contain an enormous quantity of dissolved gas: estimates suggest 250 billion cubic meters of carbon dioxide and 50–55 billion cubic meters of methane gas (Doevenspeck 2007). The waters of Lake Kivu show a stratified structure, with stable horizontal homogenous layers that have different physical and chemical properties. The highest concentrations of carbon dioxide and methane were measured in layers below a depth of 270 meters, where high-density gradients prevent mixing, thus facilitating gas accumulation.

Lake Kivu's huge gas reserves were initially only of interest to the natural sciences because of the uniqueness of the physical and chemical composition of the lake water. When a lava stream flowed through Goma and into the lake during the 2002 eruption of Nyiragongo, however, experts feared that the hot lava could have disturbed the stability of the lake, thus making a future gas outburst even more likely (Lorke et al. 2004). Such an extreme event could kill hundreds of thousands or even millions of people living on the shores of Lake Kivu, and around Lake Tanganyika if a gas cloud floated in that direction (Doevenspeck 2007). Risk assessments as of 2012 concluded that this scenario is unlikely because gas concentrations have not yet reached dangerous magnitudes, but this applies only if no significant disturbance occurs, such as a great heat input into the lake during a volcanic eruption or earthquake, events that are not unusual in the western branch of the African rift valley. People in Goma fear also the carbon dioxide–emitting fractures that are associated with the Virunga volcanic system. Very common on the entire northern shore of Lake Kivu, these dry vents are called *mazukus*, which means "evil winds" in local Swahili. Since the 1990s, numerous people have died in *mazukus*, mainly migrants and refugees to whom the phenomenon was unknown.

A Fragmented Cityscape

Situated between the Congo Basin and the densely populated highlands of Uganda and Rwanda, Goma has always been an important transit hub for long-distance trade connecting the east and the west of Central Africa. Also, because United Nations peacekeeping forces deter rebels and militias in the surrounding area, the city has been able not only to maintain but even to expand its central position in regional trade networks.

Goma today is a highly fragmented city, however. The rebuilt economic and administrative center, which was almost completely destroyed in the eruption of 2002, is the busy and vibrant heart of the city, where each person tries to gain a share of the profits from smuggling, cross-border trade, and the mineral trade (Doevenspeck 2011). The center merges into crowded popular districts, such as Murara and Mabanga, which are densely built up with small wooden houses without water or power supply. The hastily built neighborhoods on the northern periphery, such as Ngangi, developed on the former banana plantations that were destroyed by the 2002 lava flows. Landowners in the surrounding villages converted these farmlands into housing plots without any consistent land-use planning. As in similar contexts elsewhere, poverty drives people to settle close to the volcano where rents and real estate prices are low. On the city's western fringe, large refugee camps, such as Mugunga, have grown to be considered de facto districts. In contrast, the prosperous lakeside districts, such as Himbi, have new hotels, restaurants, and villas for rich Congolese and the steadily growing community of foreign experts.

An Impossible but Inevitable City: Outlook

In addition to threats from volcanoes and gas, people in Goma face other hazards to their safety and livelihood, such as dysfunctional public water supply, medical care, and education systems and, not least, a high incidence of crime because of the normalization of violence and the proliferation of firearms. Goma also shows, however, that the local result of state decline and protracted crisis need not necessarily be urban decay but "may instead result in new openings, possibilities and opportunities" (Büscher 2011, 119). Cross-border trade, new economic opportunities linked to the humanitarian industry, and enormous profits from the mineral trade all contribute to Goma's ambivalent character as an impossible but inevitable city, as the US geographer Peirce Lewis (2003) described the US city of New Orleans. War and state decline have fostered a process of "political and economic autonomisation and self-regulation" (Büscher 2011, 149). It remains to be seen how the political and economic elite will use the opportunities of alternative forms of accumulation and governance to facilitate widespread development and thus a general improvement of living conditions for the inhabitants of Goma.

Martin DOEVENSPECK
University of Bayreuth, Germany

See also Africa (*several articles*); Cape Town, South Africa; Conflict Minerals; Congo (Zaire) River; Disaster Risk Management; Immigrants and Refugees; International Conflict Resolution; Lagos, Nigeria; Migration (Africa); Mining (Africa); Nairobi, Kenya; Public-Private Partnerships (Africa); Rule of Law (Africa); Urbanization (Africa)

FURTHER READING

Büscher, Karen. (2011). Conflict, state failure and urban transformation in the Eastern Congolese periphery: The case of Goma (Unpublished Ph.D. dissertation). Ghent, Belgium: Ghent University.

Büscher, Karen, & Vlassenroot, Koen. (2010). Humanitarian presence and urban development: New opportunities and contrasts in Goma, DRC. *Disasters, 34*(2), 256–273.

Doevenspeck, Martin. (2007). Lake Kivu's methane gas: Natural risk, or source of energy and political security? *Africa Spectrum, 42*(1), 95–110.

Doevenspeck, Martin. (2011). Constructing the border from below: Narratives from the Congolese-Rwandan state boundary. *Political Geography, 30*(3), 129–142.

Favalli, Massimiliano; Chirico, Giuseppe D.; Papale, Paolo; Pareschi, Marie Teresa; & Boschi, Enzo. (2009). Lava flow hazard at Nyiragongo volcano, D.R.C. 1. Model calibration and hazard mapping. *Bulletin of Volcanology, 71*(4), 363–374.

Lewis, Peirce F. (2003). *New Orleans: The making of an urban landscape* (2nd ed.). Santa Fe, NM: Center for American Places.

Lorke, Andreas; Tietze, Klaus; Halbwachs, Michel; & Wüest, Alfred. (2004). Response of Lake Kivu stratification to lava inflow and climate warming. *Limnology and Oceanography, 49*(3), 778–783.

Smets, Benoît, et al. (2010). Dry gas vents ("mazuku") in Goma region (North-Kivu, Democratic Republic of Congo): Formation and risk assessment. *Journal of African Earth Sciences, 58*(5), 787–798.

Tazieff, Haroun. (1975). *Nyiragongo, le volcan interdit* [Nyiragongo, the forbidden volcano]. Paris: Flammarion.

von Goetzen, Gustav Adolf. (1895). *Durch Afrika von Ost nach West. Resultate und Begebenheiten einer Reise von der Deutsch-Ostafrikanischen Küste bis zur Kongomündung in den Jahren 1893/94* [Through Africa from east to west. Results and events of a journey from the German East African coast to the Congo delta in 1893/94]. Berlin: Reimer.

I

Immigrants and Refugees

Voluntary and forceful displacement have gradually increased over the years, driven by factors such as conflicts due to civil strife, development, and environmental impacts such as drought and rising sea levels. Improvements in transportation and communication have made migration easier. It is difficult to speculate how changing environments will affect migration in the coming decades and what mitigation initiatives on the effects of the changing environment will be effective.

Immigrants and refugees fall under the larger category of migrant populations: people who have left their places of habitual residence and moved elsewhere, either voluntarily or due to circumstances beyond their control.

People choose to migrate for many reasons. These are influenced by push factors (reasons that make them leave, such as drought or famine) and pull factors in the countries where they choose to move. Pull factors may include a search for better economic opportunities, education, family reunification, adventure, better living conditions, the availability of jobs, and family ties in the new country. Although people have migrated throughout history, modern voluntary migration has been made easier by factors like development in modern forms of transportation and the availability of information on other countries through the Internet and other forms of media. Globalization as a whole also has created demands for labor due to increased industrialization.

Refugees, on the other hand, are populations who are forcibly displaced from their homes as a result of conflicts or persecution due to reasons of race, ethnicity, gender, and social and religious affiliations and who cannot avail themselves of the protection of their states. These people have crossed international borders and sought asylum in countries other than their own. The United Nations High Commissioner for Refugees (UNHCR) estimates that there were 15.4 million refugees in the world in 2010 (UNHCR 2011).

In recent years, a gray area has developed between these two categories of people such that refugees have been termed immigrants, hence compromising the protection that comes with their special status.

To understand these two aspects it helps to realize that during the two World Wars many people left their countries because they feared attack. Some of these settled in far-off lands and made these lands their homes even after the war had ended. It is common to hear people say that their families emigrated from another country. These people continue to influence the culture of their new-found countries.

More recently, many families have migrated from Asian countries and settled in Europe and in Africa. Chinese farmers, for example, have been migrating to Africa since the late 1990s in the hopes of becoming landowners in Africa and paving the way for Chinese firms to find business opportunities within the African market. Although Chinese migration to Africa had been encouraged by Mao Zedong in the 1960s for political purposes, economic opportunities have driven this recent influx of farmers (Bristow 2007).

It is not unusual to find an entire community of foreigners living in capitals all over the world. Most of these communities congregate from time to time and follow closely the events taking place back home. They have left behind families and often remit finances to assist them. Many people of African descent also study, work, and live in European countries and even in Asia; they maintain ties with their countries of origin, but their new countries of residence also shape their lives.

In Europe, hundreds of thousands were displaced and became refugees with the breakup of the former Soviet Union. Europe hosts a significant population of refugees from Afghanistan, Pakistan, and Iran, and more recently from northern Africa as a result of the unrest of the Arab Spring that started in Tunisia in December 2010. Although some may return home in time, others who may have lost property and families may stay in Europe and rebuild their lives there.

According to the 2011 World Migration Report of the International Organization for Migration (IOM) (the international governmental organization that is tasked with welfare and assistance to all migrants, including immigrants and refugees), conflicts, civil wars, and environmental pressures have produced millions of refugees in sub-Saharan Africa from countries like Somalia, the Republic of Chad, the Democratic Republic of the Congo, and Sudan. Droughts in Somalia have displaced more than 52,000 people since December 2010 (IOM 2011, 53). In the Democratic Republic of the Congo, cash-for-work programs have been offered to improve infrastructure and livelihoods for migrants (2011, 146). The IOM has assisted thousands of refugees and displaced peoples in returning home: 26,000 from Chad and 17,000 from Sudan (2011, 50). Most migrant populations live in camps where international aid agencies provide food, medical care, education, and other social services.

Immigrants, Refugees, and Development

Anecdotal evidence suggests that most immigrants are driven by economic need. They leave their countries of origin and settle in second countries either permanently or semi-permanently for varying periods of time. They are engaged in productive work through which they earn a living in their new countries and also contribute toward closing the labor gap. For instance, in Europe workers from relatively poorer Eastern European countries move to wealthier Western European countries and take seasonal jobs such as harvesting fruits or jobs that are considered to be low in status, such as home care. Many are also involved in various industries, hence contributing significantly to the development of these countries. The wages and salaries are not only used in their adopted countries, but a sizable percentage is remitted back to their families, improving their socioeconomic status and supporting education, health, and other spheres of development in their countries of origin. Highly skilled professionals like doctors, information technologists, and scientists, who may not find gainful employment in their countries of origin, have also moved to other countries in search of greener pastures.

Highly skilled professionals, especially from developing countries, who emigrate to developed countries are part of the phenomenon known as the "brain drain." Highly qualified nationals who have been trained through public resources are not able to contribute directly as employees in their own countries. It can take upwards of six years of study and training to become a doctor; at the end of this time, their own system may not be able to provide wages commensurate with the number of years spent in medical school. As a result, many doctors in countries like Kenya and Malawi have left for the United Kingdom and other countries. This movement takes place even as these African countries report a lack of adequate health professionals. Without health professionals and access to health care, populations become vulnerable to rampant disease. A healthy environment becomes less of a priority when the population is in such an unhealthy state.

There are those who have argued that skills and technology transfer compensate for the brain drain. This often happens between the developed and developing countries through these immigrants as well as through remittances, which in some countries may be higher than official development assistance.

Refugees, a consequence of forceful displacement, have been a challenge for developing and developed countries alike. The state of displacement often means they are not involved in any meaningful production, especially in Africa and Asia. They depend on the states that have offered protection and assistance to provide them with all their basic needs. In Kenya, for instance, there are more than 500,000 refugees from neighboring Somalia, a country that has experienced ongoing conflict for the last two decades (UNHRC 2012b). They pose a challenge for Kenya, a far more politically stable country, but nonetheless one in which almost half of the population lives on less than a dollar per day. These refugees are settled in a refugee camp in northern Kenya, an environment with an already fragile ecosystem that has been further strained through deforestation to avail space and firewood to the refugee population (UNHRC 2012b). The same is true of refugee camps in the Republic of Chad, Pakistan, and other Asian and African countries that host large refugee populations.

In Europe, refugees may benefit from the social welfare system that is well developed in most countries there. They may also access education and employment, thereby easing the burden for the state (ECRE 2005). In Africa and Asia, mainly United Nations (UN) agencies and nongovernmental organizations (NGOs) assist refugees. Some countries, however, have made it possible for refugees to be integrated and provided them with the means of making a living. For instance, in Tanzania land may be provided for settlement by refugees (UNHCR 2012a).

Organizations, Institutions, and Conventions

Many organizations have been formed and conventions and laws passed to assist immigrants and refugees. As discussed previously, the IOM is tasked with welfare and assistance of migrants, including immigrants and refugees. The International Convention on the Protection of the Rights of All Migrant Workers and Members of Their Families is the main international instrument that governs how states should deal with immigrants. The International Labor Organization (ILO) works closely with the IOM to ensure adherence to the provisions of this convention.

The United Nations High Commissioner for Refugees is the mandated refugee agency of the United Nations. There are many other organizations, both governmental and nongovernmental, that offer protection and assistance to refugees in Africa, Asia, and Europe, as well as elsewhere in the world. The 1951 UN Convention relating to the status of refugees and the 1967 protocol relating to the status of refugees guide the UNHCR and these other organizations. At a continental level, the African Union adopted the 1969 Organization of African Unity (OAU) Convention governing the specific aspects of refugee problems in Africa. The European Union has its own guidelines on refugee management within the union. Individual states also have their own national immigration and refugee legislation.

Refugee management is to be understood in the larger context of countries working to address the reasons that lead to displacement and produce refugees in the first place. This work includes the promotion of democracy and the upholding of human rights; the cessation of conflicts, other hostilities, and wars; and the ability to address disasters that may produce refugees to ensure people can return to their homes and rebuild their lives in an amicable manner.

Immigration has always been a rather political issue in many parts of the world, but has been compounded in recent years by increasing levels of unemployment and the worldwide economic downturn. Immigrants have often been accused of reaping social benefits in the countries of destination, while people tend to forget that they too contribute to the development of these countries. Some native residents (many of whom are themselves ancestors of earlier immigrants) in the host countries have accused them of taking jobs from locals, increasing crime, and creating informal settlements. This is especially important considering that most immigrants live in communities comprised of other immigrants and refugees and tend to stay in touch with others from the same country of origin. The integration debate has been rife in many European countries, with proponents arguing that immigrants should adopt the cultures of their adopted countries, while the immigrants in turn argue that they do not want to lose their identity.

The refugees' institution is said to have been abused by some. Whereas refuge should be granted to those who cannot avail themselves of the protection of their states, there are those who seek refugee status for economic reasons. This has made refugee status determination, a process of establishing bona fide refugees, difficult. Some economic immigrants may have been granted refugee status at the expense of genuine refugees.

The side-by-side existence of refugees and communities that host them has been a challenge in Africa and Asia, especially because the international community provides assistance with food, education, and medical facilities, benefits the host community may not be able to access. Those in the host country may feel disenfranchised, which leads to tension. Refugee holding camps have also been accused of being used by insurgents to pursue war and destabilize other countries. Numerous reports by the United Nations and other organizations indicate that refugees, especially in Africa and Asia, are vulnerable to recruitment into armed groups, children are kidnapped and recruited as soldiers, and women and children provide forced labor and fall victim to sexual abuse. (For an example, see US Department of State

2012.) Governments that close refugee camps they believe are security threats deny protection to vulnerable women and children.

Climate Change

Conflict is not the only cause of displacement for immigrants and refugees. Global climate change has driven people from their homes, and the numbers of refugees are predicted to rise. By 2050, there likely will be more than 25 million refugees as a result of climate change, "replac[ing] war and persecution as the leading cause of global displacement" (Sanders 2009). Legal recognition of climate change refugees is far from comprehensive, which translates to little or no direct funding. Refugee camps that were built to house those escaping conflict have been inundated; a camp on the Kenya-Somalia border was built to house 90,000 people, but now contains more than three times that many. Many of these climate change refugees are farmers and herders who have lost land and livestock due to prolonged drought, which has an extended impact on a nation's food security (Sanders 2009).

The challenge of identifying climate change displacement lies in the lack of a universal, concrete definition and the difficulty in identifying disasters directly caused by climate change. The European Union has taken steps to address both the causes and results of climate change immigration. The EU funded a two-year study, Environmental Change and Forced Migration Scenarios, to investigate causes of environmentally forced migration in relation to social, political, and economic phenomena. In 2009 the European Refugee Fund started the "funding of projects investigating environmental degradation as [a] possible trigger for forced migration to EU Member States" (Ammer 2009).

Outlook

Climate change and population growth are creating a perpetual cycle.

> [A]s global warming accelerates, the world's population continues to grow, creating more demand for food. Tragically, the greatest population growth is projected for the poorest countries on the planet, those least able to feed the people they have now. We can expect mass starvation and mass exodus, generating waves of migration that may well overwhelm other countries, even entire regions, creating a domino effect of hunger, desperation, and violence. (Liz 2011)

There are many ways to mitigate these events, such as teaching sustainable agricultural practices that can produce abundant food in difficult climate conditions, slowing the progress of climate change, and identifying the most at-risk locations for drought and rising sea levels (Liz 2011).

Until armed conflicts are resolved and the social and environmental reasons that make people flee their homes have been addressed, many are unwilling to return home. This calls for the concerted effort of the states and the international community to find sustainable ways of resolving conflicts.

In a globalized world shaped by ease of transport and communication, among other facilitating factors, immigration will continue. The discussion on the challenge of handling the volumes of immigrants and harnessing the development potentials of this population will continue to be prominent in countries of origin and destination as well as at international forums.

Caroline Muthoni NJUKI
Intergovernmental Authority on Development (IGAD)

See also African Union (AU); Climate Change Refugees (Africa); Desertification (Africa); European Union (EU); Migration (Africa); Rule of Law (Africa); Rule of Law (European Union)

FURTHER READING

Ammer, Margit. (2009). Climate change and human rights: The status of climate refugees in Europe. Retrieved July 27, 2012, from http://bim.lbg.ac.at/files/sites/bim/ClimateChange_BIM_1.pdf

Beyani, Chaloka. (1995). State responsibility for the prevention and resolution of forced displacement in international law. *International Journal of Refugee Law, special issue*, 131–137.

Bristow, Michael. (2007, November 29). China in Africa: Developing ties. Retrieved July 26, 2012, from http://news.bbc.co.uk/2/hi/africa/7118941.stm

Duffield, Mark. (2001). Global governance and the causes of conflict. In Mark Duffield (Ed.), *Global governance and the new wars: The merging of development and security*. London: Zed Books.

European Council on Refugees and Exiles (ECRE). (2005, July). Towards the integration of refugees in Europe. Retrieved July 26, 2012, from www.ecre.org/component/downloads/downloads/125.html

European Council on Refugees and Exiles (ECRE). (n.d.). Homepage. Retrieved February 29, 2012, from http://www.ecre.org/European Council on Refugees and Exiles

European Environment Agency (EEA). Climate refugees. Retrieved July 27, 2012, from http://www.eea.europa.eu/signals/signals-2011/galleries/climate-refugees

Forced Migration Online. (2012). Homepage. Retrieved February 29, 2012, from http://forcedmigration.org/

Forced Migration Review. (1999, December). Culture in exile. Retrieved February 29, 2012, from http://www.fmreview.org/FMRpdfs/FMR06/fmr6full.pdf

International Migration Organization (IMO). (2011). World migration report 2011. Retrieved July 28, 2012, from http://www.iom.int/jahia/webdav/shared/shared/mainsite/policy_and_research/wmr2011/Chapter2-International-Migration-Annual-Review-2010-2011.pdf

Kibreab, Gaim. (1999). Revisiting the debate on people, place identity, and displacement. *Journal of Refugee Studies, 12*(4), 384–410.

Liz, Frank. (2011, November 28). Climate change and food shortage refugees. Retrieved July 27, 2012, from http://savingaplanetatrisk. org/climate-change-food-shortage/

Malkkhi, Liisa H. (1995). Refugees and exile: From refugees and humanitarian action to the new national order of things. *Annual Review of Anthropology, 24*, 495–523.

Sanders, Edmund. (2009, October 25). Fleeing drought in the Horn of Africa. Retrieved July 27, 2012, from http://articles.latimes. com/2009/oct/25/world/fg-climate-refugees25

Shum, Keane. (2011, February). A new comprehensive plan of action: Addressing the refugee protection gap in southeast Asia through local and regional integration. *Oxford Monitor of Forced Migration, 1*(1), 60–77. Retrieved July 27, 2012, from http://oxmofm.com/wp-content/uploads/2010/08/12-SHUM-OxMo-vol-1-no-1.pdf

Turk, Volker. (1999). The role of UNHCR in the development of international refugee law. In Frances Nicholson & Patrick Twomey (Eds.), *Refugee rights and realities: Evolving international concepts and regimes* (pp. 153–155). Cambridge, UK: Cambridge University Press.

Turton, David. (2003). *Refugees and other forced migrants: Towards a unitary study of forced migration* (RSC working paper 13) Retrieved February 29, 2012, from http://repository.forcedmigration.org/show_metadata.jsp?pid=fmo:2532

United Nations High Commissioner for Refugees (UNHCR). (2011). UNHCR report: 80% of world's refugees in developing countries. Retrieved July 26, 2012, from http://www.unhcr.org/cgi-bin/texis/vtx/home/opendocPDFViewer.html?docid=4df9fd696&query=2010 15.4 million refugees

United Nations High Commissioner for Refugees (UNHCR). (2012a). 2012 UNHRC country operations profile: United Republic of Tanzania. Retrieved July 26, 2012, from http://www.unhcr.org/pages/49e45c736.html

United Nations High Commissioner for Refugees (UNHCR). (2012b). 2012 UNHRC country operations profile: Kenya. Retrieved July 26, 2012, from http://www.unhcr.org/pages/49e483a16.html

United States (US) Department of State. (2012, June 19). 2012 trafficking in persons report: Sudan. Retrieved July 27, 2012, from http://www.unhcr.org/refworld/country,,,,SDN,,4fe30c939,0.html

Zetter, Roger. (1991). Labelling refugees: Forming and transforming a bureaucratic identity. *Journal of Refugee Studies, 4*(1), 39–62.

Indus River

The Indus River, the principal waterway of Pakistan and source of the word "India," is one of the world's great rivers and the source of ancient civilizations. Its flooding has created both fertile farmland and great loss of life and land. Climatic changes are causing ice melt from the Tibetan Plateau, the source of the Indus River, which may cause disastrous floods, deforestation, and damage to wildlife and vegetation.

The Indus River is the principal waterway of Pakistan and one of the geographical focal points of the Indus civilization (2500–1900 BCE), the first period of urbanization on the Indian subcontinent. The ancient name of the river was Sindhu, from which the Pakistani province of Sind takes its name. It is a simple sound shift from Sindhu to Indus, and from Indus comes the name India.

The Indus's Source and Course

The Indus basin lies in Afghanistan, China, India, and Pakistan. The Swedish geographer and explorer Sven Hedin found the source of the Indus River in 1907 at the sacred spring of Singikabab near Mapam Yumco Lake (Manasarowar Lake) in Tibet. The lake is also the source of the Sutlej River, which joins the Indus after its long course through the Himalaya and Punjab. The Indus initially flows west, then northwest, where the Gar Tsangpo joins it, past Skardu and into Gilgit, before it makes a great arcing turn to the south, at the same time dropping precipitously out of the confinement of the great mountains. Along this path many smaller mountain torrents in this vast watershed feed the river. The Kabul River joins the Indus near Attock. Passing south through the Salt Range, the Indus enters the Punjab plains near Kalabagh, where the Tochi-Kuram and Zhob-Gomal streams join

it. At this point the modern Indus, for the most part, flows within a deep entrenchment and is not a widely meandering river.

Below the Salt Range the Indus begins to be navigable, at least by small craft. Passing the city of Dera Ghazi Khan in Punjab, Pakistan, the Indus enters the central region at a point known as the *panjnad,* where the five rivers of the Punjab (Jhelum, Chenab, Ravi, Beas, and Sutlej) join the Indus.

In its lower course in Sind, the Indus flows through and has filled the geological syncline (trough of stratified rock) that formed when the main peninsular landmass of India collided with the rest of Asia. This syncline is the western edge, or scar, resulting from this intercontinental "accident." Its partner is the Ganga Valley, also a deep syncline filled with alluvium on the nose of the intercontinental collision that began in the Mesozoic era (c. 245– c. 66.4 million years ago) and continues unabated today.

The Indus and Ancient Civilization

The Indus, its tributaries, and its associated features bring prosperity to the surrounding region. The uncontrolled river inundates vast areas, making agriculture exceptionally productive. The rivers also teem with fish and other useful products like prawns (Meadows and Meadows 1999). The Indus River is also home to the endangered Indus River dolphin. Food production and the Neolithic Revolution in the subcontinent took place in the hills and piedmonts of the western Indus Valley. (The Neolithic Revolution marked the change from a hunter-gatherer society to one based on agriculture.) The productivity of the landscape generally led to the Indus civilization's establishment, which covered a million square kilometers and sent sea traders to Mesopotamia and the mouth of the Red Sea. Mohenjo Daro and Harappa are well-known cities of antiquity, but in total archaeologists are familiar with more than a thousand Indus sites.

The Indus River is reputed to have destroyed the civilization of Mohenjo Daro. Just after 2000 BCE a natural dam was believed to have formed across the Indus just below Mohenjo Daro, engulfing the city in a mass of mud and water. Archaeologists have discredited this theory, however, because they have found no trace of the dam. It has become clear that the unconsolidated alluvium of the valley could not withstand the static pressure of the water behind such an obstruction (Possehl 2002).

The Indus is considered the breadbasket of Pakistan. After their independence from Great Britain in 1947, India and Pakistan disputed the use of the water of the Indus and its five tributaries. In 1960, with the help of the World Bank, the two countries signed the Indus Waters Treaty. India took control of the three easternmost rivers: the Sutlej, the Beas, and the Ravi. The three western rivers—the Jhelum, the Chenab and the Indus—went to Pakistan.

Statistical Data

A sampler of statistics gives some impression of the size of the Indus, especially as it compares to other mature rivers. (See table 1 below.)

In comparison, the Nile, another of the rivers that gave birth to a great civilization of antiquity, inundates more steadily and more deliberately than the Indus (Buckley 1893). The Nile is measurably smaller (although much longer); it discharges an average of about 8,400 cubic meters per second. The Indus also carries significantly more silt. The total volume of silt the Indus carries during the hundred days of inundation has been estimated to be approximately 95 million cubic meters; the same statistic for the Nile would be only 32 million cubic meters.

Flooding

Within the plains of modern Sind, the Indus River is a fully mature stream. It is a powerful, violent, and unpredictable river. The winter snowfall in the Himalaya, not springtime rains, causes many floods. Flooding during any particular year leads to breaks in the upstream reaches. These breaks diminish the pressure for breach in the lower reaches of the stream. Floods moving to the east or west of the stream may leave the opposite side of the river wholly or comparatively unaffected, so that in any given year only parts of the valley flood, and some areas go dry for several years in a row. Floods are generally a blessing, and the Indus Valley has been free of famine for as long as we know.

Natural catastrophes in the Himalayan reaches of the river, not excessive snowfall and rain, cause the worst floods. The flood of 1841 began, for example, with the collapse of an ice bridge in the Shyok tributary, in the Himalaya on the upper course of the Indus in the fall of 1840. This flood formed a temporary lake 19 kilometers long, 800 meters wide, and 120 meters deep. When the dam was breached, it sent a wall of water down the river. It took two days to reach Attock in northern Punjab, where it passed as a wall of thick, muddy water 9 meters high. The 1874 flood was not linked to a natural catastrophe, but it washed away eighty towns and villages and a large portion of the city of Jacobabad. The 1942 flood left 400,000 people homeless. The floodwaters spread over 8,000 square kilometers, carrying away everything they encountered before them and destroying roads, bridges, railways, entire villages, farmsteads, and fields. The river flooded in 1973 and 1976 as well.

The 2010 flood in the Indus River began in July following heavy monsoon rains, which lasted about two months, and devastated a large area of Pakistan. Observers described the rains as the worst in this region in the last eighty years. In early August, the flood destroyed 5,665 square kilometers of cropland in the northern parts of western Punjab. The riverbank burst at

TABLE 1. Indus River Statistics

Total length	2,900 kilometers
Basin size	1,081,718 square kilometers
Total drainage area	1,165,000 square kilometers
Annual average discharge	207 cubic kilometers
Headwaters (inside Chinese-controlled Tibet)	5,000 meters above sea level
Species	25 amphibians, 147 fish

Source: Wong et al. (2007, 25–27); Kalpakian (2004, 149–182).

Sukkur in Sind Province. More than two thousand people died and over a million were left homeless as of September (BBC News 2010). The flood submerged nearly 69,000 square kilometers of fertile cropland (an area slightly smaller than Ireland) and killed 200,000 livestock.

Environmental Issues

The Tibetan Plateau, source of the Indus River, contains the world's third-largest reservoir of ice. The Chinese government has issued warnings that the Tibetan glaciers are retreating at a higher speed because of increased temperature in this region, which is four times greater than elsewhere in China. This melting will cause floods in the Indus River on a massive scale in the future. Increased deforestation, industrial waste, and global warming have affected the vegetation and wildlife of the Indus delta. These changes threaten food production in the region as well. High temperatures have caused water evaporation, which has increased salt concentration, leaving the land unsuitable for cultivation. The river may spread its course westward in a couple of centuries, a serious concern for town planning.

The government of Sind Province in Pakistan celebrated Sindhu Darya Day, or Indus River Day, on 24 January 2010 to raise people's awareness of the critical situation of the Indus River from a climatic perspective. The government will continue to celebrate the day every year.

The Indus is one of the great rivers of the world. Violent as it may be from time to time, it has been a source of food and inspiration for millennia.

Gregory L. POSSEHL
University of Pennsylvania

See also Central Asia; Middle East; Nile River; Pakistan; Transboundary Water Issues; Urbanization (Western Asia and Northern Africa); Water Use and Rights (Middle East)

This article was adapted by the editors from the late Gregory L. Possehl's article "Indus River" in Shepard Krech III, J. R. McNeill, and Carolyn Merchant (Eds.), *Encyclopedia of World Environmental History*, pp. 680–682. Great Barrington, MA: Berkshire Publishing (2003).

FURTHER READING

British Broadcasting Company (BBC) News. (2010, August 17). Pakistan floods: World Bank to lend $900m for recovery. Retrieved October 12, 2011, from http://www.bbc.co.uk/news/world-south-asia-10994989

Buckley, Robert Burton. (1893). *Irrigation works in India and Egypt.* London: E. & S. N. Spoon.

Burnes, Sir Alexander. (1834). *A voyage on the Indus.* London: John Murray.

Kalpakian, Jack. (2004). *Identity, conflict and cooperation in international river systems.* Hants, UK: Ashgate.

Lambrick, Hugh Trevor. (1964). *Sind: A general introduction* (History of Sind series, Vol. 1). Hyderabad, Pakistan: Sindhi Adabi Board.

Meadows, Azra, & Meadows, Peter S. (Eds.). (1999). *The Indus River: Biodiversity, resources, humankind.* Karachi, Pakistan: Oxford University Press.

Mughal, Muhammad Aurang Zeb. (2011). Mohenjo-daro's sewers. In Alfred J. Andrea (Ed.), *World history encyclopedia: Vol. 3* (pp. 121–122). Santa Barbara, CA: ABC-CLIO.

Pithawala, Maneck B. (1959). *A physical and economic geography of Sind (the lower Indus Basin).* Karachi, Pakistan: Sindhi Adabi Board.

Possehl, Gregory L. (2002). *The Indus civilization: A contemporary perspective.* Walnut Creek, CA: Altamira.

Shroder, John F. (1993). *Himalaya to the sea: Geology, geomorphology and the Quaternary.* London: Routledge.

Snelgrove, Alfred K. (1967). *Geohydrology of the Indus River, West Pakistan.* Hyderabad, Pakistan: Sind University Press.

Wong, C. M.; Williams, C. E.; Pittock, J.; Collier, U.; & Schelle, P. (2007). *World's top 10 rivers at risk.* Gland, Switzerland: WWF International.

International Conflict Resolution

Conflicts can potentially cause societies to disintegrate, but at the same time they offer opportunities for social change. Understanding the causes of international conflict is no less important than identifying tools for its management and resolution, which are commonly organized into three categories: peacemaking, peacekeeping, and peace building. Resolution of international conflicts reduces human suffering, strengthens the global community, and enhances sustainable development worldwide.

Peace and security create the necessary environment for sustainable social and economic development. Conflicts, depending on their severity and duration, can pose a serious threat to social and economic progress as well as to the environment. International conflict resolution helps break the conflict cycle and reestablish peace and security and so contributes to global sustainability.

Conflicts and the Environment

Conflicts are inherent in human relations and can occur between individuals or groups over issues such as religion, race, language, beliefs, values, identity, scarcity or unequal distribution of resources, contestation of central power, or colonized peoples' quest for self-determination. Human-needs theorists such as the Australian professor of conflict resolution John Burton claim that conflicts occur when certain fundamental human needs and desires are unmet (1990). These range from daily needs such as water and food to control over resources such as oil, forests, and arable and grazing lands.

Whereas before and during the Cold War the focus was on political differences, power relations, and interstate wars (Singer and Small 1972), in the post–Cold War era it was recognized that injustice and underdevelopment engender conflicts within and between states and so threaten international peace and security (Wallensteen 2007).

Conflicts are intricately connected with the environment and natural resources. The United Nations Environment Programme (UNEP 2009) claims that although the environment is seldom the only cause of violent conflicts, it can trigger, amplify, or fuel them.

Environmental resources such as land, fish, water, timber, plants, and minerals are sources of medicine, food, and fundamental raw materials for production of basic goods and services, and hence is essential for social and economic growth. The environment—air, water bodies, and land—in turn receives, recycles, and purifies waste that results from the production and consumption of goods and services, and is essential in regulating climate change. If these resources become scarce as a result of population growth, unfair sharing, and degradation and if people cannot meet their needs because of failed social, economic, and political systems, conflicts might arise. The British economics professor Paul Collier and the British expert in African economics Anke Hoeffler argue that natural resources present profitable opportunities for rebel groups to fight over them (2002). Other scholars suggest that resource-rich countries are inclined to build centralized governance structures with the aim of controlling resources. This leads to power struggles to retain or acquire control over resources (Deacon and Mueller 2004). Conflict diamonds, often called blood diamonds, from the African countries of Liberia, Sierra Leone, and Angola or illegal timber from Indonesia-Aceh corroborate these claims (UNEP 2009).

In addition, people are sometimes displaced from their lands because of extraction operations and bear the brunt of environmental pollution from these operations. Collier and Hoeffler postulate that if such people are inadequately compensated, grievances can accumulate and possibly lead to conflicts (2002). The same is true of people displaced from their lands because the lands are converted into parks and reserves to meet conservation needs. The displacement of the B'laan communities for gold mining in the Philippines is a good example (Gomez and Polinar 2012).

When conflicts break out, they wreak immense human suffering and loss of life, as well as often forcing people to migrate, sometimes across state borders. Displaced people can cause environmental degradation by cutting forests for construction material and fuel wood or to generate land for subsistence farming. This can lead to loss of biodiversity and soil erosion. The natural resource base on which livelihoods depend is thus compromised and could trigger new conflicts.

Additionally, conflicts discourage investment, and resources that would have been used for social and economic development are diverted to fund the conflicts and possibly extend their duration. The effects of bombs, land mines, and chemicals used during conflict can render lands unproductive, thereby compromising livelihoods long after the conflict has ended. Whereas failed political and social institutions cause conflicts, conversely, conflicts can exacerbate institutional problems. Postconflict reconstruction is usually costly.

If resources are of strategic importance, such as oil and uranium, they could be the object of interstate conflicts. Some natural resources, such as rivers, groundwater aquifers, oil fields, and migratory species of wildlife, do not respect state borders, making countries prone to interstate conflicts. Environmental pollution, too, knows no boundaries and creates a potential for both international and intergenerational conflict. Developing countries, for instance, argue that today's climate change is the result of greenhouse gas emissions that industrialized nations emitted during earlier phases of development. In this respect, the question of who should pay how much to mitigate and reduce dangerous climate change is fraught with conflict between states. These intra- and interstate dimensions of international conflicts, which hinder global sustainability, underscore the importance of international conflict resolution.

Conflict Resolution Efforts

International conflict resolution includes interventions geared toward reducing violence in international conflicts, reducing the chances of such conflicts resulting in violence, or establishing and reinforcing institutions for the peaceful expression of differences (Stern and Druckman 2002). The international community's toolbox for conflict resolution has evolved into three broad categories: peacemaking, peacekeeping, and peace building.

Peacemaking

Peacemaking includes activities to find a peaceful settlement to a conflict, such as coercive diplomacy, negotiation, official mediation, special envoys, arbitration, and litigation.

In *coercive diplomacy*, also called power politics or forceful persuasion, a powerful nation such as the United States or a coalition of countries such as the United Nations (UN) threatens to use force on a target state or other actor or to impose economic sanctions—or both—in order to dissuade conflict behavior. Economic sanctions can take the form of embargoing trade, halting foreign aid, or freezing a state's foreign assets. For instance, when Iraqi forces invaded Kuwait in 1990, the UN Security Council (UNSC) passed a resolution that placed an embargo on Iraqi imports and exports. When Iraq failed to comply, a US-led international coalition threatened military force and finally resorted to military intervention in 1991 to oust Iraqi forces from Kuwait (George 1991). Micah Sifry of the US-based Personal Democracy Foundation and the US author Christopher Cerf assert that the Iraqi invasion of Kuwait was an attempt to gain control over oil reserves (1991). The effectiveness of economic sanctions is contested on the grounds that they affect not only the political rulers, but also the largely innocent civilian populations. Also, unilateral use of force could be illegitimate if not backed by the international community, as was expressed by worldwide protests against the US military intervention in Iraq before the second Gulf War in 2003.

Negotiation is the process whereby conflicting parties neutralize their differences through consensus. Here, interdependence over shared resources fosters cooperation rather than competition. An example is the 1992 Convention on Biological Diversity (CBD), a legally binding international environmental agreement aiming to protect global biological resources. The CBD accommodates the needs of different country parties. For instance, industrialized country parties agree to provide financial and technological resources to support conservation efforts in developing countries.

If parties to a conflict cannot reach agreement by negotiation, they might seek *mediation*. An eminent personality (the mediator) moderates discussions between conflicting parties and encourages them to come to an agreement, which is not legally binding on the parties. For example, in Kenya in 2007, former UN secretary-general Kofi Annan helped broker a power-sharing agreement that ended postelection violence in that country.

Contrary to mediation that brings conflict parties face-to-face, a *special envoy* sometimes acts as a go-between to facilitate communication between conflicting parties that cannot talk directly to each other and paves the way for negotiation. This is sometime called shuttle diplomacy. Special envoys can be highly respected persons such as diplomats, and they can act on behalf of international organizations such as the African Union (AU) or third governments. For instance, former Ghanaian president Jerry Rawlings is the current AU special envoy for Somalia and Somaliland.

Whereas diplomacy, negotiation, and mediation are based on consensus and are less costly in terms of time and financial resources, *arbitration* is a process in which conflicting parties appoint, by mutual agreement, a third party (arbitrator) to adjudicate an issue. Contrary to mediation, arbitration is adversarial and leads to a win-lose outcome that is binding on the parties. Sessions and decisions of arbitral tribunals are usually confidential, which permits parties to discuss sensitive issues easily. Arbitration is popular in solving economic and trade-related conflict; for instance, the appellate body of the World Trade Organization (WTO) acts as an arbitrator.

Litigation as a tool of international conflict resolution involves referring a conflict to an international court. Like arbitration, litigation is adversarial and results in one party being proven right and the other wrong. Proceedings are usually public, and the judges are not appointed by the parties to the particular conflict. For example, in conflicts over the interpretation of an international treaty, such as the CBD, the parties can refer the conflict to the International Court of Justice.

Peacekeeping

Where conflict escalates into violence, peacekeeping missions serve as a buffer between conflicting parties, contain the conflict, supervise demilitarization, and pave the way for negotiations. In the post–Cold War era, the role of peacekeeping missions expanded to include delivering humanitarian aid, disarmament, and security sector reform, as well as support to electoral processes. All peacekeeping missions are authorized by the UN Security Council and operationalized by the UN Department of Peacekeeping Operations. They are established with the consent of the conflicting parties, are impartial, and sanction force only in self-defense. Such missions comprise troops and police from different countries as well as civilian staff.

As an example, on 30 November 1999, UNSC Resolution 1279 established the United Nations Organization Mission (MONUC) in the Democratic Republic of the Congo (DRC) to plan the observation of the Lusaka Ceasefire Agreement signed between the DRC and five other African countries. In a number of subsequent UNSC resolutions, the mandate of MONUC was expanded to monitor the implementation of the Ceasefire Agreement, contribute to the national program of disarmament, protect civilian populations and humanitarian workers, provide advice to the transitional government, assist in the electoral process, and prepare legal documents including a constitution. These efforts culminated in presidential and parliamentary elections in 2006. On 1 July 2010, MONUC was renamed the United Nations Organization Stabilization Mission in the DRC (MONUSCO). It should be borne in mind that the conflict in the DRC has been linked with exploitation of natural resources, such as coltan (an ore from which elements fundamental to the electronics industry are extracted) (Hayes and Burge 2003). In this way, peacekeeping converges with peace building.

Peace Building

Peace building comprises activities such as rebuilding economic, political, and social institutions. Moreover, peace building is accompanied by provision of basic services, such as water, health care, and electricity, along with basic education and peace education. These help eradicate the underlying causes of conflict and prevent postconflict societies from relapsing into violence.

In recent times, problem-solving workshops and Track II (i.e., unofficial) diplomacy have gained prominence in international conflict resolution, especially in circumstances where differences are deep-seated and historical in nature. Unofficial third parties facilitate small discussion groups between members of conflicting parties.

These facilitators could be nongovernmental organizations, academics, journalists, activists, diplomats, or other eminent personalities. The meetings are informal and take place outside government channels even if members of governments are involved. The purpose is to brainstorm possible solutions and build confidence among conflicting parties. This technique is being applied, for instance, in finding a breakthrough in the ongoing India-Pakistan conflict over Kashmir (Kaye 2005). Similarly, fact-finding missions and peace commissions are used in getting to the bottom of conflict causes. The Truth and Reconciliation Commission set up in South Africa after the first post-apartheid elections is a good example of the transitional justice process.

A discussion on international conflict resolution would be incomplete without noting the increasing role of international war crimes tribunals and the International Criminal Court (ICC). These are used to prosecute perpetrators of crimes against humanity, such as genocide and war crimes. For instance, the International Criminal Tribunal for the former Yugoslavia was set up after the Balkan wars. Likewise, Slobodan Milosevic of the former Yugoslavia and Charles Taylor of Liberia are examples of former statesmen who have been tried at the ICC for war crimes. It is noteworthy that even as fear of repercussion by the ICC can deter parties from engaging in war, it can also be a reason to prolong the war, once already started; conflict parties might refrain from engaging in peace agreements because they fear trial by ICC once peace has been achieved.

Ready markets provided by transnational corporations could extend conflicts over natural resources by rebel groups. Initiatives that ensure that conflict resources do not enter the global market are thus an important component of international conflict resolution. For instance, the Kimberly Process Certification Scheme documents the origins of diamonds and thereby ensures that blood diamonds are not sold on the global diamond market. Additionally, the UN Global Compact provides codes of conduct for transnational corporations based on corporate social responsibility strategies (for instance, contributions made by transnational corporations such as building schools or health care units, providing scholarships, or making other donations to local communities in which they operate). Finally, the Extractive Industries Transparency Initiative, which comprises private companies, governments, and civil society organizations, encourages companies to make payments public and governments to report revenue from natural resources. In this way, corruption and other socioeconomic malpractices are reduced and more funds are released for social and economic progress. These initiatives prevent grievances from accumulating and leading to conflicts.

Implications

Conflict can lead to social change, but prolonged conflict is unsustainable socially, ecologically, and economically. The importance of international conflict resolution in achieving global sustainable development therefore cannot be overemphasized.

J. Manyitabot TAKANG
University of Cologne

See also Afghanistan; Balkans; Central Asia; Climate Change Refugees (Africa); Conflict Minerals; Goma, Democratic Republic of the Congo; Immigrants and Refugees; Middle East; Mining (Africa); Pakistan; Public-Private Partnerships (Africa); Rule of Law (Africa); Rule of Law (European Union); Transboundary Water Issues

FURTHER READING

Anand, Ruchi. (2004). *International environmental justice: A north-south divide.* Aldershot, UK & Burlington, VT: Ashgate Publishing.

Banfield, Jessica; Haufler, Virginia; & Lilly, Damian. (2003, September). Transnational corporations in conflict prone zones: Public policy responses and a framework for action. *International Alert.* Retrieved May 27, 2012, from http://www.conflictsensitivity.org/sites/default/files/Transnational_Corporations_Conflict_Prone.pdf

Bartos, Otomar J., & Wehr, Paul. (2002). *Using conflict theory.* Cambridge, UK: Cambridge University Press.

Brahm, Eric. (2003). Conflict stages. Retrieved February 24, 2012, from http://www.beyondintractability.org/bi-essay/conflict-stages/

Burton, John. (1991). Conflict resolution as a political system. In Vamik Volkan, Demetrios Julius & Joseph V. Montville (Eds.), *The psychodynamics of international relationships: Vol. II. Unofficial diplomacy at work* (pp. 82–83). Lexington, MA: Lexington Books.

Burton, John W. (Ed.). (1990). *Conflict: Human needs theory.* London & New York: Macmillan & St. Martin's Press.

Collier, Paul, & Hoeffler, Anke. (2002, March). *Greed and grievance in civil war* (Center for the Study of African Economies Working Paper Series, CSAE WPS/2002-01). Retrieved March 23, 2012, from http://economics.ouls.ox.ac.uk/12055/1/2002-01text.pdf

Collier, Paul, et al. (2003). *Breaking the conflict trap: Civil war and development policy.* Oxford, UK: World Bank & Oxford University Press. Retrieved May 26, 2012, from http://homepage.mac.com/stazon/apartheid/files/BreakingConflict.pdf

Committee on International Conflict Resolution (CICR), & National Research Council (NRC). (2000). *International conflict resolution after the Cold War.* Washington, DC: National Academy Press.

Dabelko, Geoffrey; Lonergan, Steve; & Matthew, Richard. (2000, February). *State-of-the-art review of environment, security and development cooperation* (Working paper conducted on behalf of the OECD DAC Working Party on Development Co-operation and Environment). Paris: OECD. Retrieved March 22, 2012, from http://www.oecd.org/dataoecd/8/51/2446676.pdf

De Blij, Harm J., & Muller, Peter O. (2002). *Geography: Realms, regions and concepts.* New York: Wiley.

de Soysa, Indra. (2002). Ecoviolence: Shrinking pie or honey pot? *Global Environmental Politics, 2*(4), 1–34.

Deacon, Robert T., & Mueller, Bernardo. (2004). *Political economy and natural resources use* (University of California Santa Barbara Economics Working Paper No. 01-04). Retrieved March 23, 2012, from http://www.econ.ucsb.edu/papers/wp01-04.pdf

Deutsch, Morton. (1994). Constructive conflict resolution principles, training and research. *Journal of Social Issues, 50*(1), 13–32.

Dougherty, James E., & Pfaltzgraff, Robert L. (1981). *Contending theories of international relations.* New York: Harper & Row Publishers.

Downs, Anthony. (1957). *An economic theory of democracy.* New York: Harper.

Galtung, Johan. (1965). On the meaning of nonviolence. *Journal of Peace Research, 2*(3), 228–257.

Galtung, Johan. (1982). *Environment, development and military activity: Towards alternative security doctrines.* Oslo: Norwegian University Press.

Galtung, Johan. (1996). *Peace by peaceful means: Peace and conflict, development and civilization.* London & Oslo, Norway: Sage Publications & Peace Research Institute Oslo.

George, Alexander. (1991). *Forceful persuasion: Coercive diplomacy as an alternative to war.* Washington, DC: United States Institute of Peace Press.

Gomez, Kevin Mark R., & Polinar, Mila. (2012, March). Extracting options: Resolving the Philippine mining industry dilemma. *Philippine Collegian.* Retrieved May 22, 2012, from http://www.philippinecollegian.org/extracting-options-resolving-the-philippine-mining-industry-dilemma/

Hayes, Karen, & Burge, Richard. (2003). *Coltan mining in the Democratic Republic of Congo: How tantalum-using industries can commit to the reconstruction of the DRC.* Cambridge, UK: Fauna & Flora International. Retrieved May 20, 2012, from http://www.gesi.org/LinkClick.aspx?fileticket=PoQTN7xPn4c%3D

Heidelberg Institute for International Conflict Research (HIIK). (2005). *Conflictbarometer 2005: Crisis, wars, coups d'etat, negotiations, mediations, peace settlements.* Retrieved February 24, 2012, from http://hiik.de/en/konfliktbarometer/pdf/ConflictBarometer_2005.pdf

Higgins, Rosalyn. (1994). *Problems and process: International law and how we use it.* Oxford, UK: Clarendon Press.

Homer-Dixon, Thomas. (1999). *Environment, scarcity and violence.* Princeton, NJ: Princeton University Press.

Human Security Report Project. (2011). *Human security report 2009/2010: The causes of peace and the shrinking costs of war.* New York: Oxford University Press.

Kaye, Dalia Dassa. (2005). Rethinking track two diplomacy: The Middle East and South Asia (Clingendael Diplomacy Papers No. 3). The Hague, The Netherlands: Netherlands Institute of International Relations, Clingendael. Retrieved March 26, 2012, from http://www.clingendael.nl/publications/2005/20050601_cdsp_paper_diplomacy_3_kaye.pdf

Lowi, Miriam R. (2000). Water and conflict in the Middle East and South Asia. In Miriam R. Lowi & Brian Shaw (Eds.), *Environment and security: Discourses and practices* (pp. 149–171). London & New York: Macmillan & St. Martin's Press.

Lund, Michael. (1996). *Preventing violent conflicts: A strategy for preventive diplomacy.* Washington, DC: United States Institute of Peace.

Mitchell, Christopher R. (1981). *The structure of international conflict.* London: Macmillan.

O'Connell, Robert L. (1989). *Of arms and men: A history of war, weapons, and aggression.* New York: Oxford University Press.

Reimann, Cordula. (2005). Assessing the state-of-the-art in conflict transformation. In David Bloomfeld, Martina Fischer & Beatrix Scmelzle (Eds.), *Berghof handbook for conflict transformation.* Berlin: Berghof Research Center for Constructive Peace Management. Retrieved February 23, 2012, from http://www.berghof-handbook.net/documents/publications/reimann_handbook.pdf

Schelling, Thomas C. (1960). *The strategy of conflict.* Cambridge, MA: Harvard University Press.

Schelling, Thomas C. (1965). *Arms and influence.* New Haven, CT: Yale University Press.

Singer, David Joel. (1996). Armed conflict in the former colonial regions: From classification to explanation. In Luc van de Goor, Kumar Rupesinghe & Paul Sciarone (Eds.), *Between development and destruction: An inquiry into the causes of conflict in post-colonial states* (pp. 35–49). New York: St. Martin's Press.

Singer, D. Joel, & Small, Melvin. (1972). *The wages of war 1816–1965: A statistical handbook.* New York: Wiley & Sons Inc.

Smith, Dan. (2005). Trends and causes of armed conflict. In David Bloomfeld, Martina Fischer & Beatrix Scmelzle (Eds.), *Berghof handbook for conflict transformation.* Berlin: Berghof Research Center for Constructive Peace Management. Retrieved February 23, 2012, from http://www.berghof-handbook.net/documents/publications/smith_handbook.pdf

Stedman, Steven John. (2000). Spoiler problems in peace processes. In Paul C. Stern & Daniel Druckman (Eds.), *International conflict resolution after the Cold War* (pp. 178–224). Washington, DC: National Academy Press.

Sifry, Micah, & Cerf, Christopher. (Eds.). (1991). *The Gulf War reader: History, documents, opinions.* New York: Times Books/Random House.

Roberts, Mara J. (2009). *Conflict analysis of the 2007 post-election violence in Kenya.* Retrieved May 22, 2012, from http://www.ndpmetrics.com/papers/Kenya_Conflict_2007.pdf

Stern, Nicholas. (2006). *The economics of climate change: The Stern Review.* Cambridge, UK: Cambridge University Press.

Stern, Paul C., & Druckman, Daniel. (2002, December). Evaluating interventions in history: The case of international conflict resolution. *International Studies Review, 2*(1), 33–63.

Swanstöm, Niklas L. P., & Weissmann, Mikael S. (2005, Summer). *Conflict, conflict prevention and conflict management and beyond: A conceptual exploration* (Concept paper). Washington, DC & Nacka, Sweden: The Central Asia–Caucasus Institute and Silk Road Studies Program.

Trachtman, Joel P. (1999). The domain of WTO dispute resolution. *Harvard International Law Journal, 40*(333), 1–44. Retrieved May 21, 2012, from http://www.worldtradelaw.net/articles/trachtmandomain.pdf

Transparency International. (n.d.). Homepage. Retrieved March 6, 2012, from http://www.transparency.org/

United Nations (UN). (2009). United Nations mission of support for East Timor. Homepage. Retrieved March 26, 2012, from http://www.un.org/en/peacekeeping/missions/past/unmiset/index.html

United Nations Environment Programme (UNEP). (2009). *From conflict to peacebuilding: The role of natural resources and the environment.* Nairobi, Kenya: UNEP. Retrieved May 29, 2012, from http://postconflict.unep.ch/publications/pcdmb_policy_01.pdf

United Nations Global Compact Project. (n.d.). Homepage. Retrieved March 6, 2012, from http://www.unglobalcompact.org/

United Nations Organization Mission in the Democratic Republic of the Congo (MONUC). (n.d.). Homepage. Retrieved May 27, 2012, from http://www.un.org/en/peacekeeping/missions/monuc/

United Nations Peacekeeping. (n.d.). Peacekeeping operations. Retrieved May 28, 2012, from http://www.un.org/en/peacekeeping/operations/

Wallensteen, Peter. (2007). *Understanding conflict resolution* (2nd ed.). London: Sage Publications.

Wallensteen, Peter, & Stollenberg, Margareta. (2005). Armed conflict and its international dimensions, 1946–2004. *Journal of Peace Research, 42*(5), 623–635.

Lagos, Nigeria

10 million est. pop. 2010 (disputed; the figure could be as high as 17 million)

The city of Lagos is the economic nerve center of Nigeria, faced with daunting challenges of rapid population growth, slums and squatter settlements, severe traffic congestion, pollution, flooding, acute land constraint, the inability of social and physical infrastructure to match metropolitan expansion, and other threats to environmental sustainability. Government and private institutions are working in synergy, however, to improve infrastructure and increase citizens' environmental awareness.

The coastal city of Lagos is the economic hub of Nigeria and the nation's largest city and chief port. This burgeoning megacity constitutes the major part of Lagos State, one of the thirty-six states within Nigeria's federal structure. Lagos State is strategically located on the Gulf of Guinea, bounded in the north and east by Ogun State, in the west by the Republic of Benin, and in the south by 180 kilometers of Atlantic coastline. It consists of two main sections: Lagos Mainland and Lagos Island, the latter comprising the original city and adjoining areas of Ikoyi, Victoria Island, and the Lekki peninsula. Lagos was originally named Lagodi Kuramo after a port in Portugal, by Portuguese traders who visited the harbor in 1472. Notorious in the nineteenth century for its slave trade until 1861, when it was annexed by the British, Lagos became the colonial center of the protectorate of Nigeria in 1914 and the nation's capital at independence in 1960. (See chapters 10 and 11 of Mabogunje 1968 for more on the early growth of Lagos.)

Economy

The nodal position of Lagos in the national economy derives from its position as the foremost manufacturing and port city in West Africa. The boom in Nigeria's oil industry in the 1970s and the role of Lagos as the capital of Nigeria until 1991 contributed to the city's rapid urban growth. In accordance with a plan first announced in 1976, the seat of the federal government was moved in December 1991 from Lagos to Abuja, the new federal capital, 500 kilometers inland, partly in an effort to contain the city's explosive growth and also due to Abuja's more central location. Despite this change in status, Lagos remains the economic, social, and financial center of national and international communications, serving as the headquarters of major manufacturing, financial, and industrial institutions operating in Nigeria. It accounts for two-thirds of Nigeria's industrial investments and more than half of the nation's commercial activities (Lagos State 2008).

Lagos presently serves as the largest seaport in Nigeria, with the Apapa and Tin Can Island wharves handling the greater portion of the nation's imports trade, while a chunk of Nigeria's industrial capacity is located in industrial estates in the mainland suburbs of Apapa and Ikeja. In spite of the national and regional strategic position of Lagos, it ranks 137th out of 140 cities in terms of "liveability," with an overall rating of 39.0, the lowest being 37.5 for Harare, Zimbabwe. "Liveability" rankings assess the living conditions of cities around the world in five broad categories: stability, healthcare, culture and environment, education, and infrastructure. The ranking is a calculation of scores in these areas. For each city, all five categories are assessed and given a numerical value, which is then averaged to find a city's livability score. The highest possible score is 100; the lower the score, the less livable the city is (EIU 2011).

The economy of Lagos depends primarily on commerce and on industries such as food, beverages, metal work, foundries, building materials, and packaging. As the city has expanded spatially and new suburbs and centers of activity have cropped up to accommodate more immigrants, Lagos has faced problems associated with street trading and inadequate market facilities. Informal economic activity accounts for between 50 and 75 percent of the Lagos State economy and employs artisans, petty traders, mechanics, carpenters, dressmakers, hairdressers, and retail traders (Okunola 2007). Among states in Nigeria (which, at 170 million people, is the most populous nation in Africa), Lagos State has the highest number of employed people (4 million); it is also the most industrialized state and employs 45 percent of Nigeria's domestic skilled workers (NBS 2010; UN-Habitat 2010; US CIA 2012). The large number of women traders is a distinctive feature of the Lagos economy; 60 percent of Lagos women engage in sales and services, in contrast to 40 percent of men (Lagos State 2012). Notwithstanding the local and regional economic significance of Lagos, the city exhibits a striking "invisibility" in global terms, ranking low in many measures of interaction among global cities, such as air traffic, telephone traffic, and electronic communication. Partly as a result, it is omitted in many institutional and academic studies of "global city networks" (Derruder et al. 2011; Sassen 2001).

Population and Environmental Challenges

The growth of Lagos has been phenomenal, demographically and spatially: from a population of about 25,000 in 1866, it grew to 300,000 in 1950, reached 665,000 by 1963 and more than 10 million in 2010, attaining megacity status as defined by the United Nations (UN). Although population figures for Lagos are disputed, the UN projects a figure of 12.4 million by 2015, which would just exceed Cairo (UN-Habitat 2010). The 2006 census figure for the widest metropolitan area of Lagos was 7.9 million (over 9 million for Lagos State), which assuming an annual growth rate of 6 percent, would become about 10.7 million in 2012 and 12.7 million in 2015. The Lagos State government, however, regards the census figures as low, claiming an actual population of more than 17 million (Lagos State 2010). Lagos State, though the smallest state, with an area of 3,577 square kilometers (km²), or 0.4 percent of Nigeria's land area, accommodates over 6 percent of the national population.

Its initial growth having been fueled by the 1970s oil boom, Lagos must now face the enduring consequences of rapid urban population growth: slums and squatter settlements, overcrowding, poor sanitation, air and water pollution, clogged sewers, solid-waste contamination, urban traffic congestion, incessant flooding, acute land constraints, illegal conversion of land-use, unbridled

physical development without appropriate legislation, regulation, or enforcement, and other threats to environmental sustainability. Lagos exemplifies many cities of the global South, caught in an escalating crisis of inadequate basic services such as water supply, housing, and mass transit systems. In terms of spatial expansion, the city has outgrown its original lagoon setting to engulf a vast expanse of surrounding areas including over a hundred different slums and blighted areas (Adelekan 2009). The metropolitan area—consisting of sixteen of Lagos State's twenty Local Government Areas (LGAs)—accounts for approximately 1,000 km², with a census density of fewer than 8,000 people per square kilometer, although the distribution is very uneven. The fact that 17 percent of the total area consists of lagoons, creeks, and waterways, further accentuates the severe land constraints, resulting in the inability of social and infrastructural facilities to keep pace with the expansion of the metropolis and the rapid population growth.

Ongoing trade-related migration from Nigeria's hinterland and neighboring countries has fed the growth and diversity of Lagos's population. This has translated to abnormal pressure and unprecedented demand for land (Abumere 2004). And yet the vitality of the local economy and its nodal position in the national economy and in transport networks help explain the continued growth of Lagos, despite the breakdown of many basic services and infrastructure and the difficulties that this imposes on both economic enterprises and individual residents (Abiodun 1997). The phenomenon of illegal land invasions in which "undeveloped land" is taken over by immigrants to satisfy their urban land needs, is a common occurrence.

Vulnerability, Infrastructure, and Sustainability

The physical site of Lagos makes it very vulnerable to the potential impact of climate change and rising sea levels, which was one of several reasons for its replacement as national capital by Abuja. Lagos is experiencing extreme weather events with increasing frequency, and its low-lying position increases risks from flooding, exacerbated by inadequate refuse and waste disposal systems. Despite the flooding risk, 70 percent of the population lives in slums that are located mainly in the marshy lagoon areas. Single-room households with shared cooking and sanitation facilities constitute more than half of housing; 20 percent of housing is apartment blocks, and 20 percent detached houses (Lagos State 2012).

The 2006 Census indicates that 75 percent of households lived in rented dwellings, 17.6 percent in owned houses, while others were free occupiers (i.e., living rent-free). More recent data indicate 80 percent of sampled households as renters, 15 percent as owner-occupiers, and 5 percent as neither owning nor renting the dwelling. Eighty percent of households occupied one or two rooms while 13 percent occupied an average of three or four rooms and 6 percent occupied more than five rooms (Lagos State 2010). The infrastructure deficits are clear: the 2006 census data indicate that only 26 percent of the residents of metropolitan Lagos had access to piped water (Acey 2010). As for waste disposal, 53 percent of Lagos households patronized public and private refuse collectors, 22 percent used approved public dump sites, 13 percent used unapproved dump sites, and 8 percent burned their refuse (Lagos State 2012). Only 643 million liters of the 2.7 billion liters of water demanded daily are supplied. Out of 3.3 million metric tons of waste generated annually, only 1.2 million metric tons is properly collected. The number of new housing units annually is fewer than 10,000 units out of an estimated demand of one million units (Fashola 2008). Paradoxically, even as it faces this multitude of challenges, Lagos continues to grow exponentially (Gandy 2005).

Every day, seven million Lagosians commute to work by public transport or private vehicles, leading to severe traffic congestion (UN-Habitat 2010). The conventional modes of transport are buses and taxi-cabs, with rail transit and waterways (ferry services) being very limited in operational scope. The informal modes are commercial motor cycles (locally termed *okada*) and non-conventional cabs (*kabuk-abu*) (Ogunwolu and Akanmu 2004). Lagos State counts 242 vehicles per kilometer while the national average is 11 vehicles per kilometer (LOR 2008).

Megacity Planning

The re-emergence of democratic structures in Nigeria in the first decade of the twenty-first century holds great potential for the resurgence of strategic planning, policy-making, and their effective implementation. Lagos is on the verge of radical transformation, with the current state government's involvement in the Lagos Mega-City Project (LMCP). The federal government made an initial intervention with the inauguration of the Presidential Committee for the Redevelopment of Lagos Mega-City Region in 2005 and the Lagos Mega-City Region Development Authority, to address issues arising from the phenomenal growth of metropolitan Lagos across the border into adjoining Ogun State.

Acknowledging the urgent need to improve urban mobility, water supply, and waste management, the authorities are now investing extensively in infrastructure across the metropolitan area (UN-Habitat 2010). Government has shown a strong drive to attract foreign investors to participate in the LMCP, stressing the vast opportunities offered by prospective development in transportation, roads, waste management, water provision, power, tourism, property development, and bus assembly plants. Essentially the LMCP is charged with developing infrastructure, mass housing, and tourism, as well as developing the adjoining town of Badagry and linking it to the rest of the state with modern transportation systems. Other functional arms of the LMCP vision include: the Planning & Environmental Monitoring Authority (LASPEMA); the Waste Management Authority (LAWNA); the Environmental Protection Agency (LASEPA); the Waterfront & Tourism Development Corporation, the Lagos Infrastructural Improvement Program (LIIP); and the Lagos Metropolitan Area Transport Authority (LAMATA), which has engaged in a public-private partnership to create a Mass Rapid Transit System (MRTS) through the integration of urban bus, Light Rail Transits (LRTs), and water transportation networks. The state government recently pioneered the first Bus Rapid Transit (BRT) service in sub-Saharan Africa (Lagos State 2012).

The recognition by the government of the need to develop infrastructure and initiate projects in that direction is commendable, given the earlier absence of a strategic vision to manage the urban environment in the public interest. There is a need, however, for greater community inclusion and greater citizen participation in planning and managing the megacity, as well as a need for social and cultural reorientation of the population toward non-motorized modes of movement, in order to reduce traffic congestion and environmental pollution.

Adetokunbo O. ILESANMI
Obafemi Awolowo University, Ile-Ife, Nigeria

See also Africa, Western; African Union (AU); Cape Town, South Africa; Climate Change Refugees (Africa); Goma, Democratic Republic of the Congo; Immigrants and Refugees; Nairobi, Kenya; Tunis, Tunisia; Urbanization (Africa)

FURTHER READING

Abiodun, Josephine Olu. (1997). The challenges of growth and development in metropolitan Lagos. In Carole Rakodi (Ed.), *The urban challenge in Africa: Growth and management of its large cities* (pp. 192–222). Tokyo: United Nations University Press.

Acey, Charisma. (2010). Gender and community mobilisation for urban water infrastructure investment in Southern Nigeria. *Gender and Development, 18*(1), 11–26.

Abumere, Sylvester I. (2004). *The state of Lagos megacity and other Nigerian cities: Report 2004.* Lagos, Nigeria: Lagos State Ministry of Economic Planning and Budget.

Adelekan, Ibidun O. (2009, June 28–30). Vulnerability of poor urban coastal communities to climate change in Lagos, Nigeria. Paper presented at the Fifth Urban Research Symposium on Cities and Climate Change, Marseilles, France.

Derudder, Ben; Hoyler, Michael; Taylor, Peter J.; & Witlox, Frank. (Eds.). (2011) *International handbook of globalization and world cities.* Cheltenham, UK: Edward Elgar Publishing.

Douglas, Ian, et al. (2008). Unjust waters: Climate change, flooding and the urban poor in Africa. *Environment and Urbanization, 20,* 187–205.

Economist Intelligence Unit (EIU). (2011). A summary of the liveability ranking and overview: February 2011. London: The Economist Intelligence Unit Limited.

Fashola, Babatunde Raji. (2008). Public–private partnerships. *Lagos Organization Review, 5*(10), 39–42.

Federal Republic of Nigeria (FRN). (2006). *Report of the Presidential Committee on Redevelopment of Lagos Mega-city Region.* Abuja: Federal Republic of Nigeria.

Gandy, Matthew. (2005). Learning from Lagos. *New Left Review, 33,* 36–52.

Gandy, Matthew. (2006). Planning, anti-planning and the infrastructure crisis facing metropolitan Lagos. *Urban Studies, 43*(2), 371–396.

George, Catherine Kehinde. (2010). Nigeria: Challenges of Lagos as a mega-city. Retrieved July 12, 2010, from http://www.allafrica.com/stories/201002221420.html

Lagos State. (2008). Investment opportunities in Lagos State. Ikeja, Lagos: Lagos State Ministry of Information and Strategy. Retrieved April 20, 2012, from http://www.lagosstate.gov.ng/uploads/INVESTMENT%20BROCHURE.pdf

Lagos State. (2010). *Household survey 2010 edition.* Lagos Bureau of Statistics (LBS), Ministry of Economic Planning and Budget (MEPB), the Secretariat, Alausa, Ikeja. Retrieved February 7, 2012, from http://www.lagosstate.gov.ng/HOUSEHOLD%20SURVEY%202010.pdf

Lagos State. (2012). *Further analysis of Lagos State specific demographic and socio-economic data/indicators.* Lagos Bureau of Statistics (LBS), Ministry of Economic Planning and Budget (MEPB), the Secretariat, Alausa, Ikeja. Retrieved February 7, 2012, from http://www.lagosstate.gov.ng/FURTHERANALYSISOFLAGOS STATESPECIFIC DEMOGRAPHICANDSO.pdf

Lagos Organization Review (LOR). (2008). Interactive session with commissioner for transportation on Lagos Mega City. *Lagos Organization Review, 5*(10), 150–154.

Mabogunje, Akin L. (1968). *Urbanization in Nigeria.* London: University of London Press.

McNulty, Michael L., & Adalemo, Isaac A. (1988). Lagos. In Mattei Dogan & John D. Kasarda (Eds.), *The metropolis era: Mega-cities* (pp. 212–234). London: Sage.

National Bureau of Statistics (NBS). (2010). *National manpower stock and employment generation survey: Household and micro enterprise (informal sector).* Abuja, Nigeria: NBS.

Parker, George. (2006). The megacity: Decoding the chaos of Lagos. Retrieved August 12, 2010, from http://www.newyorker.com/archive/2006/11/13/061113fa_fact_packer.

Ogunwolu, Folorunso O., & Akanmu, James O. (2004). Co-operative paratransit transport schemes appropriate for a developing economy. *World Transport Policy & Practice, 10*(2), 33–40. Retrieved February 23, 2012, from http://www.eco-logica.co.uk/pdf/wtpp 10.2.pdf

Okunola, Paul. (2007). The informal economy in Lagos, Nigeria. *Habitat Debate, 13*(2), 12.

Peil, Margaret. (1991). *Lagos: The city is the people.* London: Belhaven.

Sassen, Saskia. (2001). *The global city: New York, London, Tokyo* (2nd ed.). Princeton, NJ: Princeton University Press.

United States Central Intelligence Agency (US CIA). (2012). The world factbook: Nigeria. Retrieved April 10, 2012, from https://www.cia.gov/library/publications/the-world-factbook/geos/ni.html

United Nations Human Settlements Programme (UN-Habitat). (2008). *State of the world's cities 2008/2009.* London: Earthscan.

United Nations Human Settlements Programme (UN-Habitat). (2010). *The state of African cities 2010: Governance, inequality and urban land markets.* London: Earthscan.

Lake Baikal

Lake Baikal, in southern Russian Siberia, is the world's most voluminous freshwater lake and supports a distinctive rich biota, including the only freshwater seal, the nerpa. In the 1960s the lake was at the center of an environmental struggle to protect the Soviet Union's water resources from industrial pollution and massive government hydroelectric power projects. The lake and environs were declared a World Heritage Site by the United Nations Educational, Scientific and Cultural Organization (UNESCO) in 1996.

With its 23,000 cubic kilometers of volume, Lake Baikal contains 20 percent of the world's freshwater (USGS 1993). That is as much water as in all of the North American Great Lakes combined. The lake's average depth is 730 meters, with a deepest point of 1,637 meters, and its surface lies 455 meters above sea level. Largely oriented north to south with a crescent-shaped length of 636 kilometers and an average width of just 48 kilometers, Baikal has a surface area of 31,468 square kilometers, about the size of the US state of Maryland. The flush time, the time it takes to replace all the water in Lake Baikal, is four hundred years (Di Duca 2010, 3–4). The lake's water is very clear, with visibility up to 40 meters beneath the surface. The lake freezes over from December to May with an ice crust 70–115 centimeters thick, and ice floes may persist into June.

Native Species

Biologically the lake is rich in native species. More than 2,500 freshwater biota have been recorded in Lake Baikal (Sigee 2005, 60–62). Of the 1,550 species of fauna 80 percent are native to the lake. Crucial to the food chain are the zooplankton (plankton composed of animals), especially the more than 250 species of gammarid amphipods—

shrimplike crustaceans. Of these the most important is the epischura, which maintains the purity of the water. Of the lake's 1,085 species of flora, there are 509 species of diatoms (planktonic unicellular or colonial algae) among a large number of algal species. Life, including fishes, exists at all levels of the lake. Because there is no light 1.6 kilometers below the surface, the eyes of bottom-feeding gammarids have atrophied, and they are blind, orienting by antennae. Many of the gammarid and flatworm species are marked by gigantism (abnormal largeness) or nanism (dwarfism), sometimes in the same basin; one flatworm can reach 30 centimeters in length and eats fish. Of the larger fauna, there are 52 species of fish, of which 27 are native, including the Baikal sturgeon and the omul. At the apex of the aquatic food chain is the freshwater seal, the nerpa, which breeds on the craggy Ushkan'i Islands in the middle of the lake.

The origins of the lake's distinctive biota have long intrigued biologists. Vitalii Cheslavovich Dorogostaiskii, the organizer of the Baikal Biological Station, who worked at Baikal during the 1910s and 1920s, developed the theory that most Baikal fauna evolved relatively recently from a small stock of ancestors following an evolutionary bottleneck. In the mid-Tertiary Period (25 million years ago) central Siberia was a hilly, even mountainous, area covered with lush subtropical vegetation. At first Baikal was a chain of shallower lakes. With time major tectonic shifts deepened the rift valley and united the lakes. The climate grew colder, and during the late Tertiary (from about 63 million years ago to about 2.5 million years ago) and Quaternary (from 2.5 million years ago to the present) periods, Baikal was covered in ice; shallower lakes froze to the bottom, eliminating existing fauna and flora entirely. The rich subtropical fauna began to disappear, maintaining itself only in the largest lakes such as Baikal. Only cold-hardy fauna survived. With the end of the ice ages and the onset of warming, a rapid speciation (the process of biological species formation) occurred on the basis of those few forms that had survived the climate-driven evolutionary bottleneck. Spurring this adaptive radiation was the host of new habitats that opened up for exploitation. At this time as well the Angara River provided the opportunity for a small number of Arctic fauna such as the nerpa and perhaps omul to migrate upstream (from the Arctic Ocean to the lake). Recently humans have influenced the evolution of the lake's fauna with the introduction of three species of fish (Amur catfish, the carplike Amur sazan, and perch) and, of course, with the increasingly pervasive effects of economic activity on and around the lake.

Human Interaction

Although the lake was well known to nomadic Mongol and Turkic peoples (legend has it that Mongol conqueror Chinggis [Genghis] Khan was born by the lake), Russian adventurers reached the shores of Baikal and the lake's Olkhon Island only in 1643. With the development of the salt mines at Nerchinsk and Shilka in the nineteenth century, the region around Baikal became a major destination for exiled convicts and political prisoners. One of the best-known Russian songs, "Slavnoe more, sviashchennyi Baikal" (Glorious sea, sacred Baikal), commemorates an exile's escape across the lake in the waning days of the czarist empire.

In the late nineteenth century, scientists established stations at the lake for the systematic study of its geology and biology. A. V. Voznesenskii, the director of the Irkutsk Geophysical Observatory, organized eleven hydrometeorological (relating to the study of water in the atmosphere) stations at Baikal at existing lighthouses. Previous measurements of lake levels and temperatures were collected in the period 1868–1872. In 1916 the Academy of Sciences selected a permanent site for its research station at the lake. By the late Soviet period, in the 1980s, the following institutes were among those operating at Baikal: the Limnological Institute of the Siberian Branch of the Academy of Sciences of the USSR; Kotinskaia Biological Station of the Institute of Biology of Irkutsk State University; Barguzinskii Zapovednik (inviolable nature reserve in the Barguzinsky district); Baikal'skii Zapovednik; Baikal National Park; stations of the Siberian Institute for the Study of Earth Magnetism, the Ionosphere, and the Propagation of Radiowaves; Baikal branch of the Institute of Toxicology of the Ministry of the Paper and Pulp Industry; Baikal Institute for Fish Farm Planning of the Ministry of the Fishing Industry; and the Buryat Republic Academy of Sciences.

Soviet scientists first perceived a threat to the lake's integrity in 1957, when they learned of a plan developed by S. I. Zhuk's Gidroenergoproekt (Hydropower Construction Agency) to blow up the mouth of the Angara River to allow greater water flow from Baikal to the hydroelectric power stations downstream on the Angara River, where the lake emptied. The explosion would have lowered the level of Baikal by several meters and would have been 50 percent greater than the atomic explosion at Hiroshima, Japan, during World War II. That same year the Soviet military sought to build two factories on Baikal's southern shore and main tributary, the Selenga River, to make viscose (a solution made by treating cellulose with caustic alkali solution and carbon disulfide) cord for airplane tires using the lake's pure water (Yanitsky 2011). The public was not told about the strategic nature of the proposed factories; rather, the factories were depicted as dedicated to producing high-quality paper goods, which, ironically, they eventually did.

The battle against these threats initially was waged on the pages of the pioneering publications *Literaturnaia gazeta*, *Oktiabr'*, and *Komsomol'skaia Pravda*. Prominent scientists and others wrote to the USSR Council of Ministers warning of the devastating consequences of an earthquake at the proposed factories' sites. A collective letter to *Komsomol'skaia Pravda* of 11 May 1966, entitled "Baikal Waits," was signed by some of the most important scientists and writers and described decision makers as having "taken a risk of unheard of scale, turning Lake Baikal into an experimental basin for the trials of a pollution abatement system that has never been tested in actual production conditions and which is not suited to the severe climatic conditions of the Transbaikal region" (Lapin 1987, 80). In its editorial commentary to the letter, *Komsomol'skaia Pravda* asked, "Have we really learned nothing from the countless examples when economic bureaucrats in the name of the plan devastated waterways and lakes and poisoned their currents?" (Lapin 1987, 82).

The protests remained unsuccessful. In 1966 and 1967, the two proposed factories started up, and hundreds more factories, many of them related to the military and the opening of the Baikal-Amur Mainline Railroad, also began operation in the Baikal basin during the 1970s. Other threats to the lake's natural conditions include the dumping of untreated sewage into the Selenga River and other tributaries, large-scale logging and consequent erosion on the slopes of the mountains surrounding the lake (to keep the pulp and paper factories supplied with raw materials), contamination of regional soils by toxic industrial and radioactive wastes, agricultural waste runoff, and habitat destruction. The protests of scientific and literary public opinion, which continue into the twenty-first century, have failed to close the factories or force them to delay production until all pollution-abatement facilities were running. Decades of resolutions and promises of a cleanup by the Soviet and Russian governments have been met with skepticism (Yanitsky 2011). The USSR Academy of Sciences had cautioned in 1977 that Baikal was facing irreversible degradation, and although no one knows precisely the tolerances of the lake's life forms to the growing array of toxic effluents, thermal changes, and changes in dissolved oxygen and other gases, the threats to this natural laboratory of evolution are real.

Evidence indicates that economic activity has already affected the productivity of the lake. The omul catch, which reached 9,000 metric tons in 1945, fell to 1,200 metric tons in 1967. A major die-off of nerpa seals in 1987 has not yet been explained, but is conceivably related to the decline in the omul population.

In the area, in addition to the Baykalsk Pulp and Paper Mill, which has been subject of debate regarding its environmental effect on the lake, an East Siberia–Pacific Ocean oil pipeline has been planned, and an international uranium enrichment center was proposed by the Russian government in 2006. Environmentalists are raising their voices against the possible risks of these projects to the population health and the lake ecosystem, especially if improperly implemented (Mistiaen 2008).

Protected Territories

The first protected territory on the lake, the Barguzinskii Zapovednik (established 1916 with 374,423 hectares), grew out of czarist-era concerns with protecting remaining stocks of sable and followed the recommendations of the game managers Frants Frantsevich Shillinger and O. V. Markgraf. A new reserve, the Baikal'skii Zapovednik, was proposed in 1921 but never came to be; however, a reserve bearing the same name and encompassing 165,724 hectares was established in 1969 on a different part of the lake. The Baikalo-Lenskii Zapovednik with 659,919 hectares was created in 1986. Additionally, the Pribaikal'skii (418,000 hectares) and Zabaikal'skii (245,000 hectares) national parks were established in 1986, and there are less-permanent protected areas (*zakazniki*) totaling 86,000 hectares. Finally, a Ramsar Convention on Wetlands satellite observation site occupies 12,000 hectares in the Selenga delta. The entire lake, together with a coastal protection zone of 5.6 million hectares, a total of 8.8 million hectares, was declared a World Heritage Site by the United Nations Educational, Scientific and Cultural Organization (UNESCO) in 1996 (Saunders, Meeuwig, and Vincent 2002, 32).

Douglas R. WEINER
University of Arizona

See also Biodiversity Conservation; Biological Corridors; Central Asia; Danube River; Fisheries; Lake Chad; Lake Victoria; Mediterranean Sea; Moscow, Russia; Novosibirsk, Russia; Russia and the Soviet Union; St. Petersburg, Russia

This article was adapted by the editors from Douglas Weiner's article "Lake Baikal" in Shepard Krech III, J. R. McNeill, and Carolyn Merchant (Eds.), the *Encyclopedia of World Environmental History*, pp. 745–748. Great Barrington, MA: Berkshire Publishing (2003).

FURTHER READING

Babanine, Fedor. (2006). Research of the Baikal. Retrieved January 5, 2012, from http://www.irkutsk.org/baikal/research.htm

Di Duca, Marc. (2010). *Lake Baikal: Siberia's Great Lake.* Bucks, UK: Bradt Travel Guides Limited.

Dorogostaiskaia, E. V. (1994). *Vitalii Cheslavovich Dorogostaiskii (1879–1938).* St. Petersburg, Russia: Nauka.

Fefelov, Igor, & Tupitsyn, Igor. (2004). Waders of the Selenga Delta, Lake Baikal, eastern Siberia. *Wader Study Group Bulletin, 104,* 66–78. Retrieved January 19, 2012, from http://elibrary.unm.edu/sora/IWSGB/v104/p00066-p00078.pdf

Galazii, G. I. (1988). *Baikal v voprosakh i otvetakh* [Baikal of questions and answers]. Moscow: Mysl'.

Galazii, G. I. (1993). *Baikal atlas.* Moscow: Federal'naia sluzhba geodezii i kartografii Rossii.

Helfferich, Carla. (1990). The oddities of Lake Baikal. *Alaska Science Forum,* Article 986. Retrieved December 7, 2011, from http://www2.gi.alaska.edu/ScienceForum/ASF9/986.html

Josephson, Paul R. (1996). *New Atlantis revisited: Akademgorodok, the Siberian city of science.* Princeton, NJ: Princeton University Press.

Lapin, B. (Ed.). (1987). *Slovo v Zaszchitu Baikala* [The claim in defense of Baikal]. Irkutsk, Russian Federation: Vostochno-Sibirskoe Izdatel'stvo.

Minoura, Koji. (Ed.). (2000). *Lake Baikal: A mirror in time and space for understanding global change processes.* Amsterdam, The Netherlands: Elsevier Science B. V.

Mistiaen, Veronique. (2008, May 1). Saving the Sacred Sea: Russian nuclear plant threatens ancient lake. *New Internationalist, 411.* Retrieved December 20, 2011, from http://www.newint.org/columns/currents/2008/05/01/environment/

Pryde, Phillip R. (1991). *Environmental management in the Soviet Union.* Cambridge, UK: Cambridge University Press.

Saunders, D. L.; Meeuwig, J. J.; & Vincent, A. C. J. (2002). Freshwater protected areas: Strategies for conservation. *Conservation Biology, 16,* 30–41.

Sigee, David C. (2005). *Freshwater microbiology: Biodiversity and dynamic interactions of microorganisms in the aquatic environment.* West Sussex, UK: John Wiley & Sons, Ltd.

United States Geological Survey (USGS): Marine and Coastal Geology Program. (1993). Lake Baikal: A touchstone for global change and rift studies. Retrieved January 2, 2012, from http://marine.usgs.gov/fact-sheets/baikal/

Weiner, Douglas R. (1999). *A little corner of freedom: Russian nature protection from Stalin to Gorbachev.* Berkeley & Los Angeles: University of California Press.

Yanitsky, Oleg. (2011). The struggle in defense of Baikal: The shift of values and disposition of forces. *International Review of Social Research, 1*(3), 33–51.

Lake Chad

Lake Chad is a large, shallow (seven meters at its deepest), freshwater lake in west central Africa. It supplies water to more than 20 million people. Lake Chad has been shrinking dramatically due to a combination of climatic and anthropogenic factors, creating challenges for the area's farmers, herders, and fishers, as well as environmental pressures on the rich wildlife of the lake's ecosystem. Over the last two thousand years, Lake Chad has completely dried up on six occasions.

Lake Chad lies in west central Africa and is bordered by the countries of Nigeria, Cameroon, Chad, and Niger. The lake takes its name from the local word *chad* meaning "expanse of water." With a maximum surface area of 2,500 square kilometers—approximately the size of the US state of Rhode Island—Lake Chad is the fourth largest lake on the African continent. It is located in a semiarid portion of Africa called the Sahel, which is known for its fluctuating wet and dry seasons. Freshwater from the lake supplies more than 20 million people in the region (Sesay 2011). The lake is home to a rich fauna of fish and waterbirds, plus larger creatures such as crocodiles and hippopotamuses. Severe shrinkage of the lake, especially since the mid-twentieth century, poses not only tremendous challenges for the area's peoples and governments but also threats to the area's wildlife. Although the lake was included in the Ramsar List of Wetlands of International Importance, the only protected area is Lake Chad Game Reserve, which covers half of the shore area belonging to Nigeria.

Lake Chad is fed primarily by two rivers originating farther south in the mountainous Central African Republic: the Chari and the Logone. The lake, much of which is extended wetlands, incorporates many small islands, including the Bogomerom archipelago, as well as reedbeds and mud banks. A belt of swampland across the middle, the Great Barrier, divides the lake into northern and southern halves, and the shorelines are mainly marshy. The size of the lake varies with the seasons. During the wet season (July–September), Lake Chad receives roughly 38 centimeters of rainfall. Minimal rainfall and frequent droughts characterize the dry season (October–June). The northern portion of Lake Chad, which is in an arid climate zone, often receives only half as much rainfall as the southern portion. Lake Chad is shallow compared with most African lakes, only seven meters at its deepest; evaporation during the dry season therefore has a significant impact on lake recession and total surface area.

In the past, Lake Chad occupied a much larger land area than it does today, once having been Africa's second largest wetland (UNEP 2008, 52). Climatologists and hydrologists have divided the climate history of Lake Chad into three eras: Paleo-Chad, Mega-Chad, and present-day Lake Chad. Approximately 55,000 years ago (BP, before the present), Paleo-Chad occupied a swath of land with an estimated surface area of 2 million square kilometers, making up the entire northeastern portion of present-day Africa, from Egypt to Nigeria (Sikes 1972). Between about 20,000 BP and 5000 BP, the Paleo-Chad Basin underwent multiple periods of aridity, and the lake recessed to form Mega-Chad, which was only a quarter the size of Paleo-Chad (Drake and Bristow 2006). Mega-Chad faced severe climatic conditions over time and shrank decade by decade, which climatologists believe was due to the increasing effects of the harmattan, a seasonal dry wind from the Sahara that has contributed to seasonal droughts in the region. The era of geologic Lake Chad as we know it today began around 2000 BP. In the course of the past two thousand years, Lake Chad has completely dried up on six occasions.

In 1908, a severe drought first created the Great Barrier, a ridge that has since divided Lake Chad into a northern and a southern basin; until that time the ridge was visible only during the dry season. Over the next decades, a growing population's increased water consumption plus adverse climate change contributed to water shortages. In the 1960s, there was a significant decrease in rainfall as well as an increase in the removal of water from the lake for irrigation of surrounding lands (Coe and Foley 2001). Two other drought spells from 1973 to 1974 and from 1984 to 1985 caused the lake to recede significantly and brought on widespread famine in the region. Since 1960, Lake Chad has shrunk from 25,000 square kilometers to one-tenth of that area. A combination of factors has contributed, including uncharacteristically long dry seasons and the increased use of water by large numbers of people migrating to the area (UNEP/GRID Arendal 2008).

Millions of people depend on the waters of the Lake Chad basin region. The governments of the bordering African nations have attempted to develop large-scale irrigation and water conservation projects in order to best use diminishing water supplies, developing national agricultural programs and working to supply expanding rural populations with adequate water supplies. In 1979, the Nigerian government launched the South Chad Irrigation Project (SCIP) to irrigate the 67,000 hectares of land surrounding the lake in order to achieve self-sustainability in food production, relying less on agricultural imports from other West African countries to substitute the revenue earned by oil in the region. In stage one, an 18,000-hectare area was developed by 1984, but in stage two only a 4,000-hectare area was developed out of a planned 27,000-hectare area. Stage three never started, and the project failed (Kebbeh, Haefele, and Fagade 2003, 4). Failure of this large-scale irrigation project resulted from lack of infrastructure support from the government and high failure rates at the community level, where people were used to their own methods of coping with diminishing water resources. Such traditional methods rely on indigenous knowledge about the timing and amount of fluctuation of the water and adjust farming and grazing methods according to need (Ngatcha 2009, 9). Recently, neighboring countries have continued to implement programs for water resource management, but with more grassroots participation in the design process.

Although the lake's surface area kept decreasing from the 1960s to 2007, recent studies have shown a significant improvement in the size of the lake and its water level (UNEP 2008). The overall situation of the lake cannot be compared to the situation it was in four decades ago, however. In the past, experts have proposed diverting the Ubangi River in Congo into Lake Chad to improve its extent and water level. In 2008, the member countries of Lake Chad Basin Commission (LCBC) agreed to this plan, and a Ubangi-Chad interbasin transfer project is in progress (UNEP 2010, 52).

Craig ENSTAD
Boston University

See also Africa, Central; Africa, Western; Fisheries; Lake Baikal; Lake Victoria; Nile River; Sahara; Sahel; Transboundary Water Issues; Water Use and Rights (Africa)

This article was adapted by the editors from Craig Enstad's article "Lake Chad" in Shepard Krech III, J. R. McNeill, and Carolyn Merchant (Eds.), the *Encyclopedia of World Environmental History*, pp. 748–749. Great Barrington, MA: Berkshire Publishing (2003).

FURTHER READING

Coe, Michael T., & Foley, Jonathan A. (2001). Human and natural impacts on the water resources of the Lake Chad basin. *Journal of Geophysical Research*, 106(D4), 3349–3356.

Drake, Nick, & Bristow, Charlie. (2006). Shorelines in the Sahara: Geomorphological evidence for an enhanced monsoon from palaeolake Megachad. *The Holocene*, 16(6), 901–911.

Gleick, Peter H. (2001). *The world's water 2000–2001: The biennial report on freshwater resources*. Washington, DC: Island Press.

Jakel, Dieter. (1984). Rainfall patterns and lake level variations at Lake Chad. In Nils-Axel Morner & W. Karlen (Eds.), *Climate changes on a yearly to millennial basis*. Dordrecht, The Netherlands: D. Reidel.

Kebbeh, M.; Haefele, S.; & Fagade, S. O. (2003). *Challenges and opportunities for improving irrigated rice productivity in Nigeria*. Abidjan, Côte d'Ivoire: West Africa Rice Development Association (WARDA).

Ngatcha, B. Ngounou. (2009). Water resources protection in the Lake Chad Basin in the changing environment. *European Water*, 25/26, 3–12.

Sarch, Marie-Thérése, & Birkett, Charon. (2000). Fishing and farming at Lake Chad: Responses to lake-level fluctuations. *The Geographical Journal*, 166(2), 156–172.

Sesay, Isha. (2011, March 2). Shrinking Lake Chad turning farmland into desert. *CNN World*. Retrieved January 29, 2012, from http://articles.cnn.com/2011-03-02/world/shrinking.lake.chad_1_lake-chad-lake-region-locals?_s5PM:WORLD

Sikes, S. K. (1972). *Lake Chad*. Bristol, UK: Western Printing Services.

United Nations Environment Programme (UNEP). (2008). *Africa: Atlas of our changing environment* (Lake Chad: Africa's shrinking lake, pp. 52–55). Nairobi, Kenya: UNEP. Retrieved June 12, 2012, from http://na.unep.net/atlas/africa/downloads/chapters/Africa_Atlas_English_Chapter_2.pdf

United Nations Environment Programme (UNEP). (2010). Africa water atlas. Nairobi, Kenya: UNEP.

United Nations Environment Programme (UNEP)/GRID-Arendal. (2008). Vital water graphics: An overview of the state of the world's fresh and marine waters; Lake Chad: Almost gone (2nd ed.). Retrieved January 5, 2012, from http://www.unep.org/dewa/vitalwater/article116.html

Lake Victoria

Lake Victoria, Africa's largest freshwater lake, has a large economic influence on surrounding countries. The construction of dams, pollution, and the introduction of invasive plant and fish species have damaged the lake's ecosystem. Current sustainability efforts aim to preserve the lake's biological diversity and its economic benefits, especially through sustainable fisheries. Lake Victoria is the site of international cooperation, conflict, and controversy.

Located on the borders between Uganda, Kenya, and Tanzania, Lake Victoria is Africa's largest freshwater body and the world's second-biggest lake, with a surface area of nearly 69,000 square kilometers: roughly the size of Ireland. Lake Victoria straddles the equator and is the source of the Nile, Africa's longest river. Its watershed of 184,000 square kilometers supports more than 30 million people, including the world's densest rural populations (Swallow et al. as quoted in Orindi and Huggins 2005). Although the lake basin hosts a few large cities such as Kampala, Kisumu, and Mwanza, most of the population lives in rural villages and small towns. Lake Victoria supplies this increasing population with potable water, hydroelectric power, inland water transportation, and employment through industries such as agriculture, trade, tourism, and wildlife and fishery management. The lake also serves as a home for waste disposal, pollution, and invasive species. Eighty percent of people in the Lake Victoria basin are small-scale farmers and livestock owners, while some 3 million people engage, directly or indirectly, in subsistence and commercial fishing. Situated within the East African Community (EAC), Lake Victoria is the site of international cooperation, conflict, and controversy.

Geologically young, Lake Victoria formed 400,000 years ago over ancient bedrock in a broad depression between eastern Africa's two great rift valleys. Tectonic uplift prevented the area's original rivers from flowing westward, pooling the water and turning its flow north. Lake levels have fluctuated significantly, and the lake has even dried up completely during periods of low global precipitation, including during the last glaciations some 17,000 years ago. At times, the site likely existed as a collection of smaller lakes. While large today, Lake Victoria remains shallow, with a mean depth of only 40 meters and a maximum depth of 83 meters. Uniquely, Lake Victoria receives about 80 percent of its water from rainfall onto its surface rather than from influent rivers, streams, or groundwater. As a result, the lake's water levels vacillate annually, depending on changes in precipitation, evaporation, and power generation.

Managing the Water Level

Human efforts to control Lake Victoria's water levels have met with mixed and controversial results. In 1954, Uganda constructed the Owens Falls Dam (now the Nalubaale Dam), which regulated the lake's water level at Lake Victoria's only outlet, the Nile River. A treaty between Uganda and Egypt, forged then and later revised, ensured the dam would not impact the Nile's flow. For fifty years, as the human population surrounding Lake Victoria surged, the Nalubaale Dam successfully maintained water levels and river flow. In 2000, however, Uganda added the Kiira hydropower station to the Nalubaale Dam to provide more power to its developing economy and expanding population. After the completion of the Kiira complex in 2002, the two dams supplied 90 percent of Uganda's growing electricity demands. Measurements at the complex soon revealed a dramatic water drop in Lake Victoria, with lows not seen in nearly a century (Mugabe and Kisambira 2006).

Lake Victoria's rapidly decreased water levels have since jeopardized human settlements and threatened major trade disruptions. Kenya, Tanzania, and Uganda all depend heavily on lakeborne shipping for their economic health, and nearby Burundi and Rwanda also rely on it to some extent. Lower lake levels left international ferries stranded far from their jetties and fishing boats mired in mud, and water restrictions were imposed on towns in the populated basin. In January 2006, Uganda's Directorate of Water Development blamed the primary cause for Lake Victoria's falling water level on the Uganda Electricity Transmission Company's failure to adhere to the 1954 water outflow policy (Mugabe and Kisambira 2006). Other government officials denied the allegations, blaming the region's multiyear drought. A Kenya-based hydrologist with the United Nations International Strategy for Disaster Reduction maintained that if the Ugandan dams had operated outflow as agreed, the drought would have accounted for only half the water loss that did, in fact, occur (Kull 2006; Mugabe and Kisambira 2006; Pearce 2006).

Regardless, the Lake Victoria Basin Commission (LVBC), established in 2001 by the EAC to promote, facilitate, and coordinate activities of different lake-basin actors toward sustainable development and poverty eradication, still faces rising demands for water and electricity with less water to generate power, quench human thirst, irrigate crops, or transport people and goods reliably.

Managing Fish Populations

Lake Victoria's native cichlid fishes reflect a remarkable evolutionary event: their adaptive radiation in record time from a single common ancestor into nearly four hundred species. Cichlids are small, colorful fish frequently bred for aquariums. Mitochondrial DNA evidence identifies all of Lake Victoria's cichlid species as close relatives, many of which could interbreed if not self-segregated by habitat and sexual selection based on physical characteristics like color. Speculations on how so many species evolved from one progenitor in a single lake include the hypothesis that a prior period of low water levels isolated cichlids in ponds, allowing time for genetic drift divergence (random changes in gene frequency, especially in small populations, leading to preservation or extinction of particular genes) (Johnson et al. 1996). Evidence indicates, however, that Lake Victoria's cichlids radiated into their diverse modern forms after Lake Victoria refilled some 12,000 to 14,000 years ago. If this

theory is correct, it would mark a world speed record for vertebrate evolution.

Lake Victoria and its cichlids, however, fared poorly in the twentieth century. Since the 1920s, eutrophication (the process by which a body of water becomes enriched in dissolved nutrients, often from fertilizer runoff or sewage) has made the once-clear lake increasingly murky and anoxic (oxygen poor). Eutrophication encourages algal blooms, which deprive the water and fish of dissolved oxygen. Murky, algal waters impede Lake Victoria's cichlid fishes from properly identifying mates because coloration largely determines a cichlid's sexual selection. In addition, the water hyacinth, an invasive South American plant, has colonized much of Lake Victoria's shoreline, thriving in nutrient-rich waters and creating dense mats of vegetation that destroy habitat, block sunlight, and retard travel. In the 1950s and 1960s, attempts to expand Lake Victoria's marketable fisheries resulted in the introduction of the enormous Nile perch as well as Nile tilapia. Nile perch populations exploded in the 1980s and mid-1990s, and Lake Victoria became Africa's largest source of exported freshwater fish. The predatory Nile perch further destroyed Lake Victoria's cichlid stocks, extinguishing more than two hundred species and endangering many others (Johnson 2009).

In the twenty-first century, rapid ecological and social changes in and around Lake Victoria continued. Unsustainable, ongoing exploitation of Nile perch reduced its numbers, permitting increased biodiversity of other fish species including some cichlids once thought extinct. While the Nile perch fishery lost much of its monetary value, the availability of fish to local populations increased significantly. Fisheries managers, policy makers, and local stakeholders began to negotiate the sustainable development of Lake Victoria's resources. High-level authorities include the East African Community's Lake Victoria Fishery Organization, its Lake Victoria Basin Commission, and the World Bank. Nongovernmental organizations (NGOs) like the Lake Victoria NGOs Advocacy Network–East Africa constitute a regional initiative of, among others, the Uganda Fisheries and Fish Conservation Association, Indigenous Fisherpeople's Network (from Kenya), Tanzania Fishers Union, and the Kivulini Women's Rights Organization. All these institutions work for continued economic development in the basin while meeting stakeholders' sustainability goals. For example, a recent partnership between Anova Food and Naturland resulted in surprisingly high sales for certified sustainable Lake Victoria perch, with some proceeds fostering local education programs, mobile health clinics, and regional infrastructure for clean drinking water (EIN Presswire 2011). Weak or absent institutions in rural towns throughout the Lake Victoria basin, however, do remain a major sustainability challenge.

Implications for the Future

Climate change will probably further alter Lake Victoria's ecosystems, as human population and exploitation of those systems escalate. Water commissions will face the challenge of providing power and resources to the growing influx of political and environmental refugees while replenishing the lake's water levels. Fishery managers will have to avoid the collapse of valuable Nile perch stocks while encouraging recovery of Lake Victoria's biodiversity. Despite Lake Victoria's uncertain sustainability, it will remain one of the most important transboundary natural resources in Africa. Numerous social and ecological forces at local, national, regional, and international scales will determine Lake Victoria's future health and the increasing millions who live by it.

Roger EARDLEY-PRYOR
University of California, Santa Barbara

See also Africa (*several articles*); Biodiversity Conservation; Fisheries; International Conflict Resolution; Lake Baikal; Lake Chad; Nile River; Sahel; Transboundary Water Issues; Water Use and Rights (Africa)

FURTHER READING

Awange, Joseph L., & Ong'ang'a, Obiero. (2006). *Lake Victoria: Ecology, resources, environment.* New York: Springer.

Balirwa, John S., et al. (2003). Biodiversity and fishery sustainability in the Lake Victoria Basin: An unexpected marriage? *BioScience, 53*(8), 703–715. doi:10.1641/0006-3568(2003)053[0703:BAFSIT]2.0.CO;2

EIN Presswire. (2011, May 27). Anova food surpasses expectations with sales growth of sustainable Lake Victoria perch. *Seafood News Today.* Retrieved May 27, 2011, from http://www.einpresswire.com/article/432712-anova-food-surpasses-expectations-with-sales-growth-of-sustainable-lake-victoria-perch

Johnson, Jennifer Lee. (2009). Climate change and fishery sustainability in Lake Victoria. *African Journal of Tropical Hydrobiology and Fisheries, 12*, 31–36.

Johnson, Thomas C.; Kelts, Kerry; & Odada, Erik. (2000). The Holocene history of Lake Victoria. *AMBIO: A Journal of the Human Environment, 29*(1), 2–11. doi:10.1579/0044-7447-29.1.2

Johnson, Thomas C., et al. (1996). Late Pleistocene desiccation of Lake Victoria and rapid evolution of cichlid fishes. *Science, 273*(5278), 1091–1093. doi:10.1126/science.273.5278.1091

Joost Beuving, J. (2010). Playing pool along the shores of Lake Victoria: Fishermen, careers, and capital accumulation in the Ugandan Nile perch business. *Africa, 80*(2), 224–248. doi:10.1353/afr.0.0171

Kull, Daniel. (2006, February). Connections between recent water level drops in Lake Victoria, dam operations and drought. Retrieved May 27, 2011, from www.internationalrivers.org/files/060208vic.pdf

Mugabe, D., & Kisambira, E. (2006, January 16). Lake Victoria levels at Jinja raise eyebrows. *East African Business Week.*

Orindi, Victor, & Huggins, Chris. (2005, January 26–28). The dynamic relationship between property rights, water resource management and poverty in the Lake Victoria Basin (Presentation at International workshop, African water laws: Plural legislative frameworks for rural water management in Africa). Johannesburg, South Africa: African Centre for Technology Studies (ACTS).

Pearce, Fred. (2006). Uganda pulls plug on Lake Victoria. *New Scientist, 189*(2538), 12.

Seehausen, Ole; van Alphen, Jacques J. M.; & Witte, Frans. (1997). Cichlid fish diversity threatened by eutrophication that curbs sexual selection. *Science, 277*(5333), 1808–1811. doi:10.1126/science.277.5333.1808

United Nations Environment Program (UNEP). (2006). *Africa's lakes: An atlas of environmental change.* Hertfordshire, UK: Earthprint, Ltd.

Van der Knaap, M.; Roest, F. C.; & Munawar, M. (2007). Great Lake Victoria fisheries: Changes and sustainability, and building blocks for management. *Aquatic Ecosystem Health & Management, 10*(4), 481–483. doi:10.1080/14634980701764456

Verschuren, Dirk, et al. (2002). History and timing of human impact on Lake Victoria, East Africa. *Proceedings of the Royal Society of London, Series B: Biological Sciences, 269*(1488), 289–294. doi:10.1098/rspb.2001.1850

London, United Kingdom

7.75 million est. pop. 2009

London attracts, like other capitals of past colonial empires, cultural and ethnic diversity to complement its economic diversity. The city's primary specialty is business and financial services, while mass transit has been built into London's infrastructure since the days when manufacturing dominated the economy. A trend toward more comprehensive "green" planning is now taking root as this world city tries to overcome its reputation for bad air quality (e.g., the infamous London fog and the deadly Great Smog of 1952). Its work in alternative energy, the Fairtrade Towns campaign, reduction of carbon emissions, and youth programs all strive toward a more sustainable future.

London, England, one of the world's most famous cities, immediately conjures iconic images of seemingly timeless landmarks: Big Ben, Parliament, and Tower Bridge overlooking the Thames River. London does have a long history of dominance over the British and world landscapes.

Originating as a Roman fortification and local trading center (named Londinium) around 50 CE, it grew from there to a city of substantial size but then declined after 410, when the Romans departed. Anglo-Saxons reestablished its prominence as a center of government and trade by the sixth century, eventually reusing the Roman fortified City of London walls and gates. Normans continued with new centers of political power along the Thames, westward at Westminster Abbey and eastward at the Tower of London. London's population was cut almost in half by plague in the 1300s, yet its diverse trade guilds and cottage industries quickly recovered (Ackroyd 2009).

Economics, Housing, and Transit

London's economic history, like that of other European centers, changed dramatically with the rise of mercantilism in the 1500s. Over half the city's land ownership changed from church to aristocracy through the 1500s, as trade expanded beyond Western Europe. Royal Charter established the British East India Company in London in 1600, as coastal shipping fueled economic growth.

The city's population rose from 50,000 in 1530 to 225,000 in 1605 to 630,000 by 1715. Elites founded quarters in the West End and at country estates such as Windsor. Immigration from Ireland, Scotland, France (especially Huguenots), Germany, and Poland (especially Jews) diversified the population, although in segregated neighborhoods. London reached one million in population by 1800, with a small population of blacks arriving from Africa, the Caribbean, and North America (Emsley, Hitchcock, and Shoemaker 2012a and 2012b).

Housing changed from wood to brick, stone, and stucco after the Great Fire of 1666, in the form of relatively low-density, terraced housing. Higher class areas included separate servant quarters within the same building. By the late 1700s, coach services allowed mass commuting from settlements outside the city center. This gave way to rail travel by the 1830s, which progressively uprooted poor neighborhoods as new stations were built at Euston, Kings Cross, Paddington, Waterloo, and elsewhere.

By the late 1800s and early 1900s, London had one of the world's densest transportation networks—including trams, trolleys, and underground rail—that linked a network of distinct villages such as Richmond and Wimbledon with the city center. Public planning allowed for more public spaces than those such as the once rural Hyde Park, as well as an expansion of sewer system from the once open system draining to the Thames. John Snow's famous 1850s map of well water and the London cholera outbreak (Crosier 2011), along with the Great Stink of 1858, illustrated the critical need for water sanitation that was subsequently addressed by engineer Joseph Bazalgette's sewer system design, which carried sewage east of London through 134 kilometers of main sewers and 1,770 kilometers of street sewers (Swopnet 2012). Improvements during the 1960s and 1970s to two main sewage treatment plants at Crossness in southeast London and Beckton in east London were needed to dramatically improve water quality in the still naturally murky Thames.

London's craft guilds continued into the 1800s, and most goods were hand-made, including clothing and watches. The Industrial Revolution then brought prices (and in many cases value) down through mass production. The Industrial Revolution's urbanization process also magnified the draw of London as a trading hub and center of the British Empire. It became the world's largest city by 1815 with a population of 1.4 million, and reached 3 million by 1860, when over one-third of its population was born outside the city. The city more than doubled in size again by the 1910s, reaching 7 million. The population in 2009 was 7.75 million (Emsley, Hitchcock, and Shoemaker 2012a and 2012b).

The Industrial Revolution amplified, through economies of scale, the effects of world trade that started with the British East India Company. The extraction of resources in a colonial or neo-colonial context is an important aspect of sustainability, as it allows the diverting of environmental impact to nations with less stringent standards and out of the eye of the consuming public. The introduction of global markets to agricultural systems formerly based on subsistence and local markets, which has transformed cultures and degraded resources around the globe, has been most critically analyzed through the lens of political ecology, a field promoted by the work of University of East Anglia geographer Piers Blaikie. Blaikie (1985) and other political ecologists have challenged the assumption that peasants are to blame for land degradation, when displacement from land by multinational firms and promotion of inappropriate cash crops are some of the real drivers of degradation.

Air Quality

The Industrial Revolution brought another major change directly to London—air pollution. Air quality regulations had started as early as 1306. Domestic coal use had been a source of poor air quality but, as with many sustainability

issues, was magnified with industrialization and associated population growth. By the mid-1900s, coal-fired power plants at central sites such as Battersea (which operated until 1983) added to domestic coal use. Air pollution may have culminated with the Great Smog of December 1952, which caused four thousand premature deaths (similar in number to the 1854 cholera and 1918 influenza epidemics) and resulted in the Clean Air Act of 1956 (Mayor of London 2002).

Oil and then natural gas have replaced coal as the primary energy and heating sources in recent decades. The air pollutants of primary concern have now become nitrogen dioxide and particulate emissions from automobile traffic. In 2009, 19 percent (about 790,000) of London's workforce of 4.2 million people commuted into the capital using various means, largely from East Anglia and the South East. Solutions are being sought in expanding and improving mass transit, in disincentives for auto use at peak times, and in advanced automobile technology. Recent goals were not met, but improvements were made in reducing vehicle traffic pollution based on a 2002 Mayor's Air Quality Strategy (Mayor of London 2002). More recent monitoring revealed spotty compliance with 2010 objectives.

One of Mayor Boris Johnson's more prominent initiatives is his Cycle Superhighways campaign to encourage bicycle commuting into central London. The first of many routes, complete with blue-painted bike lanes and multiple safety features, roughly follows the Northern London Underground line from Merton (in South West London) into the city center. Ridership has doubled and the goal is to increase use 400 percent between 2000 and 2025.

From Industry to Services

One other recent development, rivaling the shift from craft guilds to mass production in the 1800s, is the change from industry to services as London's economic base. This shift from manufacturing to services coincided with the move away from coal. London became a center for overseas investment as early as the 1500s, and this focus continued to increase with the peak of the British Empire and the Industrial Revolution. As with most developed nations, the latter half of the twentieth century saw the service sector dominate employment and gross domestic product.

The service sector is extremely diverse, which adds elements of resilience (and sustainability) to the economy. This sector includes both business services (e.g., capital, financial, legal, technical) and consumer services (e.g., education, entertainment, health care, tourism). Although most world cities deal in all these services to some degree, London is especially dominant in business and financial services, supporting domestic, continental, and global networks. Today London (along with New York City) serves as one of the great financial centers of the planet, dealing in investment, trading, and currency exchange in staggering amounts daily. Financial services have recently accounted for approximately one-fifth of London's economy (CEBR 2012).

One example of how the service sector contributes economically is higher education in London, which generates £12 billion (US$1.87 billion) each year in goods and services including £1.4 billion (US$2.18 billion) in export earnings; educates 433,000 students from the United Kingdom and overseas while employing 98,000 academic and nonacademic staff; has nearly £470 million (US$731 million) of research funding grant monies; attracts to the United Kingdom 102,000 international students from virtually every nation on Earth, who in turn contribute over £6 billion (US$9.33 billion) to the London economy; and produces over 130,000 skilled graduates every year, 90 percent of whom work in London, East Anglia, or the South East (London Higher 2012).

Diversity

London's present-day features of economic diversity, class division, population density, and mass transit were set in motion centuries earlier. Like other developed-nation world cities such as New York and Paris, it has also attracted a remarkable cultural and ethnic diversity that continues to grow over time.

In 2009, just over half (58 percent) of London's population was white British, concentrated in the outer ring of London. Nonwhite groups made up 31 percent of the population (compared to 5 to 14 percent in other English regions). In 2009, 1.6 million Londoners (21 percent) were non-UK citizens and came from over thirty-three different countries. At least three hundred languages are spoken in London, many reflecting roots in the British colonial empire (London Higher 2012).

Pakistanis (concentrated in northwest and northeast London) and Bangladeshis (centered in northeast central London) combined outnumber Asian Indians (concentrated in northwest London), while black Africans (central residential ring and north London) are the fastest growing sectors, outnumbering black Caribbean natives (also central residential ring and north London). Bangladeshi (58 percent), Indian (54 percent), and black African (36 percent) populations reached the highest percentages of any one London neighborhood in 2005 (*The Guardian* 2005).

European and Latin American immigration to London is also growing. Christianity (58 percent) and no religion (16 percent) were the most prevalent religious affiliations in 2001, followed by Islam (8 percent) and then Hinduism (4 percent). By 2028 London's population is projected to increase by 16 percent and reach 8.9 million people (Red Orbit 2003).

One of the more comprehensive reports of the London Sustainable Development Commission (LSDC) deals with income inequality. Important global trends are outlined, including the diminishing returns of rising income in relation to happiness. A key point is that income inequality leads to consumerism, as the "have-nots" attempt to model the "haves." This consumerism leads to increased environmental impact such as resource extraction and carbon footprint (total greenhouse gas emissions). Quality of life factors increase in more equal societies, including trust among classes and individuals as well as a list of health and social benefits such as decreases in crime, obesity, and drug use.

These factors can be improved without the consumerist model. In fact, a recent study by climate change expert Chris Goodall, "Peak Stuff," shows that the United Kingdom has been reducing its consumption levels since before the 2008 recession, indicating an economy can still grow while reducing consumption of basic resources like paper and water (Goodall 2011). This compilation of inequality research shows that, "although the benefits of increased equality are bigger nearer the bottom of society, they extend to the vast majority of the population, including people in the highest categories of income, education or occupation" (Wilkinson and Pickett 2010).

Fair Trade and Sustainable Development

Fair trade (also spelled *fairtrade*, notably by Fairtrade International, a leading proponent of fair trade) is a program and product brand designed to alter the traditional global consumption process by incorporating better prices, decent working conditions, local sustainability, and fair terms of trade for farmers and workers in the developing world. A Fairtrade Towns campaign has grown to over five hundred towns and cities in the United Kingdom that follow specific principles for promoting fair trade (Fairtrade International 2011). London is the world's largest designated Fairtrade city.

Quality of life for animals is a key part of sustainable development for many. A recent television campaign altered consumer views of living conditions for industrial chickens, resulting in such an increased demand for free-range chicken that supermarkets could not meet it. Concern for effects of urban consumption on hinterlands is high in the United Kingdom.

Another challenge in limiting urban effects on UK rural areas is the arena of alternative energy. Wind farms can be especially controversial in light of their alteration of traditional British coastal landscapes. Wealthy landowners can offer stiff challenges to installation of such infrastructure, as seen for example in 2012 with the US billionaire Donald Trump's protest against a proposed wind farm off the Scottish coast where he has recently constructed a golf resort. Germany has managed to incorporate wind turbines in less obtrusive small groups, integrated into many rural villages. Germany's flexibility in solar energy policy has led to far more private solar panels than in the United Kingdom, where requirements to connect to a public grid can act as disincentives.

The new Siemens Pavilion, near the 2012 Olympics site, offers another example of London-based sustainability initiatives. Siemens (a global giant in electronics, consumer goods, health care diagnostics, heavy industry, and energy infrastructure) is investing £30 million (US$46.8 million) in a new exhibition and conference center in East London, as a figurehead of a new Green Enterprise District. According to Siemens, the District will stretch "across East London, exploiting the potential from undeveloped plots of industrial land to attract new investment, create up to 6000 new jobs and develop new low carbon skills" (Siemens 2010). The Green Enterprise District is designed to position London as a global leader of the low-carbon (basically, reduced carbon dioxide emissions) economy, incorporating green building and alternative energy. Projections indicate the low-carbon marketplace is an opportunity for bringing "between £40 billion to

£140 billion of investment into London and creating a workforce of more than 200,000 by 2025" (Siemens 2010).

Sustainability awareness in London can be shown by the incorporation of the One Planet Olympics theme with its bid to host the 2012 games. (See the sidebar on page 190 for more on the London Olympics.) The theme summary states: "We only have one planet; London 2012 will respect its ecological limits, its cultural diversity and create a legacy for sport, the environment, and the local and global community" (London 2012, WWF, and Bioregional 2005). Initiatives include not only conservation awareness programs, green procurement policies, and encouragement of mass transit use leading up to the games, but development of locally sensitive green space and trail systems in East London and elsewhere.

London has an ambitious target to reduce carbon dioxide emissions by 60 percent by 2025. The London Sustainability Exchange (LSx), set up to play a coordinating role in making London a sustainable world city, collaborated with the southwestern London borough of Merton to comprehensively review transitions to low carbon output. Key findings include: (1) carbon savings of 60–70 percent can be reached by retrofitting (modifying with new parts), through incentives such as the Green Deal, in combination with behavioral change programs; (2) a challenge is that retrofit measures with greatest carbon savings are least attractive to residents (solid wall insulation, solar photovoltaics [PV], boiler upgrades); (3) more popular but less impactful retrofit measures could be stepping stones to bigger impact measures (LSx and Sustainable Merton 2012). Low Carbon Zones are now set up, through the mayor's RE:CONNECT program, to comprehensively look at similar transitions in other boroughs.

The borough of Merton includes the city of Wimbledon, of tennis fame, which recently joined a network similar to Fairtrade Towns, called Transition Towns. Also originating in the United Kingdom, such towns, now spread around the globe, work on transitioning to low-carbon, locally resilient communities. Resilience in this context involves not just economic diversity but transitions to low-carbon homes, alternative transportation, urban farming, and in general less reliance on global markets and fossil fuels.

Another major challenge to sustainable development in London is linking urban youth to nature. Such connection has been shown to lead to more sustainable behavior later in life as well as enhanced free-form learning and quality of life. This is the focus of another major report from the London Sustainable Development Commission. London has surprising availability of green space: "Two thirds of London's area is made up

LONDON 2012 OLYMPICS

The bid to host the 2012 Summer Olympics was a close match between London and Paris, but London won with its promise to not only "put on the biggest sporting event in the world" but to "hold the world's first truly sustainable Olympic and Paralympic Games, leaving a legacy far beyond the departure of the Olympic flame" (London 2012 Olympic and Paralympic Games 2012b).

British Petroleum (BP) was the most prominent sponsor of the 2012 games. As the supplier of the fuel for the 5,000-vehicle fleet (such as limousines for Olympic officials) and the generators powering the event, BP used the opportunity to test new biofuels, such as cellulosic fuels made from grasses, biobutanol (made by fermenting biomass), and diesel fuel derived from sugar. The BP Target Neutral program was also planned to offset the carbon footprint of official travel to, from, and around the games, as well as helping visitors to offset some of their own carbon footprint from travel to the games.

Some groups opposed the 2012 games for such reasons as the increased budget and BP's sponsorship (critics say that the company is merely attempting to improve its image after the Deepwater Horizon oil spill of 2010). The Official Protestors provide a list of promises the 2012 games make to London that the group is skeptical will be upheld, such as providing jobs for Londoners, providing more housing after the games are done, and even the claim that this will be the "greenest" games yet.

Doubts about London's ability to host the games began in 2002; most London officials were against the idea of making the bid, concerned that the games would not be an economic benefit in the long run. Barcelona, Spain, offers one of the few examples where infrastructure built to support its 1992 Olympics had long-term benefits by revitalizing the city's waterfront and improving the quality of life for residents. Some of the strongest reasons London pursued the bid were the hopes that the same would happen for East London, an industrial wasteland for many years, and that the success of the 2002 Commonwealth Games (and the infrastructure such as the Docklands Lightrail to support it) would be repeated with the 2012 games, hopes that gave the UK minister Tessa Jowell the confidence to pursue an Olympics 2012 bid (Gross 2012).

Despite skepticism and difficulties, the trend toward sustainability is rising; whether or not the current efforts will make a long-term difference in the larger picture is debatable. The 2012 Olympics promised to deliver even greater contributions to sustainability than those made by the Sydney Games of 2000 (dubbed the Green Games), or Beijing when it was required to implement drastic changes in order to host the Olympics of 2008. (In addition to undertaking a massive tree-planting campaign, the Beijing government ordered polluting industries to cease activities two months before its games began, and "seeded the sky" with silver iodide in order to induce rainfall in the city, with the hopes of reducing remaining air pollution.) Time will tell what the legacy of these games will be, but this trend of increasingly sustainable Olympic Games could be a potential leading factor in prospective host cities' hopes of winning future bids.

The Editors

LONDON OLYMPICS SIDEBAR REFERENCES

British Petroleum (BP), & Target Neutral. (2012). Offset your travel carbon footprint for free. Retrieved July 11, 2012, from https://spectatortargetneutral.bp.com/tag/start

Counter Olympics Network. (2012, June 25). The myth of the Olympic truce. Retrieved July 11, 2012, from http://counterolympicsnetwork.wordpress.com/category/the-problem-with-the-olympics/

Gross, Michael Joseph. (2012, June). Jumping through hoops. *Vanity Fair*. Retrieved July 12, 2012, from http://www.vanityfair.com/culture/2012/06/international-olympic-committee-london-summer-olympics

London 2012 Olympic and Paralympic Games. (2012a). Fuelling the games. Retrieved July 11, 2012, from http://www.bplondon2012.com/london_2012_fuelling_the_future/fuelling_the_games/

London 2012 Olympic and Paralympic Games. (2012b). Sustainability. Retrieved July 11, 2012, from http://www.london2012.com/about-us/sustainability/

London 2012 Olympic and Paralympic Games. (2012c). Target Neutral. Retrieved July 11, 2012, from http://www.bplondon2012.com/target_neutral/

Official Protestors of the London 2012 Olympic Games. (2012). Reasons why the London 2012 Olympic games are something worth protesting! Retrieved July 11, 2012, from http://www.protestlondon2012.com/10reasons.html

of green spaces or water, and ten percent is designated as Metropolitan Open Land, yet children's experiences of natural places in the capital have been in long-term decline, as a result of societal changes" (LSDC 2011). The problem is particularly acute among the poor and ethnic minorities. Abundant programs exist, such as London's City Farms, but reach a small percentage (approximately 4 percent) of the population. The report focuses on "children under the age of 12 and on nature that has the potential to be experienced as part of children's everyday lives (rather than in one-off residential trips or adventure activities)." Recommendations include to "embed children and nature aims in relevant London-wide policies and strategies," such as health, parks, schools, and transportation (LSDC 2011).

Diverse leadership is critical to implementing sustainability initiatives, many of which must cut across government, corporate, community, and individual cultures. New initiatives such as Low Carbon Zones and Cycle Superhighways continue to make London a leader on the world stage of urban sustainability. Many challenges lie ahead in "scaling up" transitions to a comprehensive green economy.

William FORBES

Stephen F. Austin State University

See also Energy Security (Europe); European Union (EU); Germany; Immigrants and Refugees; Stockholm, Sweden; United Kingdom and Ireland; Urbanization (Europe); Warsaw, Poland

FURTHER READING

Ackroyd, Peter. (2009). *London: A biography*. New York: Random House.

Barnett, Clive; Cloke, Paul; Clarke, Nick; & Malpass, Alice. (2011). *Globalizing responsibility: The political rationalities of ethical consumption* (RGS-IBG book series). Oxford, UK: Wiley-Blackwell.

Blaikie, Piers. (1985). *The political economy of soil erosion in developing countries* (Longman Development Series, No. 1). London: Longman. Reprinted by Pearson Education in 2000.

Center for Economics and Business Research (CEBR). (2012, May 8). News release: Economic test for newly re-elected mayor as London struggles to grow in 2012, held back by weakened financial services sector. Retrieved June 26, 2012, from http://www.cebr.com/wp-content/uploads/London-City-Regional-Prospects-Press-Release-May-2012-London-Economy1.pdf

Crosier, Scott. (2011). John Snow: The London cholera epidemic of 1854. Center for Spatially Integrated Social Science (CSISS) Classics. Retrieved June 26, 2012, from http://www.csiss.org/classics/content/8/

Emsley, Clive; Hitchcock, Tim; & Shoemaker, Robert. (2012a). London history: A population history of London. *Old Bailey Proceedings Online*. Retrieved June 21, 2012, from http://www.oldbaileyonline.org/static/Population-history-of-london.jsp

Emsley, Clive; Hitchcock, Tim; & Shoemaker, Robert. (2012b). London history: Material London. *Old Bailey Proceedings Online*. Retrieved June 21, 2012, from http://www.oldbaileyonline.org/static/Material-london.jsp

Fairtrade International. (2011). About us: Our partners. Retrieved June 29, 2012, from http://www.fairtrade.net/our_partners.0.html

Goodall, Chris. (2011). Peak stuff: Did the UK reach a maximum use of material resources in the early part of the last decade? Retrieved June 23, 2012, from http://www.carboncommentary.com/wp-content/uploads/2011/10/Peak_Stuff_17.10.11.pdf

The Guardian. (2005). London: The world in one city. Retrieved June 26, 2012, from http://www.guardian.co.uk/britain/london/0,,1394802,00.html. See especially Special report: London by ethnicity: http://www.guardian.co.uk/graphic/0,5812,1395103,00.html

Hickman, Martin. (2008, February 28). The campaign that changed the eating habits of a nation: Boycott of battery chickens forces supermarkets to think ethically. *The Independent.* Retrieved June 22, 2012, from http://www.independent.co.uk/life-style/food-and-drink/news/the-campaign-that-changed-the-eating-habits-of-a-nation-788557.html

London & Partners. (2012). London's city farms. Retrieved June 28, 2012, from http://www.visitlondon.com/attractions/outdoors/city-farms

London Fairtrade Capital. (2012). Fairtrade London. Retrieved June 22, 2012, from http://fairtradelondon.org.uk/

London Higher. (2012). Higher education in London: HE facts and figures; London's population. Retrieved June 21, 2012, from http://www.londonhigher.ac.uk/helondon.html

London Sustainability Exchange (LSx), & Sustainable Merton. (2012). Energise Merton Action Plan. Retrieved June 23, 2012, from http://www.lsx.org.uk/docs/page/3534/LEAF%20Energise%20Merton%20Action%20Plan%20Final.pdf

London Sustainable Development Commission (LSDC). (2010, September). London leaders 2009–10 project summary. London: Greater London Authority; LSDC. Retrieved June 23, 2012, from http://www.londonsdc.org/documents/research/London_Leaders_Summary_Final.pdf

London Sustainable Development Commission (LSDC). (2011). Sowing the seeds: Reconnecting London's children with nature. London: Greater London Authority; LSDC. Retrieved June 22, 2012, from http://www.londonsdc.org/news/4/Sowing-the-Seeds--Reconnecting-Londons-Children-with-Nature/

London 2012; World Wild Fund for Nature (WWF); & Bioregional. (2005). Towards a one planet Olympics: Achieving the first sustainable Olympic Games and Paralympic Games. Retrieved June 22, 2010, from http://www.london2012.com/mm%5CDocument%5CPublications%5CSustainability%5C01%5C25%5C66%5C62%5COne-planet-olympics-2005_Neutral.pdf

Maiteny, Paul T. (2002). Mind in the gap: Summary of research exploring "inner" influences on pro-sustainability learning and behaviour. *Environmental Education Research*, 8(3), 299–306.

Mayor of London. (2002). 50 years on: The struggle for air quality in London since the great smog of December 1952. London: Greater London Authority. Retrieved June 21, 2012, from http://legacy.london.gov.uk/mayor/environment/air_quality/docs/50_years_on.pdf

Mayor of London. (2012). Developing low carbon zones to help cut local emissions. Retrieved June 29, 2012, from http://www.london.gov.uk/priorities/environment/climate-change/low-carbon-zones

Pearce, Fred. (2011, November 28). The new story of stuff: Can we consume less? *Yale Environment 360*. Retrieved June 23, 2012, from http://e360.yale.edu/feature/the_new_story_of_stuff_can_we_consume_less/2468/

Red Orbit. (2003, December 2). London is the capital of ethnic diversity as white population falls. Retrieved June 27, 2012, from http://www.redorbit.com/news/science/24938/london_is_the_capital_of_ethnic_diversity_as_white_population/

Robbins, Paul. (2011). *Political ecology: A critical introduction* (2nd ed.). Oxford, UK: Wiley-Blackwell.

Samra, Babinder. (2011). Does resilience increase sustainability of transition towns? Retrieved June 23, 2012, from http://www.transitionnetwork.org/resources/does-resilience-increase-sustainability-transition-towns

Siemens. (2010, May 27). Mayor unveils plans for £30m Siemens Pavilion to kick-start London's "Green Enterprise District." Retrieved June 25, 2012, from http://www.siemens.co.uk/en/news_press/index/news_archive/siemens-pavilion.htm

Southwestern Opportunities Network (Swopnet). (2012). In praise of Joseph Bazalgette: History of London's sewers. Swopnet Engineering Databank. Retrieved June 28, 2012, from http://www.swopnet.com/engr/londonsewers/london-sewer-history-joseph-bazalgette.html

Wilkinson, Richard, & Pickett, Kate. (2010). The impact of income inequalities on sustainable development in London. London: Greater London Authority; Equality Trust; London Sustainable Development Commission. Retrieved June 21, 2012, from http://www.londonsdc.org/documents/The%20impact%20of%20income%20inequalities%20on%20sustainable%20development%20in%20London.pdf

Mediterranean Sea

The Mediterranean Sea is the planet's largest inland sea; it is very salty, very clear, and biologically comparatively poor. It hosts ten thousand animal and plant species; about 300 million people in eighteen countries live in its basin (locations where water drains into the Mediterranean). Industrial pollution has become a cause for concern, however, with pesticides and industrial chemicals affecting the water quality. Overfishing has also been a problem, although measures have been taken to help prevent it.

Although it does have a very narrow outlet to the Atlantic Ocean, the Mediterranean is considered to be the Earth's largest inland sea. It is very salty because evaporation is high and the freshwater influx from rivers is low. Where its waters flow into the Atlantic, at Gibraltar, its saltier water is heavier and forms an undercurrent beneath the incoming current of ocean water. It takes about eighty years for the Mediterranean's water to flush out fully. In 2007 its catchment (or basin) was inhabited by about 300 million people in eighteen countries (Conservation International 2007). The Mediterranean is home to about ten thousand species of animals and plants; however, its waters are not rich in nutrients, so its total biomass is very low. One result is that the water—where it is not polluted—is remarkably clear.

Marine pollution in the Mediterranean is nearly as old as civilization. The ancient harbors of Ostia, Piraeus, and Alexandria were strewn with wastes. Bays, estuaries, and inlets such as Turkey's Golden Horn, the Venetian lagoons, or the Bay of Naples were bustling with human activity and became unsanitary long before modern times. Since about 1960 the main pollutants in

the Mediterranean, as in many other waters, have been microbes, synthetic organic compounds such as dichlorodiphenyltrichloroethane (DDT) or polychlorinated biphenyls (PCBs), oil, and excess nutrients. Pollution has come especially from the major urban centers, the larger rivers, and a few industrial centers on the shores of the sea.

Until around 1920, raw sewage flowed into the Mediterranean unchecked and untreated. By 1990 about 30 percent of the raw sewage headed for the Mediterranean received treatment, but the total quantity of sewage has tripled or quadrupled since 1900 (McNeill 2000, 141). The risks of illness to people eating seafood from the Mediterranean or bathing in its waters have increased significantly. By the late 1980s, when the European Union developed guidelines for microbial contamination of water, beach closings due to unacceptable levels had become common from Spain to Greece.

Oil became a major pollutant when Arabian oil fields opened up after World War II. Between 1970 and 1990, about one-quarter of the world's oil shipments crossed the Mediterranean, and events ranging from routine dumping of bilge water to leakage and spills left behind one-sixth of the world's oil pollution. One-third of that oil washed up as tar on the beaches (McNeill 2000, 141–142).

Industry has been the primary contributor to the pollution of the Mediterranean. For the quarter century after 1960, industrial production in Mediterranean countries rose by about 6–7 percent annually. Despite the rapid growth of industry in northern Africa, by 1990 it still accounted for only 9 percent of Mediterranean industry; the several countries from Israel in the east around the coast to Croatia accounted for another 10 percent. Italy generated 66 percent of the industrial production of the Mediterranean basin; Spain (mostly Barcelona) 10 percent; France only 5 percent (McNeill 142). The greatest pollution problems therefore developed in the northwestern area of the basin, around the mouths of rivers with industrialized basins, such as the Ebro, Rhone, and Po, and around centers of heavy industry, such as Barcelona, Genoa, and the northern Adriatic coast.

Eutrophication—the process by which a body of water becomes enriched with nutrients—has resulted mainly from the introduction of agricultural runoff and municipal sewage. Algal blooms occur when excess nutrients allow algae populations to proliferate, sometimes covering the water surface in sheets called *algal mats*. Although they occurred in the Mediterranean prior to 1950, algal blooms happened much more often after about 1950 because of urbanization and the growing use of chemical fertilizers. The most affected areas were France's Gulf of Lion, which suffered its most serious blooms after 1980; the Saronic Gulf around Athens, which experienced its first in 1978; and the northern Adriatic. Between 1872 and 1988, the northern Adriatic recorded fifteen eutrophic blooms, their frequency increasing after 1969. Algal blooms have played havoc with fish populations, seabed life in general, and the tourist trade.

The fish population of the Mediterranean has suffered from illegal overfishing of restricted varieties, especially of bluefin tuna, of which the amount in the market exceeded the officially reported catch by 140 percent in 2010. As of 2011, a contributing factor is the investment by many Mediterranean fishermen in newer boats, which they are eager to put to use (Black 2011a). In November of 2011, the International Commission for the Conservation of Atlantic Tunas (ICCAT) strengthened protection of tuna stocks by implementing an electronic system for recording the numbers of bluefin tuna catches, as paper records made underreporting easier. It is hoped this measure will protect tuna stocks, which in recent years have been devastated by illegal overfishing (Black 2011b).

Environmental awareness and politics around the Mediterranean emerged in the 1970s. In 1975, sixteen Mediterranean countries and the European Community launched the Mediterranean Action Plan (MAP). Under the auspices of the United Nations Environment Programme (UNEP), Mediterranean countries agreed to an ongoing process of environmental management for the entire basin. The plan supported scientific research and integrated environmental planning. The plan produced several protocols that

helped limit pollution. Unfortunately, however, through poor enforcement and special dispensations, there have been setbacks, including the loss of about 2,000 kilometers of coastline to development. Although twenty-five years later the sea was more polluted than when the MAP began, it surely would have been much more so without the MAP. Some credit for improvements in the ecological health of the Mediterranean achieved by the MAP goes to the scientists who worked together, rising above international disputes and rivalries.

In the last quarter of the twentieth century, about one-third of international tourism involved visits to Mediterranean countries, usually to beaches. Thus a major incentive for cleaning up the waters of the Mediterranean Sea has been the tourist trade that brings hundreds of billions of dollars to the area. Although the economic exploitation of the Mediterranean Sea is not ecologically sustainable, mainly due to the overdraft on fisheries, the sea is not in immediate peril of environmental collapse. Continued pressures on marketable species will likely make them rare, and up to a point more valuable, but other foods and fish from other seas can easily substitute for diminished catches in the Mediterranean. Water pollution will likely neither abate nor intensify dramatically in the foreseeable future, because while population growth and further chemicalization of agriculture in the basin continue, this is roughly offset by the building of more and more water treatment plants. As of the early twenty-first century, political storms have visited the shores of the Mediterranean, at least in Greece, Syria, Libya, Egypt, and Tunisia, and more rough weather likely lies ahead. As for the sea itself, it remains and is likely to remain more placid. Its biological resources will degrade slowly, but in the near future not enough to inspire major efforts to reverse course.

J. R. McNEILL
Georgetown University

See also Biodiversity Conservation; Cairo, Egypt; Danube River; France; Middle East; Nile River; Shipping and Freight; Transboundary Water Issues; Travel and Tourism Industry; Tunis, Tunisia; Urbanization (Western Asia and Northern Africa); Water Use and Rights (Middle East and Northern Africa)

This article was adapted by the editors from J. R. McNeill's article "Mediterranean Sea" in Shepard Krech III, J. R. McNeill, and Carolyn Merchant (Eds.), the *Encyclopedia of World Environmental History*, pp. 826–828. Great Barrington, MA: Berkshire Publishing (2003).

FURTHER READING

Black, Richard. (2011a, October 18). Med bluefin tuna catch "unabated." BBC News. Retrieved December 21, 2011, from http://www.bbc.co.uk/news/science-environment-15323370

Black, Richard. (2011b, November 19). Protection boosted for tuna, sharks and swordfish. BBC News. Retrieved December 17, 2011, from http://www.bbc.co.uk/news/science-environment-15804817

Conservation International. (2007). Biodiversity hotspots: Mediterranean Basin: Human impacts. Retrieved January 28, 2012, from http://www.biodiversityhotspots.org/xp/Hotspots/mediterranean/Pages/impacts.aspx

De Walle, Foppe B.; Nikolopulou-Tamvakli, M.; & Heinen, W. J. (Eds.). (1993). *Environmental condition of the Mediterranean Sea.* Dordrecht, The Netherlands: Kluwer Academic.

Grove, A. T., & Rackham, Oliver. (2003). *The nature of Mediterranean Europe: An ecological history.* New Haven, CT: Yale University Press.

Haas, Peter M. (1990). *Saving the Mediterranean: The politics of international environmental cooperation.* New York: Columbia University Press.

McNeill, J. R. (2000). *Something new under the sun: An environmental history of the twentieth-century world.* New York: W. W. Norton & Company.

Stanners, David A., & Bourdeau, Philippe. (1995). *Europe's environment.* Copenhagen, Denmark: European Environment Agency.

Microfinance

Microfinance, the umbrella term for microsavings and microcredit, can be invaluable in breaking the poverty cycle. In a microfinance program, a recipient (typically someone without access to mainstream financial institutions) is granted money for a specific, well-defined business plan based on a budget using the income expected from the investment. The presence of such essential elements as planning and support from the microfinance providers helps ensure success.

The term *microfinance* describes small-scale savings and credit. There are two types of microfinance. *Microsavings*, as the name implies, are small-scale savings, perhaps amounting to the equivalent of a few dollars every month, for which the savers are paid interest and from which they can withdraw whenever they wish. *Microcredit* is a relatively small loan that is repayable, with or without interest; it is distinct from a grant, which is startup capital and generally not repaid. This article focuses on microfinance as it has been observed and practiced by the Irish microfinance expert Nora McNamara, first in Cork, Ireland, and in later years in Igalaland, Nigeria. This discussion provides only a brief summary of the principles and practice of microfinance; for an in-depth discussion of the procedures and issues, the reader is referred to the seminal work of British professors David Hulme and Paul Mosley (1996a, 1996b).

Microfinance's Place in Sustainable Development

The purpose of microfinance is to enable people without access to mainstream financial institutions to gain capital or materials with which to create life-changing opportunities, such as opening a small shop or buying livestock

with which to make cheese, milk, etc. Because individuals and households often lack money to invest in business opportunities, in theory, microfinance makes sustainable development (e.g., development that does not depend on exhausting resources) possible. This process, however, is long and arduous because microfinance is neither a panacea nor a quick fix. It is just one element in achieving sustainable development.

Even when users exercise good practice, microfinance may not succeed initially. People using it may be handling significant amounts of money for the first time; experience suggests a temptation to splurge. Planning is an important part of the process, and the proposed project must be clearly defined. Research, perhaps through a market survey, helps define the project. The microcredit recipient must budget realistically, and the funder must study carefully any expected profits. The funder must carefully monitor the project and stay abreast of the enterprise. Microcredit providers must provide psychological support and encouragement so that their clients stay committed through the entire process.

Experiences with Microfinance

History is full of examples of attempts to help the poor using microfinance, from the pawn shops Franciscans established in the fifteenth century to credit unions in nineteenth-century Germany to the Grameen Bank (GB) in Bangladesh made famous by the 2006 Nobel Peace Prize winner Muhammad Yunus.

Case Study: Cork, Ireland

Nora McNamara's own interest in microfinance began in a credit union in Cork, Ireland, in the 1970s. Its management and operational skills give an in-depth understanding of how microcredit succeeds. Clients in Cork committed to changing their money-management habits; they built trust with a volunteer at the credit union and received life coaching and counseling as much as microcredit. A relationship of trust with the credit union volunteer replaced a relationship of fear brought about by previous interactions with moneylenders. Clients usually would receive a loan to pay off all loans, freeing them from moneylenders. Funders charged a minimal interest rate. Dependency was not encouraged; members agreed on weekly savings, no matter how little. Local volunteers managed the program and helped to keep costs down so the credit union itself was sustainable (in the financial sense of the word).

From Cork to Igalaland, Nigeria

The credit union approach came to Igalaland, Nigeria, West Africa, during the mid-1970s (McNamara and Morse 1998). Igala women were clear that their greatest needs were water and food, but because they lacked cash for growing food and developing water infrastructure, they wanted to start an agricultural project to raise funds. A local mentor suggested they begin a microfinance program based on the traditional programs understood in Igalaland.

Africa is rich in different indigenous forms of microfinance, developed to a high level and adaptable to current needs. One of these indigenous forms is called *nonrotating* credit, where members pay a fixed or variable amount at regular intervals and repay a loan at the end of an agreed interval. Another is known as *rotating*, and while more complex, it is among the most widespread. Each member of the group pays a fixed amount of money in a given period, and the total amount is paid to each member in rotation. The local rotating type in Igalaland needed some revision to keep costs minimal and interest low. Programs developed record-keeping methods modeled on the credit union to gain credibility. Both men and women made small but regular savings, which they used to get the capital required. Canadian expatriates volunteered to record savings.

Water projects were costly at the time, but the communities anticipated grants as overseas donors acknowledged efforts women's groups made. In the 1970s, communities relied on local resources to fuel development from the bottom up (i.e., as opposed to coming from the government); local microcredit had this potential. It also matched community commitment to work with what people knew rather than attempting to impose ideas. The microfinance program in Igalaland during the 1970s also encouraged savings in parallel with credit. Women pioneered these programs, but men soon saw the advantages gained from savings. In another context, farmers began to group themselves in what were adaptations of traditional farming institutions in which savings were vital. Group members saved equal amounts weekly. Sustainability, rather than dependency, was the hallmark of development.

People initially expected that savings would increase as income from agriculture improved, but they did not realize these savings. Instead, they used the additional income for school fees, hospital bills, and home improvement. Availability of low-interest credit and an increase in income through improved returns in agriculture enhanced people's livelihoods and status. Local moneylenders charging usurious rates occasionally were put out of business, or at least challenged for the first time. This success story, often attributed to agricultural improvements, would be incomplete without recognizing the influence of microcredit.

Farmers often were asked what would happen if microcredit were not available. At no point in the project's history did increased income create a savings increase sufficient to eliminate the need to borrow. The outcome of this dialogue led to the development of a business plan called Farmers' Economic Enterprise Development (FEED). This plan aimed at making credit more efficient by adopting a more businesslike approach where borrowers had to specify how they would use the credit and show in a credible way how an enterprise would generate profit.

Sustainability

In the early days of the microfinance program in Igalaland, costs were kept low as expatriates volunteered assistance, but this system changed as workloads increased. Managing microfinance obviously was costly and demanding, which created the need to hire local and trained paid staff to manage the program. Administrative charges helped pay these costs and program changes kept operational costs as low as possible. The program was organized around groups rather than individuals. They needed small offices, however, mostly rented for meetings and document storage; the program incurred security costs related to collecting savings, issuing loans, and managing loan repayments. Discussions on how to reduce costs and maximize financial security led to groups taking more responsibility for securing savings and loans.

Another important aspect of microcredit sustainability is the repayment rate (capital plus interest). Borrowers who have not invested the money wisely may not be able to repay the loan and could default. Lack of repayment creates problems for the lender and increases costs. In the Igalaland program, defaults were rarely a major issue, largely because the program was founded upon traditional systems of microfinance and run by members themselves (loan size was determined largely by collateral held in savings). The introduction of the business-plan approach also helps minimize risks. Repayment, however, has been an issue with other microfinance projects, and this situation has resulted in a tendency to lend only to those most likely to repay. Because these people tend to be the wealthiest, programs may move away from helping the poor. The Grameen Bank has been criticized for this reason (Islam 2007). Sustainability—the balance between income and costs, with a goal of minimizing or reducing the need for subsidies (Yaron 1992)—is often a key aspect of microfinance programs (Hulme and Mosley 1996a, 1996b), and their sustainability typically relies on the financial viability of those running them.

Business Plans and Microcredit for Individuals

Microcredit for Igalaland in the 1970s focused mainly on group microcredit because of its cost effectiveness. One size does not fit all, however. Credit to poorer people, especially women, is best done on an individual basis, as in the following real-life example. A local woman named Caroline wanted a loan to raise chickens to supplement her income and thereby help to educate her children. She asked to be taught budgeting, and microcredit was provided in stages. She bought fifty chickens and recorded costs, including feeding and veterinary costs. When she sold her chickens and eggs, she checked her revenue against her income and had made a profit. The simple business plan helped her arithmetic and self-confidence, and she has often shared her early learning skills with people who lack money-management and business skills. She now manages the Money Management and Budgeting (MABS) program in Igalaland.

Outlook

Provision of microfinance in an enabling environment can work wonders. Without a supportive environment, however, success is improbable. Microfinance is not a static service, but is constantly evolving to meet ever-changing situations. Recent moves toward business plans and MABS have enhanced the potential of microfinancing, and more innovative microcredit will continue to evolve as the world shrinks. The Muslim approach of interest-free lending has potential and is attracting attention. Providing money to microcredit users without accompanying supports can do more harm than good. Diligent providers ensuring responsible use of microfinance bring enduring results and sustainability for borrowers and lenders.

Nora McNAMARA
Missionary Sisters of the Holy Rosary

See also Africa, Western; Agriculture, Small-Scale; Corporate Accountability (Africa); Diet and Nutrition; Education, Environmental; Education, Higher (Africa); Public-Private Partnerships (Africa); Rural Development; United Kingdom and Ireland

FURTHER READING

Bornstein, David. (1996). *The price of a dream: The story of the Grameen Bank*. Oxford, UK: Oxford University Press.

Hulme, David, & Mosley, Paul. (1996a). *Finance against poverty, volume 1*. London and New York: Routledge.

Hulme, David, & Mosley, Paul. (1996b). *Finance against poverty, volume 2*. London and New York: Routledge.

Islam, Tazul. (2007). *Microcredit and poverty alleviation*. Surrey, UK: Ashgate Publishing.

McNamara, Nora, & Morse, Stephen. (1998). *Developing financial services: A case against sustainability*. Cork, Ireland: On Stream Publications.

Smith, Philip, & Thurman, Eric. (2007). *A billion bootstraps: Microcredit, barefoot banking and the business solution for ending poverty*. New York: McGraw-Hill.

Yaron, Jacob. (1992). Successful rural finance institutions (World Bank discussion paper No 150). Washington, DC: World Bank.

Yunus, Mohammad. (1999). The Grameen Bank. *Scientific American*, *281*(5), 90–95.

Yunus, Mohammad, & Jolis, Alan. (2003). *Banker to the poor: The story of the Grameen Bank*. London: Aurum Press Ltd.

Middle East

The Middle East includes western and southwestern Asia as well as North Africa. Most of the population of roughly 390 million people speaks Arabic. The region is primarily desert or semi-desert, and several countries' economies depend on their abundant oil reserves. The region is facing degradation of water quality, overcultivation of marginal lands, and widespread pollution. Although deforestation and desertification have long been believed to be problems in the region, research has undermined this common misunderstanding and revealed that the Middle East has a much more resilient and dynamic environment than previously thought.

The Middle East is a highly diverse region that includes Algeria, Egypt, Libya, Morocco, and Tunisia in North Africa and the countries of the Levant and the Arabian Peninsula, including Bahrain, Iran, Iraq, Israel, Jordan, Lebanon, Oman, Qatar, Saudi Arabia, Syria, the West Bank and Gaza, the United Arab Emirates (UAE), and Yemen. Many scholars also include Turkey, whereas others consider it a part of Europe. The term "Middle East" was first used in 1902 but was not widely adopted until World War II (Adelson 2012). Along with Near East and Far East, however, Middle East is considered by many to be a Eurocentric term, although there is not, as yet, a more widespread term in English that is not considered to be Eurocentric.

This complex region has one of the longest known histories of human occupation and is considered one of the birthplaces of human societies. Consequently, the Middle East also has a long history of human use of the environment, including many important events such as the domestication of wheat, barley, sheep, and goats. It is not surprising, then, that many scholars have claimed that humans and their herds of animals long have degraded the environment of the Middle East. Research has

shown, however, that the vegetation in this region is well adapted to many human uses (and to grazing), and it is actually quite a resilient and dynamic environment (Blumler 1998; Middleton 2009; Nicholson 2011; Perevolotsky and Seligman 1998). Although in the past deforestation, overgrazing, and desertification were believed to be the most important environmental concerns, the most pressing environmental problems at the beginning of the twenty-first century are actually the degradation of available water resources, pollution of air, water, and soil, the spread of marginal agriculture, and other effects of unregulated economic development in a rapidly urbanizing region.

Overview

Despite the fact that the Middle East is often thought of as a single region, it is actually a very diverse and differentiated group of nations, peoples, languages, and physical environments. Out of a total population of almost 390 million people, the majority speaks Arabic (PRB 2011). Many people, however, speak other languages, including Turkish, Persian (mainly in Iran), Berber, Hebrew (mainly in Israel), Kurdish, Azeri, and so forth. French is the lingua franca of several former colonies and former mandate territories. Although approximately 90 percent of the population of the Middle East is Muslim, other religions include Judaism, Christianity, and Zoroastrianism. There are many different ethnicities, and local people may identify themselves by many different combinations of these languages, religions, and ethnicities; this fact further complicates the region.

The physical environment is equally complex. More than 80 percent of the Middle East is classified as desert or semi-desert. The summer temperature is usually between 30°C and 40°C, although it occasionally reaches

50°C, especially in parts of Saudi Arabia (Held and Cummings 2011, 38). Although aridity and infrequent rainfall are the norm in the region as a whole, some places, such as the mountains in Yemen, Turkey, Iran, and Morocco, receive plentiful rainfall, while some parts of the Sahara desert receive practically no rainfall at all for years at a time (Beaumont, Blake, and Wagstaff 1988; Nicholson 2011). As a result, vegetation differs greatly from one place to another, largely depending on rainfall. For the region as a whole, only approximately 7 percent of the land is capable of growing crops without irrigation (Held and Cummings 2011, 142). The majority of the local plants and animals are well adapted to arid environments, and species diversity is high in several Middle Eastern countries, especially in the Mediterranean region, including Morocco and Lebanon (Laity 2008; Middleton 2009; Woodward 2009).

Some countries in the region, like Saudi Arabia and Kuwait, mainly depend on their oil resources and oil-related products, while others, like Israel and Egypt, have well-developed cotton, textile, dairy, and leather goods industries. Although some oil-producing countries such as Saudi Arabia are very wealthy, roughly 20 to 30 percent of the population of the Middle East still lives below the poverty line, and unemployment is at an average of 15 to 20 percent, varying by country (Qadir et al. 2010; Schwedler and Gerner 2008). Literacy rates in parts of the Middle East have significantly increased in recent years, and the average literacy rate has reached 80 percent, although rates are generally lower for women and girls (UN Statistics Division 2011). The majority of the population, approximately 63 percent, lives in cities, which are concentrated along coastlines, rivers, and other sources of water (Held and Cummings 2011). The Middle East has one of the highest rates of urbanization in the underdeveloped world, second only to Latin America.

In 2003, the United States and the United Kingdom invaded Iraq, claiming that Iraq had developed weapons of mass destruction. Such weapons, however, were never found (Held and Cummings 2011). The ensuing war resulted in more than 5 million Iraqis seeking refuge in other countries, in addition to several million internally displaced persons (United Nations High Commissioner for Refugees 2008). The war caused deterioration of the infrastructure, water supplies, and food security in the country, in addition to widespread environmental contamination with uranium and heavy metals and other urgent environmental problems (Koppel 2009).

Most of the countries in the region have authoritarian governments, are highly indebted to organizations such as the World Bank and other lending organizations, and import large amounts of food. A wave of protests and revolutions, often referred to as the Arab Spring, began in Tunis, Tunisia, in December 2010. Tunisia, Egypt,

and Libya all saw the overthrow of autocratic governments; as of 2012 Syria was embroiled in a virtual civil war. These political and economic realities have a direct bearing on the state of the environment in many Middle Eastern countries today and will certainly have an impact on the environment in the future.

Land Degradation

Deforestation and overgrazing have long been blamed for land degradation in the Middle East. Research has demonstrated, however, that these two forces have not had a significant impact on most Middle Eastern environments now or in the past (Blumler 1998; Davis and Burke 2011; Davis 2012; Lamb, Eicher, and Switzer 1989; Olsvig-Whittaker et al. 2006). Rather, the vegetation in the Middle East is highly resilient and is well adapted to drought and grazing (Batanouny 2001; Debaine and Jaubert 2002; Middleton 2009; Woodward 2009). Approximately 4 to 5 percent of the Middle East's rural population is estimated to practice nomadic or semi-nomadic pastoralism. Deforestation in the region since 1990 has been only 0.1 percent (World Bank 2012a) on average, and in some places, the forested area has actually increased. Since 1990, for instance, Morocco has experienced an increase of 1.5 million hectares, and in Syria forests have increased by 82,000 hectares (FAO 2012). In Abu Dhabi, afforestation has been occurring at an astounding rate of 26 percent annually since 1980 (Davis and Burke 2011, 14). (Afforestation, as opposed to reforestation, is the practice of planting trees where they have not traditionally grown in the past, at least within recent history.) Given the desert-adapted ecology of the region, it is not surprising that there are little hard data demonstrating desertification (Thomas and Middleton 1994; Nicholson 2003; Davis and Burke 2011; Davis 2012). Many scholars see the environments of the Middle East as naturally arid lands that humans and livestock are using in a largely sustainable manner rather than as deforested, overgrazed, and desertified (Blumler 1998; Olsvig-Whittaker et al. 2006; Davis 2012).

One cause of land degradation of growing concern across the Middle East, however, is the expansion of dry-land cereal cultivation into marginal areas where average rainfall is too low to support reliable cereal harvests. The process of plowing these dry lands desiccates the soil, and most fields are soon abandoned, leaving the local vegetation severely degraded. In North Africa, for example, cereal cultivation has increased dramatically since 1980 (Swearingen and Bencherifa 1996). In other Middle Eastern countries, the area under cereal cultivation has also expanded, but not as dramatically, and varies a great deal year to year (World Bank 2012b). Much of the increase in Morocco, Algeria, and Syria has been in marginal areas that were previously grazing lands. Experts are concerned that this may produce long-term land degradation in large areas of the Middle East. Despite these problems, many Middle Eastern governments feel they have no choice but to continue to expand dryland cereal cultivation to provide basic foods to their population as their economies are squeezed by structural adjustment policies and other political/economic factors. Structural adjustment policies are enforced by the International Monetary Fund and include cutting subsidies on basic foods, privatizing business and industry (which results in job losses), cutting social services such as health care and education, and so on (Davis 2006). Such policies nearly always make the poor poorer, increase the number of people going hungry, and have a negative impact on the environment.

The amount of irrigated land has doubled in many areas in the Middle East since 1970, with some countries like Saudi Arabia seeing a fourfold increase (FAO 2012; Held and Cummings 2011). Much of this expansion has been made possible by the building of large dams on major rivers as well as by the increased pumping of groundwater and the reuse of wastewater. With this increase in irrigation, often year-round, has come a host of problems. One of the most important is salinization of agricultural soils. Because of a variety of factors including inadequate drainage, salts commonly build up in perennially irrigated soils, which is harmful to plant growth (White 1988). The growing problem of salinization from irrigation is directly related to a multitude of water resource problems throughout the Middle East.

Water Resources

Although the Middle East is home to approximately 6 percent of the world's people, it contains only about 1 to 1.5 percent of the world's freshwater supplies (PRB 2002; Qadir et al. 2010). Freshwater supply per person in the Middle East is approximately only 14 percent of the global average (1,145 cubic meters per person per year, as opposed to a global average of 8,240 cubic meters) (PRB 2002). Many countries in the Middle East have far less

water than this. Jordan, for example, one of the poorest countries and categorized as a water-stressed country, has one of the lowest per capita water supplies in the Middle East, with an average of 85 liters per person per day, compared with 600 liters per person per day in Europe and the United States (Held and Cummings 2011, 330). Agriculture uses approximately 80 percent or more of the Middle East's water, while nearly 8–10 percent goes to domestic use, and industry uses about 5–6 percent (PRB 2002; Qadir et al. 2010). Many of the countries in the Middle East use their renewable water supplies at or above the rate of natural recharge by utilizing nonrenewable sources such as fossil water aquifers and advanced technologies like desalination. With growing populations, recent data indicating downward trends in rainfall, and the specter of climate change, water shortages and water quality will likely worsen in the future (Sowers, Vengosh, and Weinthal 2011).

There is, however, an increasing attempt to manage water resources in several countries. Saudi Arabia, for example, decided in 2008 to cut its domestic wheat production by 12.5 percent annually to reduce the amount of water used for irrigation, and more than two thousand mosques in Abu Dhabi have been fitted with devices that reduce water use when people wash for prayer (Vidal 2011). In many of the Gulf countries recycled wastewater is used for landscape irrigation, and Israel has led the development and deployment of drip irrigation for agriculture for several decades. The use of wastewater, however, comes at a cost because adequate treatment is expensive, and even treated wastewater is often contaminated with salts, boron, pollutants, pharmaceuticals, and toxins like heavy metals (Qadir et al. 2010; Sowers, Vengosh, and Weinthal 2011).

Because there are few major rivers, a substantial amount of water is taken from underground water sources (aquifers). In areas such as the Arabian Peninsula, aquifers provide most of the water for domestic use, industry, and agriculture. Countries in this region currently use the water from these aquifers faster than the aquifers are being recharged, thus exceeding the renewable supply of water. Overuse has lowered the water table in many areas, causing natural springs to dry up and necessitating deeper wells. This overwithdrawal (mining) of aquifers is not confined to the Arabian

Peninsula. Other countries that mine their aquifers in an unsustainable manner include Bahrain, Kuwait, Oman, Qatar, Saudi Arabia, the UAE, Yemen, Israel, the West Bank and Gaza, Jordan, Syria, Morocco, and Tunisia (ACSAD 2000).

As a result of this overuse, the intrusion of salty seawater into many coastal aquifers has made them unusable for drinking and often for irrigation. Aquifers throughout the region are also degraded and polluted by heavy metals such as mercury, by pesticides and fertilizers, and by raw human sewage (which carries disease-causing microbes), which seep down into these aquifers from the surface (Masri 1997; Magaritz et al. 1990; Ouis 2011; Sowers, Vengosh, and Weinthal 2011). The resulting pollution is a serious threat to public health. Aquifers are very difficult to clean of these pollutants, because the rate of recharge is slow and they are largely confined in underground bodies of water. Naturally occurring radioactive contamination has been discovered in a large fossil water aquifer in Jordan, and the scientists involved hypothesize that this problem may be widespread in similar sandstone aquifers in the region (Vengosh et al. 2009). The levels of radioactive contamination detected in the Jordanian aquifer are high enough to be carcinogenic. Because of water overuse, pollution, and short supply, several Gulf countries, including Saudi Arabia and the UAE as well as Israel and several other countries, rely on desalination plants to produce water (Sowers, Vengosh, and Weinthal 2011). Desalination is expensive, and the plants create air pollution as well as water pollution from the waste products, which include concentrated brine, various toxic chemicals and heavy metals, and heat accumulation harmful to marine ecosystems (NRC 2008).

The Nile River, the Jordan River, and the Tigris–Euphrates river basin are three major river systems in the Middle East. Because of scarcity, disputes over water are an important element in Middle Eastern politics (Gleick 1994; Held and Cummings 2011). Dams have been built on the Nile, Euphrates, and several rivers in Morocco to store water and to generate electricity. These large dams have caused a host of problems, including increases in waterborne diseases such as schistosomiasis, salinization in areas of perennial irrigation, deterioration of downstream water quality, changes in the water tables downstream, siltation of the dam reservoir, adverse effects on deltas and wetlands, coastal erosion, decline in river fish populations, river channel degradation, and erosion of arable land downstream due to decreased sediment load in rivers (Gleick 1994; White 1988). The Aswan High Dam in Egypt has caused a number of serious problems of this nature, including the salinization of around 50 percent of all arable land in Egypt, significant erosion of the delta area, and an increase in schistosomiasis (White

1988; Held and Cummings 2011). A complication of schistosomiasis treatment in Egypt has been a dramatic increase in hepatitis C, spread when contaminated syringes were used to give anti-schistosomiasis drugs (Frank, Mohamed, and Strickland 2000). The environmental impact of this dam has been especially wide ranging.

Pollution

Surface waters such as rivers, reservoirs, and lakes are also suffering from pollution. Agricultural pollution with pesticides and fertilizers contaminates soils and water supplies as do industrial pollutants. Four lakes in northern Egypt, known as the Four Sisters, for example, are very polluted with a variety of industrial toxins, agricultural runoff, and sewage. High percentages of the fish caught in these lakes register alarming levels of contaminants such as dichlorodiphenyltrichloroethane (DDT), polychlorinated biphenyls (PCBs), heavy metals, and pesticides (Bush and Sabri 2000). Water pollution is also a serious problem in many other countries in the region (Sowers, Vengosh, and Weinthal 2011). Sources for 60 to 70 percent of drinking water in Lebanon are contaminated with fecal bacteria (Masri 1997). Significant water pollution is reported in nearly every Middle Eastern country from these sources and from petroleum products. As rivers discharge into seas and oceans, significant pollution of the Mediterranean, the Red Sea, the Atlantic coastal waters of Morocco, and the Persian Gulf has also occurred, negatively affecting fisheries (El-Nady 1996; Henchi 1996; Masri 1997).

Air pollution is another large and growing problem across the Middle East. The main sources of air pollution are industry and transport including shipping and automobiles, although pollution from household cooking and heating are significant in some countries (Hussein 2008; Kanakidou et al. 2011). Leaded automobile fuel is widely used and produces airborne lead that settles onto soil and water, polluting them also. The problem of lead contamination from automobiles and industries is so grave in Cairo and other parts of the Middle East that playground dust has been found to contain lead levels that exceed those for hazardous waste sites in the United States (Hopkins and Mehanna 1997). In the mid-1990s, the average blood lead level among men in Cairo was found to be 30 micrograms per deciliter, very high compared to US standards of the time (less than 10 micrograms per deciliter) (PRIDE 1994). Cairo also has some of the worst air pollution in the world (Kanakidou et al. 2011). The level of particulate matter in Cairo's air is five to ten times higher than international health standards, was higher than the level in any other large city in the world in the mid-1990s, and still rivals that of Mexico City and Tokyo (Hopkins and Mehanna 1997; Kanakidou et al. 2011). Large cities such as Casablanca, Beirut, Amman, Tunis, Tehran, and Jidda have similar air pollution problems (Henchi 1996; Masri 1997). Unregulated dumping of solid waste and industrial toxins has contaminated water and soil in many areas (Hussein 2008). Contaminated soil and water can contaminate local food with dangerous levels of bacteria, pesticides, and other toxins, thus endangering the food chain.

Outlook

In response to the Middle East's growing environmental problems, many countries have created new branches of government for the protection of the environment, and especially water, over the last two decades (Sowers, Vengosh, and Weinthal 2011). This has resulted in new environmental legislation, as well as ratification of international treaties in several countries, including Morocco, Egypt, Iran, Jordan, Lebanon, Oman, the UAE, and Tunisia. The gains from the new environmental legislation have been minimal, however. Due to high poverty levels and high rates of indebtedness across the Middle East, governments have, for the most part, chosen to put their meager financial resources toward economic development and security rather than toward regulation and enforcement of existing environmental policies (Chourou 1995; Hopkins and Mehanna 1997; Jreisat 1997; Sowers, Vengosh, and Weinthal 2011). As a result, new environmental protection laws are not often enforced, and basic regulations for industrial air and wastewater emissions are still minimal. Outside of a few major cities, organized solid waste collection and disposal do not exist. Across the Middle East, only about 43 percent of wastewater is treated; the remainder is dumped, polluting the soil and water supply (Qadir et al. 2010). Lack of basic infrastructure and industrial regulation are directly linked to political and economic problems common to authoritarian governments. Without addressing those basic underlying factors, it is unlikely that the environmental challenges confronting the Middle East will be addressed effectively, sustainably, or equitably.

Diana K. DAVIS
University of California at Davis

See also Agriculture, Small-Scale; Cairo, Egypt; Desertification (Africa); Dubai, United Arab Emirates; Fisheries; Mediterranean Sea; Nile River; Sahara; Shipping and Freight; Transboundary Water Issues; Tunis, Tunisia; Urbanization (Western Asia and Northern Africa); Water Use and Rights (Middle East and North Africa)

FURTHER READING

Adelson, Roger. (2012). British and US use and misuse of the term "Middle East." In Michael Bonine, Abbas Amanat & Michael Gasper (Eds.), *Is there a Middle East? The evolution of a geopolitical concept* (pp. 38–47). Palo Alto, CA: Stanford University Press.

Arab Centre for the Studies of Arid Zones and Drylands (ACSAD). (2000). Alternative policy study: Water resource management in west Asia. Retrieved July 9, 2012, from http://www.grida.no/publications/other/geo2000/?src=/geo2000/aps-wasia/index.htm

Batanouny, Kamal A. (2001). Plants in the deserts of the Middle East. Berlin: Springer-Verlag.

Beaumont, Peter; Blake, Gerald H.; & Wagstaff, J. Malcolm. (1988). *The Middle East: A geographical study.* London: David Fulton.

Blumler, Mark A. (1998). Biogeography of land-use impacts in the Near East. In Karl S. Zimmerer & Kenneth R. Young (Eds.), *Nature's geography: New lessons for conservation in developing countries.* Madison: University of Wisconsin Press.

Bush, Ray, & Sabri, Amal. (2000, Fall). Mining for fish: Privatization of the "commons" along Egypt's northern coastline. *Middle East Report, 30*(216), 20–23, 45.

Chourou, Béchir. (1995). The dilemma between environmental protection and economic development. In Eric Watkins (Ed.), *The Middle Eastern environment.* Cambridge, UK: St. Malo Press.

Davis, Diana K. (2006). Neoliberalism, environmentalism and agricultural restructuring in Morocco. *The Geographical Journal, 172*(2), 88–105.

Davis, Diana K. (2012). Scorched Earth: The problematic environmental history that defines the Middle East. In Michael E. Bonine, Abbas Amanat & Michael Ezekial Gasper (Eds.), *Is there a Middle East? The evolution of a geopolitical concept* (pp. 170–188). Palo Alto, CA: Stanford University Press.

Davis, Diana K., & Burke, Edmund, III. (Eds.). (2011). *Environmental imaginaries of the Middle East and North Africa.* Athens: Ohio University Press.

Debaine, Françoise, & Jaubert, Ronald. (2002). The degradation of the steppe, hypotheses and realities. *The Arab World Geographer, 5*(2), 124–140.

El-Nady, F. E. (1996). Heavy metals exchange among the aquatic environment in the Mediterranean coast of Egypt. *Indian Journal of Marine Science, 25*(3), 225–233.

Food and Agriculture Organization of the United Nations (FAO). (2012). *FAOSTAT: Production yearbook database from 1961-present.* Rome: UNFAO. Retrieved July 9, 2012, from http://faostat.fao.org

Frank, Christina; Mohamed, Mostafa; & Strickland, G. Thomas. (2000). The role of parenteral antischistosomal therapy in the spread of hepatitis C virus in Egypt. *The Lancet, 355,* 887–891.

Gleick, Peter H.; Yolles, Peter; & Hatami, Haleh. (1994). Water, war, and peace in the Middle East. *Environment, 36*(3), 6–15, 35–42.

Held, Colbert C., & Cummings, John T. (2011). *Middle East patterns: Places, peoples, and politics.* Boulder, CO: Westview Press.

Henchi, Belgacem. (1996). Pollution and the deteriorating quality of life in Tunisia. In Will D. Swearingen & Abdellatif Bencherifa (Eds.), *The North African environment at risk.* Boulder, CO: Westview Press.

Hopkins, Nicholas, & Mehanna, Sohair. (1997). Pollution, popular perceptions and grassroots environmental activism. *Middle East Report, 27*(213), 21–25.

Hussein, Muawya A. (2008). Costs of environmental degradation: An analysis in the Middle East and North Africa region. *Management of Environmental Quality: An International Journal, 19*(3), 305–317.

Jreisat, Jamil. (1997). Environmental management: The will and the way in Jordan. *Journal of Developing Societies, 13*(1), 18–30.

Kanakidou, Maria, et al. (2011). Megacities as hot spots of air pollution in the east Mediterranean. *Atmospheric Environment, 45,* 1223–1235.

Koppel, Naomi. (2009, February 11). Iraq faces "alarming" enviro problems. CBS News. Retrieved July 10, 2012, from http://www.cbsnews.com/2100-500257_162-550970.html

Laity, Julie. (2008). *Deserts and desert environments*. Oxford, UK: Wiley-Blackwell.

Lamb, H. F.; Eicher, U.; &. Switsur, V. R. (1989, January). An 18,000-year record of vegetation, lake-level and climatic change from Tigalmamine, Middle Atlas, Morocco. *Journal of Biogeography*, *16*(1), 65–74.

Magaritz, M.; Amiel, A. J.; Ronen, D.; & Wells, M. C. (1990). Distribution of metals in a polluted aquifer: A comparison of aquifer suspended material to fine sediments of the adjacent environment. *Journal of Contaminant Hydrology*, *5*(4), 333–348.

Masri, Rania. (1997). Environmental challenges in Lebanon. *Journal of Developing Societies*, *13*(1), 73–115.

Middleton, Nick. (2009). *Deserts: A very short introduction*. Oxford, UK: Oxford University Press.

National Research Council (NRC). (2008). *Desalination: A national perspective*. Washington, DC: The National Academies Press.

Nicholson, Sharon E. (2003). Desertification. In Shepard Krech, John R. McNeill & Carolyn Merchant (Eds.), *Encyclopedia of world environmental history* (pp. 297–303). New York: Routledge.

Nicholson, Sharon E. (2011). *Dryland climatology*. Cambridge, UK: Cambridge University Press.

Olsvig-Whittaker, Linda; Frankenberg, Eliezer; Perevolotsky, Avi; & Ungar, Eugene D. (2006). Grazing, overgrazing and conservation: Changing concepts and practices in the Negev Rangelands. *Sécheresse*, *17*(1 & 2), 195–199.

Ouis, Pernilla. (2011). Engineering the Emirates: The evolution of a new environment. In Stanley Brunn (Ed.), *Engineering Earth: The impacts of megaengineering projects* (pp. 1409–1423). Boston: Kluwer.

Perevolotsky, Avi, & Seligman, No'am. (1998). Role of grazing in Mediterranean rangeland ecosystems. *BioScience*, *48*(12), 1007–1017.

Population Reference Bureau (PRB). (2002). Finding the balance: Population and water scarcity in the Middle East and North Africa. Retrieved February 13, 2012, from http://www.prb.org/Publications/PolicyBriefs/FindingtheBalancePopulationandWaterScarcityintheMiddleEastandNorthAfrica.aspx

Population Reference Bureau (PRB). (2011). Population mid-2011. Retrieved February 13, 2012, from http://www.prb.org/DataFinder/Topic/Rankings.aspx?ind=14

Project in Development and Environment (PRIDE). (1994). Comparing environmental health risks in Cairo, Egypt (Report submitted to USAID/Egypt). Washington, DC: PRIDE.

Qadir, Manzoor; Bahri, Akissa; Sato, Toshio; & Al-Karadesh, Esmat. (2010). Wastewater production, treatment, and irrigation in Middle East and North Africa. *Irrigation and Drainage Systems*, *24*, 37–51.

Schwedler, Jillian, & Gerner, Deborah J. (2008). *Understanding the contemporary Middle East*. London: Lynne Reinner.

Smith, Pamela. (1999). Protecting the Arab environment. *Middle East*, *286*, 33–36.

Sowers, Jeannie; Vengosh, Avner; & Weinthal, Erika. (2011). Climate change, water resources, and the politics of adaptation in the Middle East and North Africa. *Climatic Change*, *104*, 599–627.

Swearingen, Will D., & Bencherifa, Abdellatif. (1996). *The North African environment at risk*. Boulder, CO: Westview Press.

Thomas, David S. G., & Middleton, Nicholas. (1994). *Desertification: Exploding the myth*. West Sussex, UK: John Wiley & Sons.

United Nations High Commissioner for Refugees. (2008, April 29). Iraq: Latest return survey shows few intending to go home soon (Briefing notes). Retrieved January 9, 2012, from http://www.unhcr.org/4816ef534.html

United Nations (UN) Statistics Division. (2011). Social indicators. Retrieved February 13, 2012, from http://unstats.un.org/unsd/demographic/products/socind/literacy.htm

Vengosh, Avner, et al. (2009). High naturally occurring radioactivity in fossil groundwater in the Middle East. *Environmental Science and Technology*, *43*(6), 1769–1775.

Vidal, John. (2011, February 20). What does the Arab world do when its water runs out? *The Guardian*. Retrieved January 5, 2012, from http://www.guardian.co.uk/environment/2011/feb/20/arab-nations-water-running-out

White, Gilbert F. (1988). The environmental effects of the High Dam at Aswan. *Environment*, *30*(7), 4–11, 34–40.

Woodward, Jamie. (2009). *The physical geography of the Mediterranean*. Oxford, UK: Oxford University Press.

World Bank. (2012a). Little green data book. Retrieved July 6, 2012, from http://data.worldbank.org/sites/default/files/ldb-green-2012.pdf

World Bank. (2012b). Land under cereal production (hectares). Retrieved February 13, 2012, from http://data.worldbank.org/indicator/AG.LND.CREL.HA/countries/EG-XQ-XN?display=default

Migration (Africa)

Migration is people moving from one place to the other, either between countries or within a single country. In most of Africa, the focus of migration has been on rural-to-urban movement within a single country and from one country to another within the same subregion. Migrants may leave behind all means of support to move to a new environment that may not guarantee support. It is important that migrants' activities are socially, economically, and environmentally sustainable to minimize the emergence of other forms of unsustainable migration.

Migrations range from in-country and mostly rural-to-urban delineations to international movement beyond one's country of origin (national) to another country (international boundaries). Africans have thus moved from one country to another within the same subregion (e.g., West Africa), referred to as intra-regional; between countries of different subregions (e.g., West Africa to Southern Africa), referred to as inter-regional; and across the boundaries of the African continent, referred to as intercontinental (Adepoju 2002 and 2008a). For the African, these movements represent part of the human penchant for change, development, and livelihood diversification. In Africa, migration is thus culturally constructed and based on the notions of family, home, and kinship; it is posited as one's extended household away from home (van Blerk and Ansell 2006).

As a result, the attribution of migration in some discourses to poverty, lack of employment, and over-population or high human densities may be an oversimplification. In Africa, movements are facilitated by the intertwining of deeply entrenched transnational and national social networks (Muanamoha et al. 2010), which have elicited migrants' growing interest in literacy, economic activity, and remittances (the transfer of capital from workers back to their places of origin) (Henry, Boyle, and Lambin 2003). The rural-to-rural and rural-to-urban migrations are considered a necessity to cushion migrant households from further economic and financial disability. Incomes from remittances of in-country, intra-, or inter- African regional migrants have thus been found to contribute to debt repayment, social status, shelter, and basic livelihood needs of families. It has been argued, therefore, that migration and remittances are pillars of social and economic sustainability in Africa and are contributing to the attainment of some of the United Nations' Millennium Development Goals.

Technological change and regional integration as well as cross-border trade and cultural exchange have driven African migration in recent times. Improved communication as well as transportation strategies such as air mobility bring Africans closer than before and within shorter time periods. Labor and trade mobility have traditionally dictated migration as a global phenomenon, although war and conflict in Africa have resulted in refugees as unintended migrants. Although many of the efforts to minimize migration in Africa have been through social and economic instruments such as welfare support programs, emigration laws, and trade regulations, the sustainability of these efforts may be constrained by the physical environmental resource base due to extensive occupation and changing land use (i.e., land available for farming or agriculture). The African migration dictated by spatial occupancy and available land coupled with the pressure of maintaining their livelihoods will thus lead to environmental degradation (Black et al. 2011) and create imbalances in social and economic sustainability. There is therefore the need to understand all forms of migration influences on the physical environment of Africa to avoid the creation of *environmental refugees*, who are an emerging group of displaced humans.

Origin, History, and Influence

The history of the movement of humans in Africa dates back several generations and constitutes the origin of the human race globally. Researchers argue that cultural and environmental differences, rather than racial superiority, influenced the outmigration of other races (Campbell and Tishkoff 2010; Richter et al. 2012). Migration within Africa might have been either a voluntary search for greener pastures or forced migration fueled by conflict and slavery (Singh et al. 2005). Entire communities and tribes in precolonial times moved from one part of a country to the other, from rural to urban areas, and from one part of Africa to another in search of shelter from warfare and better human security and of arable land (Adebusoye 2006; Shinn 2008). Pastoral nomads, including the Fulani, moved across the Sahel to the south in response to seasonal climatic change (de Haas 2007), and pastoralists moved between Kenya and Tanzania, Somalia and Ethiopia, and Nigeria and Cameroon in the precolonial era.

The most well known influence of migration in Africa is the emergence of new settlements such as the Ovambo in Namibia (Gewald 2003) and in many other countries or communities where migration is associated with farm labor, urbanization, and health problems associated with settling in environments unsuitable for human habitation and people performing jobs detrimental to their health in the process of diversifying livelihoods (e.g., Ndegwa, Horner, and Esau 2007; Parnell and Walawege 2011). Migrating to where there is work provides income for families of migrants (Ziesemer 2012), to the extent that there are fears that remittances from migration are creating unsustainable local and family economies as opposed to national economies for development. Additionally, the African regional "brain drain" (migration of skilled labor) is considered to have immense influence on financial and human capital transfers among Africans through short- and long-term return migration, resulting in areas where migrants have increased skill and expertise through cross-cultural experience and work in new occupations other than the ones in which they originally trained. Health workers and people in academia or education often migrate from Africa, whereas less skilled or unskilled laborers' migrations remain in Africa (Adepoju 2008b; UNDP 2009). Migration within subregional Africa has influenced labor forces in individual countries and created labor inequalities, economic imbalances for some economies, and additional pressure on access to environmental resources that affect expanding farms and settlements (Konseiga 2005). Large population movements in the early 1960s toward the expansion of cash crop plantations (e.g., cocoa in Ghana and Côte d'Ivoire, coffee in Côte d'Ivoire) attracted a workforce from other parts of West Africa, leaving labor and productivity deficits in the originating countries.

Social, economic, and political factors drive Africa's migration and thus influence development in these sectors. Development could be delayed from the overuse and abuse of the continent's environmental wealth. The ease with which Africans can readily and quickly settle in new places—due, in part, to Africans' similar cultural identities—influences the production base of areas in countries because they compete for public resources. Competition for limited resources may constitute new or nontraditional forms of migration because indigenous populations who lack targeted skills may be displaced by migrants who have these skills. Both resident and immigrant populations may migrate because of a lack of cultural identity (cultural dilution) rather than for reasons of conflict or resource depletion. Cecilia Tacoli (2009), a senior researcher at the International Institute for Environment and Development, argues that migration partly reflects the failure of society to adapt to changes in the physical environment. Yet in Africa the failed economic and political infrastructure influences the environmental factor, and the attainment of human livelihood is inseparable from the use of environmental resources. The spread of disease has been part of the African immigration as well, with HIV/AIDS migrant households found to depend largely on "free" environmental resources for their livelihoods due to loss of jobs and lack of care (van Blerk and Ansell 2006; Hunter, De Souza, and Twine 2008).

Regional Migration Dynamics

Of all the migrations in Africa, the intra-Africa emigration rate (migration within subregions) is estimated at 52 percent, while inter-Africa migrations (across borders) was 48 percent (UNDP 2009). These movements were characterized by distinctive forms of migration in the different subregions and were created mostly by increasingly differentiated economic performance and political relationships through new forms of labor (Gould 1988; Adepoju 2008b). The migration within Africa (both inter- and intra-) can be categorized into six large pools, which are not exclusive of one another (Njock and Westlund 2010). They are international migration across national borders; seasonal migration lasting for one or two seasons, and then a return home for a certain amount of time; long-term migration involving several years of settlement but eventually a return to the home country; and permanent migration with the migrant integrated into the local population of the receiving country and eventually acquiring the host country's nationality. Contractual migration involves an employment contract formally established in the country of origin with circular migration where people move fluidly, temporarily or in the long term, between countries, in a manner that benefits all involved (IOM 2008). Stopover migration means that migrants make shorter or longer stops in a place en route to their final destination. Migration flows and processes in East Africa appear to be dominated by circular migration involving temporary or semi-permanent migration from a rural area to another rural area or to an urban area as well as rural-to-urban migration intra-regionally that is generally at lower rates than in West or Southern Africa (Black et al. 2004).

The intra-African migration is generally defined by the background of colonial borders that overlooked social characteristics such as linguistic and ethnic commonalities as well as barriers. A single ethnic group hence may have found itself spanning two or more of the new countries (Balbo and Marconi 2006; Shimeles 2010). The Yoruba, one of the largest ethnic groups in West Africa, span Nigeria, the Republic of Benin, and Togo (Mullen 2004). Yet these shared characteristics have also promoted and eased movements across neighboring countries (Shimeles 2010). Movement of people within the continent has dominated cross-border migration, with almost 90 percent of the intra-African migration taking place in West Africa, followed by 65 percent in Southern Africa, the latter attracting migrant labor for the mines. The most common destination countries for emigrants in Africa are Côte d'Ivoire, Nigeria, South Africa, Sudan,

Kenya, and Tanzania, although the difference in level of per capita gross domestic product (GDP) between the location of the origination country and of the target country may be negligible; indeed, in some cases the originating countries have higher GDP per capita. The highest migration to other subregions was recorded for West Africa (38.5 percent) and the least for North Africa (6.4 percent). (See table 1 below.)

Environmental Sustainability Nexus

Increasing evidence suggests links between migration and the environment in Africa. Debates on climate change and migration focus on displacement and migration as a significant problem (Black et al. 2011; Marchiori, Maystadt, and Schumacher 2012). The environment drives migration through mechanisms characterized as the availability and reliability of ecosystem services and exposure to hazard. The availability and reliability of ecosystem services as well as exposure to hazard operating in combination with sociopolitical, economic, and demographic changes affect individual migration decisions and flows (Black et al. 2011). Weather anomalies in parts of Africa induce rural-to-urban migration that subsequently triggers migration beyond individual countries and subregional boundaries (Marchiori, Maystadt, and Schumacher 2012). Climatic change, as proxied by rainfall, has changed urbanization in sub-Saharan Africa and is linked strongly to decolonization due to the often simultaneous lifting of legislation prohibiting the free internal movement of native Africans (Barrios, Bertinelli, and Strobl 2006). Similarly, soil quality has significantly reduced migration in Kenya but is marginally increasing

TABLE I. Matrix of the Proportion of Subregional Emigration in Africa in 2010

Destination	Origin				
	East Africa	Central Africa	North Africa	Southern Africa	West Africa
East Africa	**46.6**	14.8	12.1	26.5	0.0
Central Africa	30.2	**50.3**	5.7	6.5	7.2
North Africa	51.2	26.9	**20.4**	0.0	1.5
Southern Africa	34.6	0.1	0.0	**65.3**	0.0
West Africa	3.2	6.6	0.7	0.0	**89.5**
Total (inter-regional)	26.5	14.0	6.4	14.6	38.5

Note: Bold numbers indicate migration within a subregion versus across regions. The high percentage of migration within the West African region indicates very few migrants leave the West African region for other destinations. North Africa, with the lowest migration rate within the subregion, means most migrants move to other regions in search of work or resources.

Source: Shimeles (2010, 9).

migration in Uganda, showing that adverse environmental conditions tend to increase migration (Gray 2011).

Environmental sustainability concerns the capacity of the environment to endure, remain diverse, and produce over time. Traditional arguments have portrayed migration and migrants as threats to human security, as well as to survival and development, whereas the development community has argued that human mobility is a tool likely to contribute immensely to development (Landau and Vigneswaran 2007). In both discourses, however, sustaining the environment, especially natural resources, has been empirically remote to the debate because many of the discourses on migration and development tend to focus on economic sustainability. The US climate change specialist Jürgen Scheffran and his colleagues, in a study of West Africa, argue that migration is becoming an important means of climate change adaptation (Scheffran, Marmer, and Sow 2012). It is thus possible that migration would relieve pressure on densely populated areas (Jensen and Ahlburg 2004), a form of ex ante insurance. Yet that difference in population would be added onto the destination area, which over time may also have to evolve, especially urban areas (Poelhekke 2011). Consequently, land use and land cover changes greatly impact migration in Africa, as migrants converge in fragile environments or undertake makeshift jobs in the frustration of making a living. People vulnerable to limited resources, mostly in risky and degraded environments, adopt means to diversify or self-insure risk by collective decision making based on cautious cost-benefit evaluations (Borjas 1994; Adepoju 2008b). Such decision structures can ensure the sustainable use of environmental resources.

Social and Economic Sustainability Nexus

Social and economic sustainability defines a society where people live within reasonable means and enhance the capacity of social and economic systems to endure change while people profit and prosper (e.g., through remittances). Remittances are a key element in the relationship between migration and development, especially for poor countries (Page 2009). A study of Morocco has shown that remittances are significant to economic development and improve the standard of living among ethnic groups (de Haas 2006). Internal migration has also provided avenues to facilitate the education and international migration of younger household members as well as to build social capital and transfer knowledge. While it is understood that remittances may not constitute a rising tide for development, they increase the social resilience in the communities of origin and trigger innovations across regions (Newland 2003; Scheffran, Marmer, and Sow 2012). Families of migrants directly spend remittances, unlike development aid; remittances are an efficient way to raise the incomes of people as well as the financial, human, social, and other types of capital in the receiving country (O'Neil 2003; IOM 2005). These contributions form some basis for social and economic sustainability, inform the UN Millennium Development Goals, minimize poverty incidence, and enhance sustainable development.

Some analysts worry that migration, rather than being a source for structural changes needed for development, may delay such changes through autonomous unsustainable local and family economies. Kevin O'Neil (2003), an associate policy analyst at the Migration Policy Institute in Washington, DC, draws a parallel to natural resource windfalls (benefits that are a side effect of other activities, such as trees being cut down for small-scale mining operations being sold for lumber and not accounted for in legitimate forest production) wiping out the potential of migration to raise incomes and causing wasteful environmental use. Migration can open new pathways for co-development, however, in connecting the home and host communities (Scheffran, Marmer, and Sow 2012). While the social costs of migration to the individuals, their families, origins, and destinations are known, little can be said of the social-environment linkages because data are scarce. Migrant fishers, for example, face problems of overfishing in most of West Africa, which can become a source of conflict (Njock and Westlund 2010). In Ghana, migrants whose intentions are to gain meaningful employment in the mines are faced with disappointments, and instead join local people in mining communities to undertake small-scale mining endeavors, at times as illegal surface mining (called *galamsey*) on and around the concessions of large-scale mining companies (Nyame, Grant, and Yakovleva 2009). Such unlicensed practices have polluted rivers, enhanced deforestation, displaced communities and farms, and augmented floods. Cross-border movement from Namibia due to desertification, and overgrazing and erosion in Lesotho, into South Africa has created basic natural resource scarcity and social conflicts (McDonald 1999). Human mobility thus results in rapid social and economic change with tremendous adverse effects in ecologically vulnerable or fragile biophysical environments (Codjoe and Bilsborrow 2011).

Outlook

Migration is expected to intensify on the African continent because livelihoods are insecure due to deteriorating social, economic, and security conditions and diminishing financial returns of the working class (Adepoju 2008b). Global change, which is expected to be heightened by the complexity and uncertainties associated with climate change, is projected to adversely affect life support systems, especially shared resources such as transboundary water resources, and is likely to increase cross-border mobility (Bates et al. 2008). Reduced precipitation for rain-fed agriculture will limit food systems, which will in turn diminish food security. Several forms of natural risks and associated disasters such as drought, floods, and desertification will displace human populations and become severe through climate change effects (Reuveny 2007; Dovie 2010). Environmental mobility hence is expected to significantly characterize migration of poor people on the African continent.

The interest in the impact of climate change on population distribution and mobility has attracted recent debates, which project that by 2050 the expected number of climate change–displaced people will range between 200 million (Myers 2005) and 1 billion (Christian Aid 2007). Rainfall anomalies alone caused a total net displacement of 5 million people during the period 1960–2000 (a minimum of 128,000 people every year), and future weather anomalies may lead to an additional annual displacement of 11.8 million people by the end of the twenty-first century (Marchiori, Maystadt, and Schumacher 2012). Such weather anomalies may contribute to migration factors in Africa, including the selection of destination.

In response or adaptation to the changing environmental conditions, new forms of labor will emerge. Some people will be excluded from economic activity, with the majority possibly turning to the environment for free goods. Others may go beyond Africa to other continents. Economic globalization, including recent unpredictable meltdowns in the economies of the global North combined with the impacts of climate change, means that livelihoods in most African countries will be adversely impacted. Increased migration will also mean increased exposure of the biophysical environment to unsustainable use; hence decision makers need to study and document the migration-sustainability outcomes based on a robust theory such as the state-pressure-response model for informed policy decision making.

Delali B. K. DOVIE, Samuel N. A. CODJOE, and
EnoAbasi D. ANWANA
Regional Institute for Population Studies,
University of Ghana

See also Africa (*several articles*); Agriculture, Small-Scale; Cairo, Egypt; Cape Town, South Africa; Climate Change Refugees (Africa); Fisheries; Goma, Democratic Republic of the Congo; Immigrants and Refugees; Lagos, Nigeria; Mining (Africa); Nairobi, Kenya; Rural Development; Tunis, Tunisia; Urbanization (Africa); Urbanization (Western Asia and Northern Africa)

FURTHER READING

Adebusoye, Makinwa P. (2006). *Geographic labour mobility in Sub-Saharan Africa* (IDRC Working Papers on Globalization, Growth and Poverty Working Paper Number 1). Ottawa, Canada: IDRC.

Adepoju, Aderanti. (2002). Fostering free movements of persons in West Africa: Achievements, constraints and prospects for international migration. *International Migration, 40*(2), 3–28.

Adepoju, Aderanti. (2008a). *Migration in sub-Saharan Africa.* Uppsala, Sweden: Elanders Sverige AB, Mölnlycke.

Adepoju, Aderanti. (2008b). *Migration and social policy in sub-Saharan Africa.* Geneva: United Nations Research Institute for Social Development (UNRISD).

Balbo, Marcello, & Marconi, Giovanna. (2006). International migration, diversity and urban governance in cities of the South. *Habitat International, 30*, 706–715.

Barrios, Salvador; Bertinelli, Luisito; & Strobl, Eric. (2006). Climatic change and rural–urban migration: The case of sub-Saharan Africa. *Journal of Urban Economics, 60*, 357–371.

Bates, Bryson C.; Kundzewicz, Zbigniew W.; Wu Shaohong; & Palutikof, Jean P. (2008). Climate change and water (Technical paper VI of the Intergovernmental Panel on Climate Change). Geneva: IPCC.

Black, Richard; Ammassari, Savina; Mouillesseaux, Shannon; & Rajkotia, Radha. (2004). *Migration and pro-poor policy in West Africa* (Working paper C8, November, Development Research Centre on Migration, Globalisation and Poverty). Brighton, UK: University of Sussex.

Black, Richard, et al. (2011). The effect of environmental change on human migration. *Global Environmental Change, 21*, S3–S11.

Borjas, George J. (1994). The economics of immigration. *Journal of Economic Literature, 32*(4), 1667–1717.

Boyle, Paul. (2009). Migration. In Rob Kitchin & Nigel Thrift (Eds.), *International encyclopedia of human geography: Vol. 7* (pp. 96–107). London: Elsevier.

Campbell, Michael C., & Tishkoff, Sarah A. (2010). The evolution of human genetic and phenotypic variation in Africa. *Current Biology, 20*, R166–R173.

Christian Aid. (2007). *Human tide: The real migration crisis.* London: Christian Aid.

Codjoe, Samuel N. A., & Bilsborrow, Richard E. (2011, May 11). Are migrants exceptional resource degraders? A study of agricultural households in Ghana. *GeoJournal, 1*–14. doi:10.1007/s10708-011-9417-7

de Haas, Hein. (2006). Migration, remittances and regional development in Southern Morocco. *Geoforum, 4*, 565–580.

de Haas, Hein. (2007). *The myth of invasion: Irregular migration from West Africa to the Maghreb and the European Union* (IMI research report 2007). Oxford: University of Oxford.

Dovie, Delali B. (2010). *Climate change, water and disasters: Perspectives from Ghana's three northern regions* (WRC-CCA Report Series No. 1). Accra, Ghana: Water Resources Commission.

Gewald, Jan-Bart. (2003). Near death in the streets of Karibib: Famine, migrant labour and the coming of Ovambo to Central Namibia. *The Journal of African History, 44*, 211–239.

Gould, William T. S. (1988). Government policies and international migration of skilled workers in sub-Saharan Africa. *Geoforum, 19*(4), 433–445.

Gray, Clark L. (2011). Soil quality and human migration in Kenya and Uganda. *Global Environmental Change, 21*, 421–430.

Henry, Sabine; Boyle, Paul; & Lambin, Eric F. (2003). Modelling inter-provincial migration in Burkina Faso, West Africa: The role of socio-demographic and environmental factors. *Applied Geography*, *23*, 115–136.

Hill, Polly. (1963). *Migrant cocoa farmers of Southern Ghana*. London: Cambridge University Press.

Hunter, Lori M.; De Souza, Roger-Mark; & Twine, Wayne. (2008). The environmental dimensions of the HIV/AIDS pandemic: A call for scholarship and evidence-based interventions. *Population and Environment*, *29*, 3–4.

International Organization for Migration (IOM). (2005). *Costs and benefits of international migration*. Geneva: IOM.

International Organization for Migration (IOM). (2008). *World migration report 2008: Managing labour mobility in the evolving global economy*. Geneva: IOM.

Jensen, Eric R., & Ahlburg, Dennis A. (2004). Why does migration decrease fertility? Evidence from the Philippines. *Population Studies*, *58*, 219–231.

Konseiga, Adama. (2005). *Regional integration beyond the traditional trade benefits: Labor mobility contribution: The case of Burkina Faso and Côte d'Ivoire* (Development Economics and Policy Vol. 46). New York: Peter Lang Publishing, Inc.

Landau, Loren B., & Vigneswaran, Darshan. (2007). Shifting the focus of migration back home: Perspectives from Southern Africa. *Development*, *50*(4), 82–87.

Marchiori, Luca; Maystadt, Jean-François; & Schumacher, Ingmar. (2012). The impact of weather anomalies on migration in sub-Saharan Africa. *Journal of Environmental Economics and Management*, *63*, 355–374.

McDonald, David A. (1999). Lest the rhetoric begin: Migration, population and the environment in Southern Africa. *Geoforum*, *30*, 13–25.

Muanamoha, Ramos Cardoso; Maharaj, Brij; & Preston-Whyte, Eleanor. (2010). Social networks and undocumented Mozambican migration to South Africa. *Geoforum*, *41*, 885–896.

Mullen, Nicole. (2004). Yoruba art and culture. Retrieved June 21, 2012, from http://wysinger.homestead.com/yoruba.html

Myers, Norman. (2002). Environmental refugees: A growing phenomenon of the 21st century. *Philosophical Transactions of the Royal Society B*, *357*(1420), 609–613.

Myers, Norman. (2005). *Environmental refugees: An emergent security issue* (Presented at the 13th Economic Forum). Prague, Czech Republic.

Ndegwa, David; Horner, Dudley; & Esau, Faldie. (2007). The links between migration, poverty and health: Evidence from Khayelitsha and Mitchells Plain. *Social Indicators Research*, *81*, 223–234.

Newland, Kathleen. (2003). *Migration as a factor in development and poverty reduction*. Washington, DC: Migration Policy Institute.

Njock, Jean-Calvin, & Westlund, Lena. (2010). Migration, resource management and global change: Experiences from fishing communities in West and Central Africa. *Marine Policy*, *34*, 752–760.

Nyame, Frank K.; Grant, Andrew J.; & Yakovleva, Natalia. (2009). Perspectives on migration patterns in Ghana's mining industry. *Resources Policy*, *34*, 6–11.

O'Neil, Kevin. (2003). *Using remittances and circular migration to drive development*. Washington, DC: Migration Policy Institute.

Page, B. (2009). Remittances. In Rob Kitchin & Nigel Thrift (Eds.), *International encyclopedia of human geography: Vol. 7* (pp. 329–334). London: Elsevier.

Parnell, Susan, & Walawege, Ruwani. (2011). Sub-Saharan African urbanisation and global environmental change. *Global Environmental Change*, *21*, S12–S20.

Poelhekke, Steven. (2011). Urban growth and uninsured rural risk: Booming towns in bust times. *Journal of Development Economics*, *96*, 461–475.

Reuveny, Rafael. (2007). Climate change-induced migration and violent conflict. *Political Geography*, *26*, 656–673.

Richter, Jürgen, et al. (2012). "Contextual areas" of early *Homo sapiens* and their significance for human dispersal from Africa into Eurasia between 200 ka and 70 ka. *Quaternary International*. doi:10.1016/j.quaint.2012.04.017

Scheffran, Jürgen; Marmer, Elina; & Sow, Papa. (2012). Migration as a contribution to resilience and innovation in climate adaptation: Social networks and co-development in northwest Africa. *Applied Geography*, *33*, 119–127.

Shimeles, Abebe. (2010). *Migration patterns, trends and policy issues in Africa* (Working Papers Series N 119). Tunis, Tunisian Republic: African Development Bank.

Shinn, David H. (2008). *African migration and the Brain Drain Paper*. Ljubljana, Slovenia: Institute for African Studies and Slovenia Global Action.

Singh, Kavita; Karunakara, Unni; Burnham, Gilbert; & Hill, Kenneth. (2005). Forced migration and under-five mortality: A comparison of refugees and hosts in north-western Uganda and southern Sudan. *European Journal of Population*, *21*, 247–270.

Tacoli, Cecilia. (2009). *Crisis or adaptation? Migration and climate change in a context of high mobility*. New York & London: UNFPA and IIED.

United Nations Development Programme (UNDP). (2009). *Human development report 2009*. New York: UNDP.

van Blerk, Lorraine, & Ansell, Nicola. (2006). Imagining migration: Placing children's understanding of "moving house" in Malawi and Lesotho. *Geoforum*, *37*, 256–272.

Ziesemer, Thomas H. W. (2012). Worker remittances, migration, accumulation and growth in poor developing countries: Survey and analysis of direct and indirect effects. *Economic Modelling*, *29*, 103–118.

Mining (Africa)

Africa's rich mineral endowment has not yet benefited the majority of people on the continent or the environment. Finding ways to translate mineral wealth into an engine for sustainable development is crucial. The African Union's action plan known as the African Mining Vision articulates how mining could contribute to sustainable growth and development through consideration of all five forms of capital (financial, natural, produced, human, and social), with a focus on the neglected areas of social and human capital, and the environment.

Africa is well endowed with minerals and oil, although the full extent of African mineral reserves is unknown. Geological mapping of the continent is limited, and 2012 estimates of Africa's mineral wealth are believed to be understated. In 2005, African reserves were said to account for more than 80 percent of the world's vanadium, diamonds, and manganese, as well as about two-thirds of the world's platinum and phosphate, and about half of the world's cobalt, aluminum, chromium, and gold (UNECA 2009). Other minerals produced in significant quantities include bauxite and uranium. In 2006, Africa also accounted for about 8 percent of world gas reserves and 9 percent of world oil reserves (Twerefou 2009).

Translating mineral wealth into the engine of sustainable development, however, is a complex and challenging process that requires a deep understanding of social, economic, and environmental contexts, as well as a shared vision of the desired future, and the will and means to recognize and address concerns.

Context

Africa is home to roughly 1 billion people in sixty-one nation states. From a socioeconomic perspective, the population of sub-Saharan Africa is ranked lowest on the Human Development Index (HDI). The population is young, with a large proportion of people younger than fifteen years of age. Particularly in rural areas, excluding North Africa, just more than half of the population lives below the poverty line of $1.25 per day, and more than a third does not have access to safe drinking water (UNECA et al. 2011). In such areas, people rely heavily on biodiversity and ecosystem services to support their livelihoods. Although school enrollment is generally high, with 83 percent of children (in 2008) enrolling for primary school, this is not matched by primary school completion rates which ranges from just below 20 percent to around 67 percent in different countries; up to 31 million school-aged children are not enrolled in school with disproportional numbers of children coming from poor and rural households, and around 153 million adults are illiterate and account for 20 percent of illiterate adults globally (UNECA et al. 2011). Access to information and communication technology (ICT) is low but increasing, with 41 percent of people having access to cellular phones and nearly 10 percent having access to the Internet in 2010 (UNECA et al. 2011). In Africa as a whole, the development of infrastructure for energy, transportation, and water and sanitation—typically financed from central government revenues—lags behind that of developed countries, even in the African countries that are rich in mineral resources (World Bank 2010). Links among the infrastructures of different regions are often absent, and access to infrastructure by households has not improved since 1990. This hinders access to local and global markets. Power interruptions are common in 30 of the 48 countries in Africa, and maintenance costs are high (World Bank 2010). The presence of diverse cultural and ethnic identities of African people, however, means that general facts about Africa tend to mask differences between the circumstances of people in various localities and within different groups, and thus need to be read circumspectly.

Regulatory reforms of the 1980s and 1990s geared the mineral policies of African countries towards the promotion and attraction of investment and little else. As a result, the vast majority (95 percent) of mineral products are exported without any beneficiation (UNECA 2009). Typically minerals beneficiation involves transforming an as-mined mineral, or a combination of minerals, into a product of higher value. Where this happens in the country of mineral origin, it can have a cascading effect on economic activity, with a concomitant increase in economic growth and development. Because of Africa's focus on raw mineral exports, however, mineral extraction has not tended to meet the national or regional developmental needs of the majority of African people.

Sub-Saharan Africa is a dual mining economy with a large-scale mining (LSM) sector comprised predominantly of foreign players, and an expanding artisanal and small-scale mining (ASM) sector controlled by indigenous groups (Mohammed Banchirigah 2006). ASM is largely a poverty-driven activity, notorious for its unsafe work practices, and characterized by nonmechanized, labor-intensive mining activities that often result in significant pollution and land degradation. ASM does, however, make a considerable positive contribution to African economies and to sustaining rural livelihoods (UNECA and AU 2011); the sector employs around 8 million workers, who in turn support about 45 million dependents (Benkenstein 2012). The relationship between ASM and LSM is seldom harmonious, although it is recognized that successful partnerships are necessary in order to contribute to growth and development (Benkenstein 2012; Aubynn 2009). Contestation over mineral resources is frequently at the root of conflict, with LSM holding legally acquired concessions, but small-scale miners believing they have traditional rights to work on the land, whether for mining or farming (Aubynn 2009).

By itself, mining is an unsustainable activity. Mining projects have a finite life, and even mines drawing on vast mineral reserves eventually close down. The idea that mining in Africa can lead to sustainable development therefore rests on utilizing mining as a springboard for minerals beneficiation (the process of extracting the valuable material from ore and building industries based on mineral resources), together with using revenues generated by mining activities to educate people, provide health care, build infrastructure, develop social and financial institutions, advance skills

and knowledge, and foster enterprise and choice among people. Also fundamental to the idea of sustainable development is that mining must not be allowed to irreversibly impinge upon the ecological conditions that are fundamentally essential to support life and, ultimately, all socioeconomic activity.

Expectations

In 2009, the African Union (AU) developed an African Mining Vision, which is intended to promote "broad-based sustainable growth and socio-economic development," coupled with transparency, equitability, and optimization in the exploitation of mineral resources (AU 2009). The African Mining Vision is based on the idea that mineral resources can be used as a platform for long-term, broad-based growth and development. It recognizes the importance and complexity of artisanal and small-scale mining, and its contribution to the livelihoods of millions of African people, as well as the critical areas that must be addressed to better integrate it into the economy and support sustainable development.

Local examples of applying the principles of the African Mining Vision exist. In South Africa, human resource and local socioeconomic development are promoted through mining companies' legal obligation to compile and implement a social and labor plan. Democratic Republic of Congo law requires ministerial authorization for exporting unprocessed ores for treatment outside the national territory. Such authorization will only be granted if it is "impossible to treat the substances in the National Territory at a cost which is economically viable for the mining project" (DRC 2002). Furthermore during the late 1990s and early 2000s, most major African mining jurisdictions enacted laws that vest the ownership and custodianship of minerals in the state, allowing only for time-limited concessions or licenses to prospect for and exploit minerals. Mining companies, through their corporate social responsibility (CSR) programs, also have contributed to infrastructural development, health care, education, employment, and local economic development. These local endeavors cannot, however, replace or be sustained without strong regional and national development strategies and legitimate governments supported by the rule of law.

One of the potential shortcomings of the African Mining Vision is that it understates the problems associated with mining, especially the environmental impacts that directly affect communities reliant on land and environmental resources. It also requires the existence of strong, transparent, and accountable regulatory institutions and processes to monitor the impacts of mining, enforce restrictions, and ensure that mining revenues are directed toward the appropriate development of other forms of capital. These are seldom in place in the African nations.

Impacts

While mining and mineral extraction have the potential to contribute to economic prosperity, they are often accompanied by enormous environmental degradation and social upheaval. These problems are significant and well known.

Mining has negative impacts on the natural environment through resource consumption, waste generation, and irreversible alteration of landscapes. In Africa—with its significant biodiversity, vast areas of relatively unspoiled natural habitat (including tropical rain forest), and unequal spread of resources—these impacts often are profound. Biodiverse ecosystems provide life-supporting services to communities dependent on subsistence farming and grazing.

Environmental governance has generally been weak. Since the 1990s, there has, however, been significant progress with many of the new laws in the major mining jurisdictions requiring prior assessment of environmental impacts (Twerefou 2009), along with other forms of environmental integration, such as restrictions on mining in certain areas. Enforcement and compliance regarding such obligations remain challenging, however, with artisanal and small-scale mining being largely unregulated.

The social impacts of mining are numerous and are magnified in conditions of widespread poverty. In some cases, people may need to be resettled to allow for mining in certain areas. This deeply disrupts established communities, and people may resist. Other social impacts include influx of people, creation of informal and unplanned settlements, conflict over who owns and should benefit from minerals, use of precious minerals such as diamonds to fund conflicts, loss of land and land use, and loss of access to resources and associated livelihoods. Local communities often bear a disproportionate share of the cost of mining, with the benefits being enjoyed elsewhere. Ensuring the health and safety of both employees and the neighboring communities is also a concern, and this too requires strong regulation and oversight.

Support of Sustainable Development

The importance of developing links between mining and other sectors of the economy, starting with mineral beneficiation, is emphasized by mineral economists. This paradigm falls short of the challenges of sustainable development, with its relative silence on environmental limits and the primacy of strong social institutions. Another way to frame the requirements of mining is to consider whether mining contributes to the development of natural, social, human, manufactured, and financial capital—the so-called five capitals. This model considers how various forms of capital can be transformed into durable forms of other capital, while staying within the limits posed by the natural environment (Forum for the Future n.d.).

In the absence of clear plans to develop social capital—especially governance initiatives at the global, regional, national, sub-national, and local levels—potential benefits of mining are at risk. Governance extends beyond the container of the government to encompass the sum of the multifarious processes and procedures through which individuals and institutions manage their common affairs. Enhancing the capacity of state (public) institutions acting in concert with nonstate (private) stakeholders (people with a stake in an enterprise) to govern mining and manage mineral wealth is thus crucial. Existing precedents involving African states that point to the shape of such governance initiatives include the Extractive Industries Transparency Initiative (EITI), an ambitious global governance project that aims to enhance the transparency of financial dealings among companies working with extractive resources and host states; the Kimberley Process, an initiative that originated from the desire to reduce the trade of conflict or "blood" diamonds; and the Diamond Development Initiative, an outgrowth of the Kimberley Process that seeks to address the developmental challenges in artisanal diamond mining.

Infrastructural constraints prevent Africa from realizing its natural resource potential (AU 2009) and limit opportunities for beneficiation. This is an area of focus in the African Mining Vision, and future studies should also consider how the quality of life of ordinary people can be improved through infrastructural development.

Linked to social capital is the development of human capital, which involves increasing the knowledge, skills, ability, and health of individuals in order to enable them to participate in the economy. In practice, this translates into investments into public education and health. The need for appropriate technologies, as well as research and development, within the mining sector, in particular the ASM, is another spur for developing knowledge and skills.

The beneficiation of as-mined products in the African Mining Vision reflects the AU's commitments to building manufactured capital. Given that global transportation costs are much lower than in the past, local manufacturing initiatives are not sheltered from competition from outside of Africa. Specific interventions may be needed to nurture local manufacturing, as well as to encourage and support the development of local entrepreneurs and businesses.

The revenue flow from mining is short lived. Effective taxation and ownership systems must therefore be devised to fund local development and more equitable distribution of incomes. Provisions for a post-mining future can be made by saving money generated through windfalls and resources boom times in sovereign funds for future public use. Implicit in this practice is transparency within the private and public sphere about mining-related expenditures. The EITI already exists to enable transparency in mining investments, expenditures, and payments. In the arena of international policy, the debt repayment policies of international funding institutions contributed to African countries' focus on mineral exports. The policies could be modified to promote greater economic diversity.

Finally, since the natural environment provides the bounding conditions for development, its limits must be understood and respected. This will ensure that healthy and resilient ecosystems are able to continue providing the much-needed and heavily relied-upon environmental services. Environmental governance and the capacity of environmental regulators are thus crucial to providing this assurance. In addition to improving the level and quality of mineral resource data in Africa (AU 2009), a better understanding of the biophysical environment could contribute to more effective mineral resource development.

Mavis HERMANUS, Ingrid WATSON, and Tracy-Lynn HUMBY
University of the Witwatersrand

See also Africa (*several articles*); African Union (AU); Conflict Minerals; Corporate Accountability (Africa); Goma, Democratic Republic of the Congo; Migration (Africa); Rural Development

FURTHER READING

African Union (AU). (2009). African Mining Vision. Retrieved November 4, 2011, from http://vi.unctad.org/files/wksp/oilgaswksptanz10/docs/Background%20readings/Africa%20Mining%20Vision.doc

Aubynn, Anthony. (2009). Sustainable solutions or a marriage of inconvenience? The coexistence of large-scale mining and artisanal and small-scale mining on the Abosso Goldfiles concession in Western Ghana. *Resources Policy, 34*(1–2), 64–70.

Benkenstein, Alex. (2012). Artisanal and small-scale mining in Africa: Opportunities and challenges. Retrieved March 27, 2011, from http://www.saiia.org.za/index.php?view=article&catid=78%3Adiplomatic-pouch&id=1848%3Aartisanal-and-small-scale-mining-in-africa-opportunities-and-challenges&tmpl=component&print=1&layout5default&page=&option=com_content&Itemid=230

Democratic Republic of the Congo (DRC). (2002). Law No. 007/2002 of July 11, 2002, relating to the Mining Code.

Diamond Development Initiative (DDI). (2009). Homepage. Retrieved April 12, 2012, from http://www.ddiglobal.org

Extractive Industries Transparency Initiative (EITI). (2009). Homepage. Retrieved April 12, 2012, from http://eiti.org/eiti

Forum for the Future. (n.d.). The five capitals model: A framework for sustainability. Retrieved December 5, 2011, from http://www.forumforthefuture.org/sites/default/files/images/Forum/Projects/five-capitals/The%20five%20capitals%20model.pdf

Grant, J. Andrew, & Taylor, Ian. (2004). Global governance and conflict diamonds: The Kimberley Process and the quest for clean gems. *The Round Table, 93*(375), 385–401.

Kimberley Process. (n.d.). Homepage. Retrieved April 12, 2012, from http://www.kimberleyprocess.com

Mohammed Banchirigah, Sadia. (2006). How have reforms fuelled the expansion of artisanal mining? Evidence from sub-Saharan Africa. *Resources Policy, 31*(3), 165–171.

Power, Thomas Michael. (2002). Digging to development? A historical look at mining and economic development. Retrieved December 19, 2011, from http://www.oxfamamerica.org/files/OA-Digging_to_Development.pdf

Twerefou, Daniel Kwabena. (2009). *Mineral exploitation, environmental sustainability and sustainable development in EAC, SADC and ECOWAS regions.* Africa Trade Policy Centre, Economic Commission for Africa. Retrieved December 19, 2011, from http://www.uneca.org/atpc/Work%20in%20progress/79.pdf

United Nations Development Programme (UNDP). (2011). *Human development report 2011. Sustainability and equity: A better future for all.* New York: Palgrave Macmillan.

United Nations Economic Commission for Africa (UNECA). (2009). African Review report on mining (Executive summary). Retrieved December 19, 2011, from http://www.uneca.org/csd/csd6/AficanReviewReport-on-MiningSummary.pdf

United Nations Economic Commission for Africa (UNECA), & African Union (AU). (2011). *Minerals and Africa's development: An overview of the report of the International Study Group on Africa's mineral regimes.* Retrieved April 12, 2012, from http://www.africaminingvision.org/amv_resources/AMV/ISG%20Report_eng.pdf

United Nations Economic Commission for Africa (UNECA); African Union (AU); African Development Bank Group (AfDB); & United Nations Development Programme (UNDP). (2011). Assessing progress in Africa toward the Millennium Development Goals: MDG report 2011. Retrieved December 19, 2011, from http://www.uneca.org/mdgs2011/documents/MDG2011_book_ENG.pdf

World Bank. (2010). Overview: Africa's infrastructure: A time for transformation. (Vivien Foster & Cecilia Briceño-Garmendia, Eds.). Washington, DC: World Bank. Retrieved December 3, 2011, from http://siteresources.worldbank.org/INTAFRICA/Resources/aicd_overview_english_no-embargo.pdf

Moscow, Russia

11.5 million est. pop. 2011; the figure could be as high as 13-17 million due to uncharted migration

Moscow, the largest city in Europe, is the capital of Russia and the national center for economic and scientific activities as well as trade and passenger traffic. Moscow does not rank particularly high among world cities in terms of its residents' quality of life, although it does rank well in terms of the number and quality of its research centers and its green space. Massive new office areas and old industrial areas create immense daily burdens (such as traffic congestion and noise, air, and area pollution) for its inhabitants.

Moscow appeared in the chronicles for the first time in 1147. Moscow's position as the country's national center started to assert itself in the fourteenth century, when the city was assigned the role of forming the Russian state. Even the relocation of the capital to St. Petersburg (1712–1918) could not significantly diminish Moscow's position as the national center. During the twentieth century, Moscow developed into the country's leading political, economic, and scientific center and into Europe's most populous urban region. In 1918, Moscow became the capital of Soviet Russia.

All crucial institutions concerning location and investment policies of the entire Soviet Union were concentrated in Moscow. Within the Soviet sphere, Moscow symbolized political, ideological, and military supremacy; the economic policy of the affiliated socialist states essentially was determined from here. After the collapse of the Soviet Union (over the years 1989–1991), Moscow lost its leading geopolitical role. The city also forfeited important functions in the post-Soviet region with the breakup of the Soviet Union into fifteen

sovereign national states. Moscow merely retained its role as the capital of the newly established Russian Federation.

Moscow is currently emerging as an internationally recognized political and business center again due to the country's political opening and global influence. As of 2008, it ranked fifteenth in gross domestic product among the world's largest cities (rb.ru. n.d.). Moscow is one of the world's top research centers. Its life-quality rank, however, is only seventieth among world cities (Economist Intelligence Unit 2011).

Population

Moscow is Europe's largest city and the world's seventh largest. The official figure for Moscow as of 2011 stood at 11.5 million, or 8 percent of Russia's total population (Vserossiiskaya perepis' 2011), but uncharted migration could push the real number to between 13 and 17 million. In spite of the demographic crisis at the national level, Moscow is not only a prospering resource-based region but a prominent destination of national and transnational migration.

Between 2002 and 2010, the population increased by 11 percent (Federal State Statistics Service 2004 and 2011b). During the time period from 2007 to 2009 the officially registered net migration reached 50,000–55,000.

The 2010 census shows the multi-ethnic nature of the Moscow population, with Russians making up 91 percent and other nationalities making up 9 percent. Thousands of guest workers, particularly from Central Asia and other former Soviet republics, have been living in Moscow for some years. They are employed mainly in low-wage jobs, often illegally. Over 1.5 million daily commuters come to

Moscow from its suburbs, in addition to an unknown number of temporary workers who travel from remote regions.

Economy and Living Standards

The Moscow region was the most important Soviet industrial center with a focus on technological and research-intensive industries. In the 1990s, however, due to the collapse of the socialist economic system, manufacturing shrank notably. Only an important defence subsector and related research and development facilities have been preserved. Moscow is responsible for 10 percent of Russia's manufacturing activities (Federal State Statistics Service 2011a).

Today, Moscow is characterized by an outstanding concentration of economic and innovative activities. The city's main functions now are predominantly trade, financial services, science, and administration. Moscow accounts for 18 percent of Russia's retail trade, 41 percent of wholesale trade, 40 percent of imports, and 36 percent of exports officially registered by the city's customs (Federal State Statistics Service 2011a). Moscow alone collects 22 percent of taxes for Russia's consolidated budget. In 2010, more than 260 universities and colleges, among them 155 private, as well as about 1,000 institutes of research and development were located in Moscow.

Moscow continues to be an island of economic prosperity in Russia. The unemployment rate is the lowest in the country. Living standards and the level of consumption are higher than in many other Russian regions and cities. The officially registered monthly average personal income in Moscow reached US$1,453 in 2010, while the national mean was US$582 (Federal State Statistics Service 2011a). The social stratification, however, is very strong. In 2009, about 10 percent of Moscow's population was classified as poor (23 percent in 2000). The majority of Moscow's pensioners receive US$200–400 per month, the sum that corresponds with the local subsistence minimum. The number of private cars has increased by a factor of four during the last twenty years, and in late 2010, it reached 4 million. This fact reflects the growing middle-class strata. At the same time, extremely high prices for real estate (US$4,300 to $5,800 per square meter) are encouraging an increasing social segregation.

Ecological Problems and Traffic

Moscow is a very green city when compared to other cities of comparable size. Forests, parks, and open areas cover one-third of the city's territory. The most important are Central Park of Culture "Maxim Gorki"; Izmaylovsky Park, which is six times larger than New York City's

Central Park; Sokolniki Park; and Losiny Ostrov National Park, which covers a total area of more than 116 square kilometers (Government of Moscow 2012). Sokolniki Park was Russia's first national park and is also known as the "city taiga" (the taiga is the belt of forest land bordered by the tundra on the north and the steppe in the south), where elk can be seen. Moscow has, on average, 27 square meters of parks per person, compared with 6 square meters for Paris, 7.5 for London, and 8.6 for New York (Screen n.d.).

Since the 1990s, however, the concentration of international and Russian companies in Moscow's center has been connected with large-scale investments in huge exclusive business and hotel complexes that serve the need for representation of the state, the city of Moscow, and new company groups. Investment interests have gained the upper hand in setting development priorities, in stark conflict with some of the main concepts embedded in the master plan for Moscow's long-term urban development until 2025. Major new development projects also are planned in areas designated as nature reserves. The functional and structural change of the central city districts has led to a decline in residents, an ousting of ordinary public services, and a rise in business headquarters, upmarket retailers, and office locations. The number of employees in the city center has risen by approximately 20 percent since 1990. By building spectacular large-scale projects such as Moscow City (Moscow International Business Center), which takes up around 100 hectares, whole neighborhoods have been transformed into office and commercial districts. At the same time, the unresolved privatization of state ownership results in the continuance of dilapidated industrial plants and wasteland close to the center, an enormous burden for the environment and traffic.

In the early twenty-first century, dozens of industrial zones still occupied about 20 percent of the urban land. Many of them, however, are leased partly for offices, service centers, and the like. The most environmentally dangerous enterprise in Moscow is its oil refinery plant in Kapotnya, on the southeast edge of the city; the plant, which was built in 1938, processes 9.1 million tonnes of crude oil annually (South-East District of Moscow 2011). The cleanest Moscow districts are South-West, West, and North-West; the dirtiest industrial districts are East and South-East. As in other world cities, though, Moscow's main pollution source is cars, especially along streets and in the center of the city.

One of the biggest problems the capital faces is coping effectively with its role as a national and transnational traffic hub. The city has eleven different rail lines serving nine railway terminals, thirteen national highways that converge in Moscow, and four international airports in its suburbs. The city's street system is seriously overcrowded. Business and social life is hampered severely by the extremely dense traffic and long traffic jams, especially on the main radial highways. The shortage of car parking areas aggravates the problem, particularly for the huge, newly built business complexes and residential areas.

The eleven lines of the celebrated Moscow metro (totalling 301.2 kilometers), which carry more than 10 million passengers every day, have reached their limit. To easily transport the millions of commuters and tourists through Moscow in the future, the city plans an expansion of 75 kilometers for 2016.

Plans for the City

The contemporary city covers an area of 1,070 square kilometers: slightly smaller than the land area of Hong Kong. It is divided into ten administrative divisions, or okrugs, and 125 districts. Moscow's growing significance as a national and international business center is connected with a substantial demand for space and property. Because of the depleted space reserves as well as the increasingly obstructive traffic within the existing city limits, a resolution was passed to enlarge Moscow's territory radically, by a factor of 2.4. The spatial expansion of

Figure 1. Map of New Moscow Territory

The new area of Moscow

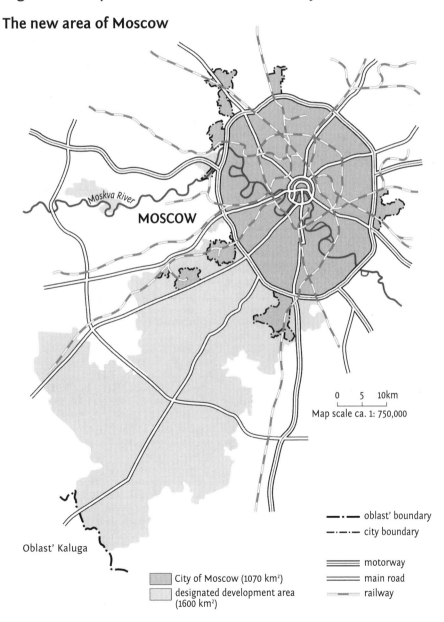

Source: Map courtesy of the Leibniz-Institut für Länderkunde, Cartographic Department. Copyright 2011 Leibniz-Institut für Länderkunde. Cartography by Romana Schwarz.

1,480 square kilometers includes the open and less urbanized spaces of the Moscow Oblast', with its twenty-two municipalities southwest of the city. (See figure 1 on page 219.)

The main motivation underpinning the massive expansion of Moscow appears to be the government's intention to subvert the trend of perimeter expansion of the capital to linear development of the newly attached territories. The strategy includes the creation of a new development axis anchored in the development of five to six independent local centers. Planners are designing the city territory with areas spacious enough to host an international financial center and the administrative complex for all federal facilities, as well as an "interdisciplinary city of innovation" similar to Silicon Valley in California.

Isolde BRADE
Leibniz Institute for Regional Geography, Leipzig, Germany

Tatyana G. NEFEDOVA
Institute of Geography, Russian Academy of Sciences

See also Novosibirsk, Russia; Parks and Preserves; Russia and the Soviet Union; St. Petersburg, Russia; Urbanization (Europe); Warsaw, Poland

FURTHER READING

Brade, Isolde, & Rudolph, Robert. (2004). Moscow, the global city? The position of the Russian capital within the European system of metropolitan areas. *Area, 36*(1), 69–80.

Brade, Isolde, & Rudolph, Robert. (2005). Moscow: Processes of restructuring in the post-Soviet metropolitan periphery. *Cities, 22*(2), 135–150.

Economist Intelligence Unit. (2011). The liveability ranking and overview February 2011. Retrieved July 17, 2012, from https://www.eiu.com/public/topical_report.aspx?campaignid=Liveability2011

Federal State Statistics Service. (2004). *Chislennost' i razmeshchenie naselenia. Itogi Vserossijskoi perepisi naselenia* [The population of the Russian Federation and its distribution] Tom 1. (Vol. 21). Moscow: Федеральная служба государственной статистики [Federal State Statistics Service].

Federal State Statistics Service. (2007). *Chislennost' naselenia Rossijskoi Federacii po gorodam, poselkam gorodskogo tipa i rionam na 1 janvarja* [The population of the Russian Federation in cities, settlements of urban type and districts]. Moscow: Федеральная служба государственной статистики [Federal State Statistics Service].

Federal State Statistics Service. (2008). *Chislennost' naselenia Rossijskoi Federacii po gorodam, poselkam gorodskogo tipa i rionam na 1 janvarja* [The population of the Russian Federation in cities, settlements of urban type and districts]. Moscow: Федеральная служба государственной статистики [Federal State Statistics Service].

Federal State Statistics Service. (2009). *Chislennost' naselenia Rossijskoi Federacii po gorodam, poselkam gorodskogo tipa i rionam na 1 janvarja*

[The population of the Russian Federation in cities, settlements of urban type and districts]. Moscow: Федеральная служба государственной статистики [Federal State Statistics Service].

Federal State Statistics Service. (2010a). *Chislennost' naselenia Rossijskoi Federacii po gorodam, poselkam gorodskogo tipa i rionam na 1 janvarja* [The population of the Russian Federation in cities, settlements of urban type and districts]. Moscow: Федеральная служба государственной статистики [Federal State Statistics Service].

Federal State Statistics Service. (2010b). Регионы России. Основные характеристики субъектов Российской Федерации [The Russian Regions: Main characteristics of the subjects of the Russian Federation]. Moscow: Федеральная служба государственной статистики [Federal State Statistics Service]. Retrieved July 17, 2012, from http://www.gks.ru/bgd/regl/B10_14s/Main.htm

Federal State Statistics Service. (2011a). Регионы России. Основные характеристики субъектов Российской Федерации [The Russian Regions: Main characteristics of the subjects of the Russian Federation]. Moscow: Федеральная служба государственной статистики [Federal State Statistics Service]. Retrieved July 17, 2012, from http://www.gks.ru/bgd/regl/b11_14s/Main.htm

Federal State Statistics Service. (2011b). *Vserossijskaya perepis naselenia 2010 goda. Predvaritel'nye itogi* [Population census in the Russian Federation 2010. Preliminary results]. Moscow: Федеральная служба государственной статистики [Federal State Statistics Service].

Government of Moscow. (2012). Moscow parks. Retrieved May 23, 2012, from http://www.mos.ru/about/parks/

Leadership for Environment and Development (LEAD) International. (2000). Moscow City environmental profile. Retrieved October 10, 2011, from http://www.leadnet.ru/mep/english/introduction.htm

Machrova, Alla G.; Nefedova, Tat'jana G.; & Trejvish, Andrej I. (2008). *Moskovskaja oblast' segodnja i zavtra* [The Moscow Oblast' today and tomorrow]. Moscow: Novy chronograph.

Osipov, Viktor I. (2006). Geological conditions of Moscow subsurface development (IAEG paper 254). Retrieved October 10, 2011, from http://iaeg2006.geolsoc.org.uk/cd/PAPERS/IAEG_254.PDF

rb.ru. (n.d.). Homepage. Retrieved May 23, 2012, from http://www.rb.ru

Rossijskoe Bisness Televidenie (RBC). (2011a). *Granicu Moskvy dovedut do Kaluzhskoi oblasti* [The borderline of Moscow will be drawn up to the Kaluga Oblast']. Retrieved September 29, 2011, from http://top.rbc.ru/society/19/08/2011/611234.shtml

Rossijskoe Bisness Televidenie (RBC). (2011b). The official published map of the new area of Moscow. Retrieved September 29, 2011, from http://top.rbc.ru/society/19/08/2011/611426.shtml?from=qip

Rossijskoe Bisness Televidenie (RBC). (2012a). Latest news. Retrieved May 23, 2012, from http://www.rbcholding.com/index.shtml

Rossijskoe Bisness Televidenie (RBC). (2012b). RBC group of companies. Retrieved May 23, 2012, from http://www.rbc.ru/company.shtml

Screen. (n.d.). Green dress of Moscow. Retrieved May 23, 2012, from http://www.screen.ru/moscow/zelen.htm

Sobyanin, Sergei. (2011). Территория Большой Москвы—курица, несущая золотые яйца [The territory of Greater Moscow—A hen that lays golden eggs]. Retrieved September 29, 2011, from http://top.rbc.ru/society/19/08/2011/611300.shtml

South-East District of Moscow. (2011, November 27). РОССИЯ-МОСКВА-НПЗ-ИНТЕРВЬЮ [Russia-Moscow refinery interview]. Retrieved July 23, 2012, from http://www.uvao.ru/uvao/ru/regions/n_1189/o_336112

Nairobi, Kenya

3.5 million est. pop. 2012

Nairobi is the capital city of Kenya and one of Africa's key financial, business, transport, communications, nongovernmental organization, and diplomatic capitals; it is also known as the "safari capital of the world" thanks to its globally known wildlife tourism industry. Because of rapid population growth and poor planning by colonial and postcolonial governments, the city (which dates from 1899) has grown haphazardly and with little regard for environmental sustainability. Although the government has formulated plans to help guide the city's future growth, its intractable environmental and development challenges persist.

Nairobi is Kenya's capital, premier city, and one of Africa's most important cities. It has an estimated population of 3.5 million and a land area of 695 square kilometers. The recently created Nairobi Metropolitan Region has an area of 32,000 square kilometers (almost as large as the US state of Maryland) and an estimated population of 6.65 million people (Ministry of Nairobi Metropolitan Development 2012). The city lies between 1,600 and 1,850 meters above sea level on the southeastern edge of Kenya's agricultural heartland at 1°16'S latitude and 36°48'E longitude; its high elevation gives the city a temperate climate despite its close proximity to the equator. Its average density of 4,515 people per square kilometer is the highest in the country, followed by that of Mombasa (4,292 people per square kilometer), Kenya's second largest city, whose 2009 population was 939,370 (Commission of Revenue Allocation 2011). The western side of the city is higher, cooler, and well-drained, whereas the eastern half is lower, hotter, and swampy.

The city is traversed by the Mathare and Ngong rivers and is subject to minor earthquakes and tremors given its proximity to the Great Rift Valley. The indigenous Karura forest lies in the north of the city, and the gate into Nairobi National Park, the only game park in the world that is close to a capital city, lies 7 kilometers south of the city center (Mitullah 2003).

Nairobi is named for the Maasai phrase *enkare nairobi*, meaning "a place of cold waters." The city originated when the railhead of the Kenya Uganda Railway (KUR) reached the site in June 1899, paving the way for the creation of the KUR headquarters there in July of that year. By year's end, the British colonial government had an administrative presence in the city that helped it become the colonial capital in 1907 and the capital of independent Kenya in 1963.

In response to the city's rapid growth, the colonial government published the Nairobi Municipal Community (NMC) regulations in 1900 and, for the first time, defined the emerging urban center's boundaries. In 1919, the NMC was replaced by the Nairobi City Council (NCC), which managed the city, with minor interruptions, until 2012. In early 2013, the NCC will transform into a county government with a popularly elected county governor and assembly as stipulated in Kenya's 2010 constitution (National Council for Law Reporting 2010).

In the colonial era, Nairobi was a racially segregated city (Otiso 2005a). Now Nairobi is a cosmopolitan and multicultural city whose three main population components are Africans (95 percent), Asians (about 4 percent), and Europeans (about 1 percent). While the last two groups are small, they do have significant influence in city and national affairs (Obudho 1997). The city's African population comes from all of Kenya's forty major ethnic groups, although most of them are Bantus (e.g., Kikuyu, Luhya, Kamba, and Gusii) and, to a smaller extent, Nilotes (e.g., Luo, Kalenjin, and Maasai) and Cushites (e.g., Somali). Although the Nairobi population is multireligious (Protestant, Catholic, African traditional religions, Islam, Hinduism, Buddhism, Judaism, and atheist), the vast majority of people are Christians (83 percent) and Muslims (11 percent). Many Nairobians are also multilingual speakers of Kiswahili, English, and other local African and foreign languages (Government of Kenya 2009).

Nairobi's population has grown rapidly since the city's founding in 1899. Specifically, it grew from 11,000 in 1906 to 30,000 in 1928, 267,000 in 1962, 828,000 in 1979, 1.3 million in 1989, and 3.1 million in 2009 (Government of Kenya 2009; Obudho 1997; UN-Habitat 2006a). As of 2012, its population is believed to be 3.7 million. In 2009, Nairobi's 3.1 million people accounted for 25 percent of Kenya's total urban population of 12.4 million and 8 percent of its 38.6 million people (Government of Kenya 2009).

The annual growth rate of the city's population has varied over time, being roughly 4 percent in 1906, 17 percent in 1928, 7 percent in 1944, and 6 percent in 1962. Between 1969 and 1989, it grew at an annual average rate of 5 percent and is currently estimated to be growing at 4–5 percent (Obudho 1997; US CIA 2012). Like the rest of Kenya, Nairobi has a very young age structure. In 2009, 87 percent of Nairobi's population was below forty years old, and nearly half of its population was between twenty and forty years of age. Also in 2009, the city's sex ratio was 51 percent male and 49 percent female, an imbalance attributable to Kenya's generally higher male rural-urban migration (Government of Kenya 2009). Although the city's population growth is mostly due to natural increase (given its young age structure) and in-migration, some of it has also come from the expansion of city boundaries in 1920, 1927, and 1963 (Obudho 1997).

Economy

Nairobi is the financial, business, industrial, transport, communications, nongovernmental organization, and diplomatic capital of East and Central Africa. The Nairobi stock exchange is the ninth largest in Africa in market capitalization as well as the eighth largest in number of listed companies (ASEA 2012). In 2008, the city's estimated economic output of $12 billion ranked it 13th in Africa and 147th in the world in terms of city gross domestic product at purchasing power parity exchange rates (Hawksworth, Hoehn, and Tiwari 2009).

Nairobi is called the "safari capital of the world" and is the main center of eastern Africa's global wildlife tourism industry thanks to its many superb hotels, tour companies, and Jomo Kenyatta International Airport, which also serves as the home base of the rapidly growing Kenya Airways (Otiso et al. 2011). Nairobi is also a key global diplomatic center that hosts the world headquarters of the United Nations Environment Programme (UNEP), UN Human Settlements Program (UN-Habitat), and the regional offices of the UN Children's Fund (UNICEF), UN Educational, Scientific and Cultural Organization (UNESCO), UN Industrial Development Organization (UNIDO), and the UN Development Programme (UNDP) (City Council of Nairobi 2007).

The city is the nerve center of Kenya's economy, contributing slightly less than 50 percent of its gross domestic product and 43 percent of its urban wage employment. In 2008, its wage employment was distributed as follows: community, social, and personal services: 39 percent; manufacturing: 19 percent; wholesale and retail trade, restaurants, and hotels: 15 percent; construction: 10 percent; finance, insurance, real estate, and business services: 10 percent; and transport and communications: 8 percent (Kenya National Bureau of Statistics 2009). Moreover, in that year, Nairobi accounted for between 36 and 66 percent of Kenya's total urban wage employment in the foregoing economic sectors. As Kenya's major industrial base, Nairobi produces processed food, beer, vehicles, soap, pharmaceuticals, construction materials, engineering products, textiles, and chemicals.

In 2009, the city's formal economy employed 20 percent of its workforce, whereas the informal (or *jua kali*) economy accounted for 80 percent (Kenya National Bureau of Statistics 2009, 72, 80). The informal economy generally consists of small-scale economic enterprises that are often undocumented, semiorganized, unregulated, reliant on low-to-simple technology, and have one to a few part- to full-time workers (City Council of Nairobi 2007; ILO 1993). Many of Nairobi's informal economy workers, whether paid or unpaid, include auto repairers, painters, carpenters, shoemakers, craftspeople, hairdressers, drivers, domestic servants, petty traders, urban farmers, and hawkers of various food commodities. Because of the informal economy's importance to the Nairobi and national economies, the Kenya government has tried to facilitate its operation in recent decades to varying degrees of success (UN-Habitat 2006a).

Entrepreneurship and employment in Nairobi's informal economy is gendered, with women mostly selling items like vegetables, fruits, and clothes, while men tend to deal in higher-profit-margin products like electronics, shoes, hardware, toys, and other assorted goods

(UN-Habitat 2006a). Even in the formal sector, women are mostly concentrated in low-paying occupations because of their historically disadvantaged access to education, land, and other productive assets (City Council of Nairobi 2007). Most of the city's poor people thus are women, even though the city's overall poverty rate is 23 percent (Commission of Revenue Allocation 2011).

Although Nairobi's informal economy is dominated by low-income residents, many in the middle- and upper-income classes also use it to diversify or bolster their income. This economic strategy of using multiple modes of livelihood became entrenched in Nairobi and in many other African cities in the tough economic times of the 1980s and 1990s (Owusu 2001).

Environmental Sustainability

Water, air, and land pollution are growing threats to Nairobi's environment, with the main contributors being explosive population growth, inadequate sanitation services, the high number of motor vehicles and commercial and industrial enterprises, and the poor coordination of the city's and nation's environmental management agencies. Because the city's poor people have traditionally had low access to sanitation services, they are especially vulnerable to the health effects of the city's weak environmental management.

Nairobi's history of inequitable service provision dates back to the colonial era when the needs of its European and, to some extent, Indian populations held higher privilege. Although many Africans are now part of the Nairobi elite, the city's practice of neglecting the needs of the majority continues. Downtown and the middle- and upper-class areas of the city are, therefore, well served by municipal and private sanitation services. Overall, the well-off areas of Nairobi host only 40 percent of the city's population. The remaining 60 percent of the city's population is left dealing with its own waste

through open-air burning, improper disposal in pits and other illegal places, and through various self-help efforts (City Council of Nairobi 2007; Otiso 2003). Because of the city's elitist orientation, it has never really developed adequate infrastructure for its rapidly growing population (Otiso 2005a).

Inefficiency in the city's waste collection and disposal is also manifested in its poor management of its sole waste dump site at Dandora, low levels of recycling, lack of waste transfer facilities, and widespread mixing of waste at the point of generation. Because most of the city's waste consists of food remains, there is an ample but unexploited opportunity for reducing the city's waste through composting (City Council of Nairobi 2007).

Another contributor to Nairobi's poor environment management is the city's high proportion of recent rural-urban migrants who have tenuous emotional and financial links to city. Because most of these migrants' sympathies are with their rural areas of origin, they tend to be apathetic toward the management of the city's environment. This "divided loyalty" originated in colonial policies that excluded the local African population from the city (Hake 1977). Nairobi will continue to deal with the negative effects of these colonial policies until most of its residents are born in the city and Kenya becomes predominantly urban in the 2030s (Otiso 2005a; Onyango-Obbo 2012).

On the brighter side, Kenya's incoming devolved government system, beginning in 2013, promises to give Nairobi a more equitable and effective waste and environment management system. This is because the new local governments, including that of Nairobi county, will have clearly defined and protected functions and sources of revenue and more accountable leaders who are popularly elected (National Council for Law Reporting 2010).

Water and Health

Nairobi's poor environmental management has compromised the city's health and water supply by polluting and contaminating many of its rivers and other surface water sources. Although the city currently produces more water than it needs, it has a growing water problem because of its rapidly growing population, inadequate water distribution infrastructure, high (50 percent) water loss to leakage and illegal connections, drought, and the growing pollution of its groundwater sources. Although an estimated 42 percent of the city's households (mostly middle- and upper-income ones) have proper water connections, they must contend with regular service disruptions. In the low-income areas of the city, where in-house water connections are rarer, residents commonly buy water from vendors by the jerry-can or fetch it from neighborhood standpipes (City Council of Nairobi 2007).

Because most Nairobi residents lack access to in-house piped water supplies, it is not surprising that only about 40 percent of them have waterborne sewerage services (African Development Bank Group 2010). Most Nairobians (60 percent) thus rely on pit latrines, septic tanks, and conservancy tanks for the disposal of their human waste, thereby contributing to their city's groundwater pollution problem. In Nairobi's many slum areas (e.g., Kibera and Mathare) toilet facilities are even rarer, and residents suffer from high levels of respiratory and digestive tract infections caused by their unsanitary living environments (UN-Habitat 2006b).

Although middle- and upper-income residents have access to indoor plumbing, the efficiency of this service is frequently compromised by erratic water supply, poor maintenance, overloaded sewer lines, illegal connections to trunk sewers, the use of toilets for the disposal of garbage, and the blocking of sewage pipes for irrigation. Moreover, the regular discharge of raw sewage into the city's streams and rivers creates a major health risk to all city residents, especially those who live in the Eastlands next to such polluted bodies of water (UNEP 2006).

Urban Planning

Nonmotorized transport (e.g., walking and cycling) is a common form of transport in Nairobi. Because city managers have over the years focused on the needs of motorized transport, however, Nairobi's nonmotorized transport sector is inconvenient, dangerous, devoid of proper infrastructure, and poorly integrated into the city's overall transport and development planning. As a

result, certain forms of nonmotorized transport, especially cycling and *boda-bodas* (bicycle taxis) are less common in Nairobi than in many similar-sized cities around the globe. Besides making Nairobi famous, the city's ubiquitous and privately operated "*matatu*" (minibus) public transport vehicles inhibit the use and growth of nonmotorized forms of transport in the city because they are a major cause of pedestrian and cyclist injuries and deaths. Ultimately, this contributes to gridlock in the city's motorized transport system (Mitullah and Makajuma 2009).

Many of Nairobi's pressing economic, social, environmental, housing, and transport problems stem from its history of poor planning and management. Although the city has had four master plans (the 1926 zoning plan, the 1948 master plan, the 1973 Metropolitan Growth Strategy, and the 2012 Nairobi Metropolitan Region Spatial Plan), it has historically either failed to implement or has poorly implemented these plans. As a result, the city lacks effective physical planning and development control and is inconvenient to live in. The key reasons for this state of affairs include insufficient capital and skilled manpower resources, rapid population growth, lack of a political will to properly plan and manage the city, and the city's continued reliance on inappropriate and outdated colonial planning and building codes (Otiso 2005a).

From 1973 to 2012, the city had no master plan and, in this thirty-eight-year period, city and national urban managers relied on various piecemeal measures to manage Nairobi. Measures included the ineffective 1970s policies of limiting urbanization, increasing urban housing through site and service programs and slum upgrading, and the development of growth-poles to disperse Kenya's urbanization and reduce population pressure on Nairobi and other major cities. Whereas the first strategy proved to be impractical and the second fizzled for lack of funding, the third failed because (1) it involved too many towns that were poorly selected and resourced, (2) it was poorly coordinated because of a lack of a national urban policy and a well-articulated urban and regional development policy, (3) it was no match for the market forces responsible for the agglomeration of economic activity in Nairobi, and (4) it tried to create a top-down urban hierarchy instead of investing in rapidly growing secondary towns (Otiso 2005b). Nairobi thus grew haphazardly for nearly four decades. By 2000, it had such a severe infrastructural and housing shortage that 50 percent of its population lived in informal settlements such as the famous Kibera and Mathare slums (Omwenga 2010).

When the National Rainbow Coalition (NARC) government came to power in 2002, on the promise of reviving Kenya's economy, it quickly became evident that the country's economic recovery required major investments in its economic engine: Nairobi. Accordingly, the NARC government initiated many investments in the city's infrastructure and housing sector. It also introduced many political and economic reforms that have since revived the city's real estate sector and greatly improved its housing supply, infrastructure, and living conditions. Nevertheless, because much of the new housing has been built by the private sector and is targeted at middle- and upper-middle-income residents, many Nairobians continue to struggle to find affordable and good quality housing even with the government's ongoing ancillary slum upgrading projects (Omwenga 2010). Moreover, because of rapid population growth, the city has a housing deficit of 2 million units that it plans to partially offset by redeveloping its older low density housing estates in Eastlands, such as Kaloleni and Shauri Moyo, into higher-density ones (Kiberenge 2012).

Another noteworthy planning development for Nairobi is the creation in 2008, by the Kenya Coalition government that took over from its NARC counterpart, of the Ministry of Nairobi Metropolitan Development (MNMD), intended to marshal more public and private resources and the political will to further hasten Nairobi's economic and social development (Omwenga 2010). In the same year, the MNMD released the Nairobi Metro 2030 Strategy with the aim of transforming the Nairobi Metropolitan Region (NMR) "into a world class African region, that is able to create sustainable wealth and offer a high quality of life for its residents, the people of Kenya, investors and offer an unmatched experience for its esteemed visitors" (Government of Kenya 2008, v). Simultaneously, to facilitate better coordination and management of the city's regional growth, the MNMD expanded the NMR from 695 to 32,000 square kilometers (Government of Kenya 2008, v). In 2012, the government sought to operationalize the Nairobi Metro 2030 Strategy by releasing the Nairobi Metropolitan Region Spatial Plan (MNMD 2012). Nairobi has seen many positive developments in the last decade, and only time will tell if it will be a better planned, managed, and environmentally sound world-class African metropolis by 2030.

Kefa M. OTISO
Bowling Green State University

See also Africa, East; African Union (AU); Cairo, Egypt; Cape Town, South Africa; Goma, Democratic Republic of the Congo; Lagos, Nigeria; Migration (Africa); Sahel; Tunis, Tunisia; Urbanization (Africa); Urbanization (Western Asia and Northern Africa); Water Use and Rights (Africa)

FURTHER READING

Achola, Milcah. (2002). Colonial policy and urban health: The case of colonial Nairobi. In Andrew Burton (Ed.), *The urban experience in eastern Africa* (pp. 119–137). Nairobi, Kenya: BIEA.

African Development Bank Group. (2010). *Nairobi Rivers Rehabilitation and Restoration Program: Sewerage Improvement Project.* Tunis-Belvedère, Tunisia: African Development Bank Group.

African Securities Exchanges Association (ASEA). (2012, April). Monthly reports. Retrieved May 20, 2012, from http://www.african sea.org/asea/Statistics.aspx

Charton-Bigot, Hélène, & Rodriguez-Torres, Deyssi. (Eds.). (2010). *Nairobi today: The paradox of a fragmented city.* Nairobi, Kenya: Mkuki Na Nyota Publishers.

City Council of Nairobi. (2007). *City of Nairobi environment outlook.* Nairobi, Kenya: UNEP. Retrieved April 14, 2012, from http://www.unep.org/geo/pdfs/NCEO_Report_FF_New_Text.pdf

Commission of Revenue Allocation. (2011, December). *Kenya: County fact sheets.* Nairobi, Kenya: Government Printer.

Government of Kenya. (2008). *Nairobi metro 2030: A world class African metropolis.* Nairobi, Kenya: Government Printer.

Government of Kenya. (2009). 2009 census. Retrieved May 11, 2012, from https://opendata.go.ke/

Hake, Andrew. (1977). *African metropolis: Nairobi's self-help city.* London: Chatto & Windus.

Hawksworth, John; Hoehn, Thomas; & Tiwari, Anmol. (2009). *Which are the largest city economies in the world and how might this change by 2025?* Retrieved April 10, 2012, from http://www.ukmediacentre.pwc.com/imagelibrary/downloadMedia.ashx?MediaDetailsID=1562

International Labor Organization (ILO). (1993). *Report of the 15th International Conference of Labor Statisticians.* Geneva: ILO.

Kenya National Bureau of Statistics. (2009). *Economic survey 2009.* Nairobi, Kenya: Government Printer.

Kiberenge, Kenfrey. (2012, May 22). City residents fear being kicked out in estate upgrade. *Standard.* Retrieved May 22, 2012, from http://standardmedia.co.ke/?articleID=2000058032&pageNo=1

King, Kenneth. (1996). *Jua Kali Kenya: Change and development in an informal economy.* Oxford, UK: James Currey.

Ministry of Nairobi Metropolitan Development (MNMD). (2012). *Development of a spatial planning concept for Nairobi metropolitan region* (Final plan, January 2012). Nairobi, Kenya: Ministry of Nairobi Metropolitan Development.

Mitullah, Winnie. (2003). Urban slums reports: The case of Nairobi. Retrieved May 11, 2012, from http://www.begakwabega.com/documenti/Nairobi-HabitatReport2003.pdf

Mitullah, Winnie V., & Makajuma, George A. (2009). Analysis of non-motorised travel conditions on Jojoo Road corridor in Nairobi. Rondebosch, South Africa: African Centre of Excellence for Studies in Public and Non-Motorised Transport (ACET).

Morgan, William Thomas Wilson. (Ed.). (1967). *Nairobi: City and region.* Nairobi, Kenya: Oxford University Press.

National Council for Law Reporting. (2010). *The Constitution of Kenya, 2010.* Retrieved May 21, 2012, from http://www.kenyalaw.org/klr/fileadmin/pdfdownloads/Acts/ConstitutionofKenya2010.pdf

Obudho, Robert. (1997). Nairobi: National capital and regional hub. In Carole Rakodi (Ed.), *The urban challenge in Africa* (pp. 292–336). Tokyo: United Nations University Press.

Obudho, Robert. (Ed.). (1983). *Urbanization and development planning in Kenya.* Nairobi, Kenya: Kenya Literature Bureau.

Omwenga, Mairura. (2010). *Nairobi: Emerging metropolitan region: Development planning and management opportunities and challenges.* 46th International Society of City and Regional Planners (ISOCARP) Congress 2010. Retrieved April 14, 2012, from http://www.isocarp.net/Data/case_studies/1662.pdf

Onyango-Obbo, Charles. (2012, May 16). How Kenya's Asian and white tribes can save the "orphan" Nairobi county. *Daily Nation.*

Otieno, Jeckonia. (2012). Current building code fit for archives. *The Standard.* Retrieved April 11, 2012, from http://www.standardmedia.

co.ke/InsidePage.php?id=2000056052&cid=470&story=Current%20building%20code%20fit%20for%20archives

Otiso, Kefa M. (2003). State, voluntary and private sector partnerships for slum upgrading and basic service delivery in Nairobi City, Kenya. *Cities*, *20*(4), 221–229.

Otiso, Kefa M. (2005a). Colonial urbanization and urban management in Kenya. In Steven Salm & Toyin Falola (Eds.), *African urban spaces in historical perspective*. Rochester, NY: University of Rochester Press.

Otiso, Kefa M. (2005b). Kenya's secondary cities growth strategy at a crossroads: Which way forward? *GeoJournal*, *62*(1–2), 117–128.

Otiso, Kefa M.; Derudder, Ben; Bassens, David; Devriendt, Lomme; & Witlox, Frank. (2011). Airline connectivity as a measure of the globalization of African cities. *Applied Geography*, *31*(2), 609–620.

Owuor, Samuel, & Mbatia, Teresa. (2011). Nairobi. In Simon Bekker & Goran Therborn (Eds.), *Capital cities in Africa* (pp. 120–140). Cape Town, South Africa: HDRC.

Owusu, Francis. (2001). Urban impoverishment and multiple modes of livelihood in Ghana. *Canadian Geographer*, *45*(3), 387–403.

United Nations Human Settlements Programme (UN-Habitat). (2006a). *Innovative policies for the urban informal economy*. Nairobi, Kenya: UN-Habitat.

United Nations Human Settlements Programme (UN-Habitat). (2006b). *Nairobi urban sector profile, HS/802/05E*. Nairobi, Kenya: UN-Habitat.

United States Central Intelligence Agency (US CIA). (2012). *World factbook: Kenya*. Retrieved May 11, 2012, from https://www.cia.gov/library/publications/the-world-factbook/geos/ke.html

Nile River

The Nile River supplies water to hundreds of millions of people in eleven countries. Utilization of its waters has given rise to controversies and conflicts since ancient times and continues to the present day to be a source of political tensions. While some observers are optimistic that finding a way to share the Nile's waters equitably could lead to peaceful negotiations and cooperation among rivals, others predict that the Nile may become a battleground for future "water wars." Sustaining this natural resource is intricately tied to the political stability and the economic development of a large portion of the African continent.

The Nile is the world's longest river, measuring 6,671 kilometers in length, and it is also seen by many as the world's most important river given the vast area and large population it affects. The Nile Basin catchment area is shared among eleven countries: Burundi, the Democratic Republic of the Congo (DRC), Egypt, Eritrea, Ethiopia, Kenya, Rwanda, South Sudan (a new nation as of July 2011), Sudan, Tanzania, and Uganda. It drains an area of more than 3.35 million square kilometers, which covers about one-tenth of the African continent. The White Nile and the Blue Nile meet in Khartoum in Sudan to form the Nile. The White Nile provides approximately 15 percent of the water to the Nile, whereas the Ethiopian tributaries (the Blue Nile, Atbara, and Sobat rivers) contribute approximately 85 percent of the water, as measured at Aswan in Egypt, where the total water of the Nile annually averages 84 billion cubic meters. Sustainable management of this immense natural resource is essential not only to the quality of life of the people of the region but also to the economic and political stability of the Nile countries.

As of 2011, there were approximately 370 million people living in the eleven Nile countries and about 200 million in the basin itself. It is estimated that by 2030 there will be about 650 million people, of which 330 million will be living in the basin (FAO n.d.). Clearly the pressure on the utilization of the water will be increasing. In addition, the prediction of global climate change raises new uncertainties regarding the amount of rainfall in the catchment area and the resulting total flow of the Nile.

Geopolitical Complexity

The development and sustainability of all the Nile countries are dependent upon the river to various degrees. For example, Egypt, as a downstream country in a desert, is totally dependent upon the Nile, and the river provides about 98 percent of the country's fresh water. In 2011, Egypt had a population of more than 80 million people, and it is expected to increase to about 130–140 million by 2050 (FAO UN n.d.). The majority of Egypt's Nile water comes from Ethiopia, which also has a population that numbers about 80 million people and one of the fastest rising population rates in the Nile Basin, expected to rise to more than 150 million by 2050. How the Nile water should be shared is a complex and sensitive question.

Sharing of the waters of the Nile River has been a controversial political issue with geopolitical consequences since ancient times and no doubt will continue to be so in the future. In 1929, Egypt and Great Britain (on behalf of the East African colonies) negotiated the Nile Water Agreement, which stated that "no irrigation or power works or measures are to be constructed or taken on the

River Nile and its branches, or on the lakes from which it flows . . . in such a manner as to entail any prejudice to the interests of Egypt, either reduce the quantity of water arriving in Egypt, or modify the date of its arrival, or lower its level." In effect the 1929 agreement gave Egypt the right of veto over any uses of the Nile that would affect its own interest.

In 1959, Egypt and Sudan signed the agreement titled For the Full Utilization of the Nile Waters, in which they divided the totality of the Nile waters between themselves without any consideration for the upstream countries, not even inviting them to the negotiations. According to this agreement, of the Nile's annual average 84 billion cubic meters of water as measured at Aswan, Egypt should receive 55.5 billion cubic meters and Sudan 18.5 billion cubic meters, and the rest evaporates mainly in Lake Nasser. This agreement thus implied that the other Nile basin countries were denied use of the Nile water, which has hindered the development of the respective countries because water is essential for hydropower projects, irrigation programs, and food security. As a consequence, upstream countries have disputed this agreement for a number of reasons (Tvedt 2010).

The 2010 Cooperative Framework Agreement

In 1999, the Nile Basin Initiative was established among the then ten Nile countries (with Eritrea having an "observatory status"). The aim has been "to achieve sustainable socio-economic development through the equitable utilization of, and benefit from, the common Nile Basin water resources" by negotiating a new agreement that included the upstream countries. In May 2010 the Cooperative Framework Agreement (CFA) was signed by Ethiopia, Rwanda, Tanzania, and Uganda; it was signed by Kenya shortly thereafter and by Burundi in February 2011. Egypt and Sudan have strongly opposed this agreement. For Egypt it means the loss of its historic dominance of the Nile's utilization as well as the veto rights with regard to Nile issues going back to the 1929 agreement. In order for Sudan to develop, they also need to use more water than was allocated in the 1959 agreement for hydropower and irrigation systems. With South Sudan as a new nation state this also puts more pressure on Sudan's water resources.

The 2010 agreement has changed the geopolitical map and altered the premises for the use of the Nile water by giving the upstream countries the right to an equitable share and use of the Nile without harming the needs of others. How a sustainable use of the Nile will take place in practice is uncertain, however, given the continuous political processes, the projected population increase, and the possibility of less water in the Nile due to climate change. Moreover, with the collapse of the regime of Hosni Mubarak in Egypt in February 2011 and the independence of South Sudan in July 2011, new factors regarding the collective use of the Nile have emerged that will have implications for future negotiations.

Possibilities

Although water is a limited and finite resource, the character of rivers has certain advantages compared to other limited resources. Within "the tragedy of the commons" paradigm developed by the US ecologist Garret Hardin (1968), a limited resource, open to all, is likely to run a course toward overuse and ruin. The use of water as a common property resource has often been interpreted from this perspective, but rivers open up possibilities for different uses that may benefit the respective parties involved. As the historian and Nile expert Terje Tvedt (2010, 240) says: "Societies along the Nile are neither equally capable of harming their common resource nor equally likely to suffer the consequences of others' behaviour, not only because some live upstream and others downstream, but also because individual action need not negatively affect other actors (although this of course may happen, and very deliberately so)." For example, Ethiopia launched the construction of the Grand Ethiopian Renaissance Dam in April 2011, a 5,250-megawatt dam on the Blue Nile, which is expected to be complete in 2014. Egypt views this dam as representing a threat to its country's national security because it will reduce the water table in Lake Nasser, the reservoir of the Aswan Dam. Egypt faces another potentially devastating threat, however: the Nile carries huge amounts of silt, which eventually could fill up Lake Nasser and destroy the Aswan Dam. The presence of other dams farther upstream should reduce the amount of silt and thus prolong the lifespan of the Aswan Dam (Tvedt 2010).

The media have often referred to the Nile as a likely place where "water wars" will take place in the twenty-first century, perhaps in response to (and remembrance of) President Anwar Sadat's famous 1978 threat to attack Ethiopia if that country diverted the Nile, and in April 2011, Ethiopia dismissed the current Egyptian commission's threat as a psychological game. With the fall of the Mubarak regime, tensions have softened, and now both Egypt and Ethiopia focus on cooperation and finding a solution amenable to both parties. A contradicting theory thus suggests that water has the potential to create greater interdependence between states, and as such is a pathway to peace through negotiation. Politicians have rhetorically used both of these positions to acknowledge that managing the use of the Nile water faces many challenges, some of which may include future cooperation or conflict among Nile states. The ways in which the Nile issues are settled politically will have profound consequences for a sustainable use of the river, the development of the Nile countries, and the geopolitics within and beyond the region.

Terje OESTIGAARD

The Nordic Africa Institute, Uppsala, Sweden

See also Africa (*several articles*); African Union (AU); Cairo, Egypt; Congo (Zaire) River; Danube River; International Conflict Resolution; Lake Victoria; Mediterranean Sea; Rhine River; Sahara; Sahel; Transboundary Water Issues; Water Use and Rights (Africa); Water Use and Rights (Middle East and Northern Africa)

FURTHER READING

Arsano, Yacob. (2007). *Ethiopia and the Nile. Dilemmas of national and regional hydropolitics.* Zurich: ETH.

Food and Agriculture Organization of the United Nations (FAO). (n.d.). Population prospects in the Nile Basin. Retrieved November 9, 2011, from http://www.fao.org/nr/water/faonile/products/Docs/Poster_Maps/POPULATIONBIG.pdf

Hardin, Garret. (1968). The tragedy of the commons. *Science, 162,* 1243–1248.

Nile Basin Initiative. (2011). Homepage. Retrieved July 20, 2011, from http://www.nilebasin.org/newsite/

Tvedt, Terje. (2004). *The River Nile in the age of the British.* New York: I. B. Tauris.

Tvedt, Terje. (Ed.). (2010). *The River Nile in the post-colonial age: Conflict and cooperation in the Nile Basin countries.* London & New York: I. B. Tauris.

Tvedt, Terje, et al. (Eds.). (2006–2010). *A history of water* (6 vols.). New York: I. B. Tauris.

Waterbury, John. (2002). *The Nile Basin: National determinants of collective action.* New Haven, CT: Yale University Press.

Novosibirsk, Russia

1.5 million est. pop. 2012

Novosibirsk is the third most populated city in Russia after Moscow and St. Petersburg. Located in a busy transport corridor of the Trans-Siberian Railway, it is one of the biggest economic, financial, academic, and cultural centers in resource-rich Siberia, leading to the city being dubbed the "Chicago of Siberia." Economic success has come at the expense of pollution from industrial and infrastructure development, chemicals, and radiation, however, which Novosibirsk is now addressing.

Novosibirsk, a city straddling the Ob River in south-central Siberia, is one of the fastest growing cities in the world. It was established in the 1690s as a settlement called Nikolsky Pogost (Nicholas Churchyard) that consisted of not much more than a small hotel with a chapel and warehouse near the Siberian road; later a cargo pier was built to serve as the main industrial facility for steamers. In the 1890s the settlement had fewer than 700 citizens, but by 1962 the city officially had 1 million, becoming one of the few cities in Russia to make the transformation from a small town to a city with more than a million inhabitants in less than seventy years. By the beginning of the twenty-first century Novosibirsk had a population of 1.5 million and was the third most populous city in Russia after Moscow and St. Petersburg, and the largest municipality by area in the country. This rapid growth was due mainly to the fact that at one point the only bridge over the Ob River along the Trans-Siberian Railway was in the area in which the settlement was located, and the city is still geographically well positioned because it lies at the crossroads of all important transportation modes (road, rail, water, and air) in Siberia (Brockhaus and Efron 1897; Tkachenko 2005).

The dramatically fast development of the city began after 30 April 1893, when the first group of bridge builders arrived and created the railroad bridge that not only linked opposite riverbanks but also led to the consolidation of a few small villages into a township (Imperial Russian Geographical Society 1894). This turning point is considered to be the official birth date of the future city of Novosibirsk, which over time has been known variously as Nikolsky Pogost, Krivoshekovskaya Village, and Novonikolayevsk (or New Nikolayevsk, after Saint Nicholas; the Chapel of Saint Nicholas was built there in 1914 and marks the geographic center of Russia). On 25 May 1925 Novonikolayevsk became the administrative center of Siberia, and on 17 November 1925 the city was renamed Novosibirsk (New Siberia).

Economy

In 1912 Emperor Nicholas II extended the Trans-Siberian Railroad southward, and overnight the city of Novosibirsk—which connected regional river, road, and railway transportation—became not only the largest multimodal hub of the Altai area (crossroads of modern Kazakhstan, China, and Mongolia), but also a transnational hub. An economic boom followed, and within a few years the city became one of Russia's biggest regional financial centers, with 70,000 people employed in seven banks. There were ten mills with a total production capacity of more than 190,000 metric tons of flour per year, a factory for producing spare parts for mill machinery and another to manufacture basic agricultural machines, and a creamery. The main Siberian office of D. S. Morgan and Company (the Brockport, New York, inventors of the grain reaping machine) was opened in the city as well. In 1917, before the Revolution, a large number of Siberian cooperative organizations (joint businesses that operate as a conglomerate in a variety of economic fields) made Novonikolayevsk a base for their regional headquarters, making the young city a "capital of cooperatives" in the vast territory, while retaining its status as the area's transportation, industrial, and commercial hub. Manufacturing—led by the flour milling industry—is currently one of the most developed economic sectors of the city (Klimenko 2004).

After the Revolution (and especially during the USSR's First Five-Year Plan) the city invested heavily in reconstructing existing enterprises and constructing new ones, the first of which were factories that produced machinery and mining equipment. Construction of the Turkestan–Siberian railway (1927–1931) and Novosibirsk–Leninsk–Kuznetsk railway line, as well as a locomotive repair factory, boosted economic growth and turned the city into a major center for Asian Russia. Because of its rapid development and industrialization, Novosibirsk was dubbed "the Chicago of Siberia."

As a center in the Siberian Federal District, Novosibirsk has housed many Siberian regional offices since the late 1990s, such as those for the railway, the inland water fleet, aviation, hydrometeorology (the study of the transfer of water and energy between the land surface and the lower atmosphere), geology, science and culture, the diocesan administration of the Russian Orthodox Church, the provinces, and so on. The city is also home to the Interregional Association of the Economic Cooperation of the Constituent Entities of the Russian Federation "Siberian Accord" (IASA), a consortium of fifteen provinces of Asian Russia whose purpose is "forming [the] necessary conditions for creating common economic, legal, industrial, and information space on the territories of . . . the IASA members" (IASA 2012), as well as executive management for the Association of Siberian and Far Eastern Cities.

Novosibirsk's economic and financial importance triggered the development of its scientific sector. During the 1930s dozens of research laboratories and research and design institutes and bureaus were established in the city, and later the USSR Academy of Sciences' West Siberian Branch (1943) and Siberian Branch (1957) followed. The famous Novosibirsk Akademgorodok (Academy Town) was established in 1957, and as one of the city's districts gave new impetus to its growth. Akademgorodok is a unique town created as a city-forest. This may be the only example of an environmentally harmonious Russian settlement: due to its design, the species composition of forest flora and fauna (except for large vertebrates) has not changed over a fifty-year period. The town meets cultural criterion number 2 of the United Nations Educational, Scientific and Cultural Organization (UNESCO) Convention Concerning the Protection of the World Cultural and Natural Heritage, which requires a city to

"exhibit an important interchange of human values . . . on developments in architecture or technology, monumental arts, town-planning or landscape design" (UNESCO 2008). Akademgorodok is a proud masterpiece of architecture and is an environmental city of the future of Novosibirsk. It is one of Russia's most important scientific and educational centers and includes dozens of research institutions, such as the Presidium of the Siberian Branch of the Russian Academy of Sciences (RAS), Novosibirsk State University, and the Physics and Mathematics School (Akademgorodok 2012). Many world famous scientists have come from Novosibirsk Akademgorodok, including the mathematicians Leonid Vitaliyevich Kantorovich (winner of the Nobel Prize for economics in 1975), Mikhail Alekseevich Lavrientyev, and Anatoly Ivanovich Maltsev; the archaeologist and ethnographer Alexey Pavlovich Okladnikov; the chemist Valentin A. Koptyug; and many others (Goryushkin 1993).

Environment

The leading industries in and around Novosibirsk are power generation, gas and water supply, metallurgy, metalworking, and machinery building; together they account for 94 percent of total industrial production and make a significant impact on the environment (Gorodetsky 2004). During its period of rapid growth in the twentieth century, the Novosibirsk urban development policy was carried out without adequate consideration of environmental factors and the policy's impact on the life of citizens. Inadequate state control of natural and industrial environments allowed high levels of pollution from chemical and radioactive substances, uncontrolled electromagnetic fields, noise, and other factors affecting people's health. Only later, when Akademgorodok and other districts were established, were attempts made to consider environmental issues. At the beginning of the twenty-first century Novosibirsk began the process of solving its many complex environmental problems, such as those related to air quality, drinking water, waste management, and greening the city. The Strategic Plan for Sustainable Development of Novosibirsk and Complex Target Programs includes many solutions to these problems (Gorodetsky 2004).

The environmental conditions in Novosibirsk derive largely from radiation in the environment and contamination of air and soil. Transportation, power plants, utility boilers, and chimneys of private houses are all major sources of air pollution, with about 60 percent of air pollution coming from cars. Air pollutants come in the form of formaldehyde, benzopyrene, nitrogen compounds, ammonia, phenol, and a high concentration of suspended particles (Breathe Freely 2012). In spite of already having a well-developed public transportation system (a public bus system appeared in 1926, tram in 1934, and trolleybus in 1957), in 1978 a decision was made to construct a metro system—the first in Siberia—in order to make public transportation more ecologically friendly. It was launched in January 1986 and is the third longest metro system in Russia. The unique metro bridge over the Ob River—the only surface-level station and track in an otherwise underground system—is the longest covered metro bridge in the world, with a total length of 2,145 meters (the span over the river is 896 meters) (Novosibirsk Metropolitan 2012). Besides the metro system, other initiatives intended to reduce air pollution include banning leaded petrol and diesel fuel with sulfur content above 0.05 percent in order to eliminate lead emissions and reducing emissions of sulfur dioxide. The city also has introduced new environmental-control procedures that provide vehicle owners with emissions certificates. Finally, a large number of cars as well as power-generating plants have been re-equipped for natural gas consumption (Breathe Freely 2012).

The soil in Novosibirsk suffers the effects of about 1.4 million tonnes of solid waste created annually (Gorodetsky 2004). By accumulating most anthropogenic and technological waste, the soil experiences extensive erosion, flooding, and long-term contamination from toxicants, salts of heavy metals, radioactive waste, petroleum, minerals, nitrates, pesticides, and human and animal pathogens.

Institutions related to the nuclear industry introduced technogenic radioactive contamination in Novosibirsk during the 1940s and 1950s. Many of these entities no longer exist, but traces of their activities are still evident in some parts of the city. After the Chernobyl tragedy in April 1986 (in what was then the Ukrainian Soviet Socialist Republic and is now simply called Ukraine), the government mandated surveys of radioactive contamination in cities with populations of more than 1 million people. In 1988 these studies were conducted in Novosibirsk, resulting in deactivation of almost all areas of radioactive contamination. As of 2012 radioactive contamination levels in the city are lower than in previous years, but Novosibirsk continues to allocate funds for activities aimed at ensuring the safety of citizens from radiation (Government of Novosibirsk 2012a and 2012b).

Freshwater availability and quality is another environmental issue. Observations of surface water quality show contamination of many water bodies in excess of what fishery regulations allow. The main pollutants are petroleum products, phenols, nitrogen compounds, and copper. In contrast, transit pollutants from adjacent areas are the primary contaminants of the Ob River, and the direct disposal of wastewater from sites in the city pollutes the smaller rivers (Government of Novosibirsk 2012b).

The Novosibirsk Center for Hydro-Meteorology and Environmental Monitoring is one of the major regional centers of the Russian Hydro-Meteorological Service and one of thirty-four regional centers of the World Meteorological Organization's World Weather Watch Programme. The center provides actual and prognostic hydrometeorological data and monitors air, water, soil, radiation, and emergency situations (CHEM-RSMC Novosibirsk 2012). Monitoring and nature conservation activities are also a concern of nongovernmental organizations such as the Siberian Environmental Center, a charitable nongovernmental organization established in 1999 that works in the Novosibirsk region, the Altaisk region, and the Republic of Altai (SibEcoCenter 2012).

Greening of the city to improve the quality of the urban environment is one of the main objectives of Novosibirsk's strategic development plan. Green areas currently cover 19,300 hectares, or about 40 percent of the urban area. Forests in the city constitute up to 53 percent of all green areas; the rest are parks, squares, boulevards, gardens, nurseries, plantations, and the like. The city's Architecture and Town Planning Council is responsible for planning green-area development through 2030 (Government of Novosibirsk 2012c).

Outlook

The 2007 Worldwide Quality of Living Survey by Mercer Human Resource Consulting (MHRC) ranks Zurich, Switzerland, number one out of 215 cities for overall quality of life. New York City (where MHRC is located) is indexed at 100, and other cities are ranked against it on factors such as medical services, levels of air pollution, the efficiency of waste and sewage systems, water potability, presence of harmful animals and insects, and infectious diseases. Novosibirsk was ranked very low at number 182, but higher than either St. Petersburg (184) or Moscow (201) because environmental indicators, relatively cheap real estate, and the growth of consumer activity make the city more attractive to businesses (MHRC 2007).

Novosibirsk looks to the future with optimism. In May 2012 a working group was created to expand on proposals for improving the regulatory framework with an eye toward developing industrial and innovative high-tech clusters in the region, in order to realize the competitive potential of the area. The priority clusters are in the fields of (1) biopharmacology, (2) ceramics, (3) information and technology (IT), (4) autonomous energy sources, and (5) power electronics and electrical engineering. These five clusters bring together 110 participants and 47 investment projects (Government of Novosibirsk 2012a and 2012b). Mikhail A. Lavrent'ev, the first president (1957–1975) of the Siberian Division of the USSR Academy of Science, was very creative and had a good sense of humor. When the city had its first May Day celebration, he organized the demonstration so that instead of flags and banners of the Communist Party leaders in the vanguard, there were young mothers with baby carriages holding the first newborns of Akademgorodok.

Victor K. TEPLYAKOV
Seoul National University

See also Central Asia; Lake Baikal; Moscow, Russia; Russia and the Soviet Union; St. Petersburg, Russia; Ukraine

FURTHER READING

Akademgorodok. (2012). Homepage. Retrieved May 3, 2012, from http://academgorodok.info/ (in Russian)

Breathe Freely: Ecology of Cities and Regions. (2012). Экология Новосибирска [Ecology of Novosibirsk]. Retrieved May 11, 2012, from http://www.dishisvobodno.ru/eco_novosib.html (in Russian)

Brockhaus, Friedrich Arnold, & Efron, Malkin. (Eds.). (1897). Энциклопедический словарь Брокгауза и Ефрона: Том XXI (41). Нибелунги—Нэффцер [Brockhaus and Efron Encyclopedic Dictionary: Vol. XXI (41). Nibelungen—Nefftser]. St. Petersburg: Publishing House of Semenovskaya.

Brumfield, William. (2011, February 21). Global scientific center rises in the midst of Siberia's forests. *Russia beyond the Headlines*. Retrieved May 3, 2012, from http://rbth.ru/articles/2011/02/21/global_scientific_center_in_siberiass_forests_12482.html

Gorodetsky, Vladimir Filipovich. (2004). Стратегический план устойчивого развития города Новосибирска и комплексные целевые программы [Strategic plan for sustainable development of Novosibirsk and complex target programs]. Retrieved May 3, 2012, from http://strateg.novo-sibirsk.ru/4-4-6.htm (in Russian)

Goryushkin, Leonid M. (Ed.). (1993). Новосибирск: 100 лет. События. Люди [Novosibirsk:100 years. Events. People]. Novosibirsk, Russia: Nauka.

Government of Novosibirsk. (2012a). В Минэкономразвития РФ поданы заявки от Новосибирской области на поддержку пяти кластеров [The Ministry of Economic Development submitted an application to the Novosibirsk region in support of the five clusters]. Retrieved May 15, 2012, from http://www.nso.ru/Lists/News/DispForm.aspx?ID=3682 (in Russian)

Government of Novosibirsk. (2012b). Создана рабочая группа по развитию инновационных кластеров [The Working Group of innovative technologies is established]. Retrieved May 11, 2012, from http://www.nso.ru/Lists/News/DispForm.aspx?ID=3847 (in Russian)

Government of Novosibirsk. (2012c). Развитие озеленения в Новосибирске [Development of greening in Novosibirsk]. Retrieved May 11, 2012, from http://www.novo-sibirsk.ru/media/news/19430.html (in Russian)

Imperial Russian Geographical Society. (1894). Записки Западно-Сибирского отдела императорского географического общества. Омск, т. XXXV [Proceedings of the West Siberian Department of the Imperial Russian Geographical Society. Omsk, Vol. 35]. Omsk, Russia: Imperial Russian Geographical Society.

Interregional Association Siberian Accord (IASA). (2012). Homepage (English). Retrieved June 21, 2012, from http://www.sibacc.ru/en/

Klimenko, Vladimir Ilyich. (Ed.). (2004). История промышленности Новосибирска: Том 1. Начало. Новосибирск [The history of industrial Novosibirsk: Vol 1. The beginning: Novosibirsk]. Novosibirsk, Russia: Издательский дом "Историческое наследие Сибири" [Publishing House "Historical Heritage of Siberia"].

Mercer Human Resources Consulting (MHRC). (2007). The 2007 worldwide quality of living survey by city. *CRA Magazine*, Article 06. Retrieved May 11, 2012, from http://www.cramagazine.com/issues/summer07/article06.htm

Novosibirsk Center for Hydro-Meteorology and Environmental Monitoring (CHEM-RSMC Novosibirsk). (2012). Monitoring of environmental pollution: Evidence. Retrieved May 11, 2012, from http://meteo-nso.ru/information.php?id=108 (in Russian)

Novosibirsk Metropolitan. (2012). Хроника строительства [Chronicle of construction]. Retrieved May 4, 2012, from http://www.nsk-metro.ru/index.php?Chronicle (in Russian)

Novosibirsk Reference Online. (2012a). Экология Новосибирска [Ecology of Novosibirsk]. Retrieved May 15, 2012, from http://www.businessnsk.ru/faq/00000042.html (in Russian)

Novosibirsk Reference Online. (2012b). Экологические проблемы Новосибирска [Environmental problems in Novosibirsk]. Retrieved May 15, 2012, from http://www.businessnsk.ru/faq/00000043.html (in Russian)

Schmadel, Lutz Dieter. (2003) *Dictionary of minor planet names: Vol 1* (5th ed.). New York: International Astronomical Union & Springer.

Siberian Environmental Center (SibEcoCenter). (2012). About us. Retrieved May 11, 2012, from http://www.sibecocenter.ru/en/about.htm

Tkachenko, Tatiana A. (2005). Новосибирск: Путеводитель [Novosibirsk: A guidebook]. Novosibirsk, Russia: Siberian Museum Agency.

United Nations Educational, Scientific and Cultural Organization (UNESCO). (2008). The criteria for selection. Retrieved July 3, 2012, from http://whc.unesco.org/en/criteria/

P

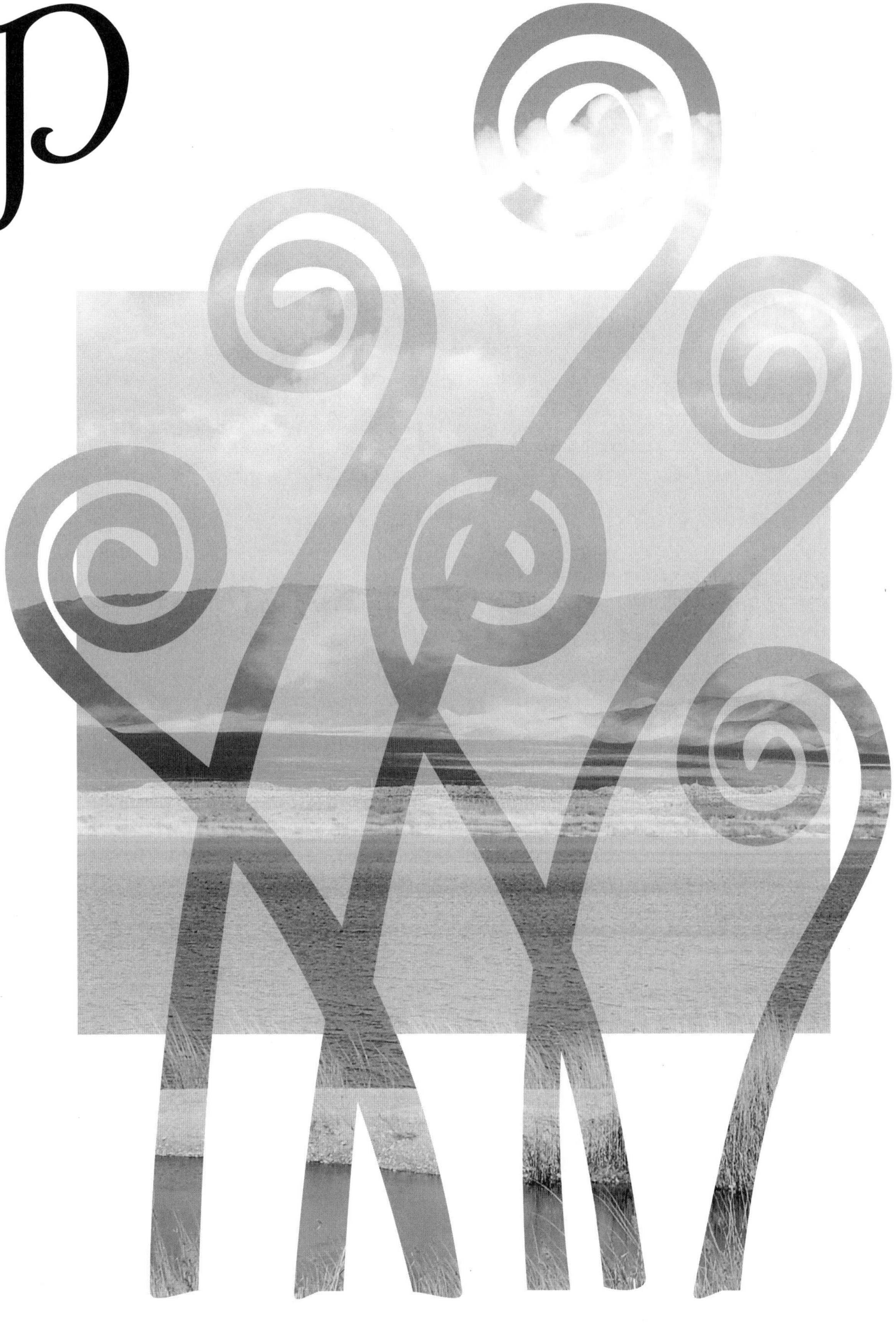

Pakistan

190.2 million est. pop. 2012

Pakistan is situated between India to the east, China to the northeast, Afghanistan to the northwest and north, Iran to the west, the Arabian Sea to the south, and is separated from Tajikistan by the narrow and rugged Wakhan Corridor (part of Afghanistan) to the north. Created in 1947, Pakistan is a relatively a new country, but it is home to the ancient Indus Valley and subsequent civilizations. It has a diverse geography and some unique species of fauna and flora. Pakistan is actively concerned with addressing environmental issues, though solutions require consideration of complex governmental and societal structures.

Situated at the crossroads of South Asia, Central Asia, and the Middle East, Pakistan (literally meaning "the Land of the Pure") was created on 14 August 1947 out of Muslim-majority territories in the northeast and northwest parts of British India. As of 2012 it has an estimated population of 190.2 million people, making it the sixth most populous country on the planet after China, India, the United States, Indonesia, and Brazil (US CIA 2012). Initially consisting of two parts separated by approximately 1,600 kilometers of Indian territory, Pakistan split in 1971, when the eastern half seceded and became the Republic of Bangladesh. The western portion, officially called the Islamic Republic of Pakistan, is a federal parliamentary republic consisting of four provinces: Baluchistan; Khyber Pakhtunkhwa (KPK), previously known as the North West Frontier Province; the Punjab; and Sind. The federal capital, Islamabad, is a separate administrative unit and lies in the central, northern part of the country. The Federally Administered Tribal Areas of Pakistan comprise seven tribal agencies and six frontier regions sharing borders with Afghanistan.

The federally administered agencies of the northern areas of Gilgit and Baltistan have been given a status of a de facto province with more autonomy according to the Gilgit-Baltistan Empowerment and Self-Governance Order in 2009 because of the people's demand to make it a province (Khan 2009; Shigri 2009). As a consequence of the partition of British India into the states of India and Pakistan, the status of the Kashmir region is still disputed, according to the United Nations, regarding its annexing to either of the states (UNMOGIP 2012). It is divided into Pakistani-administered Kashmir—a protected quasi-autonomous state called Azad (Free) Kashmir—and Indian-administered Kashmir. The Kashmir region is the source of Indus River waters, which play an important role in the agriculture of both countries. In 1960, India and Pakistan entered into the Indus Waters Treaty to regulate the use of Indus waters.

Pakistan is a member of the United Nations, the Commonwealth of Nations, and the G20 developing nations. It has the seventh largest standing armed forces in the world and is a declared nuclear weapons state, being the first and only Muslim nation to have that status. Islam plays a major role in the country's identity, politics, and day-to-day life, with Muslims making up 98 percent of the population. Pakistan is also a founding member of the Organisation of the Islamic Conference (now the Organisation of Islamic Cooperation).

Climate and Geography

Pakistan's climate is generally arid, characterized by little rainfall, hot summers, cool or cold winters, and wide climatic variations between extremes of temperature: at one end, the warm, humid coastal area along the Arabian Sea, and at the other, the frozen, snow-covered, relatively inaccessible ridges of the Karakoram Range and other mountains in the far north.

Less than a fifth of Pakistan's land area has the potential for intensive agricultural use. Nearly all of the cultivable land is actively under cultivation, and although outputs are low by world standards, agriculture is considered to be the backbone of Pakistan's economy. Barley and wheat cultivation, along with the domestication of herd animals like sheep and goats, can be traced back to Mehrgarh in Baluchistan in 8000–6000 BCE. Irrigation was developed in the Indus Valley by around 4500 BCE and is still practiced through the canals from the Indus River and its tributaries, forming one of the world's largest canal systems (Wright 2009). The existence of animal-driven ploughs is evident from around 2500 BCE.

The Indus River plain consists of two major regions, corresponding roughly to the provinces of Punjab and Sind, which combine to be Pakistan's breadbasket. "Punjab" means the confluence of five rivers: the Indus, Jhelum, Chenab, Ravi, and Sutlej. During the British colonial period, the irrigation system was improved by digging more canals in the province, facilitating the emergence of extensive cultivation despite arid conditions. Engine tube wells are used in some areas in the absence of canals, whereas some of the areas, like the northern parts of Punjab, have arid agriculture. Pakistan is one of the largest producers and suppliers of wheat, rice, cotton, sugarcane, date palm, mango, and chickpeas in the world today (Board of Investment 2012). The crops are categorized into *Kharif* (autumn harvest or monsoon crop) and *Rabi* (winter or spring harvest) crops. Livestock is an integral part of Pakistan's economy. In some areas, such as in Baluchistan, farmers raise animals without any agriculture, making the livestock their only source of income.

The Baluchistan plateau, spotted with seismic fault lines, is an austere, dry place that has been compared with the surface of the moon. It has the lowest population-density rates in the country. People living closer to the rivers and in the coastal areas of Sindh and Baluchistan largely depend upon fishing for their living. Fish farming is also a growing industry in Pakistan not only in the coastal areas but also in Punjab and northern areas.

The northern highlands region features some of the most rugged and famous mountains in the world, including the world's second-highest peak, K2, and many peaks that are snow covered year round. The northern part of the country also has high-altitude species of fauna, including snow leopards and markhors (wild goats). The northern forests in the Hindu Kush and Karakoram ranges include alpine junipers. Some of this region was once part of the old Silk Road trading system that traversed Central Asia more than a thousand years ago, whereas other parts were essentially cut off from the outside world because of the craggy and difficult terrain.

Politics and Economics

Pakistan is constitutionally a parliamentary republic. Although the head of state is the president, the prime minister usually wields greater political influence. Three parallel legal systems exist: civil, religious, and military. The Council of Islamic Ideology, a constitutionally mandated organization, ensures that the country has no laws that are contradictory to the tenets of Islam.

For the first time in Pakistan history, an elected government of the Pakistan People's Party, along with its allies, is completing its tenure in 2012. Feudal and paternalistic relations continue to dominate political processes, however, especially in rural areas. Access to resources, services, jobs, state functionaries, and other benefits is mediated through powerful influential patrons who, in most instances, are men. Although distinctions based on *qaum* (tribe) remain significant social markers in the Punjab (Lyon 2004), particularly in rural areas, they have nowhere near the authority that tribal affiliation holds in the KPK and Baluchistan. In the latter areas, patrilineal lineages are the most significant bonds, with vendettas and feuds intrinsic features of social relations. Pakhtuns (the dominant ethnic group in the KPK) and Baluchis (the dominant ethnic group in the Baluchistan province) are irredentists, tribal members who recognize no legitimate authority other than that of their immediate tribal leader. Similarly, in Sind, socioeconomic ties traditionally revolve around a few large dominant *waderas* (landholding families). The remainder of people live in persistent poverty.

With independence, many people feared that Pakistan might cease to exist; East Pakistan's secession in 1971—aided by India—further aggravated that anxiety, increasing hatred against India and an ideological and political negotiation within the state (Talbot 1998). In the 1990s, political and ethnic radical movements were largely replaced by growing sectarian terrorism, and eventually anti-West and anti-United States sentiments in the 2000s. Pakistan was suddenly thrust to the center of the global political arena in the days following the terrorist attacks on the United States of 11 September 2001. Because it had been a frontline state in the US proxy war against the former Soviet Union in Afghanistan, Pakistan now became a frontline state in the war against global terrorism, particularly against the Taliban-led government of Afghanistan and the al-Qaeda organization.

With Pakistan's unwavering support, military action succeeded in overthrowing the regime in Afghanistan in December 2001.

Throughout the 1980s and 1990s, Pakistan's economy was constantly undergoing economic restructuring, albeit unsuccessfully in the area of bringing about viable reforms. The hyperinflation and economic stagnation that hit Pakistan's economy in late 1996 contributed to lowering people's already weak purchasing power; morale was further lowered as the government was forced to introduce austerity measures to prevent the economy from going into default. Despite all these issues, Pakistan's industry, especially in sporting goods, surgical instruments, mobile and telecommunication products, and agriculture, have seen a boom (Board of Investment 2012). As of 2012, however, the last few years have seen a severe energy crisis that has reduced the national growth.

With a low human-development position that underscores what the political and economic turmoil of the past few decades has wrought, Pakistan has a literacy rate of 57 percent (69 percent male and 45 percent female literacy rates) as of 2010 (Ministry of Finance 2010). Pakistan also has a high percentage (40 percent) of underweight children under the age of five years (FAO 2010).

Society

Like its geography, Pakistan's cultural landscape is diverse. Having roots in one of the world's most ancient civilizations, the Indus Valley and then Indo-Greek Gandhara, Pakistani culture today has been shaped by various religious and ethnic factors. Its ancient society has been connected with the great civilizations of the world through trade, as revealed by archaeological evidence at Harappa and Mohenjo-daro (Mughal 2011a; Wright 2009). This region has been influenced by Greek, Arabic, Persian, Central Asian, and British cultures during its history, and resultant cultural imprints can be found on Pakistani languages, food, dress, and other forms of tangible and intangible culture.

Pakistani social life revolves around family and the honor of women. A family's traditions have considerable bearing on its members, influencing perceptions of proper gender roles, occupational choices, whether and how to pursue an education, and alliances with others. Large extended families of the past provided ample opportunity for socialization, sustenance, protection, and regulation. Isolated individuals living apart from relatives remain uncommon; even male workers who have migrated to cities generally live with a relative or a friend of a relative. Children live with their parents until marriage; sons and their families—except in the most congested urban areas in the country—tend to live with their parents for their entire lives.

After independence, the millions of Hindus and Sikhs who left for India were replaced by roughly seven million Muslim immigrants who fled from India to Pakistan at the time of partition in 1947 (Talbot 1998), the majority of whom settled in Punjab. This influx of immigration changed the demographic features of many cities, especially the then-capital, Karachi. The refugees, generally better educated than most native people, especially in Sindh, filled a vacuum in the commercial life.

Urbanization has been occurring at an unprecedented rate in Pakistan, and 35 percent of Pakistanis live in cities, according to 2005 estimates (*Daily Times* Staff Report 2007). Over half of all urban residents live in cities of more than a million people. More than 50 percent of the total urban population in 2005 lived in eight cities of Pakistan, namely Karachi, Lahore (the two largest cities), Faisalabad, Rawalpindi, Multan, Hyderabad, Gujranwala, and Peshawar (*Daily Times* Staff Report 2007). The traditional hold—both economic and political—that local landlords enjoy in rural areas, especially in Punjab and Sindh, virtually ensures the continuation of limited socioeconomic opportunities and mobility, which in turn are the greatest reasons for migration to urban areas.

Karachi has come to house the poorest slums in the country, particularly in the working-class neighborhoods of Orangi and Korangi. It was ravaged by violence in the 1990s as contending ethnic groups vied to solidify their local power and control. Since the eruption of the civil war in Afghanistan, the city of Karachi had also become a destination point for refugees from Afghanistan escaping the turmoil in that country and the poverty and dependency of the refugee camps in KPK and Baluchistan.

Environmental Issues

Pakistan has been subject to frequent natural disasters, especially earthquakes and floods. The 1935 and 1945 earthquakes in Baluchistan, the 1974 earthquake in Hunza Valley, and the 2005 large earthquake in the northern part of the country, including Kashmir, have affected millions of people and caused vast infrastructural damage (Khan 2010).

Global warming is another environmental issue affecting the natural balance in Pakistan. It has been noted that the Karakoram and Himalayan mountain ranges in the northern part of the country have grown wetter over the past century than they were over the preceding millennia. The melting of glaciers and heavy rainfall have caused the Indus River and its tributaries to overflow. Floods in the 1970s, 1980s, and 1990s, and in 2010 in various parts of the country, especially Gilgit-Baltistan, Punjab, Sindh, and central eastern parts of Baluchistan, have caused serious damage (Khan 2010).

Although the area had one of the best sewerage systems in the world during the ancient era of the Indus Valley civilization (Mughal 2011b), Pakistan is now suffering from a surfeit of solid and liquid excreta. This has caused an increase in the number of waterborne diseases like gastroenteritis. Low-lying land is generally used for waste disposal. Another issue is the contamination of shallow groundwater near urban industries that discharge wastes directly into the ground. This has largely affected the availability of clean drinking water. Air pollution from vehicles is also a major issue in big cities like Lahore and Karachi. Deforestation, soil erosion, and water shortage in dry conditions are some of the other major environmental problems that threaten humans, as well as other species.

The government of Pakistan has became increasingly concerned about environmental threats since the early 1990s and has addressed environmental concerns by starting programs such as the Pakistan Environment Protection Agency and the National Conservation Strategy. An Environmental Protection Act was passed in 1997 and recently a "green bench" of the Supreme Court has been announced to deal with the environmental issues (*The Nation* Staff Report 2012). According to the Joint Monitoring Program of the World Health Organization and the United Nations Children's Fund (UNICEF), access to an improved water source increased from 83 percent in 1990 to 91 percent in 2004 (WHO and UNICEF 2012a). Similarly, improved sanitation coverage increased from 37 percent to 59 percent (WHO and UNICEF 2012b).

Pakistan has fourteen national parks, seventy-two wildlife sanctuaries, sixty-six game reserves, nine marine and littoral protected areas, nineteen protected wetlands, and a number of other protected grasslands, shrublands, woodlands, and natural monuments. The country is actively concerned with environmental issues at national and international levels, signing international treaties like the United Nation's Convention on the Law of the Sea, and the Framework Convention on Climate Change. Pakistan has a legal framework for environmental protection but there is a need to improve its capacity to enforce these laws.

Anita M. WEISS
University of Oregon

Muhammad Aurang Zeb MUGHAL
Durham University

See also Afghanistan; Agriculture, Small-Scale; Central Asia; Indus River; Middle East; Urbanization (Western Asia and Northern Africa)

FURTHER READING

Basic Facts. (2012). Ministry of Information & Broadcasting: The information gateway to Pakistan. Retrieved April 10, 2012, from http://www.infopak.gov.pk/BasicFacts.aspx

Board of Investment, Prime Minister's Secretariat (Public) Government of Pakistan. (2012). Pakistan industries. Retrieved April 17, 2012, from http://www.pakboi.gov.pk/index.php?option=com_content&view=article&id=122&Itemid=138

Daily Times Staff Report. (2007, June 28). Pakistan's urban population to equal rural by 2030: UNFPA. Retrieved April 18, 2012, from http://www.dailytimes.com.pk/default.asp?page=2007%5C06%5C28%5Cstory_28-6-2007_pg7_9

Food and Agriculture Organization of the United Nations (FAO). (2010). Nutrition country profiles: Pakistan summary. Retrieved May 4, 2012, from http://www.fao.org/ag/agn/nutrition/pak_en.stm

Khan, Amir Nawaz. (2010). Climate change adaptation and disaster risk reduction in Pakistan. In Rajib Shaw, Juan M. Pulhin & Joy Jacqueline Pareira (Eds.), *Climate change adaptation and disaster risk reduction: An Asian perspective: Vol. 5*. Bingley, UK: Emerald Group Publishing Limited.

Khan, M. Ismail. (2009, September 9). Gilgit-Baltistan autonomy. Retrieved April 10, 2012, from http://archives.dawn.com/archives/30198

Khan, Shahrukh Rafi. (Ed.). (2000). *Fifty years of Pakistan's economy: Traditional topics and contemporary concerns*. Karachi, Pakistan: Oxford University Press.

Languages of Pakistan. (2012). Ethnologue: Languages of the world. Retrieved April 10, 2012, from http://www.ethnologue.com/show_country.asp?name=pk

Lyon, Stephen M. (2004). *An anthropological analysis of local politics and patronage in a Pakistani village*. Lampeter, UK: Edwin Mellen Press.

Ministry of Finance, Government of Pakistan. (2010). Pakistan economic survey 2010–11. Retrieved April 12, 2012, from http://finance.gov.pk/survey/chapter_11/10-Education.pdf

Mughal, Muhammad Aurang Zeb. (2011a). Harappan seals. In Alfred J. Andrea (Ed.), *World history encyclopedia: Vol. 4* (p. 707). Santa Barbara, CA: ABC-CLIO.

Mughal, Muhammad Aurang Zeb. (2011b). Mohenjo-daro's sewers. In Alfred J. Andrea (Ed.), *World history encyclopedia: Vol. 3* (pp. 121–122). Santa Barbara, CA: ABC-CLIO.

Ministry of Finance, Government of Pakistan. (2010). Pakistan economic survey 2010–11. Retrieved April 12, 2012, from http://finance.gov.pk/survey/chapter_11/10-Education.pdf

The Nation Staff Report. (2012, March 26). CJ announces "green bench" in Supreme Court. Retrieved May 5, 2012, from http://www.nation.com.pk/pakistan-news-newspaper-daily-english-online/national/26-Mar-2012/cj-announces-green-bench-in-supreme-court

The PEW Forum on Religion and Public Life. (2009, October 7). Mapping the global Muslim population: A report on the size and distribution of the world's Muslim population: Sunni and Shia populations. Retrieved April 12, 2012, from http://www.pewforum.org/Muslim/Mapping-the-Global-Muslim-Population(6).aspx

Qadeer, Mohammad Abdul. (2006). *Pakistan: Social and cultural transformations in a Muslim nation*. New York: Routledge.

Shigri, Manzar. (2009, November 12). Pakistan's disputed northern areas go to polls. Retrieved April 10, 2012, from http://www.reuters.com/article/2009/11/12/us-pakistan-election-idUSTRE5AB1ZE20091112

Talbot, Ian. (1998). *Pakistan: A modern history*. New York: St. Martin's Press.

United Nations, Department of Economic and Social Affairs/Population Division. (2011). World population prospects: The 2010, volume II: Demographic profiles: Country profile: Pakistan. Retrieved April 12, 2012, from http://esa.un.org/unpd/wpp/country-profiles/pdf/586.pdf

United Nations Military Observer Group in India and Pakistan (UNMOGIP). (2012). UNMOGIP background. Retrieved April 10, 2012, from http://www.un.org/en/peacekeeping/missions/unmogip/background.shtml

United States Central Intelligence Agency (US CIA). (2012). The world factbook: Pakistan. Retrieved April 17, 2012, from https://www.cia.gov/library/publications/the-world-factbook/geos/pk.html

Weiss, Anita M., & Gilani, S. Zulfiqar. (Eds.). (2001). *Power and civil society in Pakistan*. Karachi, Pakistan: Oxford University Press.

World Health Organization (WHO), & United Nations Children's Fund (UNICEF). (2012a). Joint monitoring programme for water supply and sanitation: Estimates for the use of improved drinking-water sources: Pakistan. Retrieved April 12, 2012, from http://www.wssinfo.org/fileadmin/user_upload/resources/PAK_wat.pdf

World Health Organization (WHO), & United Nations Children's Fund (UNICEF). (2012b). Joint monitoring programme for water supply and sanitation: Estimates for the use of improved sanitation facilities: Pakistan. Retrieved April 12, 2012, from http://www.wssinfo.org/fileadmin/user_upload/resources/PAK_san.pdf

Wright, Pita P. (2009). *The Ancient Indus: Urbanism, economy and society*. Cambridge, UK: Cambridge University Press.

Parks and Preserves

Parks and preserves are central to global conservation efforts, but their establishment and management has undergone significant transformation since their introduction in the late nineteenth century. Management approaches are now more inclusive, taking into account the position of these protected areas in the wider socio-environmental landscape, but also the contributions of a variety of interested parties to ensure the delivery of sustainable conservation and development outcomes.

Biodiversity loss continues to dominate global policy agendas driven by the desire to achieve sustainable development targets for the future. One such target, emphasized at the World Summit on Sustainable Development in 2002, sought to reduce the rate of worldwide biodiversity loss by 2010. This has not been achieved, and the Earth continues to lose biodiversity in all its facets—from genes to functioning ecosystems—and the ecological services they provide (Rands et al. 2010; Butchart et al. 2010). This rate of loss, however, would arguably have been more severe had it not been for the parks and preserves (protected areas) that were established with biodiversity conservation objectives in mind (Gaston et al. 2008, 97; Hoffmann et al. 2010, 1508).

Protected areas are the flagships of global biodiversity conservation efforts and have a long history in both developing and developed nations, including those in Africa and Eurasia. Historically, protected areas were the domain of government, which reinforced Western preservationist ideals through top-down management approaches implemented with little regard for indigenous communities or their relationship with the land, its habitats, and wildlife (Chape, Spalding, and Jenkins 2008; Mulongoy and Chape 2004). During the 1980s and 1990s there was a growing realization that these traditional management practices do not succeed when they are employed unilaterally. This is particularly true in developing nations where local communities have been excluded from conservation initiatives, both geographically and as important stakeholders (Naughton-Treves, Holland, and Brandon 2005, 221, 227). Conservation efforts now rely on cooperation between myriad stakeholders (i.e., those people who have a stake in the outcome of something) to achieve "triple bottom line" sustainability objectives: protecting the environment, boosting economic potential, and maximizing social development. When considering the role of protected areas in achieving such objectives, it is necessary to have an understanding of how these areas emerged and how their management has changed over time.

History

The classical Western preservationist approach to protection is commonly associated with the model used in the United States following the proclamation of Yellowstone National Park in 1872. This model—centrally governed public parks set aside as areas for conservation, wilderness, and aesthetic value—became the paradigm to follow when establishing subsequent parks globally (Mulongoy and Chape 2004, 7, 8). These venues were also set aside for recreation and enjoyment in sparsely populated areas of little commercial value (e.g., Yosemite) (Eagles, McCool, and Haynes 2002, 6), and enhancing the visitor experience remains a central tenet of national parks in the United States to this day. The "national park" model that is now synonymous with this approach rapidly gained momentum across the globe, and national parks were established in Eurasia: various parks in Sweden (by 1909) and in Africa (in 1926) with the proclamation of Kruger National Park in South Africa (Hall-Martin and Carruthers 2003;

Kupper 2009, 60). A key distinction between the US model and African and Eurasian models is that protected areas in Africa and Eurasia were established with a greater emphasis on conservation, and African parks, in particular, serve as a vehicle for establishing sanctuaries for wildlife. In Europe, scientific research has also been advocated as a primary park objective, initially by the Swiss but also, to a lesser degree, in other countries including Germany, Italy, and Russia (Kupper 2009, 64). Although the first African and Eurasian national parks were launched early in the twentieth century, both regions have a much longer history of setting aside areas for protection. In Eurasia, forests were set aside as hunting reserves for the aristocratic elite (e.g., Bialoweiża Forest, a primeval forest in Poland, which was added to the United Nations Educational, Scientific and Cultural Organization's [UNESCO] World Heritage List in 1979). Indigenous communities in Africa lived in tandem with wildlife for centuries, and social hierarchies (e.g., elders, chiefs, and royalty) controlled access to resources, as did cultural taboos (such as avoiding areas because of omens and spiritual beliefs) and nomadic lifestyles. In Africa, only after European colonization and the subsequent widespread utilization and "commodification" of wildlife were formal protected areas established to safeguard dwindling wildlife populations. These interventions often led to the forced relocation of local communities and a subsequent restriction on their access to areas where they had previously engaged in traditional subsistence or pastoralist practices and cultural or spiritual ceremonies (Hall-Martin and Carruthers 2003, 28–29; Turner 2004, 164).

There has been a significant paradigm shift, however, in the principles that underpin protected area governance. Protected areas are no longer seen as areas necessary simply for the protection of biodiversity, but instead aim to meet a variety of sustainable development objectives. These include the recognition of cultural and heritage values, the sustainable use of natural resources (including both consumptive and nonconsumptive uses), benefit sharing, and the active participation of local communities in governance and, specifically, in decision making (Chape, Spalding, and Jenkins 2008, 113). Protected areas also provide a range of ecosystem services essential for human well-being including, for example, the provision of water and the cultural and lifestyle benefits that are gained through the recreational use of those areas. These parks and reserves will also be increasingly important in mitigating the effects of climate change by acting as carbon sinks that "lock up" areas of natural vegetation (Dudley et al. 2010, 28–33). This mitigation effect will increase their value considerably as governments begin to grapple with the ideas of carbon trading and the need to offset carbon emissions. Park boundaries have also become blurred as surrounding landscapes are included as buffer areas or "transfrontier" parks and as management practices increasingly take the wider-reaching environmental and socioeconomic benefits of these protected areas into account.

Status and Management

Globally, the number (and extent) of protected areas continues to increase, and similar trends have been noted in Africa and Eurasia. The patterns of these protected areas, however, differ between these two regions. There are more than 71,000 protected areas that have been issued an International Union for Conservation of Nature (IUCN) designation in Eurasia—with almost 11,000 of these occurring in Russia alone (Protected Planet 2012). In contrast, the African continent has only 1,192 areas classified according to IUCN criteria. The proportion of conserved land is also considerably greater in Europe and Russia, where some 15.5 percent and 10.3 percent (respectively) of the land is protected, whereas in Africa this figure is only 8.1 percent. It is significant, however, that the average size of these protected areas in Africa is thirteen times greater than those in Russia, and more than one hundred times greater than those in the rest of Europe. (See table 1 below.) The existence of small isolated habitat remnants that persist (in "mosaics") in otherwise inhospitable habitats creates a number of problems for conservation. These issues relate to species extinction, minimum viable populations, the movement and migration of species, and the exchange of genetic materials, as well as the increasing erosion of natural habitats from the transitional environments along the edges of these remnants.

The IUCN classifies protected areas in six categories. Category Ia is for strict nature reserves; Ib is for

TABLE 1. Comparative Regional Patterns in Formal Protected Areas

Region	Land Area	Total Area of Protected Areas	Number of Protected Areas	Average Area ± Standard Deviation
Africa	29,955,346	2,447,290 (8.1%)	1,192	2,053 ± 6,668
Russia	16,911,282	1,747,109 (10.3%)	10,953	159 ± 1,776
Europe	6,792,695	1,050,112 (15.5%)	60,317	17.4 ± 263

Note: Areal extents are expressed as square kilometers. Values in parentheses represent the percentage of the region contained within these parks and reserves.

Source: Compiled by author from Protected Planet (2012).

wilderness areas. Category II sites are deemed classical national parks, managed for environmental protection and recreational values, but they are also used to foster ongoing scientific research. Category III areas are natural monuments that protect sites and features of significant natural and/or cultural value. Category IV sites are those that protect, through ongoing management interventions, either species or habitats. Category VI sites are managed-resource protected areas where local communities permit the sustainable use of natural resources in observance of biodiversity protection objectives.

Africa has a high number of sites classified as category II, IV, or VI, while Eurasian sites are predominantly classified under categories III and IV, but the areal extent within each category varies. Furthermore, although there are few strict nature reserves (Ia) and (Ib) in either region, there has been a recent resurgence and interest in establishing wilderness areas in Eurasia, as noted by the actual extent of these areas. (See figure 1 below.)

The initial management goals of many African protected areas were aimed toward species conservation objectives, particularly for wildlife. Some areas were set

Figure 1. Breakdown of IUCN Protected Area Categories

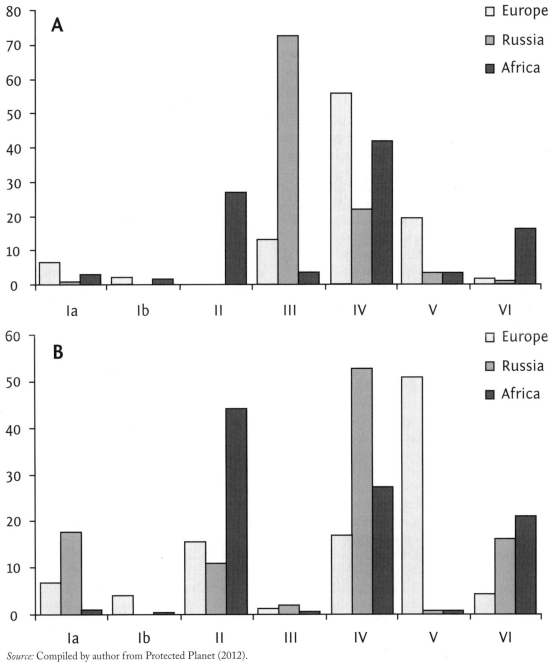

Source: Compiled by author from Protected Planet (2012).

IUCN protected area categories broken down by number (A), and areal extent (B) in Europe, Russia, and Africa. The text above explains the meaning of Ia, Ib, II, III, etc.

aside expressly for the purpose of protecting the last remaining populations of threatened or declining species, such as in the Bontebok, Mountain Zebra, and Addo Elephant national parks in South Africa. To this day, the large mammalian fauna, and in particular the "Big 5" (elephant, rhinoceros, buffalo, lion, and leopard), remain central to conservation efforts implemented throughout Africa on both public and private lands. In Europe, landscape conservation of the region's fauna, flora, and natural habitats was ratified by the 1982 Bern Convention, firmly grounding these aims as ones that specifically address biodiversity management—rather than sustainable development—objectives (Diaz 2010). Conservation efforts in Europe have also adopted a more collaborative approach following the establishment of the EUROPARC Federation in 1973 (EUROPARC Federation 2012). With 440 signatories from 36 countries (as of 2011), this organization effectively guides the implementation of biodiversity conservation strategies throughout Europe.

The early years of park management were also characterized by efforts to maintain these isolated ecological systems in a state of balance. This approach, prevalent in both Eurasia and Africa throughout the mid-to-late twentieth century, has now been superseded by adaptive management principles that recognize the dynamic nature of the environment. This adaptive management philosophy (Du Toit, Rogers, and Biggs 2003; Chape, Spalding, and Jenkins 2008, 132) is better able to assess the potential for the sustainable use of natural resources by using experimental approaches to evaluate the relative costs (e.g., impacts on biodiversity) and benefits (e.g., resources to support local livelihoods) to protected areas and their neighboring communities. This "learning by doing" approach to management also enables protected area agencies to monitor the impact of a range of threats that continue to have an impact upon the natural and cultural values of parks and reserves.

African and Eurasian parks and reserves face many similar global threats including habitat loss and the ongoing fragmentation of remaining habitats, habitat degradation, human population growth, the introduction of alien invasive species, and, of course, climate change. Many of these threats may not be prevalent within parks specifically, but their ongoing impact on surrounding landscapes can have cascading or cumulative effects on park biodiversity. Furthermore, these external threats exacerbate the isolated nature of many protected areas, ultimately affecting the long-term persistence of ecological communities.

In Africa, other threats impacting protected areas include high levels of subsistence harvesting, illegal wildlife poaching, as well as socioeconomic and governance factors such as civil or political unrest and the lack of financial support and human capital necessary for protected-area management (Suich, Child, and Spenceley 2009). Circumventing the sociopolitical issues is challenging but there are ways to minimize environmental threats. One approach is to move away from managing parks and reserves in isolation and to establish networks of protected areas (e.g., linking public and private areas and creating transfrontier parks) as a means to increase connectivity (Chape, Spalding, and Jenkins 2008, 101–106; Worboys, Francis, and Lockwood 2010). Landscape connectivity is achieved through a number of mechanisms, many of which have been used throughout Africa and Eurasia since the early 1990s to achieve sustainable conservation and development objectives.

Management across Landscapes

The overarching message of the fifth World Parks Congress in Durban, South Africa, in 2003 was that of "benefits beyond boundaries," and it recognizes the importance of regarding parks and reserves as part of the broader landscape when addressing issues of connectivity and participatory management. Similar views, voiced at previous congresses in 1982 and 1992, noted that the success and sustainability of protected areas in developing nations, including Africa, were tied to the need to address human concerns. This paradigmatic shift toward "parks for people" has given rise to various integrated conservation and development approaches. Buffer zones, corridors, and the establishment of new protected areas that serve as stepping-stones between larger areas all contribute to improving connectivity and the resilience of protected areas. There are, however, interventions aimed at consolidating expansive landscapes across Africa and Eurasia to achieve sustainable conservation and development goals. These include biosphere reserves, transfrontier / transboundary conservation areas, wilderness areas, as well as community-based natural-resource management initiatives (Brunner 2003; Suich, Child, and Spenceley 2009).

The global UNESCO Man and the Biosphere (MAB) Programme, comprising 580 sites in 114 countries (as of 2011), integrates people with the environment using participatory approaches to achieve its mission "to ensure environmental, economic, and social (including cultural and spiritual) sustainability." The biosphere concept links core biodiversity protection zones to adjacent buffer zones for education, research, and limited tourism. These in turn are surrounded by transition zones containing human settlements, tourism, and other extensive land uses. Africa and Eurasia had 74 and 195 individual biosphere reserves in 33 and 31 countries (respectively) as of 2011 (UNESCO 2011).

Transfrontier / transboundary conservation areas seek to link protected areas that share common international boundaries—which have been historically fragmented because of political circumstances, such as colonization. The philosophy driving the development of transfrontier areas emphasizes the enhanced ecological services that a unified protected area could provide for biodiversity protection through linkages with, for example, biosphere reserves. It also highlights the potential for using these areas as "peace parks" in order to improve international relations. Ideas favoring cross-border cooperation have been in place since the 1940s, but it can take much longer to finalize formal negotiations and agreements. One example of this is the Kgalagadi Transfrontier Park: an agreement between South Africa and Botswana formally opened the park as Africa's first transfrontier area in 2000. Despite its recent formal recognition, this transfrontier park has effectively been operating as a single ecological management unit since a verbal agreement was reached in 1948; formal negotiations commenced only in 1992. Although formal agreements may be somewhat redundant in these situations, in some cases political boundaries hamper transfrontier arrangements. For example, in Eurasia, where political tensions and physical barriers (i.e., fences) separate protected areas, the lack of formal agreements limits potential gains (Brunner 2003, 14).

The establishment of extensive wilderness areas that limit human access in order to protect the natural value of landscapes is gaining momentum throughout Europe through the establishment of the PAN Parks Foundation in 1999 (PAN Parks Foundation 2012). PAN Parks, operating as an independent organization, acts as an intermediary between conservation agencies, governments, local business, nongovernmental organizations, and tourism operators to provide a certification mechanism for establishing extensive wilderness areas. Those areas protect Europe's last remaining undisturbed natural landscapes while still providing sustainable tourism opportunities. The prerequisites for acquiring "wilderness-area" status include having a minimum size of 100 square kilometers, no fragmentation by linear barriers (e.g., roads or fences), and no "extractive use" (e.g., hunting, logging, infrastructure) permitted within the park boundaries. In this way, the wilderness areas conserve not only their natural character but also the ecological functioning of these systems. In 2002, the Fulufjället National Park in Sweden and the Oulanka National Park in Finland were the first European parks to receive PAN Parks' certification. Since then ten additional parks have been certified, and negotiations are ongoing to achieve PAN Parks' goal of setting aside one million hectares of wilderness across Europe (PAN Parks Foundation 2012).

Community-based natural-resource management (CBNRM) programs are commonly associated with Africa. Unfortunately it is impossible to provide a detailed review of the complexities or success of these here. Although there is much criticism of this integrated conservation and development approach (Naughton-Treves, Holland, and Brandon 2005, 239–240), there are many instances where such programs are successful (Suich, Child, and Spenceley 2009). Central to such success is the manner in which the fundamental principles that underlie these community-based operations are implemented. The CBNRM approach is multifaceted and combines economic, political, and institutional goals to collectively improve the productivity of nonagricultural systems through the adoption of higher-value land uses (e.g., wildlife). In Africa, the ability to capitalize on these alternative land use options is often predicated on the devolution of ownership rights of both land and wildlife resources to local communities. This is just a first step, however, because government support for such programs and the collective actions of individuals within communities are also key ingredients for success.

Sustainable Conservation Pathways

Protected areas have a significant role to play in sustainable development. These areas, comprised of natural environments and their constituent species, provide far-reaching social benefits underpinned by the conservation of biodiversity. Where communities actively manage these resources, support for conservation is generated, and this ensures the persistence of species and habitats through sustainable use practices that deliver socioeconomic benefits to communities. Herein exists the opportunity for parks and reserves to capitalize on one of their founding objectives, namely, to set aside areas for public enjoyment. Tourism is an expanding global industry, and nature-based tourism concentrated primarily in parks and reserves is a significant sector. Eurasia and Africa in particular are preferred destinations for nature-based tourists. In Africa the lure of the Big 5 flagship species (elephant, lion, buffalo, rhinoceros, and leopard) continues to attract millions of visitors each year. In Eurasia the natural landscapes and increasing number of designated wilderness areas form a significant component of the nature-based tourism experience. If poorly managed, tourism could threaten the parks and reserves. The sector nevertheless also offers substantial benefits that foster conservation efforts. For example, while some parks and reserves receive substantial funding (through tourism-related activities) in order to manage these areas, for many these finance streams prove to be negligible. There is therefore an opportunity for sustainable tourism to support triple-bottom-line objectives for protected areas in the twenty-first century.

J. Guy CASTLEY
Griffith University

See also Africa (*several articles*); African Union (AU); Biodiversity Conservation; Biological Corridors; Ecotourism; Education, Environmental; European Union (EU); Genetic Resources; Migration (Africa); Public-Private Partnerships (Africa); Travel and Tourism Industry

FURTHER READING

Brunner, Robert. (2003, January–June). European perspective and experience in transboundary cooperation. *Asean Biodiversity, 3*(1&2), 10–15.

Butchart, Stuart H. M., et al. (2010). Global biodiversity: Indicators of recent declines. *Science, 328*(5982), 1164–1168.

Chape, Stuart; Spalding, Mark; & Jenkins, Martin. (2008). *The world's protected areas: Status, values and prospects in the 21st Century* (Prepared by the UNEP World Conservation Monitoring Centre). Berkeley & Los Angeles: University of California Press.

Diaz, Carolina Lasen. (2010). The Bern Convention: 30 years of nature conservation in Europe. *Reciel, 19,* 185–196.

Dudley, Nigel, et al. (2010). *Natural solutions: Protected areas helping people cope with climate change.* Gland, Switzerland; Washington, DC & New York: IUCN-WCPA, TNC, UNDP, WCS, The World Bank & WWF. Retrieved May 9, 2012, from http://awsassets. panda.org/downloads/natural_solutions_climate_climate_2009.pdf

Du Toit, Johan; Rogers, Kevin H.; & Biggs, Harry C. (2003). *The Kruger experience: Ecology and management of savanna heterogeneity.* Washington, DC: Island Press.

Eagles, Paul F. J.; McCool, Stephen F.; & Haynes, Christopher D. A. (2002). *Sustainable tourism in protected areas: Guidelines for planning and management.* Gland, Switzerland & Cambridge, UK: IUCN.

EUROPARC Federation. (2012). Homepage. Retrieved May 9, 2012, from http://www.europarc.org/

Gaston, Kevin J.; Jackson, Sarah F.; Cantú-Salazar, Lisette; & Cruz-Piñón, Gabriela. (2008). The ecological performance of protected areas. *Annual Review of Ecology, Evolution, and Systematics, 39,* 93–113.

Hall-Martin, Anthony, & Carruthers, Jane. (2003). *South African national parks, a celebration: Commemorating the fifth World Parks Congress 2003.* Auckland Park, South Africa: Horst Klemm Publications.

Hoffmann, Michael, et al. (2010). The impact of conservation on the status of the world's vertebrates. *Science, 330*(6010), 1503–1509.

Kupper, Patrick. (2009). Science and the national parks: A transatlantic perspective on the interwar years. *Environmental History, 14,* 58–81.

Mulongoy, Kalemani J., & Chape, Stuart. (2004). *Protected areas and biodiversity, an overview of key issues.* UNEP-WCMC Biodiversity Series No 21. Cambridge, UK: UNEP-WCMC.

Naughton-Treves, Lisa; Holland, Margaret Buck; & Brandon, Katrina. (2005). The role of protected areas in conserving biodiversity and sustaining local livelihoods. *Annual Review of Environment and Resources, 30,* 219–252.

PAN Parks Foundation. (2012). Homepage. Retrieved May 9, 2012, from http://www.panparks.org/

Protected Planet. (2012). Homepage. Retrieved May 9, 2012, from http://www.protectedplanet.net/

Rands, Michael R. W., et al. (2010). Biodiversity conservation: Challenges beyond 2010. *Science, 329*(5997), 298–1303.

Suich, Helen; Child, Brian; with Spenceley, Anna. (Eds.). (2009). *Evolution and innovation in wildlife conservation: Parks and game ranches to transfrontier conservation areas.* London: Earthscan.

Turner, Robin L. (2004). Communities, wildlife conservation, and tourism-based development: Can community-based nature tourism live up to its promise? *Journal of International Wildlife Law and Policy, 7,* 161–182.

United Nations Educational, Scientific and Cultural Organization (UNESCO). (2011). Directory of the World Network of Biosphere Reserves (WNBR). Retrieved May 9, 2012, from http://www.unesco.org/new/en/natural-sciences/environment/ecological-sciences/biosphere-reserves/world-network-wnbr/wnbr/

Worboys, Graeme L.; Francis, Wendy L.; & Lockwood, Michael. (2010). *Connectivity conservation management: A global guide.* London: Earthscan.

Public-Private Partnerships (Africa)

Since the 2002 Johannesburg World Summit on Sustainable Development, public-private partnerships (PPPs) have emerged as preferred instruments to implement internationally agreed-upon sustainability goals. Recent evidence suggests these new mechanisms of global governance do not meet the expectations placed on them and are often overrepresented by traditional international agencies. PPPs operating in Africa are also subject to this criticism, but have a higher match than most between function and actual output.

Public-private partnerships for sustainable development (i.e., collaborative agreements between public, private for-profit, and private nonprofit actors) are often hailed as a vital new element of the emerging system of global sustainability governance. In policy and academic debates alike, partnerships are promoted as a solution to deadlocked intergovernmental negotiations, to ineffective treaties and overly bureaucratic international organizations, to power-based state policies, to corruption within elite organizations, and to many other real or perceived current problems, including stagnant economic development, environmental degradation, and health-related challenges. Public-private partnerships (PPPs) are often seen as innovative forms of governance because, at least in theory, they were established with the intention of increasing the participation of the private sector in implementing global sustainability goals. They are now ubiquitous.

Emergence of PPPs

PPPs for sustainable development were highly promoted at the 2002 Johannesburg World Summit on Sustainable Development (WSSD), where they emerged as a "type 2 outcome" (a voluntary partnership initiative), alongside the more traditional outcomes of intergovernmental diplomatic processes ("type 1 outcomes"). Because the governments participating in the 2002 summit could not agree on any new binding commitments, the idea of partnerships was introduced to effectively implement those commitments on which the international community *had already* agreed, such as the commitments comprising the Millennium Development Goals (which include specific targets and timetables for issues such as the eradication of poverty and provision of access to clean drinking water), and Agenda 21 (the blueprint for sustainable development negotiated in 1992 at the United Nations Summit for Environment and Development in Rio de Janeiro). As of August 2011, 348 partnerships for sustainable development had been registered with the United Nations Commission on Sustainable Development (UNCSD), the administrative body in charge of the partnership process.

The Promise of Partnerships

Evidence from a recent quantitative analysis of all UNCSD-registered partnerships for sustainable development suggests that these new mechanisms of global governance do not meet the high expectations that have been placed on them (Pattberg et al. 2012). While individual partnerships are highly effective and make important contributions to sustainable development, questions remain regarding the performance of the nearly 350 partnerships that were established around and after the 2002 Johannesburg summit. Approximately 37 percent of all WSSD partnerships do not generate any traceable output (Szulecki, Pattberg, and Biermann 2011, 719). In addition, the partnerships that are active do not seem to close

THE RENEWABLE ENERGY AND ENERGY EFFICIENCY PARTNERSHIP (REEEP)

The Renewable Energy and Energy Efficiency Partnership (REEEP) is a prime example of the larger universe of public-private partnerships devised and established around the 2002 Johannesburg summit. As an open-ended initiative to facilitate multistakeholder cooperation (i.e., cooperation involving a variety of interested parties) in the renewable energy, climate change, and sustainable development sector, REEEP is a cooperative platform for more than 3,500 members and 250 registered partners, among them 45 governmental actors (both national and subnational), including all of the G7 states (states belonging to the international finance group consisting of the finance ministers from Canada, France, Germany, Italy, Japan, the United Kingdom, and the United States), 180 private entities, and 6 international organizations.

REEEP represents a market-oriented group of actors working for sustainable development. Its inten-

tion is to facilitate the exchange of technologies, identify and remove policy and regulatory barriers in the renewable energy market (and also create such markets in the first place if they do not exist), and provide information for various stakeholders, including the general public. The partnership is foremost a platform for communication between the partners, and a means to streamline the idea of renewable energy into efforts of informing and educating the wider public. It is therefore both a deregulatory and a regulatory enterprise—aimed at the removal of state-level and regional barriers for the renewable energy market, yet at the same time devoted to regulation and rule setting within this relatively new and rapidly growing sector. The membership remains open, and the number of partners is constantly growing.

Source: The Renewable Energy & Energy Efficiency Partnership (REEEP). (2012). Homepage. Retrieved April 24, 2012, from http://www.reeep.org/

existing governance gaps (Haas 2004) and do not address the core functions they were originally charged with addressing and for which they were believed to be advantageously poised, namely: to initiate new global governance norms in areas where governments fail to take action; to help implement existing intergovernmental regulations more effectively; and to increase the inclusiveness and participation in global governance by bringing in actors that have so far been more or less marginalized.

Partnerships in Africa

This general assessment also holds true for partnerships active in Africa, but with a number of notable differences. African partnerships comprise a higher number of partners on average (33.6) than do other UNCSD-registered partnerships (24.8). This trend is even more pronounced in sub-Saharan Africa (SSA), where the average partnership comprises 37 partners (Pattberg et al. 2012).

There are also notable differences between the geographic scopes of UNCSD-registered partnerships: those that implement their activities in SSA are more frequently global in scope (67 percent) than the average.

They are less often regional (28 percent) or local (5 percent). (See figure 1 on page 249.) Outside Africa, the proportion of partnerships with a global focus is lower (42 percent), while the percentage of partnerships with regional or subregional focus is considerably higher (52 percent). This observation may appear to be counterintuitive, as one might expect to see more regional or locally oriented partnerships in a region with (1) distinct regional and local characteristics and (2) a history of persistent development challenges.

Against this background, it is interesting to analyze the involvement of state actors in African partnerships. It is clear that African governments show significant interest in partnerships for sustainable development. Among partnerships implementing their activities in continental Africa, 54 percent have at least one African state partner. The rate of government involvement in partnerships for sustainable development implementing activities in South America, by contrast, is lower (38 percent), as it is in those implementing activities in states that are members of non-OECD (Organization for Economic Co-operation and Development) Asian partnerships (39 percent). (See figure 2 on page 249.)

The lead partners (organizations that take responsibility for coordinating partnership activities) most

Figure 1. Geographical Scope of Partnerships

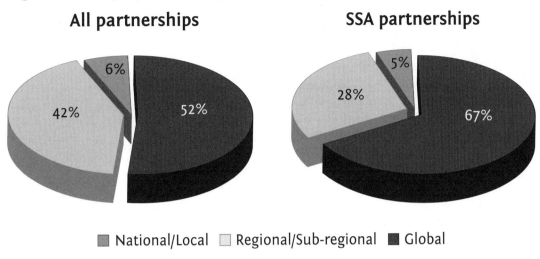

All partnerships **SSA partnerships**

■ National/Local ■ Regional/Sub-regional ■ Global

Source: Pattberg et al. (2012, 139).

Partnerships for sustainable development that implement their activities in sub-Saharan Africa (SSA) are more often global in scope than other partnerships.

Figure 2. Presence of State Partners in Partnerships Implementing Activities in Their Own Region

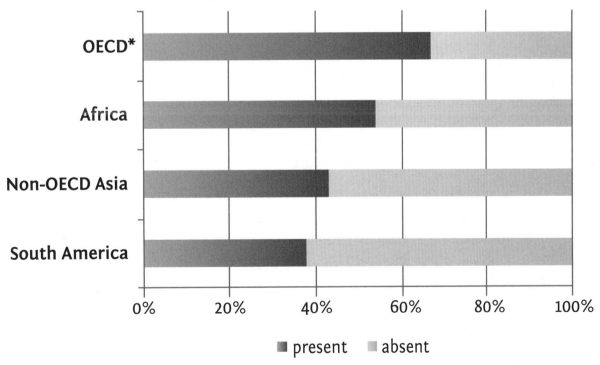

■ present ■ absent

*Organisation for Economic Co-operation and Development (OECD)

Source: Pattberg et al. (2012, 141).

The rate of government involvement in partnerships for sustainable development is highest in OECD (Organisation for Economic Co-operation and Development) member countries and lowest in South America.

frequently associated with African partnerships are international organizations such United Nations (UN) agencies. Considering this fact within the context of the robust involvement of governments in partnerships for sustainable development calls into question the likelihood that partnerships will bring new and hitherto marginalized actors (such as workers, youth, indigenous people, and women) to the fore in implementing sustainability goals, as had been originally intended. Rather, it seems that African partnerships are less public-private in nature than much of the general partnership rhetoric assumes.

Partnership Issue Areas

A partnership's potential contribution to sustainable development is often reflected in the concrete issue areas and policy domains in which it is active. Partnerships implementing action in SSA do not differ from other observed partnerships in terms of the issues on which they focus, except in four areas. Three of these (poverty, agriculture, and energy) are more popular among SSA partnerships than they are among other partnerships; a fourth area (disaster management) is less popular. (See figure 3 below.)

Figure 3. Proportions of Partnerships According to Issues in Sub-Saharan Africa and Worldwide

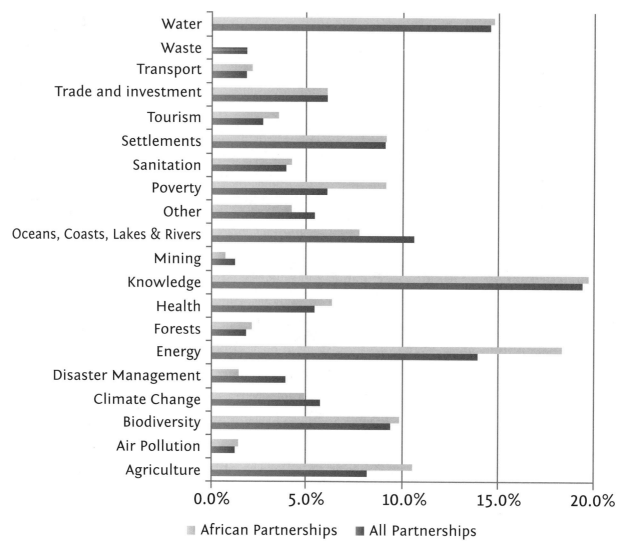

Source: Pattberg et al. (2012, 154).

Focal issues of partnerships active in sub-Saharan Africa are similar, overall, to those of partnerships elsewhere, although three areas (poverty, agriculture, and energy) are more popular among SSA partnerships than they are among other partnerships; a fourth area (disaster management) is less popular.

Partnerships established during or after the Johannesburg summit do not appear to reflect the priority concerns of African countries, such as health and adaptation issues (as, for example, stated in the Johannesburg Plan of Action, the key policy document that resulted from the 2002 summit). The explanation for the apparent mismatch lies in the global nature of most partnerships that have an African state as a country of implementation—they were set up to address sustainability in a broad sense; they were not established to address the policy priorities of African countries. This underscores the criticism that partnerships "do not necessarily match the priorities set out in the multilateral process" (Hale and Mauzerall 2004, 234) and do not contribute effectively to the implementation of widely agreed upon sustainability goals.

Are Partnerships Effective?

One way to assess whether partnerships for sustainable development are effectively addressing sustainability problems is to measure their output. The concept of output refers to the concrete and tangible results that a partnership produces. This includes organizing formal activities, training people, setting up offices and administrative structures, reporting and monitoring partnership activities, and producing and disseminating knowledge and information (for example through publications, websites, or other media). Partnerships that implement activities in an SSA country have a higher rate of output than the average. (See figure 4 below.) This is also true for African partnerships as a whole, but

is most pronounced in partnerships operating in SSA countries.

While it is possible to measure the activities of partnerships through output analyses, it is also possible to evaluate whether these activities are fulfilling the stated goals and functions of the partnerships. The observed output of a partnership, matched with its assumed function, is a measure of the fit between function (what the partnership proposes to do) and output (what the partnership actually does). Where the two do not match, the likelihood that a defined sustainability goal will be successfully implemented is questionable. Partnerships involving African countries do not have a lesser fit between function and output than the average sample. The fit between output and function among SSA countries only is even higher: 65.5 percent of relevant SSA partnerships fulfill some or all of their stated functions, against 57 percent of all observed partnerships. In comparison to other regions of the world, Africa as a whole fares better than most, although the highest percentage of partnerships fulfilling all their functions is found in South America.

Outlook for African Partnerships

Partnerships for sustainable development active in Africa are not different from the close to 350 partnerships that have emerged as a result of the 2002 WSSD in Johannesburg. While African partnerships share with most other partnerships for sustainable development a general mismatch between pressing problems and actual issue areas of implementation, and an overrepresentation

Figure 4. Comparative Proportions of Output for Sub-Saharan Africa and Worldwide Partnerships

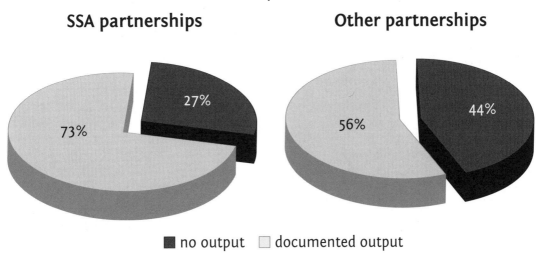

Source: Pattberg et al. (2012, 144).

The tangible results produced by partnerships in sub-Saharan Africa are higher than those produced by other partnerships.

of traditional international actors such as governments and international organizations, African partnerships have a slightly higher fit between function and output. This high fit between purported function and actual activity is good news for those that believe that the urgent challenges of transforming our unsustainable lifestyle into a truly sustainable one cannot be met without innovative governance instruments such as partnerships for sustainable development.

Philipp PATTBERG
VU University Amsterdam

See also Africa (*several articles*); African Union (AU); Biodiversity Conservation; Climate Change Refugees (Africa); Conflict Minerals; Corporate Accountability (Africa); Diet and Nutrition; Disaster Risk Management; Ecotourism; Immigrants and Refugees; International Conflict Resolution; Microfinance; Migration (Africa); Mining (Africa); Parks and Preserves; Rule of Law (Africa); Rural Development; World Bank

FURTHER READING

Biermann, Frank; Chan, Man-san; Mert, Ayşem; & Pattberg, Philipp. (2007). Multi-stakeholder partnerships for sustainability: Does the promise hold? In Pieter Glasbergen, Frank Biermann & Arthur P. J. Mol (Eds.), *Partnerships, governance and sustainable development: Reflections on theory and practice* (pp. 239–260). Cheltenham, UK: Edward Elgar.

Haas, Peter M. (2004). Addressing the global governance deficit. *Global Environmental Politics, 4*(4), 1–15.

Hale, Thomas N., & Mauzerall, Denise L. (2004). Thinking globally and acting locally: Can the Johannesburg partnerships coordinate action on sustainable development? *The Journal of Environment & Development, 13*(3), 220–239.

Pattberg, Philipp. (2010). Public-private partnerships in global climate governance. *Wiley Interdisciplinary Review: Climate Change, 1*(2), 279–287.

Pattberg, Philipp; Biermann, Frank; Mert, Ayşem; & Chan, Sander. (2012). *Public-private partnerships for sustainable development: Emergence, influence, and legitimacy.* Cheltenham, UK: Edward Elgar.

Szulecki, Kacper; Pattberg, Philipp; & Biermann, Frank. (2011). Explaining variation in the performance of transnational energy partnerships. *Governance: An International Journal of Policy, Administration, and Institutions, 24*(4), 713–736.

Rhine River

The Rhine River is the third-busiest river in the world, transporting more than 200 million metric tons of freight annually and traveling through six countries. With many important settlements on its banks, the river became increasingly polluted as industrialization increased. Initiatives such as the Rhine Action Programme (1987–2000) and its continuing body, Rhine 2020, have seen cooperation between these countries and much improvement in the river.

The Rhine originates in the Swiss Alps and flows in a northwestwardly direction to the North Sea via Switzerland, Liechtenstein, Austria, Germany, France, and the Netherlands. It is 1,250 kilometers long and has a discharge of 2,200 cubic meters per second at its delta. Its watershed is 185,000 square kilometers, over half of which lies in Germany. The Aare, Neckar, Main, Mosel, and Ruhr are its principal tributaries.

The ancient Celts named the river "Renos," from which "Rhenus" (Latin), "Rhein" (German), "Rhin" (French), "Rijn" (Dutch), and "Rhine" (English) are all derived. It has been a trade route since Roman times, although the reefs and cliffs of the Rhenish Slate Mountains (between Mainz and Bonn) acted as a navigational hindrance, as did the proliferation of German principalities and tollbooths during the medieval era. Dutch and British visitors immortalized the river in poems and paintings in the seventeenth century, giving birth to Rhine Romanticism and a still-thriving tourist industry.

In 1815, the Congress of Vienna established the International Commission for Rhine Navigation to promote flood control projects as well as the removal of in-channel hazards such as islands, reefs, and curves. The river has been under a free-trade regime since ratification of the Mannheim Acts in 1868. The coal-rich Ruhr region jump-started industrial growth on the Rhine after 1850, especially in the iron, steel, and chemical sectors. Hydroelectric dams allowed industrialization to spread upstream to the Swiss-German and French-German borders at the beginning of the twentieth century. After 1945, oil from the Middle East turned the Rotterdam harbor at the Rhine mouth into a major refining and petrochemical site. Today, the Rhine transports more than 200 million metric tons of coal, steel, chemicals, and other freight annually, making it the third-busiest river (behind the Yangzi [Chang] and the Mississippi) in the world (*People's Daily* 2006; *Asia Times* 2006).

Economic progress came at a high environmental price, and by the 1970s the Rhine channel was so polluted with chemicals and salts that it was commonly referred to as "Europe's most romantic sewer." The number and variety of plant and animal species living in or near the river had plummeted. Especially hard hit were migratory fish, notably salmon. In 1986, a fire at a Sandoz chemical facility in Basel, Switzerland, resulted in the accidental release of agricultural chemicals into the river, killing flora and fauna for hundreds of kilometers downstream. Equally troublesome were the four "hundred-year" floods (so called because floods of that magnitude are supposed to happen only once every hundred years) of 1983, 1988, 1993, and 1994, caused as much by ill-conceived land-reclamation and channel-straightening projects as by unseasonable weather.

In 1963, the riparian states established the International Commission for the Protection of the Rhine to address the river's many environmental problems. Water quality has vastly improved since then, and the channel is once again capable of supporting most life forms, a remarkable turnabout given the river's heavy usage. The large number of dams, factories, cities, and other human-built fixtures along its channel and banks, however, have hampered efforts to restore the Rhine's former floodplains and migratory routes. As long as the river remains Europe's premier navigational route, only a partial restoration will be feasible.

The Rhine Action Programme was launched in 1987. It was also called "Salmon 2000," in the hope that salmon would return to the river by that year. Never part of European Union law, the program involved the cooperation of the countries that border its route and was implemented and monitored by the International Commission for the Protection of the Rhine. The program has been very successful, with a 70–100 percent reduction in most pollutants. Since the late 1990s, salmon have also returned to the Rhine (ICPR 2012a). Levels of pollutants such as lead, ammonium, and phosphorus have sharply declined from their 1970s high levels, and numbers of trout, shad, sea bream, and other fish are up (Bernstein 2006). The ecological communities that inhabit the Rhine have also increased in recent years, and river meadows, or alluvial plains, are also increasing. Rhine 2020, a new program, was launched in 2001 to build on the sustainability successes of the countries involved. One of its core aims is not only to increase salmon numbers in the Rhine (as was the plan with Salmon 2020) but to make the salmon populations self-sustaining (when reintroduced, the salmon needed the help of humans to survive). Another aim is to have an action plan for floods so that people and communities can be better prepared for when they happen. Further improvement of water quality and groundwater protection are other important aims of Rhine 2020 (ICPR 2012b).

Mark CIOC
University of California, Santa Cruz

See also Congo (Zaire) River; Danube River; European Union (EU); France; Germany; Indus River; Nile River; Transboundary Water Issues; Volga River

FURTHER READING

Asia Times. (2006, January 11). Yangtze now world's busiest freshwater route. Retrieved May 17, 2012, from http://www.atimes.com/atimes/China_Business/HA11Cb03.html

Bernstein, Richard. (2006, April 20). Rhine has fish again, but it's not as it was. Retrieved April 16, 2012, from http://www.nytimes.com/2006/04/20/world/europe/20iht-journal.html

Cioc, Mark. (2002). *The Rhine: An eco-biography, 1815–2000*. Seattle: University of Washington Press.

Clapp, Edwin Jones. (1911). *The navigable Rhine*. Boston: Houghton Mifflin.

Heinberg, Heinz; Mayr, Alois; & de Lang, Norbert. (Eds.). (1996). *The Rhine Valley: Urban, harbour and industrial development and environmental problems*. Leipzig, Germany: Institut für Länderkunde.

International Commission for the Protection of the Rhine (ICPR). (2012a, February 14). History: Balance of the Rhine Action Programme (1986–2000). Retrieved April 16, 2012, from http://www.iksr.org/index.php?id=165&L=3&cHash=455fdab52ce6eafbf6f72632159564bf&no_cache=1&sword_list%5B0%5D=rhine&sword_list%5B1%5D=action&sword_list%5B2%5D=programme

International Commission for the Protection of the Rhine (ICPR). (2012b, February 14). Rhine 2020: Program on the sustainable development of the Rhine. Retrieved April 16, 2012, from http://www.iksr.org/index.php?id=30&L=3

People's Daily. (2006, January 6). Yangtze River becomes world's busiest freshwater route. Retrieved May 17, 2012, from http://english.peopledaily.com.cn/200601/06/eng20060106_233300.html

Rees, Goronwy. (1967). *The Rhine*. New York: Putnam.

Berkshire's authors and editors welcome questions, comments, and corrections. Send your emails about the *Berkshire Encyclopedia of Sustainability* in general or this volume in particular to: sustainability.updates@berkshirepublishing.com

Rule of Law (Africa)

Laws are the rules that bind societies and governments. They are designed to protect the rights of the people and facilitate the fair and equitable use of resources. Laws are not infallible, however, and are subject to problems of enforcement and interpretation. Environmental laws are especially vulnerable to these issues because they are often perceived to run counter to the objectives of economic development. These challenges are particularly acute in much of Africa, because a wide variety of local legal systems have yet to be unified under national and international systems, and many African legal systems lack effective enforcement capacity.

The rule of law, in its most basic form, is the principle that no one is above the law. It follows that law applies equally to everyone and that state authority may be exercised only in accordance with due process. Laws safeguard individuals against abuses, which may arise from the exercise of unrestrained power and from arbitrary governance.

The rule of law is premised on the existence of a transparent legal system, key components of which are an independent judiciary, a legislative body that follows a clearly defined procedure, and a transparent and accountable prosecution process.

There is some scholarly debate as to whether economic and social development and environmental protection are premised on the existence of the rule of law or whether economic development may lead to the development of the rule of law. This concern is particularly important in the Africa, in which many countries are characterized by uneven economic development, political instability, widespread exploitation of natural resources, and limited transparency.

The Development of National Legal Systems

Africa is often divided into North Africa and sub-Saharan Africa. States in North Africa, many of which are largely desert states, typically have a history of Arab and/or Islamic culture and legal systems, often with French colonial influences. The geography, cultures, and legal systems of the sub-Saharan African states vary widely. Many states are former colonies of Great Britain, France, Belgium, Portugal, the Netherlands, and Germany, and legal systems often reflect these colonial origins. The colonial legacy has had a significant impact on the rule of law. At the date of independence (generally in the 1950s and 1960s), most African states had limited experience of self-governance and therefore had limited legislative capacity. Generally, common law legal systems were retained in former British colonies such as Ghana, Kenya, and Sierra Leone, and civil law legal systems were retained in the former colonies of civil law states, including Angola, Namibia, and the Democratic Republic of the Congo.

Many traditional authority structures that existed, in some form, for centuries have been retained in or restored to post-independence legal systems. In several countries, customary courts were abolished by statute but later recognized constitutionally (such as in Ethiopia), reorganized into local or community courts (such as in Kenya, Malawi, and Sierra Leone), or integrated into state law (as in Uganda).

In recent years, sharia courts have been established in a number of African countries with significant Muslim populations, including Ethiopia, Gambia, Ghana, Kenya, Libya, Mali, Nigeria, Senegal, Somalia, Sudan, and Tanzania. In some countries such as Ethiopia, Kenya, and Sudan, these courts are constitutionally created or recognized. In others like Ghana, sharia law is applied in customary courts under the broad category of customary law.

Although each African state has its own legal system, there are common features. In almost all the states of sub-Saharan African, the constitution has been redrafted at least twice since independence. Each iteration is designed to better reflect the sovereign status of the state, but the body of colonial law has generally evolved little since independence. Instead, new rights (such as human rights) and obligations (like environmental protection) have in general been simply grafted onto the existing body of law. There are three main areas of recent legislative activity. First, commercial codes and laws are often taken, in whole or in part, from the body of law of former colonial powers or from new donor nations. Second, laws on new or evolving areas of criminal activity such as terrorism, narcotics, or money laundering are also often taken from donor nations. Third, draft laws protecting the status of citizens in certain regards, such as women's property rights or sexual violence, are often provided by international nongovernmental organizations (NGOs) or other donors and are based on templates that may not be particularly adapted to local conditions. This may result in limited or ineffective implementation of new law.

It is exceptionally difficult to measure and thus evaluate the rule of law. One NGO, the World Justice Project (WJP), has developed a Rule of Law Index, which is a quantitative assessment tool designed to evaluate compliance with the rule of law on the basis of nine criteria. The 2011 version of the WJP Index included sixty-five countries, but because only six of those countries are African, the data are limited (WJP 2011). Further, although failed states like Somalia may lack any effective governance, there are other states such as the Democratic Republic of the Congo that appear to have the legal and political institutions but where implementation of law may be very limited. Some states (such as Liberia) depend on the presence of a United Nations peacekeeping mission to maintain the rule of law, while others like South Sudan (formed in July 2011) are young, fragile, and at a very early stage of development. Others have long histories of relative stability but have significant disparities in income distribution and corresponding social and environmental challenges. The Republic of South Africa, for example, has a long established, mature, and sophisticated legal system, a highly educated judiciary, and law schools of global significance, but also has significant rural and urban poverty as well as high rates of urban crime. Nigeria, for example, has immense oil reserves and well developed public services such as education and health, but also has a particularly high level of systemic corruption. Exploitation of natural resources is widespread throughout much of Africa, both by subsistence communities who depend on those resources for survival and by large multinational corporations who typically export large volumes of timber, oil, or minerals to foreign markets, often in breach of (poorly enforced) national laws. As demand for energy continues to increase, it appears likely this will continue.

Access to Justice

In some African countries, access to justice may be difficult or impossible. Police, prosecution authorities, and courts may be located in inaccessible locations and/or may operate in a language that the population does not understand. Law libraries may not be readily accessible, literacy rates may be low, and law may not be available in written form. Public services salaries for police, prosecutors, or judges may be low, in which case public servants may be susceptible to undocumented capital flows.

Many donor programs like the World Bank, United States Agency for International Development (USAID), and United Kingdom Department for International Development (DFID) focus on the development of the rule of law. Typically, programs include monitoring (including the observation of trials), capacity building (such as judicial training), and legislative improvement (including the codification of property rights). Although it is difficult to evaluate the impact of individual programs, it is clear that effective law enforcement is premised on the existence of stable legal and political institutions. Legislation alone will not prevent abuse of power that, in turn, often leads to human rights violations and environmental degradation; if properly used, however, law is an important tool in the fight. A comprehensive solution will require societal change, financial resources, technological innovation, improved surveillance techniques, and above all, political will at national and international levels. If law, either national or international, is to provide a realistic foundation for its own implementation, it must provide for consultative or participatory approaches, it must facilitate transparency and accountability, and it must establish processes and requirements that are feasible and achievable.

The Westphalian legal order, which was based on independent, sovereign, and territorially defined states, allowed each state to pursue its own interests within its sovereign territory and gave each state equality within the global system. International law emerged as the rules and principles that govern relations between states. That classical view of international law distinguished clearly between international and domestic law. Public international law, the domain of sovereign states, provided a body of customary law and a series of binding instruments, the purpose of which was to govern relationships between states. National law governed all matters within states. Jurisdiction to make and enforce national law derived from the legitimacy of the state. In states where that legitimacy is lacking, such as dictatorships and failed states, law may have limited or no legitimacy and thus there may be little or no effective rule of law.

Challenges

First, according to the World Bank, good governance and the rule of law are central to economic and social development. Both are also prerequisites to the effective implementation of sustainable environmental policies. Well-drafted legislation with widespread support can further good governance by establishing stable regimes where political and economic security may develop.

Second, the World Bank has identified corruption as the single greatest obstacle to economic and social development. According to the Bank, corruption undermines development by distorting the rule of law and weakening the institutional foundation on which economic growth and environmental protection depends. Corruption has a particularly strong effect on the poor, who are hardest hit by economic decline, are most reliant on the provision of public services, and are least capable of paying the extra costs associated with bribery, fraud, and the misappropriation of economic privileges. Because corruption undermines economic development and reduces donor assistance available to end users, eliminating corruption is critical to the furtherance of the rule of law. Corruption limits the effectiveness of government action in almost every area of political life and reduces the resources available for economic and social development as well as environmental protection. Consequently, governments are unlikely to be able to implement even the most basic law if the regime is disabled by corruption on a large scale. In 2003, the United Nations Convention on Corruption was adopted by the United Nations General Assembly. There are also a number of regional anticorruption instruments, each of which exists independently of other treaties and each of which has varying degrees of effectiveness and success. To date, no single formula has been identified, and it is unlikely that the existence of a law against corruption would significantly reduce corruption in certain states unless additional anticorruption measures were also implemented.

Third, closely related to the issues of good governance and corruption are transparency and accountability. Transparency demands that the system or process be open to public scrutiny, either directly or via an institution or process to which there is public access. Accountability requires that reasons be given for government decisions and that mechanisms exist by which those decisions may be reviewed. As accountability increases, the cost to public officials of making decisions that benefit their private interests (such as unlawful sale of endangered fauna, the protection of which they are theoretically responsible for,

to a foreign buyer) at the expense of the broader public interest also increases. This provides a disincentive for them to continue with corrupt practices. The level of accountability depends largely on the effectiveness of sanctions and the capacity of accountability institutions to monitor the actions, decisions, and private interests of public officials.

One NGO, Transparency International (TI), works at the national and international level to curb corruption. TI was founded in 1993 by a small group experienced in business and international development. It now has an international administrative department and more than ninety national chapters. At the international level, TI raises awareness about the damaging effects of corruption, advocates policy reform, works toward the implementation of international conventions, and subsequently monitors compliance by governments, corporations, and banks. At the national level, chapters work to increase levels of accountability and transparency by monitoring the performance of key institutions and pressing for necessary reforms in a nonparty political manner. TI produces an annual global corruption report, together with regional reports. These reports identify standards and practices throughout the world and suggest areas in which concealment is most likely to occur.

According to TI, one of the most powerful tools for combating corruption is access to information, or transparency. International commitments implemented by national governments are usually subject to transparency and accountability via the mechanisms of administrative law, such as freedom-of-information legislation or appeal and judicial review; to whatever extent those mechanisms apply in each country. In reality, it may be difficult to detect irregularities in government processes in certain African countries because not every country has comprehensive administrative law, and even where such law exists, it may not be implemented uniformly or at all. Further, transparency may offer a solution to such disparate problems as environmental degradation, money laundering, financial volatility, and corruption. It requires power to induce disclosure or to restructure incentives, however. Revelation of information shifts power from the former holders of secrets to the newly informed, and these relationships may create social and/or political instability in already fragile regions.

Fourth, central to the political agendas of many African countries, international organizations, and donor agencies is the reduction of poverty. It appears that increasing access to preventative health services, education (particularly girls' education), and vocational training are key to economic and social development. Such economic and social development may be the catalyst for better implementation of the rule of law and corresponding improvements in environmental protection. It may therefore be more effective for donors to focus on policies to stimulate economic and social development than on policies that aim to strengthen the rule of law but do not provide for poverty reduction.

Fifth, democracy can promote compliance with national and international law, but it does not necessarily do so. Stable democracies may foster respect for the rule of law, encourage public participation in national and international affairs, have an independent legal system with effective enforcement mechanisms, and be characterized by transparency and accountability at all levels of government. Not all democracies (such as in Liberia), however, are stable. Not all stable democracies have the financial resources necessary to implement their international agreements (such as in Seychelles), and in stable democracies in which those resources do exist, public opinion may not support international commitments. Consequently, national commitment to the implementation of national law, together with the capacity to implement that commitment, is more important than the precise form of government.

Sixth, it is important to avoid legislation that overreaches. In developing countries, overreaching tends to occur in three areas: provisions may exceed capacity for implementation (i.e., there may be an imbalance between the activities, procedures, and institutional arrangements prescribed by legislation and the human and financial resources available to implement that legislation nationally, locally, or both); provisions may exceed what is necessary to achieve reasonable and legitimate objectives (i.e., legislation may prohibit activities that are unrelated to the goal of the legislation); and provisions may exceed what is socially acceptable (i.e., legislation may prohibit local practices and norms and may require immediate social and institutional change for insufficient reason or without providing incentives to facilitate that change). For example, in several East African countries, legislation has restricted activities that may be undertaken in forests but has not defined *forest* or has defined the term so broadly that the definition bears little resemblance to what exists on the ground. In some jurisdictions *forest* includes all land that is not privately occupied, marginal land, or both, and the categorization of land as forest may be a matter of administrative convenience or a political tool for national or local bureaucracies. This may limit the land-use options of local people, undermine local traditions and practices, and threaten already fragile livelihoods. It may also require that limited government resources be divided among many areas, in consequence of which none will receive the resources it requires for adequate land management.

The balance of the three elements overreaching will be different in each location where legislation is implemented. Consequently, legislation, which is to be implemented in a variety of locations each with different characteristics, must be designed in a manner that allows for regional variation. It should, for example, be drafted by lawyers who have at least some knowledge of the political, economic, and social conditions of each location and who are familiar with the resources that will be available in each location to support implementation. Legislation that overreaches is not inherently flawed, because it has an aspirational value, but aspirational legislation is almost impossible to implement. Because ineffective implementation is likely to squander scarce resources and may also cast doubt on the legitimacy of the legislature, it is better to draft more restricted legislation that can be implemented rather than broader legislation that may be ignored.

Prospects

Sub-Saharan Africa is one of the fastest-growing regions in the world. Seven of the world's ten fastest-growing economies are in that region (Stromsem et al. 2009). Foreign direct investment in Africa approaches US$80 billion per year, trade has tripled over the last decade, and twenty new democracies have been established since 1989 (Stromsem et al. 2009). Yet the rule of law is not universally recognized, and there are significant disparities in economic and social development as well as environmental protection. Approximately 75 percent of Africans live on less than US$2 per day, nearly half of all child deaths globally occur in Africa, and some regions remain critically unstable (Stromsem et al. 2009). Liberia, Africa's oldest democracy, currently depends on a United Nations peacekeeping mission for stability and was, for many years, ruled by Charles Taylor, a dictator currently on trial at the International Criminal Court for crimes against humanity. Nigeria had a strong infrastructure and vibrant trading ports but is now one of the most corrupt states globally. The Republic of South Africa has world class universities, law and medical schools, but also has one of the highest rates of HIV/AIDS globally. Tremendous economic progress is being made; until the rule of law is not simply established, however, but also nurtured and allowed to develop in a manner that corresponds with local social and economic conditions throughout the African continent, it is likely that environmental degradation and threats to, and breaches of, the peace will continue.

Catherine P. MacKENZIE
University of Cambridge

See also Africa (*several articles*); African Union (AU); Climate Change Refugees (Africa); Corporate Accountability (Africa); Education, Higher (Africa); International Conflict Resolution; Mining (Africa); Public-Private Partnerships (Africa); Rule of Law (European Union); Transboundary Water Issues; Water Use and Rights (Africa); Water Use and Rights (Middle East and North Africa); World Bank

FURTHER READING

African Commission on Human and Peoples' Rights. (2012). Homepage. Retrieved August 15, 2012, from http://www.achpr.org/

African Development Bank (ADB). (2012). Homepage. Retrieved August 15, 2012, from www.afdb.org

African Human Security Initiative. (n.d.). Homepage. Retrieved August 15, 2012, from http://www.africanreview.org/

African Legal Information Institute (ALII). (n.d.). Homepage. Retrieved August 15, 2012, from http://www.africanlii.org/

African Union (AU). (n.d.). Homepage. Retrieved August 15, 2012, from http://www.au.int/en/

Africa Peace Forum (APFO). (2012). Homepage. Retrieved August 15, 2012, from http://www.amaniafrika.org/

Brierly, J. L. (1963). *The law of nations: An introduction to the international law of peace* (6th ed.). New York & Oxford: Oxford University Press.

Cassese, Antonio. (2008). *International criminal law* (2nd ed.). Oxford, UK: Oxford University Press.

Council of Europe. (1990, November 8). Convention on Laundering, Search, Seizure and Confiscation of the Proceeds from Crime. Retrieved August 15, 2012, from http://conventions.coe.int/Treaty/en/Treaties/Html/141.htm

Council of Europe. (1999, January 27). Criminal Law Convention on Corruption. Retrieved August 15, 2012, from http://conventions.coe.int/Treaty/en/Treaties/Html/173.htm

Food and Agriculture Organization of the United Nations (FAO). (2001). *Trends in forestry law in Europe and Africa* (FAO Legislative Study Number 72). Rome: FAO.

Fox, Gregory H., & Roth, Brad R. (Eds.). (2000). *Democratic governance and international law.* Cambridge, UK: Cambridge University Press.

Institute for Human Rights and Development in Africa (IHRDA). (n.d.). Homepage. Retrieved August 15, 2012, from http://www.ihrda.org/

International Bar Association. (n.d.). Rule of Law Action Group Home. Retrieved August 15, 2012, from http://www.ibanet.org/PPID/Constituent/Rule_of_Law_Action_Group/Default.aspx

International Bar Association Legal Brief Africa. (n.d.). Homepage. Retrieved August 15, 2012, from http://www.legalbrief.co.za/index.php?page=Legalbrief_Africa

International Legal Assistance Consortium (ILAC). (2012). Homepage. Retrieved August 15, 2012, from www.ilac.se

Ku, Charlotte, & Jacobson, Harold K. (Eds.). (2003). *Democratic accountability and the use of force in international law.* Cambridge, UK: Cambridge University Press.

Michel, James. (2010, October 15). *Alternative dispute resolution and the rule of law in international development cooperation* (Justice and development working paper series no. 12). Washington, DC: World Bank.

Organization of American States. (1996, March 29). Inter-American Convention against Corruption. Retrieved August 15, 2012, from http://www.oas.org/juridico/english/treaties/b-58.html

Organization for Economic Co-operation and Development (OECD). (2011). 1997 Convention on Combating Bribery of Foreign Public Officials in International Business Transactions: Adopted by the Negotiating Conference on 21 November 1997. Retrieved August 15, 2012, from http://www.oecd.org/investment/briberyininternationalbusiness/anti-briberyconvention/38028044.pdf

Samuels, Kirsti. (2006). *Rule of law reform in post-conflict countries: Operational initiatives and lessons learnt* (Social development papers conflict prevention and reconstruction no. 37). Washington, DC: World Bank.

Stapenhurst, Rick, & Kpundeh, Sahr. (Eds.). (1999). *Curbing corruption: Towards a model for building national integrity.* Washington, DC: World Bank.

Stromsem, Jan, et al. (2009). *Africa regional rule of law status review.* Washington, DC: USAID.

Transparency International. (2012). Homepage. Retrieved August 15, 2012, from www.transparency.org

United Kingdom Department for International Development (DFID). (2012). Homepage. Retrieved August 15, 2012, from www.dfid.gov.uk

United Nations (UN). (2004). United Nations Convention against Corruption. Retrieved August 15, 2012, from http://www.unodc.org/documents/treaties/UNCAC/Publications/Convention/08-50026_E.pdf

United Nations Department of Peacekeeping Operations. (n.d.). Homepage. Retrieved August 15, 2012, from http://www.un.org/en/peacekeeping/about/dpko/

United Nations and the Rule of Law. (n.d.). Homepage. Retrieved August 15, 2012, from http://www.un.org/en/ruleoflaw/index.shtml

United States Agency for International Development (USAID): Africa. (n.d.). Homepage. Retrieved August 15, 2012, from http://www.usaid.gov/where-we-work/africa

World Bank. (2000). *Anti-corruption in transition: A contribution to the policy debate.* Washington, DC: World Bank.

World Bank. (2002). *The world development report 2002: Building institutions for markets.* Washington, DC: World Bank.

World Bank. (2003). *Legal and judicial reform: Strategic directions.* Washington, DC: World Bank.

World Bank. (2004). *The world development report 2004: Making services work for the poor.* Washington, DC: World Bank.

World Bank. (2011). *Legal vice presidency annual report financial year 2011: The World Bank and the rule of law.* Washington, DC: World Bank.

World Bank. (2012). Homepage. Retrieved August 15, 2012, from www.worldbank.org

World Justice Project (WJP). (2012). Homepage. Retrieved August 21, 2012, from http://worldjusticeproject.org/

Rule of Law (European Union)

European Union (EU) law is an important driver in the development of environmental law across the twenty-seven member states of the Union. Through its institutional supra-structure, the EU passes and enforces laws affecting the environment. It aims for a high level of protection of the environment and has established key principles, which determine how to apply environmental laws and require a precautionary approach to be integrated across the policies of the EU. Problems of harmonized enforcement approaches to environmental law across the European Union mean that a lack of compliance with the rule of law remains an issue.

The key objective of the European Union (EU) is the establishment of a single market, and one of the mechanisms for achieving and maintaining this objective is the harmonization of laws across the member states. Environmental law is one of the areas where the European Union has competence to legislate. It seeks not only to harmonize existing laws, but has been markedly proactive in driving forward the environmental laws and policy of all the member states.

Institutional Structure of the EU

The European Union is rare among international organizations in that it has power to regulate the actions of its members as well as to bring enforcement mechanisms against defaulting members. It has a sophisticated bureaucracy with complex institutions. Its various institutions bring together the leaders of the national governments (Council of Ministers), provide a full-time administration (European Commission), provide a democratically elected representative body (European Parliament), and provide a court that has power to

adjudicate the legality of the actions of the member states (European Court of Justice).

As the civil service of the community, the commission is organized into different departments known as directorate-generals. Directorate-General XI (DG XI) is responsible for the environment. Within DG XI there is a unit dealing with enforcement, infringements coordination, and legal issues and that deals with complaints and generates enforcement action.

The European Environment Agency was established by Council Regulation EEC/1210/90 and is located in Copenhagen, Denmark. It has no regulatory function but was set up to coordinate an information network. It collects national data on the environment and provides information to form the basis for new EU legislation. It also provides information to the public (subject to rules on the confidentiality of information) on the state of the environment. It is responsible for drawing up expert reports on environmental issues and establishes uniform criteria to ensure the harmonization of environmental controls across the member states of the European Union.

Membership of the European Union means, therefore, that each member state must implement EU law into its national legal system, or enforcement action may be forthcoming. EU environmental law is thus a major force in the development of national laws relating to the environment in each of the member states.

Development of the EU and Its Environmental Policy

The devastation of the Second World War led to a desire to integrate the European economies to avoid the conflicts that had dogged Europe for more than a hundred years and to achieve a level of industrial stability and prosperity that would ensure the quality of life of the citizens of the European states.

The Treaties

After the Second World War, France, the Federal Republic of Germany, Italy, the Netherlands, Belgium, and Luxembourg signed the first of the treaties in Paris on 18 April 1951. This was the European Coal and Steel Community, which emphasized the need for "world peace." The attempt to integrate the coal and steel industries came as a result of their importance in wartime as well as from the concern for ensuring that no individual state could dominate and acquire the capacity to make war independently of the others. The Treaty of Paris was the first attempt to establish a separate institution at a supranational level with legislative and administrative powers.

This treaty was followed in 1957 by the two Treaties of Rome, which established two more communities: the European Economic Community (EEC) and the European Atomic Energy Treaty (Euratom) (Europa n.d.c). The objectives of the treaty establishing the EEC furthered the resolution of the Congress of Europe at The Hague in May 1948 for "a united Europe throughout whose area the free movement of persons, ideas and goods is restored" (Pledge 1, Hague Congress 1948). It was originally entered into by Belgium, France, Italy, Luxembourg, the Netherlands, and the Federal Republic of Germany, which declared their determination "to lay the foundations of an ever closer union among the peoples of Europe" (HR-Net 1957).

It is possible for any European state that respects the "principles of liberty, democracy, respect for human rights and fundamental freedoms, and the rule of law" (Article 6, Treaty on European Union) to seek membership of the European Union, and the conditions for membership (known as the Copenhagen criteria) were set down in 1993. As of 2012, there are twenty-seven member states, which include a number of Eastern European states, with more currently applying for membership. The European Union thus forms one of the largest trading communities in the world.

The Euratom Treaty, which established the European Atomic Energy Community and was concluded on the same day as the European Economic Community, 25 March 1957, also emphasized raising the standard of living for ordinary people: "It shall be the task of the Community to contribute to the raising of the standard of living in the Member States and to the development of relations with the other countries by creating the conditions necessary for the speedy establishment and growth of nuclear industries" (Article 1, Euratom Treaty 1957).

Environmental issues, insofar as they were considered at all, would have been specifically relegated to the imperative requirement of reorganizing industry and reestablishing shattered economies. The establishment of the European Economic Community created a structure, however, that was eventually to make the rise of environmental issues possible. The Treaty of Rome did not establish simply a series of common objectives; it also established a structure with institutions and a bureaucracy to enforce and execute those objectives.

A further thirty years were to elapse before any significant amendment was made to the EEC Treaty, and it was not until the passing of the Single European Act in 1987 that environmental issues were formally incorporated into the treaty. Five years later, on 1 November 1993, the Treaty on European Union (known as the Maastricht Treaty) came into force. Two further amending treaties followed—the Treaty of Amsterdam, passed in 1997, followed by the Treaty of Nice in 2001, with the current treaties now contained in the Treaty of Lisbon, which entered into force on 1 December 2009 and established the Treaty of European Union (TEU) and the Treaty on the Functioning of the European Union (TFEU) (Official Journal of the EU 2008b). This treaty replaced the term *community* with *union*—it is no longer correct to use the term *EC law* except when making historical references.

Legal Basis of EU Environmental Law

The objectives of the European Union are contained in Article 3 (TEU), which, among a range of other objectives, also specifies that the "Union . . . shall work for the sustainable development of Europe based on balanced economic growth and price stability . . . and a high level of protection and improvement of the quality of the environment." Article 3 also provides that the Union "shall contribute to peace, security, the sustainable development of the Earth, solidarity and mutual respect among peoples, free and fair trade, eradication of poverty and the protection of human rights." The impact of the environmental objectives is enhanced by the integration principle in Article 11 (TFEU), which requires that environmental protection requirements "must be integrated into the definition and implementation of the Union policies and activities, in particular with a view to promoting sustainable development" (Official Journal of the EU 2008a, 53).

The main environmental provisions are contained in Title XX, Articles 191–193 (TFEU), which contain more detail and specific requirements including the protection of the quality of the environment, the protection of human health, the prudent and rational utilization of natural resources, the promotion of measures at the international level to deal with regional or worldwide environmental problems, and in particular to combat climate change.

Of great interest are the principles established in Article 191: that the EU environmental policy shall aim at a high level of protection and be based on the precautionary principle; that the policy shall be based on the principles that preventive action should be taken; that environmental damage should as a priority be rectified at source; and that the polluter should pay.

None of these principles are further defined in the treaties, but they have been applied with varying degrees of success in the European Court of Justice and national courts.

The precautionary principle was added subsequent to its adoption as Principle 15 of the Rio Declaration of 1992 (United Nations Conference on Environment and Development [UNCED], Rio de Janeiro, Brazil, 1992) "Where there are threats of serious or irreversible damage, lack of full scientific certainty shall not be used as a reason for postponing cost-effective measures to prevent environmental degradation" (UNEP 1992).

Unlike the preventive principle, the precautionary principle is intended to be used in circumstances where, even though clear scientific evidence is not available to support a particular theory, it is felt that precautions should still be taken. The presumption to be adopted is against the discharge or use of potentially harmful or accumulative substances even where the exact nature of the risk is not known. Where there is evidence of possible risk, rather than actual risk, the precautionary principle thus indicates that steps should be taken to prevent it. In *R v. Secretary of State for Trade and Industry ex parte Duddridge and others* (1996 Environmental Law Reports 325), a case that came before the Court of Appeal in the United Kingdom, it was held that this principle did not place any direct obligation on any organ of a national government. The court held that the principles were designed to underpin such policy on the environment as the institutions of the community should decide to promulgate, and only where that was so done would an obligation be imposed on a national government.

The European Court of Justice, however, has been more specific about the application of the principle. In *Pfizer Animal Health SA/NV v. Council* (2002, Case T-13/99), it was relied on to justify the banning of an antibiotic developed by Pfizer on the basis that there was some potential for harm to human beings. *United Kingdom of Great Britain and Northern Ireland v. Commission of the European Communities* (1996, ECR I-3903) gives another example of its use in the bovine spongiform encephalopathy (BSE, a disease caused by prions in cattle, commonly called "mad cow" disease) context and the potential for harm to humans. Further expositions of the principle can be found in the Communication from the Commission on the Precautionary Principle (COM [2000]1) (Commission of the European Communities 2000), General Principles of Food Law (COM [97]176) (Commission of the European Communities 1997), and Royal Commission on Environmental Pollution Report "Setting Environmental Standards" (1998).

The preventive principle emerged at the earliest stage in the development of European environmental policy in the first Action Programme and is based on the maxim that prevention is better than cure. The Environmental Impact Assessment Directive (Council Directive on the assessment of the effects of certain public and private projects on the environment, 85/337; [1985] OJ L175/40 as amended) is a prime example of this principle in that it requires an assessment of the environmental effects of major construction projects to be assessed before they are approved and given the go-ahead. The Registration, Evaluation, Authorisation and Restriction of Chemicals (REACH) Regulation (1907/2006) is another example. It requires chemicals to be tested not only for their health effects but also for their effect on the environment in general before being launched on the market.

The proximity principle advocates that environmental damage should be rectified as close to its source as possible. Its effect was considered by the European Court of Justice in *Commission v. Belgium* (Case C-2/90, [1992] 1 ECR 4431, [1993] 1 CMLR 365), where a decree by the Walloon Regional Executive banning the import of waste into the region was, in relation to waste other than hazardous waste, held to be effective. The court cited the proximity principle as an appropriate reference point for such an environmental protection measure.

The "polluter pays" principle underlies much EU legislation and is designed to ensure that environmental damage is paid for by the polluter. Industry can no longer use natural resources freely without taking account of the external costs of the damage they cause to the environment. This principle encourages the use of economic and fiscal instruments aimed at influencing the behavior of producers and promoting technologies and processes that are consistent with resource conservation.

Development of EU Environmental Policy

EU laws are implemented at a domestic level. Member states sometimes take a grudging approach toward implementing EU laws, even though they are mandated to do so by the accession treaties. The precise manner of implementation of EU law at the domestic level is usually left to the member states (except when the applicable EU law is in the form of an EU regulation, which then takes effect in the exact form in which it is written).

The enforcement of EU environmental law may be through the medium of criminal law with its array of penalties—typically the case in the member states with a common law system (United Kingdom and the Republic of Ireland). Where the system in force in the member state is a civil law system, then enforcement may be through a civil or administrative law system—typical of all other member states. Inevitably this results in a great variety of sanctions and penalties across the twenty-seven member states.

The problem of environmental crime can be a cross-border problem, and the potential for corporate activities to be highly profitable while causing significant harm to the environment is a matter of great concern. Such breaches of environmental law can involve atmospheric emissions, water contamination, and illegal trade in endangered species, to name a few problems. Although the European Union has developed an extensive body of law concerning the environment, with more than two hundred directives in force, there are still significant areas of noncompliance. A number of studies ordered by the commission show that the variation in penalties and the lack of sufficiently severe sanctions mean that compliance can be poor (European Commission 2012c). In 2008, Directive 2008/99/EC was passed in light of increasing concern at the rise in environmental offenses on a cross-border basis and the failure of the extant system of penalties to ensure compliance. The objective of the directive was to achieve improvement of compliance by making criminal penalties more widely available, thus signifying the social unacceptability of environmental crime. Not only would unacceptability be signaled by the introduction of "effective, proportionate and dissuasive criminal penalties," but common rules on offenses would improve investigation across borders (Official Journal of the EU 2008a, 30). The type of activities covered by the directive include discharges into air and water; waste activities including its shipment; dangerous activities in operating plants; use of nuclear materials; protected wild fauna and flora including trading; habitat destruction; and ozone-depleting activities.

Despite the implementation of this directive and other EU efforts on improving implementation of the laws, there remain problems about enforcement and compliance. It is estimated that failure to comply with environmental laws costs approximately 12 billion euros (US$14.7 billion) in health and environmental costs (European Commission 2012a). This cost was reported in a 2012 Commission Communication entitled "Improving the Delivery of Benefits from EU Environment Measures: Building Confidence through Better Knowledge and

Responsiveness" (COM/2012/095), which the European Commission issued, advocating improvements through better tools for achieving compliance. It followed the 2008 Commission Communication on implementing European Community Environmental Law (which established the enforcement strategy for dealing with breaches) (COM/2008/0773 final) and the 2007 Commission Communication: "A Europe of Results—Applying Community Law" (COM (2007) 502 final). The 2012 Commission Communication seeks to improve the collecting and sharing of information and knowledge on environmental problems and deal with them more effectively at a local level involving the "European citizen."

European environmental policy is developed through the medium of the Action Programmes. These are documents that establish a proposed action plan for environmental developments over a period of time, usually about five years. They form the basis for policy development in the environmental arena. The Action Programmes are resolutions of the Council of the European Communities and of the representatives of the governments of the member states. There have been six Action Programmes starting with the first in 1973 to the current, the sixth (for the years 2002–2012 [COM (2001) 31]) (Europa 2001). The seventh is in preparation.

The first Action Programme set out eleven general principles.

1. Prevention is better than cure. (This principle appears in all the Action Programmes and is now in the TEU.)
2. Environmental impacts should be taken into account at the earliest possible stage in all decision making.
3. Exploitation of nature that causes significant damage to the ecological balance must be avoided.
4. Scientific knowledge should be improved to enable action to be taken.
5. The "polluter pays" principle; that is, that the cost of preventing and repairing environmental damage should be borne by the polluter.
6. Activities in one member state should not cause deterioration of the environment in another.
7. Environmental policy in the member states must take into account the interests of the developing countries.
8. The European Community (as it was known prior to the establishment of the European Union in the Treaty on European Union) and its member states should promote international and worldwide environmental protection through international organizations.
9. Environmental protection is everyone's responsibility; therefore, education is necessary.

10. Environmental protection measures should be taken at the most "appropriate level," taking into account the type of pollution, the action needed, and the geographical zone to be protected. This is known as the "subsidiarity principle."
11. National environmental programs should be coordinated on the basis of a common long-term concept and national policies should be harmonized within the community, not in isolation.

In 1992, a Report on the State of the Environment (COM (92) 23 final—Vol. III) was published, which concluded that despite the two decades of community action and the many pieces of legislation on the environment, there continued a "slow and relentless deterioration of the general state of the environment of the Community." The report blamed the increase in economic and social activity and the deficiencies in the data available for decision making on environmental policies. The Fifth Programme responded to these concerns with a markedly different approach. It was influenced both by the Report of the State of the Environment and by the United Nations Conference on Environment and Development (UNCED) meeting in Rio de Janeiro in 1992, which adopted the Rio Declaration, and Agenda 21, a program aimed at achieving sustainable patterns of development worldwide that clearly reflects a global perspective. The European Council subsequently adopted the UNCED measures. This perspective, however, was tempered by the counterbalancing political objective of subsidiarity. The Fifth Programme was colored by these two approaches. On the one hand there was a much broader view of the need to protect the environment, while on the other it was recognized that such measures as the program proposed should not necessarily be carried out at the community level. Nevertheless, this did not affect the underlying themes of the program, which indicated that certain courses of action should be taken at *some* level of the community. This idea is known as *subsidiarity*, which is presented as a mechanism for ensuring that EU environmental policy will be made more effective by ensuring that actions are taken at the appropriate level.

The other context that influenced the Fifth Programme was the political developments across Central and Eastern Europe as well as the wider international level. Although the program did not specifically refer to the possibility of the extension of the European Union across the geographical European territory, it stated that environmental measures currently in place were insufficient to deal with developments across states beyond the EU member states. Reference was made to the need to play a positive role in the formulation of sustainable development programs in the developing countries as well as the countries of Central and Eastern Europe.

The Sixth Programme, the latest, is entitled "Environment 2010: Our Future, Our Choice," which identifies overall objectives and priority actions for the EU's future environment policy. It developed seven thematic strategies in the field of soil and the marine environment (in the priority area of biodiversity), air, pesticides and urban environment (in the priority area of environment, health, and quality of life), and natural resources and waste recycling (in the priority area of natural resources and waste). The thematic strategies constitute the framework for action at EU level in each of the concerned priorities. Planning is under way in 2012 for the seventh Action Programme.

Outlook

The European Union is a powerful force for the development of environmental law not only in the twenty-seven member states but also on the international field. Through the legal process of its bureaucratic supra-institutions, it is capable of passing and enforcing laws within the member states that harmonize the approach to environmental protection across Europe. Furthermore, that approach is based on important and far-reaching principles and on a precautionary approach and is aimed at achieving a high level of protection of the environment.

Rosalind MALCOLM
University of Surrey

See also E-Waste; Energy Security (Europe); European Union (EU); European Union Greenhouse Gas Emission Trading Scheme (EU ETS); Fisheries; France; Germany; Rule of Law (Africa); United Kingdom and Ireland

FURTHER READING

Bell, Stuart, & McGillivray, Donald. (2010). *Environmental law* (7th ed.). London: Oxford University Press.
Cardwell, Paul; French, Duncan; & Hall, Matthew. (2011). Tackling environmental crime in the European Union. *Environmental Law and Management, 23,* 113–121.
Commission of the European Communities. (1997). The general principles of food law in the European Union. Retrieved August 1, 2012, from http://eur-lex.europa.eu/LexUriServ/LexUriServ.do?uri=COM:1997:0176:FIN:EN:PDF
Commission of the European Communities. (2000). Communication from the Commission on the precautionary principle. Retrieved August 3, 2012, from http://ec.europa.eu/dgs/health_consumer/library/pub/pub07_en.pdf
Commission of the European Communities. (2007, September 5). Communication from the commission: A Europe of

results–Applying community law. Retrieved July 27, 2012, from http://ec.europa.eu/eu_law/eulaw/pdf/com_2007_502_en.pdf

Commission of the European Communities. (2008, November 18). Communication from the commission to the European parliament, the council, the European economic and social committee and the committee of the regions on implementing European community environmental law (COM/2008/0773 final). Retrieved July 27, 2012, from http://eur-lex.europa.eu/LexUriServ/LexUriServ.do?uri=COM:2008:0773:FIN:EN:PDF

EurActiv. (2011). Homepage. Retrieved July 27, 2012, from http://www.euractiv.com/

Europa. (n.d.a). Communication from the commission to the European parliament, the council, the European economic and social committee and the committee of the regions improving the delivery of benefits from EU environment measures: Building confidence through better knowledge and responsiveness (COM/2012/095 final). Retrieved July 26, 2012, from http://eur-lex.europa.eu/LexUriServ/LexUriServ.do?uri=COM:2012:0095:FIN:EN:HTML

Europa. (n.d.b). Environment. Retrieved July 27, 2012, from http://europa.eu/legislation_summaries/environment/index_en.htm

Europa. (n.d.c). Euratom Treaty (1957) establishing the European Atomic Energy Community: Text of the treaty. Retrieved July 31, 2012, from http://eur-lex.europa.eu/en/treaties/dat/12006A/12006A.htm

Europa. (2001). Communication from the Commission to the Council, the European Parliament, the Economic and Social Committee and the Committee of the Regions on the sixth environment action programme of the European Community "Environment 2010: Our future, Our choice": The Sixth Environment Action Programme (COM/2001/0031 final). Retrieved August 6, 2012, from http://eur-lex.europa.eu/LexUriServ/LexUriServ.do?uri=CELEX:52001DC0031:EN:HTML

Europa. (2012). Enlargement 2013: Croatia. Retrieved July 27, 2012, from http://eur-lex.europa.eu/en/index.htm

European Commission. (2012a). Communication from the commission to the European Parliament, the council, the European economic and social committee and the committee of the regions (COM(2012) 95). Retrieved August 1, 2012, from http://eur-lex.europa.eu/LexUriServ/LexUriServ.do?uri=COM:2012:0095:FIN:EN:PDF

European Commission. (2012b). Environment: Highlight. Retrieved July 27, 2012, from http://ec.europa.eu/environment/index_en.htm

European Commission. (2012c). Environmental crime: Studies. Retrieved July 27, 2012, from http://ec.europa.eu/environment/legal/crime/studies_en.htm

Hellenic Resources Network (HR-Net). (1957, March 25). Treaty establishing the European Community as amended by subsequent treaties: Preamble. Retrieved August 6, 2012, from http://www.hri.org/docs/Rome57/Preamble.html

Horspool, Margot, & Humphreys, Matthew. (2012). EU law (7th ed.) (Core texts series). London: Oxford University Press.

Hughes, David. (1995). The status of the "Precautionary Principle" in Law: R v Secretary of State for Trade and Industry ex parte Duddridge. Journal of Environmental Law, 7(2), 224–244.

Kramer, Ludwig. EU environmental law (7th ed.). London: Sweet & Maxwell.

Official Journal of the European Union (EU). (2008a). Directives: Directive 2008/99/EC of the European parliament and of the council of 19 November 2008 on the protection of the environment through criminal law. Retrieved August 1, 2012, from http://eur-lex.europa.eu/LexUriServ/LexUriServ.do?ur=OJ:L:2008:328:0028:0037:EN:PDF

Official Journal of the European Union (EU). (2008b). Treaty on European Union and Treaty on the Functioning of the European Union. Retrieved July 31, 2012, from http://eur-lex.europa.eu/LexUriServ/LexUriServ.do?uri=OJ:C:2008:115:0047:0199:EN:PDF

Royal Commission on Environmental Pollution. (1998). Twenty-first report: Setting environmental standards. London: The Stationery Office.

United Nations Environment Programme (UNEP). (1992). Rio Declaration of 1992 (United Nations Conference on Environment and Development [UNCED], Rio de Janeiro, 1992). Retrieved July 31, 2012, from http://www.unep.org/Documents.multilingual/Default.asp?DocumentID=78&ArticleID=1163

COURT CASES

Commission v. Belgium
Pfizer Animal Health SA/NV v. Council
R v. Secretary of State for Trade and Industry, Ex parte Duddridge and others
United Kingdom of Great Britain and Northern Ireland v. Commission of the European Communities

Berkshire's authors and editors welcome questions, comments, and corrections. Send your emails about the *Berkshire Encyclopedia of Sustainability* in general or this volume in particular to: sustainability.updates@berkshirepublishing.com

Rural Development

Rural development is traditionally a practical approach used by governments to boost economic development in rural areas. Since becoming entrenched in the sustainability discourse, it has, on the surface, abandoned macro "top-down" programs based on the agricultural sector, favoring localized and participative actions. It still carries a heavy economic and political component, which is the heritage of both capitalist politics and totalitarian regimes worldwide, and is particularly linked to the post–World War II era and the Cold War.

Rural development is an elusive concept, the definition of which depends on many variables and on the understanding of other related words. For instance, without agreements on the tangible meaning of words and expressions such as development, sustainable development, rural, rural poor, and resilience, little can be done to define rural development in a constructive and consequential way. Furthermore, most of these expressions acquire different meanings and interpretations according to historic period, geographic area, political ideology, and economic status of a given country.

For all these reasons, therefore, it is difficult to provide an agreed-upon definition of the expression. In fact, most experts claim that there is no comprehensive definition for rural development at all (van der Ploeg et al. 2000). Consequently, they are only able to provide themes, issues, and focal points that have characterized the concept over time (Ellis and Biggs 2001).

Perhaps the most practical and realistic definition was provided by the World Bank in 1975, defining rural development as "a strategy designed to improve the economic and social life of a specific group of people—the rural poor. . . . It involves extending the benefits of development to the poorest among those seeking a livelihood in the rural areas. . . . It is concerned with the monetization and modernization of society, and with its transition from traditional isolation to integration with the national economy" (quoted in Dixon 1990, 56–57) While this is among the most quoted definitions of rural development, it is also one of the most criticized, especially in light of extensive study and change in rural development during the nearly four decades since the definition was written. Popular criticisms that reflect modern views on rural development include:

1. Many rural poor do not have an alternative to "seeking a livelihood in the rural areas." Furthermore, most rural development initiatives since the 1990s have been aimed at preventing rural-urban migrations, which were causing enormous social problems worldwide.

2. The extension of benefits, once known as a *trickle-down effect*, often never materializes because it would involve a conscious economic and political decision to share benefits with the poor (i.e. the majority of the world's population). What rural development has become concerned with, therefore, is how to create economic development and new socioeconomic and environmental benefits from interventions in rural areas (Dixon 1990).

3. The definition's mention of "modernization of society" implies Westernization under a capitalist economic system. This is often portrayed as the key to successful rural development programs, regardless of local realities and other governmental priorities.

4. The mention of "national economy" is not completely pertinent; in most developing countries, questions of ethnicities, tribe, and class often supersede the construct of nations (Dixon 1990). At the local level, many believe traditions contribute to survival, and external forces endanger the process.

The beneficiaries of rural development are, in this view, "small-scale farmers, tenants and the landless" (Dixon 1990, 57). Rural poor, therefore, are people whose livelihoods depend on land and its resources, whether as landowners, workers, or members of common-pool institutions. This establishes the direct link between rural areas and poverty, but it also implies the link to environmental conservation and sustainable development. The common assumption in the 1970s and 1980s, was that "poverty, inequality and environmental degradation are a self-reinforcing triangle leading to greater . . . poverty" (Duffy 2000). In more recent times, however, concerns over increasing poverty in developing countries are linked to ecological disasters, such as drought cycles, floods, resource consumption, and civil wars, which must be taken into account when designing and implementing sustainable rural development programs.

Historical Background

The history of rural development in Europe is very much linked to the events that followed World War II and the continent's need for economic development. In Africa, rural development has been influenced by the decolonization process, which led to a wave of political independence for numerous countries between 1957 and 1975. During these decades, the two powers of the Cold War, the Soviet Union and the United States, succeeded in establishing agriculture-based rural development programs (RDPs). Similar programs had been implemented in colonial Africa affecting the rural communities, particularly nomadic pastoralists in a drive toward sedentarization. While the initial programs focused exclusively on agricultural development aimed at feeding the rural areas, the 1970s saw a move toward "integrated" RDPs, which attempted to address structural services like infrastructure, health, and education, in response to rural needs. The impact of these programs, however, was arguably not as successful as intended. It lacked the capacity to include in the planning the communities concerned, particularly in developing areas such as Africa. Overall, the early to mid stages of rural development exemplified a top-down socioeconomic reform that, it was expected, would be accepted and implemented by the selected beneficiaries. This did not happen, and its sustainability began to be questioned.

Many of the current principles and working concepts related to sustainability derive from either the Brundtland Report, published in 1987 by the United Nations World Commission on Environment and Development (also known as the Brundtland Commission), or the subsequent UN World Conference on Environment and Development,

or Earth Summit, held in 1992 in Rio de Janeiro. Rural development, however, predates both events. The Brundtland Report in fact refers to a further elaboration of the concept—integrated rural development—without providing a definition (World Commission on Environment and Development 1987, S. 5.3) This is because rural development is firstly a governmental policy that aims to provide supporting economic growth in rural areas by enlisting them to produce nourishment for the whole country, and perhaps for the export market. In the words of the Bangladeshi rural development activist Farida Akhter, rural development implies "state-mediated policy and programs to shape the rural to meet the urban need" (Akhter 2006, 92). Hence, the current connection between sustainability and rural development must be understood in its historic and geographical perspectives.

Part of post–World War II economic reconstruction in Europe, as well as in the United States and the Soviet Union, was the boosting of essential productive sectors. Support for agriculture was meant to provide food for the nations, and it manifested either as capitalist programs to support private farmers or communist-based government-owned communal farming initiatives. In either case, rural development served the double purpose of feeding the nations and extending the power of the state to remote areas and peripheral citizens. In many ways, it became a way of connecting the nations. This is evident in the key words associated with the concept in the 1950s: modernization, dual-economy model, community development (Ellis and Biggs 2001). In the international domain, such terms must be associated with events following World War II, specifically the political and territorial divisions between the capitalist West and the communist East, as well as the ensuing postcolonial period. Both systems entered into industrial, agricultural, and scientific competitions that were implemented through top-down approaches to economic systems at home, which included rural development. In contrast to the views of the Indian development specialist M. C. Behera (2006), rural development was never solely directed to the third world.

Nonetheless, the main political and economic battlegrounds for the Cold War were developing countries. Africa, for instance, was once again divided according to political affiliation with the world's economic and political giants. Regardless of the economic system, however, the end result was the continuation of government-owned or private large-scale farming, which further reduced the possibility for sustainable small holdings, or allotments, for local consumption. In some parts of Africa, particularly in areas near European settlements, African natives who had previously been farm owners became farm laborers, working in a system that aimed at controlling rural areas, rather than developing them, in an effort to boost urban and export markets nationally and globally.

This so-called interventionist approach continued through the 1960s and well into the 1970s, although new buzzwords were introduced, and a closer look at the developing world changed the focus of the practice. The British economists Frank Ellis and Stephen Biggs (2001) insist that the first and most important paradigm shift in rural development was the acknowledgement of the "basic needs" approach and the strategy for the developing world (Hoadley 1981). Rural development began to be associated not only with the Western world, but with friendly poorer countries, through aid programs created in an attempt to counteract the spread of communism into postcolonial developing countries. The apparent dissociation between rural development and agriculture, in favor of its association with other forms of socioeconomic development, stands clear in the words of the US economist Bruce Johnston, spoken in 1970:

> Rural development is essentially a part of structural transformation characterized by diversification of the economy away from agriculture. This process is facilitated by rapid agricultural growth, at least initially, but leads ultimately to a significant decline in the share of agriculture to total employment and output and in the proportion of rural population to total population. (as quoted in Anriquez and Stamoulis 2007, 3)

Here began the divergence in the application of rural development between wealthy and developing countries. In the former, it remained essentially a structural program for agricultural efficiency to supply urban areas, basically implying that other basic needs were being met by the state. In and for developing countries, however, it became part of wider development plans that targeted the majority of their population: the peripheral and rural poor. Agriculture continued to be viewed as the key to rural development, although the implementation scale changed. In a general view, the developing world was to become the granary of the wealthy, be they represented by the national middle and upper classes, or by the great political powers in the East and the West.

After the downfall of the Soviet Union in 1991 and the rise of environmental and social justice theories on the political scene, the world globalized (at least in spirit, if not with significant political commitment) under the banner of sustainable development. As environmentalism and human rights became important social—and economic—issues, the door opened for rural development to shift once again toward more socially aware implementation approaches that could fit under the sustainability umbrella. The sustainable livelihoods approach (SLA), participatory rural appraisal (PRA), and stakeholder analysis became relevant methods for planning rural development programs around the best interests of rural residents. SLA analyzes relationships among the factors that affect the livelihoods of those living in rural areas, and how a rural development program might impact those relationships and adapt to suit the local social and natural environment. PRA gives rural people a voice in the development planning process through various opportunities to express their opinions and share their knowledge. In the same vein, stakeholder analysis examines groups and individuals targeted by development projects and provides guidelines for how their interests should be addressed. These methodologies, along with new objectives such as poverty reduction, then eradication, and good governance, gradually entered the rural development scene during the 1970s and 1980s, and succeeded in shifting its focus. This is when rural development increasingly was applied to developing countries (Ellis and Biggs 2001), with the exception of programs like LEADER (Liaisons between Actions of Development of Rural Economy, translated from the original French), which was funded by the European Union in the 1990s for EU countries (Moseley 2003).

As a consequence of these historical transformations, rural development continues to have three major political linkages: traditionally with agriculture, as seen in many government departments; occasionally with land reform; and rarely with social affairs. Still, there is no widespread agreement over the actual interpretation of rural development as a practice. The globalization of economic, technological, political, and social systems has only managed to confuse an already complex scenario (Behera 2006). The global economic system shifted to a widespread liberalized capitalistic style, which in many African countries penetrated the communist political systems that were in place, creating a fusion of liberal economics and communist politics. Globalization created a world in which economic inequalities are spread across scales (i.e., areas of influence that may be, for example, geographical, social, economic, or political) and geographic areas). Global environmental governance, which aims to achieve sustainability through the holistic involvement of political, social, and economic bodies worldwide, facilitated the spread of nongovernmental organizations for development, including rural development, and the displacement of vast sums of money in a decision-making system that some call "complex multilateralism" (discussed in O'Brien et al. 2000). It has also increased its flexibility in theory and practice, which has characterized development interventions, to the point of instability. This, in turn, has led to rising insecurity in rural communities about the use of real participatory, or bottom-up, approaches (Dixon 1990). As a result, rural development has not found a unifying theoretical approach, nor has it been able to follow a sustainable, or Gandhian, development model that includes the preservation of resources for future generations (Behera 2006).

The Modern Outlook

An attempt to provide a meaning for rural development should acknowledge that, as is the case for many development concepts, only by understanding its historical and geographical progress could one derive an idea of what it entails in the present (Behera 2006). In the twenty-first century, rural development is considered an intrinsically localized process based on *sustainability*, based on *innovation and value-adding implementation*, achieved through *community involvement, social inclusion, and partnership*, through *strategic planning* (Moseley 2003). This is a rather unspecific description, which implies both a generalist approach and an uncertainty in implementation, given by the use (in italics) of development jargon created over the past decades. It does, however, take into account historical paradigm shifts and geographical applications that have constructed the present concept as applied globally, but is unable to differentiate between the implementation policies and politics.

It also presents rural development as a unified theory and practice, which it is not. In the Western world, with the notable exception of the European Union's LEADER Programme (Moseley 2003), rural development has remained "*a new developmental model for the agricultural sector*" (van der Ploeg et al. 2000, 392, italics in the original). In the developing world, however, it has changed and adapted in its applications, most notably because of the links established between rural development and social welfare, land distribution, and sustainability (Ellis and Biggs 2001), with all three being linked to the political goals of national politics. Globalization, however, entails that local process and national decision making in developing countries be guided by international economics and the approaches of international organizations; at this scale, agriculture is still a major driver for rural development programs. In this context, Farida Akhter (2006) calls rural development "predominantly an interventionist tool of post-colonial states with the support of multilateral and bilateral aid agencies targeting by its very design the southern countries and their people." Her observations, it should be noted, do also apply to rural development programs of the past, and place rural development practice in a global economic context that has little to do with sustainable development and its principles. Rural development is a tool that merges political and economic scales in order to manage people and natural resources at the local level. The real success of its implementation rests more on the people implementing the project than on the intentions and theories offered by development agencies and governments. This is particularly true when it is still focused on land distribution and intensive agriculture, as is the case in Latin America and East Asia (Dixon 1990).

In Africa, particularly south of the Sahara, land issues are still very complex and changeable. It is, however, like various other areas around the world, a battleground for donor agencies that work to renegotiate and implement localized, sustainable practices for modern rural development programs that aim to increase food security, given the steady rise in global food prices and an increasingly urban-centric population worldwide. Zimbabwe is one example of a major regional challenge for donor agencies. Once the cradle of community-based rural development programs, Zimbabwe endured a decade of political and economic strife beginning in the late 1990s. In 2012, Zimbabwe is a crucial country for rural development, given the dualistic relationship between government and nongovernmental organizations, as well as its social and environmental potential for development.

Rural Development in Developing Countries

In the 1970s and 1980s, the triangulation between poverty, development, and environment prompted the entry of rural development into the sustainability discourse, whereby the economic development of the rural poor was deemed essential in order to conserve natural resources, which were diminishing in quantity and quality (Anderson and Grove 1987). For developed countries and international institutions, rural development became the way to formalize otherwise fuzzy systems and networks in developing countries, such as nomadic pastoral groups, with the aim of collecting both socioeconomic and environmental benefits. Two important realities pertaining to the developing world, however, are discounted by such assumptions:

1. Rural poor rely on subsistence agriculture, or self-sustaining farming, as well as other survival strategies that are not land based or directly resource based; seasonal and permanent employment migration in Africa is a widespread and important source of income.
2. Western-type modernization may not be directly absorbed in local systems unless it provides equal or better yields than traditional agricultural systems and crop varieties.

Sustainability, therefore, has managed to provide clear justifications for rural development practices that were primarily economically and politically driven in developing countries. For instance, land distribution that would promote medium- and large-scale farming has allowed for more defined land-use planning, and contained use of natural resources. On the other hand, it has displaced subsistence farmers and increased the number of landless workers, who are thus reduced to employment on the larger farms for survival; increased environmental stresses on water tables from extraction and use of chemical products; and contributed to land clearance in order to increase the quantities of land available for agricultural rural development.

The objective of rural development experts to create community-based enterprises has rarely been achieved, and never without external support. In southern Africa, this has been strictly related to nonagricultural activities under the umbrella of the Sustainable Use of Natural Resources (SUNR), where nature conservation and safari hunting initiatives in Namibia and Zimbabwe are clear examples of sustainable rural development through devolution, or the transfer of power and access to land from governmental to local organizations.

Since the early 1990s, evaluations of rural development programs and policies in developing countries have consistently produced similar criticisms. Akhter (2006, 99) has summarized these criticisms as five common outcomes of rural development policies:

- breakdown of rural families [and of traditional socioeconomic systems];
- emergence of "female headed households" in rural areas [because husbands had to look for formal employment elsewhere, including urban areas]
- migration of rural people, particularly women, to urban slums

- influx of commodities into the rural market from urban areas [including mobile phones and satellite television]
- high cost and nonavailability of food in the villages [due to the increased amount of imports and the reduction in subsistence farming]

Indeed, there is a clear disconnect between sustainability objectives and the reality at the local level, although sustainable and rural development programs seem to have the same goals: economic development, social welfare, and environmental protection.

The expected results on all three points, however, are what determine the degree of implementation. In developed countries, rural development can afford to be a policy based on territorial uniqueness and become a further selling point for the existing economic sectors within the formal economic system. In developing countries, rural development aspired to be a sustainable poverty eradication strategy, but was sidetracked by global political and economic interests. Though the world began to discuss sustainable development in the 1980s, the Brundtland Report's suggestion to change the economic system to one that is more equitable and socially just has yet to be implemented, and the results yielded by rural development programs worldwide demonstrate a widening gap with sustainability. Even the use of integrated rural development programs advocated by the Brundtland Commission has been disjointed and unable to ensure participation and devolution.

In essence, rural development as a practice has not moved far from its initial vision of promoting and financing formal intensive and extensive agricultural programs in order to support urban areas and their hinterland. On a global scale, developing countries represent rural areas and the industrialized countries represent urban areas. Despite contemporary approaches focused on environmental sustainability, localization, and participative methodology, national governments and international organizations have yet to consistently and completely adapt rural development programs to the needs of the people they target in developing countries.

Clara BOCCHINO
North-West University, Potchefstroom, South Africa

See also African Union (AU); Agriculture, Small-Scale; Immigrants and Refugees; Microfinance; Migration (Africa); Public-Private Partnerships (Africa); Urbanization (*several articles*); World Bank

FURTHER READING

Akhter, Farida. (2006). Rural development in the era of globalisation: Fragmented realities. In M. C. Behera (Ed.), *Globalising rural development: Competing paradigms and emerging realities* (pp. 92–107). New Delhi, India: Sage Publications India.

Anderson, David, & Grove, Richard. (Eds.). (1987). *Conservation in Africa: People, policies and practice.* Cambridge, UK: Cambridge University Press.

Anriquez, Gustavo, & Stamoulis, Kostas. (2007). *Rural development and poverty reduction: Is agriculture still the key?* (ESA working paper no. 07-02). Washington, DC: Agricultural Development Economics Division, Food and Agriculture Organization of the United Nations.

Behera, M. C. (Ed.). (2006). *Globalising rural development: Competing paradigms and emerging realities.* New Delhi, India: Sage Publications India.

Dixon, Chris. (1990). *Rural development in the third world.* London: Routledge.

Duffy, Rosaleen. (2000). *Killing for conservation: Wildlife policy in Zimbabwe.* Oxford, UK: International African Institute (IAI) & James Currey.

Ellis, Frank, & Biggs, Stephen. (2001). Evolving themes in rural development 1950s–2000s. *Development Policy Review, 19*(4), 437–448.

Fernando, Nimal A. (2008). Rural development outcomes and drivers: An overview and some lessons. Mandaluyong City, Philippines: EARD Special Studies & Asian Development Bank.

Hoadley, J. Stephen. (1981). The rise and fall of the basic needs approach. *Cooperation and Conflict, 16*(3), 149–164.

Moseley, Malcom J. (2003). *Rural development principles and practice.* London: SAGE Publications.

O'Brien, Robert; Goetz, Anne Marie; Scholte, Jan Aart; & Williams, Marc. (2000). Contesting global governance: Multilateral economic institutions and global social movements. Cambridge, UK: Cambridge University Press.

United Nations General Assembly. (1992). Report of the United Nations Conference on Environment and Development, Annex I: Rio Declaration on Environment and Development. A/CONF.151/26 (Vol. I). Rio de Janeiro: United Nations.

van der Ploeg, Jan Douwe, et al. (2000). Rural development: From practices and policies towards theory. *Sociologia Ruralis, 40*(4), 391–408.

World Commission on Environment and Development. (1987). *Our common future.* New York: United Nations Environment Programme.

Russia and the Soviet Union

Russia is a huge nation, and the Soviet Union, of which Russia was once a part, was even bigger. Early agrarian expansion, which stretched to the Pacific Ocean when the railroad was extended to the east, led to the extinction of a number of native species, and large-scale industrialization during the Cold War resulted in large environmental degradation in many locations. The most well known environmental disaster occurred in 1986, when the Chernobyl nuclear power station in Ukraine exploded. Although many nongovernmental organizations have established themselves in twenty-first-century Russia, destruction of the environment and industrial pollution remain significant challenges.

Occupying one-sixth of the Earth's land area, the former Soviet Union, which included the Russian Soviet Federal Socialist Republic (presently the Russian Federation), occupied 22.2 million square kilometers and embraced eleven time zones. Although dominated by the European Russian and western Siberian plain, its enormous territory variegated geologically and topographically as well as by soil type, climate, vegetation, and fauna. Major geographical subdivisions include the Arctic tundra desert, a broad belt of coniferous taiga (a moist subarctic forest dominated by conifers that begins where the tundra ends), mixed deciduous (leaf-dropping) forests, wooded steppe, steppe, extensive mountainous regions, major deserts and semideserts, and pockets of humid subtropical lowlands.

As late as the early seventeenth century, unbroken grassland stretched from the Danube River to Mongolia. For centuries, nomadic herders had pastured their flocks on this ocean of grass. These groups were often mixtures of clans and ethnicities. Ecologists and biogeographers continue to debate the degree to which these groups affected steppe vegetation. At the same time, however, large tracts of the steppe were frequently burned during war to deprive enemies of pasture, which would have reinforced the trend toward xerophilic (thriving with minimum water) vegetation.

During the sixteenth and seventeenth centuries, the Muscovite state constructed an elaborate defensive line along its southern forests bordering the steppe, consisting of abatis (barriers of cut trees) and palisades to bar nomadic horsemen from invading and raiding its towns and farmsteads. Although they were no longer needed by the end of the eighteenth century, the defensive lines remained undeveloped, becoming dense islands of forest that were rich in wildlife amid agricultural and parklike landscapes (the Tula abatis was preserved as the Tul'skie zaseki zapovednik, or "inviolable" nature preserve from 1935 to 1951, when it was eliminated by the Stalinist regime; the Kaluzhskie zaseki nature reserve was established in 1992 to protect another segment of the sixteenth-century defensive forest line).

By the middle of the nineteenth century, all of the cultivable land on the steppe had been converted to cereal farming on gentry estates. As a result, the herds of European bison (*Bison bonasus L.*) and tarpan (*Equus ferus ferus*), or wild horse, disappeared (the last one died in 1877). The last tur, an ancestral form of the domesticated cow, was killed in 1644, and the saiga antelope (*Saiga tatarica*), once found as far west as Moldavia, was driven back eastward beyond the Don River. The steppe was cleared of beaver (*Castor fiber*) and moose (*Alces alces*) as well. The once-extensive ranges of the greater bustard (*Otis tarda L.*) and lesser bustard (*Otis tetrax L.*), common cranes (*Grus grus L.*) and Demoiselle cranes (*Anthropoides virgo L.*), and other species of steppe avifauna (birds of a region) are now contracted to isolated spots.

The Lure of Furs

Russians originally were drawn east by the lure of furs. Expansion, first pursued by the Republic of Novgorod in the eleventh through fifteenth centuries, followed trapping grounds. The port of Vladivostok served as a springboard for Russian whaling, sealing, and fishing in the North Pacific and for the eventual establishment of bases in Alaska and on the California coast. Among the early mammalian casualties of the Russian presence in the Pacific was the Steller's sea cow, which was exterminated by 1783. By 1917, sea otter populations were also endangered, as were those of sable and beaver on the mainland. Of greater environmental impact was the construction of the Trans-Siberian railroad (1892–1916) and the great expansion of peasant migration in its wake. An estimated 7 million peasants moved to Siberia from crowded areas of European Russia in the period from 1801 to 1916. Most of these settled in western and central Siberia, in the fertile steppe of the western Altai.

Although the Russian empire remained overwhelmingly rural, during its last half-century a remarkable process of urbanization and industrialization occurred. St. Petersburg grew from 500,000 people in 1858 to 1.5 million in 1914, and Moscow grew from 400,000 in 1858 to 1.2 million by that same year. One major environmental issue of the late imperial period was the decline of forest cover in European Russia from 213.4 million hectares (52.7 percent of the territory) in 1696 to 172.3 million in 1914 (35.2 percent). There was no single cause but rather a multitude: industrialization; railroad, home, and telegraph construction;

impoverishment of the landed gentry; and, not least important, peasant land hunger.

Led by eminent field biologists, a Russian nature protection movement emerged in the 1890s. The soil scientist Vasilii Vasil'evich Dokuchaev had proposed as early as 1894 that the few remaining islands of steppe be protected to allow scientific study and to serve as baseline references (etalons) of what the original vegetation was like. This idea was further developed by the zoologist Grigorii Aleksandrovich Kozhevnikov, who argued that representative tracts embracing all the various surviving pristine ecological communities in the Russian empire and, later, the Union of Soviet Socialist Republics (USSR), should be protected as zapovedniki, or permanently inviolable nature reserves. Because experts thought the ecological community of the zapovednik represented healthy nature, degraded land—that is, land altered by human economic activity—could also be restored using the etalon as a model.

Kozhevnikov and other leading activists such as the botanist Ivan Parfen'evich Borodin and the entomologist (a biologist who studies insects) Andrei Petrovich Semenov-tian-shanskii were also concerned with ethical and aesthetic aspects of nature protection, but these arguments were downplayed in favor of scientific and utilitarian ones after the Bolsheviks assumed power in November 1917.

The institutionalization of nature protection began during the last decade of czarist rule. In 1910, the first citizens' conservation group, the Khortitsa Society of Defenders of Nature, was established to save picturesque cliffs on the Dnepr River, and a year later the botanist Valerii Ivanovich Taliev founded a nature protection society in Kharkiv, also in Ukraine. In 1911, the Permanent Nature Protection Commission under the auspices of the Imperial Russian Geographical Society was organized. The thirty-one prominent scientific and government leaders who were members of the society constituted an advisory body to the regime. Russia's first state nature reserve, the Barguzinskii *zapovednik,* was established in 1916 to protect the habitat of sable (*Martes zibellina*). Borodin and Kozhevnikov also represented Russia at the First International Conference for the Protection of Nature, held in Bern, Switzerland, in 1913.

Nature Groups

In 1924 the All-Russian Society for the Protection of Nature was founded, reaching fifteen thousand members by 1932 and publishing a bimonthly journal, *Okhrana prirody* (Protection of nature). Another strong nature protection organization was the Central Bureau for the Study of Local Regions (Tsentral'noe biuro kraevedeniia), established in 1925, which united sixty thousand members of local affiliates.

During the 1920s, Anatolii Vasil'evich Lunacharskii, the RSFSR (Russian Soviet Federated Socialist Republic) people's commissar for education, created the Department of Nature Protection within that ministry, responsible for the first network of protected territories exclusively dedicated to ecological and scientific study (*zapovedniki*). The Interagency State Committee for Nature Protection, which had a mandate to assess the environmental impact of economic policies, existed from 1925 to 1931, when it was closed after it opposed the targets of the Soviet regime's First Five-Year Plan. The First Five-Year Plan (1928–1932, because it was completed in four years) was the first comprehensive attempt to directly manage the entire economy, including all investment, production, and distribution. Nature protection activists bravely advanced arguments against hydropower projects, collectivization, and the "transformation of nature" (including mass introductions of nonnative species). Miraculously, the All-Russian Society for the Nature Protection and the *zapovedniki,* although they were attacked, managed to survive as relative islands of autonomy within the Soviet state, probably because the regime did not think they were important.

After the Interagency State Committee for Nature Protection was closed, control of the reserves passed from the RSFSR People's Commissariat of Education to the VTsIK (RSFSR legislature) and then to the RSFSR Council of People's Commissars (later, Ministers), or cabinet. Other USSR republics had their own network of *zapovedniki,* and by 1951 there were 128 reserves with an aggregate area of 12.6 million hectares across the Soviet Union. That year, however, Soviet political leader Joseph Stalin signed a decree obliterating 88 reserves and turning them over to logging concerns. The 40 remaining "inviolable" *zapovedniki* occupied a territory of only 1.4 million hectares, barely 0.06 percent of national territory. Acclimatization of exotics (introduction of nonnative species), which had been forced on the *zapovedniki* during the 1930s, intensified, and the *zapovedniki* were heavily logged and deforested.

With the early Soviet period came the emergence of a scientist-led field of public health and pollution control. At its core were 1,600 public health physicians and environmental chemists who actively pursued novel technical means of treating industrial wastes. Like the nature protection activists, they insisted that the regime proceed with caution in its drive to industrialize. They proposed wastewater recycling as early as 1934, for example. In the later 1930s, however, the government severely repressed scientists, physicians, and public figures active in this movement.

Stalin's Policies

Stalin's agricultural and industrial policies literally changed the face of the Soviet Union. Collectivization eliminated what was left of the natural landscape as monocultures were planted over enormous areas of leveled land. A network of irrigation canals was built in the arid southern steppe belt of the country and, later, in the central Asian deserts. To protect the fields from deflation (erosion of the soil by wind), the Great Stalin Plan for the Transformation of Nature, launched in October 1948, planned a vast network of shelterbelts, similar to those planted in the United States in the 1930s. The shelterbelts were not successful for a number of reasons (including the mandatory selection of oak), however, and they were abandoned in 1954.

The First Five-Year Plan (1928–1932) included the completion of a major hydroelectric power station on the Dnepr River (DneproGES) as well as the Baltic to White Sea Canal, which was largely dug by hand by hundreds of thousands of deportees. This first gulag (Soviet penal system) project, like the Ukhta rail line that sank into the permafrost and other projects, did not have any economic or military value once completed, and it was destroyed during the German invasion in 1941. A country more than 80 percent rural on the eve of industrialization, the USSR had an urban majority (those living in centers of more than ten thousand) by 1959.

Reacting to programs under way in Germany and the United States, Stalin in 1942 initiated a Soviet atomic program, which was overseen by the secret police chief Lavrentii Beria and led by the physicist Igor' Kurchatov. The program exploded an atomic bomb in August 1949 and tested a hydrogen bomb in 1953. A year later, the first atomic power plant in the world was inaugurated at Obninsk. Atmospheric and underground tests resulted in radioactive contamination of more than 260 sites within Russia alone. The explosion of nuclear wastes at a secret nuclear weapons–processing plant near Kyshtym, 70 kilometers from Cheliabinsk, in September 1957, for example, released 2 million curies (units of radioactivity). As a result, ten thousand people were evacuated, and a large area was contaminated, including the watershed of the Techa River. Although the Soviet scientist Zhores Aleksandrovich Medvedev first deduced that this ecological disaster had occurred, it was not until 1989 that Soviet authorities admitted that it had happened.

Other legacies of the Soviet nuclear program include the explosion onboard the nuclear submarine *Kursk* in the Barents Sea in 2000 in which all 118 submariners died, and the dumping of spent nuclear fuel in the Arctic Ocean. The world's biggest single industrial accident was the 27 April 1986 explosion of nuclear reactor 4 at Chernobyl. Among the complex mix of causes was the lack of sophistication of Soviet industrial welding, which dictated a vulnerable design (RMBK-1000 graphite reactor), promoted by a politically connected scientific insider (Academy of Sciences president A. P. Aleksandrov); the increasing view among Soviet leaders that nuclear power represented a fix for a system that squandered energy against a backdrop of steeply increasing costs for extraction of hydrocarbons and coal; and a culture of fear and distorted information flow that impeded the safe testing of a retrofitted emergency cooling system. It is estimated that the accident affected 3.5 million people, including 1.25 million children and 300,000 cleanup workers (UN 2004). According to the World Health Organization (WHO), 600,000 liquidators (cleanup workers) were exposed to radiation, some at high levels; 200,000 residents received doses of radiation significantly higher than normal; and 5 million received doses a little above normal levels. Sickness levels, however, are difficult to calculate due to the fact that "[i]n addition to the lack of reliable information provided to people affected in the first few years after the accident, there was widespread mistrust of official information and the false attribution of most health problems to radiation exposure from Chernobyl" (WHO 2006).

Developments after Stalin

In the late 1950s, Soviet leader Nikita Sergeevich Khrushchev initiated a campaign to make the Soviet Union self-sufficient in processed chemicals, especially fertilizers. The spread of chemical plants and later biochemical plants increased pollution as well. Continued military buildup also brought additional sources of pollution.

Although the All-Russian Society for the Protection of Nature survived threats to close it during Stalin's last three years in power, Communist Party functionaries took over its leadership in the mid-1950s after its merger with the All-Russian Society for the Promotion and Protection of Urban Green Plantings. Despite its huge numerical growth—the All-Russian Society for the Protection of Nature had 29 million members by the early 1980s, and its Belorussian analog had 3.4 million, or 34.5 percent of that republic's population—the society played no further important role in environmental activism.

The Moscow Society of Naturalists (MOIP), the Moscow Branch of the Geographical Society of the USSR, and student movements that emerged in the late 1950s gradually superseded the All-Russian Society for the Protection of Nature. Most important of the student movements were the independent-minded Nature Protection Brigades (*druzhiny po okhrane prirody*), which appeared first at Tartu State University (Estonian Soviet Socialist Republic) and Moscow State University, with branches ultimately functioning in about 140 higher education institutions by the mid-1980s with a total of five thousand members. Some students went to the Altai during the early 1960s to organize a model sustainable forest (the Kedrograd movement). Also during the

1960s, a powerful movement of scientists, journalists, writers, and students formed to stop the construction and operation of ecologically damaging pulp and paper mills at Baikal.

The grand plans of the administration of Leonid Brezhnev, notably the construction of a gargantuan earthen-and-stone dam across the Gulf of Finland to protect the city of Leningrad (St. Petersburg) from hundred-year floods from the Baltic Sea, elicited resistance as well. Owing to later protests during the Mikhail Gorbachev administration, the final kilometer of the dam was never connected. Another project of unimaginable scale—the diversion of the northward-flowing rivers of Siberia and European Russia to the south to irrigate crops in the arid steppe belt—was canceled by Gorbachev's premier, Nikolai Ryzhkov, after leading scientists, writers, and citizen activists objected strenuously.

With the freer atmosphere in Russia initiated by Mikhail Gorbachev, numerous outside nongovernmental conservation organizations established branches in Russia and many of the other successor states to the USSR. They include the International Crane Foundation, World Wildlife Fund (now known as the World Wide Fund for Nature [WWF]), Greenpeace, International Fund for Animal Welfare, the Biodiversity Conservation Center, and the Sacred Earth Network. Among Russian organizations, the Socio-Ecological Union, led by the biologist Sviatoslav Zabelin, has played a central role in coordinating environmental activism since 1987.

Ministries Abolished

Since 1991, Russia and Uzbekistan have both abolished special ministries for environmental protection, in the Russian case merging environmental protection into the Ministry for Natural Resources, an incarnation of the former Soviet Ministry of Geology.

Environmental restoration has been pursued in a number of areas, notably on the site of the Kursk Magnetic Anomaly, a large iron deposit. During open-pit excavation, the area's topsoil was set aside and replaced after the deposit was mined out. The area has been partly revegetated. Another major success story has been the cleanup of the Moscow River.

Nevertheless, success stories are overshadowed by large-scale crises: Chernobyl, the Aral Sea, Cheliabinsk Oblast and the Urals, the Sea of Azov, the Donbas, the Kuzbas, the Black Sea and its coast, the Fergana Valley, the Kola Peninsula, Noril'sk, eastern Kazakhstan, Kalmykia, the western Siberian oil and gas fields, Novaia Zemlia and the Kara and Barents Seas, and the highway

through the Khimki Forest linking Moscow and St. Petersburg. Everywhere in Eurasia, dangerously toxic stockpiles of banned farm chemicals and nuclear waste in huge quantities await appropriate disposal. Foreseeing the scope of the decomposition of effective state power and the ensuing chaos, the professors Igor Altshuler, Yuri Golubchikov, and Ruben Mnatsakanyan (1992, 211) have pondered, "How much collapse of the USSR is environmentally safe for the rest of the world and . . . even for mankind's survival?"

Douglas R. WEINER
University of Arizona

See also Central Asia; Danube River; Lake Baikal; Moscow, Russia; Novosibirsk, Russia; Parks and Preserves; St. Petersburg, Russia; Ukraine; Volga River

This article was adapted by the editors from Douglas R. Weiner's article "Russia and the Soviet Union" in Shepard Krech III, J. R. McNeill, and Carolyn Merchant (Eds.), the *Encyclopedia of World Environmental History*, pp. 1074–1080. Great Barrington, MA: Berkshire Publishing (2003).

FURTHER READING

Ahlander, Ann-Mari Satre. (1994). *Environmental problems in the shortage economy: The legacy of Soviet environmental policy.* Aldershot, UK: Edward Elgar.

Altshuler, Igor I.; Golubchikov, Yuri N.; & Mnatsakanyan, Ruben A. (1992). Glasnost, perestroika, and eco-sovietology. In John Massey Stewart (Ed.), *The Soviet environment: Problems, policies and politics.* Cambridge, UK: Cambridge University Press.

Bassin, Mark. (1999). *Imperial visions: Nationalist imagination and the geographical expansion in the Russian Far East, 1840–1865* (Cambridge Studies in Historical Geography No. 29). Cambridge, UK: Cambridge University Press.

Bater, James H., & French, R. A. (Eds.). (1983). *Studies in Russian historical geography.* London: Academic Press.

Danilova, L. V., & Sokolov, A. K. (Eds.). (1998). *Traditsionnyi opyt prirodopol'zovaniia v Rossii* [Traditional experience in the treatment of nature in Russia]. Moscow: Nauka.

DeBardeleben, John. (1985). *The environment and Marxism-Leninism: The Soviet and East German experience.* Boulder, CO: Westview Press.

Edberg, Rolf, & Yablokov, Aleksei. (1991). *Tomorrow will be too late: East meets West on global ecology.* Tucson: University of Arizona Press.

Ely, Christopher. (2002). *This meager nature: Landscape and national identity in imperial Russia.* DeKalb: Northern Illinois University Press.

Goldman, Marshall I. (1972). *The spoils of progress: Environmental pollution in the Soviet Union.* Cambridge, MA: MIT Press.

Gustafson, Thane. (1981). *Reform in the Soviet Union: Lessons of recent politics on land and water.* Cambridge, UK: Cambridge University Press.

Gustafson, Thane. (1989). *Crisis amid plenty: The politics of Soviet energy under Brezhnev and Gorbachev.* Princeton, NJ: Princeton University Press.

Karimov, Alexei. (1999, December). Russian cadastral surveys before and after Peter the Great. *The Cartographic Journal, 36*(2), 125–132.

Komarov, B. (1980). [Ze'ev Wolfson]. *Unichtozhenie prirody v sovetskom soiuze* [The destruction of nature in the Soviet Union]. Armonk, NY: M. E. Sharpe.

Lemeshev, Mikhail. (1990). *Bureaucrats in power: Ecological collapse.* Moscow: Progress Publishers.

Medvedev, Zhores A. (1979). *Nuclear disaster in the Urals.* New York: W. W. Norton.

Medvedev, Zhores A. (1990). *The legacy of Chernobyl.* New York: W. W. Norton.

Moon, David. (1999). *The Russian peasantry, 1600–1930: The world the peasants made.* New York: Longmans.

Organisation for Economic Co-operation and Development (OECD). (1999). *Environmental performance reviews: Russian federation.* Paris: OECD.

Pallot, Judith, & Shaw, Denis J. B. (1990). *Landscape and settlement in Romanov Russia, 1613–1917.* Oxford, UK: Oxford University Press.

Peterson, D. J. (1993). *Troubled lands: The legacy of Soviet environmental destruction.* Boulder, CO: Westview Press & RAND.

Pryde, Philip Ruste. (1991). *Environmental management in the Soviet Union.* New York: Cambridge University Press.

Pryde, Philip Ruste. (Ed.). (1995). *Environmental resources and constraints in the former Soviet republics.* Boulder, CO: Westview Press.

Rywkin, Michael. (Ed.). (1988). *Russian colonial expansion to 1917.* New York: Mansell.

Smith, Jeremy. (Ed.). (1999). *Beyond the limits: The concept of space in Russian history and culture* (Studia Historica No. 62). Helsinki, Finland: Finnish Historical Society.

United Nations (UN). (2004). United Nations and Chernobyl: Ukraine. Retrieved March 15, 2012, from http://www.un.org/ha/chernobyl/ukraine.html

Weiner, Douglas R. (1999). *A little corner of freedom: Russian nature protection from Stalin to Gorbachev.* Berkeley & Los Angeles: University of California Press.

Weiner, Douglas R. (2000). *Models of nature: Ecology conservation and cultural revolution in Soviet Russia* (2nd ed.). Pittsburgh, PA: University of Pittsburgh Press.

World Health Organization (WHO). (2006). Health effects of the Chernobyl accident: An overview. Retrieved March 15, 2012, from http://www.who.int/mediacentre/factsheets/fs303/en/index.html

Yanitsky, Oleg N. (2000). *Russian greens in a risk society.* Helsinki, Finland: Kikimora Publications.

Yemelyanenkov, A. (2000). *The Sredmash Archipelago.* Moscow: IPPNW.

Sahara

Approximately 9 million square kilometers in area, the Sahara is the largest hot desert on Earth; it covers most of North Africa, and it is expanding. The ecosystems of the Sahara have been relatively little disturbed by human intervention because the climate is so inhospitable. In areas where water is available, however, such as oases, human presence makes severe demands on the limited resources.

The Sahara desert covers most of North Africa including major parts of Algeria, Chad, Egypt, Libya, Mali, Mauritania, Morocco, Niger, Sudan, Tunisia, and Western Sahara. This huge area is almost as large as China or the United States. It can be divided into the western Sahara, the central Ahaggar Mountains, the Tibesti Mountains, the Air Mountains, the Ténéré desert, and the Libyan desert (Gearon 2011, xi–xx). Most of the Sahara consists of rocky hamada (exposed bedrock) with some area covered by ergs (sand dunes), which may rise to 180 meters. At 3,415 meters high, Emi Koussi in the Tibesti Mountains in northern Chad is the highest peak in the Sahara. On its south, the Sahara is delimited by semiarid savanna called the Sahel.

The Sahara has one of the hottest climates in the world. The mean annual temperature usually exceeds 30°C and can rise to more than 50°C during the summer. Nighttime temperatures can fall below freezing in the winter. During summer, the Sahara also experiences hot and dust-filled winds. The rains in the region are rare and unpredictable; annual rainfall is less than 25 millimeters, and even less than 5 millimeters in the eastern part of the desert. Extensive aquifers underlying many parts of the Sahara in some places are close enough to the surface to produce natural oases, called wadi(s).

History

Under the force of natural climate change, the Sahara evolved from an ocean of grassland that supported pastoralism to an imposing arid vastness that separated sub-Saharan Africa from the societies that surrounded the Mediterranean Sea. Early communities of human hunter-gatherers and fishers lived in the Saharan basin from before the sixth millennium BCE. Around the fifth millennium BCE, these developed into agricultural and pastoral communities, and those living along the riverbanks focused on fishing. These ways of life spread from the Nile River valley into the vast grasslands of what would later become the Sahara desert (Ehret 2002). From the middle of the third millennium BCE, the Sahara began to desiccate, and by the beginning of the second millennium BCE the Sahara as we know it today had formed (Kröpelin et al. 2008).

In the first millennium CE North African peoples adopted the use of the dromedary camel, which originated in northeastern Africa. The camel made it possible for human groups both to develop a nomadic culture in the extremely arid sections of the desert and to make regular crossings of the Sahara, linking North Africa with the areas and societies to the south. Saharan camel pastoralism existed in its purist form only in the most arid regions; elsewhere pastoralists had mixed herds of camels, sheep, and goats, and toward the fringes of the desert it was possible to herd cattle as well (Tristram 1860, 377–382). The Sahara has been inhabited by Berbers, predynastic Egyptians, and Nubians since millennia ago. Greeks, Phoenicians, Arabs, Ottomans, and French also invaded and occupied the region in later periods (Gearon 2011).

Saharan slave traders benefited during the long era of the trans-Saharan slave trade, from the ninth through the nineteenth century. Millions of people enslaved in interstate warfare below the Sahara were taken by Saharan traders to North African and Mediterranean markets (Savage 1992). Saharan societies also absorbed large numbers of sub-Saharan captives, who served as slave workers in the salt mines, the oases, or the livestock sector.

Environmental Concerns

France invaded Algeria in 1830 and later colonized other parts of the Sahara region, including Tunisia in 1881 and Morocco in 1912. French colonizers blamed the environmental decay of North Africa, "the granary of Rome," on the mismanagement of the land by the local pastoralists. This narrative was used to justify the colonial rule, but recent studies suggest otherwise, that the environment of the region had been stable during this part of its history (Davis 2007). British rule started in Egypt in 1882 while Italy colonized the present-day countries of Ethiopia, Libya, Eritrea, and Somalia. Spain also colonized what is now known as Western Sahara (a territory whose sovereignty has been in limbo since Spain withdrew in 1976). During this era, the whole Saharan region experienced extensive agriculture and industrialization as the British, French, Italians, and Spanish introduced modern agricultural methods and railway networks. After the Second World War, the Saharan countries became independent, and during the course of the twentieth century, some Saharan regions were discovered to be rich in mineral resources such as iron ore, oil, and uranium. The Algerian, Egyptian, and Libyan regions of the Sahara are rich in oil, while iron ore is found in great quantity in Algeria and Mauritania. Morocco and Western Sahara are rich in phosphates (Azevedo 2003). The exploitation of these mineral resources increased economic development and rapid industrialization. Because of increased industrialization, natural gas is being used extensively in Algeria, Tunisia, Libya, and Morocco (Hagget 2002, 2240). In the 1960s, the French set off aboveground and subterranean nuclear test explosions in the Algerian Sahara and contaminated the desert with radiation at those sites.

In addition to global climate change, some of the factors causing desertification in the Sahara are deforestation leading to airborne dust storms, more pressure on its natural resources by the local population, and less rainfall. It is estimated that the Sahara is expanding southward at a rate of 48 kilometers every year (McLaughlin and Purefoy 2005). This means that more and more semidesert or cultivable area in the region is turning into desert with diminishing resources for the survival of life. Many national and international agencies have claimed that in the last decades of the twentieth century, under pressure from drought, many nomads gave up pastoralism and settled in desert towns and cities. Some researchers have challenged such claims. They suggest that politics and power relations have led to this misleading information, and that the actions of the local people over decades, such as planting forests around settlements (thus increasing forest cover), should be taken into account (Fairhead and Leach 1996). Satellite images and modern studies have shown an increase in the grazing areas and the number of trees in the Sahara between 1982 and 2002 (Owen 2009).

Although people have made use of the great Sahara desert, the hot, arid, windy climate is so inhospitable that it has discouraged significant development, and this has to some extent protected the natural environment and ecosystems. The Sahara comprises several ecoregions, which harbor distinct species of flora and fauna due to their variations in temperature, rainfall, elevation, and soil (Williams and Faure 1980). In addition to dromedary camels and goats, the Sahara supports animals like the monitor lizard, hyrax, sand viper, crocodile, African wild dog, and ostrich. Birds such as the African silverbill and black-throated firefinch are typical to this region. Not more than five hundred species of plants have been reported in the whole Sahara. Acacia trees, palms, succulents, spiny shrubs, and grasses are among those that have managed to adapt to its environment (Le Houérou 1990). There is continually more pressure on the local natural resources, especially water, to meet the needs of the increasing human population, which also results in a lack of food and water available for wildlife, threatening the stability of their populations (Haggett 2002, 2206–2211). Underground aquifers have been used for irrigation purposes in many countries of the region, especially Algeria, Morocco, and Tunisia, but in the 1990s more water was pumped from underground aquifers for irrigation to increase agricultural production, which led to soil degradation and salinization (Kassas 2008).

Outlook

Today the Sahara faces water shortages due to less rainfall, desertification, and increasing temperatures. All these conditions eventually contribute to the suffering of local human populations as well as pose a threat to the survival of Saharan animal and plant species. On the other hand, the Sahara may soon contribute to global sustainability and clean energy production, as initiatives are under way—such as the Sahara Solar Breeder Project, a joint project between Japan and Algeria—to harness the desert's abundant sunlight to supply power to other parts of the world.

The Editors

See also Africa (*several articles*); Agriculture, Small-Scale; Cairo, Egypt; Climate Change Refugees (Africa); Desertification (Africa); Mediterranean Sea; Nile River; Sahel; Tunis, Tunisia; Water Use and Rights (Africa); Water Use and Rights (Middle East and North Africa)

This article was adapted by the editors from James L. A. Webb Jr.'s article "Sahara" in Shepard Krech III, J. R. McNeill, and Carolyn Merchant (Eds.), the *Encyclopedia of World Environmental History*, pp. 1085–1088. Great Barrington, MA: Berkshire Publishing (2003).

FURTHER READING

Allan, John Anthony, & Barker, Graeme. (Eds.). (1981). *The Sahara: Ecological change and early economic history.* Boulder, CO: Westview Press.

Azevedo, Mario J. (2003). Geo-economy and history. In Emmanuel Nnadozie (Ed.), *African economic development* (pp. 47–63). London: Academic Press.

Barrillot, Bruno. (2002). *L'héritage de la bombe. Sahara, Polynésie (1960–2002)* [The heritage of the bomb. Sahara, Polynesia (1960–2002)]. Lyon, France: Centre de Documentation et de Recherche sur la Paix et les Conflits.

Cloudsley-Thompson, J. L. (Ed.). (1984). *Sahara Desert.* Oxford, UK: Oxford University Press.

Davis, Diana K. (2007). *Resurrecting the granary of Rome: Environmental history and French colonial expansion in North Africa.* Athens: Ohio University Press.

Ehret, Christopher. (2002). *The civilizations of Africa: A history to 1800.* Charlottesville: University Press of Virginia.

Fairhead, James, & Leach, Melissa. (1996). *Misreading the African landscape: Society and ecology in a forest-savanna mosaic.* Cambridge, UK: Cambridge University Press.

Gearon, Eamonn. (2011). *The Sahara: A cultural history.* Oxford, UK: Oxford University Press.

Haggett, Peter. (Ed.). (2002). *Encyclopedia of world geography: North Africa.* New York: Marshal Cavendish Corporation.

Kassas, Mohamed. (2008). Aridity, drought and desertification. In Mostafa K. Tolba & Najib W. Saab (Eds.), *Arab environment: Future challenges, 2008 report of the Arab Forum for Environment and Development* (pp. 95–110). Beirut, Lebanon: Arab Forum for Environment and Development.

Kröpelin, Stefan, et al. (2008). Climate-driven ecosystem succession in the Sahara: The past 6000 years. *Science, 320*(5877), 765–768.

Laroui, Abdallah. (1977). *The history of the Maghrib: An interpretive essay.* Princeton, NJ: Princeton University Press.

Le Houérou, Henry Noël. (1990). *Recherches écoclimatique et bio-géographique sur les zones arides de L'Afrique du Nord* [Ecoclimatic and biogeographical research on arid zones of North Africa]. Montpellier, France: CEPE/CNRS.

Lovejoy, Paul E. (1986). *Salt of the desert sun.* Cambridge, UK: Cambridge University Press.

McLaughlin, Abraham, & Purefoy, Christian Allen. (2005, August 1). Hunger is spreading in Africa. *The Christian Science Monitor.* Retrieved January 30, 2012, from http://www.csmonitor.com/2005/0801/p01s02-woaf.html

Owen, James. (2009, July 31). Sahara desert greening due to climate change? *National Geographic News.* Retrieved July 26, 2012, from http://news.nationalgeographic.com/news/2009/07/090731-green-sahara.html

Savage, Elizabeth. (Ed.). (1992). *The human commodity: Perspectives on the trans-Saharan slave trade.* London: Frank Cass & Co, Ltd.

Tristram, Henry Baker. (1860). *The Great Sahara: Wanderings south of the Atlas Mountains.* London: John Murray.

Webb, James L. A., Jr. (1995). *Desert frontier: Ecological and economic change along the western Sahel, 1600–1850.* Madison: University of Wisconsin Press.

White, Kevin, & Mattingly, David J. (2006). Ancient lakes of the Sahara. *American Scientist, 94,* 58–65.

Williams, M. A. J., & Faure, H. (Eds.). (1980). *The Sahara and the Nile.* Rotterdam, The Netherlands: A. A. Balkema Publishing Co.

The Sahel

Spreading horizontally across North Africa in a narrow strip between the Atlantic Ocean and the Red Sea, the Sahel is a region of geographic, climatic, and ecological transition between the extremely arid Sahara in the north and the semiarid savanna in the south. Although the region has long been subject to drought and famine, a combination of climate factors and human land use in the area since the 1960s has contributed to severe droughts, famine, and aridification, often leading to conflict. The Darfur region of Sudan in particular has been the site in recent years of warfare that has claimed between 200,000 and 500,000 lives.

The Sahel is a band of semiarid land, varying in north-south extent from several hundred to a 1,000 kilometers, running roughly 5,400 kilometers across the full width of the African continent. The Sahel region includes parts of Senegal, southern Mauritania, Mali, Burkina Faso, southern Algeria, Niger, northern Nigeria, Chad, Sudan, South Sudan (which voted to split off from Sudan in July 2011), northern Ethiopia, and Eritrea. The strip of land is more than 3 million square kilometers in area, nearly one-third the size of the continental United States. Its name comes from the Arabic *sahel*, meaning "shore" or "border," because of its location between the fuller aridity of the Sahara to the north (the "sea" of sand) and the greater humidity of the grassland savanna to the south. In a broad ecological sense, the entire Sahel is a transitional zone that has been endowed with floral and faunal elements from both the Saharan and savanna ecological zones. The biotic composition of the Sahel has also been profoundly changed by millennia of human land-use practices, including the introduction of domesticated livestock and the use of fire for clearing agricultural fields and for eliminating the bush habitat of the

tsetse fly (bearer of the parasite that carries trypanosomiasis, also called sleeping sickness). Early human settlements developed near the flat floodplains of the Senegal and Niger rivers and their tributaries, which flow through these semiarid lands (McIntosh 1993, 181–185).

Through overhunting and competition with livestock, many Sahelian mammals have been reduced in population in recent years, while some have already gone extinct (like the scimitar-horned oryx) or are endangered (like the African wild dog, the cheetah, and the lion). Overgrazing, overfarming, and natural soil erosion have led to desertification. During the long dry seasons, the annual grass species in the region (e.g., *Cenchrus biflorus*, *Schoenefeldia gracilis*, *Aristida stipoides*) wither and die.

At least since the introduction of the camel sometime in the second half of the first millennium CE, which allowed for mixed (camel, cattle, sheep, goat) pastoralism under arid conditions, the Sahel has evolved as a transitional cultural zone between the largely pastoral livestock economies of the western Saharan peoples and the largely agricultural economies of the African savanna peoples, who plant crops such as millet, sorghum, and indigenous rice. The pastoral and agricultural economies were often complementary; livestock herders traded salt from desert mines in addition to animal products (meat, milk, hides) for cereals grown by settled cultivators. Pastoralists, however, often had the upper hand militarily and during times of duress were able to employ force to secure their access to resources. The recent conflict in Darfur, discussed in the section on Darfur below, is an example of this conflict in human activities. As an alternative to raiding, many pastoral groups established relationships of dominance over agricultural villages, from which they drew tribute grain. During the precolonial era, the Sahel's principal exports into the Atlantic sector were human captives for the slave trade and gum arabic;

during the colonial era, the principal export was peanuts, and peanuts have continued to be a staple export during the postcolonial period (Webb 1995; Brooks 1993).

Threats to Water Resources and Food Production

During the colonial period, French experts undertook a large-scale and unsuccessful intervention to develop the middle valley of the Niger River in the Sahel. The drive for large-scale development programs remained a core theme into the early twenty-first century (van Beusekom 2002). In recent decades, the rapidly expanding and urbanizing Sahelian populations have incurred a very large cereal deficit that has been met through massive food purchases and international food aid (Raynaut 1997).

During the last decades of the twentieth century, some of the postcolonial Sahelian states undertook the controversial construction of dams along the Senegal and Niger rivers in order to harness water resources for irrigated agriculture and hydropower production. These dams have altered the natural flooding patterns upon which floodplain agriculturalists have depended, and the impoundment of water and its use in irrigation has created conditions conducive to the transmission of malaria, schistosomiasis, and other diseases. On the other hand, these projects have also offered new agricultural options to some farmers. The goals of sustained intensive agriculture and food self-sufficiency have remained elusive.

Droughts and Other Calamities

The Sahel has a long history of droughts, the causes of which have been the source of much speculation. In 1914, because of a shortage of rainfall, there was a major drought in the region, causing a large-scale famine. In the early 1960s, when there was a considerable increase in the rainfall in the northern part of the region, the region's governments encouraged, and sometimes forced, people to move to the northern part, which resulted in overgrazing in those areas. Subsequently, during the late 1960s the Sahel suffered a severe drought, which experts at the time attributed to local human agency, alleging that the desert was expanding as a result of deforestation and the overgrazing of Sahelian pastures. This perspective has been compromised by evidence that the Sahel has historically been subject to cycles of drought and that processes of climate change such as global warming are not necessarily generated locally (for details see Fairhead and Leach 1996; Swift 1996; McIntosh 2005).

Darfur

The Darfur region of Sudan is a prime indication of the kind of conflict that climate change, and its associated movements of people, can provoke. The Darfur conflict erupted in 2003, claiming between 200,000 to 500,000 lives before a tentative peace treaty was signed in 2005; a peace treaty that proved far from permanent. Although the conflict in Darfur stems from complicated and interwoven social, religious, and political factors, the United Nations Environment Programme (UNEP) argues that climate change is the leading catalyst. Prolonged periods of drought and famine, the spreading of the desert farther south (by approximately 100 kilometers since the late 1960s), and decreases in rainfall have forced nomadic herders (the aforementioned pastoralists) to encroach on sedentary farmers' land (UNEP 2007). The UNEP also cautioned that if issues such as climate change and desertification go unchecked, conflicts like that of Darfur could spring up in other areas of Sudan, and that "no peace will last without sustained investment in containing environmental damage and adapting to climate change" (Borger 2007; UNEP 2007).

Outlook

The Sahel continues to be subject to severe ecological stress. The Sahelian farming systems have been the focus of a great deal of applied research, and most experts now seek ecological solutions that take into account the local ecological knowledge of Sahelian farmers.

The Editors

See also Africa (several articles); African Union (AU); Agriculture, Small-Scale; Climate Change Refugees (Africa); Desertification (Africa); Diet and Nutrition; Lagos, Nigeria; Migration (Africa); Nile River; Rural Development; Sahara; Transboundary Water Issues; Water Use and Rights (Africa)

This article was adapted by the editors from James L. A. Webb Jr.'s article "Sahel" in Shepard Krech III, J. R. McNeill, and Carolyn Merchant (Eds.), the Encyclopedia of World Environmental History, pp. 1086–1088. Great Barrington, MA: Berkshire Publishing (2003).

FURTHER READING

Borger, Julian. (2007, June 22). Darfur conflict heralds era of wars triggered by climate change, UN report warns. The Guardian. Retrieved July 10, 2012, from http://www.guardian.co.uk/environment/2007/jun/23/sudan.climatechange

Brooks, George E. (1993). Landlords and strangers: Ecology, society, and trade in western Africa, 1000–1630. Boulder, CO: Westview Press.

Fairhead, James, & Leach, Melissa. (1996). Misreading the African landscape: Society and ecology in a forest-savanna mosaic. Cambridge, UK: Cambridge University Press.

Foy, Henry. (2010, June 21). Millions face starvation in west Africa, warn aid agencies. *The Guardian.* Retrieved January 5, 2012, from http://www.guardian.co.uk/world/2010/jun/21/millions-face-starvation-west-africa

Gritzner, Jeffrey Allman. (1988). *The West African Sahel: Human agency and environmental change.* Chicago: University of Chicago Press.

McIntosh, Roderick J. (1993). Pulse model: Genesis and accommodation of specialization in the middle Niger. *Journal of African History, 34*(2), 181–200.

McIntosh, Roderick J. (2005). *Ancient Middle Niger: Urbanism and the self-organizing landscape.* Cambridge, UK: Cambridge University Press.

Mortimore, Michael. (1998). *Roots in the African dust: Sustaining the sub-Saharan drylands.* Cambridge, UK: Cambridge University Press.

Moseley, W. G. (2008). Strengthening livelihoods in Sahelian West Africa: The geography of development and underdevelopment in a peripheral region. *Geographische Rundschau International Edition, 4*(4), 44–50.

Raynaut, Claude. (Ed.). (1997). *Societies and nature in the Sahel.* London: Routledge.

Swift, Jeremy. (1996). Desertification: Narratives, winners and losers. In Melissa Leach & Robin Mearns (Eds.), *The lie of the land: Challenging received wisdom on the African environment* (pp. 73–90). Portsmouth, NH: Heinemann.

United Nations Environment Programme (UNEP). (2007). Environmental degradation triggering tensions and conflict in Sudan. Retrieved July 10, 2012, from http://www.unep.org/Documents.Multilingual/Default.asp?ArticleID=5621&DocumentID=512&l=en

van Beusekom, Monica M. (2002). *Negotiating development: African farmers and colonial experts at the Office du Niger, 1920–1960.* Portsmouth, NH: Heinemann.

Watts, Michael. (1982). *Silent violence: Food, famine and peasantry in northern Nigeria.* Berkeley & Los Angeles: University of California Press.

Webb, James L. A., Jr. (1992). Ecological and economic change along the middle reaches of the Gambia River, 1945–1985. *African Affairs: The Journal of the Royal African Society, 91*(4), 543–565.

Webb, James L. A., Jr. (1995). *Desert frontier: Ecological and economic change along the western Sahel, 1600–1850.* Madison: University of Wisconsin Press.

St. Petersburg, Russia

4.8 million est. pop. 2012

St. Petersburg, Russia—known as Leningrad during the Soviet era—has confronted a number of economic, social, and environmental challenges since the end of the Soviet Union in 1991: a catastrophic economic decline in the 1990s, a legacy from the Soviet period of high levels of industrial pollution, and rapid and in some cases unregulated growth that threatens the city's rich architectural and cultural heritage. The city, called "the Venice of the North" due to its large network of canals, was designated a UNESCO World Heritage Site in 1990: the world's largest such site in an urban setting.

St. Petersburg (formerly Leningrad, 1924–1991, and Petrograd, 1914–1924), was the capital of czarist Russia for almost two centuries and became an industrial and manufacturing powerhouse at the end of the nineteenth century. It was one of the ten largest cities in the world by 1900, and later became an important part of the Soviet Union's powerful military-industrial complex. Heavy industry and manufacturing were developed largely within city limits during the Soviet period. At the same time, the city emerged as a worldwide tourist destination due to preservation of its large-scale architectural ensemble in the city historic center, as well as other cultural attractions (e.g., the Hermitage Museum, the Kirov Theater). The city, together with Moscow the only two in Russia with federal status, covers 1,400 square kilometers and is the second largest in the Russian Federation with a population of 4.8 million residents. The Constitutional Court was moved from Moscow to St. Petersburg in 2008. In the early twenty-first century, St. Petersburg is dealing with such environmental issues as new pollution from increased automobile traffic, decline of public transportation, and loss of green space to new construction.

Soviet Environmental Legacy

In Russia's transition from central planning to a market economy after the collapse of the Soviet Union, air and water industrial pollution levels began to decline in St. Petersburg in the mid- and late-1990s as industrial production declined sharply. Yet an improving economy beginning in 2000 reversed that trend and has led to increasing levels of pollution, which continue to pose environmental challenges and risks to the city today.

The city's source for drinking water is the Neva River, into which Lake Ladoga (Europe's largest lake) flows before it reaches Neva Bay and the eastern Baltic Sea. Quality of the drinking water in the city remains poor, due in part to an antiquated delivery system; city residents boil all tap water before drinking it. Until the 1970s the city relied on the large and fast-flowing Neva River to flush the city's largely untreated wastewater into the Baltic Sea. As of 2012 only 10 percent of the city's wastewater is released without treatment, thanks to the completion of wastewater treatment plants and improvements in their efficiency. The Russian Federation is a signer of the Helsinki Convention and has faced pressure from its Scandinavian neighbors on the Baltic Sea to improve its environmental record, including reducing the high levels of phosphorus released into Neva Bay and the Gulf of Finland.

Two industry-related dangers remain largely unchanged from the Soviet period. The town of Krasny Bor, located immediately to the south of the city, contains a large number of toxic chemicals and other pollutants. Leaks from the depository are reported regularly. Similarly, the Leningrad Nuclear Power Plant, located in Sosnovy Bor, lies within 80 kilometers of St. Petersburg (and has the same type of reactors as were involved in the Chernobyl nuclear power plant disaster of 1986). While the plant's safety record has been criticized, its operating license has been extended to 2026. A second nuclear plant (Leningrad Nuclear Power Plant-2) is now under construction in proximity to the first. One of the most controversial projects in the city has been the 25-kilometer-long flood barrier in Neva Bay, under construction for more than two decades and completed in August 2011. City ecologists have feared the barrier will disrupt natural circulation patterns and aquatic environments close to the city. An equally controversial initiative has been large-scale land reclamation on Neva Bay and the Gulf of Finland.

Transition 2000–2010

Transportation problems, loss of green space, and development threats to the city's architectural heritage emerged as challenges to the city's environmental and social sustainability during the decade 2000–2010, the city's second decade of transition from central planning to market economy.

Public Transportation Collapse

Public transportation was highly developed and well subsidized during the Soviet period, but large segments of it fell into disrepair beginning in the 1990s. Private automobile ownership grew dramatically, and traffic congestion, unknown during the Soviet period, became ubiquitous in the city center after 2005. The city's rapidly expanding private automobile fleet is now the largest source of air pollution in the city. At the same time, public transportation has suffered sharply reduced levels of investment. Tramway rails have been torn up, and trolleybus and bus lines have been sharply cut back, in part to clear roads for automobile use. The city's subway system, the Metro, with some of the deepest stations in the world, has been expanded, though at a pace much slower than originally planned. The completion of the city's ring road in 2008 removed some traffic from the city's center, but the ring road has also been widely

criticized for its poor construction and has been plagued by accidents.

Loss of Green Space

New construction of commercial and residential buildings has led to a sharp loss of green space in the city. This is particularly evident in the historic center, where green space has long been in short supply. Parks, children's playgrounds, and inner courtyards have become the sites of highly controversial infill construction. Similarly, the city's outer green belt inherited from the Soviet period is being actively dismantled as commercial centers and suburban residences are built. Road construction has also impacted those green belts, such as the building of the widely criticized Western High-Speed Diameter through Yuntolovsky Zapovednik (Yuntolovsky nature reserve). Expropriation of private property, including ironically the former territory of private automobile garages, for road construction has also been the source of much controversy.

Threats to Architectural Heritage

With its large number of museums, theaters, and educational institutions, St. Petersburg continues to be considered Russia's cultural capital. After the Nazi siege of the city (then Leningrad, 1941–1944), the city's historic center was largely restored to its previous condition and is a showcase of eighteenth- and nineteenth-century architecture by Western European architects. Indeed, the city is called "The Venice of the North" by its residents due to its large network of canals and its neoclassical architecture. The city is also famous for its "white nights" during the period of near all-day light in the summer months due to its far northern latitude. The city's designation in 1990 as a World Heritage Site by the United Nations Educational, Scientific and Cultural Organization (UNESCO) made it the world's largest such site in an urban setting. Despite the designation, beginning in 2005 developers constructed a large number of disharmonious glass and steel buildings within the city's historic center that have been the source of much public criticism. (See figure 1 on page 288.) More than one hundred historic buildings were demolished during that same period. Nevsky Prospect, the city's central street, has lost six historic buildings to new construction since 2005. New high-rise buildings have significantly altered the previously low horizontal panoramas along the Neva River in the city center. Loss of the city's architectural heritage has become a highly politicized topic, and it is cited as one of the reasons for which city governor Valentina Matvienko was replaced in August 2011. Reconstruction of the New Holland Island by the New York City firm WORKac, the

Figure 1. New Construction

Photo: Nathaniel S. Trumbull.

This 2010 photo shows the new Nevsky Shopping Center, across from St. Petersburg's neo-Renaissance Moscow Train Station. St. Petersburg governor Valentina Matvienko had promised that the Center would look identical to the buildings in the two blocks demolished to make way for it, but the glass and steel of the top of the building was entirely new.

modern design of an expansion of the Mariinsky Theater by the Toronto firm Diamond+Schmitt, and the planned superskyscraper Okhta (now Lakhta) Center of a new Gazprom headquarters in the city have been subjects of intense architectural and political debate in the city.

Positive Trends and Ongoing Challenges

A few recent positive environmental trends have emerged in St. Petersburg. The city's combined heating and power plants have been converted from coal to cleaner-burning natural gas. The completed flood barrier serves also as support for a highway by which truck and automobile traffic now pass by Neva Bay, and the ring road allows traffic to pass around rather than through the city center. Residential water metering and natural gas metering are slowly being implemented. New rules for paid parking in the city center may help alleviate traffic congestion.

Other social problems loom large, however. As elsewhere in Russia, public health care is of poor quality. City residents' average longevity is far below Western standards. As in most other cities making the post-Soviet transition to a market economy, St. Petersburg has witnessed an increasingly growing divide between a small wealthy class and much larger lower-income portion of the population. Civil society is only in its infancy and faces a system of highly prejudicial courts. Environmental and social nongovernmental organizations remain marginalized. Corruption and cronyism among city leaders is recognized to be a persistent obstacle to improving effective city governance.

Nathaniel S. TRUMBULL
University of Connecticut

See also London, United Kingdom; Moscow, Russia; Novosibirsk, Russia; Russia and the Soviet Union; Scandinavia; Stockholm, Sweden; Urbanization (Europe); Warsaw, Poland

FURTHER READING

Bater, James. (1996). *Russia and the post-Soviet scene: A geographical perspective.* New York: John Wiley & Sons.

Blinnikov, Mikhail. (2011). *A geography of Russia and its neighbors.* New York: Guilford Press.

Dixon, Megan. (2010). Gazprom versus the skyline: Spatial displacement and social contention in St. Petersburg. *International Journal of Urban and Regional Research, 34*(1), 35–54.

Gillmor, Don. (2010). Red tape. Retrieved September 15, 2011, from http://www.walrusmagazine.com/articles/2010.05--red-tape/

Golubchikov, O. (2010). World-city-entrepreneurialism: Globalist imaginaries, neoliberal geographies, and the production of new St. Petersburg. *Environment and Planning A, 42*(3), 626–643.

Lonkila, Markku. (2011). Driving at democracy in Russia: Protest activities of St. Petersburg car drivers' associations, *Europe-Asia Studies, 63*(2), 291–309.

May, Rachel; Ignatieva, Maria; & Rolley, Nikolai. (2011). The Neva Project: Ecology and cultural history in an urban river. Retrieved on September 15, 2011, from http://enspire.syr.edu/nevaproject/Nevahome.html

Ruble, B. (1990). *Leningrad: Shaping a Soviet city.* Berkeley: University of California Press.

Salisbury, H. E. (2003). *The 900 days: The siege of Leningrad.* New York: Da Capo Press.

Shaw, D. J. B. (1978). Planning Leningrad. *Geographical Review, 68*(2), 181–200.

Trumbull, Nathaniel. (2007). Pressures on urban water resources in Russia: The case of St. Petersburg. *Eurasian Geography and Economics, 48*(4), 495–506.

Scandinavia

34.9 million est. pop. 2010

Scandinavia has a varied environmental and geographical makeup—from mountains in Norway and Sweden, to forests in Finland, agricultural land in Denmark, and extensive barren areas (yielding geothermal heat in many places) in Iceland. Although the region ranks high in terms of quality of life, it does have environmental problems, such as air and marine pollution. Green politics are supported across the region, although in Norway whaling and oil reserves remain divisive issues. Recent efforts in Scandinavia have reduced sulfur emissions from local industries to less than half from their peak in the 1970s, but pollutants from outside the region continue to affect forests.

Scandinavia consists of five nations in Northern Europe: Norway, Sweden, Denmark, Finland, and, far off in the North Atlantic, Iceland. (The term *Nordic* is also sometimes used for roughly the same region, especially with reference to the Nordic Council—Norway, Sweden, Finland, Denmark, Iceland, Greenland, and the Faroe Islands.) The Scandinavian Peninsula is (technically) made up of only Norway and Sweden, although Finland is usually included in the term, as well. Denmark is the only one of the countries directly connected to Europe and is separated from the peninsula by the Baltic Sea and the Skagerrak and Kattegat straits.

Scandinavia's climate varies from tundra and subarctic—with parts of Norway, Sweden, and Finland lying north of the Arctic Circle, and Iceland coming very close to the circle—to milder temperate zones in Denmark and southern Sweden. The terrain varies, with mountains in Norway and Sweden more than 2,000 meters tall, to heavily forested lake regions in Finland and flat coastal plains in southern

Sweden and Denmark. Iceland possesses a unique landscape marked by treeless, grassy plains and large barren, rocky areas created by recent geological activity, and the island has several active volcanoes.

Despite their geographical separation, the five Scandinavian countries share strong linguistic, historical, and cultural ties dating back centuries. Sweden is the most populous country, with just under 9 million inhabitants, followed by Denmark (5.2 million), Finland (5.1 million), Norway (4.4 million), and Iceland (only 266,000). All five countries are modern industrialized societies, with some of the world's highest standards of living. Principal economic activities include heavy manufacturing, mining, shipping, electronics, telecommunications, forestry, and fishing. Norway possesses a large petroleum and natural gas industry based on the country's North Sea oil fields. Agriculture plays a minor role in the Scandinavian economy, with the exception of Denmark, much of whose land is intensively farmed.

Environmental Challenges

Like other industrial countries, the Scandinavian countries face a variety of environmental challenges. The region has more uninhabited wilderness than other areas of Europe, especially in Iceland and the Arctic territory; population growth over the twentieth century, however, has put pressure on the remaining wilderness areas. Principal endangered species in Scandinavia include the Arctic fox, lynx, wolf, and wolverine. Also, the Saimaa freshwater seal, a rare species found only in one isolated Finnish lake, is all but extinct, with fewer than one hundred left in the wild.

Given the importance of fishing to the Scandinavian economies, marine pollution is a particular concern.

Pollution levels in the Baltic Sea have risen to the point that many of the fish are no longer edible, and the Scandinavian fishing industry has thus sharply declined since the 1970s. Oil pollution from shipping and offshore drilling has caused numerous problems, with a blowout at Norway's Ekofisk oil field in 1977 releasing 22,000 metric tons of oil into the marine environment. The leaching of fertilizers into the sea led to eutrophication that caused a large algal bloom off the Swedish coast in 1988; it killed thousands of fish and was one of the worst cases on record.

All Scandinavian countries are wrestling with ground and water contamination, especially from heavy metals and chemicals. Denmark's agricultural industry has also resulted in fertilizer and pesticide contamination in that country.

Air pollution is also a problem, and the region was among the first to recognize the threat of acid rain. Recent efforts in Scandinavia have reduced sulfur emissions from local industries to less than half from their peak in the 1970s, but pollutants from outside the region continue to affect forests.

Iceland has some of the cleanest air in the world, due in part to the fact that a large percentage of the country's energy (apart from motor vehicles) is generated from geothermal sources, and that the island is generally quite windy. Volcanic eruptions, however, do occasionally cause spikes in particulate matter, especially from windborne ash. The newsworthy eruptions of Iceland's Eyjafjallajökull volcano in April and May 2010, while relatively small, disrupted air traffic for hundreds of thousands of travelers, mainly going to and from northern Europe. The United Nations Environment Programme (UNEP) estimates that the grounding of European flights during this time meant that around 344,000 tonnes of carbon dioxide (CO_2) emissions from airplanes per day were avoided; the UNEP estimates that the volcano itself emitted around 150,000 tonnes of CO_2 per day during this period (UNEP 2011, 2).

Environmental Activism

Scandinavia has some of the highest levels of environmental activism in the world. The region has a long history of protecting wilderness areas, its first nature reserves having been established in the early 1900s. More recently Scandinavia's Arctic regions have become popular destinations for environmental tourism. Most Scandinavian cities have regulations pertaining to urban growth and recycling. Scandinavian countries have also led the way in renewable energy sources, with Denmark investing heavily in wind turbine technology, and Iceland relying almost exclusively on geothermal sources.

Since the late 1970s, green politics has become increasingly influential, and a majority of Scandinavians now favor environmental protection over economic growth. The Swedish Green Party (Miljöpartiet de Gröna), formed in 1981, enjoyed its first electoral successes in 1988, sending several members to the parliament. In 1995 a member of the Finnish Green Party (Vihreä Lütto) was named Finland's environment minister. The green parties in Denmark and Norway have been less successful, though in Denmark, the Red-Green Alliance helped elect a center-left coalition government in September 2011 (Nichols 2011). Norway, in particular, is deeply divided over the issue of whaling; it has not agreed to calls for a ban on commercial whaling and still engages in small-scale whaling for scientific purposes.

In Sweden, trees are the most abundant natural resource after iron ore. An investigation in late 2011 into forestry practices in Sweden revealed that clear-cutting is common. The forestry rules in the country are lax after restrictive legislation was replaced in 1993 with a more voluntary system. At one particular plot, 95 percent of all trees were witnessed to have been cut down for lumber, fuel, and paper. Locals are doing something about this—having observed that conservation trumps industry, they are educating themselves and others in biodiversity, identifying rare species in the forests, and highlighting these to forestry companies and the government before they are cut down. Despite these actions, there is still a fear for the future of Swedish forests (Hoffner 2011).

Outlook

Scandinavia is in the forefront of environmental stewardship. In Copenhagen, a "cycle superhighway" opened in April 2012, the first of twenty-six such planned routes. The "highway" links twenty-one local municipalities whose governments collaborated to ensure that there were contiguous, standardized (i.e., with similar lighting and road surfaces) bike routes into the city, across distances of up to 22 kilometers (McGrane 2012). (See the sidebar on page 347.) In Stockholm, with its easy access to green space and clean water even in the city center, carbon dioxide emissions have decreased by nearly 600,000 tonnes per year since 1990, in part due to an innovative district-wide (as opposed to individual) heating and cooling system; this system is the world's largest of its kind (Stockholm Business Region 2010, 18). These are but two examples of many in a region well known for its progressive attitudes toward the environment. The world will continue to look to Scandinavia for inspiration for a more sustainable future.

James H. LIDE
History Associates Incorporated

See also Biodiversity Conservation; Ecotourism; Education, Environmental; Energy Security (Europe); Fisheries; Parks and Preserves; Stockholm, Sweden; Svalbard Global Seed Vault

This article was adapted by the editors from James H. Lide's article "Scandinavia" in Shepard Krech III, J. R. McNeill, and Carolyn Merchant (Eds.), the *Encyclopedia of World Environmental History*, pp. 1097–1099. Great Barrington, MA: Berkshire Publishing (2003).

FURTHER READING

Agger, Peder, & Utzon-Frank, Tine. (Eds.). (1995). *Nordic nature: Prior requirements and principles of nature conservation in the Nordic countries.* Copenhagen: Nordic Council of Ministers.

Alanen, Arnold R. (1995). *Nordic environment: Historical and contemporary perspectives.* Madison: University of Wisconsin Department of Scandinavian Studies.

Bernes, Claes. (1993). *The Nordic environment: Present state, trends, and threats.* Copenhagen: Nordic Council of Ministers.

Bernes, Claes. (1996). *The Nordic environment: Unspoiled, exploited, polluted?* Copenhagen: Nordic Council of Ministers.

Historical Atlas. (n.d.). Population of Scandinavia: Official population statistics. Retrieved June 12, 2012, from http://www.tacitus.nu/historical-atlas/population/scandinavia.htm

Hoffner, Erik. (2011, December 28). A green veneer: Sweden's forestry industry gets low marks despite reputation. *National Geographic.* Retrieved January 27, 2012, from http://newswatch.nationalgeographic.com/2011/12/28/a-green-veneer-sweden%E2%80%99s-forestry-industry-gets-low-marks-despite-reputation/

McGrane, Sally. (2012, July 17). Commuters pedal to work on their very own superhighway. *The New York Times.* Retrieved August 8, 2012, from http://www.nytimes.com/2012/07/18/world/europe/in-denmark-pedaling-to-work-on-a-superhighway.html?pagewanted=all

Munk, Peter. (Ed.). (1996). *Governing the environment: Politics, policy and organization in the Nordic countries.* Copenhagen: Nordic Council of Ministers.

Nichols, Dick. (2011). Denmark: Red-Green Alliance triples vote as right thrown out. Retrieved December 16, 2011, from http://www.greenleft.org.au/node/48860

Stockholm Business Region. (2010). Green Stockholm 2010. Retrieved August 9, 2012, from http://www.investstockholm.com/Global/Investment%20promotion/Dokument/green%20cap%20LR.pdf

United Nations Environment Programme (UNEP). (2011). Year book 2011: An overview of our changing environment. Retrieved August 8, 2012, from http://hqweb.unep.org/yearbook/2011/pdfs/events_and_development.pdf

Shipping and Freight

Water-based transportation modes are considered more environmentally "friendly" than other modes such as road haulage and aviation. Nevertheless, the shipping industry faces several severe sustainability issues, including greenhouse gas emissions, ocean contamination, and ship disposal. Shipping in Africa and Europe is marked by the difficulty of enforcing international regulations and by the fact that the national laws with which ships have to comply change as ships change territorial waters.

Among the five fundamental modes of transportation—air, road, rail, pipeline, and sea—sea transportation is normally considered to be the one with the second lowest carbon emissions per tonne-kilometer (World Economic Forum 2009), surpassed only by pipeline cargo transportation.

Although levels of carbon emissions and associated problems of climate change rank among today's most debated topics, the environmental impact of shipping is more diverse than the current general debate on sustainability in logistics and transportation suggests. There are three main environmental issues facing the modern shipping industry: carbon dioxide (CO_2) and other greenhouse gas (GHG) emissions, contamination of the ocean (with its concomitant destruction of oceanic biodiversity), and shipbreaking (the disposal of ships at the end of their lifetime). While Europe has enforced regulations promoting cleaner ship disposal practices and is contemplating expanding its emission trading system to the shipping industry, African countries are struggling to cope with the environmental damage the shipping industry creates.

Water-based transportation clearly includes inland navigation as well as sea transportation, but the focus of this article is on sea transport. The reason for this is two-fold. Transportation by sea for one thing far exceeds transportation by inland navigation: while the absolute amount of tonne-kilometers transported has risen almost continuously since the beginning of the century (European Commission 2010), the relative share of inland transportation in the European Union (EU) has dropped to 5.9 percent (Eurostat 2011). Secondly, most of the sustainability issues relevant to sea transportation apply equally to inland waterways and do not require a separate consideration.

Contamination of the Sea

Contamination of the sea and destruction of oceanic biodiversity have several roots, among which are ship accidents at sea where the crew is forced to lighten cargo (intentionally disposing of cargo at sea, under duress, to prevent loss of the entire ship), garbage disposal at sea (illegal dumping of refuse), and the accidental release of cargo (often chemical) from sunken or damaged ships. A sunken ship is a disaster waiting to happen because, if its cargo was not released before the sinking, it will eventually be released into the sea. In Africa, for example, almost all of the 260,000 tonnes of heavy crude oil on board the oil tanker *ABT Summer* were released into the sea when the ship sank off the coast of the Republic of Angola in 1991 (IncidentNews 2012). Similarly, the oil tanker *Katina P*, which sank off the coast of Mozambique in 1992, released approximately 72,000 tonnes of crude oil into the ocean. Both incidents caused severe environmental damage. In 2009, between 1,500 and 2,000 tonnes of oil were accidentally spilled in EU waters alone (European Maritime Safety Agency 2010). There is no estimate on amounts of illegally discharged oil.

Our oceans have been labelled the world's biggest garbage dump (McLendon 2010). Garbage floating in the oceans can easily be seen on satellite photos; in the Pacific there is a dump twice the size of the US state of Texas (McLendon 2010). Sea disposal of shipping refuse has historically been common practice due to the mistaken belief that the ocean's immense size ruled out the possibility of contaminating its ecosystem. Furthermore, it is far less expensive than regular disposal, or even recycling. And, because tracing back sea pollution to its specific originator is virtually impossible, the fear of being caught is not a deterrent when it comes to the practice of illegal dumping at sea.

Emissions

Shipping activities account for approximately 3.3 percent of total global CO_2 emissions (Zahedi 2011). In the EU, navigation is the source of 15.3 percent of the carbon emissions produced by transportation (European Commission 2010). For Africa, equivalent data from reliable sources are hard to come by, possibly because of the lack of awareness of sustainability issues within the shipping industry. It is important to consider, however, that shipping not only produces carbon emissions but also sulphur oxides (SO_x) and nitrogen oxides (NO_x), both of which contribute to climate change, perhaps even more so than carbon emissions.

The problem with emissions is exacerbated by the inherent difficulties associated with the enforcement of regulations. As ships regularly change territorial waters, so also do the national laws with which they must comply; in addition, national laws cannot be enforced in international waters, and international agreements have been hard to reach. Currently, sea traffic is mostly excluded from any fiscal burdens related to emissions. It is not included, for example, in the European Emissions Trading System that grew out of the Kyoto Protocol, part of an international environmental treaty initiated by the United Nations to fight global warming.

One of the chief culprits contributing to environmental pollution in the shipping industry is so-called bunker fuel, which is a heavy residue of oil processing and the most prevalent ship fuel in use. Bunker fuel is the most environmentally damaging of all the fuels because of its high sulphur content.

Another culprit is port congestion, the equivalent of traffic congestion in urban areas. Because ports have only a limited amount of dockage and limited number of cargo and container cranes, ships often have to queue up and lie at anchor outside the harbor while they await their turn to discharge and pick up cargo. In Durban, South Africa, Africa's busiest port, the amount of cargo that is moved in and out of the port has surpassed the port's handling capacity. The same holds true for the port of Tema, Ghana, where the number of containers that require handling forces carriers to wait for hours upon hours to complete

their business (USAID 2005). The consequences of this congestion are not only economically devastating for the domino effect delays they effectuate, but also because longer lead times translate to higher costs as a result of port congestion surcharges. Moreover, the port congestion also leads to higher fuel consumption, due to standby times, which, in turn, leads to higher environmental pollution.

Ship Disposal

Shipbreaking—a common type of ship disposal that involves the scrapping of all reusable parts of the ship—is reminiscent of recycling and therefore may, at first sight, appear to be environmentally friendly. But the process of shipbreaking itself leads to both environmental and social problems. The deconstruction of a ship is costly, owing to its labor-intensive nature and, in many regions, to legislation governing the handling of different types of waste materials. The long-distance cargo sector, however, has managed to take advantage of the unregulated spaces of international trade to avoid compliance with local regulations. In order to avoid European laws, for example, the shipbreaking sector moved from Europe to China and Taiwan, where enforcement was lax. When enforcement of regulations in these countries was strengthened, the shipbreaking sector moved again, this time to South Asia. Although most vessels today are broken down in India and other Asian countries, such as Bangladesh and Pakistan, where labor costs and costs for garbage treatment are low, some experts believe that the industry is once again getting ready to move, this time to ports in Africa (The Ecologist 2010). One of the world's largest shipbreaking yards is already in Nuadibú, Mauritania. The workers there are often unqualified—a factor that increases the likelihood of accidents with the highly toxic materials—and are exploited under terrible working conditions. Toxic effluents and other wastes are dealt with inappropriately and, consequently, significantly contaminate beaches, oceans, and the workers themselves (Vardar et al. 2005).

Because it is difficult for governing bodies to regulate the shipping industry, efforts to reduce environmental damage by the shipping industry are introduced either by international entities, or they are introduced as port initiatives. Private firms have introduced some scattered attempts, either on their own or in association with other firms.

International Maritime Organization

The most prominent and potent international body dealing with ship traffic is the International Maritime Organization (IMO), a United States–based agency of the United Nations responsible for the safety and security of shipping and the prevention of marine pollution by ships. While its main responsibility was originally the provision of international safety standards, the IMO has become an important driver of more sustainable shipping practices and has contributed greatly to providing internationally accepted rules for global sea freight since its foundation in 1948 (IMO 2011a).

In 1973, the IMO adopted the International Convention for the Prevention of Pollution by Ships (known as MARPOL), which addresses several types of pollution by ships and applies to 99 percent of the world's merchant tonnage (IMO 2011b). Among other things, MARPOL prohibits the disposal of plastics anywhere into the sea and obliges governments to provide garbage reception facilities at ports and terminals. All large vessels are required to have a Garbage Management Plan that includes written procedures for collecting, processing, storing, and disposing of garbage. This thorough process ensures that the whereabouts of any items brought onto the vessel can be determined at any given moment. It is now almost impossible to get rid of garbage at sea as this would reduce the expected weight of garbage at the point of destination. Similar approaches are taken to reduce the amount of sewage drained from vessels into the oceans.

The IMO has also set safety standards for building and operating oil tankers that will minimize oil spills in the event of an accident, or in the event that cargo must be intentionally discharged at sea to avoid loss of the entire ship. A similar approach has been taken for transportation of potentially hazardous chemicals such as those that are flammable, toxic, corrosive, or reactive. The IMO helped define standards for vessels that should be used in the transportation of different types of chemicals to ensure their safe transport.

Finally, in 2009, the IMO adopted the Hong Kong Convention for the Safe and Environmentally Sound Recycling of Ships, a resolution that regulates the design, construction, operation, and preparation of ships in order to facilitate safe and environmentally sound recycling. The convention also regulates ship recycling facilities to make sure they are run in a safe and environmentally sound manner and includes an enforcement mechanism that includes certification and reporting requirements. Every ship must carry a Green Passport, an inventory of all the ship's materials that are potentially hazardous to the environment, and every ship recycling yard must provide a Ship Recycling Plan that explains in detail how each ship will be recycled. The IMO works on the implementation of this resolution.

Industry Initiatives in Africa and Europe

National states continually struggle with the definition and global application of internationally written rules and regulations for environmental protection and safety, and the IMO seeks to arbitrate in this area, independent of the home country from which a vessel originates. Another promising avenue for fostering environmental protection is that of industry initiatives. The Green Award Foundation, one such initiative, is dedicated to promoting the safe and environmentally friendly operation of ship, crew, and management. Originally founded in 1994 by the port authority of Rotterdam, the Netherlands, and the Dutch Department of Transport, the now-independent foundation issues the Green Award certificate as a reward for high safety and environmental standards in shipping. The certificate integrates the expectations from multiple international conventions, legislations, and developments in the area of ship layout, equipment, crew, operations, and management. The certification procedure consists of an office audit and an audit of each individual ship applying for certification. The document is valid for three years and is subject to annual verification. The drawback has been its limited applicability. To date, only oil tankers and bulk carriers are eligible to apply, but future plans will include liquid natural gas tankers as well. Around two dozen international ports (including most ports in South Africa) and several port service providers grant price reductions for ships holding this certificate. Some major European ports, in an effort to better handle capacity and promote sustainability, now charge higher rates and port dues for vessels that do not hold a Green Award certificate. In addition, some government institutions and private companies set out financial incentives for vessels that do hold the certificate.

A more recent initiative is the World Ports Climate Initiative (WPCI), launched in 2008. Fifty of the most important ports and port authorities worldwide participate in this association. These include the four largest ports in Europe: Rotterdam, Le Havre, Bremerhaven, and Hamburg; and, in Africa: the Ministry of Transport of Kenya, the national port authority of Kenya, the authorities of Lagos State (an administrative division of Nigeria), and the national port authority of South Africa, all of which are among the ten busiest ports on the African continent. The aim of the WPCI is to raise awareness, initiate projects to reduce GHG emissions, and provide an information exchange platform for the maritime sector (WPCI 2011). One of their projects, an initiative similar to the Green Award certificate, is the Environmental Ship Index which grades ships on the basis of their environmental performance and awards them points. As of the beginning of 2012, fifty ships belonging to different companies and seven ports participated in this voluntary system. Although this initiative does take sulphur dioxide and nitrogen into account, its shortcoming is that it has no punitive component but rather only grants rewards to participants in the form of discounts on port charges.

Shipping Firm Initiatives

The shipping sector is a global and very competitive one, in which cost reduction and "race-to-the-bottom" (in this case, meaning the tendency of some multinational corporations to cut costs by changing the location of their operations to countries that have little or no environmental regulations) play a fundamental role. In regions like the EU, especially in countries like Germany or the Scandinavian countries where environmental sensitivity is high and corresponding claims for environmental protection are higher, many firms would willingly embrace the new approaches in order to become more sustainable. Sustainability frequently comes at a cost, however, for example by making the investment in modern, low-emission vessels. Consequently, and for as long as international competitors do not do the same, firms have to look for ways to avoid losses and competitive disadvantages by seeking to pass on the costs for sustainable technologies to their customers.

Even so, many of the activities that companies undertake to promote sustainability do have the added advantage of reducing costs. During the economic crisis beginning in 2008, for example, speed reduction was widely implemented as a measure to decrease fuel usage and costs. Other measures that can reduce costs are load optimization and improved fleet planning to avoid standby time and losses incurred when vessels are less than fully loaded. Ever mindful of good customer relations, most major shipping companies offer a CO_2 calculator on their websites, which enables customers to calculate the carbon footprint of their cargo.

Other companies bank on technical innovations to save fuel. Among the latest inventions are large foil kites that can be attached to a vessel to deliver additional power. Ships employing this technology become hybrid vehicles with two types of propulsion. The first commercial cargo ships to be equipped with kites have already been tested, reportedly reducing annual fuel costs by 20 percent (BBC News 2008).

Future Outlook

While public debate concentrates mostly on emissions from aviation and road transportation, sustainability issues are pressing in the shipping industry as well. As national regulations have limited power, it will continue to be up to international organizations and private firms to take the initiative. Both the scientific community and international regulatory bodies will have to be involved. Scientists need to continue their efforts to develop new fuel compositions to replace the environmentally damaging bunker fuel. The European Commission, meanwhile, is working along these lines by suggesting that, from 2013 on, air and sea traffic be included in the emissions trading system.

Anna GROBECKER and Julia WOLF
EBS Business School, Germany

See also African Union (AU); Corporate Accountability (Africa); European Union (EU); European Union Greenhouse Gas Emission Trading Scheme (EU ETS); Germany; Rule of Law (Africa); Rule of Law (European Union); Scandinavia

FURTHER READING

British Broadcasting Company (BBC) News. (2008, January 22). Kite to pull ship across Atlantic. Retrieved February 24, 2012, from http://news.bbc.co.uk/2/hi/7201887.stm

The Ecologist. (2010, March 2). Shipbreaking: Clampdown in Asia will send it to Africa. Retrieved February 6, 2012, from http://www.theecologist.org/News/news_analysis/430969/shipbreaking_clampdown_in_asia_will_send_it_to_africa.html

European Commission. (2010). *EU energy and transport in figures: Statistical pocketbook 2010.* Luxembourg: Publications Office of the European Union.

European Maritime Safety Agency. (2010). Maritime accident review 2010. Retrieved September 4, 2011, from http://www.emsa.europa.eu/implementation-tasks/accident-investigation/item/1219.html?cuscat=141

Eurostat. (2011). Sustainable development: Transport. Retrieved February 27, 2012, from http://epp.eurostat.ec.europa.eu/statistics_explained/index.php/Sustainable_development_-_Transport#Greenhouse_gas_emissions_from_transport

IncidentNews: Office of Response and Restoration. (2012). Homepage. Retrieved February 7, 2012, from http://www.incidentnews.gov/

International Maritime Organization (IMO). (2011a). Brief history of IMO. Retrieved September 5, 2011, from http://www.imo.org/About/HistoryOfIMO/Pages/Default.aspx

International Maritime Organization (IMO). (2011b). Pollution prevention. Retrieved September 5, 2011, from http://www.imo.org/OurWork/Environment/PollutionPrevention/Pages/Default.aspx

International Maritime Organization (IMO). (2011c). Recycling of ships. Retrieved September 7, 2011, from http://www.imo.org/OurWork/Environment/ShipRecycling/Pages/Default.aspx

McLendon, Russell. (2010, February 24). What is the Great Pacific Ocean Garbage Patch? Retrieved September 4, 2011, from http://www.mnn.com/earth-matters/translating-uncle-sam/stories/what-is-the-great-pacific-ocean-garbage-patch

United States Agency for International Development (USAID). (2005). Trade developments. Port congestion in Africa. Implications for competitiveness and economic growth. Retrieved February 6, 2012, from http://pdf.usaid.gov/pdf_docs/PNADH133.pdf

Vardar, Erdem, et al. (2005). End of life ships: The human cost of breaking ships (A Greenpeace-FIDH Report in Cooperation with YPSA). Amsterdam, The Netherlands: Greenpeace International.

World Economic Forum (WEF). (2009). *Supply chain decarbonization: The role of logistics and transport in reducing supply chain carbon emissions.* Geneva: WEF.

World Ports Climate Initiative (WPCI). (2011). About us: Mission statement. Retrieved September 5, 2011, from http://www.wpci.nl/about_us/mission_statement.php

Zahedi, Kaveh. (2011). The emissions gap and the potential role of shipping. Third intersessional meeting of the working group on GHG emissions from ships. United Nations Environment Programme.

Stockholm, Sweden

2.1 million est. pop. 2011 Stockholm County; 864,000 est. pop. 2011 Stockholm municipality

Across Europe, and indeed across the world, Stockholm is well known for its endeavors toward urban sustainability. In 2010, Stockholm was the first city to receive the European Green Capital award from the European Union Commission. The city has been noted for improving energy efficiency in buildings, diverting all household waste from landfills, and developing ecodistricts. In a European perspective, however, Stockholm is a fast-growing metropolitan area, which creates challenges for its environmentally sensitive approach to urban and regional planning.

In comparison to countries like the United Kingdom, the Netherlands, or Germany, space is not necessarily a limiting factor in Swedish urban development because of its low population density (around 21 inhabitants per square kilometer on average). Urban sprawl indeed became one of the defining characteristics of Swedish urban development in the twentieth century and is still a major challenge for sustainable urban planning. Population growth and a renewed interest in the inner city, reflected in market pressure, however, have ensured that land in the inner city is at a premium. This has led to increased efforts at densification during the past two decades, although sprawl is still a threat in some outlying areas. Given the climatic conditions in the Nordic countries, it is not surprising that the overall energy consumption per capita is high. Rising living standards, especially in large urban areas, have contributed to increasing energy consumption, not only in terms of heating and electricity consumption but also transport, because cars have become a more common choice.

The urban area of Stockholm has spread outward over the centuries from the Old Town (Gamla Stan), on a ridge between Lake Mälaren and the Baltic Sea. Clearly identifiable annual rings show where development has jumped over to the next island and/or next municipality. As of 2012 the larger Stockholm urban agglomeration is marked, morphologically (i.e., regarding its physical urban form) and functionally, by a monocentric layout, shaped by the inner city of Stockholm and a number of neighboring dense urban areas with a relatively high concentration of workplaces. Nevertheless, as communication infrastructure was enhanced (in close connection to the construction of the Stockholm's subway system), urban settlements spread outward, creating suburbs. (See figure 1 on page 298.)

The characteristics of Stockholm's physical environment—a series of islands and the bodies of water around them—contribute to both the concentration of population and the transport challenges; distances are longer, and the basic transport infrastructure is extremely costly to build, in particular due to the need to build bridges or tunnels through rock. At the same time, Stockholm's urban environmental quality is perceived to be high, with many blue and green wedges throughout the central city.

Stockholm has seen almost continuous growth, albeit at varying pace during the twentieth century. In recent years the population in particular has increased relatively quickly in the city of Stockholm, as well as across Stockholm County, with an annual growth rate of 30,000 inhabitants per year—3.5 percent higher than the rest of the country. At the end of 2010, the population of Stockholm County was 2.1 million, while the city of Stockholm had 847,000 inhabitants. The latest forecasts predict that the population of Stockholm County will reach 2.4 million inhabitants by 2030 (maybe even higher

Figure 1. Urbanization in Stockholm, 1945 to 2004

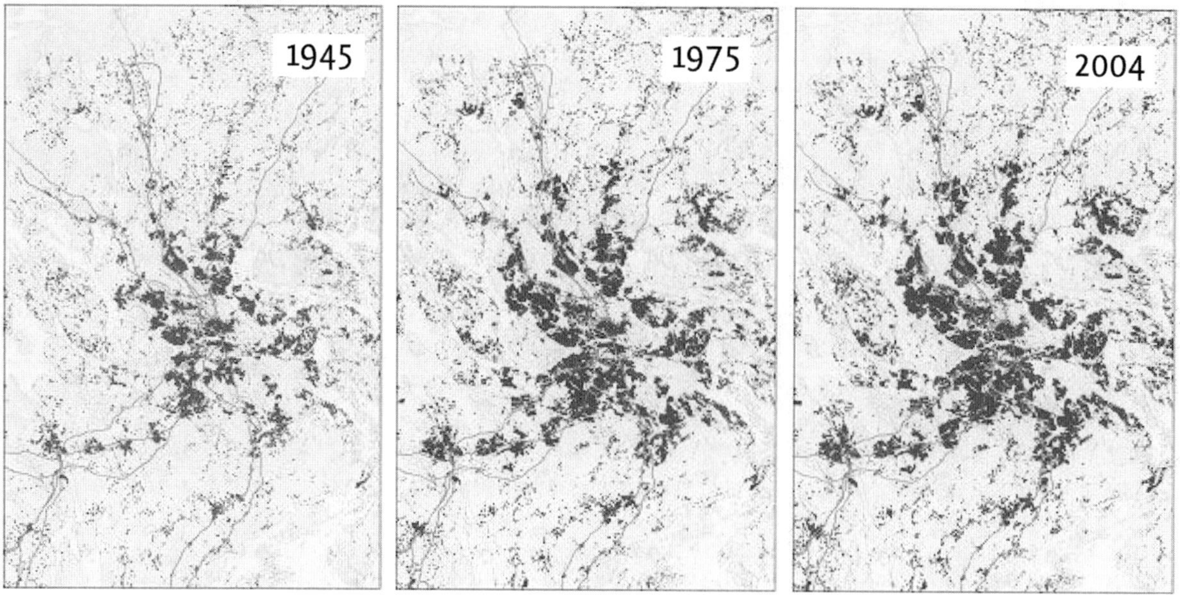

Source: Provided courtesy of Stockholms läns landsting (Office of Regional Planning) (2010).

The growth of population, the rise of car ownership, and distinct topography (expanses of water punctuated with islands) have contributed to Stockholm's rapid expansion in the past sixty years.

at the current rate of growth). Contributing to population growth are the ongoing migration into Stockholm County (from other parts of Sweden, but also from abroad) and the current baby boom (around 2.1 children per woman in Stockholm County) (Office of Regional Planning 2010).

Sustainable Urban and Regional Planning

For many decades, the interplay between enlarging housing and labor markets and improving the regional transport system has defined the regional planning discourse. According to the Office of Regional Growth, Environment and Planning (until 2010 called the Office of Regional Planning), the transport system in the Stockholm region is close to its capacity limits: road traffic has increased by 80 percent since 1970, while the road surface area has increased by only 10 to 20 percent. Examples of short-term improvements to the transport infrastructure are the extension of the local tram network and the construction of a third track for the north-south light railway through the city (Stahre 2007, 99). Meanwhile, the congestion charge, an environmental tax for roadway users, permanently implemented in 2007, has helped reduce commuter trips by private car (Dymén and Henriksson 2009).

Densification and polycentric development are the operative words in the current urban planning discourse in Stockholm. Such concepts can be found in current planning documents at the municipal and county levels in Stockholm (Office of Regional Planning 2010; RUFS 2010; Stockholm Stad 2010). The city of Stockholm aims to strengthen a handful of centers outside the inner city by improving public transport and by creating higher densities and a better functional mix of services and jobs. The region, too, has a polycentric development strategy, aiming to develop eight so-called regional centers at a distance of fifteen to forty kilometers from the inner city of Stockholm; the selected municipal and regional centers differ, however, which means competition in some cases. The regional plan argues that in addition to offering a number of functional and economic benefits, a polycentric strategy will enable land consumption and energy use related to transport to be minimized.

The most recent municipal and regional development plans identify spatial and land-use planning as important factors for mitigating and adapting to climate change. Stockholm has an ambitious goal to be free of fossil fuels by 2050; further densification, effective district heating, and improved public transport systems are central to reaching this goal (Stockholm Stad 2010). This goal is at odds, however, with the ongoing debate over regional enlargement in East Central Sweden, which would integrate the Stockholm region with its larger hinterland.

The idea here is that through better transport connectivity (in particular, an improved road network), it would be possible to enlarge the daily urban system and hence the potential labor market for Stockholm's core (Office of Regional Planning 2010).

The city of Stockholm implemented the Stockholm Environment Programme for 2012 to 2015, which takes account of the city's growth and aims to maintain Stockholm's high-quality environment. The program promotes sustainability in six key areas: (1) Environmentally efficient transport, intended to reduce the city's impact on climate, the environment, and residents' health, is to be realized through improvements in technology, efficient public transport, and incentives to use alternatives to the private car. (2) To ensure that goods and buildings are free of dangerous substances, the city will identify and avoid using dangerous substances itself and will encourage the safe handling of chemicals. The city of Stockholm will also ensure that 25 percent of the food it purchases is organic. (3) The program will promote sustainable energy use through more energy-efficient technology and a shift to renewables and through the city's overall aim of being climate-neutral and fossil fuel–free by 2050. (4) Sustainable use of land and water will be promoted in several ways. Land and water areas of particular attraction for biodiversity or recreation will be preserved and developed. Development of other land and water areas will be minimized and compensated for; where development occurs, it will be designed with future climate changes in mind. (5) In encouraging waste treatment with minimal environmental impact, the city aims to minimize waste and increase the percentage that is reused and recycled. Waste management is intended to help close eco-cycles and save energy and natural resources. (6) Finally, the goal is to realize healthy indoor environments and reduce the percentage of people adversely affected by their indoor environment. The city will lead by example through efforts to improve indoor environments in schools, preschools, care institutions, and municipally owned housing.

In addition to the Stockholm Environment Programme goals, the Stockholm City Plan, the document that guides all development in the city, focuses on promoting a walkable city while harnessing the strengths of its natural surroundings, promoting business and education, fostering social cohesion, and meeting housing needs in a growing city (City of Stockholm 2012c).

The City of Stockholm has been successful in diverting waste from landfills. Through incineration, a method that has been in use in Stockholm since 1909, recycling, and biological processes, 10 percent of total municipal waste generated went to landfills in 2010. More impressively, 0 percent of the city's household waste went to landfills. Currently, 59 percent of municipal waste and 73 percent of household waste is incinerated for energy recovery. Stockholm has also emphasized biological food waste treatment, with the aim of collecting 35 percent of restaurant and grocery and 10 percent of household food waste for this treatment (European Commission 2010).

Another focus of the Stockholm municipal plan is to densify the urban landscape in order to meet the high demand for more offices, hotels, and other facilities in the city center. The plan also aims to increase the provision of housing in the inner city and in inner-ring suburbs.

Efforts at densification are exemplified by the Stockholm Royal Seaport project, a development recognized for its innovation by the Clinton Climate Initiative. Once completed, the area will offer 10,000 new apartments, 30,000 office spaces and 600,000 square meters of commercial space, thereby having a considerable impact on growth in the inner city. Building on the tradition of Hammarby Sjöstad, a nearly completed environmentally sustainable brownfield redevelopment area in Stockholm, construction on Stockholm Royal Seaport formally began during the winter of 2010 and has a completion date of 2025. The area is designed to be a mixed-use district that will help mitigate housing shortages in the inner city, provide opportunities for business development, promote technological innovation, and continue in its role as a port of entry and departure for cruise ships traveling across the Baltic Sea. In pursuing a strategy of densification on a formerly polluted brownfield site, the development is in accord with contemporary notions of environmentally friendly development associated with compact city design. Environmental sustainability and climate change mitigation are heavily emphasized in plans for the site. This focus is evident in the three overall environmental goals for Stockholm

Royal Seaport: carbon emissions below 1.5 tonnes per capita per year by 2020, freedom from fossil fuels by 2030, and adaptations to future climate change challenges.

Recent studies indicate that the area is on its way to achieving its desired aims (Galera Lindblom et al. 2011). As part of the process there has been a great emphasis on technological innovation, energy reduction, and locally based solutions.

The maintenance or improvement of existing urban qualities and the city's attractiveness remain an overarching concern. These issues have activated a local debate about the pros and cons of high-rise buildings in the city center as well as a degree of concern regarding green areas within the municipality of Stockholm. As a result, there is a great deal of media coverage of issues related to sustainability and urban development, a factor that in turn encourages a high level of awareness of such issues among the public. Furthermore, a diverse number of groups actively promote their perspectives on development in Stockholm. Some would conservatively allow minimal growth in the city to preserve its existing character; others ask where, not if, skyscrapers should be built. Even as opinions on Stockholm's future differ greatly, there is widespread agreement that the city of Stockholm needs to be more transparent and inclusive in its planning practices.

The densification goal also raises the controversial issue of "greenfield" development; particularly controversial are decisions regarding which green areas are to be maintained and which are to be used for densification. It will be interesting to see how greenfield development is carried out in practice because it poses a modest contradiction to Stockholm's former municipal plan, which emphasized the preservation of unbuilt land in the city (Stockholm Stad 1999).

Hammarby Sjöstad

One of the biggest urban development projects currently taking place in Stockholm, Hammarby Sjöstad involves the redevelopment of a former industrial area into an environmentally sustainable, mixed-use area. Covering 250 hectares, it will be made up of 11,000 apartments housing 20,000 to 25,000 people with an additional 10,000 people working in the area (Hammarby Sjöstad 2011). It is expected to cost approximately 20 billion Swedish kronor (approximately US$3 million) and is slated for completion in 2017 (Energy-Cities 2006). Using the Hammarby Model, the area strives to integrate energy flow, waste, drinking water, and sewage into a single system to promote the reuse and recycling of outputs wherever possible. (See figure 2 on page 301.)

In 1992, an economic upsurge coupled with population growth brought an increase in housing demand in Stockholm (Vestbro 2005). Shortly thereafter, a decision to bid for the 2004 Olympic Summer Games was approved. Planners foresaw the Hammarby Sjöstad area as an ideal location for Olympic facilities that would be unsurpassed in terms of environmental performance (Energy-Cities 2006). Despite losing the Olympic bid to Athens, continued economic and population growth ensured that the project continued. Cleanup efforts prior to construction led to the removal of 130 tonnes of oil and fuel and 180 tonnes of heavy metals.

Hammarby Sjöstad involved an integrated planning approach, unusual in Swedish planning at the time. In following this approach, different agencies and administrations that normally act separately worked closely together in all of the planning stages. When an unexpected abundance of families with young children appeared in the area, prompting a shortage of schools, for example, the city was able to respond quickly; within several years it changed the zoning for certain buildings to increase the number of schools and day care centers, thereby alleviating the problem.

The project was also an early example of the city of Stockholm's policy of building inward through the reuse of former industrial sites. By doing so, Stockholm can achieve higher densities, which can (at least potentially) lead to greater resource efficiency in a variety of ways, including better access to public transit, reduced dependence on automobiles, and greater proximity to employment and services (SUME 2011). Continuing its efforts to promote environmental sustainability, the city of Stockholm recently began construction on Norra Djurgårdsstaden, a former industrial site located two kilometers northeast of the city center. It will build on the lessons learned at Hammarby Sjöstad.

Although the development has achieved recognition, it has faced some criticism in Sweden. Critics point out that the building standards have been surpassed by new legal standards for all buildings, and that a lack of behavioral change among residents and employees in the area has led to a relatively limited reduction in energy consumption. The vast majority of area residents have relatively high earnings, and few have foreign backgrounds, particularly from outside of Europe—factors that are detrimental to the area's social sustainability.

Outlook

While Stockholm aspires, in its planning ambitions, to continue the city's focus on environmental sustainability, the rapid, long-term population and economic growth that is forecast for the region poses challenges. The

Figure 2. The Hammarby Eco-Cycle Model

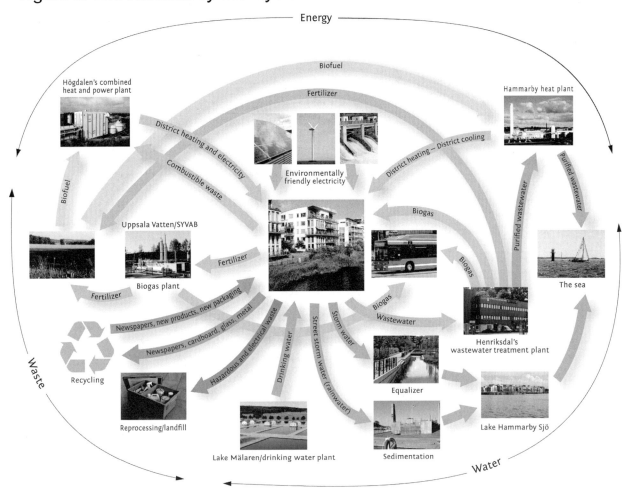

Source: GlashusEtt (2006).

The Hammarby Model is designed to create an urban environment that is based on sustainable resource use, minimizing energy consumption and waste output while promoting resource savings, reuse, and recycling.

current planning discourse pays considerable attention to the densification potentials and public transport challenges of the inner city. Recent research, however, indicates that Stockholm's future performance in terms of resource efficiency and long-term sustainability depends more on suburban areas and their capacity to accommodate people and jobs, to develop access to public transport, to upgrade the quality of the built environment, and, finally, to improve the thermal quality of buildings. To realize this it will be essential to implement Stockholm's regional plan for polycentric development. Only through this wider perspective will Stockholm be able to maintain its image as an attractive, healthy, and environmentally friendly region, as befits its designation as the first European Green Capital.

Peter SCHMITT and Mitchell REARDON
Nordregio (Nordic Centre for Spatial Development), Stockholm, Sweden

See also Energy Security (Europe); European Union (EU); London, United Kingdom; Moscow, Russia; Scandinavia; St. Petersburg, Russia; Urbanization (Europe); Warsaw, Poland

FURTHER READING

Andersson, Magnus. (1998). Stockholm's annual rings: A glimpse into the development of the city. Stockholm: Stockholmia förlag.

City of Stockholm. (2012a). A sustainable city: The Stockholm Environment Programme. Retrieved April 3, 2012, from http://international.stockholm.se/Stockholm-by-theme/A-sustainable-city/

City of Stockholm. (2012b). The final report from the European Green Capital project. Retrieved April 3, 2012, from http://international.stockholm.se/Stockholm-by-theme/European-Green-Capital/Final-report/

City of Stockholm. (2012c). Stockholm Environment Programme 2012–2015. Retrieved May 17, 2012, from http://www.stockholm.se/KlimatMiljo/Klimat/Klimatanpassning/

Dymén, Christian, & Henriksson, Anu. (2009). Spatial planning and its contribution to climate friendly and sustainable transport solutions. *Nordregio Working Paper*, 4.

Energy-Cities. (2006). Hammarby Sjöstad: Sustainable districts. Retrieved April 2, 2012, from http://energy-cities.eu/IMG/pdf/Sustainable_Districts_ADEME1_Hammarby.pdf

European Commission. (2010). Stockholm: European Green Capital 2010. Retrieved July 4, 2012, from http://ec.europa.eu/environment/europeangreencapital/docs/cities/brochure_stockholm_greencapital_2010.pdf

Galera Lindblom, Patrick; Weber, Ryan; Reardon, Mitchell; & Schmitt, Peter. (2011) Planning for resource efficient cities. *Nordregio Working Paper*, 8.

GlashusEtt. (2006). *Hammarby Sjöstad: En unik miljösatsning i Stockholm* [Hammarby Sjöstad: A unique environmental project in Stockholm]. Stockholm: GlashusEtt. Retrieved April 2, 2012, from http://www.hammarbysjostad.se/miljo/pdf/HS_miljobok_sv.pdf

Hammarby Sjöstad. (2011). *Stadsdelen* [The district]. Retrieved on April 2, 2012, from http://www.hammarbysjostad.se/

Office of Regional Planning. (2010). *RUFS 2010: Regional Utvecklingsplan för Stockholmsregionen 2010 (Rapport 1:2010)* [RUFS 2010: Regional development plan for Stockholm, 2010 (Report 1:2010)]. Stockholm: Office of Regional Planning.

Stahre, Ulf. (2007). *Den globala staden: Stockholms nutida stadsomvandling och sociala rörelser* [The global city: Stockholm's contemporary urban transformation and social movements]. Stockholm: Bokförlaget Atlas.

Stockholm Stad [City of Stockholm]. (1999). *Översiktsplan* [Comprehensive plan]. Stockholm: Stockholm Stad.

Stockholm Stad [City of Stockholm]. (2010). *Promenadstaden: Översiktsplan för Stockholm* [Walking city: A comprehensive plan for Stockholm]. Retrieved April 3, 2012, from http://www.stockholm.se/oversiktsplan

Sustainable Urban Metabolism for Europe (SUME). (2011). Planning resource-efficient cities (SUME synthesis report). Retrieved March 18, 2012, from http://www.sume.at/project_downloads

Swedish Central Statistical Office. (2011). Homepage. Retrieved May 31, 2012, from http://www.scb.se/

Vestbro, Dick Urban. (2005). Conflicting perspectives in the development of Hammarby Sjöstad, Stockholm. Retrieved April 3, 2012, from http://www.infra.kth.se/bba/HamSjostad.pdf

Svalbard Global Seed Vault

The Svalbard Global Seed Vault, opened by the Norwegian government and its partners in 2008, stores backup agricultural seed collections, ensuring global food security and genetic diversity. Its Arctic location keeps frozen seeds in conditions that permit long-term storage, although not all seeds can be frozen. To secure global crop diversity, the world needs both ex situ (off-site) storage and preservation of seeds in farmers' fields.

The Svalbard Global Seed Vault contains frozen and dried agricultural seeds that in many ways constitute the foundation of global food security. The vault, opened in 2008, is a cold storage carved into a mountainside in the Arctic archipelago of Svalbard. It holds backup copies of collections already stored in seed banks around the world that can be used to restore these collections in cases of emergencies or accidents.

Importance of Seed Banks

Seed banks provide easy access to genetic material and play a vital role in the conservation of agricultural seeds. Farmers and plant breeders all over the world depend on access to a wide diversity of seeds, because these can be used to breed new varieties that can cope with evolving diseases and pest attacks. The seeds stored in seed banks around the world may contain genetic material that can help meet future challenges such as crops that can grow under hotter, drier, or wetter conditions. The principle of the long-term storage of seeds is to dry them to a 5–8 percent moisture content and store them at $-10°C$ to $-20°C$, which secures their longevity for up to a hundred years.

Not all types of plants can be conserved in this way. Those that cannot be are (1) plants that do not form seeds (e.g., potato); (2) seeds that are recalcitrant, which means

that they cannot survive such a dried and frozen state (such as avocado, mango, rubber, and cocoa); (3) species with slow seed production (such as many tree species); and (4) crops that reproduce vegetatively (e.g., banana). Such species are therefore conserved in *field gene banks*, which are large areas of land where the plants are grown and looked after. The United Nations Food and Agricultural Organization (FAO) has estimated that more than 525,000 samples are stored in field gene banks around the world. The disadvantages of field gene banks are that they require large areas of land and frequent maintenance and that they are vulnerable to natural disasters and climate-related events such as droughts and floods. This method is also expensive compared with other methods—for example, seed bank storage—and it is normally used when there are no alternatives. Other means of conservation have therefore been sought through biotechnology, such as *in vitro storage*, which refers to storage in laboratory conditions. Species stored in field gene banks or by in vitro methods are, however, not included in the Svalbard Global Seed Vault because it is a cold storage for dried and frozen seeds.

Seed banks have proven to be of great importance in reconstruction work after natural disasters such as the tsunami that hit South and Southeast Asia in 2004. The International Rice Research Institute provided farmers with salt-tolerant rice varieties for use in fields that were inundated with saltwater. Similarly, the International Centre for Tropical Agriculture in Colombia provided improved bean varieties to farmers in Honduras and Nicaragua in the aftermath of Hurricane Mitch in 1998 (CGIAR 2007–2008).

Many seed banks struggle with limited budgets, which affect their ability to meet international standards for the long-term storage of seeds. In addition to financial limitations, many of the world's most important seed banks are located in politically unstable regions such as Ethiopia, Colombia, Nigeria, Syria, and Côte d'Ivoire. Two tragic examples of valuable seed collections that were destroyed due to war are Afghanistan's national collection, which was obliterated in 1992, and the Iraqi collection at Abu Ghraib, wiped out during the US invasion of 2003. By storing duplicates of existing seed collections at Svalbard Global Seed Vault, the world's seeds are less vulnerable to such incidents.

Svalbard Global Seed Vault

The Svalbard Global Seed Vault has a storage capacity of 4.5 million seed samples and can house all the unique seed samples that today are conserved in facilities in more than a hundred countries (Ministry of Agriculture and Food 2010). In 2010, about 6.5 million seed samples were conserved in seed banks around the world, but only 1 million to 2 million samples were considered distinct (Fowler 2008a, 11). Most of these are crops important to agricultural production and global food security, such as rice, wheat, barley, sorghum, maize, soybean, and pearl millet. The most substantial collections are kept in International Agricultural Research Centers under the Consultative Group on International Agriculture Research. These collections are held in trust by the United Nations system and are freely available to plant breeders, farmers, and scientists all over the world on the condition that no recipient seeks intellectual property rights to the material. Such availability is not the case for all seed collections; many national seed banks are more restrictive with the access to their seeds and genetic material. At the Svalbard Global Seed Vault, the depositor owns the stored samples and is the only one who has access to the stored material. Because the vault is located deep inside a mountain just a thousand kilometers from the North Pole, the deposited seeds are to be accessed only in emergencies.

Several partners have made the implementation of the seed vault possible. Three Norwegian ministries—the Ministry of Foreign Affairs, the Ministry of Environment, and the Ministry of Agriculture and Food—have financed the construction of the facility. The management and operations are taken care of by the Nordic Genetic Resource Center, while the Global Crop Diversity Trust provides support for ongoing costs such as assisting developing countries to prepare and transport their seed samples. The security of the seed vault is handled by the governor of Svalbard.

The Svalbard archipelago, situated between latitudes 74° and 81° north, was selected as the location for the seed vault for several reasons. The permafrost ensures that temperatures in the cold storage would never rise above −3.5°C if the environmental equipment were to fail. The seed vault's official website states that "low temperature and the limited access to oxygen will ensure low metabolic activity and cause a delay in the aging of the seeds" (Ministry of Agriculture and Food 2010). Its isolated location provides better security compared with most other seed banks in the world. Despite this isolated location, the infrastructure such as roads, communications, and electricity is good. In terms of geology, the seed vault has been constructed in stable sandstone that has low radiation levels. Finally, the vault's location deep inside a mountain ensures that neither rising sea levels nor melting permafrost are risks.

Origin and History

The idea of making a secure storage for seeds in the permafrost was inspired by the Nordic Gene Bank (now called the Nordic Genetic Resource Center), which since 1984 has stored duplicates of its seed collection in an abandoned coal mine at Svalbard. The seeds were naturally cooled at −3°C or −4°C, and viability tests after the first twenty years showed promising results (Qvenild 2008).

In the early 1990s, international experts, the FAO, and Norwegian authorities started planning an international secure storage that could help protect some of the world's most important agricultural seeds. At the time, these plans were impossible to realize due to technical, financial, and political constraints. The proposed facility was to be based on natural permafrost cooling, and several scientists pointed out that this did not meet international standards for long-term conservation at −18°C. This severely undermined the credibility of the proposed international storage at Svalbard. The main obstacles against finding donors and realizing the international seed storage facility, however, were political.

At that time, polarized discussions occurred among member countries of the FAO regarding access to seeds and the use and patenting of their genetic qualities. Plants collected in several developing countries, which were naturally rich in biological diversity, were used for commercial purposes and protected by intellectual property rights by the seed industry. The Neem tree from India, the Enola bean variety from Mexico, and the Hoodia cactus from South Africa are examples of the commercial industry patenting qualities of local plants without giving economic compensation to the countries of origin. Conservation efforts such as the Svalbard initiative were difficult to implement because the legal status of the seeds was lacking. To ship off seeds to a storage facility in a developed country without legal clarification about the ownership could, in the eyes of some developing countries, mean losing the material. In this international climate of little mutual trust, the idea simply had to be abandoned.

A New Try

A renewed interest to secure the world's agricultural heritage awakened in 2004 when the FAO's International Treaty on Plant Genetic Resources for Food and Agriculture came into force. This treaty settled the legal status for more than sixty-four major agricultural crops and forages. The countries that have signed the treaty have agreed that these plants will be accessed and exchanged freely and that claims to intellectual property rights over the material are prohibited. Together with a group of Nordic experts, the Norwegian Ministry of Foreign Affairs and the Norwegian Ministry of Agriculture and Food made a new proposal to the member countries of the FAO's Commission on Genetic Resources for Food and Agriculture. This time international seed bank standards of −18°C were followed and sufficient funding was secured. The Svalbard Global Seed Vault was officially opened on 26 February 2008 with people such as Wangari Maathai, the African Nobel Peace Prize winner, and José Manuel Barroso, the president of the European Commission, taking part in the ceremony.

Critical Voices

Critical voices against the seed vault itself are difficult to find. The seed vault is, however, part of a quite costly ex situ strategy of conserving seeds, which means that seeds are conserved in an artificial setting such as a botanical garden or a seed bank. Another way to conserve seeds is in situ within farmers' fields, where they are exposed and adapted to such things as changing climate conditions. In addition, the seeds that are conserved in situ form natural parts of biological and social systems and practices. The environmental anthropologist Thom van Dooren notes that frozen seeds stored ex situ at the Svalbard Global Seed Vault will not adapt to new conditions caused by climate change (van Dooren 2009b, 102). In addition, ex situ storage tends to contain only the most commercially

interesting seeds. Van Dooren writes that seed banks "primarily provide genetic resources to plant breeders and other gene storage facilities. They are simply not designed to be of direct benefit to farmers. . . . [M]ost of the world's farmers live 'in areas with poor and/or inaccessible road and electronic services,' and so could not make use of these banks even if they did know that they existed" (van Dooren 2009a, 381). In situ conservation is perhaps of more use to subsistence farmers than ex situ storage. The tendency, however, has been to invest more money in the more commercially interesting ex situ conservation. The international civil society organization ETC Group (known formally as the Action Group on Erosion, Technology and Concentration) writes that "[a]lthough some are sympathetic, few scientists are working with farmers to improve local conservation technologies, strengthen local breeding strategies, or to access far away seed accessions. In this unhappy environment, the Doomsday Vault becomes a lightning rod for everybody's discontent" (ETC Group 2008, 6). The ETC Group stresses the urgent need of supporting on-farm conservation in addition to ex situ storage. The world needs both strategies in order to preserve our agricultural heritage for the future.

The Future

The conservation of crop diversity is of crucial importance to both commercial plant breeders and subsistence farmers. The plants that constitute the foundation for the food on our tables have acquired their special qualities through hundreds of years of careful selection and cultivation in farmers' fields. While agricultural production in most industrialized countries is based on a handful commercial species, the subsistence farmers of the Southern Hemisphere are growing a wide variety of species in order to meet their monetary and dietary needs. In the years to come, commercial and subsistence farming will be exposed to pests and diseases as well as extreme weather conditions such as drought, flooding, and tropical storms. Against such threats, it is comforting to know that a large part of the global crop diversity is stored ex situ in national or regional seed banks. In both developed and developing countries, new crop varieties that can tolerate and thrive under the surprises and trends associated with climate change will increasingly be required. Seed banks have played and will continue to play a central role in maintaining and developing crop diversity for the future, in addition to playing a key role in restoring agriculture after climate-related emergencies. Whatever the future may bring, the new Svalbard Global Seed Vault is a step in the right direction toward securing global crop diversity in an era of rapid climate change.

Marte QVENILD

Norwegian Institute for Nature Research

See also Agriculture, Small-Scale; Biodiversity Conservation; Diet and Nutrition; Disaster Risk Management; Genetic Resources; Scandinavia

FURTHER READING

Charles, Daniel. (2006). A "forever" seed bank takes root in the Arctic. *Science, 312*(23), 1730–1731.

Consultive Group on International Agricultural Research (CGIAR). (2007–2008). Thousands of crop varieties from four corners of the world depart for Arctic seed vault. *CGIAR Newsroom*. Retrieved March 3, 2008, http://www.cgiar.org/news/seedtransfer_svalbard.html

Dworkin, Susan. (2009). *The Viking in the wheat field: A scientist's struggle to preserve the world's harvest.* New York: Walker.

ETC Group. (2008). Svalbard's doomsday vault: The global seed vault raises political/conservation debate. Retrieved April 5, 2010, from http://www.etcgroup.org/en/node/5077

Food and Agriculture Organization of the United Nations (FAO). (2010). Global issues: Biodiversity. Retrieved April 6, 2010, from http://www.fao.org/biodiversity/biodiversity-home/en/

Fowler, Cary. (2008a, February). The Svalbard Global Seed Vault: Securing the future of agriculture. Retrieved March 30, 2010, from http://www.croptrust.org/main/arcticseedvault.php?itemid=211

Fowler, Cary. (2008b, March). The Svalbard seed vault and crop security. *BioScience, 58*(3), 190–191.

Fowler, Cary. (2008c, November). Crop diversity: Neolithic foundations for agriculture's future adaptation to climate change. *Ambio, 8*, 498–501.

Global Crop Diversity Trust. (2010). Svalbard Global Seed Vault Retrieved March 29, 2010, from http://www.croptrust.org/content/svalbard-global-seed-vault

Johnson, R. C. (2008). Gene banks pay big dividends to agriculture, the environment, and human welfare. *PLoS Biology, 6*(6), 1152–1155.

Ministry of Agriculture and Food (Norway). (2010). Svalbard Global Seed Vault. Retrieved April 5, 2010, from http://www.regjeringen.no/en/dep/lmd/campain/svalbard-global-seed-vault.html

NordGen. (2010). Seed orchards. Retrieved April 6, 2010, from http://www.nordgen.org/index.php/en/content/view/full/2/

Qvenild, Marte. (2008). Svalbard Global Seed Vault: A "Noah's Ark" for the world's seeds. *Development in Practice, 18*, 110–116.

van Dooren, Thom. (2009a). Banking seed: Use and value in the conservation of agricultural diversity. *Science as Culture, 18*(4), 373–395.

van Dooren, Thom. (2009b). Genetic conservation in a climate of loss: Thinking with Val Plumwood. *Australian Humanities Review, 46*, 101–110.

Williams, Nigel. (2008). Deeper and down. *Current Biology, 18*(6), 230–231.

T

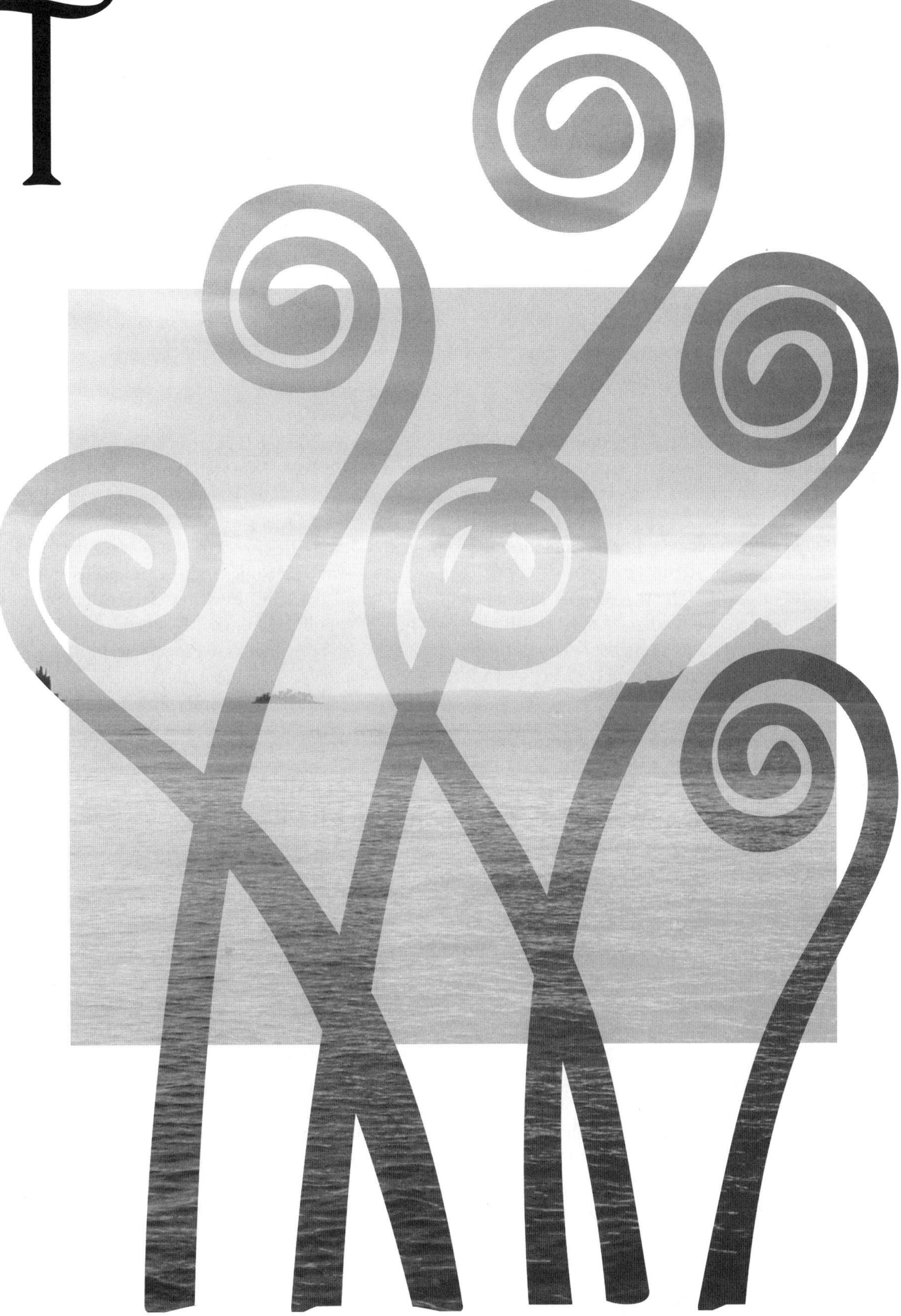

Transboundary Water Issues

The Jordan River, the Dead Sea, the Mountain Aquifer, and the Nile River basin are a few examples of aquatic ecosystems that cross political borders. Millions depend upon them for water, but history, power, and politics have resulted in uneven access and environmental degradation. As such, these ecosystems provide concrete examples of not only the conflicts that arise in managing and maintaining transboundary ecosystems, but also how the shared goal of ecological rehabilitation can be a tool for overcoming political conflict.

Borders are socially, politically, and culturally constructed but have profound material effects on both humans and the environment. Politics play a vital role in ecosystem management, and historical struggles and shifting boundaries greatly shape the natural environment. The issues facing ecosystems today are often transboundary, as neither nature nor environmental issues are constrained by political borders. Ecosystems traverse these delineated spaces, often from one state to another, and even across entire continents.

Aquatic ecosystems that cross international borders are especially contested, meaning water politics can provide a critical lens to further understand the effects of borders on ecosystems. Water is vital to the existence of both nature and society, and as such represents a pressing environmental issue in the world today. Climate change and the threat of increased water scarcity only exacerbate the issue. Many riparian (bordering a body of water) states and countries are involved in conflicts because of uneven access and unrecognized rights to shared water sources. Power and politics alter the distribution and management of bodies of water, oftentimes resulting in negative consequences for both people and the environment. This relationship is increasingly evident in the Middle East, as water security and water scarcity have come to define the water politics of the region. Shifting boundaries from decades of conflict have guaranteed that parties in the region have different levels of access to water, leading to disputes and tension. Jordan, Israel, and the Palestinian territories share ecosystems shaped by political borders. By examining three prominent ecosystems in this region—the Jordan River, the Dead Sea, and the Mountain Aquifer—as well as the Nile River basin, it becomes easy to see how borders transform ecosystems in various ways.

Borders and Ecosystems in the Middle East

Jordan, Israel, and the Palestinian territories make up an area in the Middle East with common borders and shared ecosystems. A political border is a geographic area established by law or treaty at any level of governance that defines the boundary of a specific area, such as a country, state, or territory. Conflicts arise when several areas share a water supply that is unevenly allocated, when there is no treaty in force to govern how water should be shared, or when one jurisdiction is more vulnerable to losing water because the other has an economic, political, or military advantage. An ecosystem includes all the organisms living in a particular environment; those shared by Jordan, Israel, and the Palestinian territories include the Jordan River basin, the Mountain Aquifer (an underground layer holding water in soil, rock, or other material), and the Dead Sea.

The environmental degradation within these areas is an environmental issue affecting all three states because of the shared nature of the water. As mentioned previously, environmental conflicts arise due to uneven power relationships and control over resources, in addition to historical legacies of conflict. Yet the environment also can be a tool for overcoming the tension created by boundaries through the promotion of both political and ecological rehabilitation. There are several organizations in the Middle East working to bring together people to solve these shared environmental issues. EcoPeace / Friends of the Earth Middle East (FoEME) is one environmental peacemaking organization that brings together Jordanians, Palestinians, and Israelis to cooperate on addressing shared environmental issues in order to promote peace in the region and to protect their common environmental heritage. Other partnerships in the region include the Arava Institute for Environmental Studies, an environmental studies program in which future Jordanian, Palestinian, Israeli, and international leaders work on regional environmental problems (Arava Institute 2012). Additionally, the Israel Palestine Center for Research and Information contains an Environment Department that studies communication and cooperation issues between Israeli, Palestinian, and Jordanian environmental organizations (IPCRI n.d.). These organizations demonstrate how cooperation can aid in tackling environmental issues that transcend borders.

Jordan River

The Jordan River valley is a historically, culturally, and religiously significant geographic wonder situated in the Great Rift Valley that stretches from Jordan across eastern Africa to Mozambique in southern Africa. The upper Jordan River rises on the Syria-Lebanon-Israel border and flows south through Israel to the Sea of Galilee, where the lower Jordan River (LJR) flows south to the Dead Sea. The LJR and its tributaries are shared by Syria, Jordan, Israel, and the Palestinian territories

and is made up of three sections: the first from the Sea of Galilee to the Yarmouk River (running through Israel), the second from the Yarmouk River confluence to the Bezeq Stream (bordering Israel and Jordan), and the third from the Bezeq Stream to the Dead Sea (bordering Jordan and the Palestinian West Bank).

The LJR used to have an annual average water flow of 1.3 billion cubic meters going to the Dead Sea, but unregulated human activity in the region has caused vast environmental degradation to the river. More than 98 percent of historical flow has been diverted by Israel, Jordan, and Syria for urban and agricultural usage (Gafny, Talozi, and Al Sheikh 2010). In 1964 Israel built a major pumping system to divert water from the Sea of Galilee for drinking and agricultural purposes, and during the same period Syria and Jordan built dams and weirs to divert water from the Yarmouk River. Adverse human effects on the river only have been heightened because of the increased diversion of water for water-intensive crops (such as bananas) grown in the desert. Overexploitation of the Jordan River for domestic and agricultural purposes and its contamination with pollution, sewage, saline waters, and agricultural runoff are examples of the human activities that have led to the loss of more than 50 percent of its biodiversity (Gafny, Talozi, and Al Sheikh 2010). The Jordan River is also an important religious site for baptisms, yet those who enter the water at the historical baptism site called Qaser al Yehud face possible health risks because of the high pollution rates.

Many stretches of the lower LJR will remain dry unless all parties take drastic action to return freshwater to the river. The average annual flow diverted by Israel is approximately 46 percent, by Syria 26 percent, and by Jordan 23 percent—as compared to the 5 percent diverted by the Palestinian territories (Gafny, Talozi, and Al Sheikh 2010). The politics of the management of the LJR not only affects the health of the ecosystem, but has denied the weakest stakeholders, the Palestinians, a fair share of riparian rights.

In the absence of solutions crafted by governments in the region, the FoEME has served as a model for best practices in environmental peacemaking with respect to transboundary resource management. Its collaborative approach in management of the LJR has been shown to lead to dialogue, peacemaking, and environmental rehabilitation. Transboundary projects such as the Good Water Neighbors (GWN) project and the Jordan River Peace Park have created opportunities for cross-border cooperation in a politically conflicted region. The GWN project identifies cross-border communities that can work together to advocate for fair and sustainable water management. From the local to the national level, GWN is comprised of adults, youths, and mayors who have come together and agreed upon concrete programs to share water more fairly and manage it better. The proposed Jordan River Peace Park, a potential transboundary protected area, is a case in point. (Transboundary protected areas, also known as peace parks, are established primarily to preserve animal migration routes. These protected areas promote the environmental conditions necessary to support biodiversity while creating a space for cooperative management, joint research and educational programs, and opportunities for collaborative nature-based tourism.) The proposed park is located where the Jordan River and the Yarmouk River meet at the Jesir al Majami / Gesher Three Bridges site. Cooperation between Jordan and Israel to develop such a site for tourism and environmental education creates a space for transboundary engagement.

Dead Sea

Another shared ecosystem in this region is the Dead Sea, the world's lowest body of water, which borders Jordan, Israel, and the Palestinian territories. The level of the Dead Sea has dropped 25 meters since the 1960s because of diversion of the Jordan River (the sea's natural water source) and activities of the mineral extraction industry. As stated previously, the water flow from the Jordan River to the Dead Sea is now only 2 percent of its historical volume. Adding further to the contraction of the Dead Sea is the overexploitation of minerals for industrial purposes: factories sprawled across the southern end of the Dead Sea evaporate water to extract minerals for use in production, such as potash for fertilizer. This extraction contributes 30–40 percent of the total evaporation of Dead Sea waters. Since the Jordan River is now but a trickle of sewage, there is no water to replace this depletion. Consequently the Dead Sea has lost one-third of its surface area and continues to drop one meter per year (Turner et al. 1999).

The governments of Israel, the Palestinian territories, and Jordan, as well as the international community, have taken note of the Dead Sea's endangered ecosystem. A proposed conduit would bring 1.9 billion cubic meters of water from the Red Sea to the Dead Sea in order to replenish the latter; development plans include a 180-kilometer pipeline and a desalination plant, in addition to proposed tourism expansion in both regions (Glausiusz 2010). Although some Israeli, Palestinian, and Jordanian ministers believe the conduit will ease political tensions in the Middle East by creating a great deal of new water, environmentalists are concerned that the conduit not only ignores the root cause of demise of the Dead Sea, but also presents a technological fix that could lead to greater ecological disasters for the Dead Sea, the Red Sea, and the Arava Valley. The less dense, sulfate-rich water of the Red Sea, when mixed with the denser, calcium-rich water of the Dead Sea, will create calcium sulfate (gypsum), possibly turning the color of Dead Sea water white, then green. Furthermore, the ecosystem of the Red Sea may be threatened by the scale of the pumping required for this project, placing the diverse coral reefs in the Gulf of Aqaba at risk. In this case, collaboration may threaten long-term regional stability if cooperation leads to further environmental degradation.

In 2008 the World Bank began funding both a feasibility study and an environmental and social assessment to examine the potential impacts of the proposed conduit. The resulting reports do not provide a final recommendation, but instead consider three scenarios: (1) no project (projected Dead Sea decline without the conduit), (2) base case (predicted outcomes of implementing the project), and (3) base case plus (predicted outcome of implementing the project plus the transmission of potable water to Jordan, Israel, and the Palestinian territories) (World Bank 2009). In contrast, FoEME recommends regional cooperation in restoring the area's natural systems through partial rehabilitation of the LJR, reducing impacts of the mineral extraction industry, and forming a Dead Sea commission to jointly manage the area.

Mountain Aquifer

The Mountain Aquifer is one the largest sources of drinking water for Israelis and Palestinians in the region and is a highly contested water source. The Mountain Aquifer's recharge area (where rain falls) is located primarily in the West Bank, while its discharge area is located mainly in Israel. More than 3 million people live in the recharge area, including more than 2 million Palestinians and more than 200,000 Israeli settlers. The Palestinian population in the West Bank depends on springs, wells, and water extracted from the aquifer for drinking and agriculture. Although this is an important water source for both Israelis and Palestinians, Israel allocates 80 percent of the water extracted to itself, leaving the Palestinians with only 20 percent (Tagar and Qumsieh 2006).

The Mountain Aquifer is vulnerable to groundwater pollution from sewage and solid waste as well as agricultural effluents, all of which can contaminate drinking water. Untreated sewage and leakage of sewage from cesspits is increasing toxicity levels in groundwater sources for the recharge area's 3 million residents. Yet the Palestinians have built only one sanitary landfill site to date in the aquifer's recharge area, in the Jenin district. Political hurdles and lack of funding have delayed considerably the building of sanitary landfills and sewage treatment plants in the Palestinian territories, and it could be argued that the interest of Palestinians in investing in such facilities is diminished given their less than equitable share of Mountain Aquifer water. A more equitable division of aquifer water likely would go a long way in highlighting the long-term mutual interest of both parties in avoiding pollution of already scarce water resources.

Nile River Basin

Although river basins and aquifers within the borders of Jordan, Israel, and the Palestinian territories provide superb examples of how political borders shape ecosystems, there are other examples of this relationship in Afro-Eurasia. Perhaps the best-known example is the Nile River basin.

The Nile River basin, situated in Africa, spreads over ten countries and represents more than 10 percent of the area of the continent. The Blue Nile and its tributaries in Eritrea and Sudan flow from Lake Tana in Ethiopia, while the White Nile and its tributaries in Rwanda, Burundi, Congo, Tanzania, and Kenya flow from Lake Victoria in Uganda. The Blue Nile and the White Nile meet in Khartoum, Sudan, and from there the Nile flows upstream through Egypt to the Mediterranean Sea. Although 86 percent of the Nile originates in Ethiopia and 46 percent of its waters come from the White Nile (Kendie 1999), only two riparian countries, Egypt and Sudan (the former of which does not

supply any water source to the Nile), have sole rights and control of the water source.

The hydropolitics of the Nile River basin are highly contested because of the historical dualistic—rather than incorporative—nature of its water rights. An agreement signed in 1929 by Britain and Egypt, followed by the 1959 Agreement of November, granted Egypt and Sudan exclusive rights to the Nile River and left the other eight riparian countries out. More than 80 percent of the Nile's water source originates from Eritrea and Ethiopia, but more than 90 percent of the Nile's waters are used by Sudan and Egypt (Kendie 1999). The Nile Basin Initiative was formed in 1999 to create a framework for cooperation and management of the Nile by all ten riparian countries at various levels of society; water scarcity, overpopulation, and drought make such cooperative water management a necessity.

Implications for Transboundary Cooperation

Ecosystems are complex and diverse areas that are not bound by socially or culturally constructed borders. Political borders greatly influence the environment within delineated spaces, which may have negative consequences on the biodiversity of a region. These consequences include uneven allocation of resources, depletion of water sources, and unregulated sewage pollution. This relationship between political borders and ecosystems varies across the globe as historical legacies of conflict, environmental laws and treaties, and different types of land use shape the consequences of environments altered by humans.

The ecosystems of the Jordan River, Dead Sea, and Mountain Aquifer overlap the borders of Jordan, the Palestinian territories, and Israel and are shaped greatly by the struggles for power that directly influence environmental decision making. Although political entities in the region share the blame for pollution and overexploitation of resources, it is evident that the political situation in the region underlies the actions of these entities. Transboundary cooperation is vital if ecosystems that span borders are to be rehabilitated. In Jordan, the Palestinian territories, and Israel, ecological rehabilitation can lead to political and social rehabilitation on many levels, from the regional to the national. Groups such as FoEME have shown that cross-border collaboration in research and in carrying out projects can be implemented at both grassroots and governance levels, and that such collaboration can overcome political boundaries between communities while creating conditions for long-lasting peace in the region. This model of engagement can be applied in communities and regions around the world.

Not all environmental issues occur within areas of conflict such as the Middle East, but the region's experience does illustrate the importance of transboundary cooperation in addressing environmental issues. In order to overcome political differences, change must center on environmental issues beyond political borders. The creation of transboundary commissions, treaties, and laws among parties in conflicted regions is a vital and necessary solution to preserve, rehabilitate, and manage ecosystems threatened by overexploitation, pollution, and degradation from human activity.

Environmental issues, such as deforestation and water scarcity, are not bound to single countries but rather to entire regions and continents. The tension between politics and the environment is only exacerbated by wanton consumption, pollution of resources, disputed boundaries, and uneven allocation of resources. Collaboration among regions on multiple levels can lead not only to sustainable and healthy ecosystems, but also to a long-lasting peace in regions such as the Nile River basin and the Jordan River basin. For the benefit of both society and nature, neighboring areas should act together to solve common environmental problems rather than being constrained by political borders. Through cooperation, a region can work toward repairing both the environment and its politics, within shared ecosystems and beyond borders.

Gidon BROMBERG and Jessica C. MARX
EcoPeace / Friends of the Earth Middle East

See also Biological Corridors; Congo (Zaire) River; Danube River; Fisheries; Indus River; International Conflict Resolution; Lake Baikal; Lake Chad; Lake Victoria; Mediterranean Sea; Nile River; Rhine River; Volga River; Water Use and Rights (Africa); Water Use and Rights (Middle East and North Africa)

FURTHER READING

Al-Jayyousi, Odeh, & Bergkamp, Ger. (2008). Water management in the Jordan River Basin: Towards an ecosystem approach. In Olli Varis, Cecilia Tortajada & Asit K. Biswas (Eds.), *Management of transboundary rivers and lakes* (pp. 105–121). Berlin: Springer.

Alkhaddar, Rafid; Sheey, William; & Al-Ansari, Nadhir. (2005). Jordan's water resources: Supply and future demand. *Water International*, *30*(3), 294–303.

Amer, Salah El-Din, et al. (2004). Sustainable development and international cooperation in the Eastern Nile Basin. *Aquatic Sciences–Research Across Boundaries*, *67*(1), 3–14.

Arava Institute. (2012). Homepage. Retrieved May 25, 2012, from http://www.arava.org/

Beyth, Michael. (2007). The Red Sea and the Mediterranean–Dead Sea canal project. *Desalination*, *214*(1), 365–371.

Bromberg, Gidon, et al. (Eds.). (2007). *Good water neighbors: Identifying common environmental problems and shared solutions*. Amman, Jordan; Bethlehem, Palestine; & Tel Aviv, Israel: EcoPeace / Friends of the Earth Middle East. Retrieved September 22, 2010, from http://foeme.org/uploads/publications_publ69_1.pdf

Brooks, David B.; Trottier, Julie; Bromberg, Gidon; & Al Khateeb, Nader. (2008). *Draft agreement on water cooperation between the state of Israel and the Palestinian National Authority*. Amman, Jordan; Bethlehem, Palestine; & Tel Aviv, Israel: EcoPeace / Friends of the Earth Middle East. Retrieved September 22, 2010, from http://foeme.org/uploads/publications_publ104_1.pdf

Gafny, Sarig; Talozi, Samer; & Al Sheikh, Banan. (2010). *Towards a living Jordan River: An environmental flows report on the rehabilitation of the Lower Jordan River*. Amman, Jordan; Bethlehem, Palestine; & Tel Aviv, Israel: EcoPeace / Friends of the Earth Middle East. Retrieved September 22, 2010, from http://foeme.org/uploads/publications_publ117_1.pdf

Glausiusz, Josie. (2010). Environmental science: New life for the Dead Sea? *Nature*, *464*(7292), 1118–1120.

Gleick, Peter H. (1993). Water and conflict: Fresh water resources and international security. *International Security*, *18*(1), 79–112.

Israel Palestine Center for Research and Information (IPCRI). (n.d.). Projects. Retrieved May 25, 2012, from http://www.ipcri.org/IPCRI/E-Projects.html

Israel, Rebekah. (2009, November). A comparative analysis of peace parks. (Paper presented at the annual meeting of the Southern Political Science Association, Atlanta, GA). Retrieved September 22, 2010, from http://www.allacademic.com/meta/p396152_index.html

Kameri-Mbote, Patricia. (2007). *Water, conflict, and cooperation; Lessons from the Nile River basin. Navigating Peace Series: Vol. 4.* Washington, DC: Woodrow Wilson International Center for Scholars.

Kendie, Daniel. (1999). Egypt and the hydro-politics of the Blue Nile River. *Northeast African Studies*, *6*(1–2), 141–169.

Lubarr, Tzipora. (2005). *Good water neighbors: A model for community development programs in regions of conflict: Developing cross-border community partnerships to overcome conflict and advance human security*. Amman, Jordan; Bethlehem, Palestine; & Tel Aviv, Israel: EcoPeace / Friends of the Earth Middle East. Retrieved September 22, 2010, from http://foeme.org/uploads/publications_publ19_1.pdf

Peterson, Richard B.; Russell, Diane; West, Paige; & Brosius, J. Peter. (2008). Seeing (and doing) conservation through cultural lenses. *Environmental Management*, *45*(1), 5–18.

Shuval, Hillel I., & Dweik, Hassan. (Eds.). (2007). *Water resources in the Middle East: Israel-Palestinian water issues—from conflict to cooperation*. Berlin: Springer.

Swain, Ashok. (2002). The Nile River basin initiative: Too many cooks, too little broth. *SAIS Review of International Affairs*, *22*(2), 293–308.

Tagar, Zecharya, & Qumsieh, Violet. (2006). *A seeping time bomb: Pollution of the mountain aquifer by solid waste*. Amman, Jordan; Bethlehem, Palestine; & Tel Aviv, Israel: EcoPeace / Friends of the Earth Middle East. Retrieved June 30, 2012, from http://foeme.org/uploads/publications_publ59_1.pdf

Tagar, Zach; Keinan, Tamar; & Qumsieh, Violet. (2005). *Pollution of the mountain aquifer by sewage: Finding solutions.* Amman, Jordan; Bethlehem, Palestine; & Tel Aviv, Israel: EcoPeace / Friends of the Earth Middle East. Retrieved June 30, 2012, from http://foeme.org/uploads/publications_publ29_1.pdf

Turner, Michael; Fariz, Gaith; Faris, Husan Abu; Hoermann, Sefan; & Bromberg, Gidon. (1999). *Let the Dead Sea live: Concept document: Moving towards a Dead Sea basin biosphere reserve and world heritage listings.* Amman, Jordan; Bethlehem, Palestine; & Tel Aviv, Israel: EcoPeace / Friends of the Earth Middle East. Retrieved September 22, 2010, from http://foeme.org/uploads/publications_publ25_1.pdf

Turner, Michael; Nassar, Khaled; & Al Khateeb, Nader. (2005). *Crossing the Jordan: Concept document to rehabilitate, promote prosperity and help bring peace to the lower Jordan River valley.* Amman, Jordan;

Bethlehem, Palestine; & Tel Aviv, Israel: EcoPeace / Friends of the Earth Middle East.

Whittington, Dale, & McClelland, Elizabeth. (1998). Opportunities for regional and international cooperation in the Nile Basin. *Water International, 17*(3), 144–154.

Wolf, Aaron. (1998). Conflict and cooperation along international waterways. *Water Policy, 1*(2), 251–265.

World Bank. (2009). *Red Sea–Dead Sea water conveyance study program feasibility study: Options screening and evaluation report: Executive summary.* Retrieved May 25, 2012, from http://siteresources.worldbank.org/INTREDSEADEADSEA/Resources/C-B_Options_Screening_Jan2009.pdf

Woube, Mengistu. (1994). Environmental degradation along the Blue Nile River basin. *Ambio, 23*(8), 519–520.

Travel and Tourism Industry

The travel and tourism industry has been responsible for significant economic, social, cultural, and environmental impacts in the Afro-Eurasian region. Consequently, assessing sustainability and providing solutions to sustainability challenges have been at the forefront of academic research on tourism. The concern has filtered into the industry, with corporate social responsibility and accreditation programs, as well as cases of best practice in sustainable tourism, developing worldwide.

Given its regular use as a development tool, travel and tourism has come under great scrutiny in the sustainability literature, and one could argue that refinement of the concept has, to some extent, occurred within this specific industry. With this refinement, however, has come the recognition of two important factors: one, that sustainability, as a future-based concept, is very difficult to define; and two, that it is highly context dependent. Indeed, many authors have pointed to these problems in tourism, because of the ability of sustainability to be "variously interpreted or appropriated" (Sharpley and Telfer 2002, 325). In a tourism context, it has been argued that the various interests of a tourist destination can be loosely grouped into four categories: host population, tourist guests, tourism organizations, and the natural environment (Cater 1993). All four of these groups have the common aim of ensuring long-term sustainable development of their destinations, although the potential for each group to act independently and consult only its own self-interests is likely, and in fact common, ultimately to the detriment of themselves and their peers.

One of the major difficulties in dealing with the industry is its diverse nature and the complexity of its interconnections. This underlines the fact "that the major role-players in tourism all have a stake in sustainable tourism and that their present and future interests are in many ways tied to one another and to sound environmental practice" (Cater 1993, 22). Thus one must recognize that understanding context requires an acknowledgement of interconnectedness, for the idea of tourism being able to achieve sustainable development "independently of other activities and processes is philosophically against the true nature of the concept, as well as being unrealistic" (Butler 1998, 28).

Sustainable Tourism Planning in Afro-Eurasia

Awareness of the impacts of tourism, particularly the unplanned mass tourism of the post–World War II period in Europe, led to greater attention to effective tourism planning. According to Donald Getz, of the University of Queensland's School of Tourism, tourism planning has moved through several paradigms, from post-war Boosterism, an economic, industry-oriented approach in the 1950s and 1960s, and a physical/spatial approach in the 1970s (the "golden age" of planning), to a community-oriented approach in the 1980s (Getz 1987). C. Michael Hall, professor of marketing at the University of Canterbury, suggests, however, that starting in the mid-1990s a greater concern with the impacts of tourism has led to the prevalence of an emerging sustainability paradigm (Hall 2008). This paradigm integrates economic, environmental, and sociocultural objectives, with sustainability as a core objective supported by tourism planning and other planning processes and a requirement that planners act as facilitators with explicit strategic remits. Hall (2008) points to the challenges of such an approach, which requires a value reorientation by tourists and the industry, consideration for the scale and context-specific solutions, an awareness of global influences, and strong community control of resources. Furthermore, the sustainability paradigm requires patience, diligence, and long-term commitment, which is not always present in the time horizons of short-term Western political and capitalist thinking. Indeed, community-based resource management is a long-term undertaking (Calumpong 2000) that requires sustained commitment. Tourism consultant Zena Hoctor's observations of West Clare's marine ecotourism project in Ireland suggest that there was a need to move beyond the consultative to the self-mobilization level to ensure long-term sustainability of the project, from objects of development to empowerment. She recognized this to be a long-term process requiring the sustained commitment of all the stakeholders (i.e., those people who have a stake in the outcome of an enterprise) involved (Hoctor 2003).

Early project work on developing more-sustainable forms of tourism in Afro-Eurasia was largely initiated by nongovernmental organizations (NGOs) active in the tourism sector. Some NGOs have been particularly concerned with the dependency relationships reinforced by international mass tourism and the exploitation of less developed peoples and places and their resources. A good example of this is Tourism Concern, which has been instrumental in promoting a rights-based approach to tourism development since 1988 and has run a number of successful campaigns on issues such as gender exploitation. Other NGOs, such as Gambia Tourism Concern, have taken a more destination-based approach, assisting specific communities, because, as professor of development studies Regina Scheyvens contends, "in an ideal world, communities would devise and initiate sustainable and successful tourism ventures entirely by themselves, but at present the reality is that they often lack the experience, network and skills to be able to do this, and thus appropriate outside assistance is often required" (Scheyvens 2002, 210).

The Sustainable Livelihoods Approach (SLA) offers a useful integrative framework for assessing the sustainability of tourism at a community level, on peoples' assets (Ashley 2000). Although the SLA was developed during the 1990s as a new approach to poverty reduction (Carney et al. 1999), it has been central to the emphasis on "pro-poor tourism" in recent years (Ashley, Goodwin, and Roe 2001). The SLA facilitates a systematic appraisal of how tourism impacts livelihoods. The approach is people-centered, designed to be participatory, and emphasizes sustainability. Also, as professor Miranda Cahn, a specialist in rural development, suggests, it "is positive in that it first identifies what people have rather than focusing on what people do not have. The [sustainable livelihood] approach recognizes diverse livelihood strategies:

it can be multi-level, household, community, regional or national, and can be dynamic" (Cahn 2002, 3).

Sustainable Livelihood Approaches

At the heart of the SLA lies an analysis of five types of asset upon which people draw to build their livelihoods (HSRC 2002). These are natural capital (the natural resource stocks upon which people draw for livelihoods); human capital (the skills, knowledge, ability to labor, and good health important to be able to pursue different livelihood strategies); physical capital (the basic enabling infrastructure such as transport, shelter, water, energy, and communications); financial capital (the financial resources that are available to people such as savings, credit, remittances, or pensions, which provide them with different livelihood options); and social capital (the social resources such as networks, group memberships, or relationships of trust upon which people draw in pursuit of their livelihoods). Professors of tourism Erlet Cater and Carl Cater (2007), however, suggest that to this classic pentagon should be added cultural capital, which can be defined as the cultural resources (heritage, customs, and traditions) that are a feature of local livelihoods (HSRC 2002; Glavovic, Scheyvens, and Overton 2002).

Although initially applied in less-developed settings, the SLA has also proven to be useful in assessing sustainability in tourism in more-developed locations in Europe. Reidar Mykletun, professor in the Norwegian School of Hotel Management at the University of Stavanger, for example, uses the model to examine the sustainability of festival tourism in Norway, offering the addition of administrative capital to explain "the regulation of public goods and welfare, the organization of civil servants and officers employed to enforce these rules, and the political bodies elected to be in charge of major decisions and developments" (Mykletun 2009, 25). Administrative capital, however, is essentially a temporary organizational structure, such as one set up to operate a sports event (Mykletun 2009), and lacks the constituent depth to be a factor discussed in the context of the more complicated relationships of power and benefit conflicts in the host community. C. Wang and Carl Cater (2011) therefore explore political capital as a more permanent expression of a community's power structure in assessing sustainable livelihoods in tourism.

Best Practice in Sustainable Tourism

The rising profile of sustainability in Eurasia and Africa reflects a shift in position toward sustainability being a goal to be achieved rather than a barrier to development, with some authors suggesting that sustainability has attained significant consumer value (Weeden 2011). Indeed, positive moves toward sustainability have come through actively sharing best practice. For example, the Tourism for Tomorrow awards were established in 1989 by Britain's Federation of Tour Operators to encourage action from all sectors of the industry to protect the environment. The awards were taken over by British Airways in 1992 and further developed to encompass all aspects of sustainable tourism, with the aim of leading the industry in this field. Awarded since 2003 by the World Travel & Tourism Council (WTTC), the global peak industry body for the tourism sector, the accolades now cover demonstrations of sustainability for destinations, communities, conservation, and businesses. In 2011, three of the four categories were won by entrants in Afro-Eurasia: Singita Pamushana Lodge in Zimbabwe won the Conservation Award for its successful partnership with the local Malilangwe Trust in helping rehabilitate and protect almost 50,000 hectares of degraded wildlife habitat that had suffered from years of poaching; Guludo Beach Lodge in Mozambique won the Community Benefit Award for having demonstrated direct and tangible benefits to local people, a strong contribution to community development, and enhancement of cultural heritage in the area; and Alpine Pearls, a nonprofit organization headquartered in Austria, won the Destination Stewardship Award, having successfully demonstrated sustainable tourism management at a regional destination level.

Accreditation and Regulation

As well as best practice, there is still a requirement for accreditation and regulation. One of the longest-running programs has been Green Globe, a sustainability brand created by the WTTC following the United Nations Conference on Environment and Development, known as the Earth Summit, in Rio de Janeiro in 1992. Although initially emerging from an interest in sustainable tourism, Green Globe seeks to cover all aspects of sustainability at a variety of scales. Green Globe has been criticized, however, for an aggressive expansion strategy to achieve a dominant position and a lack of concrete obligations required for initial accreditation (Honey and Rome 2001). The primary focus of the certification provided by Green Globe is an environmental management system, with an emphasis on energy use, waste, and pollution management based on ISO 14001 from the International Organization for Standardization. (ISO, the abbreviation for the International Organization for Standardization, derives from the Greek word *isos*, meaning "equal.") Criticism of Green Globe, however, has continued because of ongoing confusion over whether the brand should be considered a marketing tool or a genuine measure of sustainable practice. In 2011 the numerous global accreditation programs for sustainable tourism and ecotourism thus came together to form the Global Sustainable Tourism Criteria, administered by the Global Sustainable Tourism Council. These criteria were developed with the knowledge of twenty years of sustainable-tourism thinking in the field and are aligned with the United Nations Millennium Development Goals (Bricker, Black, and Cottrell 2012).

Education for Sustainable Tourism

The dynamic nature of sustainability in tourism and the importance of creating discursive educational environments led to the creation in 2001 of the BEST Education Network. This an international consortium of educators, with significant representation from Eurasia and Africa, committed to furthering the development and dissemination of knowledge in the field of sustainable tourism. The network accomplishes this by holding annual three- to four-day think tank workshops at various universities around the world. Some of the principal outputs from these workshops are teaching resources on sustainable tourism case studies that can be used by educators. This shift in academic thinking on sustainability has been mirrored in the tourism industry, with most organizations in Afro-Eurasia embedding sustainability within broader policies on corporate social responsibility (CSR). Although the sustainability discourse has led the debate on matters such as community integration and environmental concerns, CSR has moved this forward to some degree, enabling a responsibility-based ethical approach to these issues. Being central to the tourism product in Africa and Europe, hotel chains and tour operators have instigated a number of initiatives in this area. Paulina Bohdanowicz (sustainability manager for Hilton hotels) and Piotr

Zientara (professor of human development) review the significant place of CSR in top hotel chain operations in Europe, suggesting that "the entire sector can be held up—to firms from other industries—as a model of responsible behaviour" (Bohdanowicz and Zientara 2011, 34). The Travel Foundation is the UK travel industry's own charity, set up in 2003 to respond to concerns over the sustainability of travel and tourism. Since then, it has helped the travel industry understand, manage, and take effective action on sustainable tourism, through undertaking research and education projects in Cyprus, Egypt, Kenya, Morocco, the Greek island of Rhodes, South Africa, the Gambia, and Turkey. Individual tour operators such as Thomson and First Choice, both part of the Touristik Union International (TUI) group, have highlighted twenty commitments to aspects of sustainable tourism through their Holidays Forever program. Operating largely within the Afro-Eurasian hemisphere, they commit to initiatives in carbon footprint reduction, destination stewardship, living values, and consumer education. The dominance of TUI in the package tourism sector in Africa and Europe, providing over 30 million holidays a year, means that they can make significant strides in sustainability education. For example, they aim to educate over half a million children annually in sustainability principles through their resort kids club programs.

Degrowth and Sustainability

One of the major challenges in the sustainability of the travel and tourism industry in Afro-Eurasia will be coping with the huge forecasted growth from emerging markets. This may require a revision of the unchallenged mantra among governments and industry that continued growth is the only path forward for tourism development. Indeed, in common with many other industries, tourism holds up growth as the key measure of success, evident in almost all government and industry reports, conferences, and development objectives. Almost universally, "high (tourism) growth is a cause of national pride; low (tourism) growth attracts accusations of incompetence in the case of rich countries and pity in the case of poor countries" (Hamilton 2003, 1). As previous authors have suggested, the international structures of tourism are somewhat to blame; for example, the United Nations World Tourism Organization in particular needs more and more tourism activity on a global scale to continue to justify its existence (Hall 2008).

There are countless examples of destinations and nations that have not benefitted from growth in tourism numbers, precisely because of the dependency structures of the global industry (Scheyvens 2007; Mowforth and

Munt 2008), for example mass package tourism. Destinations in Afro-Eurasia would perhaps be better placed to examine more cautious growth strategies and consider recent work on steady-state tourism, for example the concepts of degrowth (Hall 2009) and demarketing (Holden 2009)—scaling back consumption and demand—for sustainable tourism. Indeed, some African nations such as Botswana and Namibia are pursuing high-yield tourists rather than mass-growth strategies, and luxury destinations such as the Maldives are searching for alternatives to intensification. In this regard, critical work on the perceived value of sustainability in tourist products (Low 2010) will be of importance.

Carl Iain CATER
Aberystwyth University

Tiffany LOW
University of Bedfordshire

See also Corporate Accountability (Africa); Ecotourism; Education, Environmental; Parks and Preserves; Rule of Law (Africa); Rule of Law (European Union)

FURTHER READING

Ashley, Caroline. (2000). *The impacts of tourism on rural livelihoods: Namibia's experience* (Working paper 128). London: Overseas Development Institute.

Ashley, Caroline; Goodwin, Harold; & Roe, Dilys. (2001). *Pro-poor tourism strategies: Expanding opportunities for the poor.* Greenwich, CT & London: CERT, IIED, ODI.

BEST Education Network. (2012). Homepage. Retrieved May 2, 2012, from http://www.besteducationnetwork.org

Bohdanowicz, Paulina, & Zientara, Piotr. (2011). CSR-inspired environmental initiatives in top hotel chains. In David Leslie (Ed.), *Tourism across Europe: Steps towards sustainability: Tourism enterprises and the sustainability agenda.* London: Ashgate.

Bricker, Kelly; Black, Rosemary; & Cottrell, Stuart. (Eds.). (2012). *Ecotourism and sustainable tourism: Transitioning into the new millennium.* Sudbury, MA: Jones & Bartlett.

Butler, Richard. (1998). Sustainable tourism: Looking backwards to progress? In Colin Michael Hall & Alan A. Lew (Eds.), *Sustainable tourism: A geographical perspective* (pp. 25–34). Harlow, UK: Longman.

Cahn, Miranda. (2002). Sustainable livelihoods approach: Concept and practice (Paper given at Development Studies of New Zealand Conference). Retrieved January 11, 2012, from http://www.mendeley.com/research/sustainable-livelihoods-approach-concept-practice/

Calumpong, H. (2000). *Community based coastal resources management in Apo Island.* Dumaguete City, Philippines: Silliman University.

Carney, Diana, et al. (1999). *Livelihood approaches compared: A brief comparison of the livelihoods approaches of the UK Department for International Development (DFID), CARE, Oxfam and the UNDP.* London: Department for International Development.

Cater, Carl Iain, & Cater, Erlet. (2007). *Marine ecotourism: Between the devil and the deep blue sea.* Oxford, UK: CABI.

Cater, Carl Iain, & Garrod, Brian. (Eds.). (2013). *The encyclopedia of sustainable tourism.* Oxford, UK: CABI.

Cater, Erlet. (1993). Ecotourism in the third world: Problems for sustainable tourism development. *Tourism Management, 14*(2), 85–90.

Getz, Donald. (1987). Tourism planning and research: Traditions, models and futures (Paper presented at Australian Travel Research Workshop, Bunbury, Western Australia).

Glavovic, Bruce; Scheyvens, Regina; & Overton, John. (2002). Waves of adversity, layers of resilience: Exploring the sustainable livelihoods approach (Paper given at Development Studies of New Zealand Conference, Palmerston North, New Zealand, Massey University).

Global Sustainable Tourism Council (GSTC). (2011). Homepage. Retrieved May 2, 2012, from http://new.gstcouncil.org/

Hall, C. Michael. (2008). *Tourism planning: Policies, processes and relationships* (2nd ed.). Harlow, UK: Pearson Education.

Hall, C. Michael. (2009). Degrowing tourism: Décroissance, sustainable consumption and steady-state tourism. *Anatolia: An International Journal of Tourism and Hospitality Research, 20*(1), 46–61.

Hamilton, Clive. (2003). *Growth fetish*. St. Leonards, Australia: Allen & Unwin.

Hoctor, Zena. (2003). Community participation in marine ecotourism development in West Clare, Ireland. In Brian Garrod & Julie C. Wilson (Eds.), *Marine ecotourism: Issues and experiences*. Clevedon, UK: Channel View.

Holden, Andrew. (2009). The environment-tourism nexus: Influence of market ethics. *Annals of Tourism Research, 36*(3), 373–389.

Holidays Forever. (n.d.) Homepage. Retrieved May 8, 2012, from http://www.holidaysforever.co.uk

Honey, Martha, & Rome, Abigail. (2001). *Protecting paradise: Certification programs for sustainable tourism and ecotourism*. Washington, DC: Institute for Policy Studies.

Human Sciences Research Council (HSRC). (2002, March). Sustaining livelihoods in southern Africa: Social capital and sustainable livelihoods (Issue 5). Retrieved May 10, 2005, from http://www.cbnrm.net/pdf/khanya_002_slsa_issue05_sc.pdf

Leslie, David. (Ed.). (2011). *Tourism across Europe: Steps towards sustainability: Tourism enterprises and the sustainability agenda*. London: Ashgate.

Low, Tiffany. (2010). Sustainable luxury: A case of strange bedfellows? (Paper presented at Tourism and Hospitality Research in Ireland Conference, County Clare, Ireland, Shannon College of Hotel Management).

Mowforth, Martin, & Munt, Ian. (2008). *Tourism and sustainability: Development and new tourism in the third world* (3rd ed.). Oxford, UK: Routledge.

Mykletun, Reidar J. (2009). Celebration of extreme playfulness: Ekstremsportveko at Voss. *Scandinavian Journal of Hospitality and Tourism, 9*(2–3), 146–176.

Scheyvens, Regina. (2002). *Tourism for development: Empowering communities*. Harlow, UK: Pearson Education.

Scheyvens, Regina. (2007). Exploring the tourism-poverty nexus. *Current Issues in Tourism, 10*(2–3), 231–254.

Sharpley, Richard, & Telfer, David J. (Eds.). (2002). *Tourism and development: Concepts and issues*. Clevedon, UK: Channel View.

Tourism Concern. (n.d.). Homepage. Retrieved May 2, 2012, from http://www.tourismconcern.org.uk

Tourism for Tomorrow. (2012). Homepage. Retrieved May 2, 2012, from http://www.tourismfortomorrow.com

Travel Foundation. (2012). Homepage. Retrieved May 8, 2012, from http://www.thetravelfoundation.org.uk/

Wang, C., & Cater, Carl Iain. (2011). Exploring the political changes of community-based ecotourism development after a crisis (Paper presented at New Horizons in Tourism Research, Shangri-La, China).

Weeden, Clare. (2011). Responsible tourist motivation: How valuable is the Schwartz value survey? *Journal of Ecotourism, 10*(3), 214–234.

Tunis, Tunisia

2.7 million est. pop. 2011

Tunis, the site of ancient Carthage and the capital of the modern nation of Tunisia, is a city with an extremely long history, blending continuity and change. It also occupies a very distinctive site environmentally. On both counts—historical and geographical—it exemplifies many sustainability issues and challenges. In late 2010, Tunisia saw the beginning of what would become known as the Arab Spring.

In some respects Tunis, the capital city of Tunisia in North Africa, is an "ordinary" city; in other ways it is truly exceptional. Its population of 2.7 million is close to the median size among the world's national capitals. It is growing, but not exceptionally fast. In terms of prosperity or affluence, as measured by the United Nations (UN) or World Bank, Tunisia is again close to the median among the world's nation-states (94th among 187 countries on the UNDP 2011 Human Development Index [UNDP 2012]), and conditions in Tunis City reflect this.

Conversely, Tunis as the site of ancient Carthage has an exceptionally long history, demonstrating the extremes of "sustainability." Not only does it occupy an environmentally distinctive location, but, culturally, the population is exceptional in its homogeneity, with more than 95 percent describing themselves as Arab and Muslim. Although most cities are firmly placed in one continent, Tunis lies within at least three "worlds": Middle Eastern, Mediterranean, and African. On the global political stage, Tunis seemed very ordinary until late 2010, when it shot to world attention with the sudden overthrow of Tunisia's president, Zine el-Abadine Ben Ali, and his government, in what has been widely seen as the start of the 2011–2012 Arab Spring.

Location and Site

Tunis dominates Tunisian life from the extreme northeast corner of the country, itself part of the North African region known as the Maghreb, which links Tunis physically and culturally with cities in Algeria and Morocco and, more ambiguously, to Libya (Nouschi, bi-al-Hammamat, and Social Science Research Council 1996). The city's distinctive site includes a historic core that lies 10 kilometers inland, separated from the Mediterranean Sea by the Lac de Tunis, a 35-square-kilometer lagoon with a narrow sea outlet. This core, which was the whole city until the 1920s, occupies a 3-kilometer-wide isthmus between Lac de Tunis to the east and the salt lake (sebkhet) Sejoumi to the west. The city now extends from this cramped core for more than 20 kilometers north, west, and south, although it is constrained by another sebkhet to the north and by rocky hills (jebels). (See figure 1 on page 320.)

The shallow Lac de Tunis is traversed by a causeway dating from Roman times and now used by the light railway linking the city center and the coast. Parallel to this is a canal 450 meters wide and 6 meters deep, built by the French in the late nineteenth century but little used today. These features present challenges and opportunities for environmental management.

The western part of the city's core comprises the old walled medina, with more than one thousand historic buildings separated by narrow alleys, including the *souk* with micro-scale shops and craft workshops. Between this area and the lagoon is another small area that was the French city of the nineteenth and twentieth centuries. The duality of the city's core is not unusual in cities of former colonial countries.

At the same time, this cramped dual core contrasts sharply with extensive but diverse inner and outer

Figure 1. Tunis

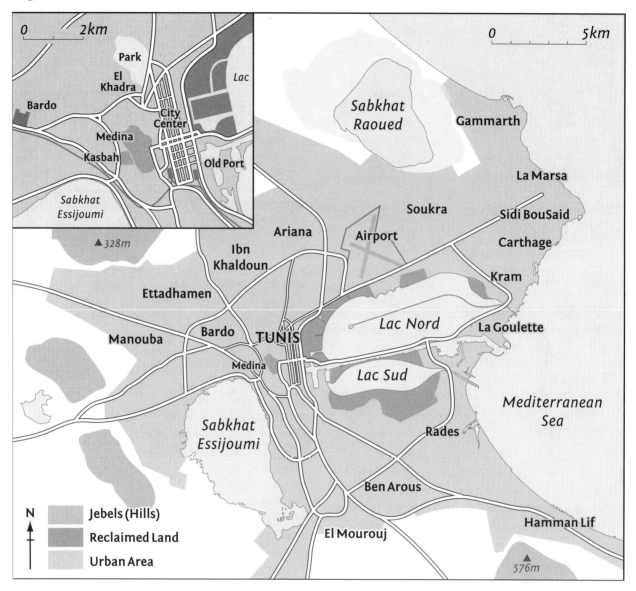

Source: Map courtesy of Miles Irving, University College London Department of Geography.

suburbs. Bardo, the innermost northwest suburb, is largely commercial and residential, but its palace (dating from 1420) houses a museum with one of the world's finest collections of Roman and Carthaginian art, as well as the Tunisian parliament. The suburbs of Ariana *gouvernerate* to the north and Ben Arous to the south now have more than half a million inhabitants each (Hamzaoui Oueslati 2004). Particularly rapid growth has taken place over the past twenty years in Ettadhamin and Manouba to the west. Carthage, 12 kilometers northeast of the city center, is now the most exclusive suburb, with very low density housing. The presidential palace is located there.

The small port built near the city center in the nineteenth century was connected to the sea by the canal through the Lac de Tunis. It was replaced in the early twentieth century by a new port at La Goulette, at the seaward end of the canal. Since the 1990s this port has been replaced, for all but passenger-ship and cruise-ship berths, by deep-water docks at Rades, east of the canal entrance.

History

According to academic histories and current guidebooks (e.g., Jacobs 2009, 69–134), the most important fact about Tunis is that its small suburb of Carthage is the site of a major settlement dating from 814 BCE, when the Phoenicians established an independent city-state that traded around the Mediterranean and extended its authority well inland (Lancel 1995). Famous Carthaginians included Hannibal, the great general, born in 247 BCE. The settlement was destroyed in 146 BCE by the Romans, who plowed over its site "to create a wasteland" according to the Roman historian Tacitus. But a new city was established, which became the third largest in the Roman Empire, after Rome and Alexandria, and its hinterland was the main granary supplying Rome.

The present city dates from the Muslim conquest of 700 to 750 CE, during which time remnants of ancient Carthage were abandoned and the Great Mosque was built. The city thrived in the ninth century, replacing Qairwan/Kairouan, 120 kilometers south-southwest, as the administrative center of the emerging Tunisia. The character of the city was fully documented by the renowned geographer Ibn Khaldun, born in Tunis in 1332 (Lacoste 1984). A further boom came between 1350 and 1500, when the fortified Qasbah was built as the seat of government, and the population reached between 50,000 and 100,000. The inhabitants included refugees from the Christian reconquest of Spain, as well as many Sicilians and Maltese. At this time Tunis had strong links with Marrakech and Fez in Morocco, to the west, and with Cairo, to the east.

The Ottomans gained control in the sixteenth century, and the population hovered between 100,000 to 120,000 for three centuries. The city's administrative and commercial roles were maintained into the nineteenth century as the French established colonial control. When independence was granted in 1956, Tunis automatically became the national capital (Sebag 1998; Akrout-Yaiche 2006). For several hundred years, therefore, the city experienced continuity amid change.

Population and Society

The city's population was recorded as 150,000 in 1901, and it grew slowly to 220,000 in 1936 (nearly half were Europeans), plus 40,000 in the suburbs. The medina was occupied almost entirely by Arabs, while 100,000 French lived in the colonial New Town to the east. By the time of independence in 1956, the population had reached 400,000 (still including 120,000 Europeans), plus 150,000 in the suburbs. The next census in 1966 recorded 470,000 (with only 20,000 Europeans) in the city, plus 210,000 in the suburbs.

The 2004 census recorded a population of 730,000 in the administrative city, 1.3 million in the urban agglomeration including inner suburbs, and 2.4 million in the 2000-square-kilometer greater metropolitan area. The 2.4 million represented 25 percent of Tunisia's total population, and 35 percent of its urban population. Tunis dominates the Tunisian urban system (Signoles 1985), being far larger than the leading provincial cities of Sfax (270,000), Sousse (170,000), and Kairouan (120,000). The population is now growing by about 1 percent a year, roughly half by excess of births over deaths, and half by excess of in-migration over out-migration. The in-migration is from rural areas and from smaller cities, while the out-migration includes legal and illegal migration to Europe. Many of the 200,000 Tunisians in France, 100,000 in Italy, and 50,000 in Germany come from the Tunis suburbs.

The 2004 census indicated an age structure with 25 percent under fifteen and just 5 percent over sixty-five. The average fertility rate has dropped well below 2 births per woman (compared with more than 2.5 births in Morocco's cities and in Cairo). The rate of school enrollment is almost 100 percent up to age sixteen; at the several universities in the city, enrollment is 55 percent female, far higher than in most Arab cities. Indeed, the role of women in civic life and in the urban economy has advanced rapidly since the 1980s, and females now make up one-third of paid employees and more than 40 percent of civil servants (Holmes-Eber 2003).

Tunisia's population as a whole enjoys better health and education than the rest of the African continent and better than in most Middle Eastern countries. United Nations sources indicate that life expectancy at birth is 74 (the world average is 68; the European average is 80 [WHO 2012]). The under-five mortality figure is 16 per thousand (the figure for all of sub-Saharan Africa is 121; the world average is 57 and industrialized countries is 6 [UNICEF 2011]). Unpublished official figures show all such indicators for the Tunis agglomeration to be even better than the national averages (UNICEF 2010).

Cultural homogeneity is a striking feature of the Tunis population. More than 98 percent describe themselves as Arab, and more than 98 percent describe themselves as Muslim—and as following the same Sunni branch of Islam (US CIA 2012). In this respect Tunis stands in contrast to Beirut, the similarly sized "cosmopolitan" capital city of Lebanon, where several forms of both Islam and Christianity are well represented. It also contrasts sharply with the Tunis of 1956, on the eve of independence, when almost half of the population were Europeans, mostly from France. The French legacy remains powerful culturally, especially in terms of language, but the underlying homogeneity is such that Arabic is the first language of the population.

The Urban Economy

Tunis is the undisputed focus of the national economy. What is disputed is whether its dominance is detrimental to regions to the west and south. Official statistics suggest that the city's economy accounts for more than one-third of the national gross domestic product, which grew by 3 percent to 5 percent a year between 2000 and 2010. In the 1980s the city accounted for more than 90 percent of all bank deposits in Tunisia (Signoles 1985), and it is unlikely that this has changed.

The national administration is highly concentrated in the city, in addition to a municipal administration employing many thousands; social services represent another important economic sector. Commerce, however, is the most visible part of the urban economy: wholesale, retail, services, and finance. Tunis houses the headquarters of almost every large Tunisian company and the Tunisian headquarters of almost every foreign company operating in the country.

Manufacturing plays a major part in the city's economy and has a larger impact than commerce on its environment. Traditional crafts survive on a small scale in the central medina, but in terms of employment and value of output, they are vastly outweighed by factories in suburban areas such as Ben Arous and Rades since 1960 and in peripheral areas such as Utique to the north and Grombalia to the south since 1980. Some, including flour mills, furniture factories, and cement works, serve national markets. Others are geared to export markets, including factories making clothing and shoes mainly for European Union countries, but also electronic goods, and automobile and aircraft components. Tunis and its periphery account for roughly half of the country's manufactured goods, which in turn account for a large percentage of Tunisia's exports.

Tourism matters to the Tunisian economy as a provider of employment and as a source of more than 10 percent of foreign exchange. Some tourists come to Tunis from France, and more from Arab countries such as Algeria, Libya, and Saudi Arabia. Other visitors arrive on cruise ships, primarily to visit the ruins of Carthage.

Tunis is not only Tunisia's capital city but its main port. For a while, new dock facilities at Rades, between the southeast shore of the lagoon and the sea, represented successful environmental management. Rades largely replaced La Goulette and now handles more than five thousand ships a year, most carrying cargo to and from Marseilles in France and Genoa in Italy. An entirely new port is now planned for Enfidha, 90 kilometers to the south, to handle the new generation of container ships.

The key economic problem facing Tunisia and Tunis City is a very high youth unemployment rate, which was a factor in recent political change. By 2010 the total number of urban unemployed included a high proportion with higher education qualifications. New jobs in call centers set up in Tunis by French firms have made only a dent in these numbers. Few countries devote more than

6 percent of all public expenditure to education, and some question whether this expenditure on Tunisia's part is sustainable in relation to work opportunities. Indeed, well-educated people or "experts" may become one of Tunisia's leading "exports."

Key Environment and Sustainability Issues

Tunis's distinctive site has provided both challenges and opportunities throughout its history, and this remains true today. In recent years, for example, a sewerage system was installed that has transformed the Lac de Tunis. In the 1990s and early 2000s extensive new land was reclaimed from the lagoon, permitting development of a zone of administrative and commercial buildings, halfway between the old city core and the sea (Barthel 2003). This reclamation process continues on the north and south shores of the lagoon.

Much of the housing in Tunis is at a low density compared with Cairo or Beirut, with very little high-rise building as yet. Most new housing consists of apartments, but in three-story blocks that increase the need for land and contribute to low overall population densities and urban sprawl.

From the 1930s to the 1950s many migrants arriving in Tunis settled, often as renters, in densely packed, illegal, flimsy dwellings on the city fringes. These were all demolished in the 1960s, after independence, when a massive program of new public housing began. According to the 2004 census less than 1 percent of housing in Tunis consisted of slums with inadequate services. Access to electricity, clean water, and sewerage is almost universal. Sanitation is generally up to European standards and vastly better than in most African cities.

In the 1980s the state was much engaged in home building but has ceased in this almost entirely. Most new housing is privately built, with between 10 and 20 percent considered in some sense "informal" (far less than in Cairo). A government agency remains active in regulating private-sector housing and providing water and sanitation. Supplying the city with water presents severe challenges.

Tunis boasts an exceptionally extensive (and inexpensive) and efficient public transport network, in sharp contrast to other cities of the Arab world such as Beirut. The Société des Transports de Tunis operates two hundred bus routes and a tram (métro-léger) network that was initiated in 1985 and then extended to some outer suburbs. A much older railway links central Tunis to the coastal suburbs of La Goulette, Carthage, and La Marsa, while the main-line railway system serves the southeastern suburbs and links Tunis to other cities. Low fares on public transport may help to explain the almost total absence of bicycles.

The road system includes the narrow alleys of the medina, suitable only for pedestrians and motorbikes, and a north-south highway fringing the former port that leads to new motorways, linking Tunis to other cities. As in any city, congestion increases during rush hours and construction work, but the density of private cars is far lower than in most middle-income cities. Tunis-Carthage Airport, located only 8 kilometers from the city center, handles 10 million passengers a year. Tunis is far ahead of most North African cities with respect to cell phone use and Internet access, factors that contributed to the speed of political change in early 2011.

From 2006 to 2008 detailed plans were prepared by Middle Eastern entrepreneurs for large-scale multi-use private "developments" on new land reclaimed from the Lac de Tunis as well as on land now occupied by the salt lakes. Five-star hotels and a massive sports complex were also proposed. The stated aim was to create a mini-Dubai.

Global recession and political change in Tunisia have largely put these plans on hold, although some infrastructure work continues. Major questions arise as to whether even half the proposed development is sustainable, either in terms of pressures on the environment, especially water supply, or in terms of the capacity of the Tunisian economy to absorb within the foreseeable future all the new retail and office space and high-cost housing.

The city's long-term prospects will inevitably depend in part on climate change. Sea-level rise will present challenges and could eventually cause physical devastation as much of the land is low-lying. Increasing aridity could profoundly affect the Tunisian economy by reducing crop yields and making water provision more costly.

Global Links and Immediate Prospects

Far from being restricted to one continent, Tunis continues to have diverse links with Europe and the Middle East as well as Africa (O'Connor 2004). For one hundred years its strongest tie was to Paris. This tie remains strong, as do its links with other French cities, although for the most part its political and economic connections to Europe are now more dispersed. Tunis maintains links with Tripoli and Benghazi in Libya, with Algiers and Cairo, and with Gulf and Saudi cities (which provide the wealthiest tourists). It has housed the headquarters of the Arab League (1979–1990), and of the Palestine Liberation Organization (1973–2003).

For the Romans, what is now Tunisia was not just *in* Africa—it *was* "Africa" or "Ifriqiya"—but Tunis today tends to look north to Europe and east to the Middle East. Tunis is physically rooted in Africa, but its human links to Africa south of the Sahara are weak. Tunis airport has scheduled flights to 36 European, 7 Middle Eastern, 7 North African, and just 4 sub-Saharan African destinations (200, 20, 40, and 2 weekly flights, respectively). For many citizens of Tunis the most important "African" dimension of life is probably the fifty-member Confédération Africaine de Football.

Tunis was marked by extreme, perhaps excessive, political stability for more than fifty years under the authoritarian rule of presidents Bourguiba and Ben Ali. A comparison of writings on Tunisia under Ben Ali (Alexander 2010; Hibou 2011) demonstrates clearly the well-ordered but undemocratic nature of the regime. There was an effective civil service, with little low-level corruption compared with many Middle Eastern and African countries, but the government had become dictatorial and repressive, while the Ben Ali family increasingly took personal control of key sectors in the economy and looted state finances. A protest movement originating in a poor inland town in late 2010 spread quickly to Tunis City, bringing crisis for three weeks before toppling the regime. The challenge of restoring order and building new political institutions through 2011 at the national level can be seen in the life of the capital city, which for most of the population soon returned to "normal," except in vital areas such as free speech. It is too early to assess the possible impact of the Arab Spring on environmental issues.

Tunis is many cities: a North African city, a Middle Eastern city, and a Mediterranean city; an ancient city, a former colonial city, a postcolonial city, and a thriving modern city; an Arab city and a Muslim/Islamic city. It would also like to see itself as a "global city." Indeed, in late February 2012, Tunis hosted an international crisis meeting on Syria, with representatives of sixty countries attending.

Anthony M. O'CONNOR
University College London

See also Africa (*several articles*); Cairo, Egypt; Dubai, United Arab Emirates; Mediterranean Sea; Middle East; Urbanization (Africa); Urbanization (Western Asia and Northern Africa)

FURTHER READING

Abdelkafi, Jellal. (1989). *La Médina de Tunis* [The Medina of Tunis]. Paris: CNRS.

Akrout-Yaïche, Sémia. (Ed.). (2006). *Tunis 1800–1950: Portrait architectural et urbain* [Tunis 1800–1950: Architectural and urban portrait]. Tunis, Tunisia: Elyzad-Clairefontaine.

Alexander, Christopher. (2010). *Tunisia: Stability and reform in the modern Maghreb.* London & New York: Routledge.

Barthel, Pierre-Arnaud. (2003). Les lacs de Tunis en projets: Reflets d'un nouveau gouvernement urbain [Developing the lakes of Tunis: A new approach in urban governance]. *Annales de Géographie, 633,* 518–536.

Belhareth, Taoufik. (2004). *Transport et structuration de l'espace tunisien* [Transport and Tunisia's space]. Tunis, Tunisia: University of Tunis.

Belhedi, Amor. (1979). L'espace tunisois [The spatial structure of Tunis]. *Revue Tunisienne de Géographie, 4*, 9–39.

Belhedi, Amor. (1983). Différenciation sociale de l'espace urbain: Le cas de Tunis [Social contrasts across urban space: The case of Tunis]. *Etudes Méditerranéennes, 5*, 27–52.

Bilas, Charles. (2010). *Tunis: L'orient de la modernité* [Tunis: Oriental modernity]. Paris: Eclat.

Binous, Jamila; Bechr, Fatma Ben; & Abdelkafi, Jellal. (1985). *Tunis.* Tunis, Tunisia: Sud-Editions.

Chabbi, Morched. (2001). La croissance du grand Tunis [The growth of greater Tunis]. In Jacques Vallin & Thérèse Locoh (Eds.), *Population et développement en Tunisie* [Population and development in Tunisia] (pp. 311–326). Tunis, Tunisia: Cérès.

Fakhfakh, Mohamed. (1989). Croissance urbaine et environnement dans le district de Tunis [Urban growth and environment in the district of Tunis]. *Géographie et Développement, 8*, 57–76.

Hamzaoui Oueslati, Najet. (2004). *Centres urbains secondaires dans le district de Tunis* [Secondary urban centers in the Tunis area]. Tunis, Tunisia: University of Tunis.

Hibou, Beatrice. (2011). *The force of obedience: The political economy of repression in Tunisia.* Cambridge, UK, & Malden, MA: Polity.

Holmes-Eber, Paula. (2003). *Daughters of Tunis: Women, family and networks in a Muslim city.* Boulder, CO & Oxford, UK: Westview.

Jacobs, Daniel. (2009). *Rough guide to Tunisia* (8th ed.). London, New York, & Delhi: Rough Guides.

Jedidi, Mohamed. (1990). Le projet d'aménagement des berges septentrionales du Lac de Tunis [Management project for the northern edge of the Lac de Tunis]. *Revue Tunisienne de Géographie, 19*, 15–50.

Lacoste, Yves. (1984). *Ibn Khaldun: The birth of history and the past of the Third World.* London: Verso.

Lancel, Serge. (1995). *Carthage: A history.* Oxford, UK: Blackwell.

Lawless, Richard, & Findlay, Alan. (1981). Tunis. In Michael Pacione (Ed.), *Problems and planning in Third World cities* (pp. 94–126). London: Croom Helm.

Miossec, Jean-Marie. (1999). La mosaïque urbaine Tunisienne [The Tunisian urban mosaic]. In Pierre Signoles, Galila el-Kadi & Rachid Sidi Boumedine (Eds.), *L'urbain dans le monde Arabe* [The city in the Arab world] (pp. 87–118). Aix-en-Provence, France: CNRS.

Nouschi, Andre; bi-al-Hammamat, Markaz al-Thaqafi al-Dawli; & Social Science Research Council. (1996) *Système urbain et développement au Maghreb* [The urban system and development in the Maghreb]. Tunis, Tunisia: Cérès.

O'Connor, Anthony. (2004). How African is Tunisia? In Ray Harris & Khalid Koser (Eds.), *Continuity and change in the Tunisian Sahel* (pp. 74–87). Aldershot, UK & Burlington, VT: Ashgate.

Robinson, Jennifer. (2006). *Ordinary cities: Between modernity and development.* London: Routledge.

Sebag, Paul. (1998). *Tunis: Histoire d'une ville* [Tunis: History of a city]. Paris: L'Harmattan.

Sethom, Hafedh. (1992). *Pouvoir urbain et paysannerie en Tunisie* [Urban power and the peasantry in Tunisia]. Tunis, Tunisia: Cérès.

Signoles, Pierre. (1985). *L'espace tunisien: Capitale et état-région* [The capital city and Tunisian space]. Tours, France: Laboratoire URBAMA.

Signoles, Pierre; Belhedi, Amor; Miossec, Jean-Marie; & Dlala, Habib. (1980). *Tunis, Évolution et fonctionnement de l'espace urbain* [Evolution and functioning of the urban space of Tunis]. Tours, France: Laboratoire URBAMA.

Tlatli, Salah-Eddine. (1978). *La Carthage punique: Etude urbaine* [Punic Carthage: An urban study]. Paris: Librairie d'Amérique et d'Orient.

United Nations Children's Fund (UNICEF). (2010). Tunisia: Statistics. Retrieved July 27, 2012, from http://www.unicef.org/infobycountry/Tunisia_statistics.html

United Nations Children's Fund (UNICEF). (2011). Childinfo: Monitoring the situation of children and women. Retrieved July 27, 2012, from http://www.childinfo.org/mortality_underfive.php

United Nations Development Programme (UNDP). (2012). Human development reports. Retrieved July 22, 2012, from http://hdr.undp.org/en/statistics/

United States Central Intelligence Agency (US CIA). (2012). World factbook: Tunisia. Retrieved July 27, 2012, from https://www.cia.gov/library/publications/the-world-factbook/geos/ts.html

Woodford, Jerome S. (1990). *The city of Tunis: Evolution of an urban system.* Wisbech, UK: Middle East & North African Studies Press.

World Health Organization (WHO). (2012). Global health observatory (GHO): Life expectancy at birth. Retrieved July 27, 2012, from http://www.who.int/gho/mortality_burden_disease/life_tables/situation_trends/en/index.html

Ukraine

45.7 million est. pop. 2010

Ukraine, long known as the "bread basket of Europe," is a large and fertile country in Eastern Europe that is perhaps best known, unfortunately, for the meltdown of a nuclear reactor at Chernobyl nuclear power station in 1986, which caused huge amounts of radiation (over 100 times the amount released by the bombings of Hiroshima and Nagasaki) to travel as far as Northern Europe and eventually the entire world. In recent years, however, Ukraine has attempted to improve its environmental standing.

Ukraine has been an independent nation in Eastern Europe since 1991. Formerly a republic within (member nation of) the Soviet Union, it is now a member of the Commonwealth of Independent States. Ukraine shares borders with Poland, Slovakia, Hungary, Romania, Moldova, Russia, and Belarus. It is bordered by the Black and Azov seas on the south. Ukraine encompasses 603,700 square kilometers—for comparison, France covers 643,000 square kilometers—and administratively is divided into twenty-four regions, one autonomous republic (Crimea), and two urban centers (Kiev and Sevastopol).

About 73 percent of the population is Ukrainian and 21 percent Russian. The remainder is divided among 110 ethnic groups including Jews, Belarusians, Moldovans, Bulgarians, Poles, Greeks, Hungarians, Crimean Tatars, Armenians, Germans, and Gypsies (Romani). Ukrainian is the official language, and Eastern Orthodox Christianity the dominant religion.

About 95 percent of Ukraine is flatland, of which about 70 percent is lowlands. Ukraine is divided by its main river, the Dnieper, into two sections—Right Bank Ukraine (Volyns'ko-Podil's'ka highland, eastern Carpathy, Polyssia) and Left Bank Ukraine (Dnieper lowland, Donets'ka highland). The Black Sea lowland is situated at the south. The two major mountain ranges are the Crimea Mountains and the Carpathians (the highest point in Ukraine is Mount Goverla at 2,061 meters). The most important rivers are the Dnieper, Pivdenny Bug, Dniester, and Danube (all of which empty into the Black Sea) and their tributaries, including the Psel, Goryn, Desna, and Ingulets. Natural lakes are concentrated in Ukrainian Polyssia and in the lower Danube region; along the Black Sea coast there are numerous brackish (semi-saltwater) estuaries. *Chernozem* (rich humus) is the most widespread soil type.

Ukraine has more than thirty thousand natural floral species and about forty-five thousand natural faunal species. The four main geographical zones are forest (average afforestation level is 14 percent; mixed forests dominate), mixed forest-steppe, steppe (arid and semiarid, about 40 percent of the territory of Ukraine), and the Crimea Mountain zone. The climate is moderate, warm (with moderately cold winters), and continental, being located at the southern part of the Crimea littoral-subtropical zone. Average temperatures in January are −8°C in northeastern Ukraine and 4°C in Crimea; in July, 17°C in northwestern Ukraine and 23°C in southern Ukraine. Average annual precipitation is 300–500 millimeters in the Black and Azov seas region, 600–700 millimeters in northeastern Ukraine, 1,000–1,200 millimeters in the Crimea Mountains, and more than 1,500 millimeters in the Carpathians.

Combustible mineral resources (hard coal, oil, natural gas), metals (iron, manganese, uranium, titanium, mercury), ores, and nonmetallic mineral sources (graphite, fireclays, rock salt, building materials) create a natural

326

resource base and determine the direction of international trade and national production development. The country established its first nature reserve, Askaniya-Nova, in 1921 and stresses the conservation of natural resources as a national priority (US Department of State 2011).

In matters of environment, Ukraine is well known as the site of the 1986 Chernobyl nuclear power station accident, which contaminated 21 percent of the territory of Ukraine, as well as neighboring nations, with cesium isotopes. On 26 April 1986, one of the four reactors at Chernobyl nuclear power station exploded. The accident released at least one hundred times more radiation into the atmosphere than the dropping of atomic bombs on Hiroshima and Nagasaki. Most of the radiation hit other areas of Ukraine, Belarus, and Russia, but much of Northern Europe was also affected (BBC News 2006). The diffused radiation eventually spread to the entire world. The last reactor at Chernobyl was shut down in 2000. A new shelter surrounding the original one, which covers the damaged reactors that caused the accident, is scheduled to be completed in 2014.

Ukraine is a signatory of the international Kyoto Protocol calling for reduced greenhouse gas emissions. Ukrainian soil is considered a national asset thanks to its excellent fertility and agricultural quality; the country has long been known as the "bread basket of Europe." Agriculture comprises 72 percent and forests 17 percent of total land area (UNDP 2011). The country has a pollution fee system, whereby taxes are levied on air and water emissions and solid waste disposal; enforcement of this tax, however, is lax. Issues of natural environment protection, water pollution, and air pollution are discussed by representatives of the Ukrainian Ecological Association "Green Light" and by members of the Ukrainian Green Party. The Green Party was represented in the Ukrainian Parliament after the elections of 1998, though it failed to gain seats in the 2002 elections.

Since the end of the 1990s a major environmental concern has involved the Danube estuary, which covers a total area of 7,000 square kilometers—roughly half the size of Puerto Rico. As waterways from several states feed into the Danube river (it is Europe's second longest river), this has caused pressure on the river's watershed, and the runoff into the Black Sea is controlled by dams.

Levels of chemicals, especially nitrates and phosphorus, have increased in the estuary in recent years, causing the over-enrichment known as eutrophication, which encourages plant growth to the point of depleting oxygen. Water quality and sediments have deteriorated in the estuary and northern part of the Black Sea, causing fish numbers and biodiversity to decrease. An international organization, the International Commission for the Protection of the Danube River, is a body set up to sort out the transnational problems affecting the river.

Olena V. SMYNTYNA
Odessa I. I. Mechnikov National University

See also Balkans; Central Asia; Danube River; Mediterranean Sea; Russia and the Soviet Union; Scandinavia; Transboundary Water Issues; Volga River

This article was adapted by the editors from Olena V. Smyntyna's article "Ukraine" in Shepard Krech III, J. R. McNeill, and Carolyn Merchant (Eds.), the *Encyclopedia of World Environmental History*, pp. 1227–1228. Great Barrington, MA: Berkshire Publishing (2003).

FURTHER READING

Berlinsky, Nikolai; Bogatova, Yulia; & Garkavaya, Galina. (2006). Estuary of the Danube. In Peter J. Wangersky (Vol. Ed.), *Estuaries. The handbook of environmental chemistry: Vol. 5* (pp. 233–264). Berlin: Springer.

British Broadcasting Company (BBC) News. (2006). The Chernobyl disaster. Retrieved December 21, 2011, from http://news.bbc.co.uk/1/shared/spl/hi/guides/456900/456957/html/nn1page1.stm

International Commission for the Protection of the Danube River (ICPDR). (2011). Homepage. Retrieved January 28, 2012, from http://www.icpdr.org/icpdr-pages/home.htm

Naulko, V. I. (1998). *Khto i vidkoly zhive v Ukrayini* [Who and since what time lives in Ukraine]. Kiev, Ukraine: Golovna Spezializovana Redakcia Literatury Movamy Natzionalnyh Menshin.

Popov, V. P. (Ed.). (1968). *Fiziko-geographicheskoye rayonirovanie Ukrainskoi SSR* [Natural geographic demarcation of Ukraine SSR]. Kiev, Ukraine: Naukova Dumka.

Smoliy, V. A. (Ed.). (1998). *Ukraina kriz' viky* [Ukraine throughout the centuries]. Kiev, Ukraine: Alternativy.

United Nations Development Programme (UNDP): Ukraine. (2011). Energy and environment. Retrieved December 21, 2011, from http://www.undp.org.ua/en/energy-and-environment

United States Department of State. (2011, April 25). Background note: Ukraine. Retrieved December 21, 2011, from http://www.state.gov/r/pa/ei/bgn/3211.htm

Wangersky, Peter J. (Ed.). (2006). *The handbook of environmental chemistry, Volume 5: Water pollution/estuaries*. Berlin: Springer.

United Kingdom and Ireland

United Kingdom (including Northern Ireland): 63 million est. pop. 2012;

Republic of Ireland: 4.7 million est. pop. 2012

The United Kingdom and Ireland (split between the independent nation of Ireland and Northern Ireland, part of the United Kingdom) lie on the very edge of Europe and offer a landscape that is biologically and geographically diverse. The isles' history, also diverse, has had an international impact as a leading proponent of the Industrial Revolution and with an empire covering a fifth of the globe at its height. This has led to many environmental problems, but in recent years consecutive governments in both nations have attempted to deal with these issues.

The conglomeration of islands on the northwestern periphery of the continent of Europe known collectively as the United Kingdom and Ireland (which is split between the independent republic of Ireland and Northern Ireland, which is part of the United Kingdom) has wielded a disproportionate influence over the human history of the planet. (This article will refer to the island of Ireland in its entirety, rather than Northern Ireland and Ireland, unless specifically stated otherwise.) The British Empire, which once boasted control over one-fifth of the Earth's land surface, helped to stimulate, directly or indirectly, the exploitation of natural resources on an unprecedented global scale. Industrialization, a process that has fundamentally altered the ability of humans to harness the Earth's resources, caused the removal of most of the inhabitants of these islands from a rural, predominantly agricultural environment into an urban, industrialized one. At the same time, that rural environment—or perceptions of what it had once been— became associated with a nostalgic sense of identity that

partly informs contemporary environmentalism within the United Kingdom and Ireland. This view of the past also influences such diverse aspects of public policy as planning, forestry, recreation, and the allocation of resources to agriculture.

Raw Materials

If the latitudes of the United Kingdom and Ireland are compared with the eastern coast of North America across the Atlantic, the northernmost limit of these islands (Shetland) is on a level with Labrador and the southernmost limit (Isles of Scilly) with Newfoundland. Most of the islands, however, share the temperate climate of the European mainland and also benefit from the warming effects of the North Atlantic drift (the warm ocean current flowing from northeastward from Mexico toward northwest Europe under the influence of prevailing winds), which allows even palm trees to grow on the northwest coast of Scotland.

Within the main islands of the United Kingdom and Ireland is a significant east-west divide in terms of rainfall. The west endures increasing amounts of warm, wet weather throughout the year, perhaps as a result of global warming, whereas the east can struggle with periods of drought in the summer. Some parts of the British Isles, particularly the mountainous regions of Scotland, northern England, Wales, and Ireland, are at the limits of cereal cultivation. They are not inherently marginal, given that the ability to maintain large numbers of animals, the vagaries of climate change, the existence of significant mineral resources, and participation in international trade over the last millennia have all contributed to a complex and varied history.

In terms of resources, the mountains, plains, rivers, and seas of the United Kingdom and Ireland have played host to a large number of valuable—and exploitable—assets, from gold to salt to herring to sheep to oil, and much in between. Most of the human history of the United Kingdom and Ireland encompasses determined efforts to extract and utilize these resources, which, though they may have seemed limitless at one time, unfortunately have not proved to be so. Having recently recognized the human contribution to the degradation of these resources, sometimes to the point of extinction, has led to parts of the United Kingdom and Ireland finally making strenuous efforts to harness the power of renewable resources. These include technology related to wind power and wave power, both abundant in these areas.

As with climatic conditions, there is considerable environmental variation across the main islands of the United Kingdom and Ireland. Ecological conditions have continually interacted with the cultural attributes of the human populations who live within them to create the environmental histories of these islands.

From Tundra to Farming

The great glaciers that pressed down on the landmasses of northern Europe during the last ice age, gouging out many of the landforms still evident today, also wiped out most of the traces of human history prior to that date. There are only a few such traces in the United Kingdom, all in the east of England. In the first millennia after the retreat of the ice, environmental conditions dictated the course of history. Temperatures rose, causing the replacement of the tundra landscape of boulders, light soils, and scrubby plants such as juniper, with warmth-loving trees. This was a gradual process, and there were also environmental limits to the changes taking place. Deciduous forest did not spread beyond the highland line (a geological fault cutting across Scotland from the southwest to the northeast, and effectively dividing the country into a mountainous highland region to the northwest and lowland plains to the southeast). By 7000 BCE, most of the United Kingdom and Ireland was covered in forest of one kind or another.

With the arrival of trees, many of the large animals of the tundra, such as reindeer and wild horse, disappeared. The transition from birch and pine to oak forests also provided a better environment for some animals over others, although the fact that different parts of the country had different types of tree cover ensured some diversity. Red and roe deer, wild pig, and beaver were all particularly at home in the oak forests. These are the environments that the newly arrived human populations found as they spread across the land bridge that attached mainland Britain to Europe until about 6000 BCE. Many settled around the coasts, supplementing the

more unreliable hunting of animals with the collection of berries and other vegetation, and the extremely healthy fruits of the rivers and seas. Around 3500 BCE the peoples of these islands became aware of the techniques associated with a rather different way of life. Farming had made its way across Europe from the Middle East. Now humans began to have a much more direct impact on the environment, manipulating species to create domesticated cereals and animals, dividing land into field systems and designated areas for animal husbandry, developing permanent settlements, and constructing visible symbols of their existence and relationship with the universe.

Farmland and Forests

An example of the impact of prehistoric human predecessors on the visual appearance of the landscape comes from the Céide (pronounced *kayje*) Fields in County Mayo in the west of the Republic of Ireland. It represents the oldest enclosed farmland discovered in the Western world (older than the Egyptian pyramids), built about five thousand years ago. Mosaics of stone walls crisscross a huge area, dividing it into fields. The move to settle down probably had the greatest effect on the forest, as large swaths were chopped down to make way for agriculture. Environmental historians in the United Kingdom and Ireland have devoted much attention to woodland history because there is so little forest left, but the blame for much of the reduction lies at the feet of prehistoric human ancestors, rather than more recent entrepreneurs.

The increasing evidence for the activities of prehistoric farmers, particularly the great monuments related to the dead, lets one see how they viewed themselves as part of a bigger picture. The heavens played a key role in their belief systems, perhaps not surprisingly considering that so many sources of difficulty seemed to relate to the skies, whether it was too much or too little rain, or an eclipse, which was often viewed as a portent of disaster such as disease. This suggests that these early peoples saw themselves as part of the environment that they occupied and were well aware of the need to placate nature, which had the power of life or death.

Although a hierarchy in society had evolved long before the arrival of the Romans to conquer Britain in 43 CE, the newcomers showed the natives from parts of these islands (mostly England—Ireland, Wales, and most of Scotland were not conquered) just what could be achieved with the centralization of power. The harnessing of the Roman Empire's resources, including human slaves, provided wealth for citizens and the environment in which to develop the technology that brought about the famous bathhouses, aqueducts, road systems, and basic central heating.

As one empire began to decline, another—technically of a spiritual rather than a secular nature—began to rise. Christianity arrived in Britain in the fifth century CE, taking various routes and forms. It was the reformation of the Roman Catholic version of Christianity from 1000 onward, however, that led to the dominance of the view that humans are masters on Earth. The medieval chroniclers continued to interpret the activities in the skies as portents of disaster or retribution for bad behavior here on Earth, but they had little to say about the environment in general.

Innovations

By the later Middle Ages, the regulation of access to resources—from the rights of the tenantry to take wood, peat, and other essentials of existence to the privilege of the nobility to hunt for deer and game in specially designated areas known as "forests" (which did not explicitly involve trees)—was also long established. Salt and coal extraction, the mining of metals such as tin and even gold, and the harnessing of rivers by means of waterwheels were some of the host of activities that attested to the practical abilities of humans to increasingly control the environment.

Disease affecting humans, animals, and crops, however, was also a major aspect of the Middle Ages, with Bubonic plague being only one type, though the repeated bouts of it from 1348 onward were devastating. Pollution was already affecting some of the denser populations, especially in London, due to the burning of coal. Also, by 1300 the population had expanded well beyond the carrying capacity (the population that an area will support without deterioration) of existing settlements, prompting the conversion to agriculture of "unproductive" land such as woodlands and heaths, thus showing some of the basic effects that demographics can have on the course of environmental history.

Throughout the historic period, the United Kingdom and Ireland have never been closed systems, self-sufficient and isolated. The peoples of these islands were inclined to travel, as well as to accommodate newcomers,

willingly or unwillingly. The early modern period, however, witnessed a new expansion of horizons with the discovery of the New World far to the west. The British Empire was beginning.

At the same time, science was advancing in all directions, challenging religious versions of how the world had come about, how it operated, and where it might be going. This led to the Age of Enlightenment, and scientists and thinkers from the British Isles were at the forefront of it.

The Goal of Improvement

The drive for rationality, rather than a reliance on traditional assumptions, spilled over into almost every aspect of life, and agriculture was not immune. Improvement was the practical expression of Enlightenment thinking and involved the application of scientifically established principles to farming. Higher productivity was achieved through fertilizers, primarily manure but also marl, lime, and chalk, on acidic soils. New crops, such as turnips and clover, also improved yields.

Like the monastic orders before them, the devotees of improvement understood that, in order to effect the changes they believed were absolutely necessary for progress, as much land as possible needed to be brought under their full control. During the eighteenth century this meant that common land, which had housed the animals of the peasantry for centuries, became regarded by landowners as "waste" because they could not do with it what they liked. The process of enclosure, which had begun in England under the direction of individual landowners as early as the sixteenth century, was now sanctioned by Parliament in the eighteenth century as absolute property rights became more clearly enunciated in law.

The draining of the fens (wet lowlands), a constant refrain in the history of southeast England, continued, but experiments took place elsewhere, most particularly in the *carse* (floodplain) lands around the river Forth near Stirling, Scotland, which were transformed from a peat bog into productive, arable land. Interestingly, the remnants of this bog at Flanders Moss are now a national nature reserve. One era's wasteland is another era's prime ecological area.

The process of agricultural improvement took place at different times and in slightly different ways in the various parts of the United Kingdom and Ireland. In some parts, however—most notably the western parts of Ireland and the northwestern part of Scotland—improvement was often also associated with a time when the land was managed in such a way as to fail to meet the basic dietary needs of the expanding population. The famines of the eighteenth and nineteenth centuries caused immense psychological damage to the people involved and their successors. The problem lay less with the environment itself, however, and more with, for example, the decision to rely entirely on the potato crop or to move people to marginal coastal areas and replace them with sheep. In both places, the result of difficult conditions was an exodus of people, partly to the growing urban centers of England and lowland Scotland, and partly by emigration to other countries. The places they left behind, often still containing poignant relics of past settlement, are now regarded as some of the best wilderness in the country. It seems fitting, somehow, that the last wolf in the British Isles was shot during the eighteenth century.

Industrialization

The transformation of the British Isles did not end there. The entrepreneurialism that thrived within the empire with its plethora of cheap resources, when combined with scientific and technological innovation, brought about something radically new: industrialization. This is not meant to imply that there had been no industry before. Mining of coal, salt, and tin was already centuries old, and it could be argued that the sheep ranching of the later Middle Ages was industrial in scale, even before the domestic cloth industry—especially in England during the same period—is mentioned.

Modern industrialization, beginning in the eighteenth century, was different because now, finally, mechanization began to supplant human muscle power. Once that happened, the circle of acquiring and consuming sufficient food only to fuel directly the range of activities needed to ensure the production of enough food and so forth, was finally broken. Although humans still had to work, they could now sign up to an ever-increasing range of jobs, develop new skills that differentiated them from others, and, eventually, embrace a new set of activities associated with the concept of leisure time.

The first major industries revolved around textiles, with cotton, grown in the colonies by slaves taken in British ships from Africa, shipped to the United Kingdom to be worked into cloth. Those who worked the spinning jenny (an early fiber-spinning machine) and other mechanized aids to industry often still lived within the rural environment. The direct connection with the land, however, had been broken because the resource they exploited was not grown there.

The implications of this triumph of machines over muscle also had serious implications for the impact of human activity on the environment. Thanks to agricultural improvements, the land began to produce more food of better quality and greater reliability. The demand for more products, using a larger number of raw materials and more energy to produce and transport them, emphasized both the human ability to transcend almost any restrictions that nature might try to place on them as well as an increasingly inventive talent for destruction.

By the nineteenth century the population began to rise beyond any previous level, placing unprecedented pressure on, for example, housing space, water supplies, food production, and the transport infrastructure. Human ingenuity and initiative overcame many of these problems, particularly the supply of clean water to inhibit diseases such as cholera. The serious flooding of more recent years has made it clear that diverting river flows and reclaiming floodplains over the last few centuries have not been without serious consequences.

As industrialization began in earnest, with the creation of factories and the accompanying rapidly expanding urban environment, coal emissions became both visible and deadly. Although coal emissions were associated with every major industrial city, London's "peasoupers" (dense, dirty yellow fogs) in particular gave considerable added atmosphere to many literary works of the period. The power of the industrialists ensured that legislation to curb industrial emissions was slow in coming, though progress was made after the Alkali Act of 1863. Nevertheless, domestic emissions, a far greater source of pollution, were not curbed through the law until 1956 and 1968. Here cultural inbreeding played its part: the British refused to ditch their inefficient, polluting, open coal-burning hearths in favor of closed continental ones simply because of the firm belief that their system was bound to be best.

Artistic Community

The profound changes to the landscape and way of life associated with industrialization affected even the artistic community. Some, such as writer Emily Brontë in *Wuthering Heights,* although celebrating the wildness of preindustrial rural England, also saw the potential of change for those sections of the population trying to eke out a living from difficult conditions. The belief in the all-encompassing benefits of progress was also seriously challenged, however, though those who did so had mixed motives. Poet William Wordsworth and other writers, enamored with the Lake District in northwest England, lamented not only the crisscrossing of the country by the railways with their infernal racket and ungodly appearance by the middle of the nineteenth century, but were also concerned that the access of the lower classes to railway travel might mean an influx of insensitive souls to such rural idylls. Not everyone, they apparently thought, had sufficient sensibility to appreciate the poetry in these wildernesses.

Ironically, the success of these writers has frozen the Lake District into an image of dry-stone walls, neat fields, and sheep, as well as daffodils—a perfect improver's landscape and illustrative of a comparatively recent history. Nevertheless, it is an icon of English identity, and woe betide anyone trying to change it, from the Forestry Commission that attempted to grow plantations of trees there in the 1930s, to the force of nature itself, decried eloquently by one farmer during the 2001 foot-and-mouth disease crisis, who predicted that, if all the sheep were culled, there would be scrub within five years and trees within ten. It was clear that, unlike in Scotland, the restoration of trees was most unwelcome.

Concern for the environment was not restricted to those of an artistic bent. Experience out in the colonies led to the first direct appreciation of the power of nature to hit back, and led to theories about deforestation, climate change, and desiccation as early as the mid-eighteenth century. These theories were then imported back to the British Isles, where, even if they were not directly applicable, at least generated discussion about the potential impacts of the exploitation of resources.

Twentieth Century

The twentieth century brought perhaps the greatest impact of human activity on the environment in absolute terms. Ironically, however, the same century also brought a huge upsurge in concern for the environment, associated in part with the rise of democracy and grassroots movements from the 1960s. For some, the pressures of twentieth-century life, the inescapable everyday symbols of the never-ending human capacity to use up fossil fuels and other irreplaceable resources, forged a sense of a past golden age, when humans and nature lived in harmony. The truth, inevitably, is far less simple.

Another potentially positive aspect of the twentieth century was the growth of the state's willingness and ability to intervene, both in the United Kingdom and in the Republic of Ireland (which became a separate state in 1921), often thanks to pressure from conservation organizations. In particular, the 1947 Town and Country Planning Act, followed by the National Parks Act of 1949, provided the legislative basis for regulation of both the built and the natural environment within the United Kingdom.

Despite some positive trends, however, the twentieth century also brought the increasing globalization of economies and therefore the globalization of the impact of human activity, particularly by industrialized nations such as the United Kingdom. This has sometimes meant that policies designed to clean up Britain's environmental record have been achieved at the expense of the continuing exploitation of someone else's resources; the move to restore seminatural woodlands while still importing large amounts of softwoods from Canada and Scandinavia is a case in point. The United Kingdom is also no longer the world's leading industrial nation, although it has been called the "Dirty Man of Europe" because of its continuing pollution.

Recent Issues

Both the United Kingdom and the Republic of Ireland are in the forefront of responding to many environmental issues, including those involving energy, food, and climate change. In 2008, the United Kingdom government signed the Climate Change Act, which capped carbon dioxide levels. The act called for an 80 percent cut in carbon dioxide levels by 2050 (to 1990 levels) and a reduction of 34 percent by 2020 (Department of Energy and Climate Change 2012). These are some of the strictest environmental controls in the world. The Scottish Parliament (which was recreated in 1999) has gone for even higher targets than the rest of the United Kingdom when it comes to renewable energy.

Nuclear Energy

In the wake of the Fukushima nuclear disaster in March of 2011, which occurred after an earthquake and its resulting tsunami devastated the northeastern coast of Japan, the ongoing economic crisis that started in 2008 and a change in political winds is threatening the United Kingdom's nuclear program, with uncertainty hanging over all five of the new proposed nuclear power stations. There is also concern as all of Britain's nuclear power stations are due to stop working within ten years. In addition, Britain's energy security is in jeopardy because of concern over levels of North Sea oil. Observers are looking across the channel to Germany, which has reduced the number of its nuclear power stations in the wake of the Japan disaster, and to France, traditionally more friendly to nuclear energy than Germany. The newly elected socialist president of France, François Hollande, campaigned in part on the issue of closing twenty-four of France's fifty-eight reactors (Wright 2012). Although England will almost certainly build new reactors, the

Scottish government refuses to contemplate this north of the border (while this is a UK issue, it is a sensitive political one, given that Scotland will vote on whether or not to become independent in 2014).

As of 2012, in the Republic of Ireland there are no nuclear power stations, and nuclear power is prohibited by legislation. Although the topic has long been considered somewhat taboo, debates do occur as to whether Ireland should become a nuclear nation in the future. Although the future (if any) of nuclear energy in the nation is uncertain, polls show that an overwhelming majority of people in Ireland wish that they had more information on the subject (Lynch and Wright 2012).

The Local Food Debate

Global focus on energy consumption has naturally extended to food consumption. In cities such as Galway City, Ireland (and in fact all over the British Isles), signs in restaurants and public houses with phrases such as "local," "seasonal," and "organic" are common. Eating locally sourced meat and produce, once a necessity on the islands, is now a trend supported by chefs (who often have an influential role as tastemakers), consumers, farmers, and tourists. The question of exactly what "local" means, and what food production methods are the most sustainable, is the subject of much debate. In the example of Galway City, which has a mild climate and access to a relatively large and agricultural hinterland as well as to the Atlantic coast, buying local produce year-round is a more realistic option for consumers than it might be in other locations. As an example of the debate over what "local" means, some chefs in Galway City consider artisanal foods, such as cheeses and wines (some produced elsewhere and shipped into the city) to be preferable to food that is mass produced—even if the mass-produced food is technically more "local"—and consider these imported artisanal items to be local (Duram and Cawley 2012). Trends of eating local continue to be a primary influence on consumer choices; a 2008 study in the United Kingdom showed 60 percent of respondents preferring restaurants using local ingredients over those not (Ball 2008).

Outlook

Adjustment to the new world order in the twenty-first century in part means understanding how the environments contained within the islands of the United Kingdom and Ireland have evolved. There has been almost no point during the last ten thousand years when humans have not had an impact, and that is something that must be accepted as intrinsic to the human relationship with the rest of the natural world. The human role

as master of technology, however, has proved to be as double-edged as that of human nature itself. Millions of people in this area have been lifted out of the physical hardship and drudgery of subsistence living into the psychological difficulties of a world containing weapons of mass destruction and the knowledge of their own responsibility for the degradation of the planet that sustains them. These islands northwest of the European continent have experienced a full, rich, and varied environmental history. It is vital that people learn from the past so that the future can also be full, rich, and varied.

Fiona J. WATSON
University of Dundee

See also European Union (EU); Fisheries; France; Germany; London, United Kingdom; Scandinavia; Urbanization (Europe)

FURTHER READING

Aalen, Frederick H. A.; Whelan, Kevin; & Stout, Matthew. (Eds.). (1997). *Atlas of the Irish rural landscape.* Cork, Ireland: Cork University Press.

Allanson, Paul, & Whitby, Martin Charles. (Eds.). (1996). *The rural economy and the British countryside.* London: Earthscan.

Andrews, Malcolm. (1989). *The search for the picturesque: Landscape aesthetics and tourism in Britain, 1760–1800.* Stanford, CA: Stanford University Press.

Ball, Stephen; Rowson, Bill; & O'Toole, Sean. (2008). Report on consumer perception of organic, ethical and local foods served in restaurants in the Sheffield area. Sheffield, UK: Centre for International Hospitality Management Research, Sheffield Hallam University.

Bell, Jonathan. (1992). *People and the land: Farming life in nineteenth century Ireland.* Belfast, Northern Ireland: Friar's Bush.

Brimblecombe, Peter. (1987). *The big smoke: A history of air pollution in London since medieval times.* London & New York: Routledge.

Bunce, Michael. (1994). *The countryside ideal: Anglo-American images of landscape.* London & New York: Routledge.

Chambers, Jonathan David, & Mingay, Gordon Edmund. (1966). *The agricultural revolution 1750–1880.* London: Batsford.

Clapp, Brian William. (1994). *An environmental history of Britain since the industrial revolution.* Harlow, UK: Longmans.

Coleman, David, & Salt, John. (1992). *The British population: Patterns, trends and processes.* Oxford, UK: Oxford University Press.

Cook, Hadrian F., & Williamson, Tom. (1999). *Water management in the English landscape: Field, marsh and meadow.* Edinburgh, UK: Edinburgh University Press.

Department of Energy and Climate Change. (2012). Climate Change Act 2008. Retrieved January 26, 2012, from http://www.decc.gov.uk/en/content/cms/legislation/cc_act_08/cc_act_08.aspx

Dodghson, Robert A., & Butlin, Robin A. (1990). *An historical geography of England and Wales.* London: London Academic.

Duram, A. Leslie, & Cawley, Mary. (2012). Irish chefs and restaurants in the geography of "local" food value chains. *The Open Geography Journal,* 5, 16–25. Retrieved June 18, 2012, from http://benthamscience.com/open/togeogj/articles/V005/16TOGEOGJ.pdf

Edwards, Kevin J., & Smout, T. Christopher. (2000). Perspectives on human-environment interactions in prehistoric and historical times. In George Holmes & Roger Crofts (Eds.), *Scotland's environment: The future* (pp. 3–29). East Linton, UK: Tuckwell Press.

Evans, E. Estyn. (1992). *The personality of Ireland: Habitat, heritage and history*. Dublin, Ireland: Lilliput.

Foster, Sally, & Smout, T. Christopher. (Eds.). (1994). *The history of soils and field systems*. Aberdeen, UK: Scottish Cultural Press.

Foster, Chris, et al. (2006). Environmental impacts of food production and consumption. Report to the Department for Environment, Food and Rural Affairs (Defra). Manchester, UK: Manchester Business School.

Fraser Darling, Frank. (Ed.). (1955). *West highland survey: An essay in human ecology*. Oxford, UK: Oxford University Press.

Garnett, Tara. (2008). Cooking up a storm: Food, greenhouse gas emissions and our changing climate. Food Climate Research Network, University of Surrey. Retrieved June 18, 2012, from http://www.fcrn.org.uk/sites/default/files/CuaS_web.pdf

Grove, Richard H. (1995). *Green imperialism: Colonial expansion, tropical island Edens and the origins of environmentalism 1600–1860*. Cambridge, UK: Cambridge University Press.

Grove, Richard H. (1997). *The evolution of the colonial discourse on deforestation and climate change, 1500–1940*. Cambridge, UK: Cambridge University Press.

Hassan, John. (1998). *A history of water in modern England and Wales*. Manchester, UK & New York: Manchester University Press.

Howell, David W. (1978). *Land and people in nineteenth century Wales*. London & Boston: Routledge and Kegan Paul.

Huckle, John, & Martin, Adrian. (2001). *Environments in a changing world*. Harlow, UK: Pearson Education Ltd.

Johnson, James Henry. (1994). *The human geography of Ireland*. Chichester, UK & New York: Wiley.

Lamb, Hubert H. (1988). *Weather, climate and human affairs*. London & New York: Routledge.

Linnard, William. (1982). *Welsh woods and forests: History and utilization*. Cardiff: National Museum of Wales.

Mackenzie, John M. (1997). *Empires of nature and the nature of empires: Imperialism, Scotland and the environment*. East Linton, UK: Tuckwell Press.

Lynch, Declan, & Wright, Angela. (2012). Managing the future energy policy for Ireland: Examining the role of nuclear power. *American International Journal of Contemporary Research*, *2*(2), 40–50. Retrieved May 21, 2012, from http://www.aijcrnet.com/journals/Vol_2_No_2_February_2012/6.pdf

Mitchison, Rosalind, & Roebuck, Peter. (Eds.). (1988). *Economy and society in Scotland and Ireland 1500–1939*. Edinburgh, UK: John Donald.

O'Flanagan, Patrick; Ferguson, Paul; & Whelan, Kevin. (Eds.). (1987). *Rural Ireland 1600–1900: Modernization and change*. Cork, Ireland: Cork University Press.

Parry, Martin L. (1978). *Climatic change, agriculture and settlement*. Folkestone, UK: Dawson.

Perry, Richard. (1978). *Wildlife in Britain and Ireland*. London: Croom Helm.

Peterken, George F. (1996). *Natural woodland: Ecology and conservation in Northern temperate regions*. Cambridge, UK: Cambridge University Press.

Rackham, Oliver. (1976). *Trees and woodland in the British landscape*. London: Dent.

Rackham, Oliver. (1986). *The history of the countryside*. London: Dent.

Roberts, Neil. (1989). *The holocene: An environmental history*. Oxford, UK: Blackwell.

Rose, Chris. (1991). *The dirty man of Europe. The Great British pollution scandal*. London: Simon & Schuster.

Sheail, John. (2002). *An environmental history of twentieth-century Britain*. Basingstoke, UK: Palgrave.

Simmons, Ian. (2001). *An environmental history of Britain*. Edinburgh, UK: Edinburgh University Press.

Smout, T. Christopher. (1993). *Scotland since prehistory*. Aberdeen, UK: Scottish Cultural Press.

Smout, T. Christopher. (2000). *Nature contested: Environmental history in Scotland and Northern England since 1600*. Edinburgh, UK: Edinburgh University Press.

Smout, T. Christopher. (Ed.). (2002). *People and woods in Scotland. A history*. Edinburgh, UK: Edinburgh University Press.

Stephenson, Tom. (1989). *Forbidden land: The struggle for access to mountain and moorland*. Manchester, UK: Manchester University Press.

Thirsk, Joan. (Ed.). (1967–2000). *The agrarian history of England and Wales* (vols. 1–8). Cambridge, UK: Cambridge University Press.

Thirsk, Joan. (1997). *Alternative agriculture: A history from the black death to the present day*. Oxford, UK: Oxford University Press.

Thomas, Keith. (1983). *Man and the natural world: Changing attitudes in England 1500–1800*. London: Allen Lane.

Trinder, Barrie. (1987). *The making of the industrial landscape*. London: Phoenix.

United States Central Intelligence Agency (US CIA). (2012a). The world factbook: United Kingdom. Retrieved August 9, 2012, from https://www.cia.gov/library/publications/the-world-factbook/geos/uk.html

United States Central Intelligence Agency (US CIA). (2012b). The world factbook: Ireland. Retrieved August 9, 2012, from https://www.cia.gov/library/publications/the-world-factbook/geos/ei.html

Wheeler, Dennis, & Mayers, Julian. (Eds.). (1997). *Regional climates of the British Isles*. London & New York: Routledge.

Whyte, Ian, & Whyte, Kathleen. (1991). *The changing Scottish landscape, 1500–1800*. London & New York: Routledge.

Woodell, Stanley Reginald John. (Ed.). (1985). *The English landscape: Past, present and future*. Oxford, UK: Oxford University Press.

Wright, Oliver. (2012, May 16). Power politics: French threat to UK energy. *The Independent*. Retrieved May 21, 2012, from http://www.independent.co.uk/environment/green-living/power-politics-french-threat-to-uk-energy-7754470.html

Wrigley, Edward Anthony. (1988). *Continuity, chance and change: The character of the industrial revolution in England*. Cambridge, UK: Cambridge University Press.

Urbanization (Africa)

Urban growth in Africa, especially tropical Africa, is the world's fastest, with excess of births over deaths and net in-migration. Cities with 1 million inhabitants in 1960 had more than 4 million by 2010. Africa is still becoming more urbanized, although less rapidly than in the period from 1960 to 1990. Some cities have long histories but more date from the 1880s–1960s (the colonial era) and have changed greatly since independence. Because urban growth takes place in conditions of extreme material poverty for the majority of people, it presents both governments and families with great sustainability challenges.

Africa is the least urbanized continent, but it is also where urban growth is taking place most rapidly. United Nations sources indicate urban population growth in Africa of 3.4 percent per year from 2000 to 2010, compared with 2.2 percent for the whole world and 2.4 percent for India. In sub-Saharan Africa, annual growth was almost 4.0 percent. Lagos, Nigeria, may have grown from the world's twenty-eighth largest city with around 7 million inhabitants in 2000 to eighteenth largest with more than 10 million in 2010, and it is forecast to rise to twelfth largest with a population of 14 million by 2020. (See table 1 on page 336 and figure 1 on page 337.) Kinshasa in the Democratic Republic of the Congo (DRC) follows close behind, and growth rates are similar in cities such as Abidjan in Côte d'Ivoire (Ivory Coast), Addis Ababa in Ethiopia, Nairobi in Kenya, and Dar es Salaam in Tanzania (UN 2011). In South Africa, already more urbanized by the mid-twentieth century, urban growth has been, and is likely to remain, slower.

Urban growth is not the same as urbanization, but African urban population growth has been faster than national growth, so urbanization has been taking place in terms of an increasing proportion living in cities. In sub-Saharan Africa the rise was from 10 to 15 percent in 1960 to 30 to 40 percent in 2010. Both urban growth and urbanization have slowed since their 1960s and 1970s peak as both natural increase and net in-migration have slackened. The British geographer Deborah Potts (2012a and 2012b) has shown that in many countries urbanization has slowed far more than is generally acknowledged.

Precise population numbers are not given here because they would certainly be wrong: reliable census figures are lacking in every country, and administrative boundary changes can distort reality. Lack of data is, in fact, a greater problem for urban management across most of Africa than elsewhere in the world, especially serious in rapidly changing situations. Although Nigerian government sources indicate 10 to 11 million inhabitants in Lagos, the Lagos state government insists on more than 15 million city dwellers. Furthermore, although most international statistics tell us that the urban share of Africa's population rose from 20 percent in 1960 to more than 40 percent in 2010, the population in 2010 might be better described as 30 percent urban, 50 percent rural, and 20 percent either urban fringe/peri-urban or constantly moving between urban and rural areas. A simple rural-urban dichotomy is more misleading in Africa than in most of the Middle East or South Asia, where rural-urban physical and social distinctions are often sharper.

Recent decades have potentially brought change to the data situation as a result of satellite photography. Much of this material is as reliable, and even "accurate," as elsewhere in the world, even if not as detailed, but researchers have undertaken little analysis of it yet. Even a casual inspection of sequences of images shows rapid physical

TABLE 1. Africa's Largest Cities

City	Population in Millions			Annual % Growth 2000–2010
	Estimate 2000	Estimate 2010	Projection 2025	
Cairo, Egypt	10.2	11.0	13.5	0.8
Lagos, Nigeria	7.2	10.6	15.8	3.8
Kinshasa, DRC	5.6	8.8	15.0	4.5
Khartoum, Sudan	4.0	5.0	8.0	2.8
Luanda, Angola*	2.6	4.8	8.1	6.1
Alexandria, Egypt	3.6	4.4	5.6	2.0
Abidjan, Côte d'Ivoire	3.0	4.1	6.3	3.1
Johannesburg, South Africa	2.8	3.6	4.1	2.9
Nairobi, Kenya	2.2	3.5	6.2	4.6
Dar es Salaam, Tanzania	2.1	3.4	6.2	4.6
Kano, Nigeria	2.7	3.4	5.1	2.5
Addis Ababa, Ethiopia*	2.4	3.0	4.8	2.2

Source: UN World urbanization prospects, the 2009 revision & UN 2011.

**Note:* The low 2000–2010 growth rate figure for Addis Ababa is puzzling, and the high figure for Luanda perhaps exaggerated. The former may allow for boundary change, the latter not.

expansion of cities, which undoubtedly reflects growth of population and activity. But how closely it reflects growth in each part of Africa has yet to be explored.

Urban Origins and Growth

Among Africa's giant cities, Cairo and Alexandria in Egypt have the longest history but are growing more slowly than most. Because both the history and the current circumstances of North African cities, from cities in Egypt to cities in Morocco, have much more in common with Middle Eastern cities than with those south of the Sahara, they are considered in another article.

Some cities in sub-Saharan Africa, such as Kano and Katsina in northern Nigeria, have existed for many centuries (Mabogunje 1968) while others, such as Ibadan in southern Nigeria and Addis Ababa in Ethiopia, although more recent, are also wholly indigenous in origin. The majority of African cities, and even of provincial towns, however, are of colonial origin, even if they incorporate indigenous smaller settlements (O'Connor 1983). Very few are postcolonial creations, with the major exception of the new Nigerian national capital, Abuja. Census data from about twenty countries indicate that recent rapid urban growth has changed the geographical pattern of towns and cities very little. Academics and the media sometimes

suggest increasing primacy of national capital cities, but there is little firm evidence of this. Small towns have often grown equally fast.

Natural increase has contributed around 50 percent of recent African urban population growth, net in-migration around 30 percent, and transformation of rural settlements into either small towns or peri-urban zones around 20 percent. Fertility rates are lower in cities than in most rural areas, but this is offset by age profiles marked by a preponderance of young adult and school-leaver teenager in-migrants. Many of the older in-migrants remain strongly attached to rural home areas, hoping to retire there (or at least to be buried there), and this outflow reduces urban death rates. Rapid growth through natural increase in future decades is almost guaranteed by a median age between seventeen and nineteen in most cities.

At one time urban male-to-female sex ratios showed a huge male majority in southern Africa, although not in western Africa, and a change to a more even balance has been a notable feature of recent decades. Although this represents a significant improvement in African urban society, it involves an economic cost in countries where women play the larger role in agriculture, contributing to falling per capita food production in many countries. Townspeople more often find some land on which to grow maize or cassava than in Middle Eastern or Asian cities, and micro-agriculture is an important element in

Figure 1. Sub-Saharan Cities with More than Half a Million Residents

Source: Map courtesy of Miles Irving, University College London Department of Geography.

Few institutional and academic discussions of world cities or global city networks acknowledge the existence of any cities in tropical Africa. In 2010, however, there were 52 cities in sub-Saharan Africa with between half a million and 3 million people, and 10 cities with more than 3 million residents: Abidjan, Côte d'Ivoire (Ivory Coast); Kano and Lagos, Nigeria; Kinshasa, DRC; Luanda, Angola; Khartoum, Sudan; Addis Ababa, Ethiopia; Nairobi, Kenya; Dar es Salaam, Tanzania; and Johannesburg, South Africa.

urban economies (Obudho and Foeken 1999), but this is becoming more difficult as urban population densities increase.

The broad pattern of urban growth is similar across most of tropical Africa, but migration to towns and cities has been accelerated in some countries, including Sudan, the DRC, and Angola, by intense conflict turning rural areas into war zones. Although Tanzania has been more peaceful, rural-to-urban migration has remained at a high level for decades, partly as a result of "villagization," a government plan to move people from scattered

settlements and small villages into nucleated villages (roughly circular villages arranged around a central place). Many people decided instead to move on to cities. Urbanization has long been much slower in South Africa, while Deborah Potts (2010 and 2012a and b) has demonstrated recent slowing, and even reversal, in Zimbabwe, Zambia, and beyond.

In terms of urban spatial structure, Africa presents extreme contrasts. It has some of the world's most divided cities, with huge disparities of income and well-being between neighborhoods, notably in South Africa, but extending north to Harare in Zimbabwe and, to some extent, Nairobi in Kenya. It also has some of the world's most homogenous cities, such as Addis Ababa in Ethiopia or Ibadan in Nigeria. Even in Ibadan spatial structures are important, but they are scarcely visible because they are based on clan and lineage rather than class or income.

Urban Economy and Social Welfare

Recent urbanization in Africa has increased the income and material well-being of most migrants, despite limited national economic development, but the influx of poorer people from rural areas has lowered the *average* urban income levels and greatly intensified urban material poverty (O'Connor 1991; Gebre-Egziabher 2011). Because migrants often join kin in town, this pressure also applies widely at the household level. Journalistic figures of 50 percent or even 70 percent "unemployment" levels are meaningless, especially where there is no system of social security benefits. Most employment is microscale and undocumented (Bryceson and Potts 2006), and there is massive underemployment, with many households in most African cities surviving on incomes of under US$2 a day. Large-scale manufacturing and trade do exist in African cities, but at most they employ well under 10 percent of the working population.

Wealth is substantial and highly visible in Johannesburg and Cape Town, both in South Africa, but is restricted to a few and is much less visible in Lagos, Nigeria, and Khartoum, Sudan. The United Nations has published "Gini Coefficient" figures, which measure income disparities on a scale of 0 to 1, for various cities. While the 0.75 for Johannesburg is among the world's highest, those for Kinshasa in the DRC (0.39), Dakar in Senegal (0.37), and Dar es Salaam in Tanzania (0.34) are among the world's lowest, indicating widely shared poverty rather than gross inequality (UN 2011, 260).

The impact of urbanization on social welfare is often complex. For instance, there is usually better access to health care than in rural areas; but there are also greater health risks, especially due to inadequate sanitation facilities—a far more serious issue at high population densities (Kebbede 2004). In addition, while the scourge of HIV/AIDS is present in many African rural areas, incidence is higher in the cities. In this case, the problem is more extreme in South Africa than in most cities of tropical Africa. Recent years have brought some steps toward drug treatment for HIV/AIDS, however, even beyond South Africa. UNICEF data show that very high child mortality rates are at least dropping gradually in most countries. Access to education is one motive for African teenage rural-to-urban migration, because children have much greater access to secondary education in most cities than in most rural areas. Enrollment rates are rising rapidly; but schools are often poorly equipped and grossly overcrowded.

Problems of Growth

Cities such as Nairobi have quadrupled in population with little physical expansion, giving rise to some areas of intense residential overcrowding. Although large areas of African urban housing are often described as "shantytowns," building materials may be better than in most rural areas; the majority of residents are renting, however, often just one room for the household, while large numbers of people may be lodging with kinfolk for many months. Insofar as these are also "squatter settlements" (i.e., the owners have no legal rights), provision of services, such as water supply and refuse disposal, is especially problematic (Kebbede 2004). In many cities the majority of dwellings, legal or illegal, do not have piped water— it has to be fetched from standpipes or bought from vendors (Larsson et al 2009).

Lack of adequate toilets is an Africa-wide problem greatly magnified by the urbanization process and consequent high-density living (Black and Fawcett 2008). The garbage disposal challenge has been examined in depth for Africa by the US geographer Garth Myers (2005) and in a set of case studies brought together by the Nigerian geographer Adepoju Onibokun (2000). Waste disposal problems are not just a by-product of growth, but also of the widespread shift from biodegradable packaging, such as banana leaves, through extensive use and reuse of metal cans, to the current proliferation of plastic.

The state can do little to provide shelter for most of the poor in African cities, such as Addis Ababa in Ethiopia, Bamako in Mali, or Dar es Salaam in Tanzania. Governments are unwilling to build housing at standards so low that most people could afford it, and there can be no question of subsidized housing when there is no possibility of this for rural dwellers. (The situation in more prosperous South Africa is, of course, different.) In most cities, the state's role lies more in planning than in housing, in designating areas for people to house themselves, and in providing some services. But planning for ongoing poverty is extremely difficult: the planning profession has little experience of this.

Transport provides similar dilemmas. Whereas Cairo has a new underground/metro system, there is no prospect of financing this in the cities of tropical Africa. There is also very little municipal intracity transport of the type operated effectively in Tunis, so for most people movement involves either walking, often long distances, or minibuses that are hugely overcrowded, as they must be if they are to operate cheaply enough to be afforded. Light motorcycles are increasingly used in some cities, often as taxis; but the World Bank database confirms that only in South African cities do more than 5 percent of households have private cars (Gwilliam 2011).

The rapid spread of mobile phones, faster than anywhere in the world and replacing no phone rather than fixed lines, provides some relief to ever-increasing transport problems. For traders in particular this cuts out the need for some physical movements. An equally rapid spread of the Internet may prove the greatest change in African urban life in the second decade of this century, affecting almost everyone indirectly, whether for local interaction or for contact with the wider world.

Since the 1990s, increasing emphasis has been placed on issues of "governance," both within Africa and by external agencies such as the World Bank. This is as relevant to sustainability as it is to economic and social development. Although academic fashion has stressed "urban bias" in African development, at least an equal case can be made for acknowledging "urban neglect." Organizations from the World Bank and charity aid agencies to African political elites with both family roots and rural political support have often devoted far more than half their attention to rural areas. Specifically urban administration and management has been notoriously weak. Governance is as important at the municipal level as it is at the national level, and has been problematic both in cities such as Nairobi and in thousands of small towns. Independence in the 1960s brought great change in the nature of national governments across Africa, but not much change at city level.

Apart from anachronistic and dysfunctional administrative structures, corruption provides the only possible explanation of much municipal decision making. Although corruption is, sadly, part of the image of Africa for many foreigners (and Africans also) (Mbaku 2007), its intensity varies greatly from one city to another. Transparency International perception data, endorsed by the United Nations and the World Bank, show it to be a far greater issue in the DRC and Sierra Leone (and hence in Kinshasa and Freetown) than in Tanzania and Ethiopia (and hence in Dar es Salaam and Addis Ababa).

African Cities in Broader Context

One important element in recent "African urbanization" is that some of it has been taking place outside the continent (Simone 2004; Konadu-Agyemang, Takyi, and Arthur 2006). For instance, there has been substantial migration to North America, Europe, and the Middle East, most of it city focused. Among immigrant groups in Britain, Africans are the most highly concentrated in London. Mostly unskilled workers are involved in the North African exodus, but migration from Ghana, Nigeria, or Cameroon includes the much-documented "brain drain" of doctors and teachers. This constitutes a serious loss to Africa, but it is partly offset by remittances migrants make to support their kinfolk, whether in towns or in rural areas, while some are investing in houses or businesses in African cities (Smith 2007).

Despite the importance of such a diaspora taking people away from tropical African cities, a distinctive feature of these cities is their limited contact with cities elsewhere in the world. Inflows of foreigners to Lagos, Kinshasa, and most other cities (except those in South Africa) are small. There is also little interaction among these tropical African cities, whatever measure is used. These cities are almost invisible in most global mapping of telephone traffic and electronic communications. Some institutional and academic discussions of world cities or global city networks exclude even Cairo and Johannesburg (Taylor et al 2001); few acknowledge the existence of any cities in tropical Africa. At a more cultural level, a volume called *Cities: The World's Top 100 Meaningful Cities* (Murray 2010) includes Cairo, Alexandria, Cape Town, and Johannesburg, but nowhere in between. It might be argued that one of the main problems of most African cities is their image in the eyes of the rest of the world.

China has become a partial exception to this ignoring of African cities, so that contacts between Beijing or Shanghai and cities from Khartoum in Sudan to Lusaka in Zambia are beginning to appear on maps of world city linkages. A distinctive feature of Chinese operations in Africa, however, is that they are often self-contained, involving limited interaction with local communities. Overall, cities such as Lagos, Kinshasa, and Kampala (in

Uganda) remain very "African" rather than cosmopolitan, and most provincial towns even more so.

The cities are more cosmopolitan than most rural areas, of course, and most links between these areas and the rest of the world are channeled through the cities. Whereas this was highly relevant to management and sustainability issues when the flows involved mainly bulky exports of coffee or cocoa, and imports of manufactures, the relative importance of such flows has decreased. Flows of migrant remittances or of electronic messages between other continents and rural Africa do involve the cities, but they do not have much direct physical impact on them.

Urban Sustainability in the Future

Climate change may have greater impacts on Africa than on any other continent in the decades ahead. This is despite the fact that its cities, with the world's lowest per capita consumption of electricity and other energy sources, produce the world's lowest emissions of carbon (UN 2011). Many sustainability issues are likely to intensify, but accurate forecasting of either the direct impacts on African cities or the indirect impacts through increased migration from rural areas is unviable. From an urban perspective, the most dramatic consequence may take the form of sea-level rise. Africa is an elevated continent, and less than 1 percent of its area is directly at risk; but that area includes 7 percent of its population and 12 percent of its urban population (McGranahan, Balk, and Anderson 2007). Some coastal cities, such as Dakar in Senegal and Accra in Ghana, are sufficiently elevated to be largely immune, but others, such as Lagos in Nigeria, Cotonou in Benin, or Mombasa in Kenya, are at risk of widespread devastation unless they undertake very costly protection works or relocate the population on a massive scale (Dossou 2007; Awuor, Orindi, and Adwera 2008).

In terms of physical well-being and material poverty, the picture of African cities is bleak, with no clear evidence of improvement in recent decades on many criteria. Not only is urban poverty almost as severe as poverty in most rural areas, with many people regularly going to bed hungry (if they have a bed); but also many people *feel* poorer in the city because the affluence of a few is visible nearby. Most African countries have experienced more economic growth since 2000 than in the 1980s and 1990s, bringing real benefits to an expanding urban middle class; but this improvement has had little impact on the majority. All dimensions of future sustainability are highly problematic when the present is a condition of extreme physical hardship, especially in such matters as water supply and sanitation (Satterthwaite 1999).

None of this gloom, however, should be interpreted as indicating cultural or spiritual poverty. Churches, mosques, football grounds, and music venues are essential parts of the African urban scene. So are the extended family networks that provide a means of survival in the absence of state social security and, in many places, a strong sense of neighborhood solidarity and cohesion (Tostensen, Tvedten, and Vaa 2001; Konings and Foeken 2006). Perhaps someone, sometime, will attempt to assess both how African cities compare with cities elsewhere in the world, and how they are changing, in terms of happiness.

Anthony M. O'CONNOR
University College London

Author's note: There is substantial, separate literature on cities in South Africa.

See also Africa (*several articles*); Cairo, Egypt; Cape Town, South Africa; Climate Change Refugees (Africa); Goma, Democratic Republic of the Congo; Immigrants and Refugees; Lagos, Nigeria; Microfinance; Migration (Africa); Nairobi, Kenya; Rural Development; Urbanization (Europe); Urbanization (Western Asia and Northern Africa); Water Use and Rights (Africa); World Bank

FURTHER READING

Awuor, Cynthia; Orindi, Victor Ayo; & Adwera, Andrew Ochieng. (2008). Climate change and coastal cities: The case of Mombasa, Kenya. *Environment and Urbanization, 20*(1), 231–242.

Black, Maggie, & Fawcett, Ben. (2008). *The last taboo: Opening the door on the global sanitation crisis.* London: Earthscan.

Bryceson, Deborah, & Potts, Deborah. (Eds.). (2006). *African urban economies: Viability, vitality or vitiation?* Basingstoke, UK: Palgrave Macmillan.

Dossou, Krystel. (2007). The vulnerability to climate change of Cotonou (Benin): The rise in sea level. *Environment and Urbanization, 19*(1), 65–79.

Douglas, Ian, et al. (2008). Unjust waters: Climate change, flooding and the urban poor in Africa. *Environment and Urbanization, 20*(1), 187–205.

Frayne, Bruce; Moser, Caroline; & Ziervogel, Gina. (Eds.). *Climate change, assets and food security in southern African cities.* Abingdon, UK, & New York: Earthscan.

Gebre-Egziabher, Tegegne. (2011). *Livelihood and urban poverty reduction in Ethiopia.* Addis Ababa, Ethiopia: OSSREA.

Godard, Xavier. (Ed.). (2002). *Les transports et la ville en Afrique au sud du Sahara* [Transport and the city in Africa south of the Sahara]. Paris: Karthala.

Grant, Richard. (2009). *Globalizing city: Urban economic transformation of Accra, Ghana.* Syracuse, NY: Syracuse University Press.

Gwilliam, Kenneth. (2011). *Africa's transport infrastructure.* Washington, DC: World Bank.

Kebbede, Girma. (2004). *Living with urban environmental health risks: The case of Ethiopia.* Aldershot, UK, & Burlington, VT: Ashgate.

Konadu-Agyemang, Kwadwo; Takyi, Baffour K.; & Arthur, John. (Eds.). (2006). *The new African diaspora in North America.* Lanham, MD: Lexington.

Konings, Piet, & Foeken, Dick. (Eds.). (2006). *Crisis and creativity: Exploring the wealth of the African neighbourhood.* Leiden, The Netherlands, & Boston: Brill.

Larsson, Petter; Kirumira, Edward K.; Steigen, Andreas L.; & Miyingo-Kezimbira, Anne. (Eds.). (2009). *Sharing water: Problems, conflicts and possible solutions; The case of Kampala.* Oslo, Norway: Universitetsforlaget.

Lelo Nzuzi, Francis. (2008). *Kinshasa: Ville et environnement* [Kinshasa: City and environment]. Paris: Harmattan.

Locatelli, Francesca, & Nugent, Paul. (Eds.). (2009). *African cities: Competing claims on urban spaces.* Leiden, The Netherlands, & Boston: Brill.

Mabogunje, Akin L. (1968). *Urbanization in Nigeria.* London: University of London Press.

Mbaku, John. (2007). *Corruption in Africa.* Lanham, MD: Lexington.

McGranahan, Gordon; Balk, Deborah; & Anderson, Bridget. (2007). The rising tide: Assessing the risks of climate change and human settlements in low elevation coastal zones. *Environment and Urbanization, 19*(1), 17–38.

Murray, Kim. (2010). *Cities: The world's top 100 meaningful cities.* Quebec, Canada: Patrick Bonneville Society.

Murray, Martin J., & Myers, Garth A. (Eds.). (2006). *Cities in contemporary Africa.* New York & Basingstoke, UK: Palgrave Macmillan.

Myers, Garth A. (2005). *Disposable cities: Garbage, governance and sustainable development in urban Africa.* Aldershot, UK: Ashgate.

Myers, Garth A. (2011). *African cities: Alternative visions.* London: Zed Press.

Ngware, Suleiman, & Kironde, J. M. Lusagga. (Eds.). (1996). *Urbanising Tanzania: Issues, initiatives and priorities.* Dar es Salaam, Tanzania: Dar es Salaam University Press.

Obudho, Robert A., & Foeken, Dick. (1999). *Urban agriculture in Africa: A bibliographical survey.* Leiden, The Netherlands: African Studies Centre.

O'Connor, Anthony M. (1981). *Urbanization in tropical Africa: An annotated bibliography.* Boston: G. K. Hall.

O'Connor, Anthony M. (1983). *The African city.* London: Hutchinson, & New York: Holmes & Meier.

O'Connor, Anthony M. (1991). *Poverty in Africa.* London: Belhaven.

Onibokun, Adepoju. (Ed.). (2000). *Managing the monster: Urban waste and governance in Africa.* Ottawa, Canada: IDRC.

Potts, Deborah. (2010). *Circular migration in Zimbabwe and contemporary sub-Saharan Africa.* Woodbridge, UK: James Currey, & Rochester, NY: Boydell & Brewer.

Potts, Deborah. (2012a). Challenging the myths of urban dynamics in sub-Saharan Africa: The evidence from Nigeria. *World Development, 40,* 1382–1393.

Potts, Deborah. (2012b). *Whatever happened to Africa's rapid urbanisation?* London: Africa Research Institute.

Rakodi, Carole. (Ed.). (1997). *The urban challenge in Africa.* Tokyo: United Nations University Press.

Satterthwaite, David. (Ed.). (1999). *The Earthscan reader in sustainable cities.* London: Earthscan.

Simon, David. (1992). Cities, capital and development: African cities in the world economy. London: Belhaven.

Simone, AbdouMaliq. (2004). *For the city yet to come: Changing African life in four cities.* Durham, NC, and London: Duke University Press.

Simone, AbdouMaliq, & Abouhani, Abdelghani. (Eds.). (2005). *Urban Africa: Changing contours of survival in the city.* Dakar, Senegal: CODESRIA, and London: Zed Press.

Smith, Lothar. (2007). *Tied to migrants: Transnational influences on the economy of Accra, Ghana.* Leiden, The Netherlands: African Studies Centre.

Stren, Richard, & White, Rodney. (Eds.). (1989). *African cities in crisis: Managing rapid urban growth.* Boulder, CO: Westview.

Taylor, Peter J.; Hoyler, Michael; Walker, David R. F.; & Szegner, Mark J. (2001). A new mapping of the world for the new millennium. *Geographical Journal, 167*(3), 213–222.

Tostensen, Arne; Tvedten, Inge; & Vaa, Mariken. (Eds.). (2001). *Associational life in African cities: Popular responses to the urban crisis.* Uppsala, Sweden: Nordiska Afrikainstitutet.

United Nations (UN). (2011). *The state of African cities 2010.* Nairobi, Kenya: UN Habitat.

United Nations Department of Economic and Social Affairs (UN DESA), Population Division. (2010, March). World urbanization prospects: The 2009 revision. Retrieved June 21, 2012, from http://www.ctc-health.org.cn/file/2011061610.pdf

Berkshire's authors and editors welcome questions, comments, and corrections. Send your emails about the *Berkshire Encyclopedia of Sustainability* in general or this volume in particular to: sustainability.updates@berkshirepublishing.com

Urbanization (Europe)

Assessing key factors such as urban emissions and land-use patterns and their effect on local and global scales is required to effectively measure urban sustainability. The environmental quality of urban areas (and management of their open green spaces and waste) is crucial to the health and well-being of their populations. Eastern and southern Europe will face some of the most significant challenges (e.g., the region's fastest urban-growth rates) in the coming decades.

With 73 percent of its population living in cities, Europe ranks as the third most urbanized region in the world following only North America and the Latin America–Caribbean region (see table 1 on page 343). Although it is home to some of the world's most vibrant, resilient, and sustainable cities, the continent is characterized by significantly different levels of urbanization (defined as the percentage of a country's total population living in urban areas) and a wide variation in related indicators that measure sustainability throughout its forty-eight countries and territories. This article outlines the state of contemporary urbanization and environmental sustainability across the northern, southern, western, and eastern sub-regions of Europe (including Russia), with a particular focus on the continent's varying historic and future trajectories of urban growth and decline, as well as on local and global environmental concerns.

Overall, while Europe is widely understood to be a highly urbanized region, it is critical to note that historic and contemporary estimates and measures of urbanization vary significantly depending on the definition of *urban* that is employed. Notably, the majority of statistical comparisons relating to urbanization rates and levels, even within Europe, suffer from inconsistencies not only in the accuracy of data collection but also in each country's definition of *urban* and the conflation of statistics relating to a city's population versus that of its larger metropolitan area. For example, as the United Nations Statistics Division's annual *Demographic Yearbook* explains, the national census in the United Kingdom defines *urban* as a "settlement with a population of 10,000 or above," while in France it is defined as "an agglomeration of more than 2,000 inhabitants living in contiguous houses or with not more than 200 meters between houses, also communes of which the major portion of the population is part of a multi-communal agglomeration of this nature." In Iceland, an urban area is simply one defined as housing more than 200 inhabitants (UN Statistics Division 2011, 107–108). In addition, while the city of Paris, France, is estimated to have a population of just over 2 million, when the surrounding metropolitan area is taken into account that number increases to almost 11.8 million, highlighting the significant variation between city and metro-area indicators.

Historic Trends

Though the tradition of European urban development began with the cities of the ancient Greek and Roman empires, rapid urbanization did not begin in Europe until the Industrial Revolution in the late eighteenth and the nineteenth centuries. As industrialization spread from its epicenter in Great Britain, it stimulated a massive influx of rural-to-urban migration to cities where factories were located near population centers and markets; nations became more prosperous and cities flourished; incomes increased; transportation costs dramatically decreased; and new technologies led to a rapid growth in agricultural yields. Due to the dominance of its manufacturing sector,

TABLE I. Level of Urbanization per Region and "Tipping Points*" (Urban vs. Rural Population)

Region	Tipping Points* before 2010 (year)	2010 Urban (%)	Tipping Points* after 2010 (year)	2050 Urban (%)
World		*50.6*		*70*
Europe	*Before 1950*	*72.6*		*83.8*
Eastern Europe	*1963*	*68.8*		*80*
Northern Europe	*Before 1950*	*77*		*86.5*
Southern Europe	*1960*	*67.5*		*81.2*
Western Europe	*Before 1950*	*77*		*86.5*
Africa		40	2030	61.8
Asia		42.5	2023	66.2
Latin America and the Caribbean	1962	79.4		88.7
North America	Before 1950	82.1		90.2
Oceania	Before 1950	70.6		76.4

Source: UN-Habitat (2010).

*Note: "tipping point" refers to the point in time when the population of a given region or country became, or will become, more than 50 percent urban.

the majority of the continent's early urban growth took place in England, whose total population growth of just over 100 percent between 1600 and 1800 paled in comparison to its urban population increase of 600 percent (Wrigley 1990, 107).

Despite the primacy of urban Britain in the early decades of the Industrial Revolution, centers of employment and habitation grew throughout Europe at a rate much higher than the global average. In other early industrializing countries, such as Germany, the annexation of neighboring towns and villages, through the expansion of established economic centers, led to the growth of large cities (more than 100,000 inhabitants), thus creating considerable regional conurbations (defined as a continuous network of urban communities) (Kollmann 1969, 62). As a result, by 1910 Europe housed nearly 50 percent of the world's total urban population and over half of the world's one hundred largest cities (Satterthwaite 2007, 1–5).

While the concentration of industrial and residential uses that characterized nineteenth- and twentieth-century urbanization in Europe drove economic and social development, it also led to serious problems of pollution, crime, overcrowding, and disease in Europe's industrial capitals. These problems, accompanied by a global shift in manufacturing away from Europe, and a period of counter-urbanization (itself precipitated by the increase in automobile ownership, improved communications infrastructures, and lifestyle preferences

which favored suburban sprawl) drastically slowed the region's urbanization rates in the twentieth century. Subsequently, between 1950 and 2000, none of the world's one hundred fastest-growing large cities were located in Europe; instead, the continent has been home to a majority of the world's slowest-growing and/or shrinking cities (Satterthwaite 2007, 5). With an annual urban population growth rate of only 0.4 percent between 2005 and 2010, Europe's urban population growth rate was the slowest in the world (UN DESA, Office of the Population Division 2011; see table 3 on page 346).

Present-Day Urbanization and the Environment

In the twenty-first century, demographers anticipate that the world's less developed regions will urbanize rapidly while Europe will urbanize slowly, so that by 2050 its urban population will rise only 11 percent to 84 percent. (See table 1 above.) Moreover, significant regional variation is expected to persist, with the fastest rates of urbanization anticipated in eastern and southern Europe, which have traditionally lagged behind the rest of the region in levels of urban population due to the comparatively late adoption of industrial technologies, especially in the agricultural sector.

Though domestic rural–urban migration will constitute the majority of urban population increases in the forty-eight European countries, especially in eastern and southern Europe, international migration will also partially contribute. These drivers of urbanization vary significantly from city to city, depending mainly on the economic performance of individual urban centers (especially given the significant freedom of movement aided by the evolution of the European Union's visa policies among the twenty-six countries known as the Shengen Zone) and various national immigration policies (European Commission 2010). In addition, while overall levels of urbanization remain lower in eastern and southern Europe, the two regions are, in fact, characterized by relatively high average urban densities, and are home to some of Europe's most populous urban areas, with Russia alone accounting for two of Europe's three largest cities. (See table 2 below.) The two regions are also home to the largest overall urban population. (See table 3 on page 346.)

In addition to their varying rates and levels of urbanization, Europe's cities have significantly different levels of performance in environmental sustainability as measured by indicators of energy consumption and efficiency, carbon emissions, natural resource management, and density.

Defining Urban Sustainability

Considerable disagreement remains about how to measure the impact of urbanization on the environment. Despite comprising only 2 percent of the world's land area, European cities and others across the globe produce the majority of the world's carbon emissions, probably 70–80 percent of the total. Cities, however, also house more than 50 percent of the global population and in fact tend to have lower per capita carbon footprints than their countries' national averages (UN-Habitat 2011). Many attribute this discrepancy to the fact that cities are regional—and increasingly global—centers of industrial, economic, and service-sector activities that serve populations well beyond their city limits.

As a function of their ecological footprints (the amount of Earth's resources that a defined geographic area consumes), Europe's cities also outperform national averages. In London, for example, each individual inhabitant requires natural resources equivalent to those produced by 2.8 hectares of land, while the average European requires 3 hectares, and the average North American somewhere between 4 and 5 hectares for the same requirements (Dodman 2009, 185). In addition, high-density urban settlements provide efficiencies of scale that allow urban dwellers to benefit from shared infrastructures (water and sanitation, public transportation, and energy) in ways that rural residents cannot.

Ultimately, measuring urban sustainability requires assessing key factors at multiple scales, ranging from weighing the impact that urban emissions and land-use patterns have on global-level climate change to examining the impact at a local scale, where urban environmental quality (measured by such indicators as air and water pollution, the availability of open green space, and waste management practices) plays a major role in the health and well-being of urban populations.

Europe's urban development in the pre- and early industrial eras centered on compact, multiuse settlements equipped with pedestrian and horse-drawn transportation

TABLE 2. Europe's Largest Cities

European Rank	World Rank	City	Country	City Population	Metro Population
1	10	Moscow	Russia	10,524,000	14,800,000
2	23	London	United Kingdom	7,557,000	12,200,000
3	43	St. Petersburg	Russia	4,661,000	4,900,000
4	68	Berlin	Germany	3,432,000	3,943,000
5	73	Madrid	Spain	3,213,000	5,300,000
6	90	Rome	Italy	2,732,000	3,555,000
7	133	Paris	France	2,113,000	11,769,000
8	140	Bucharest	Romania	1,994,000	2,151,000
9	155	Minsk	Belarus	1,831,000	N/A
10	166	Hamburg	Germany	1,775,000	3,260,000

Source: City Mayors (2011).

networks that served its cities well, strengthening modern-day aspects, such as density and walkability, which contribute to lower overall energy consumption. While it should be noted that since 1950 nearly all of Europe has experienced decreasing densities and increasing urban sprawl, average urban densities remain twice as high as those in comparably urbanized and developed regions such as North America and Australia (Angel et al. 2011).

Variations in Urban Sustainability

Europe has done far more than rely on its urban heritage to attain high levels of urban sustainability. Over the past decades, many countries have instituted national and regional policies, bolstered by effective regional cooperation and planning, to advance urban environmental sustainability. Perhaps the most significant move has been to slow the spread of the automobile through the implementation of high gas taxes and strong investment in pedestrian and public transit networks (Glaeser 2011, 178). In addition, high-level regional agreements, such as the 1994 Aalborg Charter of European Cities and Towns Towards Sustainability and the subsequent European Sustainable Cities and Towns Campaign (launched the same year), have helped build consensus around critical issues of urban sustainability and to establish agendas and support networks that allow participating local authorities to engage in long-term urban and regional sustainability planning. These policies and plans, however, have been carried out (as of 2012) to different degrees and with markedly different success rates in many cities throughout Europe. (See the sidebar on page 347.)

In order to measure the variation in urban sustainability from city to city, the Green City Index, compiled by Siemens and the Economist Intelligence Unit (2009), provides a useful indicator set for making broad comparisons of urban environmental performances in Europe. The index's methodology prioritizes performance in the theme areas of carbon dioxide emissions, energy, buildings, transport, water, waste and land use, air quality, and environmental governance; it then provides city rankings based on category-specific and overall performance. Broadly speaking, the report, and others like it, point to clear regional disparities in urban sustainability, with northern and western European cities, the Nordic cities in particular, tending to be top performers, while eastern European cities are characterized by significant challenges. The study also makes apparent the close link between wealth (as measured by gross domestic product [GDP]) and sustainability, as the top performers were consistently economic powerhouses as well.

The dominance in the Green City Index of cities in wealthy nations in fact demonstrates a promising trend for global urban development. While increasing GDP has traditionally been linked not only to high levels of urbanization, but also to increased greenhouse gas emissions and environmental degradation, European cities are now leading the way in establishing the mutually beneficial relationship between economic, social, and environmental sustainability in postindustrial urban development. This trend, however, obscures the substantial variation in environmental performance based on 2011 levels and rates of urbanization and percentages of urban land cover—even among Europe's wealthier nations (as demonstrated in table 3 page 346)—as well as the broader energy production context (i.e., some regions and countries are better positioned to take advantage of low-impact, renewable energy sources despite high levels of per capita usage).

Future Challenges

Given their dual challenge of facilitating the region's fastest rates of urban growth while also struggling to consolidate economic development gains, the cities of eastern and southern Europe will likely face the most significant difficulties with regard to sustainable urban development in the region in the coming decades. In particular, the eastern European sub-region is faced with overcoming a history of heavy industry in many of its cities that are also encumbered by relatively outdated and poorly maintained infrastructure (Siemens

TABLE 3. European Urbanization and the Environment in a Selection of Nations

	Urban Population (Thousands) 2010	% Urban (2010)	Average Annual Growth of Urban Population 2005–2010	Urban Settlements as % of Total Land Area	Carbon Dioxide Emissions (metric tons per capita)	Motor Vehicles in Use (per 1,000 population) 2007–2008	Energy Consumption (kg of oil equivalent per capita—2008)
Eastern Europe							
Belarus	7,167	75	0.2	3.9	6.9	282	2,907
Bulgaria	5,355	71	−0.3	5.5	6.8	353	2,595
Czech Republic	7,717	74	0.4	14.7	12.1	513	4,282
Hungary	6,798	68	0.3	12.2	5.6	384	2,636
Poland	23,333	61	−0.2	8.7	8.3	495	2,567
Romania	12,348	57	0.6	6.3	4.4	219	1,830
Russian Federation	104,598	73	−0.3	1.1	10.8	245	4,838
Slovakia	3,002	55	−0.1	14.2	6.8	319	3,385
Ukraine	31,263	69	−0.4	4.6	6.8	152	2,943
Northern Europe							
Denmark	4,821	87	0.5	22.6	9.1	477	3,460
Finland	4,565	85	0.7	6.4	12.1	534	6,635
Ireland	2,769	62	2.3	8.3	10.2	534	3,385
Lithuania	2,226	67	−0.9	7.9	4.5	546	2,733
Norway	3,878	79	1.4	6.4	9.1	575	6,222
Sweden	7,943	85	0.6	8.7	5.4	521	5,379
United Kingdom	49,404	80	0.7	22.9	8.8	526	3,395
Southern Europe							
Croatia	2,542	58	0.3	8.6	5.6	388	2,047
Greece	6,976	61	0.6	14.2	8.8	560	2,707
Italy	41,393	68	0.7	24.9	7.7	673	2,942
Portugal	6,480	61	1.4	14	5.5		2,274
Serbia	5,525	56	0.6	7.4		227	2,181
Spain	35,662	77	1.2	13.9	8	606	3,047
Western Europe							
Austria	5,670	68	0.7	13.4	8.3	562	3,988
Belgium	10,435	97	0.6	41.3	9.7	543	5,471
France	53,527	85	1.4	13.7	6	598	4,279
Germany	60,780	74	0	17.3	9.6	554	4,083
Netherlands	13,766	83	1.1	36.7	10.6	515	4,845
Switzerland	5,643	74	0.5	20	5	567	3,491

Source: This is a condensed version (showing only those nations with an urban population over 200,000 people) of the United Nations Population Division's "Urban Population, Development, and the Environment 2011 Wall Chart."

Denmark's Bicycle Superhighway

In many countries like the United States, bicycles are legally defined as vehicles despite their overwhelming use for recreational rather than commuting purposes. Yet the only designated bike paths are often limited to strips of pavement alongside busy motorized traffic (although some cities and states are more bike-friendly than others). Even in countries like Japan, where cycling is more prevalent, paths meant exclusively for bikes are rare. Mexico City has boosted commuting by bike by installing bicycle rental stations strategically around the city, but cyclists must still compete with cars for space on streets. Denmark, however, has made the first steps toward providing large-scale bike paths specifically for commuting purposes.

In April 2012, Denmark completed construction of the first of twenty-six planned "cycle superhighways" surrounding Copenhagen. The idea was to boost bicycle commuting of suburb dwellers, who mostly use cars or public transportation; the latter, while vastly preferable to cars from an environmental standpoint, still emit some carbon dioxide into the atmosphere and don't help with health issues such as obesity. Although many bike paths already existed, standards in paving, maintenance, and lighting could be inconsistent across municipalities. Officials from Copenhagen and twenty-one local governments in the surrounding area collaborated to ensure the new bike routes would be standardized and well maintained. The similarity to an automobile highway was intentional, to encourage use along longer distances—up to twenty-two kilometers in some areas (McGrane 2012).

The intended benefits include safer travel for bicyclists, less air pollution from vehicles, and a healthier population. Statistics show that every ten kilometers biked instead of driven saves approximately 1.6 kilograms of carbon dioxide emissions and nine cents in health care costs. Further innovations planned for ease of use include angled trash cans that can catch a cyclist's litter more easily, and "conversation lanes" for travelers riding together to have enough room to ride abreast and chat without impeding faster-moving traffic (McGrane 2012).

This transition may be natural in a city where half the commuters bike already—the population is densely settled—and the landscape is flat, but may pose a challenge elsewhere. Issues of urban sprawl and cultural values are especially difficult to overcome. In many nations car ownership is a coveted status symbol and bikers are often looked down on as being obstacles to motorized vehicles. Dense infrastructure may impede the ability of city planners to design safe bike paths away from motorized traffic. The rest of the world may be slow to follow Denmark's example until issues of urban design evolve to incorporate these kinds of changes in a way that makes them convenient for the majority of users. Denmark has set a fine example, in the meantime, in demonstrating how complicated issues of transportation, public health, and climate change may have a very simple solution.

The Editors

Further Reading

McGrane, Sally. (2012, July 17). Commuters pedal to work on their very own superhighway. *New York Times*. Retrieved August 29, 2012, from http://www.nytimes.com/2012/07/18/world/europe/in-denmark-pedaling-to-work-on-a-superhighway.html?_r=2&pagewanted=all

and The Economist Intelligence Unit 2009). That said, the vast majority of European cities, despite relatively high levels of public transportation ridership, are likely to suffer with regard to future environmental sustainability if urban sprawl and the often related effects of increased automobile ownership are not reduced (EEA 2006).

Many of these concerns are being addressed through the development and propagation of low- and zero-carbon towns—such as the Hammarby Sjöstad district of Stockholm, Sweden—that integrate high efficiency building materials, a heavy reliance on renewable energy sources, "walkability" and integrated transportation, and innovative water and waste management. Major threats to European cities remain, however, due to the broader, long-term ramifications of global climate change. In particular, due to a long history of urban development along rivers and coast lines, 70 percent of Europe's most populated urban areas are situated roughly 9 meters (or less) above sea level, making the region's urban populations especially vulnerable to overall sea level rise, increased rainfall, and flooding (ESPON 2010).

Ultimately, however, given Europe's low rate of urbanization, high average levels of economic, social, and political development, as well as already globally high levels of renewable energy use registered in the first decades of the twenty-first century, future urban development in Europe is likely to be among the most environmentally sustainable in the world. That said, in light of a decreasing share of the global economy, of aging populations, and in some cases of shrinking cities, the future health of Europe's overall urban development will probably be dictated by the region's ability to simultaneously address aspects of its cities' social, economic, and environmental vitality in the twenty-first century.

Eugenie L. BIRCH, Alexander M. KEATING,
and Susan M. WACHTER
University of Pennsylvania

See also European Union (EU); European Union Greenhouse Gas Emission Trading Scheme (EU ETS); London, United Kingdom; Moscow, Russia; Russia and the Soviet Union; St. Petersburg, Russia; Stockholm, Sweden; United Kingdom and Ireland; Urbanization (Africa); Urbanization (Western Asia and Northern Africa); Warsaw, Poland

FURTHER READING

Angel, Shlomo; Parent, Jason; Civco, Daniel L; & Blei, Alejandro M. (2011). *Making room for a planet of cities.* Cambridge, MA: Policy Focus Report, Lincoln Institute of Land Policy.
Birch, Eugenie L., & Wachter, Susan M. (Eds.). (2010). *Global urbanization.* Philadelphia: University of Pennsylvania Press.
City Mayors. (2011). Largest cities and their mayors 2011 (Cities ranked 1–150). Retrieved April 3, 2012, from http://www.city-mayors.com/statistics/largest-cities-mayors-1.html
Dodman, David. (2009). Blaming cities for climate change? An analysis of greenhouse gas emissions inventories. *Environment and Urbanization, 21*(1), 185–201.
European Commission. (2010, November). Second state of European cities report (Research project for the European Commission, DG Regional Policy). Essen, Germany: German Institute of Urban Affairs.
European Commission. (2012). Environment: Sustainable development. Retrieved April 3, 2012, from http://ec.europa.eu/environment/eussd/
European Environmental Agency (EEA). (2006). Urban sprawl in Europe: The ignored challenge (EEA report no. 10/2006). City of Luxembourg, Luxembourg: Office for Official Publications of the European Communities.
European Observation Network on Territorial Development and Cohesion (ESPON). (2010). First ESPON 2013 synthesis report: New evidence on smart, sustainable and inclusive territories. Retrieved April 3, 2012, from http://www.espon.eu/main/Menu_Publications/Menu_SynthesisReports/
Glaeser, Edward. (2011). *Triumph of the city.* New York: Penguin Books.
International Institute for Environment and Development (IIED). (2011). Homepage. Retrieved April 3, 2012, from www.iied.org
Kollmann, Wolfgang. (1969). The process of urbanization in Germany at the height of the industrialization period. *Journal of Contemporary History, 4*(3), 59–76. Retrieved April 19, 2012, from http://www.jstor.org/discover/10.2307/259731?uid=3739696&uid=2&uid=4&uid=3739256&sid=47698901376337
Kotkin, Joel. (2005). *The city: A global history.* New York: Modern Library Chronicles.
Marcotullio, Peter J., & McGranahan, Gordon. (Eds.). (2007). *Scaling urban environmental challenges: From local to global and back.* London: Earthscan.
Population Reference Bureau. (2012). Homepage. Retrieved April 3, 2012, from www.prb.org
Satterthwaite, David. (2007, September). *The transition to a predominantly urban world and its underpinnings.* London: International Institute for Environment and Development (IIED). Retrieved April 3, 2012, from http://pubs.iied.org/10550IIED.html?k=The transition to a predominantly urban world
Satterthwaite, David; McGranahan, Gordon; & Tacoli, Cecilia. (2010). Urbanization and its implications for food and farming. *Philosophical Transactions of the Royal Society B, 365*(1554), 2809–2820.
Siemens, & The Economist Intelligence Unit. (2009). European Green City Index: Assessing the environmental impact of Europe's major cities. London: Siemens & The Economist Intelligence Unit, London. Retrieved April 3, 2012, from http://www.nwe.siemens.com/denmark/internet/dk/presse/Documents/Green_City_Index_report.pdf
Sustainable Cities and Towns Campaign. (n.d.). Homepage. Retrieved April 3, 2012, from http://sustainable-cities.eu/index.php
United Nations Department of Economic and Social Affairs (UN DESA), Office of the Population Division. (2012). World urbanization prospects, the 2011 revision. Retrieved April 3, 2012, from http://esa.un.org/unpd/wup/index.htm
United Nations Department of Economic and Social Affairs (UN DESA), Office of the Population Division. (2011). Urban population, development, and the environment 2011. Retrieved April 3, 2012, from http://www.un.org/esa/population/publications/2011UrbanPopDevEnv_Chart/urbanpopdevenv2011wallchart.html
United Nations Human Settlements Programme (UN-Habitat). (2010). State of the world's cities 2010/2011: Cities for all: Bridging the urban divide. Nairobi, Kenya: UN-Habitat.
United Nations Human Settlements Programme (UN-Habitat). (2011). Cities and climate change. London: Earthscan.
United Nations Human Settlements Programme (UN-Habitat). (n.d.). Homepage. Retrieved April 3, 2012, from www.unhabitat.org
United Nations (UN) Statistics Division. (2011). *Demographic yearbook 2009–2010.* New York: UN.
Wrigley, E. Anthony. (1990). Brake or accelerator? Urban growth and population growth before the Industrial Revolution. In A. D. van der Woude, Akira Hayami & Jan de Vries (Eds.), *Urbanization in history: A process of dynamic interaction.* Oxford, UK: Oxford University Press.

Urbanization—Western Asia and Northern Africa

The process of turning urban centers into somewhat rural-seeming places through new migrants' practice of urban or peri-urban agriculture is widespread in most countries of western Asia and northern Africa. Urbanization has been left to codified law, but the region is in a position to inspire countries toward more environmentally sustainable behavior as it reassesses customary law practices, such as aflaj, a traditional water management system, and himās, a traditional system of multipurpose land use and protection.

Rapid urbanization is one of the critical trends shaping the future in most countries of West Asia and North Africa (abbreviated as WANA). The urbanization process is fueled by population growth and a range of compounding factors, such as desertification, climate change, drought, and a general flight of people from rural poverty toward towns and cities in search of better services and livelihoods. Those new residents are in dire need of appropriate living conditions, but waiting lists for housing are long and funding is often lacking—and often there are simply no houses or other infrastructure. The result is sprawling, informal settlements, which in turn are associated with changes in the structure of the space organization, along with intense pressure on the environment and its resources.

As more rural people move to towns and cities, they bring their ways with them and turn urban centers into more rural-seeming places through the practice of urban or peri-urban agriculture. This has occurred in the cities of Algiers (Algeria), Beirut (Lebanon), Cairo (Egypt), Damascus (Syria), Khartoum (Sudan), Mogadishu (Somalia), Moroni (Comoros), Nouakchott (Mauritania), and Sana'a (Yemen). Such agriculture is diverse, thriving, and sometimes a profitable activity in towns and cities all over non-oil-producing countries of WANA for both poor and affluent urban dwellers. Food production is increasing, but it has been associated with serious environmental damage, especially as a threat to scarce water resources (Abaza, Saab, and Zeitoon 2011).

The combined effects of ruralization and chaotic urban expansion significantly modify landscapes and thus the hydrological cycle, as in, for example, Beirut, where water-related problems, including reduced capacity for water retention (e.g., the waste of green water—rainfall that infiltrates and remains in the soil), are increasing in the new urban environment. Rapid development of urban landscapes is often accompanied by modification of natural habitats, which could result in the degradation of ecosystems. In addition, urbanization often causes the environment and its resources to deteriorate, creating acute water shortages and shrinking the green space offered by nature reserves and parks, such as has occurred in Beirut, Cairo, Damascus, Kuwait City, Nouakchott, and Sana'a.

The question remains how are urban dwellers in WANA supposed to raise their standard of living without further damaging the already vulnerable urban environment. The old adage "Example is better than precept" addresses that question. In WANA, several uncodified traditional systems, with cultural roots that predate Christianity and Islam, deal directly with resource challenges posed by urban development. Now that more of WANA's population lives in urban rather than rural areas, the need to understand and implement sustainable customary law practices has never been more urgent.

Since sustainability involves managing the impact of human activity on the environment, with intergenerational equity taken into account, we look at two creative strategies for improving the urban environment through conservation of the natural environment and its resources. Several WANA countries have concurrent societal arrangements (i.e., customary law and codified law) that regulate land and water resources through different frameworks. Examples of customary law practices include *aflaj* and *himnās*, discussed below; and examples of codified law include town development and housing and planning law.

Traditional Systems of Sustainable Urban Development

Traditional systems are living monuments of humanity's ingenuity and testify to the importance attached to sustainability. Throughout the centuries, Middle Eastern ancestors contributed much to the regional environment and its resources, working out some of the finest examples of sustainable urban development.

A better understanding of traditional systems can help address current urban challenges related to water and green space. In several WANA countries, access to land and water is regulated according to systems of customary law, such as *aflaj* and *himās*, which are practiced, respectively, in Oman and Saudi Arabia.

Falaj: A Long-Standing Indigenous Water Management System

The word *falaj* (pl. *aflaj*), which in Arabic means a fracture or fissure on the ground, is derived from an ancient Semitic term meaning "to divide." The *falaj* system is an indigenous method of using slopes and gravity to force the flow of water downward via canals, thus minimizing the financial cost and avoiding the use of mechanical equipment to convey water.

The *aflaj*, estimated to be about 2,500 years old, is considered the main traditional water system in the Sultanate of Oman. Despite the introduction of underground and surface wells, the *aflaj* still plays the major role in irrigation, drinking water, livestock watering, and other domestic purposes.

Though such a water system is known by different names throughout the world (e.g., *karez* in Afghanistan and Pakistan; *foggara* in Algeria and Libya; *galeria* in the Canary Islands, Spain, and Latin America; *kanerjing/kanjing* in China; *surangam* in India; *qanat* in Iran; *ingruttato* in Italy; *mappo* in Japan; *khattara/khettara* in Morocco; and *felledj* in Yemen), the philosophy behind a *falaj* remains consistent: to entrust the water supply to the water users themselves, for the sake of the community and the environment. Although the

water distribution system is complex, it is both effective and fair.

A *falaj* length varies; it may reach 17.3 kilometers. Its structure comprises a main well that may reach a depth of 20 to 60 meters, a central canal, and access shafts that are built every 50 to 60 meters along the central canal. Each farmer is entitled to a share of water based on cultivated plot size and contribution to the *falaj* construction. Although most *aflaj* are fully owned by farmers, the government owns some, in full or in part. If the government contributed to the construction of the *falaj*, it normally owns some shares of land or water.

Typical large *falaj* administration consists of a *wakeel* (agent or manager), two *areefs* (foremen to deal with technical problems), a *qabidh/amin aldaftar* (treasurer/bookkeeper), a *dallal* (auctioneer), and *beedars* (daily laborers). The *Sheikh* (head of the village) assigns the *wakeel* to his job based on a recommendation from the *falaj* owners. Depending on the size of the *falaj* system, a *falaj* can have some or all of the above administration. At the least, the *falaj* should have a *wakeel*.

In every *falaj*, water shares are not owned by individuals but are allocated to the community. Water shares for one water rotation are sold in an open auction.

In the case of disputes, either the *wakeel* or the water shareholder can file a complaint with the *Sheikh*. If the latter cannot settle the dispute, it is put before the *walee* (governor), who transfers it to ordinary courts (though this rarely occurs). Water distribution has been accepted by the shareholders without any apparent problems. One of the *areefs* arranges the schedule of the water rotation among water shareholders. The *qabidh* is in charge of the *falaj* income (water shares, plot, and/or crops). As the *amin aldaftar*, the *qabidh* organizes water shareholder sale auctions with the help of the *dallal*. The *beedars'* job consists of canal and tunnel cleaning and repairing minor collapses. Generally, water rents provide most of the *falaj* income.

The Sultanate of Oman regularly intervenes to maintain and preserve the *aflaj* through laws, by-laws, and ministerial orders. The *aflaj* system in Oman illustrates how codified law interacts with customary law practices.

Aflaj have survived for more than two thousand years for three main reasons. First, as freshwater is considered the source of life within Omani society, and *aflaj* play a major role in sustaining life, therefore abiding by the *falaj* organization maintains and safeguards the source of life. Second, the *falaj* system is managed and maintained by the grassroots water users through a top-down approach and a time-honored system embedded in societal values. Third, the system is based on the dominant, sacrosanct religious obligations—honor of ancestral traditions, tribal loyalty, and human respect (person to person, family to family, and family to community).

Himā: A Tradition of Conservation

Himā (pl. *himās*) is a community-managed natural resource system. It has shaped national approaches to environmental sustainability through stabilizing and controlling nomadic grazing, restoring rangelands, protecting biological diversity, and managing water catchment areas. The *himā* originated in Saudi Arabia about two thousand years ago as a private sanctuary, and religion embraced the concept but transformed it into a public asset in which all community members had a share and a stake. Later, the *himā* concept disseminated throughout Asia under different local names.

Himā means "protected or forbidden area," with its living and nonliving resources receiving special protection. Within the Islamic tradition, scholars have identified four conditions that must be met for an area to be considered a *himā*: (1) It must be established in the way of God for the public welfare; (2) it must be recognized by a religious authority to ensure that it is not being established for the wrong reasons (e.g., by the rich for the rich); (3) it should avoid causing undue hardship to the community (e.g., depriving local people of indispensable resources); and (4) the actual benefits to society must be greater than its societal cost.

The concept of *himā* largely disappeared in the post-European era of the WANA region. Currently just a few *himās* are being managed actively; many have been abandoned because of major political, economic, and social changes stemming from rapid population and economic growth. As a state-centric approach emerged, "*himās* were engulfed by ministry-controlled swaths of public land" (Verde 2008). One consequence has been the drifting of rules and regulations for land protection away from a local community focus.

Nature reserves and parks face tremendous resistance from local people who see them as intrusive to their rights without bringing any tangible benefits. The *himā*, which preserves resources for both animals and humans, is designed to protect the numerous goods and services provided by land and can contribute significantly to bettering livelihoods. Using *himās* instead of creating reserves that exclude people sends the message that a government is taking the people's welfare into consideration—as, for example, with the Saudi Decree of 1954 declaring *himās* as public lands (Gari 2008). Conservationists tout the benefits of the *himā* system.

Scholars and organizations are reviving the ancestral tradition and revisiting *himās* throughout WANA (e.g., Jordan, Lebanon, Oman, and Saudi Arabia). They are considering how best to merge and adapt the *himā* concept with other international systems of conservation, in a way that complements the established modes of sustainable urban development for the benefit of the people. As part of this intent, they are trying to link biodiversity conservation with economic development by changing the blanket prohibition of nature reserves and parks to an area of zoning and management.

Possible Adoption of Traditional Systems

Several challenges confront urban sustainability in WANA, requiring various measures to address them, especially invigorating customary law practices and encouraging the harmonization of societal arrangements.

With their concentration of human and economic activities, the urban environments in WANA can cause intensive environmental degradation. Conversely, the vitality of towns and cities has the potential to improve the quality of life and minimize stresses on the natural environment. So WANA countries could build on their traditional systems in the urban environment and foster synergies in the actions of customary and codified law.

Multiple forms of customary law practices coexist and sometimes conflict with prevailing codified law. The WANA countries need to take the best of customary law and the best of codified law to create, in the interest of the poorest of their urban dwellers, a sustainable urban development paradigm that is based on the needs and culture of their societies. One way forward would be to develop a methodology to operationalize this challenge, possibly in the form of guidelines or a checklist that WANA countries could use to compile and assess the customary law practices and codified law. This challenge is an important issue in the discourse on sustainable urban development.

Complementarity between Customary and Codified Law

Because urban expansion usually reduces green space—resulting in reduced rainfall-absorbing capacity of the soil, infiltration, and recharge, as well as increased groundwater and surface runoff—the revisited *himās* could directly reduce the pressure on the remaining green space covers. Developing the revisited *himās* could mitigate negative impact on the hydrological cycle and improve the quality of both the natural and urban environments.

Moreover, the revisited *falaj* would remain consistent with its original philosophy—to entrust the supply of water to grassroots water users—for the sake of the new urban dwellers and the environment. As noted in *aflaj* irrigation systems, the construction of irrigation canals and furrows would be controlled by the head of the district or headman, and, although a single individual could tap a stream for individual use without first consulting the head of the district, the latter could prohibit the construction or use of any such canal or furrow. Once constructed, the canal or furrow would be the exclusive property of the people who constructed it until they abandoned it. Then it would revert to the district authorities.

Both examples focus on the possible complementarity between customary law practices and codified law in the processes of sustainable urban development. They are not offered as ready-made answers for all cases, but rather as a suggestion that it is always useful to acknowledge working examples for urban management. Most peoples of WANA can benefit from "living" (i.e., existing) customary law practices. These appear very resilient in the areas of housing, town development, and planning. A key issue is the extent to which these customary law practices can be incorporated into codified law.

Codified law in most WANA countries is often set in conformity with that applied in water-rich developed countries, so in many cases is not suitable for addressing prevailing conditions and economic or technical situations in WANA. Furthermore, codified law has a centralizing mission; but the equation of "one country, one legal system" for sustainable urban development is less a descriptive than a prescriptive set of assumptions about sustainability and society, and is particularly irrelevant in the broader picture of codified law as a societal process. Codified law is not above societal dynamics. Rather, societal context shapes and conditions the role of codified law.

Pros and Cons of Concurrent Societal Arrangements

Some WANA countries are challenged by the ideology of legal centralism. Most do not possess a single legal system for sustainable urban development, but have as many legal systems as there are societal organizations (e.g., tribe, clan, family, associations) and arrangements.

The dilemma faced by those engaged in sustainable urban development has been how to reconcile the existing societal organizations at the district, provincial, and central government levels. There is much resentment among new urban dwellers about attempts by codified law to assert its authority regarding allocation and preservation of water resources. The new urban dwellers find it incomprehensible that they would be subject to the obligations of the codified law.

Societal arrangements can integrate new urban dwellers into the existing urban environment. Municipal law in WANA countries should somehow address the issue of customary law practices and strike a balance between codified law and customary law. People in the WANA region cannot do away with societal processes that deform the best devised law and set new hurdles for the most-determined policy makers and powerful legislators; however, customary law practices are insufficiently incorporated into municipal law in most WANA countries, giving precedence to codified law.

Codified law and the societal context in which it operates must be examined together. There has been new recognition of the important and irreplaceable role that ancestral traditions play in human interactions with the rest of the natural world. Moreover, municipal law in most of the WANA region is multilayered, reflecting different societal dynamics and priorities as well as customary law practices and codified law.

Several WANA countries have focused on the use of codified law to solve environmental problems, although some of them rely on a blend of codified law and customary law practices. Each country has yet to assess the consequences that recognition of customary law practices may have on its political scene and on the utilization of the environment and its resources.

Future Research Directions

Can traditional systems help secure sustainable urban development? Roman philosopher and statesman Marcus Tullius Cicero addressed that question: *"Historia est testis temporum, lux veritatis, vita memoriae, magistra vitae, nuntia vetustatis*" ("History is the witness of time, the light of truth, the essence of remembrance, the teacher of life, the messenger from times past"). Looking at the past is essential for sustainable urban development in WANA; nevertheless, the overall goal is to fuse traditional practices with recent developments in conservation science.

The need to grasp and rethink the basics of traditional systems may not be seen as a priority by some policy makers. Yet ruralization and its impacts on the hydrological cycle and living conditions ensure the need for a fresh look at urban development. The fact that most urban centers are likely to be adversely affected in the not-too-distant future, even though some may benefit from ruralization, should ensure that a national consensus can be progressively built. This makes it imperative to start thinking about the future of sustainable urban development now.

Ancient systems like the *aflaj* and *himās* have proven their efficiency and demonstrate their potential contribution to sustainable urban development. While traditional systems could be updated to sustain urban development in WANA, many of the countries are lacking some of the essential factors that contributed to sustainability in the past (e.g., top-down approach and sacrosanct religious obligation). Research in this field needs to continue until a suitable urban development paradigm is adapted to accommodate today's realities of sustainable development and cities.

While great urban challenges lie ahead, towns and cities around the WANA region are drawing from a wealth of traditions regarding urban governance found in the pre-Islamic heritage. With some modest political or legislative support, the possibilities for improving access to water and better living conditions in the urban environment are considerable. Revisiting traditional systems to make them more responsive to local conditions may provide one suitable starting point for improving quality of life and well-being and meeting the needs of most urban dwellers. In sum, WANA countries could lead other countries toward more environmentally sustainable urban environments by reviving and reconsidering *aflaj* and *himās*, which in turn could inspire millions of urban dwellers around the world.

Tarek MAJZOUB
Beirut Arab University

Fabienne QUILLERÉ-MAJZOUB
IODE—University of Rennes 1

See also Agriculture, Small-Scale; Biological Corridors; Middle East; Migration (Africa); Public-Private Partnerships (Africa); Rural Development; Transboundary Water Issues; Urbanization (Africa); Urbanization (Europe); Water Use and Rights (Middle East and North Africa)

FURTHER READINGS

Abaza, Hussein; Saab, Najib; & Zeitoon, Bashar. (Eds.). (2011). *Arab environment: Green economy: Sustainable transition in a changing Arab world.* 2011 Report of the Arab Forum for Environment and Development (AFED). Retrieved January 31, 2012, from http://www.afedonline.org/Report2011/main2011.html

Al-Ghafri, Abdullah; Inoue, Takashi; & Nagasawa, Tetuaki. (n.d.). Irrigation scheduling of *Aflaj* of Oman: Methods and modernization. Sapporo, Japan: Hokkaido University Graduate School of Agriculture. Retrieved August 31, 2011, from http://www.inweh.unu.edu/drylands/docs/Publications/AlGhafri.pdf

Al-Hassani, Salim T. S. (2009). 1000 years amnesia: Environment tradition in Muslim heritage. Retrieved August 31, 2011, from http://muslimheritage.com/topics/default.cfm?ArticleID=1167

Al-Hathloul, Saleh. (1996). *The Arab-Muslim city: Tradition, community, and change in the physical environment.* Riyadh, Saudi Arabia: Dar al-Sahan.

Al-Shaqsi, Saif Bin Rashid. (1996). *Aflaj* management in the Sultanate of Oman: Case study of Falaj Al-Hamra (Dawoodi) and Falaj Al-Kasfah (Aini) (Graduate thesis). Cardiff, UK: University of Wales, Centre for Arid Zone Studies.

Bagader, Abubakr A.; El-Chirazi El-Sabbagh, Abdullatif T.; As-Sayyid Al-Glayand, Mohamad; Samarrai Mawil Y. I.-D.; & Llewellyn, Othman Abd-ar-Rahman. (1994). *Environment protection in Islam.* Gland, Switzerland, & Cambridge, UK: IUCN & MEPA, IUCN Environmental Policy & Law Paper No. 20 Rev. Retrieved August 31, 2011, from http://cmsdata.iucn.org/downloads/eplp_020reven.pdf

El-Ashry, Mohamed; Saab, Najib; & Zeitoon, Bashar. (Eds.). (2010). *Arab environment. Water: Sustainable management of a scarce resource.* 2010 Report of the Arab Forum for Environment and Development (AFED). Retrieved August 31, 2011, from http://www.afedonline.org/Report2010/main.asp

Foltz, Richard C.; Denny, Frederick M.; & Baharuddin, Azizian. (Eds.). (2003). *Islam and ecology: A bestowed trust.* Cambridge, MA: Harvard University Press.

Foltz, Richard, & the Forum on Religion and Ecology. (2004). *Islam and ecology bibliography.* Center for the Study of World Religions. Retrieved August 31, 2011, from http://fore.research.yale.edu/religion/islam/islam.pdf

Gari, Lutfallah. (2008). Ecology in Muslim heritage: A history of the himā conservation system. *Environment and History, 12*(2), 213–228. Retrieved August 31, 2011, from http://www.muslimheritage.com/topics/default.cfm?ArticleID=916

Hodge, A. Trevor. (2000). Qanats. In Örjan Wikander (Ed.), *Handbook of ancient water technology: Technology and change in history: Vol. 2.* Leiden, The Netherlands: Brill Academic Publishers.

Llewellyn, Othman. (2000). *The importance of traditional conservation practices in Saudi Arabia.* Riyadh, Saudi Arabia: National Commission for Wildlife Conservation and Development.

Majzoub, Tarek. (2005, November 14–18). Potential "legislative water governance" in the ESCWA region. Seminar on Water governance: The role of stakeholders and civil society institutions. Beirut, Lebanon.

Majzoub, Tarek; Mokorosi, Palesa Selloane; García-Pachón, Maria del Pilar; Leendertse, Kees; & Indij, Damian. (2010). Streams of law: A training manual and facilitators' guide on water legislation and legal reform for integrated water resources management. Pretoria, South Africa: Cap-Net. Retrieved August 31, 2011, from http://www.cap-net.org/node/2354

Ministry of Regional Municipalities & Water Resources. (2008). *Aflaj Oman in the world heritage list.* Muscat, Oman: Sultanate of Oman.

Nair, V. Sankaran. (2006). India-centric hydraulic civilization of the old world. Retrieved August 31, 2011, from http://www.boloji.com/index.cfm?md=Content&sd=Articles&ArticleID=5256

Nizwa.net. (n.d.). The traditional aflaj irrigation system. Retrieved August 31, 2011, from http://www.nizwa.net/agr/falaj/chapter4.html

Regional Office for Science and Technology for the Arab States (ROSTAS). (1986). *The major regional project on rational utilization and conservation of water resources in the rural areas of Arab states with emphasis on traditional water systems.* Paris: UNESCO-ROSTAS & the Arab Center for Studies of Arid Zones and Drylands (ACSAD). Retrieved June 22, 2012, from http://unesdoc.unesco.org/images/0007/000721/072165eb.pdf

Rovere, Marta Brunilda, & Iza, Alejandro. (Eds.). (2007). *Prácticas ancestrales y derecho de aguas: De la tensión a la coexistencia* [Ancestral practices and water rights: From stress to coexistance]. Gland, Switzerland, & Bonn, Germany: IUCN, Environmental Policy & Law Paper No. 68. Retrieved August 31, 2011, from http://www.iucn.org/dbtw-wpd/edocs/EPLP-068.pdf

Van Koppen, Barbara; Giordano, Mark; & Butterworth, John. (Eds.). (2007). *Community-based water law and water resource management reform in developing countries.* Wallingford, UK: CAB International.

Verde, Tom. (2008). A tradition of conservation. *Saudi Aramco World, 5*(6), 10–16. Retrieved August 31, 2011, from http://www.saudiaramcoworld.com/issue/200806/a.tradition.of.conservation.htm

West Asia–North Africa (WANA) Forum. (2010). Report of the Second WANA Forum: Pursuing supranational solutions to the challenges of carrying capacity. Amman, Jordan: WANA Forum Secretariat. Retrieved August 31, 2011, from http://www.slideshare.net/WANAforum/report-of-the-second-wana-forum-2010

United Nations Educational, Scientific and Cultural Organization (UNESCO); Man and Biosphere (MAB) Division of Ecological and Earth Sciences; & International Hydrological Programme (IHP) Division of Water Sciences. (n.d.). Water cycle in urban areas. Retrieved August 31, 2011, from http://www.aquatic.unesco.lodz.pl/index.php?p=water_cycle

World Resources Institute (WRI); United Nations Environment Programme (UNEP); United Nations Development Programme (UNDP); & World Bank. (1996). *World resources 1996–1997: A guide to the global environment: The urban environment.* New York: Oxford University Press. Retrieved August 31, 2011, from http://pdf.wri.org/worldresources1996-97_bw.pdf

Volga River

The Volga River, rising near Moscow and draining into the Caspian Sea, is Europe's longest river. It serves a quarter of Russia's industry and almost half its population. In recent years, the river has become contaminated, polluted, and heavily dammed. As a result, the river basin has sustained considerable environmental damage. In August 2011, the Russian president identified the river as a key environmental concern.

At 3,700 kilometers in length, the Volga is the longest river in Europe, comparable in length to the Mississippi in the United States. The Volga and its basin are located in western Russia, and the river has been Russia's most significant waterway throughout history. As such, the river has been referred to as "the Soul of Russia," "the Mother Volga," and "Russia's Main Street." The river supports a quarter of the country's industry and almost half of its population. Sixty percent of the Volga's water comes from snowfall in the north. Despite its length and the many tributaries that flow into it, each winter the river freezes along its entire length (McNeese 2005, 8).

The Volga River originates at an elevation of only 225 meters above sea level in the Valdai Hills, which are situated northwest of Moscow. This low elevation is sometimes cited as the reason the river lacks the capacity to "flush" itself clean; a history of excessive diversions and extreme contamination from a variety of sources is the more probable reason the river has problems with pollution. From its source, the Volga flows northeast of Moscow to the Rybinsk Reservoir. Through the Rybinsk Reservoir and a set of canals one can travel from the Volga River all the way to the Baltic Sea by water. Indeed, most of the Volga is navigable. Yearly statistics typically cite the Volga as carrying at least half of all river-borne freight in Russia. Fifty million tonnes of freight and 800,000 passengers travel along the Volga annually (Medvedev 2011).

From Yaroslavl' the Volga River begins to flow southward, eventually forming a large delta of almost three hundred channels and emptying into the Caspian Sea. On its course southward it passes through or near several significant cities, such as Nizhniy Novgorod, Kazan, Samara, Saratov, Volgograd, and Astrakhan. Among its many tributaries are the Oka, Belaya, Vyatka, and Kama rivers.

Throughout the twentieth century, the Volga was manipulated and contaminated. Most notable among early diversions of the river was the Great Volga project, which Soviet leader Joseph Stalin promoted. Because the country's leadership, beginning with Russian communist leader Vladimir Lenin, was fond of large-scale water projects, the Volga and its tributaries were dammed under the Great Volga project, and thirty-four hydroelectric stations were constructed. The reservoirs created along the Volga are immense and are sometimes referred to as "inland seas." During storms, the ocean-sized waves produced on these reservoirs jeopardize the fragile soils of the area's shorelines. The dams also reduce spawning grounds of fish by obstructing their natural runs. The consequence has been a dwindling fisheries industry. Deforestation to make way for agricultural land has also been a problem, with the resulting soil erosion amounting to the loss of nearly 10 percent of the Volga basin's land area in the last thirty years.

Urban, agricultural, and industrial effluents pollute the river and its reservoirs. Many of the cities along the Volga's course discharge polluted wastewater from inadequate sanitation facilities. In the middle Volga region near Samara, the Volga-Ural oil fields and former state farms also contribute their share of pollution. In the lower Volga region, dioxin pollution from the agricultural use of herbicides and insecticides and from chemical production has been high for decades. Dioxin contamination is demonstrated to be harmful to humans, threatening especially their reproductive, endocrine, and immune systems. It is also a problem for the fauna of the region. Heavy-metal contamination, including copper, manganese, and lead, is also at a high level. Sixty-five of Russia's one hundred most polluted cities are situated on the banks of the river, where access to fresh water for locals is limited (Medvedev 2011). In the region's agricultural sectors, runoff of nitrates from fertilizers into the reservoirs of the river causes rampant algae growth in the summer. Chemical contamination from agricultural and industrial sectors has eradicated much of the wildlife from the area. Because water from reservoirs is used for irrigation, food crops in the wider region are also affected. An additional source of contamination is the petrochemical industries in the vicinity of Astrakhan. Runoff of industrial by-products in this region is severe, and pipelines and refineries leak frequently.

The river basin contains 42 percent of the vegetation types of Russia, with vegetation varying along the length of the river. Forest cover in particular changes depending on the geographic region; in the east, oak, maple, and ash trees are plentiful, whereas the west has more firs, larch, and pine trees. Deciduous trees line the forested steppe zone across the middle of the Volga from the Urals to the Don River basin. This region also contains multitiered forests—oak, ash, elm, and maple in the upper tiers, pear, apple, and hazelnut in the lower tiers (Saiko 2001, 190–191). Human activity places stresses on the river basin especially in the extreme cold of the north and the aridity of the south; the large forested central areas of the river basin are more resilient to human stresses. The situation worsens the farther south the river travels, as contaminants accumulate. As a result, the southern steppe region is the most vulnerable of the river's ecosystems. Air pollution is also a problem: the cities and industries in the Volga basin are responsible for more than a quarter of the air pollution in Russia.

Although organizations such as the 1989 Public Committee to Save the Volga have made efforts to control pollution and overexploitation of the river and increasing rates of water consumption, environmental concerns were a low priority in the early years of the twenty-first century. Even national reserves and wetlands that the international Ramsar Convention identified as significant are in a precarious situation. Despite this, the Volga River continues to be an important route for trade to the interior of Russia (McNeese 2005, 96). In August 2011, Russian President Dmitry Medvedev declared that fisheries, water resource protection, and waterway development are some of the biggest issues that he was aiming to tackle. He announced that money would be spent on cleaning the river and its drainage systems and repairing and protecting hydroelectric facilities. A new federal program targeting Russia's waterways will coordinate these issues, with assistance from the government and the natural resources ministry (Medvedev 2011).

Kyle T. EVERED
Michigan State University

See also Danube River; Fisheries; Mediterranean Sea; Moscow, Russia; Russia and the Soviet Union; Shipping and Freight; Transboundary Water Issues; Ukraine

This article was adapted by the editors from the article "Volga River" in Shepard Krech III, J. R. McNeill, and

Carolyn Merchant (Eds.), the *Encyclopedia of World Environmental History,* pp. 180–1281. Great Barrington, MA: Berkshire Publishing (2003).

FURTHER READING

Kur'yakova, A. N. (2011). Balance of heavy metals in the Volga River delta. *Doklady Earth Sciences, 493*(2), 1186–1189.

McNeese, Tim . (2005). *The Volga River.* Philadelphia: Chelsea House.

Medvedev, Dmitry (Chair). (2011, August 17). *Meeting on developing the Volga's water resources.* Retrieved November 8, 2011, from http://eng.kremlin.ru/news/2713

Mordukhai-Boltovskoi, F. D. (1979). *The river Volga and its life.* The Hague, The Netherlands: W. Junk.

National Public Radio (NPR). (2010, November 1). Russia's troubled waters flow with the mighty Volga. Retrieved June 15, 2012, from http://www.npr.org/templates/story/story.php?storyId=130837658

Pryde, Philip R. (1991). *Environmental management in the Soviet Union.* Cambridge, UK: Cambridge University Press.

Roberts, Geoffrey. (2003, February 28).Victory on the Volga. *The Guardian.* Retrieved June 15, 2012, from http://www.guardian.co.uk/world/2003/feb/28/russia.comment?INTCMP=SRCH

Saiko, Tatyana. (2001). *Environmental crises: Geographical case studies in post-socialist Eurasia.* Harlow, UK: Pearson Education.

Warsaw, Poland

1.71 million est. pop. 2012

Violence and destruction in Warsaw throughout the twentieth century created economic, social, and political instability that prevented the city from focusing attention on becoming environmentally sustainable. Poland's independence in 1989 and its membership in the European Union in 2004 improved conditions, allowing Warsaw to work on infrastructure, public transportation, and developing energy efficient buildings. Despite all the improvements, environmental sustainability is not, as yet, within Warsaw's grasp.

Warsaw is located in the eastern central part of Poland, where it straddles the Vistula River, covering an area of 517.9 square kilometers. Approximately 1.71 million people live in Warsaw as of 2012, and in 2009 some 10 million tourists visited the city. Warsaw is an important destination point for leaders seeking to bridge the economic, political, and environmental policies of Eastern and Western Europe, while it also serves as both the capital and political center of Poland—a country that since 1989 has evolved from a Communist-controlled Soviet satellite state to become an independent nation with full-fledged membership in the North Atlantic Treaty Organization (NATO) and the European Union (EU). Since joining the EU in 2004, Poland has been criticized by other member states for not emphasizing environmental issues. Poland has made efforts to improve the city's environmental record, however, particularly in the area of transportation modernization and green building. But the destructive past that Warsaw and the rest of Poland witnessed in the first half of the twentieth century has made it all the more challenging to emphasize the type of green development needed to create an environmentally sustainable city.

History

During the Warsaw Uprising of 1944 thousands of local residents came together to fight the German soldiers who had occupied the city since Poland was invaded in 1939. The uprising was quickly defeated in what would be one of the most destructive periods the city ever witnessed. After engaging in street battles, looting, and setting fire to buildings, German soldiers systematically blew up the city's most culturally and historically important buildings with dynamite, destroying the most important ones first (Project InPosterum n.d.). In total, approximately 180,000 Varsovians (Warsaw residents) were killed; it is estimated that, over the entirety of World War II, 600,000 to 800,000 Varsovians died. In January 1945, following the destruction of the city, Soviet soldiers, who stood on the other side of the Vistula River during the uprising, marched into the ruins of Warsaw to become the city's new occupiers. The Soviet Union largely controlled the city and the rest of the country until Poland's independence in 1989.

While under Soviet control and under the guidance of the office of reconstruction, Varsovians undertook the huge task of rebuilding their city. Warsaw grew into a large industrial base filled with factories and large housing blocks. With most of the efforts being placed on clearing rubble, mines, and munitions, and rebuilding historically important buildings, little attention was paid to environmental concerns during the reconstruction.

Since becoming independent and transitioning from a command economy to a free market, Warsaw became sufficiently stable—economically, socially, and politically—to be in a position to pay attention to creating a modern and environmentally sustainable city. In 2008 Warsaw was ranked number eight out of sixty-five cities in MasterCard's Worldwide Emerging Market Index. In

2007 Warsaw's per capita gross domestic product (GDP) was 94,200 złotys (about US$32,180) a year, about 160 percent of the European Union's average (MasterCard 2008; *The Warsaw Voice* 2009).

Warsaw was one of eight cities in Poland and Ukraine chosen to host the 2012 Union of European Football Associations (UEFA) Euro Cup, a soccer tournament for which 1.4 million tickets were available, and that brought an aggregate total number of 1,402,538 fans to Warsaw's "fan zone" over the course of the final matches (UEFA 2012). It was estimated that for the month of June, during which the majority of matches took place, the Warsaw Chopin Airport would need to accommodate an additional 320 flights and an increase in passenger traffic by 120,000 people, many of whom would add to the already congested streets by using rental cars and other forms of private transport after exiting the airport's terminals (Warsaw City Council Press Department 2012). Although many visitors used public transportation to travel in and around the capital, a deadly 3 March 2012 train accident that occurred along the Krakow-Warsaw line led many officials to question the safety of the public rail system before the tournament began (Scislowska and Gera 2012). Although a considerable amount of money has gone into improving Warsaw's public transportation system in preparation for the Euro Cup, the city still has some catching up to do before it is on a par with other European capitals, as does the country as a whole, which is far behind the rest of Europe in terms of rail speed, safety, and efficiency. Implementation of new environmental laws has delayed progress in some areas of public transportation modernization because of the extra time it takes to ensure the more stringent regulations are being followed and that environmental impact assessments are being conducted (*The Warsaw Voice* 2011b). These delays may cause some stress and congestion during the upsurge of visitors during events like the Euro Cup, but over the long term the stricter regulations will require city planners to develop cleaner and more sustainable ways for improving public transportation, which in turn will help the city to be a more environmentally friendly destination.

Transport and Air Quality

In 2009 Warsaw had 24 tram lines, 284 bus lines, 8,500 taxicabs, and 200 kilometers of bike trails (Wolff 2009). These figures will increase as infrastructure and public transportation projects are completed. Between 2007 and 2010, however, for every 1,000 Varsovians there were 555.6 registered cars congesting the city's streets and polluting its air (Eurostat 2012). The concentration of particulate matter (PM_{10}) that must not be exceeded in order to meet EU air quality standards is 50mg/m³ (50

microgram per cubic meter) with an allowance of 35 days of permitted exceedences per year (EC 2012). For the same time period as above, the number of days per year that PM_{10} concentrations exceeded 50mg/m³ was 30.6. Although this is within allowable limits, this number is expected only to increase as the economy grows despite all the access to public transportation. By comparison, Berlin, Germany, had 285.6 registered cars for every 1,000 inhabitants and during only 8.8 days of the year were particulate matter concentrations above 50mg/m³. Oslo, Norway, had 378.4 registered cars per 1,000 inhabitants and saw only 4 days out of the year where particulate matter exceeded 50mg/m³. Vilnius, Lithuania, had 437.5 registered vehicles for every 1,000 inhabitants but saw only 5 days out of the year where particulate matter was above 50mg/m³, and in Budapest, Hungary, there were 350.4 registered vehicles per 1,000 inhabitants with 39 days out of the year where particulate matter exceeded 50mg/m³ (Eurostat 2012). As in many other parts of Europe, walking, bike riding, and using public transport are popular ways of moving about in Warsaw, but traffic congestion and air pollution will likely remain a barrier to environmental sustainability in the city for many years to come.

Green Building

Green buildings can help metropolises like Warsaw become more environmentally friendly and even self-sustaining through their eco-conscious designs. In Warsaw, as in many other cities in Europe, developers constructing new ecofriendly buildings see them not only as energy efficient, but also as profitable.

The Green Corner building, to be completed by late 2012 at the intersection of Chłodna and Wronia streets, is seeking platinum Leadership in Energy Environmental Design (LEED) certification, which means, if achieved, the building will have met the highest standard for environmental friendliness by an internationally recognized system. An example of another green building in Warsaw is the Deloitte House, located by the ONZ traffic circle. The building, developed by Skanska Property Poland, received silver LEED certification and GreenBuilding certification by the European Commission. Deloitte House consumes 30 percent less electricity than other office buildings, maximizes the use of sunlight for energy efficiency, and uses carpet made from recycled materials (*The Warsaw Voice* 2011a). The Rondo 1 building, located near Deloitte House, is another building in Warsaw that is LEED certified. Rondo 1 reduced water consumption by 30 percent since becoming certified and now uses biodegradable cleaning agents. The building also produces 10 percent of its electricity from wind turbines.

Although the popularity of green buildings is increasing in Warsaw, it will be some time before these eco-friendly developments become the norm. Long-term social, political, and economic stability could help increase the number of green buildings constructed in Warsaw, but this stability is not guaranteed, which makes for a riskier investment environment for green developers seeking business there.

The Future

Although Warsaw is slowly becoming more environmentally conscious, there still remain many roadblocks to sustainability. The economy is expected to grow, which is an indicator of stability and increased environmental awareness, but this can also lead to larger consumption rates of resources, which can offset any progress toward environmental sustainability. The government is making efforts to improve the urban terrain so that sustainability can be achieved, but in the absence of long-term government commitments and a lack of alternative ways to obtain resources other than from outside the city, Warsaw may never be a self-sustaining, environmentally friendly city on which the rest of the world can model itself.

Scott M. ALBRIGHT
University of Hawaii at Hilo

See also European Union (EU); France; Germany; London, United Kingdom; Moscow, Russia; Rule of Law (European Union); Russia and the Soviet Union; St. Petersburg, Russia; Stockholm, Sweden; Ukraine; Urbanization (Europe)

FURTHER READING

European Commission (EC). (2012). Environment: Air quality. Retrieved March 10, 2012, from http://ec.europa.eu/environment/air/quality/standards.htm

Eurostat. (2012). Database: Urban audit: Key indicators for core cities. Last updated June 3, 2012. *European Commission*. Retrieved March 15, 2012, from http://epp.eurostat.ec.europa.eu/portal/page/portal/region_cities/city_urban/data_cities/database_sub1

MasterCard Worldwide. (2008). MasterCard Worldwide Centers of Commerce: Emerging markets index. Retrieved November 3, 2011, from http://www.mastercard.com/us/company/en/insights/pdfs/2008/MCWW_EMI-Report_2008.pdf

Project InPosterum. (n.d.). Warsaw Uprising 1944. Retrieved November 3, 2011 from http://www.warsawuprising.com

Scislowska, Monika, & Gera, Vanessa. (2012, March 5). Polish train crash puts spotlight on rail safety. Retrieved March 7, 2012, from http://hosted.ap.org/dynamic/stories/E/EU_POLAND_TRAINS_COLLIDE?SITE=AP&SECTION=HOME&TEMPLATE=DEFAULT

Statistical Office in Warsaw. (2011). Warsaw statistics. Retrieved March 11, 2012, from http://www.stat.gov.pl/cps/rde/xbcr/warsz/ASSETS_komunikat_ang_01_waw_2011.pdf

The Warsaw Voice. (2009, November 18). Catching up with rich nations. Retrieved November 3, 2011, from http://www.warsawvoice.pl/WVpage/pages/article.php/21297/article

The Warsaw Voice. (2011a, March 31). Rising demand for green offices. Retrieved November 3, 2011, from http://www.warsawvoice.pl/WVpage/pages/article.php/23332/article

The Warsaw Voice. (2011b, September 15). New environment-friendly laws to delay infrastructure projects. Retrieved March 7, 2012, from http://www.warsawvoice.pl/WVpage/pages/article.php/18024/news.

Union of European Football Associations (UEFA). (2011, March). UEFA Euro 2012 Poland-Ukraine ticket sales. Retrieved March 7, 2012, from http://www.uefa.com/MultimediaFiles/Download/EuroExperience/competitions/Publications/01/60/27/94/1602794_DOWNLOAD.pdf

Union of European Football Associations (UEFA). (2012, July). Fan zone figures dazzle. Retrieved July 30, 2012, from http://www.uefa.com/uefaeuro/news/newsid51839435.html.

United States Central Intelligence Agency (US CIA). (2012). The world factbook: Poland. Retrieved July 27, 2012, from https://www.cia.gov/library/publications/the-world-factbook/geos/pl.html

Warsaw City Council Press Department. (2012). Warsaw—The host city of UEFA EURO 2012. Preparations for the tournament. Retrieved July 30, 2012, from http://uefaeuro2012.um.warszawa.pl/sites/euro2012.um.warszawa.pl/files/newsletter_nr_11_eng.pdf

Wolff, Grzegorz. (2009, October 31). Warsaw by numbers. *Warsaw—The official website of the capital of Poland.* Retrieved November 3, 2011, from http://www.um.warszawa.pl/en/articles/warsaw-numbers/

Wolff, Grzegorz. (2010, August 11). Cranes on the Vistula River. *Warsaw—The official website of the capital of Poland.* Retrieved November 3, 2011, from http://www.um.warszawa.pl/en/articles/cranes-vistula-river

Water Use and Rights (Africa)

Water is a fundamental ingredient for poverty allevia-tion and sustainable socioeconomic development in Africa. Low availability and access to this life-sustaining resource have important implications for its develop-ment and use. As population growth, rapid urbaniza-tion, and industrialization lead to an even greater demand for water, unambiguous water rights will determine the course of future water development and use across the continent.

Africa is a continent of extremes in matters of water resources. It is one of the driest regions on Earth, but it also experiences large amounts of rainfall. The Congo (Zaire) River is one of the world's largest rivers by vol-ume, while the Nile is the world's longest. Abundant rainfall in Central Africa supports the Congo Basin for-ests, the second largest intact tropical rain forest block in the world; meanwhile, the Sahara in the north and the Kalahari and Namib in the south are among the world's largest deserts.

Africa's Freshwater Resources

In sub-Saharan Africa (SSA), rainfall patterns that determine freshwater abundance vary from one subre-gion to the other, and so does the occurrence of other freshwater sources such as rivers, lakes, streams, springs, and groundwater aquifers. To underscore these subre-gional differences, the Food and Agricultural Organization's (FAO) division of Africa into seven sub-regions is used here, with the concentration on the sub-regions that make up SSA. (See figure 1 on page 364.) Water statistics throughout this article, except where otherwise mentioned, are derived from FAO–

AQUASTAT Information Systems on Water and Agriculture Database. (See table 1 on page 365.)

Major freshwater basins in SSA include the Senegal and Volta river basins in the Gulf of Guinea; Lake Chad and the Niger River basin in the Sudano-Sahelian region; Lake Turkana and the River Nile basin in eastern Africa; the Ogooué and Congo river basins in central Africa; and the Zambezi and Orange river basins in southern Africa. These freshwater basins are predominantly transboundary. Indeed, two or more countries share more than fifty fresh-water water basins and numerous groundwater aquifers in Africa. Water allocation among competing uses and users in Africa therefore necessitates interstate cooperation.

Put together, SSA accounts for 9 percent of global internal renewable water resources, compared to 28.9 per-cent for Asia and 15.2 percent for Europe. With about 12 percent of the global population, SSA is therefore not water-poor by global standards.

This regional overview, however, masks important subregional disparities. For instance, central Africa is twelve times richer than the Sudano-Sahelian subregion in freshwater resources. (See table 1 on page 365.)

Conventional freshwater sources aside, some coun-tries, especially those in the southern, northern, and Sudano-Sahelian subregions, practice reuse of treated water and desalination of seawater, albeit to a very lim-ited extent.

Water Development and Use

Water is useful for domestic and municipal purposes: for industry, including hydropower generation, for agricul-ture, and for waste disposal. It plays an important role in transport, tourism, and cultural practices. Water is vital

Figure 1. Africa's Subregions

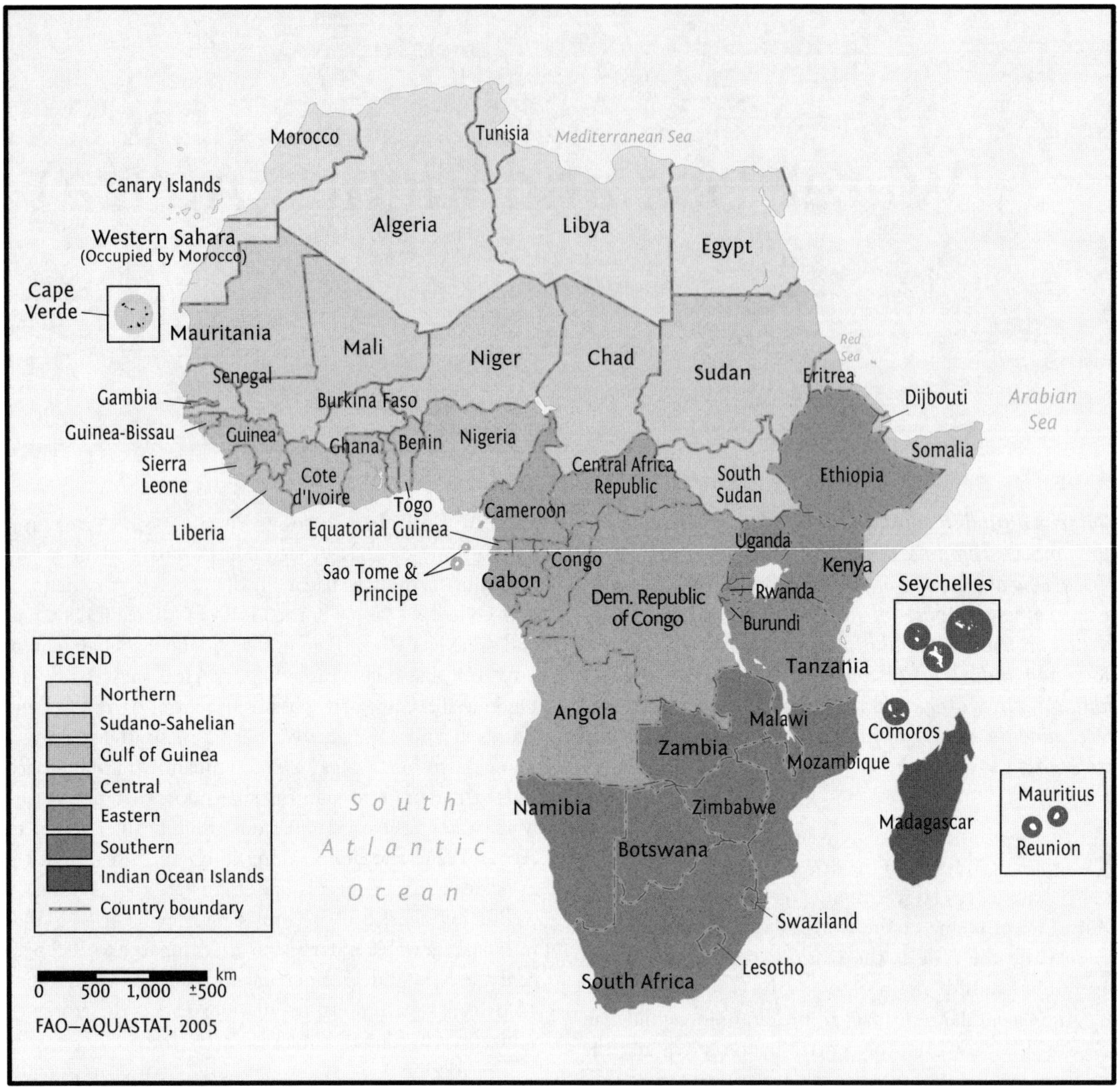

Source: Adapted from FAO–AQUASTAT (2005).

Note: Sudan and South Sudan were still one country (Sudan) in the original version of this map, from 2005. South Sudan became an independent country in July 2011.

The Food and Agricultural Organization divides Africa into seven subregions, which are shown here. The concentration in this article is on the sub-Saharan subregions.

for the survival of natural ecosystems such as forests, mangroves, and wetlands, on which many livelihoods in SSA are dependent. The higher the level of development of water resources, the more it will be available for consumption. Water development entails rainwater harvesting, diversion of river flows, and abstraction of other surface and groundwater for domestic, industrial, and agricultural purposes. Water development thus can take the form of dam and reservoir construction for hydropower generation and storage of water during high flow to ensure its availability in times of scarcity. Other common techniques for water development in SSA include

TABLE 1. Basic Water Data for Africa and Comparison with Europe, Asia, and the World

Continent/Region		Total Population (1,000 in habitants)	Total Area (1,000 ha)	Agricultural Sector Water Use (km³/year)	Municipal / Domestic Sector Water Use (km³/year)	Industrial Sector Water Use (km³/year)
Northern Africa		163,969	575,289	80	9	5
Sub-Saharan Africa	Subregions	817,158	2,429,279	105	13	4
	Sudano-Sahelian	127,193	859,221	52.4	2.1	0.4
	Gulf of Guinea	231,036	211,927	8.8	2.5	1.1
	Central Africa	111,587	532,868	1.1	0.7	0.2
	Eastern Africa	211,414	292,718	12.4	1.5	0.2
	Southern Africa	114,603	473,405	15.1	5.2	1.3
	Indian Ocean islands	21,325	59,140	14.8	0.6	0.3
Africa		981,127	3,004,568	184	21	9
Asia		4,081,022	3,241,673	2,012	217	227
Europe		732,396	2,300,711	109	61	204
World		6,741,605*	13,370,063	2,710	429	723

Source: Adapted and condensed from FAO–AQUASTAT (2010).

*Note: The world's population surpassed 7 billion in 2012.

the construction of wells, ponds, and irrigation channels and the use of wetlands and plains during flood recession.

A high level of water development contributes to positive socioeconomic development. It guarantees water availability for irrigation, for example, ensuring food security. The low level of water development in SSA nevertheless has resulted in limited availability and use, as reflected in the poor performance of key economic sectors such as agriculture and energy. According to the FAO, only 3.2 percent of all land under cultivation in SSA is irrigated, compared to 39 percent in Asia and 7.7 percent for Europe. It should be stressed here that 59 percent of the population of SSA is employed in agriculture, a value that exceeds other major regions such as Europe and Asia.

Surface irrigation is the most widespread irrigation technique used in SSA, although sprinkler techniques are also common. The International Hydropower Association notes that while Europe has developed 75 percent of its hydropower potential and Asia 22 percent, Africa has developed only 7 percent of its vast hydropower potential. According to the World Commission on Dams, Europe and Asia have about the same storage capacity, while that of SSA is less than

half that value. SSA is storing only 11 percent of its total actual renewable freshwater resources. Donor funding for large dams declined in the post-1980s because of observed socioecological impacts, which include changes in water and food security as well as disruption from construction and involuntary resettlement (WHO 2012). Smaller dams, irrigation programs, and reservoirs, mainly funded by private capital, are commonplace today. Within SSA, subregions with the least shares of freshwater resources have developed their water resources the most. Southern Africa, with 38.4 percent of continental dam capacity, is home to over 50 percent of all dams in Africa. Conversely, central Africa, the most water-rich subregion, has only 0.6 percent of Africa's dam capacity. The eastern Africa statistics underscore the importance of water development, especially storage as a coping strategy. With only 7 percent of Africa's freshwater resources and 3.4 percent of storage capacity, this subregion is prone to droughts and food crises, such as the one experienced in 2011.

By global standards, SSA accounts for the lowest per capita water use for domestic and municipal purposes. This can be traced back to the fact that more than 60 percent of Africans still live in rural areas that grossly lack access to safe drinking water and basic sanitation. In fact, the Joint Monitoring Program of the World Health Organization (WHO) and the United Nations Children's Fund (UNICEF) asserts that 330 million people in Africa lack access to safe drinking water, and 565 million people lack access to basic sanitation. Social effects of this poor water development include malnutrition due to food insecurity and high morbidity and mortality due to waterborne diseases like diarrhea and cholera. In addition to these, lack of access to basic sanitation leads to pollution, while limited access to water sources exacerbates competition, unsustainable use patterns, and conflicts. According to the Intergovernmental Panel on Climate Change (IPCC), these socioeconomic factors will be amplified by the impacts of climate change on the quantity and quality of freshwater resources in Africa.

It is clear that water development is a prerequisite for different water uses, which in turn contribute to socioeconomic development. The questions of who uses how much water, from which source, when, and for what purpose depend on allocation of water to different users and for different purposes. Allocation of water is therefore at the core of any water rights regime because it sets priorities for water use and rights.

Role and Sources of Water Rights

In Africa, water rights take the form of formal or informal entitlements to use water from a freshwater source. When clearly defined, water rights reduce water degradation by encouraging the protection of water resources and development of water infrastructure like reservoirs, wells, or irrigation programs. Furthermore, guaranteed access to freshwater for the whole society through water rights helps to reduce conflicts and to resolve them when they occur. Water law; be it statutory, customary, or other, usually establishes water rights.

Water law in SSA has been heavily influenced by European concepts and principles as well as Islamic law,

such that today the sources of water law that establish rights, procedures to acquire these rights, and dispute resolution mechanisms include international agreements, national constitutions, statutes, regulations, orders, other administrative sources, and customary law. All co-exist, interact in space and time, and influence each other in a mix best described as legal pluralism.

Historically, a body of unwritten but common knowledge rules and practices generally recognized as binding on members of an indigenous group emerged in different parts of the continent. Whereas these customary water laws are not uniform, they reflect the context in which they evolved— for example, water scarcity or abundance, farming practices as opposed to pastoralist modes of life, and tenure systems. Notwithstanding variations within different groups, a number of similarities stand out. Water rights are intricately linked with land rights insofar as water is found on land. Land is the common property of the family, tribe, or village and is held in trust by the head of the family or tribal (village) chief. Water rights are thus acquired by owning a piece of land that borders a water body or by belonging to a village or other community through which a river or stream flows (Ramazzotti 1996). Abstraction of water from small water sources (e.g., springs, streams) on family land requires the head of the family's permission. In contrast, all members of the village, tribe, or clan are granted access to larger freshwater sources such as rivers. A point for collecting water for drinking and household needs is defined and is usually upstream from the point for bathing and for watering livestock.

In the past decades, African states have undertaken several reforms in the water sector. These reforms have mostly entailed formalizing water law and formulating explicit water rights by means of constitutional changes, legislative acts, and administrative decisions. Key among these has been to situate water within the public domain, which is evident in water legislation in African countries. The state thus holds public rights that legitimize allocation of water and serve as the basis for regulation and control of water uses and users and for adjudication in times of dispute. Ghana's Water Resources Commission Act of 1996, for instance, states that water resources are vested in the president of the state on behalf of and in trust for the people. In Uganda's Water Resources Act of 1995, water resources are placed under the superior use right of the state.

In some countries, water rights are part of basic rights as expressed in the national constitutions. The 1996 Constitution of the Republic of South Africa explicitly recognizes the fundamental right of access to sufficient food and water. Thirty-seven countries in SSA presently have a water code or act, while others such as Sudan and Gabon deal with water-related issues as part of environmental and natural resources legislation. In others, such as the Democratic Republic of the Congo and Swaziland, water rights and related issues can be found in regulations. Sierra Leone, Somalia, and a few others lack specific water laws but have administrative water management bodies in place.

Overall, government agencies are responsible for the implementation and administration of statutory and administrative water rights in African countries. For instance, Cameroon's Water Code of 1998 established the National Water Committee as an institution within the Ministry of Water Resources.

The predominantly transboundary nature of its freshwater basins complicates water law in Africa. In this regard, countries are adopting the 1992 Dublin Principles and Integrated Water Resources Management as the standard for managing freshwater basins across the continent. Moreover, other international norms enshrined in global treaties such as the 1997 United Nations Convention on the Law of the Non-navigable Uses of International Watercourses are being applied in sharing Africa's transboundary rivers. A good example of this is the adoption of the principle of *equitable and reasonable use* in the River Nile Co-operative Framework Agreement of 2010, which is an attempt to replace the colonial Nile Water Agreements of 1929 and 1959. The latter agreements provide for water allocations only to Egypt and Sudan and give Egypt veto power on water development projects upstream.

Water Rights Types and Features

The types of water rights are as diverse as the water laws that establish them. Customary water law in Africa generates communal water rights, while statutory water law generates public and private water rights.

Water is treated in African customary law as common property of the clan, village, or community. Local norms and traditions thus legitimize ensuing communal water rights. Customary water law thus equally establishes decision-making processes for access rights, in this case communal water rights and obligations. Communal water rights establish clear rules on local water use for household, irrigation, livestock, and other needs. These rights are not static; rather, they are adaptable to times of water scarcity and other local socioeconomic realities. Communal water rights do not specify what quantity of water each individual is entitled to have. Instead, members of the community collect as much water as needed while ensuring there is sufficient water left for everyone else. Right holders may not exclude other rightful users from the resource, and everyone has the responsibility of protecting and maintaining it. Users may contribute in labor or money. The family head or the clan or village council or chief, as the case may, resolves disputes. Rule violations are punished by fines payable to a local authority, such as a chief. Communal rights are transferred through lineage from one generation to another.

The second type of water rights observed across Africa is the public water right. Such rights emanate from the nature of water as a public good in water legislation of most African countries. Public water rights are held by the state in trust for its citizens. An important feature of public water rights lies in their disentanglement from land rights. Noteworthy is the fact that in most African countries, everyone has a right to access water for basic household needs. For example, a primary goal of Uganda's Water Statute is to promote the provision of a clean, safe, and sufficient supply of water for domestic purposes to everyone; Nigeria's 1993 Water Resources Decree declares that all may take water without charge for domestic purposes or for watering stock from any water source to which the public has free access. The definition of what constitutes basic needs varies from country to country. Section 2 of Uganda's Water Statute, for example, defines domestic use as water for basic human consumption; watering up to thirty livestock units (amounting to forty-three cattle or fifty horses or seventy-five donkeys or two hundred goats or two hundred sheep or a mixture of these); for subsistence agriculture; and for watering subsistence fishponds.

Third, African governments are increasingly issuing private water rights to individuals, through designated water authorities, for purposes other than personal and household needs. These rights are required for water used for commercial purposes and large-scale irrigation strategies and for discharging wastewater into freshwater bodies, as exemplified in the water codes of Cameroon, Nigeria, and South Africa. Individuals or corporations can hold private water rights and obtain them from the state by acquiring a license, permit, lease, concession, permission, authorization, or other title at a fee and for a fixed number of years. Private rights are not land based, but specify the volume of water associated with the entitlement, the purpose of use, and conditions associated with the right. In the case of discharge of wastewater, for instance, the right specifies the point at which the wastewater may be released. Such rights are use or usufructuary rights rather than ownership rights. Based on the conditions to which private rights are subject, they can be sold, leased, or transferred to other users. In this sense, these rights are a form of property rights.

Private rights are arguably more secure when their duration of validity is long. This outlook, alongside economic thinking that profit improves efficiency, led to the privatization of water utilities in much of Africa in the 1990s. A serious challenge in Africa therefore is to reconcile water as both an economic and public good. Failure to do this will jeopardize efforts geared at meeting the United Nations' Millennium Development Goals target of halving the number of people without sustainable access to safe drinking water and basic sanitation by 2015. African states' failure to guarantee access to water for basic human needs violates international norms such as the 1996 International Covenant on Economic, Social and Cultural Rights (ICESCR), which recognizes the right to an adequate standard of living including food and physical health. These norms imply a human right to water, as the 2002 General Comment number 15 of the United Nations Committee on Economic, Social and Cultural Rights demonstrates.

Trends, Future Perspectives, and Challenges

The total annual water use in Africa is on the increase. Although agriculture still takes up the largest share, increases in population and rapid urbanization are also contributing factors. The United Nations Economic Commission for Africa estimates that some eighteen African countries will experience water stress by 2025. To meet the water demands for food security and human needs, hydropower generation, and industry, the African Water Vision estimates an increase in water development by 25 percent by the year 2025. Unconventional methods such as interbasin water transfers, already seen today in the southern region, could become commonplace.

Formalization and introduction of private rights notwithstanding, water use in Africa remains principally a matter regulated by customary law. Africa still has a large rural population, and access rights in rural settings are based on customary practices. Procedures for the acquisition of formal water rights are cumbersome and costly, such that only corporations and individuals who can command the necessary resources can obtain such water rights. The legal status of customary water law in African statutory water law therefore is not always clear. In practice, formal water rights can be defended in court and hence can override communal rights should a conflict between the two arise. Reconciling customary law with statutory law remains a central challenge in ensuring water rights of local communities.

J. Manyitabot TAKANG
University of Cologne

See also Africa (*several regions*); African Union (AU); Agriculture, Small-Scale; Congo (Zaire) River; Desertification (Africa); Disaster Risk Management; International Conflict Resolution; Lake Chad; Nile River; Rule of Law (Africa); Sahara; Sahel; Transboundary Water Issues; Water Use and Rights (Middle East and North Africa)

FURTHER READING

Burchi, Stefano. (2005). The interface between customary and statutory water rights: A statutory perspective (Food and Agriculture Organization Legal Papers Online No. 45). Retrieved May 25, 2012, from http://www.fao.org/legal/prs-ol/lpo45.pdf

Center for Research on the Epidemiology of Disasters (CRED). (2009). EM-DAT: The OFDA/CRED international disaster database. Université Catholique de Louvain-Brussels-Belgium. Retrieved November 3, 2011, from http://www.emdat.be/database

Food and Agriculture Organization of the United Nations (FAO). (2003). Review of world water resources by country (FAO water reports 23). Retrieved August 26, 2011, from ftp://ftp.fao.org/agl/aglw/docs/wr23e.pdf

Food and Agriculture Organization of the United Nations (FAO). (2004). FAOLEX legislative database. Retrieved November 3, 2011, from http://faolex.fao.org/faolex/

Food and Agriculture Organization of the United Nations (FAO) AQUASTAT. (2005). Irrigation in Africa in figures: AQUASTAT Survey 2005. Retrieved May 31, 2012, from http://www.fao.org/nr/water/aquastat/countries_regions/africa/figurescontinent.pdf#fig6

Food and Agriculture Organization of the United Nations (FAO) AQUASTAT. (2010). Population, areas, gross domestic product (GDP) (2008). Retrieved May 31, 2012, from http://www.fao.org/nr/water/aquastat/dbase/AquastatWorldDataEng_20101129.pdf

Food and Agriculture Organization of the United Nations (FAO) AQUASTAT. (2011). AQUASTAT: FAO's information system on water and agriculture. Retrieved November 3, 2011, from http://www.fao.org/nr/water/aquastat/main/index.stm

Frenken, Karen. (Ed.). (2005). Irrigation in Africa in figures: AQUASTAT survey—2005. (FAO water reports 29). Food and Agriculture Organization of the United Nations (FAO). Retrieved July 28, 2011, from ftp://ftp.fao.org/agl/aglw/docs/wr29_eng.pdf

Global Water Partnership. (n.d). Retrieved May 25, 2012, from http://www.gwptoolbox.org/index.php?option=com_content&view=article&id=8&Itemid=3

Hodgson, Stephen. (2006). Modern water rights: Theory and practice; FAO Legislative Study 92. Rome: Food and Agricultural Organization of the United Nations. Retrieved May 20, 2012, from ftp://ftp.fao.org/docrep/fao/010/a0864e/a0864e00.pdf

International Hydropower Association (IHA). (2003). The role of hydropower in sustainable development (IHA white paper). Retrieved July 30, 2011, from http://www.carbosur.com.uy/archivos/Hydropower%20in%20sustainable%20world,%20IHA%20white%20paper,%202003.pdf

International Water Law Project. (2010). Agreement on the Nile River Basin cooperative framework. Retrieved May 25, 2012, from http://www.internationalwaterlaw.org/documents/regionaldocs/Nile_River_Basin_Cooperative_Framework_2010.pdf

Kundzewicz, Zbigniew W., et al. (2007). Freshwater resources and their management. Climate Change 2007: Impacts, Adaptation and Vulnerability In. M. L. Parry, O. F. Canziani, J. P. Palutikof, P. J. van der Linden & C. E. Hanson (Eds.), Contribution of Working Group II to the Fourth Assessment Report of the Intergovernmental Panel on Climate Change (pp. 173–210). Cambridge, UK: Cambridge University Press.

Meinzen-Dick, Ruth, & Nkonya, Leticia. (2005, January 26–28). Understanding legal pluralism in water rights: Lessons from Africa and Asia (Paper presented at the international workshop "African water laws: Plural legislative frameworks for rural water management in Africa"). Johannesburg, South Africa. Retrieved March 20, 2012, from http://www.nri.org/projects/waterlaw/AWLworkshop/MEINZEN-DICK-R.pdf

Mensah, Kwadwo. (1999). Water law, water rights and water supply (Africa). Ghana: Study country report (DFID KaR Project R7327). Cranfield University Silsoe, UK Department for International Development (DFID). Retrieved May 20, 2012, from http://allafrica.com/download/resource/main/main/idatcs/00010041:6ab9fe24570074a47d2595d7b8d0be3a.pdf

National Environmental Authority (NEMA–Uganda). (1995). Uganda Water Act. Retrieved May 25, 2012, from http://www.nemaug.org/regulations/water_act.pdf

The Nile Basin Initiative. (n.d.) Homepage. Retrieved May 25, 2012, from http://www.nilebasin.org/newsite/

Obitre-Gama, Judy. (1999). Water law, water rights and water supply (Africa). Uganda: Study country report. (DFID KaR Project

R7327). Cranfield University Silsoe, UK Department for International Development (DFID). Retrieved July 20, 2011, from http://www.dfid.gov.uk/r4d/PDF/Outputs/R73275.pdf

Pachauri, Rajendra K.; Reisinger, Andy; & Synthesis Report core writing team. (Eds.). (2007). Climate change 2007: Synthesis report. Contribution of Working Groups I, II and III to the Fourth Assessment Report of the Intergovernmental Panel on Climate Change (IPCC). Geneva: Intergovernmental Panel on Climate Change (IPCC).

Pradham, Rajendra, & Meinzen-Dick, Ruth. (2010). Which rights are right? Water rights, culture, and underlying values. In Peter G. Brown & Jeremy J. Schmidt (Eds.), Water ethics: Foundational readings for students and professionals. Washington, DC; Covelo, CA; London: Island Press.

Ramazzotti, Marco. (1996). Readings in African customary water law. (FAO Legislative Study 58). Rome: Food and Agriculture Organization of the United Nations (FAO).

Ramazzotti, Marco. (2008). Customary water rights and contemporary water legislation: Mapping out the interface (FAO legal papers online, No 76). Retrieved May 25, 2012, from http://www.fao.org/legal/prs-ol/lpo76.pdf

Republic of Ghana. (1996). Water Resources Commission Act (Act 522). Retrieved May 25, 2012, from http://www.epa.gov.gh/ghanalex/acts/Acts/WATER%20RESOURCE%20COMMISSION%20ACT1996.pdf

Republic of South Africa. (1996). Constitution of the Republic of South Africa, 1996. Retrieved May 22, 2012, from http://www.info.gov.za/documents/constitution/1996/index.htm

Republic of South Africa. (1998). National Water Act. (Act No 36 of 1998). Retrieved May 22, 2012, from http://www.dwaf.gov.za/IO/Docs/nwa.pdf

Scanlon, John; Cassar, Angela; & Nemes, Noémi. (2004). Water as a human right? Gland, Switzerland, & Cambridge, UK: IUCN.

Scott, Anthony, & Coustalin, Georgina. (1995). The evolution of water rights. Natural Resources Journal, 35(4), 821–979. Retrieved July 28, 2011, from http://lawlibrary.unm.edu/nrj/35/4/05_scott_evolution.pdf

Shiklomanov, Igor A. (2000). Appraisal and assessment of world water resources. Water International, 25(1), 11–32.

Smets, Henry. (2000). The right to water as a human right. Environmental Policy and Law, 30(5), 249.

United Nations Committee on Economic, Social and Cultural Rights (CESCR). (2002). General comment No. 15 on the International Covenant on Economic, Social and Cultural Rights (on the Right to Water). Retrieved April 20, 2012, from http://www.unhchr.ch/tbs/doc.nsf/0/a5458d1d1bbd713fc1256cc400389e94/$FILE/G0340229.pdf

United Nations Development Programme (UNDP). (2006). Human development report 2006: Beyond scarcity: Power, poverty and the global water crisis. New York: Palgrave Macmillan for UNDP.

United Nations Economic Commission for Africa (UNECA). (n.d.). The Africa water vision for 2025: Equitable and sustainable use of water for socioeconomic development. Retrieved August 5, 2011, from http://www.uneca.org/awich/african%20water%20vision%202025.pdf

United Nations Economic Commission for Africa (UNECA). (2000). Transboundary river/lake basin water development in Africa: Prospects, problems, and achievements. Retrieved July 22, 2011, from http://www.uneca.org/awich/Reports/Transboundary_v2.pdf

United Nations Educational, Scientific, and Cultural Organization (UNESCO). (2003). The United Nations world water development report: Water for people, water for life. Paris: UNESCO.

United Nations Educational, Scientific, and Cultural Organization–World Water Assessment Programme (UNESCO-WWAP). (2006). The United Nations World Water Development report 2: Water a shared responsibility. Paris: UNESCO.

United Nations Environment Programme (UNEP). (2000). Global environment outlook 2000 (GEO-2000). Retrieved August 5, 2011, from http://www.unep.org/GEO2000/index.htm

UN-Water/Africa. (2003). African water journal: Pilot edition. *United Nations Economic Commission for Africa*. Retrieved July 24, 2011, from http://www.uneca.org/sdd/African_Water_Journal_rev.pdf

White, W. R. (2010). World water: Resources, usage and the role of man-made reservoirs. *Foundation for Water Research*. Retrieved August 2, 2011, from http://www.fwr.org/wwtrstrg.pdf

World Commission on Dams (WCD). (2000). Dams and development: A new framework for decision-making. (The report of the World Commission on Dams). London; Sterling, VA: Earthscan. Retrieved August 26, 2011, from http://www.internationalrivers.org/files/world_commission_on_dams_final_report.pdf

World Health Organization (WHO). (2012). Health and social impacts of dams. Retrieved June 29, 2012, from http://www.who.int/hia/examples/energy/whohia020/en/index.html

World Health Organization (WHO), & United Nations Children's Fund (UNICEF). (2010). Progress on sanitation and drinking water: 2010 update. WHO/UNICEF Joint Monitoring Programme for Water Supply and Sanitation (JMP). Retrieved August 3, 2011, from http://whqlibdoc.who.int/publications/2010/9789241563956_eng_full_text.pdf

World Health Organization (WHO), & UN-Water. (2010). UN-Water global annual assessment of sanitation and drinking-water (GLAAS) 2010: Targeting resources for better results. WHO/UNICEF Joint Monitoring Programme for Water Supply and Sanitation (JMP). Retrieved August 8, 2011, from http://www.who.int/water_sanitation_health/publications/UN-Water_GLAAS_2010_Report.pdf

World Wide Fund for Nature (WWF). (2007). Allocating scarce water: A WWF primer on water allocation, water rights and water markets. Gland, Switzerland: WWF.

Water Use and Rights (Middle East and North Africa)

The Middle East and North Africa region, the most water-scarce populated region in the world, faces critical challenges for providing water to its ever-increasing population and protecting its agricultural economy, which demands colossal amounts of water for irrigation. The political turbulence in the region threatens efforts to build cooperation between the region's countries. Water-demand management is the only solution to the enormous water challenges the Middle East region faces, but implementation is uncertain.

People generally take for granted that when they turn on the tap, water will flow. This is not the case in the Middle East, the world's most water-scarce populated region. Almost all people living in this region have experienced hours or days when, because of problems with water-supply systems or prolonged drought periods, the taps run dry. A schedule specifying how much water the city will supply during the daytime is common in many Middle Eastern cities. The Arab world unrest in 2011 (known as the Arab Spring, a revolutionary wave of demonstrations and protests) emphasized the importance of water in this region. The Maplecroft Waterstress Index in 2011 calculated the ratio of domestic, industrial, and agricultural water consumption against renewable water supplies from precipitation, rivers, and groundwater; the index rated seventeen countries as being at "extreme risk," with the highest rated being the Middle East and North Africa (MENA) nations of Bahrain, Qatar, Kuwait, Saudi Arabia, Libya, the disputed territory of Western Sahara, Yemen, Israel, Djibouti, and Jordan (Maplecroft 2011). Water as a resource has determined the development and human settlement patterns in the Middle East since ancient times. The great civilizations of Mesopotamia flourished because their geographical location benefited from the Tigris and the Euphrates,

two of the main rivers in the Middle East. The pharaonic dynasties could develop only by using the Nile River. The Middle East has five main water bodies: the Euphrates-Tigris basin, the Jordan River basin, the Arabian Peninsula basin, the Nubian Sandstone aquifer, and the Nile basin.

Water in the Middle East always has been a scarce resource. Consequently, the development and management of water have assumed strategic and political importance. Per capita availability is the lowest, and rates of withdrawal the highest; the region already has installed more water storage than any other world region. Pathways out of poverty for millions, however, will rely on access to and use of water. Reducing poverty will increase water use (Jägerskog et al. 2009).

The challenges of water resource management in the Middle East are manifold, but the main challenge is to provide enough water for an increasingly growing population. The question is if the Middle East water resources can provide enough water to safeguard the region's food security. According to the British geographer Tony Allan, the Middle East has been running out of water since the 1970s (Allan 2002). Food imports, specifically staple foods like wheat, are an important indicator of the rising water deficit in the Middle East. The water needed to grow imported wheat is called "virtual water," and by diversifying the regional economies, Allan suggests the region can reduce water stress and use existing water resources more efficiently. Most countries in the Middle East region, however, are agricultural economies, and a macroeconomic change at that scale will not happen without resistance. Wealthier countries like Saudi Arabia, Qatar, and Israel can afford expensive desalination plants, which introduce new water to the system and help meet the demands. Using fossil fuel to desalinize water (remove salt and other minerals) is not a long-term, sustainable solution, however. The region therefore needs other more sustainable solutions like rainwater harvesting and wastewater reuse alongside highly technical water-use efficiency methods.

Water Resources of the Middle East

The Middle East region is the world's most water-scarce region (World Bank 2009). The World Bank states that the average global water availability per person is close to 7,000 cubic meters per person per year (m³/person/year); the Middle East region, however, has only about 1,200 m³/person/year, and the population is expected to grow from about 300 million in 2012 to about 500 million in 2025. Per capita availability is expected to halve by 2050 (World Bank 2009). The Middle East has 6.3 percent of the world's population and contains only 1.4 percent of the world's renewable freshwater. The agricultural sector in the MENA region needs more than 70 percent of its water resources for irrigation (Allan 2002; World Bank 2009; Wessels 2009). Water-demand management is essential to the enormous water challenges the Middle East region faces; this solution requires decreasing the amount of water used in agriculture and irrigation requirements.

The region's water resources include river systems, groundwater basins, and seawater bodies. Most of the rivers have experienced a reduction or change in flow, and industrial and agricultural pollution severely affects some, like the Jordan River and the Nile River basin. Most groundwater basins are depleted, and the high investment costs of desalination prevent the large-scale introduction of new water into the system to reduce pressure from the demand. Other solutions like wastewater reuse and rainwater harvesting, as well as rehabilitation of sustainable and traditional water systems, are implemented but have had only a marginal effect so far.

The Middle East water resources are overstretched and depleted, and this situation poses a great risk for the region's security. According to AQUASTAT data, the nation of Bahrain uses "only" 220 percent of its available renewable water reserves, compared to 943 percent in Saudi Arabia and a remarkable 2,465 percent in Kuwait (AQUASTAT 2012). Some sources show slightly different percentages. (See table 1 at right.)

Looking at the ratio of water used as a percentage of renewable resources and the available renewable resources per capita per day, Carboun data vary from the AQUASTAT data; in both datasets, however, a clear discrepancy exists between those countries relying mainly on fossil water and desalination versus those who are using renewable sources. Data from Carboun (2012), an initiative that advocates for sustainable cities in the Middle East, show that countries like Saudi Arabia, the

TABLE 1. Water Use Per Capita in the Middle East and North Africa

	Water Use Per Capita As Percentage of Renewable Resources (%)
Major oil-exporting countries	
Oman	181%
Bahrain	270%
Saudi Arabia	951%
Libya	798%
Qatar	624%
United Arab Emirates	1,600%
Resource-poor countries	
Iraq	80%
Syria	55%
Lebanon	33%
Morocco	43%
Egypt	127%
Tunisia	54%
Algeria	39%
Yemen	124%
Jordan	151%
Palestine	93%

Source: Carboun (2012).

Note: some sources show slightly different percentages.

United Arab Emirates, and Libya rely heavily on fossil water or new water. ("Fossil water" refers to groundwater that has remained in an aquifer for a long time; it is also known as *paleowater*. "New water" refers to freshwater "created" from the desalination process.) In the countries of the Arabian Peninsula, desalination introduces the new water. Desalination gives relief in the short term, as well as providing possibilities for both economic and population growth; the use of fossil fuels to desalinize water, however, is not a sustainable method of using water resources. Supplying large amounts of fossil water or desalinated water gives a false sense of environmental sustainability and water security. Libya has, since the development of the Great Man-Made River project, experienced a dramatic increase in water resources supply. The Great Man-Made River is a large network of pipes that supplies fossil water from the Nubian Sandstone Aquifer System to populated areas in the coastal zones. The network comprises 2,820 kilometers of underground pipelines and aqueducts, and supplies 6.5 million cubic meters of freshwater per day. It is the world's largest irrigation project.

The lack of renewal for both types of water resources will have environmental consequences in the long term. At some point in the future, the fossil water or desalinized water will run out, just as the fossil fuels that power modern economies will run out. By then, however, the populations of the Middle East will have grown considerably, and the social and economic impact will be on a wide scale.

Water Uses, Economy, and Limitations

Water is used for drinking, domestic activities, industry, and agriculture. Agricultural use, such as irrigation, constitutes the main demand in the water sector. Because of the demands the largely agriculturally based economies place on the region, social change, to diversify the economy, is a slow process. At the same time, the region's farmers struggle to make a sustainable and viable livelihood from agriculture. Since the mid-twentieth century, industrialization and population growth have led to a rapid urbanization that strongly affects socioeconomic structures in the rural areas. The overall revenue of agriculture at the household level decreased, while the demand rose because of a rapid population growth.

The increasing demand because of population growth has caused overexploitation of groundwater resources and diminishing surface water availability. The region's overexploitation of groundwater has been considerable. Examples are the Great Man-Made River project in Libya mentioned earlier, the exploitation of fossil aquifers in Saudi Arabia and Jordan (Disi Aquifer), and the uncontrolled individual pumping for irrigated agriculture throughout the region that caused a rapid decline of the groundwater levels. Notably, the Sana'a Basin in Yemen has known a steady decline of the groundwater levels of about one to two meters annually. Because it is a closed basin, this decline will take decades to replenish. In the meantime, urbanization, population growth, and the use of water for local qat (a shrub whose buds and leaves are chewed or brewed as tea to produce a stimulant effect) production have been increasing.

The efficiency of irrigated agriculture always has been a major factor in the economies since ancient times. One example of arguably the most sustainable way to bring water to the desert is the invention of underground water tunnels called *qanats* in the Achaemenid (Persian) Empire some 3,000 years ago. Qanats bring water to the surface using only gravity. Some of these systems are still functional, and rehabilitation work is under way in countries like Oman, Morocco, Algeria, Syria, Iraq, and Iran. These countries find the rehabilitation of these ancient but still sustainable systems beneficial from both a technical and a social point of view. The continuous practice of qanats systems in ancient times suggests that the system was ecologically "balanced" because of a highly centralized, bureaucratic society devoted to a policy of water control and the development of irrigated agriculture. A considerable number of officials ran qanats in ancient Persia. During the Achaemenid Empire, carefully planned and managed systems of administration, land and water distribution, tax collection, communication, and post backed the Persian expansion of their empire and established a wide network of qanat settlements. Government offices were in charge of construction, digging, and maintenance of qanats (Wessels 2012).

One of the solutions to the Middle East water crisis lies in the rehabilitation of traditional water systems like qanats. Between 2009 and 2011, the United Nations Educational, Scientific and Cultural Organization (UNESCO) started a major qanat rehabilitation project in North Iraq, where qanats are called *karez*. UNESCO found that the drought of 2005–2009 and lack of karez upkeep had caused 70 percent of karez to dry up and contributed to the displacement of an estimated 100,000 people in the region (Walther 2011). In 2009, the UNESCO Iraq Office started to rehabilitate qanats in cooperation with the Ministry of Irrigation and Water Resources. One of the pilot sites was the village of Sheikh Mamudian, north of the town of Shaqlawa. A team of US, Dutch, and Iranian experts documented the area and the ultimate execution of the rehabilitation works (Walther 2011).

Regional Dynamics, Religion, and Culture

December of 2010 marked the beginning of the Arab Spring, a major social upheaval in the Arab world that started with a fruit seller setting himself ablaze in the south of Tunisia. The Egyptian revolution followed, as well as the downfall of the regime of Muammar Muhammad al-Gadhafi in Libya. Syria and other Arab countries, such as Yemen, also have known serious social upheaval. As of September of 2012, Syria has descended into a civil war in all but name. The revolution in Syria reflects also the diversity of peoples of the Middle East. This diverse region has many different ethnic, religious, and cultural groups. The majority of ethnic groups are Arabs, and then Druze, Kurds, Jews, Berbers, Africans, and other major ethnic groups. Arabs are peoples originally from the Arabian Peninsula, from Bedouin tribes who spread throughout the region during the advent of Islam. Not all Arabs are Muslims, however; they fall into different religious subgroups including Islam, Christianity, Druze, and Judaism. In addition to religious Arabs, a large part of the younger generation is nonreligious and secular. The national boundaries of the current states in the Middle East are mainly the result of the Western colonial activity, which peaked after the fall of the Ottoman Empire at the beginning of the twentieth century. Italy, France, and Britain governed the area and determined the borders between states or mandate areas. The Western colonialization of the Middle East effectively ended in 1956 after the second Arab-Israeli War. These regional dynamics influence hydropolitical relations that exist between the people and countries in the Middle East. Specifically, water rights are a contentious issue between various groups and countries.

Rights, Transboundary Management, Security, and Peace

A clear distinction exists between water rights and patterns of water use. Water utilization reflects facts on the ground, while water rights are agreed-upon principles to which people in the region must adhere. The 1997 United Nations (UN) convention on the Law of Non-navigational Uses of International Watercourses and the 2002 International Covenant on Economic, Social and Cultural Rights (ICESCR) give general principles to water legislation in the Middle East. The main principle from the ICESCR is the entitlement of every human being to access to safe and clean drinking water, which is a basic human right.

According to the 1997 UN Watercourse Convention, a watercourse is a "system of surface waters and groundwaters constituting by virtue of their physical relationship a unitary whole and normally flowing into a common terminus" and an international watercourse is a "watercourse, parts of which are situated in a different state" (Green Cross International 2000; Loures, Rieu-Clarke, and Vercambre 2010).

Only Iraq, Jordan, Lebanon, Libya, Qatar, Syria, and Tunisia officially ratified the convention, however (Loures, Rieu-Clarke, and Vercambre 2010). The two main principles between co-riparian states (those co-located on banks of watercourses) follow the Helsinki rules on the Uses of the Waters of International Rivers dating from 1966: (1) reasonable and equitable sharing of water resources and (2) no harm principle to avoid unnecessary waste in the use of the water of the basin (Phillips et al. 2005; Scheumann and Schiffler 1998). A certain legal pluralism concerning water rights exists throughout the region. On the one hand, these states have implemented the principles of the Helsinki rules and the UN Watercourses Convention, as well as

governmental water management plans and policies; on the other hand, they follow informal legal systems and traditional water rights in parallel with the formal, institutionalized systems. One of the main challenges for groundwater protection and conservation is keeping individual farmers from uncontrolled pumping for irrigation. All states have legislation to curb illegal well drilling, but they find the implementation and control on the ground difficult to verify. A specific situation occurs in the Occupied Palestinian Territories (OPT), where the stalled peace negotiations between the Israelis and the Palestinians resulted in an interim situation of water agreements that are to be finalized in the last stage of the peace negotiations between the two parties. The vacuum created after the Oslo Peace Agreements in 1994 has resulted in an asymmetrical power relationship between the occupying power (Israel) and the occupied territories (Palestine) (Allan 2002; Selby 2005; Zeitoun 2008).

River basin management and transboundary water management in the Middle East is a challenge for all major river riparians. With an average discharge of 300 million cubic meters a day, the Nile is shared by eleven countries (Egypt, South Sudan, Sudan, Eritrea, Ethiopia, Uganda, the Democratic Republic of the Congo, Rwanda, Kenya, Tanzania, and Burundi). (See figure 1 on page 375.) The major dams along the Nile River are Roseires Dam, Sennar Dam, Aswan High Dam, and Owen Falls Dam (Scheumann and Schiffler 1998). The former Egyptian president Anwar Sadat said, "The only matter that could take Egypt to war again is water." The Nile basin countries had aimed to have a full Cooperative Framework Agreement by the late 1990s, but they failed to reach a full agreement (Scheumann and Schiffler 1998), until 14 May 2010, when they signed the Agreement on the Nile River Basin Cooperative Framework (The States of the Nile River Basin 2010). The World Bank, however, has been keen to unite the Nile countries in an initiative called the Nile Basin Initiative (NBI), which seeks to achieve sustainable development through equitable and common use of the Nile Basin resources (NBI 2011). The initiative is an ambitious plan, but merits credit. Safeguarding the future of the Nile and the region's security after the Egyptian revolution is important. In fact, the Egyptian revolution of 2011 indirectly has affected the diplomatic relationship between Ethiopia and Egypt concerning the Nile River management. In March 2011, Ethiopian government officials announced the start of construction on what was then called the Grand Millennium Dam and Millennium Hydropower Plant. (On 15 April 2011 the dam was renamed the Grand Ethiopian Renaissance Dam.) The dam was dubbed "the largest dam we could build at any point along the Nile, or indeed any other river (Grand Millennium Dam 2011). The dam is planned to be 145 meters tall and 1,800 meters wide and to have an artificial lake of 40 kilometers width. Previously, an announcement such as this one by the Ethiopian

Figure 1. The Nile River Basin

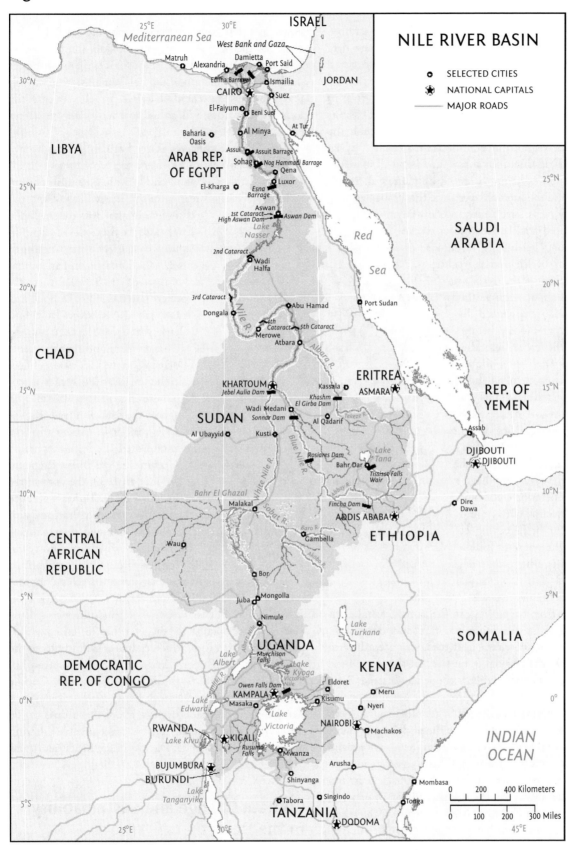

NILE RIVER BASIN

- ⊙ SELECTED CITIES
- ✴ NATIONAL CAPITALS
- — MAJOR ROADS

Source: Nile Basin Initiative (2011).

Note: This map was produced by the Map Design Unit of the World Bank. The boundaries, colors, denominations, and any other information shown on this map do not imply, on the part of The World Bank Group, any judgment on the legal status of any territory, or any endorsement or acceptance of such boundaries. The map (from 2000) predates the creation of South Sudan in July 2011.

This map shows the rivers of the Nile basin, as well as main roads; it does not show country boundaries.

government would have inspired tensions between both countries; Egypt's reaction this time was to request data sharing about the impact of the dam in an effort to start a transparent relationship with Ethiopia.

Another controversial and much fought-over river in the region is the Jordan River. The Jordan River basin is shared by five different riparians in what is arguably the most violent basin in the Middle East; Lebanon, Syria, Jordan, the Palestinian territories, and Israel all share the same basin (Jägerskog et al. 2009; Zeitoun et al. 2012). The demise of the Jordan River since the 1960s has been rapid; many parts have almost no flow anymore, just a polluted trickle. According to the regional nongovernmental organization Friends of the Earth Middle East, 97 percent of the river's original flow of about 1,258 million cubic meters is diverted by Israel, Syria, and Jordan before it reaches the Dead Sea. The remaining flow is polluted because of uncontrolled industrial and agricultural activity, and the river has lost more than 50 percent of its original biodiversity (FoEME 2011). The Dead Sea is sinking at a rate of at least one meter per year, but better regional cooperation could help reverse its decline (Brown and Crawford 2009; Jägerskog et al. 2009). The ongoing Israeli-Palestinian conflict is hampering regional efforts to establish a river basin organization and preventing all riparians from cooperating in the basin. Several plans have emerged for allocation and transboundary water management of the river basin resources according to principles of international water law, but they have been unfruitful and riparians will not cooperate. Instead, Syria has diverted part of the flow through the Yarmouk River.

Israel, the basin's main hegemon (dominant authority), has not cooperated in adhering to the principles of international water law; Israel's policies have prioritized national interests over the overall basin interests for sustainable water management (Zeitoun 2008; Scheumann and Schiffler 1998). Israel's solution to the impending water crisis in the basin has been to focus on the water supply through desalination and high-tech, efficient irrigation rather than through cooperation with its neighbors. Reports name a new Israeli desalination plant in Hadera on the northern coast as the largest of its kind in the world. The structure of the Israel-Palestinian Joint Water Committee (JWC) as of the early 2010s allows

Israel, as the hegemon, effectively to veto even the most basic drinking-water projects inside the Occupied Palestinian Territories as well; in 2011, a French report dubbed the occupation of the Palestinian territory a policy of water apartheid, because Israel prevents the Palestinians from full access to their water resources (Glavany 2011).

The Tigris-Euphrates River basin is shared by five countries: Turkey, Syria, Iraq, the Kingdom of Saudi Arabia (Euphrates), and the Islamic Republic of Iran (Tigris). With its springs in southeast Turkey and the final mouth in the Persian Gulf, the Euphrates is the longest river in southwestern Asia with a length of 2,700 kilometers and an annual volume of 35.9 billion cubic meters (Biswas 1994; Bulloch and Darwish 1993, 60). In 1946, Turkey and Iraq agreed on the rivers' control and management, focusing on the regulation of flow in the source areas. Turkey began monitoring the two streams and shared the data with Iraq (Biswas 1994). In 1980, Turkey and Iraq established the Joint Technical Committee (JTC) on Regional Waters; in 1982, the committee included Syria. Turkey's alliance and military cooperation with Israel has strained relationships between the riparians, however. The establishment of the Turkish Southeastern Anatolia Development Project (GAP) project, an extensive irrigation system based on twenty-two dams and nineteen hydroelectric power plants in the river, has raised concerns, particularly with Iraq, which claims ancient rights to the river water (Scheumann and Schiffler 1998). Iraq has demanded, therefore, through the JTC, that Turkey should guarantee the release of between 500 cubic meters per second (m^3/s) and 700m^3/s, about two-thirds of the water flow, to have a "reasonable and equitable" sharing of the flow (Biswas 1994; Daoudy 2005; Scheumann and Schiffler 1998).

Climate Change and Sustainability in the Desert

In an already water-scarce region, climate change models predict a hotter, drier, and less predictable climate, and the effects could be devastating. The Intergovernmental Panel on Climate Change (IPCC) models predict that temperatures will increase as will water variability in various countries in the Middle East, leading to a drop in precipitation of nearly 30 percent by the year 2050 (World Bank 2009). Between 2007 and 2008, about 160 villages were emptied because of prolonged drought periods, producing climate-change refugees, mainly farmers from the plains of northeastern Syria who arrived in the greater urban area of its capital, Damascus. This influx put high pressure on the urban population and its water supply. The impact of climate change poses real security concerns to the region. It could lead to increased militarization of strategic natural resources, complicating peace agreements (Brown and Crawford 2009). According to geologists and researchers Oli Brown and Alec Crawford, the countries in the region have the power to prepare, such as by promoting a culture of conservation in the region and helping communities and countries adapt to the impacts of climate change. Besides conservation, the countries could work to reduce greenhouse gas emissions and establish better cooperation, both nationally and internationally, on their shared resources (Hattam 2009).

The Arab Spring was an attempt to break free from repressive regimes; not only political and economic stresses—and thus the population's general frustration—caused it, but environmental, population, and climatic stresses also influenced it. The social unrest is a direct response to the increasing environmental and climatic pressure the population is suffering. The food security situation has deteriorated since the onset of several severe droughts since 2006. Between 2006 and 2011, for example, Syria experienced one of the worst droughts and most severe crop failures in history (Friedman 2012). According to the 2011 United Nations Global Assessment Report on Disaster Risk Reduction, herders in the northeast of Syria lost about 85 percent of their livestock, affecting 1.3 million people. Some climatic developments that have affected water supply and thus food security partly explain the current crisis in Syria.

Innovations and Sustainable Solutions

The modern innovation experts mention most often as a technical solution to tackle the Middle East water crisis is the highly efficient technology of irrigation and desalination. Drip-irrigation technology is environmentally sound, but the desalination of seawater is expensive and environmentally unsustainable in the long term unless solar energy powers desalination plants. A main and recent example of high-tech solutions is the possible implementation of the Red-Dead Canal, a proposed project that entails pumping one billion cubic meters of water annually from the Red Sea into the rapidly depleting Dead Sea (Namrouqa 2012).

The Red-Dead Canal project requires cooperation between Israel, Jordan, and the Palestinian Authority. A feasibility study the World Bank conducted is due to be published in 2012. The study raises many questions about these types of megaprojects and their environmental and political consequences. High-tech solutions seem to be a quick fix for an urgent situation, but most of them focus on supply management. Demand management approaches are far more sustainable; examples of demand approaches include reuse of wastewater, rainwater harvesting, the use of dry toilets, reduction and higher efficiency of irrigated agriculture, the import of food (i.e., virtual water), and rehabilitation of traditional water-management systems. In light of the impending climate-change effect, the states of the Middle East increasingly are cooperating on water management, which is vital for this region to cope with the water crisis effectively.

The Future

On 30 May 2012, Iraqi prime minister Nouri Maliki, in an interview with the BBC, warned that "Arab states could be headed towards a future war over water if they do not act quickly to tackle shortages" (BBC 2012). Thirteen of the world's fifteen most water-scarce countries—Algeria, Libya, Tunisia, Jordan, Qatar, Saudi Arabia, Yemen, Oman, the United Arab Emirates, Kuwait, Bahrain, Israel, and the Palestinian territories—are in the Middle East, and one-third of the overall population is under fifteen years old (Friedman 2012). Climate change may increase competition for water resources, as well as complicate peace agreements (Brown and Crawford 2009). Because the overall population in the Middle East is projected to grow, however, the annual growth rates and fertility in the region are declining from an average of 2 percent in the 1990s to 1.7 percent in the early twenty-first century. The United Nations projects that the annual growth rate in 2050 would fall further to 0.71 percent (UN DESA 2007). With the impeding climate change, however, whether the countries in this region will choose to cooperate for a more sustainable future or violently compete over water resources remains to be seen. Optimists wish for cooperation and believe that the scarcity will be a "common enemy" that will join countries together, but pessimists, considering the developments on the ground in the early 2010s (such as the Arab Spring), predict that competition will provoke full-out water wars. Others put their faith in high technology, but as long as fossil fuels are the main energy source that drives the technology, extraction and use of water is not and will not be sustainable environmentally in the long run.

Joshka WESSELS
Lund University, Sweden

See also Climate Change Refugees (Africa); Immigrants and Refugees; Middle East; Nile River; Sahara; Sahel; Urbanization (Western Asia and Northern Africa); Water Use and Rights (Africa); World Bank

FURTHER READING

Allan, Tony. (2002). *The Middle East water question: Hydropolitics and the global economy.* New York: I. B. Taurus.

AQUASTAT. (2012). UN Food and Agricultural Organisation. Rome, Italy: FAO.

Biswas, Asit K. (1994). *International waters of the Middle East: From Euphrates-Tigris to Nile.* New York: Oxford University Press.

British Broadcasting Company (BBC). (2012, May 30). Iraq's PM warns Arab states may face "water war." Retrieved July 23, 2012, from http://www.bbc.co.uk/news/world-middle-east-18262496

Brown, Oli, & Crawford, Alec. (2009). *Rising temperatures, rising tensions: Climate Change and the risk of violent conflict in the Middle East.* Winnipeg, Canada: International Institute for Sustainable Development (IISD).

Bulloch, John, & Darwish, Adel. (1993). *Water wars: Coming conflicts in the Middle East.* London: Victor Gollancz.

Corboun. (2012). Homepage. Retrieved June 22, 2012, from http://www.carboun.com/

Daoudy, Marwa. (2005). *Le partage des eaux entre la Syrie, l'Irak et la Turquie: Négociation, sécurité et asymétrie des pouvoirs* [The watershed between Syria, Iraq and Turkey: Negotiation, security and assymetry of power]. Paris: CNRS.

Friedman, Thomas L. (2012, April 8). The other Arab Spring. *New York Times.* Retrieved June 22, 2012, from http://www.nytimes.com/2012/04/08/opinion/sunday/friedman-the-other-arab-spring.html?pagewanted=all

Friends of the Earth Middle East (FoEME). (2011). *Roadmap for the rehabilitation of the Lower Jordan River.* Amman, Jordan: FoEME.

Glavany, Jean. (2011). *Rapport d'information sur la géopolitique de l'eau. Ministère des Affaires Étrangères* [Information report on the geopolitics of water: Ministry of Foreign Affairs]. Paris: National Assembly.

Grand Millennium Dam. (2011, April 2). The dam speech. Retrieved September 14, 2012, from http://grandmillenniumdam.net/the-dam-speech/

Green Cross International. (2000). *National sovereignty and international watercourses.* Geneva: Green Cross International.

Hattam, Jennifer. (2009, June 10). Global warming makes Syrian villages ghost towns. Retrieved June 22, 2012, from http://www.treehugger.com/climate-change/global-warming-makes-syrian-villages-ghost-towns.html

Jägerskog, Anders, et al. (2009). Water resources in the Middle East. Stockholm: Stockholm International Water Institute. Retrieved June 22, 2012, from http://www.worldwaterweek.org/documents/WWW_PDF/Resources/2009_18tue/Backg_report_Water_ME_Water_n_Energy_Seminar.pdf

Loures, Flavia; Rieu-Clarke, Alistair; & Vercambre, Marie-Laure. (2010). Everything you need to know about the UN Watercourses Convention. Gland, Switzerland: WWF International. Retrieved June 22, 2012, from http://www.unwater.org/downloads/wwf_un_watercourses_brochure_for_web_1.pdf

Maplecroft. (2011). Global risks portfolio. Bath, UK: Maplecroft.

Namrouqa, Hana. (2012, May 19). Red-Dead project studies ready. *The Jordan Times.* Retrieved June 22, 2012, from http://jordantimes.com/red-dead-project-studies-ready

Nile Basin Initiative (NBI). (2011). Nile Basin Initiative corporate report 2011. Entebbe, Uganda: Nile Basin Initiative.

Phillips, David J. H.; Attili, Shaddad; McCaffrey, Stephen; Murray, John S.; & Zeitoun, Mark. (2005). *The water rights of the co-riparians to the Jordan River Basin.* London: Adam Smith Institute.

Scheumann, Waltina, & Schiffler, Manuel. (1998). Water in the Middle East: Potential for conflicts and prospects for cooperation. Berlin: Springer Verlag.

Selby, Jan. (2005). The geopolitics of water in the Middle East: Fantasies and realities. *Third World Quarterly, 26*(2), 329–334.

The States of the Nile River Basin. (2010, May 14). Agreement on the Nile River Basin cooperative framework. Retrieved July 23, 2012, from http://www.internationalwaterlaw.org/documents/regionaldocs/Nile_River_Basin_Cooperative_Framework_2010.pdf

United Nations (UN). (2011). Global Assessment Report on Disaster Risk Reduction: Revealing risk, redefining development. Retrieved June 22, 2012, from http://www.preventionweb.net/english/hyogo/gar/2011/en/bgdocs/GAR-2011/GAR2011_Report_Prelims.pdf

United Nations Department of Economic and Social Affairs (UN DESA). (2007). *World population prospects: The 2006 revision.* Retrieved June 22, 2012, from http://www.un.org/esa/population/publications/wpp2006/English.pdf

United Nations Department of Economic and Social Affairs (UN DESA). (2008). *World urbanization prospects: The 2007 revision.* Retrieved June 22, 2012, from http://www.un.org/esa/population/publications/wup2007/2007WUP_ExecSum_web.pdf

United Nations General Assembly (UNGA). (2010, July 27). The human right to water and sanitation (Sixty-fourth session of United Nations General Assembly A/64/L.63/Rev.1). New York: UNGA.

Walther, Casey. (2010). Rehabilitation and conservation of Kahrez systems in the Northern Governorates, project reports. Retrieved August 4, 2012, from http://www.unesco.org/new/fileadmin/MULTIMEDIA/FIELD/Iraq/pdf/Reports/Annual/UNESCO%20A5-21%20Karez%202010%20Annual%20ITF%20Report.pdf

Wessels, Joshka I. (2009).Water crisis in the Middle East: An opportunity for new forms of water governance and peace. *The Whitehead Journal of Diplomacy and International Relations, 10*(2), 131–142.

Wessels, Joshka I. (2012). Qanat rehabilitation as a viable tool for collective action for social development and conflict resolution in rural communities in arid areas (Paper presented at UNESCO-ICQHS conference on traditional knowledge and resource management). Yazd, Iran: UNESCO.

World Bank. (2009). Water in the Arab world: Management perspectives and innovations. Washington, DC: World Bank.

Zeitoun, Mark. (2008). Power and water in the Middle East: The hidden politics of the Palestinian-Israeli water conflict. London: I. B. Taurus.

Zeitoun, Mark; Eid-Sabbagh, Karim; Dajani, Muna; & Talhami, Michael. (2012). Hydro-political baseline of the Upper Jordan River. Norwich, UK: University of East Anglia (UEA) Water Security Research Centre. Retrieved June 22, 2012, from http://www.uea.ac.uk/c/document_library/get_file?uuid=f1991713-060a-4960-9a87-1b67aafce8dd&groupId=40159

World Bank

World Bank governance was intended to balance creditor and debtor nations, but European nations are still overrepresented and African nations underrepresented. The World Bank has promoted policies favored by European nations, most notably during the era of "structural adjustment" loans in the 1980s and 1990s. External pressure forced it to moderate but not fundamentally change its positions. The rise of emerging markets may make the institution less central to development policy than in the past.

The World Bank was founded in the United States in the peaceful New Hampshire resort town of Bretton Woods in 1944, while fighting was still under way in Asia and Europe as the Second World War reached its bloody conclusion. The conference founded the International Bank for Reconstruction and Development (IBRD) and the International Monetary Fund (IMF) and also set up the precursor to the World Trade Organization (WTO). In 1960, the International Development Association (IDA) was formed to subsidize loans to low-income country governments. Together with IBRD, these two institutions are commonly known as the World Bank. There is also a suite of private sector–focused institutions, however, which together with IBRD and IDA make up the World Bank Group (WBG). The International Finance Corporation (IFC), which lends to private firms investing in developing countries, was formed in 1956; the International Court for the Settlement of Investment Disputes (ICSID) was founded in 1966; and the Multilateral Investments Guarantee Agency (MIGA) was added in 1988. Together, the IMF and World Bank Group are often known as the Bretton Woods Institutions. Although the WBG is a global institution, the focus here is on Africa and Europe, because the

relationship between these two continents within the WBG is emblematic of the shifts in power that have shaped the institution.

Beginnings

The economists John Maynard Keynes, representing the United Kingdom, and Harry Dexter White, representing the United States, are normally ascribed the principal roles in the achievements of Bretton Woods, although actually more than seven hundred delegates from forty-four countries attended, and the outcomes were the culmination of several years of work, driven forward by the US government (Mason and Asher 1973). The delegates from Africa, however, were representatives of colonial rulers. While the IMF was intended to regulate exchange rates and provide a stable macroeconomic environment for economic growth and expanding trade, the IBRD—principally a US idea (Mason and Asher 1973)—was mandated to provide the finances needed to rebuild war-ravaged economies, principally in Europe.

The national political interests of powerful countries were at play at the founding of the WBG, but they were also tempered by an unusually high degree of internationalism. The United States, the main military and financial power, was the central element of the institution: it was the largest shareholder, IBRD headquarters were in Washington DC, and it raised its money in US capital markets. Partly because the United States saw the reconstruction of its allies in Europe as an essential bulwark against the rising communist power of a militarily resurgent Soviet Union and partly for more noble motivations, an attempt was made, however, also to construct institutions that would guard against dominance by one power and that would adopt a technocratic approach to developing economies. This approach was based on the then-dominant economic principles famously set down by Keynes in his book *The General Theory of Employment, Interest and Money* (1936).

At the core of Keynes's vision for regulating the global economy was the idea that surplus and deficit countries should be given equal responsibility for fixing the problems caused by trade and financial imbalances. The IMF hence was intended to regulate exchange rates to prevent trade imbalances from growing too large. This principle extended to the World Bank, where debtor countries—principally Europeans—had equal weight with creditor nations, principally the United States. The top jobs were also divided according to an unwritten "gentleman's agreement" that the head of the Bank would be from the United States and the head of the IMF would be a European. This agreement is still respected today—despite recent promises to institute fair and merit-based selection processes (G20 2008).

This principle of balancing creditors and debtors, however, has eroded over time, as World Bank lending became exclusively focused on the developing world, including a large number of borrowers in Africa, yet developed countries, particularly Europeans, held on to a majority of the voting shares and board seats.

Part of the problem stems from the fact that the Articles of Agreement make no clear provision for how voting shares would be realigned (IBRD 1989). Without such a mechanism, it has proved extremely difficult to persuade those governments with strong voting rights to give up or dilute their shareholding to give greater say to developing countries. Because the United States and Europe have consistently held a majority of the votes, no change can happen without their approval. Alternative proposals for a reflection on democratic principles in vote shareholding have been ignored (Woodward 2010).

An independent examination of voting shares in the wake of the 2010 round of governance reforms confirmed that this trend persists (Bretton Woods Project 2010). High-income countries—as defined by the Bank in its country classifications—still maintain more than 60 percent of the vote. The United States still chooses the president of the Bank, and high-income countries hold a majority of seats on the Bank's executive board. African countries hold only three board seats, while European countries currently hold nine. Indeed, Luxembourg (population 509,074 [US CIA 2012c]) has a greater voting share than Uganda (population 35.9 million [US CIA 2012d]). This imbalance is most striking at IDA, which lends to only low-income countries. Those countries have only 11 percent of the vote, and eleven countries in sub-Saharan Africa actually suffered a reduction of their voting shares in the 2010 reforms.

Power and Policies—Structural Adjustment

It is not only the inadequacies of voting reform mechanisms, however, that have prevented African countries from gaining more influence within the World Bank: the Bretton Woods Institutions were designed, since their inception, to influence policy in any countries they lent to, and hence the dominant Western nations have used them as a tool of influence (Woods 2006). Loans came with policy conditions attached. The starkest demonstration of this occurred during the era of "structural adjustment" in the 1980s and 1990s. Until then, the Bank had been primarily an infrastructure bank, designing large projects in transport, energy, rural development, and other industrial sectors. With the advent of structural adjustment loans in the 1980s, the Bank and the IMF attempted to exert far greater control across the full range of economic policy making. The increasing indebtedness of countries in Africa and elsewhere also meant that the importance of the World Bank and IMF to those countries increased, making it hard for countries to resist demands from the Bretton Woods Institutions to change their policies.

The blend of policies advocated by the Bank during the era of structural adjustment has often been dubbed the "Washington Consensus" (GTN 2003) and included privatization of state-run industries and firms, liberalization of trade and the reduction and elimination of tariffs, the removal of subsidies, and the retreat of the state from active industrial intervention.

The Rise of Protest Power

These policies proved extremely contentious and provoked a furious backlash across the developing world. Mass movements opposing the IMF and World Bank sprang up as the impacts of these policies became apparent: rising unemployment, impacts on marginalized communities, and severe impacts for women (Sparr 1994). The precise effect is of course disputed, with supporters of structural adjustment policies claiming that they were designed to impose short-term pain but also to create more competitive economies in the long run, and they often failed only because of poor implementation (Dollar and Svensson 2000). Opponents noted the disastrous impacts of these adjustments on the poorest (Jolly 1991) and also that countries that were subject to the adjustments effectively de-industrialized themselves (Rodrik 1990).

The Bank responded not so much by changing its policies, but, during the course of the 1990s, by becoming much more aware of and involved in the political economy of developing countries' decision making. This emphasized more and more the need to reform governance processes in developing countries, and eventually, toward the end of the 1990s, their rhetoric changed to one that privileged developing country clients' "poverty reduction strategies" over the imposition of the Bank's solutions (Pender 2001). Critics rightly pointed out (Stewart and Wang 2003) that the international financial institutions (IFIs) had enormous influence in the design and approval of these strategies, but their emergence was evidence of a significant shift in the power dynamics at the Bank—that is, the increased power of external actors.

There were two main reasons for this shift. The first was structural adjustment—which was so vehemently opposed by citizens and governments in developing countries that the Bank was forced to change, as noted above. The second issue was the social and environmental impacts of Bank megaprojects. During the 1980s and 1990s, a powerful coalition of civil society groups, allied with communities adversely affected by Bank projects (e.g., people displaced by dams, affected by power plants, and deprived of livelihoods by deforestation) forced the issue onto the public agenda of the Bank's major shareholders (Fox and Brown 1998). The Bank became a hot political topic in Western capitals, precipitating reform—during the 1990s a suite of mandatory environmental and social safeguards were introduced to prevent the worst damage caused by Bank projects, and the Bank created a series of internal bodies to improve its accountability, including the Inspection Panel (IEG 2010).

In a way then, civil society groups and mass movements had used the Bank's Western-dominated governance to force it to change. By pressuring rich-country shareholders through public campaigning, the Bank had shifted its policies, not radically, but significantly. Central to this pressure had been the movements and complaints of developing countries' citizens and governments, but without their alliance with Western civil society groups, it is doubtful that that change would have happened. It is also important to remember that the change was one of emphasis and degree, not a significant change in the Bank's overall policy framework, which remains guided by the policy prescriptions supported by Western capitals. In both cases, outside pressure managed to force the Bank to moderate its position but did not change it fundamentally.

Rise of the Middle Income Countries

Emerging market economies are increasing in economic and political power, as is reflected by the G8's expansion to become the G20—the world's principal economic discussion forum. At the Bank, however, as noted above, the difficulties in getting European governments to give up

voting shares is preventing a significant increase in the emerging markets' formal voting power. Although the Europeans did agree to reduce their number of board seats by two at the IMF in 2010, they made no such commitment at the Bank. The 2010 voting shift delivered only a 2.6 percent shift to emerging markets (Bretton Woods Project 2010).

To defend their position, European governments have increasingly employed the argument that the number of voting shares they are granted reflects the cash contribution they make to the Bank. Although the World Bank's capital base is comprised of contributions made in order to buy voting shares—that is, those who have the greatest number of votes are those who have contributed the most capital—this does not pay for the running costs of the Bank, which are funded from loan repayments. In other words, developing countries pay for the Bank's day-to-day operations. High-income countries have contributed more through issuing subsidies to low-income country loans through IDA. The pot of money available for these subsidies is replenished every three years, traditionally by grants from rich-country donors. In recent years, these grants have been less significant. In the last IDA replenishment in 2010, almost half the funding came from a reallocation of World Bank Group profits and from middle-income countries, including through agreements by middle-income countries to change the terms of outstanding loans owed to them, including that of early repayment (IDC 2011).

Despite their lack of formal power, emerging markets are exerting their influence in other ways, including by blocking change. For example, in 2011, they prevented a new energy strategy from being agreed upon because they did not approve of a proposed ban on lending for coal-fired plants (Bretton Woods Project 2011). Many civil society actors worry that a World Bank influenced by more powerful emerging-market governments will not be as open as it previously was to external pressure and may marginalize low-income countries—the majority of which will increasingly be African.

Outlook

What direction will the World Bank follow? In a best case scenario, radical changes in governance could allow the Bank to refocus itself on the world's poorest countries (most of which are in Africa), thus giving them a real voice in running the institution. The increased legitimacy gained from this reform would also allow the Bank to play a supportive role in major global challenges, including on issues related to climate change. It is more likely that governance reform will proceed at a slow pace. Middle-income countries will gradually gain more power, but Western countries, particularly European ones, will continue to be overrepresented for many years to come. Low-income countries in Africa may discover that the Bank will continue to be used as a political influence tool, however, this time in a struggle between emerging and advanced economies. It is also true that the Bank is becoming less important than it used to be; its lending power is dwarfed by that of private finance, and it finds itself challenged by new rivals, including state development banks such as the Brazilian Development Bank (BNDES, from the Portugese Banco Nacional de Desenvolvimento Economico e Social), which is already more important than the Bank in lending terms, and alternatives such as the recently proposed BRICS (Brazil, Russia, India, China, and South Africa) bank (BRICS Summit 2012). It could be that the Bank will move away from its historically central role in international development and play a supporting role instead.

Jesse GRIFFITHS
European Network on Debt and Development (Eurodad)

See also African Union (AU); Disaster Risk Management; European Union (EU); International Conflict Resolution; Microfinance; Rule of Law (Africa); Rule of Law (European Union)

FURTHER READING

Bretton Woods Committee. (2012). About: Bretton Woods institutions. Retrieved April 27, 2012, from http://www.brettonwoods.org/index.php/180/Bretton_Woods_Institutions

Bretton Woods Project. (2010). Analysis of World Bank voting reforms. Retrieved May 28, 2012, from http://www.brettonwoodsproject.org/art-566281

Bretton Woods Project. (2011). World Bank energy strategy stalled. Retrieved May 28, 2012, from http://www.brettonwoodsproject.org/art-568577

BRICS Summit. (2012). Fourth BRICS summit Delhi declaration. Retrieved May 28, 2012, from http://pmindia.nic.in/press-details.php?nodeid=1404

Chang, Ha-Joon. (2008). Bad Samaritans: The myth of free trade and the secret history of capitalism. New York: Bloomsbury Press.

Dollar, David, & Svensson, Jakob. (2000, October). What explains the success or failure of structural adjustment programmes? *The Economic Journal, 110*(466), 894–917.

Fox, Jonathan A., & Brown, D. L. (1998). The struggle for accountability: The World Bank, NGOs, and grassroots movements. Cambridge, MA: MIT Press.

Global Trade Negotiations (GTN). (2003). GTN homepage: Washington Consensus. Retrieved April 27, 2012, from http://www.cid.harvard.edu/cidtrade/issues/washington.html

G20 Research Group. (2008). G20 Communiqué. Retrieved May 28, 2012, from http://www.g20.utoronto.ca/2008/2008washington1011.htm

Independent Evaluation Group (IEG). (2010). Safeguards and sustainability policies in a changing world: An independent evaluation of World Bank Group experience. IEG Studies Series. Washington, DC: IEG & World Bank.

International Bank for Reconstruction and Development (IBRD). (1989, February 16). IBRD Articles of Agreement. Retrieved May 28, 2012, from http://siteresources.worldbank.org/EXTABOUTUS/Resources/ibrd-articlesofagreement.pdf

International Development Committee (IDC). (2011). International Development Committee: Fourth report. The World Bank. London: Parliament, House of Commons.

International Monetary Fund (IMF). (2012). Homepage. Retrieved April 27, 2012, from http://www.imf.org/external/index.htm

Jolly, Richard. (1991, December). Adjustment with a human face: A UNICEF record and perspective on the 1980s. *World Development, 19*(12), 1807–1821.

Keynes, John Maynard. (1936). *The general theory of employment, interest and money.* Cambridge, UK: Cambridge University Press.

Mason, Edward S., & Asher, Robert E. (1973). The World Bank since Bretton Woods. Washington, DC: The Brookings Institution.

Pender, John. (2001). From "structural adjustment"' to "comprehensive development framework": Conditionality transformed? *Third World Quarterly, 22*(3), 397–411.

Rodrik, Dani. (1990, July). How should structural adjustment programs be designed? *World Development, 18*(7), 933–947.

Sparr, Pamela. (1994). Mortgaging women's lives: Feminist critiques of structural adjustment. Washington, DC: United Nations.

Stewart, Frances, & Wang, Michael. (2003). Do PRSPs empower poor countries and disempower the World Bank, or is it the other way round? (QEH working papers, No. qehwps108). Oxford, UK: Queen Elizabeth House, University of Oxford.

United States Central Intelligence Agency (US CIA). (2012a). The world factbook: Belgium. Retrieved April 27, 2012, from https://www.cia.gov/library/publications/the-world-factbook/geos/be.html

United States Central Intelligence Agency (US CIA). (2012b). The world factbook: India. Retrieved April 27, 2012, from https://www.cia.gov/library/publications/the-world-factbook/geos/in.html

United States Central Intelligence Agency (US CIA). (2012c). The world factbook: Luxembourg. Retrieved April 27, 2012, from https://www.cia.gov/library/publications/the-world-factbook/geos/lu.html

United States Central Intelligence Agency (US CIA). (2012d). The world factbook: Uganda. Retrieved April 27, 2012, from https://www.cia.gov/library/publications/the-world-factbook/geos/ug.html

Woods, Ngaire. (2006). *The globalizers: The IMF, The World Bank, and their borrowers.* Ithaca, NY: Cornell University Press.

Woodward, David. (2010, March). Democratizing global governance for sustainable human development. *Development, 53,* 42–47.

World Bank Group. (2012). Homepage. Retrieved April 27, 2012, from http://www.worldbank.org/

Index

A

Afghanistan, 2–6
    armed conflict and, 5
    drug trade in, 4
    minerals in, 4–5, 68
    multilateral environmental agreements
        (MEAs) and, 5
    transportation in, 4
    water availability in, 3
Africa, Central, 7–10
    Bantu speakers, 8
    European colonization in, 9
    Kariba hydroelectric dam, 9
Africa, East, 11–15
    agriculture and, 12–13
    European colonization in, 13–14
    Sirikwa people, 12
Africa, Southern, 16–18
    colonization in, 17
    current threats to the environment in, 17–18
    mining in, 17
    population growth in, 17
    precolonial settlement, 16
Africa, Western, 19–21
    deforestation in, 20–21
    gold mining in Ghana, 21
    petroleum production and oil spills, 20
African Union (AU), 22–26
    Abuja Treaty of 1991, 23
    New Partnership for Africa's Development
        (NEPAD), 23, 24
    Organization of African Unity (OAU), 22, 23
    Pan-Africanism, 22, 25
  Agenda 21, 113, 121

Agriculture, Small-Scale, 27–31
    African Conservation Tillage Network (ACT), 28
    conservation agriculture, 28, 30
    crop rotation, 29
    herbicide-resistant soybeans, 28
    Roman influence, 27–28
    Zimbabwe and, 29
  Arab Spring, 201, 373, 377
    See also **Tunis, Tunisia**
Architecture, 32–34
    African architecture, 32–33
    efficiency and sustainability labels, 34
    European architecture, 33, 34
    Fathy, Hassan, 33
    See also Masdar City, Abu Dhabi

B

Balkans, 36–38
    deforestation, 36–37
    Green Balkans, 37
    socialist period in, 37
    water security and contamination in, 37
Biodiversity Conservation, 39–42
    biodiversity hotspots, 39, 40, 41
    International Union for Conservation of
        Nature and Natural Resources (IUCN)
        Red List, 39
    protected areas, 39, 40, 41
    See also EU's Natura 2000 initiative of 1992 (France)
        under **European Union (EU)**
Biological Corridors, 43–46
    International Union for Conservation of Nature
        (IUCN) European Green Belt Initiative, 45

Bold entries and page numbers denote encyclopedia articles.

Bold entries and page numbers denote encyclopedia articles.

Bold entries and page numbers denote encyclopedia articles.